Stepping Stones

STEPPING STONES

part of the *Silence Within* series by
The International Library of Poetry

Laura Michele Diener, Editor

Stepping Stones

Library of Congress
Cataloging in Publication Data

ISBN 0-7951-5025-3

Proudly manufactured in the United States of America by
Watermark Press
One Poetry Plaza
Owings Mills, MD 21117

poetry.COM
The International Library of Poetry

FOREWORD

Throughout life, we store information collected from experiences and try in some way to make sense of it. When we are not able to fully understand the things that occur in our lives, we often externalize the information. By doing this, we are afforded a different perspective, thus allowing us to think more clearly about difficult or perplexing events and emotions. Art is one of the ways in which people choose to externalize their thoughts.

Within the arts, modes of expression differ, but poetry is a very powerful tool by which people can share sometimes confusing, sometimes perfectly clear concepts and feelings with others. Intentions can run the gamut as well: The artists may simply want to share something that has touched their lives in some way, or they may want to get help to allay anxiety or uncertainty. The poetry within *Stepping Stones* is from every point on the spectrum: every topic, every intention, every event or emotion imaginable. Some poems will speak to certain readers more than others, but it is always important to keep in mind that each verse is the voice of a poet, of a mind that needs to make sense of this world, of a heart that feels the effects of every moment in this life, and perhaps of a memory that is striving to surface. Nonetheless, recalling our yesterdays gives birth to our many forms of expression.

Melisa S. Mitchell
Senior Editor

Editor's Note

As women began to enter the work force, their roles in society vastly changed. However, there are some ways in which women's status has remained the same. The roles of feminine sexuality, for instance, have changed little since biblical times. A dualism exists in stereotypes of how women should behave sexually. Religious icons, like the Virgin Mary and Mary Magdalene, epitomize the extremes of sexual stereotype—the virgin and the prostitute. Procreation is also seen in two opposite ways—while some see childbirth as a gift, others see it as the punishment handed down from God to Eve for seducing Adam into eating the forbidden fruit.

The cultural fear of women's sexual power has created many conflicting stereotypes for women. Women are placed into confining roles where no middle ground exists, such as woman/child, harlot/virgin, and seductress/victim.

"Io"(1), by Alexandra Wynn Griffin, describes a mythological tale of one seductress/victim. Zeus raped Io, the daughter of Inachus, taking the form of a cloud to deceive not only Io but also his wife, Hera. Griffin then parallels the mythological story and that of the persona, who was also raped. The first three stanzas of the poem retell the myth of Io and Zeus, creating the expectation that the persona relates personally to Io's situation. The poem begins with Io's escape from Zeus:

> *There you go again*
> *Crossing the green briny Mediterranean*
> *Into the swift brown river Nile*
> *To escape him . . .*

Escape is not as easy as it seems. While physically escaping is as simple as crossing a river, the emotional release is much more difficult. Griffin describes the fear Io and presumably, the persona feels, describing "[y]our toga swelling about your waist / [t]wisting around you like thick white rope." There is terror "swelling" inside both victims, confining them.

As if the internal battle being fought were not enough, Io also must reckon with "gadflies" and a hundred-eyed monster, Argus, both sent by the jealous Hera:

> *Gadflies stick in your hair and bite*
> *Your scalp, the insides of your ears*
>
> *. . .*
> *His wife sets a hundred eyes to follow you . . .*

The gadflies and Argus were sent to pester Io for the rest of her life. Hera felt the girl deserved to be punished, although it was Zeus who actually committed the wrongs. To the persona, the gadflies and the "hundred eyes" represent the people who often blame rape victims stating that what they were wearing or doing brought on the attack. In both cases, the women are left unable to protest, their voices silenced by their attackers: "He gives you the dull tongue of a cow."

In the final stanza, Griffin pulls together the stories of Io and the persona:

> *They offer the name of a sea to you, but*
> *Somehow the Ionian Sea is no comfort to me*
> *As I'm pinned to the cool ground of your*
> *Clean temple by a man who thinks himself*
> *To be Jupiter or Zeus*

Although the persona knows the story of Io, it is no consolation to her in the present. The "clean temple" represents the untarnished self-image that women have of themselves, or the purity of their bodies before they are raped. The persona is being violated by a man who, like Zeus, thinks he can take advantage of women.

In "The Nude Black Trees" (1) by Deborah J. Schwing, we see more evidence of feminine duality as the persona's mother is thrown into dual roles of the giver of life and of death. The poem, told through the eyes of a newborn, uses many opposing descriptions that represent both life and death. The title, for instance, employs the words "Nude" and "Black." "Nude" represents birth; it is the way we enter the world. "Black," on the other hand, connotes death. This juxtaposition illustrates the belief that as soon as we are born we begin to die; thus, by giving birth to her child, the mother condemns the child to death. This point is made again later in the poem:

> *with my mother's screeching*
> *pleas for death or release, one being*
> *the same as the other*

Death and release are the same for the mother, as death would bring the mother release from the pain of childbirth, and the only thing that can truly release us from the pain of life is death.

Schwing applies one final opposing description to solidify the theme of her poem:

> *an elated doctor yelled my sex*
> *but the Chinese nurse whispered in my ear*
> *you have bought death*
> *in your first breath*

The "elated doctor" represents the joy felt when a new child is brought into the world.

The "Chinese nurse" is the antithesis, telling the newborn that with one breath, it is destined to die simply because it has taken a step into life.

Lydia Rose Sifferlen's "Burning Down" (1) depicts the woman/child stereotype and how a woman's sexuality can be seen as something dangerous that should be feared:

> *the night my parents told me about sex*
> *was the same night they told me about our*
> *garage burning down.*

That the persona's mother told her about sex and the garage burning down on the same night; illustrates how a woman's sexuality is viewed as both passionate and frightening.

The mother, the woman figure in this poem, symbolizes women's sexuality:

> *I imagined her in a long white Victorian*
> *nightgown, somehow, pregnant, her permanent*
> *falling into a loose wave*

After learning about sex, the persona in "Burning Down" sees her mother as a sexual being, imaging her in a "Victorian nightgown" and "somehow pregnant." The woman is juxtaposed with the child persona to show the polar opposites of a sexual being and a non-sexual being:

> *that night I lay in bed and stared and stared*
> *and stared at my window with rainbow curtains like a puppet show.*

This description of "rainbow curtains like a puppet show" exhibits the child's innocence. The persona is not like her mother, but she knows one day she will be. This revelation alarms the child, because she realizes that she will not be a child forever; she too will become a sexual being:

> *I thought each and every noise was the rip*
> *of a match, the hiss of sulfur,*
> *the whispered chaos of flame and smoke.*
> *and I lay in bed thinking, I am the evidence.*

The fear of the fire represents the child's fear that she will become just like her mother. She realized that she is the "evidence" that little girls do grow up and with that comes sexuality. Or perhaps, associating the idea of sex with the burning garage, the persona fears sexuality, but she knows that her existence is the "evidence" that it occurs.

Women's sexuality has been feared throughout the ages; because of this, women are often categorized by conflicting stereotypes. If you are not a virgin, you are promiscuous; if you are not a mother, you are a child. Through poetry, women and men alike can break down stereotypes and barriers created by our culture.

Within this anthology, many societal walls are deconstructed. I encourage you to read each of the poets' thoughts to better understand yourself as well as other people. Do not forget to read such memorable works as "I Never Did Mind the Little Things" (3) by Guy Champagne, "The Duck" (3) by Jane Becker Fischer, "Gemini"(4) by Lauren McLoughlin, "Sixteenth Floor Ginger Ale" (4) by Jeromy Biazzo, "Air for One" (3) by Rachel Uchman, "To Be Clear of a Day" (4) by Dana Hegar, and "Four" (3) by L. A. Parker.

I would like to extend sincere thanks to all the poets featured in this anthology. Congratulations, and good luck in all of your future endeavors.

This anthology would not have been possible without the hard work of our judges, editors, assistant editors, customer service representatives, graphic artists, layout artists, office administrators, data entry staff, and mail-room personnel. I would like to thank all of these people for their contributions to this anthology.

Vanessa Hairfield

Editor

Cover artwork: "Mudding Around" by Teresa Kemp

Io

There you go again
Crossing the green briny Mediterranean
Into the swift brown river Nile
To escape him
Your toga swelling about your waist
Twisting around you like thick white rope

Gadflies stick in your hair and bite
Your scalp, the insides of your ears, and
Your pink peeling forehead, and
You can scratch or drown

His wife sets a hundred eyes to follow you
He gives you the dull tongue of a cow
They do everything short of blaming you outright

They offer the name of a sea to you, but
Somehow the Ionian Sea is no comfort to me
As I'm pinned to the cool ground of your
Clean temple by a man who thinks himself
To be Jupiter or Zeus.

Alexandra Wynn Griffin

The Nude Black Trees

I was blown out of my mother's womb
on a cold March morning while
the wind wrapped itself around the
building, screaming its banshee shriek
in harmony with my mother's screeching
pleas for death or release, one being
the same as the other
I brought with me freshets of blood
that jetted out of my mother
and left Chinese ideograms on
pristine white sheets

The Chinese nurse wiped her eyes
as she read our doomed futures
an elated doctor yelled my sex
but the Chinese nurse whispered in my ear
you have bought death
in your first breath

Deborah J. Schwing

Burning Down

the night my parents told me about sex
was the same night they told me about our
garage burning down.
my mom had a scared laugh in her eye when
she said she got up out of bed that night
and stood there in the bathroom, watching it burn.
I imagined her in a long white Victorian
nightgown, somehow pregnant, her permanent
falling into a loose wave, her eyes
pressing so close to the flames that it
melted the crusty corners of dream and caul of sleep.
that night I lay in bed and stared and
stared and stared at my window with rainbow
curtains like a puppet show.
I thought each and every noise was the rip
of a match, the hiss of sulfur, the
whispered chaos of flame and smoke.
and I lay in bed thinking, I am the evidence.

Lydia Rose Sifferlen

I Never Did Mind the Little Things

On my wife's moody days
she gathers spiders

Carefully fitting them with dragon fly wings
my daughter collected from corpses
found floating
on the surface of our pond

The two of them orchestrate
these spinners
as they drape the yard
with silken tapestries

The next day wings fall off
like helicopter seeds
dropping spiders onto
precarious places

While flies abducted without webbing
litter the lawn

Guy M. Champagne

The Duck

Faded brown kimono flapping
in the newly chilled wind,
the bent and dry skinned woman
creeps beside the pond.
She is wandering
in a windowpane of thought.
Stooping where minuscule waves
meet the too-large shore,
her oversized wedding ring
slips carelessly to the ground.
It will be retrieved by someone with elastic skin
and silken threads.
Crumbling bread in her hand,
she throws it on the water's metallic surface
and watches as a swan and duck indulge in battle
for its life giving rights.
Her chapped lips curve into a secret smile
as the duck squawks its victorious cry.

Jane Becker Fischer

Winged

I draw wings on my stick figures
So they can fly away
And bring me back shiny objects
From the outside world.
I have a pebble
And three little coins,
This piece of foil, smooth from rubbing,
And the glass, edged in my own darkened blood.
Me and the trinkets hide where the light
Comes pale and seldom anymore.
But the nights are not so dark.
So when one of my angels tumbles in
And whispers to me things I see as shadows,
I can nod my head and grin.
If I am lucky, they will drag some fire in.
I will burn this hole into something brighter.
When the smoke clears and the stones fall,
The sunshine dances in on slippered feet.
I will feel this tug and my feathers ruffle.
The sky is not so far away anymore.

Heather Marie Thompson

Four

Screen door screamed a Southern song
Mama's big browns watched, hands pressed against the mesh
Four years old and I knew all the words
Daddy called me Suzy-Q in an accent thicker than humidity
Thicker than the Spanish moss

Two doors down the neighbor boy kept snakes
In a vacant room at the top of his house
We sat as balls
On chairs
In circles
And endured the snakes' release
I squirmed more than most

Dirt road home hid many things
Broken bottle sliced my foot; I did not cry
In the tub, Mama used sugar to stop the bleeding, and I
Delighted in Daddy's love offering
Cinnamon hots in a cooler cup
From Uncle Charlie's gas station

L. A. Parker

Sister

She is sister
temporal breath, cotton breasts, iron tongue
throat grazed crimson, feet nailed bleeding
to the soil of her birth, dirt of her death

Spit from the belly of naked laughing stars
she is moon brushed, earth doomed
eyes burning twilight

There are traces of archaic shores
in the fragile sands of her skin

Nameless, chanting, she is
sinking into the canvass of her own
mysterious smile

She is a silhouette of her mother's
greatest gift

She has fire in her eyes and rampant rivers
in her soul

Born and birthing, she is
the beginning and the ceaseless definition
of life

Carina Lois Rumrill

Air for One

Breathing in a box,
Air for one.
And then you came—
Gagging—
Expecting some of it.

Watching your skeletal huffs,
Collapsing lungs,
My heart softens—
Extending,
Unlatching the lid.

Yet flickering in my view,
Ten Virgin Lamps.
God's Parable to me—
Retracting,
Leaving the box locked.

Stumbling your frailty elsewhere
Foolishly received.
I watch you steal her life away—
Wondering
If Heaven awaits her while I prolong my entrance to Hell.

Rachel Ann Uchman

Going South

Once I cut myself on your tangents
and bled with the language of tomatoes
I was roughened inside curved pools
of cool denim, migrating like mad ducks
    going south
I wrote to you one time about witches
on graffiti scraps of attic books, but
were you gone? I can't remember how long
I first lost the memory of summer
    or when
there were laters full of kitchen pots &
old dogs wrapping slowly around our feet the
year your father died while capturing sleep
the same year our children's hands began
    to speak
I remember you, naked as butterflies,
speaking of the Greek weather in July
driving, tight, tight within the lines while
someone became the first man on the moon
    to die
    Andrew Morokoff

Sixteenth Floor Ginger Ale

Sixteenth floor ginger ale
looking out onto Bronx river barges
passing over fossils of urban salt bed estuaries
It was the Ganges, it was the Nile

House plant jungles somewhere between Serengeti
and Bronx River Parkway
occupied our time until the next tides a living room monsoon

There were Mallow-Mars on our return from expeditions
behind a green coach in a sea of red shag rug
We unearthed yellowing copies of daily worker,
a tarnished bust of Marx
costume jewelry stuffed closets with jars of pennies for the rolling,
manifestors and Bakelite symphonies
It was Chinese checkers under a glass coffee table

A Samovar rendered in oil hung above relics of grandpa
paperweights and enameled ashtrays
It was all on lazy susan sour eyes spun
It could have been out of Asimov
It was another world in that co-op city courtyard
In the co-op city apartment
    Jeromy Biazzo

Untitled

Trying to breathe you in through my pillow,
my heart beats incessantly in my stomach,
and I know that in hours mine will be the face of a girl
who has been playing with her mother's makeup.
These other faces I take on,
completed by red toenails,
accented by countless bottles of bubble bath and Spanish wine,
create hours of entertainment for the cat and my roommate.
With piggy banks full and debt insurmountable,
I notice my slowly clearing conscience—consciousness,
and as the silk falls away graciously at the foot of my bed—
mounted on what I do and do not remember—
I fall back on your pillow
and find the peace in my bed that you cannot.
    Sara Jaine Davis

Suddenly Everything Was Wrong

Elsie was painting in reds again.
And Joe was on the couch
putting the moves on a pug-nose girl
who'd been dead for days.

Daddy was crouched on the windowsill
speaking in tongues,
while Mother stood in the kitchen, afraid to move
lest the baby remember she was there
and climb out of its jar to get her.

And someone
I didn't know was in the room above me,
pacing back and forth until
his feet wore down to nubs
and he had to lie on the floor whispering
things to me through the boards.

And where was God, you ask, in all of this?
He was there,
in the tub,
scrubbing himself until he bled.
    Rebecca Cross

Gemini

She sleeps like a conjoined twin
recently separated from her sister.
Limbs holding on to what was once there.
Left arm crumpled awkwardly under her body,
right arm hugging her sibling's down filled chest,
left leg curled up slightly behind her,
right leg draped over her mirror's feathered thigh.

No tears are tonight for her lost half;
the first in many weeks.
Consciously, she forgets what
it feels like to share the bed.
She slumbers soundly with the corners of her
mouth drawn up in a tiny smile.
Perhaps dreaming of a night months before,
when Gemini was there,
giggling and smiling back,
holding her in a similar embrace.
    Lauren Alene McLoughlin

To Be Clear of a Day

You know that day when you hit my car with your fists,
I wear a creeping fear as a slip against my skin
It slides silkily down against my skin as slips do
And keeps me just knowing it is there

I needed it you know because life was killing me and it was my life

I want to take it off now but it hides
And wraps around my blood vessels, coiling,
And, yes, it is inside of me a whining

To be clear of a day of caffeine and wine and this, this, oh—

Its gift a screaming awareness, a token
As it loops flowered through membrane and muscle
And finds a lung—
Sweet breath!—its food (to breathe for it)

(To write of the smallest thing,) this fear, this chocolate moment
    Dana S. Hegar

On the Muni in San Francisco

I remember the murals of the SS in the subbasement
of the caserne in Nuremberg
you shoveling coal into the furnace that heated us all
Hemingway and Castro were your heroes
Jesus and Kennedy mine
you, Theo, and I would recite poetry
behind the lectern in the marble-rich chapel
discuss politics in front of a National Geographic world map
we wandered around the infamous wall
and filled our heads with futile fantasies unfulfilled
rendezvoused with our favorite Friday-night frauleins
and took leave to Amsterdam, Paris, and Rome
that was a simpler time
when we'd unearth Nazi artifacts and discover their bold
and embossed belt buckles with the outrageous insignia:
"Gott Mit Uns"
that was a simpler time for us
not quite comprehending the bellowing smoke
that shrouded Dachau
blinding the eyes of the Bishop
Philip Hackett

I Owe You

Never goes a moment,
when I don't think about you,
'cause you are in my heart, my soul and in everything I do.
I see you in my shadow,
I see you in my mirror.
I close my eyes and yet,
I see you in my thoughts . . . in my dreams,
'cause what I shared with you
is no less than precious,
'cause what you are
is no less than beautiful.
You gave me what I never had before,
you made me what I never was before.
For all you have done for me,
I owe you something.
And what I owe you . . .
. . . is no less than devotion
. . . is no less than loyalty
. . . is no less than love,
my heart, my sweetheart!
Manish Vohra

I am a Watcher

I watch you spin your useless web
Cause pain, and ruin lives
You walk oblivious to your destruction

I am a Watcher

I watch you stare vacantly at meaning
You are a blank slate unwilling to be filled

I am a Watcher

You allow yourself to be infected by others
Let them spill their thoughts into your head
You are a sponge soaking up black water

I am a Watcher

Greed and Envy rule you; they are your gods

I am a Watcher

You do not paint your own life
You let others crudely sketch it

I am a Watcher

And I know what you are

I am a Watcher

And I will not be like you
Shannon Brooke MacKenzie

"It Hurts Too Much to Remember"
and "It Hurts Too Much to Forget"

It is my sincere hope that my thoughts of looking *forward* . . .
and yes, to the *past* . . .
to remember that I have experienced MIRACLES . . .
as well as vivid DREAMS . . .
knowing that I have an special little ANGEL in Heaven,
possibly looking down on me,
her Mother, who misses her more than *mere words can express!*
It is my belief, that only those, living on Earth,
who have *lost* loved ones through death,
then *found* . . . through FAITH, LOVE and TRUST,
in our HEAVENLY FATHER, can know, that these loved ones,
may be replaced with SPIRITUAL GROWTH,
as directed to us, in our Holy Word, **THE BIBLE**.
this is my prayer, today.
Marjorie M. Bartlett

Anger

One day a young woman is told

—*You really are a slave of your passions!*

The uncomfortable truth
darkens a shady inner landscape
where reminiscences of an unresolved past prevailed.

—*You threaten my identity!*
—*My existence dissolves by such talk!*

she says. And in this moment of upheaval
she races out the door,

letting an inner monologue accelerate to
a boisterous train of justifying thoughts
that ends in masses of good reasons for being right.

The heated state of mind veils the thoughts
with an illusion of power and invulnerability.
Words and deeds come without thoughts
of the inexorable existence of the consequences . . .

When the anatomy of rage
eventually reveals in all its ugliness,
she had to deal with another truth;

—*You have just proved exactly what I mean!*
Lise Skaalerud

The Light Will Guide You Right

Why can't people understand me?
It's like I wasn't meant to be.

People laugh and play tricks on me.
Instead of living I'd rather drown myself in the sea.

My self-esteem is low.
I just want everyone to go.

Can't anyone in this dang world see?
Can't they see what they are bestowing upon me?

I want this to be my last day.
What's that you're saying? Everything is going to be okay?

How would you know?
You think you would cause your glow.

I'm God—listen to what I have to say,
No, everything won't stop today.

What you are going through is just a fork in the road.
Everyone must carry their own load.

At times that load may hurt.
Just wait and everything would be as good as dessert.

You must not go today,
'Cause deep in everyone's heart, we want you to STAY.
Matt Russell Dooley

I Am Rescued

Set my cheek to your cheek
to feel the equator pulsate
I heard Pharaoh scream, "what was I thinking?!"
Crow feathers fall announcing a celebration
when I set my cheek to your cheek
I see the lessons I've learned
while standing between the rain drops
flood waters rise beneath my feet
and I hold tight to your spirit
that lives freely inside of me
and it is my cheek to your cheek
that placed me back on the mountain
as I serve . . .
the justice, the hope, a lot of love
just like I get when I am in order
when I stay on the mountain
as I set my cheek to your cheek
I am rescued

Wanda C. Outlaw

untitled

some days i wonder about you
and all i would've said if only i knew
I love you and you're my best friend
even when you're gone it won't end

but this i never got to say . . .
and now it's too late because you've gone away
some people wonder how i could miss you still
but my heart has an empty spot that just won't fill

a puppy is running so fast
it seems his energy will always last
i see this as i close my eyes
this memory, unlike you, never dies

sometime i wonder if the pain will ever cease
and if my heart will ever somehow find peace
maybe it's selfish of me to want you near
but every thought of you brings a new tear

if i had known that was to be your last day
i would've held you tighter before you went on your way
but there are memories of you that can never disappear
and they help me to know you are near

Heather Peace

Steadfast Love

In celebration of Keith and Mavis Rau's 50th wedding anniversary
As the years go by, their gate grows slower,
The time to complete a task
Grows longer;
But love that grows in sincere resolve
Gets deeper, more fixed
With passing time.

The excitement of seeing each other
Is not as bold as it used to be,
But the comfort of being together
Is greater than the sweetest love story
Ever told.

In quietness they affirm each other
With little love offerings,
Often without a touch, without a word,
But given with a kind affection
That transcends young love.

It is not in intensity
That love ultimately finds its place,
But in the steady, enduring flow
Of affectionate care each for the other.

Clifford Van Sickle

His Name Is Vietnam

He can sit at a typewriter
while his enemies reduce his wife and boy
to gobbets of flesh
wallowing in pools of blood on his doorstep.
He can sit in a jail cell,
lean his forehead on its blood-stamped walls,
reach out to the departing cries of beaten souls,
and recite the names
of each comrade who was missing
at least half of his body,
at least three halves of his hope,
at least two mothers, three grandmothers,
and 40 little cousins.
He is a man who knows how to shed his future,
who knows how to shed his tears,
how to shed his blood and shed his life.
He is a man who wants to free his people,
but war has told him that
freedom is not free.

Helene Tuong Vy Nguyen

American Millennium

1000: Only one church, Earth is "flatten,"
    The Pope in Rome, the tongue Latin.
    The Ages were Dark, very Medieval;
    American's not known as a port of call.

1500: Columbus sails the big ocean blue,
    Earth is round, this much is true.
    Luther would soon swing a hammer—
    Soon America Europeans would clamor!

1750: A restless colony in a New Land
    Against a mighty nation took its stand.
    Soon upon Freedom, Liberty, and Justice
    Great value America would place.

1900: After a mighty Civil War
    America would soon march to the fore!
    Inventions and advances to boggle the mind—
    The United States of America—one of a kind!

2000: Standing upon the threshold of time,
    A nation seeks peace and a rhyme.
    Merging of culture, mixing of race—
    And power to explore the great outer space.

John L. Hoh Jr.

My Best Friend

I remember . . .
Swinging on the birch trees,
Having Noxzema put on my skinned knees.

Catching butterflies in a homemade net,
Watching Lawrence Welk every Saturday night on the TV set.

Fishing trips where laughter abound,
Keeping a stray kitten that we found.

Taking summer trips to a South Carolina beach,
Being told that nothing in life was out of my reach.

Putting lightning bugs in a mason jar,
Going for a spin in my new car.

Being tucked in bed and taking time to pray,
Getting a helping hand during a hospital stay.

So many life memories I have on my list—
They're not all written here, many have been missed.

Our ability to love sets us apart—
We keep our fondest memories locked up tight in our hearts.

A variety of memories, ever happy and glad—
I have of my best friend; I call him my Dad.

Janet Marie Sharp

The Reason I Dance

My heels bleed, like cherry juice
Spilling from a burnt pie crust.
Drops tickle my chin before they meet
The back of my damp hand,
My brow crying hot tears of sweat,
Gluing cotton/polyester to my back.
Exasperated muscles throb and mutiny,
Yielding to movement like old taffy.
The waterfall enclosed in white ceramic
Washes away all the disease and rust,
Letting the fatigue slip off my shoulders,
Dragging it down the drain.
Snuggled neatly between the sheets
Like a baloney sandwich, sleep
Is no stranger, but finds me instantly.
Things slow down for several minutes
Before I am awakened by the next morning.
I stumble out of bed like a newborn giraffe,
And then I dance again.

Liz Pimentel

In-Between

My life with manic depression
It's in-between the highs and low
That makes me cry and ask why.

At times I dance and sing,
So full of life, the world is mine!
I'm free to be me to do all I am able (and more).

I know [we all know] it's tainted though,
For from the highs, there come the lows.
The real sting—to see all I could have
Snatched away with such force, to tumble so far, so fast.

I had it all, not for long, it was a taste, a tease
Of what could be me, my head spins.
Just who am I meant to be?

At times instead of everything I crave, nothing.
I pray to die before I wake,
I wish the sun were rain.
Mere breath wears me, if only I could melt away.

Strangely it's the in-between where I suffer most,
Having experienced what could truly be my life,
Fearing the impending depths of despair, I'm waiting.
Which way will the wind blow?

Paige Ellen Jones

And Now I See

To my special friend who has seen the Holy Spirit too
As a man thinketh, so shall he be.
As it was written, soon we will come to see.
Behind the veil of mystery
that covers only truth and divinity.

Take me to the rivers of reflection.
I look into my heart. I look inside my soul.
I promised I would return
to the rivers of reflection.

I look into the stream.
My reflection is not my own.
My heart sings of too much love.
My face is not my own.

There is a calmness taking over.
So I see now . . . it is you, I said to this mirage.
I took my focus off this faint reflection
to see this fish beneath the surface.

I leaned back against this tree
finding myself in complete harmony.
Reflecting off the rivers of reflection
was the Son I had come to see.

William Michael Robinson

Dreams

Upon the threshold of reality
I step into the blinding light
Nothing is true here and nothing imagined
Hope does not reign there
Nor Heaven, Nor Hell
Rain does not linger, Nor mirrors show reflection
Sweet are the flowers
and dim is the sea
While here it is all negated
Here nothing may be seen
the same as one moment before
Here oceans roar, and time clicks on
But none, not time nor tide
None, not evil, nor love
Stands same assured on foot
All is neither darkness, nor light
In this selfsame world I wish to exist, and run to
All in the light of the first dawn
With the hour awakened, and thrust into the light

Laura Levenhagen

True Love

Sadly, I feared the day would never come.
But there I stood heart pounding and my body numb.

Suddenly, I hear a piano making a beautiful sound.
I take a deep breath, as the pressure begins to mound.

My stepfather gently takes my arm to lead me to the door.
This is the moment I've been waiting my whole life for.

The doors open and we begin to walk down the aisle.
Each step I take seeming more like a mile.

I gaze upon the faces of all the people most dear to me.
Then finally I'm looking into the eyes of my husband to be.

We're about to begin our new life together.
Making new memories that will last forever.

We pledged our faith and love in the presence of God.
Our family, and friends.
These feelings, we promised, never to stretch, break or bend.

After our vows I felt slightly dazed.
As I cried, my new husband sang to me the song "Amazed."

We'll always remember that day in the blistery July sun,
When our two hearts were forever united as one.

Brandee Shellhase

Be Silent and Listen

To all who have cancer and are afraid like I was
Lord, I cannot hear your voice; my mind is filled with thought,
How can I learn what you want me to do, the things that I ought?
I spend my time in prayer, asking for your love and healing,
Yet I do not allow you to come in, my head is reeling!

My body is frail, and now I have cancer.
I look to you, My God, for an answer.
Be silent, and listen, and my voice will be heard,
I may be in thought, but not in word.

Sit quietly, with a lit candle a flicker.
As soon as you are quiet, it will be quicker.
For you have done nothing but did all the talking,
I searched for a silent moment in you, as I was stalking.

But, My Lord! *No! No more words will do.*
As your Father in Heaven, I know all about you.
Now sit and listen, and maybe you will hear
An answer to your prayers, and ease your fear.

The moral of this prayer, is that we are too busy,
To do the right thing to hear God, it is so easy.
I will stop talking now, and put down my pen.
And listen, listen, and let the Lord in.

Paul Michael Phelan

I Saw an Angel

I saw an angel, in a long, white, flowing gown.
Her hair was blond and long.
There was a symphony in the stars surrounding her,
humming a beautiful song.

Her wings were open and flowed softly through the clouded air.
Her eyes were shiny, loving, and warm with her glowing stare.

I did not feel frightened, calmness and contentment to me she did send.
For this angel, she, had once been my life long friend.

She talked to me, and said everything is all right.
You will be okay, your future, can still be bright.

I'm happier than ever where I'm at, I have at last peace.
So please don't cry for me, and let your worries cease.

I smiled and nodded, and a feeling of sadness,
Yet warm relief was felt so keen
Some things have to be believed, to be seen!

Sherry Poisson

Just Another Day

To a dear friend—may she make the right choices
As the sun sets each night
You think about the day gone by
Did you live it to the fullest
Or was this day another lie

Did you stop to enjoy its beauty
And all that it had to give
Or was it just another day
Where you missed the chance to live

Did you stop to smell the flowers
Touched by fresh morning dew
Did you feel the sun caress your face
From a sky that's, oh, so blue

Or was your day filled with dark clouds
With an impending storm that won't go away
If so, my friend, you must remember
After the storm comes the bright sunny day

Don't let your heart be discouraged
In whatever you may choose to do
For only you can make the choices
to make all your dreams come true

Piera Fico

A Memo from My Heart

Dedicated to Aaron S. Curtis—my special someone
I don't know how else to tell you,
'Cause the words get in the way.
Every single chance I get
I can never say what I want to say.

I'd like to tell you face to face
And say the words so clear.
But every time I look in your eyes,
My heart is filled with fear.

I think about it night and day
And it's driving me insane.
I long to say these words to you,
Though you might not feel the same.

You won't be here for much too long
And I know we'll be apart.
So take these words I'll say to you,
They're coming straight from my heart.

While you are far away from me
Know that I'll always be thinking of you.
And before you leave I want to say
That baby . . . I love you.

Jennifer B. Loanzon

The Birds

God gave the birds the power to fly,
To fly so high in the sky,
To spread their wings among the trees
In summer sun and winter breeze,
Through valleys, plains and distant lands.
The birds do fly without a plan.

Agnes Roberts

Smoker's Life

The day was warm
The air was right
And I couldn't have felt higher
Oh, the mistakes I've made
To bring myself back would be to destroy myself
Once again

Christian Bixler

I Am

To those who can't wash away the dirtiness or the memories
I am a scared little girl on the inside
I hear the screams echoing from within
I see the nightmares every time I sleep
I feel the pain flowing too deep to forget
I am a scared little girl on the inside

I am a woman who is misunderstood
I hear the disgust in your tone
I see the way you judge me
I feel the awkwardness you have around me
I am a woman who is misunderstood

I am a mother too afraid to tell it
I hear my child's questions, still years away
I see the curiosity of youth in her eyes
I feel the need to hide her from your shadows
I am a mother too afraid to tell it

I am growing stronger in spite of you
I am learning to trust again
I am dreaming of better times
I am living without your sickness around me
I am, I am a child, a woman, a mother, I am me

Pamela Riedy

My True Love

You are my first true love,
My dream come true.

Right then I knew I loved you.

Your beauty wasn't only on the outside but within.

When I talked to you,
It was hard to keep my feelings inside.

Your lips are soft and beautiful,
Your smile brightened my day.

You are the love of my life,
I knew I couldn't let you get away.

Your personality so beautiful,

I couldn't help but dream about you.

I loved you then
And even more now.

Then one day,
My dream of holding you came true.

In my bed I lay
Thinking, remembering
That one day, that beautiful day.

Jennifer Kristen Loeffler

Ryan

Two tormented souls, as they watch his life's breath
Fade away and to know that it's final; it's death.
Christian was only six weeks old, Lord; they ask, "Why?"
If he were with them now, he'd be the apple of their eye.
Then God blessed two little girls and sent them their way
Hard times came, trials; help them, Lord, to overcome I pray.
Oh, no, Lord, not again, not another mouth to feed.
Their little girls, Lord, what about what they need?
So, she picked up the phone on that dreadful day.
An appointment was all set, nothing more to say.
As fate would have it, they were late by twenty.
The doctor was gone and they had to rethink plenty.
Distressed, longing for joy; then an audible voice said
"If you'll keep your child, I'll send you another baby boy."
She actually heard from God . . . there was no distortion
She was completely awake, there would be no abortion.
And when the time came, God kept his word
As the angels sweetly sang, they strummed each cord.
God's wonderful plan kept this mother's heart from dying.
Now, how truly thankful they are for their son, Ryan!

Martha Mass

Golden

My Grandmother's hands were ringed with gold
And stones of every hue,
White like milk and soft like breath,
Delicate and delightful to the view.

A manicure every Monday,
the nails always perfectly lacquered,
But never a dish she washed nor ever a child she hugged,
And that was all that mattered.

I looked down at my mother's hands,
Rough and scratched with love,
With kisses and squeals and thorns and scrapes—
From healing when push had come to shove.

As a child I wished for hands like Mamma had,
But then I thought about my mother's
And realized I'd much rather live with my hands
Then keep them for display like so many others.

Well now I'm grown and as I watch my child play,
I hope when she looks back that it won't be forgotten,
How worn and used her mother's hands were
From the great love she had for those she had begotten.

Caeli Elizabeth Christianson

Strain in My Brain

Stress and strain living in my brain,
Coming on like a freight train;
The smoke of steel and all the wheels,
Clouds of pain moving in my veins,
Directing all my shame that moves down the tracks,
Just to attack my senses that remain
Full of steam coming straight at me
Metal emotion coming as fast as it can.
One more town to see my head,
One more face to leave no trace.
Over the clouds and out of the still smoke,
The freight and strains moving in my brain,
Shaking the wheels moving down the track,
Into the station
of the imagination,
I see me standing there waiting
For the trip into the still smoke of wheels.
Metal emotion, shaking my brain
& the strain in my veins,
Directing my steam like the freight that stress my,
Train of movement that you see in my head,
Tracking down the way of
direction unknown.

D. L. Walker

The Lady of the Rainbow Light

I am the lady of the rainbow light to all nations that believe.
I know not from whence I come, it is a mystery,
Every ear must listen,
Every eye must see,
That we must save the children and all humanity.
You know, you have the key,
Mankind need to stop the hating,
Hurting and the destroying of each other,
And try to make life better for all,
My family, my friends, my foes and anyone that I did not call.

I'm composed of every element from space and every sphere,
For billions of light years I've been here.

Life is just a sparkle in the sand,
A line imbedded in your hand,
You pass this way, just once so wise men say,
But, I have passed this way a million times and a day.

I have traveled in paces through a million places,
Recalling a trillion faces,
Seeing all the plight,
Children crying in the night to the lady of the rainbow light.

Sue Bivins

December Day

The cold snow glistens as the sun
Creates a wonderland of fun,
And children hurry up the hill,
With sleds behind and voices shrill.
Then down they come on winter's sleigh,
Content that they may play all day.

Suddenly a sled goes awry!
Like snow angels the children fly
Through the sky and over the hills,
As I laugh with joy to see their thrills.

All is well, and off they go
To win their races forged in snow.
Soft wet mittens touch cold pink faces
As they imagine warmer places.

To those homes, they trudge along,
Singing together a playful song,
But return they will in a while
For one more race down the icy aisle.

As the moon shines they fall into warm beds;
May pleasant dreams fill their precious heads.

Mary Cecilia Erickson

Love

I love you much, you are my boy,
being with you brings me joy.
I love it when you hug me tight,
so I'll kiss you through the night.

We've been together so very long,
I love the way you wrote our song.
I want to be in your embrace,
won't rush too fast, we'll keep our pace.

I love you more than anyone can,
someday I hope that we can make plans.
But for now, I hope nothing will change,
even though they think I'm deranged.

I want to love you even more,
that would truly make my heart soar.
Your love is pure, and that brings bliss,
you're so kind and thoughtful when we kiss.

You are this way, though I know you're not real,
and this envelope soon will be sealed.
I am writing this poem, to my guy as it seems,
he doesn't exist, but he's there in my dreams.

Erika Ingram

Our Angel of Motherhood

To my beautiful mother

You were our angel; we thought you hung
The silver stars and lit the golden sun.
No problem too large, nor hurt too small
With loving care you would mend them all.
You diapered ten bottoms and nurtured us all
Taught us to walk and hugged when we'd fall.
There was always enough food for us, no doubt
But many were the days you went without.
You warmed our home, you made our beds
And you tucked in ten little sleepy heads.
You taught us to love God, which lit up our souls
You taught us values and to achieve our goals.
You made clothes, doll clothes, drapes in our home
Ice cream and shoveled sand for a beach of our own.
Whether dancing, singing, gymnastics or football
You made our costumes and attended them all.
You gave us comfort whenever we were sad
And you defended us when times were bad.
You were so brave and, of course, we knew
We would all be safe, because we had you.

     Linda D. Kilgore

As I Look into My Inner Soul

What does it tell me to say and do?
Only God will let me know
Freedom to explore my deep emotions
And bring to surface is not any easy task

Have you been chosen as my guide?
Is reason due to your strength and patience?
And, will your support make my journey easier?

There lies only honesty through this search
What is locked inside can only bring happiness
Remembering the words that will be spoken
Comes from the reflection of my thoughts

This has been a road less traveled, one many would not take
Yet, your spirit represents safety
In being vulnerable to my feelings

Despite the unknown, with you by my side
I vow to gather strength
To help release these unspoken words
The journey through this new world
Will bring treasures for you and for me
As I look into my inner soul

     Nora DeJesus

Heart of Gold

There is someone that I hold dear.
I'm happy to say
That she's always near.

I know that this is not an obsession.
I've been lost in love before,
And I've learned my lesson.

It's best to take your time to decide,
Unless you're ready for
Your worlds to collide.

That's why when there's friendship,
With trust, honor, and love,
You know . . .
the ones that start rising above.

A friendship
That starts to take on a new meaning,
That fills your heart with this feeling
Of love, long existing, but never been told,
It's there, all around you, it never grows old.
She's the one that you long for,
For she IS that heart of gold.

     Mike Manzi

To Be

What silence we find in the break of shore
As our minds flow softly to the crest
A never-ending life where there is no beginning
No sight of ending . . .

As the breeze breaks with spray upon my face
the fragrance of life is in the air
finding it with never ending pursuit
alas, the race for life has begun once again . . .

Seeing but only with feeling
the touch of which we see
we find this far from reach within the dusk of life . . .

It seems that more and more, the endings that
are beginnings . . . only to find in the worst
of times, something we couldn't see . . .

Join with the worst of points
the light you find within the end . . .
Hidden but now alive . . .
The moments of yesterday that
were all worth while . . .

     Johnie William Vereen III

Leaving

Those beautiful eyes that drive me mad
Your smiling face I need to see so bad
They came to me for this short time
to let them go felt like a crime

Your presence here made my house a home
my only wish now: for us never to roam
to be together and never to part
A wonderful life, a fresh new start

Our time together, I cannot define
here, then gone, but you'll always be mine
When we are together, I stand so tall
it lasted forever and no time at all

Although I know for now we must part
we're always together here within my heart
after the pain and the tears that flow
our love will shine and bring a new glow

So happy thoughts my sweet, sweet love
remember our good times, my precious dove
they'll come again to brighten our days
and we'll be together then for always

     Terry J. Sandgathe

My Love for You

My love for you will never die.
And to my love, I shall not lie,
About the way I feel each day;
The pain I feel when you're away.

I need to have you in my life;
Not just as friends, but as your wife.
It may not happen when we thought,
But it doesn't matter, 'cause my heart you've caught.

I'm yours forever, if you'll have me;
To love, to cherish, and having your baby.
Just ask of me and I'll do for you,
Because that's how strong my love is for you.

I love you so much—
Your kisses, your touch;
The love that we make
As sweet as cheesecake.

What do you feel for me?
Tell me now and tell me true;
Because all this poem tells is . . .
My love for you.

     Tamara LaRae Harrington

La Casita

Tio's music comes with pops and crackles
from the speakers on the wall.
It mingles with the heavy scent of pollo sizzling on the stove
and Don Crystal on the breath of the men.

From the kitchen window, it pours onto
the verandah. The guitar's spicy tempo
driven by the women's melodic laughter
warms the cooling evening.
It pools on the porch and swells with
the high-pitched of los ninos and
the deeper tones of maternal correction.

Soon la musica overflows and spills
down the stairs, picking up glissandos
of los perros whining and the rumbling bass
of los sarros arriving, before rolling along
the fence line that embraces the farm.
Even Alex can hear it down by the goats
as it picks up speed and launches in the wind.
It flies over the trees that cover the mountain
and finally comes to rest in the valley below

Jessica C. M. Gonzalez de Sather

Not the Same

If I buy you a car
Will it be all right?
If I give you the world
Will you still haunt my dreams at night?

I want to know,
Where will I go?
How will I know?

Give me your voice, give me your strength.
I'm tired, I'm weary, and I'm all worn out.
Let me scream out and shout that I'll fight it out.

Tell me what to do.
Tell me where to turn,
How to smile,
How to burn,
But never tell me how to learn.

I don't think you know what I've been through.
I'm not some wall you're speaking to.
You think I am, but I'm not.
You're the one who showed me; I'm the one you taught.
And I'm all worn out.

Afton Charlotte Boyd

My Father, My Life

To wake up every morning, to find no one around,
I fall to my knees and they crash into the ground.

Memories of you spin around my mind;
They cause me such pain, because you are far behind.

"Daddy," I just want to yell,
Why did you leave me?
Why did you have to go?
When asked, you should have said no.

All the wonderful times we shared,
All the places that we went,
I never thought this day would come.
That angel . . . Jesus should have never sent.

I will never forget you,
Not your face, nor your smile.
I just wish you could have been here
For more than just a while.

So I guess now all there's left to say is good-bye.
There will always be this empty place in my heart.
I will always love you, Daddy;
Your spirit will never keep us apart.

Olivia Vavica Poota

Why I Went to the Well Each Day

At four p.m and returned after eight p.m.
Each day I wore the same dress
I had worn for the past eight months.
And each day he looked at it like
he was only seeing it for the very first time.

Each day I went to the well to collect water
And each day, with my water drenched face,
He looked at me like I was his royal princess.

Each day I went to the well,
I scrubbed my feet so hard, they bled,
But the price for this pain was worth it.
And each day, with my rugged feet,
I stood before him like a humbled sinner,
Begging for his divine love.

Each day at four p.m.
I stealthily made my way to the well
To receive my daily doze of true, pure love.
And each day at eight p.m.
I smilingly left the lonely well with
the joy of the unsaid words that transpired between him and I.

Milka Marilyn Agbara

The Demons Within

So many things to think about
All rattling around in my mind
I'll never be able to make sense of it all
Wishing I could leave all of the hurt behind

The voices won't be hushed
Maybe it would be better to be dead
It's hard to sleep at night
Franticly trying to quiet the demons in my head

I can't let it all show
A battle's raging deep inside
It's tearing me apart
Just another thing I'm forced to hide

The demons haunt me constantly
Ruining any chance of thought
They are slowly wearing me down
Before I've always been the one who fought

I'm slowly getting weak now
My soul begins to bend
The demons have finally won
My life is coming to an end

Jennifer A. Carver

Three Valley Gap

The grass was so green, the creeks very clear,
there were little walking bridges, all very near.
The flowers were plenty and so many types;
surrounding the grounds were small, tiny lights.

We gazed across the lake, it was just like glass,
as we tried hard to imagine those days long past.
When those pioneers were many who opened the way,
so that we may travel easy on roads that were laid.

When we looked out at the castle tops into the sky,
we saw the reflection of God through our eyes.
As Heaven is beautiful, so is this grand place;
it's a coming together, no matter your race.

The beautiful Bell Gardens, what a sight to see;
it belongs in this place—this Valley of three.
As we stood on our balcony, we didn't speak;
the clouds were so white—nothing was bleak.

Three Valley Lake and the scenic Eagle Pass
will be etched in our memories, as those of the past.
I took many pictures starting right then;
besides being beautiful, we made many friends.

Millie Nelles

Experience

Life is me, love is me,
peace is me, harmony explains me.
Fun and pride, courage and fear.

I am the faith which does not believe in religion,
for my beliefs lie towards the love of a people.
I am the minion that does not serve the master,
for I am a faceless number, yet I own my own soul.
I am the voice that is never heard.
I am the dark in the closet,
as the loneliness battles my strong heart.

I am the thought that speaks aloud.
I am the aorta that was forgotten.
I am the diamond that does not shine.
I am beauty in disguise.

I am a ponderer, I am a wanderer,
I am the horse who roams
the land with only thoughts to guide him.
I am the fish who swims with the school,
yet is alone and defenseless.
I am experience.

Nicholaus Patrick Byrd

Picture Perfect

Not afraid to ever be poor . . .
How does it feel to never need more?

The polished path you walk upon . . .
A picture that shall never be gone.

Where everything's a fairy tale,
Where all the rest but you will fail.

You mirror your beautiful face,
Dress yourself in expensive lace.

Don't bother trying to lie,
Everyone knows you never cry.

Life will never do you wrong,
You'll never need to be strong.

You know others want to walk your way
Wondering when it's their big day.

Would you ever strain . . .
To take away someone else's pain?

Is your picture perfect life the only thing you care for?
And everything else you choose to ignore?

Lori Ann Proskurnia

You Are the One I Chose . . .

Yes, it's true I love you,
Yes, I think of you all day;
True you mean a lot to me,
True I just can't stay away.

But deep down I know
I would be lying if I say,
I can't live without you
That I will die if you go away.

For love is anything but addiction,
It doesn't mean to kill you;
It enters your life, so you learn to care,
It tries to teach you faith, not fear.

So, my friends, you must remember
That love that you need is all around,
That your happiness doesn't depend on one person,
In many little things it can be found.

I want you to know, my love,
That I am strong enough to survive without you,
But if given a choice by God above
I would sure choose to live my life with you.

Kiran Mushtaq Piracha

Just a Number

This is Bhuj (after an earthquake in India on January 26, 2001).
Death has no respect for creed or color
When buried under a dense rubble,
For time has taken its toll
And the world has seen it all.
Once a human, now just a number,
With amorphous identity without recognition.
Ten, twenty, or thirty thousand and one!
Alas! shared pyres.
Should be sharing love.
Was I at the top or at the bottom,
Or does it really matter?
Burning side by side
And on top of each other.
Male, female, rich or poor,
Unfortunate to have any rituals.
Abused and slandered
'Cause of your occult obliteration.
Hoping not be known as a number
Perished in this chaotic jumble!

Pauline Sharma

You Could've Been Mine

Tiny little hands and tiny little feet,
Innocent eyes staring up at me,
Precious face with a sweet little grin,
These are the things you should've been.

Lullabies sung softly in the darkness of your room,
Feeding you breakfast with a tiny silver spoon,
Going for walks in the afternoon sun,
These are the things we should've done.

Birthday parties, days at the park,
Swimming lessons, hide & seek in the dark,
Bicycle riding and scraped-up knees,
These are the things that will never be.

I'll never get to hold you or hear your gentle sigh.
I'll never get to answer when you ask me "why?"
I'll never get to hear your voice crying out for me.
I'll never get to see you because you weren't meant to be.

The world will never know what a blessing you would've been.
No one will ever see the smile that could've been.
And no other soul will feel this pain more than me
Because I was the one that said you couldn't be.

Stephanie Renée Ard

Our Handyman's Retirement

Good-bye, Tom, put your tools away.
The time has come for your retirement day;
We will miss you lots, but don't despair
You leave us knowing, that we always cared.

About you, our little handy gnome,
Who did so much in this old people's home.
You did your job, with such perfection;
But most of all, you loved our affection.

Especially when we pinched your bottom
For this, we will not be forgotten.
But not one time did you complain or wince;
You truly enjoyed, having your bottom pinched.

All joking aside, you will be greatly missed;
But what will we do with the handyman's list?
Leave it and hope for a younger handyman
With a gorgeous body and great looking tan.

Take care, Tom, and have a long life;
Enjoy your retirement with your lovely wife.
You deserve good luck and good health, too.
So, all the best to the both of you.

Janet Fagan

And God Said

Dear world,
I am disheartened by the way you
worship (things) AND forsake thy neighbor.
There are people starving,
there are people dying!
Take time to help a friend in need,
take time to help a stranger.
Love your things, BUT
DON'T worship them, PLEASE!
Human life is precious, I put it here for you.
I gave you the world so that you
could learn—not every wish comes true!
I'm sorry for the hardships,
I'm sorry for the pain.
BUT learn from these and be better,
don't live your life in vain!
I know that (things) can't hurt you,
and sometimes people do!
Try to overcome the bad, and
LET THE GOOD SHINE THROUGH . . .
I love you, GOD
Sarah E. Harter

Death

All I am is poetry, and without it I probably wouldn't be here.
Dead, like you don't exist to the world,
Because your world is dead, like you.
I know you feel like you have no one.
You are like a once vibrant and radiant rose.
You once were so lovely and full of life,
Soon you turned dark.
Like a rose, you went too long without love,
Without a family that cares, without friends.
Alone, cold, ashamed, scared, desperate;
You hate the world with a passion.
Because your mother and father are in it.
Your father beats you, your mother yells at you.
You are too young to think about suicide,
But you think it anyway.
It's only one more scar to add to the collection,
Like the one on your arm, your leg, your head
And the biggest one of all . . . your life.
Dark, unseen, ugly, unloved, misplaced, childish;
I know you feel these feelings,
Because I feel them, too.
Susan Nicole Rogers

I Do Love Thee

The sky is gray, the wind bloweth cold,
Green leaves do sway on tree limbs old;
The earth crieth out, the sky doth weep—
But thou livest, and I do love thee.

Great tomes of knowledge beckon me,
Replete with words of fantasy;
Colossal cogitations nigh—
But thou livest, and I do love thee.

Strong edifices stalwart stand,
Grave structures straddle o'er the land;
Like august hosts they shout on high—
But thou livest, and I do love thee.

The trumpet's brazen lungs resound,
The organ's pipes grand themes propound;
The world they grasp in one fell sound—
But thou livest, and I do love thee.

Thou art the wellspring of all life,
The Earth's own fertile, fruitful wife;
How could it lacking you abide—
But thou livest, and I do love thee.
Jonathan Michael DePeri

Scott

To my son, Scott
As I sit here at my desk,
looking at your pictures through my mess.
I see your coats hanging on the hook,
sometimes I stop and take a second look.
They tell us that you are gone,
and we have to try to go on.
The pain in out hearts is unbearable,
the hurt and loneliness irreparable.
A four-wheeler to ride if you must,
it's not a vehicle that I really trust.
You always took the time to call,
and say "Mom I'm here, don't worry at all."
You left behind family and friends,
who cannot believe that this is the end.
I know we have to go on,
without the son that we've loved for so long.
Because of the love in our hearts,
I know we'll never be far apart.
I'm trying to say Good-bye for now,
I know we'll be together again somehow.
Trish A. Nester

The Impossible Battle

A galloping steed, a knight in full mail.
Hears the cry of the people, an unearthly wail.

Heading the troops, toward that bloodcurdling sound.
The cursed village sits, atop the next mound.

A magical fog, settles around.
The stubborn knights are, still village bound.

In the midst of the village, sit the powerful mages.
They control the fog, and all of its phases.

"Charge!" is the cry, heard throughout the land.
The knights rush forward, swords in hand.

Alas, the knights are no match, for the magic of the mages.
They are slain one by one, the fallen knights create mazes.

One is left standing, the leader of the pack.
His Gift has protected him, he refuses to turn back.

"I'll kill you or die trying," is the knight's last vow.
He's hit, and falls, his last thought is How?

The rain pours down, it comes in waves.
This once peaceful village, now serves as many men's graves.
Katie Solberg

Not to Fear

I've become to wonder about a feeling,
I've done some thinking about this sense of healing.
Many get worried and in a fright,
To me it's as simple as saying good night.
It shouldn't be complicated or difficult to bear,
For we know not the time, nor place;
Know not when, nor where.
In this darkness in the night,
It's in my mind, in my sight.
It's reality at the fore,
Forever in my presence knocking at my door.
Till darkness is all I see custom delivered just for me,
The time has come, the time is now.
Darkness is here to show me how.
The lesson was easily taught,
It's an experience readily sought.
Now, I know; now, I've seen.
Now, it's time for the blade to gleam.
Through the softness, through the mesh,
Through the thickness, through the flesh;
Darkness now is here.
Now, I'm not, do you fear?
Heather J. Starr

On the Streets of New York

Screamingly yellow tape
whipped in the wind,
back and forth, snakelike
with black-lettered tongue
"Caution"-ed
biting punishment
to any who dare
break the swelling crowd.
"It looked like someone threw a laundry bag out the window."

The police and paramedics
worked hard to clean the scene.
"Twenty Stories?"

The sunlight found
what the building shadows
tried to hide.
"I can't see, watch out!"

An uncooperative wind
tugged off the red sheet,
showing all
what we're made of.

Jeremy M. Manjorin

Doors

There once was a stranger
knocking on my mailbox door,
at first offering nothing more
than gentle words of friendship,
a shoulder to cry on,
an ear to unload my thoughts.
Then came a friend of mine,
knocking at my heart's door.
I was hesitant and scared, asking, will he hurt me?
Should I open that door?
Or keep my heart locked up?
Soon came offerings of artwork and oh, so sensuous poetry,
absorbing through the steel walls
of the bolted door to my heart.
So when the love of my life knocked ever so sweetly
at the door to my heart,
hesitating not for an instant, without even a second thought,
I gently slipped the key under that steel-bolted door,
a slight turn of the key, and the gentle touch of his kiss,
the door to my heart slowly fell open,
like the blooming of a rosebud
into a magnificently beautiful rose.

Stephanie Anne Poulton

My Purpose in Life

What's my purpose in life?

Making lots of money?
OK! That sounds good, but it doesn't
last forever.
Then, what?

Being strong and healthy?
OK! That sounds good, but it doesn't
last forever.
Then, what?

Having lots of good friends?
OK! That sounds good, but it doesn't
last forever.
Then, what?

Helping out those people who are in need?
OK! That sounds good, but it doesn't
last forever.
Then, what?

Preaching the gospel?
Yes! That sounds excellent, because it
lasts forever!

Bo Young Chung

A Glance at Who

Occasionally, glancing to the left of me
then to the right of myself,
perhaps even below, above, or behind
may help me find where I am,
but it's going to take more than a glance
to find out who. . . .

And so you've seen
what I do with my hands,
and you've observed first hand
the methods I use to survive.
And maybe you've even heard words
come out my mouth that weren't mine;
still . . . I would suggest
before you dare to guess
concernin' who, what, or why, just ask.

'Cause you won't see me
glancin' to the left or right of myself.
Not below and, though I may glance behind,
I'm lookin' up, within, I look ahead.
Your turn.

Vernon "Jo'El" Whitehead

Twinkle, Twinkle Little Star (A New Version)

How I wonder what you are
I see you in my thoughts, I do
And I wonder why it is, don't you
I saw a shooting star and wished and wished
That you would arrive here and rescue me
My heart is safe in your care

My mind is free, when I think of you
Come and take me away
Away to a place of make believe

Twinkle, Twinkle Little Star . . .
How I wonder where you are
When will I see your bright, starry face
That sparkle of a twinkle I did wish
Would grant my one wish this eve
So that I may sleep sound till day

You shine each day and each night
In my mind and in my heart
Please, grant my wish
For this will be the last I ask of thee

Kristin A. Vaast

Admiring Star

The stars in the sky
Light it up so beautiful and bright
That you would never be lost
Even in the middle of the night

They will guide you on your path
And be your guardian on your shoulder
Fill you up with confidence and security
That can't even be broken by a boulder

You just can't help but to admire them
Even though there are so many at rest
But there is always that one
That is always better than the best

And that one is the one
That makes you feel the way you do
And that's when you know
That that star was meant for you

The point that I'm getting at
Is that star represents you
And I'm the one doing the admiring
Wondering, if you're looking down, doing it too

Shawn Derek Hicks

One Dozen of Scented Silk Roses

One dozen of scented silk roses
for your many intriguing poses.
Long-stemmed and so picturesque;
such style and elegance, I must confess.

The fragrance, guaranteed to attract.
Majestic brilliance, a known fact.
Inspiration of love and that of romance;
long walks and a memorable slow dance.

Like one dozen of scented silk roses, I say
eternal feelings with a purpose, I truly pray.
Long lasting, the emotion shall never die.
To covet its value, I will always try.

A longing quest, to one day be together;
takes unity to survive life's stormy weather.
The boat's sinking, but water I continue to bail;
for this longing quest, I would hate to fail.

Like one dozen of scented silk roses
arranged so beautifully together,
we too, my sweet, will last forever and ever!

Wilson L. Williams

Heart Whisperings

Daylight breaks with a flaming, red sun;
Mountains and clouds as a backdrop looking like one.

Colorful birds are chirping their sweet, melodious songs,
Cormorants diving for fish all day long.

Cars and bikes cram the tight city streets,
Looking for a parking spot you only find defeat.

Ladies wrapped in kimonos shuffling here and there,
Looking so small and dainty with their skin so purely fair.

Two years in Japan is the place I have come
To teach the school children and to have fun.

Shhh! I hear soft whispers, but from where do they come?
My heart is awakened, my pulse rises some.

Kansas, sweet Kansas, I now hear the words clear;
Kansas is what my heart holds so dear.

My home, family, and friends all await for me there;
Fields of sunflowers and wheat gently sway through the fresh air.

Kansas, sweet Kansas, is calling to me.
Kansas is where my heart longs to be.

Cynthia Louise Schuck

The Pillow

If I seal my eyes snuggly
And take in the scent of the flower;
I feel no longer lonely,
But in your presence, your power.

Your image; incredible, luminous,
As if you were next to me.
Your eyes leave me enchanted and curious;
So expressive, brightly they beam.

I stretch to grasp your hand,
You lunge to obtain mine, too.
Like a plane coming into land,
But brush, they never do.

The image is just a dream,
The aroma of you a reminder;
It rose from a pillow it seems,
I surrender myself to its power.

Whenever you aren't around,
And not seeing you is a fact;
I secure my eyes and lay my head,
So the scent will take me back.

Brandon David Honza

Almost Like Nod

Inspired by the song "Morning's Dawn"
I hear a waterfall in this dreamland paradise,
the ocean and birds are also quite nice.
It is sunny and cool in this dream of mine,
the water clear as crystal, oh, divine.
Angels are up in their homes made of clouds,
playing their beautiful harp music aloud.
I'm not the only one in this dream of mine,
mumblings of other people are in the background, behind.
In this world I fly like a feather,
to where Winken, Blinken, and Nod and I stand together.
High in the clouds I float in their boat,
surrounded by a dazzling, starry watered moat.
We're having such fun when the moon says to us,
"Sorry my friends, it's now time to hush.
For down on the Earth the children all sleep,
so please, do not make but a peep."
Saying our good-byes I heave a great sigh,
then we're caught by the wind, and away we all fly.
Suddenly this vision of mine is gone!
Then I wake up in the Morning's Dawn.

Morgan Canclini

My Friend Has a Garden

My dear friend has a garden
that is really neat to see,
plants grow there by the dozens
there are plants by every tree.

There is a squash, the biggest I've seen
and her beets are yellow gold,
the herbs peek out around the tank
at the strawberries bright and bold.

It is like a magic journey
when she takes you for a stride,
through and around the growing plants
while they just stretch with pride.

The cucumbers are long, lean and green
the peppers match their shade,
The potatoes play peek-a-boo
with the sweetest radishes ever made.

So if your heart needs an extra pat
to make life seem more worthwhile,
a stroll through my friends garden
will help your heart to smile.

Marilynn Jean Van Well

Endless Search

Erectly standing on the edgy cliff,
winds blowing on angelic face,
will God hear my desirous cries,
for I stand alone against the world

There is nothing I want,
but there is something I lack,
what emptiness overshadow within

Like a rock without emotion
my tears washed all feeling
only a void encapsulates
and abyss everywhere

Suddenly, a light so bright
warms my heart in the deathly cold
of winter
where shall I move
only the enduring clock will tell

Lonely walking
unexpectedly seeking
then upon great insight
overflowing power and comfort dwells in my heart

Jimmy Thung Nguyen

Relish the Beauty

The most beautiful thing in life is different things to all people,
Some love the sunrise over the ocean with the reflection
On the smooth waters and think,
If only life could be calm, and the beauty stay,
It would be perfect, but there is always the storms
That turn the waters into crashing waves with the white peaks,
The dark rolling clouds that mask the sun,
The flashing of lightning, the roar of thunder,
It makes your mind numb at the power of God,
Then all of a sudden you see a ray of light,
It sneaks through a break in the clouds,
Lines the hole with silver and gold,
The ray beams down the smooth waters, and all is calm again.
Other people may think a thing of beauty
Is a majestic tree in the mist of a forest, reaching for the sun,
Only to find the lightning in the storm.
A rose the perfect flower has thorns is beauty.
Every day has beauty. God gives us these days as a gift.
If you want to brood about the darkness, that is your gift.
If you want to relish the beauty,
No matter how large or how small, that is your gift.

Yvette Reynolds

Endless Heartbreak

I've been holding on to you so long,
I've done all I can to hold on.
But every day we grow farther apart,
Believe me, my words come from the heart.

You keep saying "It's over."
But I'm not ready to let go.
All the things I've done to make this work,
Mean nothing right now.

My grasp is slipping from your hand,
The tears are streaming down.
You can't bare to say "good-bye,"
So you close the door.

Angry and sad at the same time,
My heart sinks to the ground.
I feel so lonely and afraid,
I just can't get myself to accept that you're gone.

My breath is short,
My heart skips a beat.
One last vision of you flashes before my eyes,
And my heart stops.

Britney Dawn Biethman

Untitled

I awake up in heat
every day walking in a burning fire of
flames.

Can't walk into the water because that's
not the easy way out.

My love wanting to be
Stuck in a place . . .

Are you a friend or a foe?

No one knows.

I'm left alone to be

Can't make moves because too many obstacles
are in the way.

Can't break free.

Trying to get from behind these walls and
yet, I make things worse.

They claim to be purgers and only nothing is
being done.

Alexis Outlaw

Sunlight and Shadows

Everything in life assumes color rather fast
And just as quick, in a surge, it will become past
The lessons it teaches sometimes come slow
While voices and memories stay behind so one can always know
That feelings are unique and change with the day
For if everything stayed monotonous
Love would not teach its lessons today

One discovered change in the death of his mother
And strength when he played football with his younger brother
Isolation when his one and only true love left
And sorrow when he realized there is no one else
Fortitude as he received a ride with his father piggyback
And feeling energetic after them long kindergarten naps
Invincibility after the party at senior graduation
And guilt when indulging in the night's sweet temptations
Joy when he saw his child pull up on the corner of a table to stand
And loneliness when he watched him leave home finally a man

Everything in life assumes color rather fast
And as love settles realize each moment
Before love of itself also becomes past

Dwight Anthony Walker

The Mask of Truth

We all must wear a mask sometimes,
We do not know when, or how, or why,
But, these masks, they only make us cry,
Yet, no one sees, for they hide our eyes.

We have masks for pleasure, and for pain,
There are some for loss, and some for gain.
But, the masks don't help, they only strain,
They hide the truth that we've lost the game.

I have many different masks, myself,
Though they're detrimental to my health.
The things I feel, you have never felt
So I use my masks with panthers' stealth.

Oh! But will there ever come a day
When we all may throw our masks away?
Hear what others feel the need to say
Are our masks glued forever, to stay?

I wonder, when will it be the last,
Time I have to wear a dreadful mask?
When can we all put away the past
And make our love like His, ever last?

Cecilia Kay Pinion

Why

I don't understand why you chose to leave this place.
Your hurt and pain wouldn't have been disregarded.
You were well surrounded by gauzy lace.
I do regret how our friendship was parted.

If only I could go back, so much I would change.
I loved you more than any words can say.
To think you're unreachable is so strange.
I just don't know why you thought you couldn't stay.

I'll miss you forever because you were one unique soul.
I see your eyes and face every time I wonder "why?"
Now in my life I feel a large hole.
I can't help but to think of you and cry.

The great lesson here is only life.
Live, Learn, Love, Die.
I can tell you one thing, I'm glad I never picked up the knife.
If you die for yourself then your life only seems a lie.

For you I will always mourn.
An awakening is to be expected.
Your memory I will not be shorn.
I may not understand but I will learn to accept it.

Katherine Alicia Tillotson

Silence

On mean streets, a young man dies;
Hear, the silence
A battered woman in the hush of night cries;
Hear, the silence
A hungry child weeps, a city sleeps;
Hear, the violent, pleading, negligent sounds of silence

Poor men dreams while rich men scheme;
Hear, the silence
Workers can't cope, the homeless hope;
Hear, the silence
Students can't read, pushers breed;
Listen to the ambivalent, regressive, relative sounds of silence

Cancer, multiple sclerosis, Alzheimer's, AIDS;
Guns, violence, deferred hope, rage;
Abortions, drugs, teenage pregnancies, assisted suicides;
Aggression, oppression, transgression, overt genocide;
Wars, terrorism, hunger, apathy;
Division, corruption, exploitation, poverty;
Commercialized, diversified, monopolized, vain;
I hear the deafening silence, I can feel the pain.

Johnny L. Gooden Jr.

Oh, That Noise!

Is there nowhere I am safe?
Is there nowhere safe to hide?
Where on this Earth, in this city, my home
Can I go to get away from that noise?

It comes, constant as the sun and moon
Shattering the night, rattling 'round my head.
That sound, incessant sound, stopping to rest
Then, buzzing bee-like in my ears.

You come in the morning, during rest.
In the daytime, when I am not at home.
You interrupt the evening and my quick dinner.
While I relax with my poetry, you enter!

Are you evil or good, necessary to quality of life?
Why is it when you arrive I shutter with disgust,
Feel the tension in the nape of my neck and the
Pounding in my head and ringing in my ears?

Wicked instrument of electrical technology;
Dreaded intrusive vehicle of noise and clamor.
Surely you were meant for good when came the vision,
Now, telephone, yes, again, you ring and ring and ring!

Joyce L. Kaestner

Our Soldiers

For all who serve
Our soldiers left to fight a war,

It's really hard to tell what for.
The family's tears and hearts are pained,

Will there ever be some peace again.
To the husband boy did he work hard,
The son who last year mowed the yard,
With our mother gone our hearts are sad,
My brother and sister and yes my dad.
It's hard to sit and wait for the news,
We keep on praying it's the least we can do.
Packages and letters are mailed to you,
knowing you'll get them it's the best we can do.
If war should come this you should know,
to all our soldiers we love you so.
Peace is what you tried to defend,
You did it with pride until the end.
Once the war's over then you can come home,
We hope not far you have to roam.
It's been such a long time since we saw your face,
Our soldiers are home again healthy and safe.

Fay Henderson Dean

Wilted Egos

Wilted egos abound.
Durable as dried parchment.
Malleable as clay,
but transparent as glass.

Hearing echoes from within,
it moves out to touch a face
to prove its case,
carefully not divulging
its empty space,
whilst silently protecting its fragile side,
from who it must hide.
Move aside morality, ego must survive
if not to please, most surely to tease!

Anxious for power it ignores what's lower,
sighting that lofty tower.

With internal armor burning with ardor
it exposes a fiery shield for all to see . . .
yet to wilt like a sunburst flower
confronted by another power
greater than he.

Thomas Edghill

So in Love . . .

I am so in love with you, this feeling deep inside.
I am so in love with you, a feeling I can't hide.
I am so in love with you, I just want you to see.
I am so in love with you, your the only one for me.

When I fell in love with you, it was meant to be.
When I fell in love with you, I never felt so free.
When I fell in love with you, I knew you were the one.
When I fell in love with you, I knew the looking was done.

Now that I'm so in love with you, I fear the very worst.
Now that I'm so in love with you, I always put you first.
Now that I'm so in love with you, I want you to know.
Now that I'm so in love with you, I'll never let you go.

We are oh, so meant to be, nothing will stand in our way.
We are oh, so meant to be, my love will never sway.
We are oh, so meant to be, we will make it to the end.
We are oh, so meant to be, not just a lover, but a friend.

Don't forget I love you, no matter where you go.
Don't forget I love you, I know it has to show.
Don't forget I love you, and would give the world to you.
Don't forget I love you, no matter what you do!

Schaloe K. Comyns

Cloud

I drift from place to place,
God forgot to allocate me a fixed space.
He set me free, said, go . . . travel the world over.
May you stop in your path never.

The farmers, I delight
When I'm black, laden, and heavy.
They make merry, rejoice,
When I burst my offerings on them, a part of my duty.

The desert waits for me to kiss it,
Even if it's just a passing kiss.
My absence is missed; I'm even worshipped
By all the thirstees devoted.

When I'm light and fluffy,
I look very pretty.
Often, lovers delight in seeing me,
As they sit hand in hand beneath a tree.

If you haven't guessed,
By now my identity,
Just look up at the sky,
And you'll see me as I pass by. . . .

Miraz Vazifdar

Even the Deer

The glistening pond wakes the forest
to the bitter cold morn.
All of the creatures of the nighttime
shadows open their eyes to Winter
being born from Autumn. All is calm, all is peaceful.

The deer struts randomly through the frozen
diamonds to take a sip of the crystallized brook
not yet completely hardened by the cold.
It stands their in awe of the glamorous sunrise, then drinks.
Even the animals give due respect to their creator.

And as for us, do we truly have appreciation
of these awesome wonders?
Do we give gratitude to that of what
The Almighty God in Heaven has given you and I?
Questions we may think are answered with
true honesty, but in reality we know we are at fault.

So, when you get the chance to gaze
upon a flowered field, or watch a flock
of geese go by, admire it and
in fact realize how fortunate you and I are.
Jeanie Marie Miller

Real Emotions

Tears shed over broken hearts,
Laughter found in embarrassing moments,
Humbled by a lost competition,
Emotions that are felt time and again.

Hatred toward those that are different,
Angry words shouted out with impatience,
Greed of inheritance rather than mourning over the lost,
Emotions that are passively taught by generation.

Loving and being loved by that certain someone,
Not contemptuous, yet proud of accomplishments,
Peace within one's inner being,
Emotions that are appropriate and deserved.

Startled and awakened from a nightmare,
Overwhelming excitement with the thought of an upcoming event,
Uncontrollable sadness when a loved one perishes,
Emotions that come forth naturally.

Broad smiles regarding humor,
Looks from deep within,
Compassion for those that are suffering,
Emotions that are beautiful.
Natalie Suzanne Rickard

Why a Church Cries

Have you ever heard a church cry with its
heart broken in two? That's how it is when
your people, Lord, turn their back on you.

There can never be gladness or joy, just
heartache and pain. All because "so-called
Christians" seek for worldly gain.

We're not concerned with lost souls, or the
empty pews each Sunday. We only strive for
self-worth, and the glory that comes our way.

We never pray "Lord, thy will be done."
We only pray "Lord, do it my way."
We need more time on our knees
and heed what God has to say.

We don't want the Bible preached by a God
called man. We only want our praises sung by
anyone who can.

Our babies will be grown one day and serve a
god, too. Do you want to serve "The Living
God," or one picked out by you?
Shirley Ray Walker

C.F.S./M.E.—A Sufferer's Nightmare

For my daughter, Simone
It's been three long years now that I've had "M.E.,"
My life-style's changed, since it took hold of me.
The sweats, the pains, the headaches, too,
The exhaustive fatigue, sore throats, and "yuppie flu."
Maybe one day I'll wake up and scream
Is this a reality or but a dream?
Or is it possibly just my fate,
The finality for which there's not a date?
Often I have tingles in my fingers and toes,
Sweat with fevers and get emotional highs and lows.
I get swollen thyroids causing me much pain,
With aches behind the eyes driving me nearly insane.
In contrast, my body is often like ice,
My immune system seems to have thrown in the dice!
I have pains in my joints and my muscles ache, too;
I also get sore throats, like a perpetual flu.
No one should be cursed with this malaise,
Which imposes its whims on a mortal's days.
Hopefully its sufferers are but few,
And its victims do not include you.
Fred Place

Choices

Each day that dawns, as we walk through this life,
Is filled with decisions to make;
Full of uncertainties, looking ahead,
Unsure of which path we should take.

The forks in the road that arise up before us
Appear out of nowhere it seems;
One looks familiar and beckons us forth,
While the other is strange and unseen.

How can we know if the way that seems right
Does not lead to destruction and harm?
And what if the road that appears so unsure
Provides safety from all that alarms?

We are but human and easily swayed
By emotions so rampant and strong;
If we are not careful to seek our Lord's will,
Our choice can be seriously wrong.

Before pressing on, we must kneel at the Crossroad,
And listen to His still, small voice;
By only receiving direction from Him,
Can we confidently make the right choice!
Carolee J. Taninecz

What Is an Angel?

What is an angel, how do they look?
With feathered wings, as shown in a book?

Do they sit on your shoulder or fly high above?
Do they cover you warmly with Heavenly love?

Can they fit in your pocket to be carried around?
Or do they have feet that walk on the ground?

Are they sent by our Savior to watch over us?
Are they felt in a breeze or heard with a hush?

Only they can tell us and secrets they hold.
They're there for the young and even the old.

They can even look human, all tattered and torn,
Their face sunburned and withered and worn.

They come out of hiding whenever the need
To plant happiness in what is God's seed.

So, always smile back when someone gives forth,
No matter their stature or measure of worth.

For blessings are many, if only we see,
The angels are here for you and for me.
Judith L. Hussey

Remembering

For Michael Cuccione
Remembering the good and not the bad
Remembering the happy and not the sad
Remembering all the wonderful memories we shared
Remembering all the time we lost when no one was there

Remembering his heart of gold and smile like a child
Remembering a voice that drove girls wild
Remembering a talent that's like no other
Remembering the boy who got through all the suffer

Remembering the times he'd always made us happy
Remembering the ways he made us all sappy
Remembering the struggle he went through when he was so young
Remembering the cherished songs he'd always sung

Remembering a boy who changed many lives
Remembering a hero, who in a heart will never die
Remembering a boy, who lived his life fully
A boy, who lost his battle to cancer and living his dreams out truly
Remembering and loving
Michael Cuccione
Always

Felicia Nichole Hinnershitz

A Simple Longing

As I lay my head down to sleep
I look up and see the stars shining high above
I look over, see the peaceful, shimmering pond
I dream of that place, there she is but a dove

She is but the center of my world
She, who walks on water only for me
I who flies to the heavens for only her
And only she can set me free

She is beautiful, that girl of mine
Her might unknown and unstoppable
Her genus unparalleled, except by her beauty
And that beauty, it is immeasurable

This is a great new day
My view of the world is altered
I have a new life this great day
And no, I've not, no, I have not faltered

I recognize her unending beauty
I feel her overriding power
I want to be part of that presence
Oh, how I long for that hour

Matt Stevens

How Special You Are

How special you are, do you know?
I learn so much from watching you grow.

I notice your breathing is slow and deep.
That's just the right rhythm for me to keep.

I watch you stretch, and wiggle and run.
I follow your lead and it's so much fun.

I hear you singing and chanting in rhyme.
My voice joins with yours and we sound so sublime.

I listen to the stories that you love to share.
Your dreams and your wishes, I keep them with care.

I see the attention you give to your play.
It reminds me to focus on my work that way.

I feel the love that you have in your heart.
It keeps us connected even when we're apart.

So, little one, I hope that you know that we
learn from each other, and together we grow.

Maryanne C. Kufs

Alone

As she came to the end of her day,
She had nothing more to say.
Her life was a mess, she felt only depressed,
For the future she longed to caress.

Life had dealt her a hand of bad cards.
Hiding her lies turned her life into shards.
Where were the roses, instead of the thorns.
A taste of the good life, for that now she morns.

Promises echo, in the back of her mind.
The men, were they loyal, were some of them kind?
Who knows the future, she has only the past.
How long is a lifetime, how long can she last?

A lover is gone, a husband is dead.
The music of yesterday plays in her head.
Tomorrow's a day, she knows never will come.
The song they danced to, she now only hums.

Good-bye to the dreamers, so many, so few.
She'll dance on their graves, and sleep in the dew.
For the echo's have drown her, depression has found her, ALONE.

Lynda B. Taylor

Eternal Friend

You know my every footstep,
because you traveled there before me.
You control my every breath,
my life lies in your hands.

I long to see your face,
to memorize its every feature.
I long to experience your glory in full,
to praise your name forevermore.

I love the way you dry my tears
with sweet promises of what's to come.
I love the way you dance around me,
when blessings fill my life.

You saved me from Satan's grasp,
and I want to be with you,
to worship you with all I am;
for you alone are God.

Your creation awes me,
my heart leaps, when I realize your divinity.
I can't, nor will I, ever forget you,
because you are in my heart.

Ashley Elizabeth Chandler

Truth of Elixirage

He swooped like a robin and grabbed my neck;
his lips are beaks, scraping my vex,
so sashay in wit,
my reticence on his tail, a

vengeance,
to feel abducted;
lithe medicine,
he quelled my tone,
dicey, fresh.
Slow thoughts
in skull;
his tender flesh
so little over,
snug to the bone;
my viperess,
of all hot

distress,
creeping tail, in ignorance.
All is lost, market effect;
I'm on tiny toes, mind
chicken-scratch.

Indigo Agni Myrhh

House

Hold me close, hand in hand.
Don't let me go, try to understand.
I do not have the words to say it,
But to your heart I deeply plea it.

Wander through these blackened halls,
Running, chase the crying calls.
Hellish guards will try to scare you,
Fear them not you pass right through.

Lightning flashes through a window,
Turn quick to see a fleeing shadow,
Search the room find it hallow,
"Is this a game?" you croak then swallow.

Find a book on the floor,
Is this a book or is it more.
Winds blow, and nature rages,
Watch the flipping, untouched pages,
Read the stories, watch the faces,
Memories in unmapped places.
The pages stop to show you, you,
The quote beneath I'll leave to you.

Phillip Thomas Howell

The Sailor Man

I look at my past with a navy eye.

I borrowed a pencil and calculator,
but slept through the SAT.
I wrote in cursive and dreamed
about new school supplies.
I played high school ball, beat church drums,
and drank red Kool-Aid.

I ran away with a garbage bag
full of toys.
I saw witches fly through the kitchen,
tacked Jet Beauties on my ceiling,
and wore print vests and Sunday shoes.

But out here, everything mists
to blue black.

I am E-5; I tattooed an anchor on my forearm.
At sea, a Master at Arm's hairline does not
quite recede, and a keg counts as "just two beers."
We marry Abercrombie and Fitch,
Bob Marley, Birkenstock, and Budweiser.

A sailor's delight.

Carissa Nicole Morris

To Allen Ginsberg

You were obsessed with Kerouac, wanted his charisma?
I'm in love with your words; what does that say about me?
I read your poetry, proudly proving your words to myself,
making the most of my quiet voice
in an empty, lonely, staring room.

But then I read your descriptions of my own world:
of Clinton Administration, fast food, Iraq and its oil.
No longer passionate musings about the Depression
and your schizophrenic mother and the 1960s in Tangiers.

Only bitter old man talk.

I miss crazy rants about Neal Cassady.
Nostalgia not the same as archaic transcriptions—
insane beats and junkies,
eternally distended by your vulgar words.

Reading your dying, ailing, final reflections, I feel
my own death-illness creeping, lurking, slinking up
behind my eager eyes and crooked spine.
My immortal idol dead only three years—
it's easy to destroy yourself by saying too much.

"I'm talking to myself again."

Jen H. Seminatore

The Fire

Burning in fire with a mighty laughter,
Knowing the more you laugh
The more you burn,
To let out your feelings is to stop the fire,
And to save yourself is yet painful
To your desire,
So you keep laughing and you keep burning,
To when will you stop the fire.

Tania Noorda

The Final Journey

Left behind are the family's tears,
Cherished memories of bygone years.
Of love and laughter, a life wellspent
And now to God he has went.

Up high on angels' wings, a Heavenly flight;
Taking the journey home towards the brilliant light.
To those on Earth who weep, a life is gone;
But in God's eternal love, 'tis but the dawn.

Roger A. Beltz, M.S.

A Poem by Me

I had to read a book called *Eats*
There were a lot of poems, but no repeats
I read by day, I read by night . . .
With all this reading my brother had a fright!
Tomorrow this book report is due,
Maybe I will get the flu . . .
If I can't fool my mom, I'll guess I'll have to go
Hey but . . . it just might snow

James John Angelo Bolloli

Time to Come

It's all over as the leaves slowly drift to the ground,
its all over as the day turns into night.
The memories that last forever,
the heart that broke that day.
The dreams that won't come true,
the decisions to be made.
The time we had forever ours,
the dreams I keep forever mine.

Shari Suzanne Boyd

Mother Dear

To my dear mother
Clouds may gather in the sky,
And friends leave me by and by.
But when I see your smiling face
All the flowing tears erase.

Sometimes the road seems long and drear,
But then I see you, Mother Dear.
I feel I'm falling into a pit
But then I look up and there you sit.

Moving your lips in a silent prayer,
I know that you will always be there.
Friends are golden, I am told,
And will sometimes lend you a hand to hold.

But when I feel I can't go on,
You are there with a happy song.
You mother dear, are my very best friend
For you're always there when I'm at my end.

I just think of all your loving care
And I still see you smiling there.
Friends are golden, I must agree,
But you, Mother Dear, are dearest to me.

Tracy Elizabeth Wisdom

Strings of Our Hearts

We hold on by the strings of our heart,
Keeping our love from falling apart.
Every second feeling like an eternity
But our love always coming back . . . and we,
Keep holding on by the strings of our hearts
Day by day making new starts.
Our never ending love,
Sent to us from up above.
We hold on by the strings of our heart,
Keeping our love from falling apart.
Sarah Anne Mallozzi

As I Look

As I look into your eyes for the first time,
I see depths so unknown to me.

The sensuality of your sight enthralls me;
Comforts me, slowly drawing me into you.

Unsaid passions;
Unspoken words fill my vision
Stretching to my fingertips . . .
Tracing images of you into the center of my soul.
Lisa Marie Jankowski

Second Chances

Christ floated into my room
in a brightly colored, carnival balloon

smiling with blood dripping
from hands and feet
and collecting at the stem of the balloon
he told me i must die to live

smiling, i laughed
pushed him out of the window
and watched him float away
who said life is living?
David Michael McGuire

Not You and I

Had life been kinder, had life been true,
I'd spend more time with you.
I'd lay down my defense, open my heart,
And that could be a start.
But my needs are hollow, the wall is high.
There will not be you and I.

Tenderly you try to touch me,
But I am yet not free.
I do not allow a longer moment to share.
I have no courage to care,
Not for one moment, not for any time.
There will not be you and I.
Phyllis Adele McFarlane

Composed upon Lisa's Arm

A simple touch,
A gentle roll
Upon your skin I deposit my soul.
Windows blue,
Your eyes true, and I know exactly what to do.
Until today 'twas indecisive,
But you see just how my mind slices.
A kiss from your lips; priceless!
No words could frame my crystal bliss you tame
With only a whisper of my name.
My life has come white to be repainted in the night.
And your colors, they are just right!
Donald Thomas Scott

When She Is Still, I See Her as Bones and Parchment Skin

A cat's claw slid through her arm,
the skin falling cleanly to each side.
Weeks later it is still held together by tape.
I hesitate to touch her, thinking
this slight pressure will leave marks too,
deep brown-red bruises that will never stop growing.
They will swell and join the others
that are now the size of fists,
the size of irons.
Susan Dunavan

It's What's Inside

As we all ask our self why each day
we are silent with nothing to say.
When everything seems to be going very well,
here it is, it's coming, that damn dry spell.
It seems it finds us in those hard places,
everyone sees it in our heart and faces.
We all need somebody special in our life,
our mom, dad, friend, or wife.
Sometimes when it's rough and deep,
you want to climb out, but looks too steep.
So you go and try to make things right,
it might be a long one, but it's worth the fight.
It's hard, but we learn from our mistakes,
even when we get the bad intakes.
Tommy Leon Pilkerton

The Ache of Good-Bye

What if I told you I'm not sure I could live without you?
Would it scare you? It scares me.
'Cause I think of my grandmother
After my grandfather left us.
I've never seen her cry,
But I know she has.
She's never told me that she died inside that day,
But I know she did.
I've seen her eyes when she gazes at
His big, empty chair beside her.
I've seen her face when others talk
About him in the past tense.
And it scares me to know that the more
Deeply you love, then the more deeply you
Feel the ache of good-bye.
So what if I told you I'm not sure I could
Live without you?
'Cause I'm not sure I could.
Karen Elizabeth Elligson

To a Rich Man from a Poor Girl!

Sisters of blood can be the tightest they can be
Without any difference for the world to see;
However, the odds be it changed with this world estranged
From its old customs at hand.
This is what I wanted you to understand:
The story is long which mimics an old country song,
Or even stories of fantasy and desire
With you as the prince setting hearts on fire,
Which included many of maidens, even me.
If only I could have made you see
That none of my sisters are like me.
I worked hard to try to get to you;
I did all that I could do.
Now, you'll never know the secrets I keep inside,
The ones I was forced to hide,
Of what went wrong and could have been.
What a waste,
What a sin!
BJ

To You

This disease that you have is taking you away,
but how I so badly wish that you could sit and stay
and talk for awhile.
Not a night goes by when I don't cry myself to sleep,
holding myself together from the pain that cuts so deep
leaving a wound to never heal.
You're gone now and my mind won't seem to comprehend
that the torment I am feeling is just the beginning of the end
of life without you.
I know that you still love me even though we're far apart
and you're looking down on me from Heaven to mend my broken heart
that's bleeding without you.
I love you, Dad, because you were all that you could be,
and I hope one day that people tell me that they see you through me.

Angee Marie Malohn

A Dream's Journey of the Soul

As night beckons closing my eyes in sleep,
A field of wide flowers into my mind creeps.
Vibrant hue's of yellow, blue, pink, lavender, and white,
Bathing in their aromatic scents, a sheer delight.
Dancing softly in nature's beauty sent,
All this lent with Heaven's consent.
Mind and soul in harmony with the universe,
Reconnecting with my spirit as I converse.
Comprehending the totality of my own being,
As my existence in this lifetime is but one of many seeing.
The peaceful sleep into the realm of dreams I transverse,
To dream the dreams that are never rehearsed.
In this timeless journey peering into eternity,
For in this moment is all infinity.

Betty Lou Herman

To the Man Who Changed It All . . . My Dad

Every day I sit and pray that your life has
not been a crying shame.
With God by your side and the Heavens above,
there must not be any worries, just lots of love.
I remember the times you held me tight in
the middle of the night.
You said everything would be all right.
I remember the times your hands were tough,
only to eventually show me I was loved.
Dad, you showed me how to love.
Your open hands and your tough love
have showed me no greater love.
If I die tomorrow, it would be okay, because
I know that you will be there at those golden gates.

Catherine Marie Doolittle

Sweet Sixteen

They sent him into battle
They gave him a tot of rum
He died young
Sweet tender youth of sixteen
His whole life before him
The officers, the casualty figures they don't care
They bore them
Sweet sixteen years
His mother and sweetheart cry futile tears
Sweet sixteen
Years in the hell of the trenches he experienced
Unimaginable fear
Sweet sixteen years
He said his prayers, it did not save him
Governments and politicians, I blame them
For those who died in their millions,
Those they look on with contempt
And tread as minions

Derek Sandford

Innocence Lost

We emerge from the woods, tired and peaceful,
Leaving our childhood behind in that moment of bliss.
Yet the iron has not been fully forged,
And we have broken the gate to adulthood.

Christopher Dorian

Angel in Disguise

She believed in me and loved me, though, nothing I was
She forgave all that I did, and gave herself to me
She had no material things, yet her heart was greater than life
She shared the little she had, and only knew how to give
She believed in humankind, and loved all around
Oh, how I strive to be like her! But—yet, fall far behind
I often look at her and wonder—Is she an earthly being?
And I try to emulate her style, Yet, I don't come even close
But—no one ever has, Not even those who strive
And . . . Only then, I realize, She's an angel in disguise
An my whole body trembles, and my face cracks a smile
When I'm enlightened with the knowledge that the angel is my mom
Amazed—I close my eyes to thank my lucky stars
For I've been chosen, I've been blessed
To have an Angel for a mom
For all these years I've lived
With an Angel in Disguise!

Jennifer Rivera

Just Like Me

Can it be, all I see
Is all there is to reality?
Is something hid, perhaps not rid,
By someone else, just like me,
Who also thought this is all there would be?

When it rains, the clouds feign
To be all there is, but can it be?
Of course it is!
Behind the grey, springtime clouds,
The sun remains, as always,
A loving touch of warmth, light.
Without the clouds, a rainbow of infinite
Colors and shades there would never be.

So it cannot be that all I see
Is all there is to reality!
Too much hid, never really rid,
Just there for the wondering by all of us,
Just like me.

John F. Oster

Shenandoah

I open my eyes
and am greeted by the sun and the riverbed.
I look up into the lilies and have my perfect rest.
I stand up and hear them calling,
oh, the angels say it's time to rest.
And I look upon the river and see my soul is blessed.
All is calm beside the river, all is peaceful and in sheer bliss.
No storm is raging here, all is calm and at rest.
And I look up into the Heavens, oh, Father, my soul is blessed,
and he says to me, my daughter, your soul has rest.
And I look out at the river, I see the sparkling face of beauty,
true glory, and feel truly blessed.
The angels are singing louder and they sing this sweet ballad,
oh, daughter, your body's tired, and it's time to be at rest
and fly into the Heavens and receive your holiness.
I look out upon the valley and see the wondrous power of my
Savior,
and know it's time for rest.
I feel closer to my Father and place my hand in his
and am guided into the Heavens and have eternal rest.

Dara Octavia Grinton

I Wonder

The world is full of wonders . . .
many in which you cannot see.
All you have to do is . . .
close your eyes, open your mind, and you'll find plenty.
Tobi Milo

Equality?

YOU GO THERE.
This is the place in which you'll stay . . . there.
Away from me to live as you wish, until it bothers me.
Then I'll create a new rule to protect myself from you.
My attitudes will tarnish you and pound you downward
into a self-hate you cannot escape.
Then I'll say you're awful . . . that whenever you move into
a neighborhood, it is ruined.
I'll classify you as worthless,
and then offer you humiliating charity
since I won't employ you.
Here, for your welfare, since you're not good enough
to live in my neighborhood.
Then I'll complain that you're violent,
and swear you threaten public safety.
I'll call you militant and leftist . . . and make your image
the ingredient of my children's nightmares,
so they can rule your children.
Joseph Scalia

Crazy

They called me crazy,
because I dared to believe
if only in certain fleeting moments
that I could soar,
that the irrepressible voice inside me,
which had been screamed down to a whisper,
punished into a dark corner,
was telling me the truth that, yes,
I might possibly me miraculous magic
and not just a hunk of flesh
to be moved to the rhythm of other people's music.

They described me as weird,
because I challenged myself
to scan the higher horizon
beyond the ugly, the routine, the tragic,
to glimpse the startling majesty of being
vehemently denied by all those all striving,
scrounging like beggars for only corporal rewards,
while dying the desperate death of the soul.
Linda Marie Popolano

Your Birthday

My phone rings and I hear, "I'm ready"
I jump up and dart over to your room
I grab a bag of goodies for you that I stashed
Before handing it to you, I stand motionless
Not wanting to miss a moment of your beauty
I present you with the gifts I wanted to give you
I watch, as your smile begins to grow and glow
In anticipation I watch, as you peer into the bag
You notice the basket, which makes me smile
But you can't see the CD's below
And knowing this makes me smile even more
You grab me and kiss me saying thank you, but
I point at the bottom of the basket, which makes
You smile even more, as you look to see
What else I got for you, as you begin to glow more than before
You kiss me again and then wipe your lipstick off
Only to kiss me again, making me smile and glow
As much as you did before and still are even now
Making it seem like it was my birthday, too
William Robert Davy

Christmas Eve

Candy canes and gingerbread men,
it's Christmas Eve and there's helping hands.

Christmas treats and TV shows,
you'll have a great Christmas if you have ho, ho, ho's.

Time is ticking, it's getting late,
for Christmas day I cannot wait.
Trista Poletski

To Be One

To be one with nature is to be a nomadic creature.
To live beyond the serenities of nature, in the wild untamed future,
With no bounds and no common ground,
To live of the land, using only your hands,
To be wild and pure as a child,
To fly free, high within the trees,
To have no beginning and no ending,
To never need tending,
To live mightily above society,
To be one with yourself is to live better than wealth.
Ashley Wanschek Imperato

This Word Love

Love is a word that has been taken for granted
before trying to understand just why it's been planted.
Without this word Love it would be impossible to exist.
This world would be lonely and Love would surely be missed.

Where did this word Love actually begin?
Or was it just a word that has been lost in the wind.?
To those who have planted this word Love in their hearts,
always remember this word Love will never part.
For those who may not know and think this word Love is quite odd,
you, too, must remember this word Love is my God.
Genetra Hickson

Once Lovers

No regrets, not a single one.
Never forget the things we did for fun.
Time does pass, life continues on,
memories flash, even after you've gone.
Childish games we would always play;
things aren't the same, but I'll cherish those days.
Long hours all alone with you, never cowered,
all our dreams once came true.
Remember? The way that it felt,
both surrendered . . . two hearts at once did melt.
Jennifer Knotts

Watch

I haven't worn a watch for nine years.
I used to love the smell of my skin
when I took the watch off
and of the damp leather strap.
It reminded me of something simple and honest
like clay—forest moss—my pet dog—or my mother.
A circle on my wrist showing where
the watch had been pressed
that was smoother and colder than
the skin around it.
A tan mark embossed with "Stirling Silver."

I don't know when exactly—or why I stopped wearing my watch
but now each day seems to hold some small victory over me.
I catch myself stealing glimpses
of other people's watches,
staring down streets at church steeples and town halls,
asking strangers the time.
Perhaps that's why time seems to fly so fast now.
Dave Vane

Seasons of Lost Love

To Erin—I'll always love you.
As the gap between us grows,
You'll see the effects of the snows.
The budding rose steadily takes on frost,
And hope for new seeds is all but lost.
Its memories of spring wilting away,
It seems it was only here for a day.

Adam S. Francis

Dark Train

I hear the train at night roll by,
Interrupting thoughts long enough to sigh.
The feeling in my heart keeps time with the wheels.
Listening for a moment, to the silence you've killed.
Dark mystery, comin' from nowhere, going the same way.
Why don't you capture me like this in the day?
Gone as fast as you came.
Soon as you're gone, my thoughts are the same.
Silence and I wait for you to break us again.
Sitting here wondering, are you a foe or a friend?

Melinda Kay Ewert

love will show

when I started love was new
for fourteen years love lasted
but then she wanted to find new love
and on the net she did
so with four kids and myself she left
two thousand mile away the grass looked greener
she now regrets, as the grass wasn't greener
but my love for her now long dead and over
new love I have found better than ever
rather it be true only time will show

Clifford Gowen

Midnight Prayer

Oh, my goddess, hear my pleas
Take my worries home with thee
And whisper in my children's ears
Promises of protection to ease their fears
And for all who dwell within this home
Help to guide us away from where evils roam
Happiness, hope, and love, I plea
But most of all I ask of thee
Deep in your heart I hope to find
Peace, love, and hope of all kind

Denise Blair

Untitled

They say I'm white
I'm not
They make fun of me for being light
I am a light-skinned Puerto Rican
They say I don't belong
I do
They say I don't look Puerto Rican
I am
I might have been born here
but that doesn't mean I'm white.
I am a light-skinned Puerto Rican
What people see is the outside that looks white
They don't see the inside that is who I am
And that's Puerto Rican
I don't care what people see
I don't care what people think
I am Puerto Rican
White is just a color

Ashley Marie Ruiz

Last Kiss

Last flower I have given her was forgotten
Last Kiss I have given her faded away
Last eyes met between us was not remembered
Yet the pain continues in this heart of mine

Azad Ashraf

From the Outside

I dreamt last night
in my white-linened bed
that I was in your head.
And for the first time I saw me
from the outside, in.

I didn't look like I thought I would,
thinner than I ever wished I could,

with blackened eyes and bloodied hands,
a heaving chest and two bruised breasts.

Five a.m. and I'm awake,
with a violent chill that I just can't shake.
How is it that I'd never realized
the thoughts that are flashing
behind your opaque eyes?

Please don't hit me!
I was wrong—I apologize. . . .

Sarah Elaine Tennent

Jewels of Time

Is it founded in truth, and is this buried
in the midst of polished illusion?
Or do you like I reside in a whirlpool
of colorfully decorated confusion?

Is it like a passion fruit seed
cocooned in the bliss of an unjudging,
all-encompassing jelly of love?
To think it creates its existence
nearer to our source of curiosity.

Could this very thought be our origin?
That spirals into jubilation, as it is
impregnated with intent, then blossoms into
creation, and evolves through the intense
joy of experience?

Oh, father, mother, friend, and lover,
I burn and yearn with a relentless belief;
are we not the sacred jewels of time?

George Helou

To the Founder of Love . . .

How did you come to that conclusion?
You must have been wrong
There's no such thing
All it leads to is confusion
I've been looking for it for so long.
Then I get dropped off that swing.

You say love is forever.
How can you say that?
Do you really know what it is?
If you do, you must know all the games people play.
You start to think all love is like that.
So I ask again, do you really know what love is?

But I guess we all have our point.
We all have our own thoughts and feelings.
And no one ever feels the same.
But you thought of it, so I guess you know what you meant.
You may know more about feelings than I,
But I know more about shame.

Christina Cosman

Living Life's Path

Love is a beacon that lights up the path of Life!
Walk slowly and gather the flowers and friends
For it's a long, long walk before the path ends.
With Nature's fabulous beauty all around,
Let's enjoy the moon and the stars and every flower found.
The Love of friends complements each day!
Which helps us light up the way.
As this byway extends, it becomes so enticing;
Sometimes joys, other times depressed!
What's significant and foremost it never ends!
It will change direction, but not your destiny.

Anthony J. Giuliano

Perfection

When I told my mother, she did not believe.
Did not believe that I could see,
Did not believe that I could feel.
But I could.
I could see through the window to perfection.
I was afraid of metal and dark.
I was afraid to bleed, to breath, even to be.
I was afraid of my mother.
I was afraid of myself.
But that was only when I could see.
But that was only when I could feel.

Elizabeth Rose Merker

Why We Cry

I read the letters of past gone by
I wonder, wonder why we cry
From what I don't know why
We love, we care, we share but yet we cry
I love you dear I told you why
But all you seem to do is cry
I can only still wonder why
No it's me, now I cry
Because of you, I know not why
I love you dear but still I cry
I know now dear, you said good-bye.

Bradford G. SImpson

All above the Sky

Written at age 10
All above the sky
Moon and stars always Shy.

Where they go at the day,
Maybe they sleep all the way.

Waking all night,
Moon and Stars shine so bright.

All above the sky
They are shy from the day,
But when the night comes, they smile all the way.

Fizza Zaidi

To Be Forgotten

To be forgotten is to be remembered in reverse,
As when the stars arise and the sun's dispersed.
When the last drop of day is engulfed in mere space,
And the daytime creatures slow their pace.
To be forgotten is of remorseless sin,
Like the evil hung from a loved one's chin.
So as the day fades to night,
That of wrong is then made right.
And although to some, it may seen absurd . . .
It's forgiven and forgotten
With apologies unheard.

Angella Joy Miller

Why?

Why does your voice thrill me so?
Why do I long for your touch?
Why do I need and want you so much?
Why does your kiss melt me away?
Why do you invade my thoughts night and day?
Why do I wonder about things that cannot be
For these are forbidden to me.
These are the things I need to know,
For the answer lies deep within my soul,
Fear of what I may see.
I keep it hidden within me.

Deb DeVore

Dreams Not Experienced

Sitting here contemplating things that could be but are not
Give my mind seclusion in a world that has not been introduced
To the realization of a completely woven dream.
Endless possibilities wait yet to be discovered
But lie covered by fear and inadequacy
Loosely held by my inward conviction for normalcy
In a world that craves singleness and inspiration
Differences made only by the effort of individuals
Desiring to succeed
Differences made by those that allow dreams
To consume them

Andrew Grover

The Horsemen

For Strength, For Light, For Love go forth,
Riding not upon a pale white horse.
In time of need and need of life,
Cause not what is your usual strife.

For if she rides at the side of pain,
Your time will run thin and break in twain,
Leaving you without even misery to wrack your brain.

So steady on your path,
Ride with mercy and stay your course
For Strength, For Light, For Love go forth.

Andrew Michael Claude

Always Alone

Always Alone
Last to be picked for anything
Wanting a friend
Alone I still am
You say you're my friend
Still alone I am

Asking no pity on me
Last thing I want is that
Only one thing I want
Not pity
Everyone should know I just want a friend to talk to

Adam Charles Rhode

Forever

I hate being with you . . . such bliss and happiness are foreign to me.
I hate the way you touch me
in a way no one has ever touched me before.
You rock my world and I hate that, too.
I hate it that you make me vulnerable.
I hate it that you make me real.
It was easier hiding within myself with no feelings and no pain.
I hate the way I can't stop thinking of you.
I will focus my energy on getting over you.
It will be the last thing that I do.

Bellezza

My Loved One

My loved one, the dawn is breaking
on this our wedding day.
Soon you'll be mine, and I'll be thine
from now on and then forever.
To thee I pledge my sacred love,
my dreams and my hopes, my trust and understanding.
Let our love be everlasting,
and let me closer to thee be—
for I want to comfort you, dear,
in your sorrows and your anguish forever!
Lord, let it be!

Joanne Sims

A Dog of My Own

Mom and Dad, I want you to know,
I'm a little saddened, a little low.

For I truly want a dog of my own.
He or she can be puppy size or full grown.

That is not quite the point, you see.
I want a doggie just for me.

I'll feed and care for it all the time.

Now, I told you what I would like,
Please answer my poem!

Tracy Rawls

Dedicated to Great Uncle Werner

The big day arrives slowly and smoothly.
But now his time is up.
I feel the dark, grim hand of death hovering over him,
as he lays in his death bed.
The hand is ready to steal his soul from his body.
But his soul cries not for mercy,
for it knows that it is time to enter a patiently waiting heart.
Now his final breath, and the hand
swoops down to carry the soul away.
The pain is here with us, but joy is with his soul,
who knows that the hand is slowly coming once again.

Matthew C. Graham

Touching

Touching is for me, for you
A thing we most like to do
Important to us, oh, it's true
Our touch speaks of love and in volumes, too
And every touch it seems, well . . . new
It is one thing that will never get old
Your touch it reaches my very soul
Our love speaks in many ways
Your touch, my touch, oh, what it says
Touching is for you, for me
Touching is like this . . . see

Curtis Micheal Reaves

My Flock

I'm crazy, insane,
stupid, no pain.
My flock goes wild,
like a flower child.
Camera lights, flash,
dash, my flock.

Is cool, it's all good.
Freak, you're two!
My flock, it rises, like rags in summer sun,
But tell me;
what could you have done?

Michaela Verity

What Do You See?

What do you see?
A colorless form or a tangible entity?
I want to be found in your sight, to be just as . . .
But I cannot seem to make the right form.

What do you want me to be?
Will it satisfy all the requirements
That you do not meet?

I wish I could make myself to be the kind
Of human that you want me to be,
But then I would not be the one whom I truly see.

Michelle Lynn Johnson

Why Me and My Family?

I lost my life because of you,
I am sometimes feeling really blue,
Why did you do this to me?
Only if you could see
What my life meant to me.
I wish you knew how I felt, but oh, well.
Now you're in prison, how does it feel?
I should be glad, but I am very sad,
My family's gone because of you,
One day you'll know how I feel,
And overdose on these very same pills.

Michelle Koehl

When You Say You Love Me

When you say you love me
I get a warm feeling in my heart,
and I get the feeling we will never be apart.

When you say you love me
I feel as if I will never die,
and the whole world revolves around you and I

When you say you love me
I feel like I could fly,
because when you say you love me,
you make me feel alive.

Stephanie Diane Lauffer

Revelation

You glow, like a full moon on a warm desert night
Your hair sparkles, as a flawless diamond
Your every breath makes my heart quiver
Your smile burns in my eyes
Your every word tickles my mind
You hold my heart, and you own my soul
I live for you
I would die for you
I know this now
As I have ever know anything in my life
You are my life

Steve Roche

Sisters Are Special

When we were small, we played games of
hide 'n' seek and ring around the rosie.
As we begin to grow, we shared secrets and each other's clothes.
We had our share of arguments, not knowing what life would bring.
We have now grown to be more than sisters, we are friends.
Sisters know when you are down and out.
They know when you are happy and when you are sad.
Sisters are there when you need someone to talk to.
Your friends may come and go,
but no matter what life brings, sisters are forever.
Thank God for sisters.

Sandy Denise Miller

Race to Freedom

She would tickle my cheek,
stubbly whiskers on a soft, gray muzzle;
nibble at my hands for treats.

I stood in the stall with her
before the race,
not knowing it would be her last.

I can still see her lying on the ground,
motionless, eyes fixed,
legs stretched, as if she were running.

She raced to eternal freedom.

Deborah Caroline Rowe

A Midnight Breeze

I look to the blackened sky,
Clouds billow above my head
Lined with the dust of the heavens.
Daffodils glisten with dew,
Swaying to a warm midnight breeze.
The sweet smell of honeysuckle
Brings me to a cliff over looking the ocean,
The stars shimmer brightly and reflect in the calm water.
Waves lazily roll to shore.
I lie down in the cool sand
And dream of the wonders of tomorrow.

Christine Marie Torda

Jewels

it sparkles like fire.
ignites my every desire.
beauty lies in your sweet simplicity.
your radiance lights up a city.
you are worn around my neck for the sole reason of attraction.
your caress comforts me when i am depressed,
as you hang lying upon my chest.
its smooth glassy strings run along my rose petal perfumed body.
i am offered sweet smelling creams but,
i don't want them . . .
i long for JEWELS.

Solange Kisha Robertson

Searcher

I continue to run down this road
Not knowing where it goes
Not understanding . . .
I can't see anything to tell me where to start
or where to go.
If this battle is not physical,
Then why do I feel so unspiritual?
I feel little in this heart.
I can't find that missing part.
I can't find that peace of mind.
I'm forsaking my convictions all of the time.

Nicholas P. Snyder

To Be or Not to Be

The choice is yours—they say,
But how? you say.
Life has so many choices—so many
Decisions—be a lawyer, be a doctor,
Be a gardener, be a chief, be a
Mother or father—just be.
Surrender to your Higher Self
And enjoy life filled with love, compassion,
And forgiveness and all answers will
Come—but—the choice is yours
To Be or Not to Be!

Jane B. Duca

Returning Home

Born in a footprint of Ganesh,
Lord of Beginnings,
Nourished on diatoms, ostracods,
and cladocerans,
I left my small pool, seeking the air,
All my siblings returned to mud.

Years of rain cycles, asleep in dry times,
I grew to froghood, avoiding the hornbill,
the snake, and the crow.
It is the monsoon and the elephants
Are treading the mud.

S. Clement Anderson

If I Were a Rose

If I were a rose and the flower was all wilted,
the leaves have sagged, the stem bent over,
the roots decaying and the ground all dry,
I would not be beautiful, because there is no one around
to take care and water me.
But if there is someone to care and water me,
the ground would be moist, my roots would be growing,
my stem would be strong, my leaves would be green,
my flower would be blooming, and I would look beautiful.
Would you be the one to be there
and water me with love?

Kenneth Lyle Akkerman

Our Grandson

Pitter-Patter, Pitter-Patter, hear those little feet.
Coming 'cross the kitchen floor, they don't skip a beat.
"Pop Pop, come play with me," he says in all his glee.
He doesn't like to be alone, for he is only three.
So I get down and play with him, because he's so much fun.
Sometimes it's Cars and Trucks, sometimes it's just to run.
But I don't mind the time it takes, or where he wants to go
'Cause he's our family's shining light, and we love him so,
Just like we do our Daughters as we watched them grow.
The years have passed for his Nana and me, time just seems to fly.
And now we have our Grandson, a treasure you can't buy.

Anthony Pitt Jr.

Just a Feeling . . .

There's this feeling I have when
I'm not around you,
A feeling I get when it's just me and you.

A passion that I've never felt before.
It was you that unlocked the door.
My love, strength, thoughts, and cares are what it stores.
You found the key that no one has ever bothered to look for.

With you, it feels so meant to be.
You opened my eyes, and I began to see.
Just a feeling I get when it's just you and me.

Jessica Summer Salisbury

True Friend

When I needed you,
you were always there
to show how much you care.
Whenever I'm sad and out of place,
you're always there to put a smile on my face.
You've always been there for me,
through thick and thin.
And that's why I'm so glad to say
that I can call you a true friend.
Because I know that you'll always be there
from the beginning until the end!

Kelly S. Paavola

Crystal Clear

I dive down into the paradise,
A place I'd only seen in my dreams.
The fish swim by; friendly and curious.
I feel the cool water floating past me.
The coral I touch is rough, but oddly smooth.
A strange beeping sound;
So alien to this world, so unlike the sounds of water.
Everything gets foggy, so different from my crystal clear paradise.
I open my eyes.
It is dark when I sit up.
Once again, a dream-filled night leads to a brutal awakening.

Elena Ines Ortega

Controversial

Chastise truth spoken unique and strong
It's crude, vulgar, yet intriguing
But we're told that it's wrong
Nasty and ugly and horribly said
Lacing our thoughts, as if needle and thread
Explicit and detailed
Though life proves it real
Truth is unwanted thus explains its appeal
What is said is in papers and news
Movies and music don't create who we are
Unless, that's what we choose

Megan Christine Hamblin

Wondering River

Endless sleep fills my eyes
Like a thick, wondering river sludge
Crippled eyes
Desperately fighting to keep ajar
Distant dreams
Where walls become liquefied
And the trees never stop swaying
And people aren't really there
Sound is muffled by clouds of distant irony
Strange faces speaking fading
Whispering their mellow breath

Gene Anthony-Ray Davila

I'm Not

I'm not a beggar, I am not a thief
I'm not a hooker for sale on the streets
I'm not a dog barking at your heels
I'm nothing, nothing but real

I'm not a Power Ranger flying through the air
I'm not a Ninja Turtle or Smokey the Bear
I'm not Luke Skywalker, no force field or shield
I'm nothing, nothing but real

Your looking for a savior with the magic hook
A big, fat deposit for your little check book

Megan Leigh Romanovitz

Untitled

Complicated interest
raise their hands
to be immortal.
Shown how to feel for others
by the soul of the common rain
It drops by our side,
and kisses our feet.
Come crying to me,
by beautiful defeat.
It rarely ever matters if we step in the way,
our footsteps are running quietly away.

Raechyle Sedlisky

Reflection

Why should I tell you how I feel
when all you have to do to see the hurt
in my eyes, the pain in my heart, and hear
the silence of my suffering

is take a good look at yourself?

Beverly A. Auten

Other Things . . .

We were watching the moon and the stars
The sun and the sky
The world spinning around in a chocolate box
The lights in our eyes, as they shimmered and shone
A myriad of pools in a paper cup
Sign posts on the highway of our minds
Endless illusions spread far and wide
A universe of prose written on clouds
The moon spinning around in a daisy chain
A face so familiar we had forgotten the name
The stars in the hands of statues entwined
We were watching people explode into a million lights
And nature escaping the racing wind
A rainbow of colors painted over the sky
And the love that existed between the lines
Of a poem written on the parchment of our lives
We were watching the moon and the stars
And the sun and the sky. . .

David Edward Barnett

My Grandmother, My Best Friend

My best friend is forty years older,
And has wisdom unknown.
My best friend is prettier by far,
Then I'll ever be.
Her hair is gray,
Her eyes not as bright,
She's a little slower,
but always willing to go wherever I ask.
She'll lend a helping hand to all those without,
for her heart is solid gold.
She'll praise my accomplishments,
and dry my tears when I fail.
She'll go to the fair,
and not a complaint will you hear when my bumper car hits hers.
She's there when I need her,
no matter the time, day or night.
For she's my best friend,
Grandmother and all.

Sandy J. Yates

A Father's Shame

One night of love made many years of joy,
Wondering if the baby would be a girl or a boy.

Then you walked out on us with only one choice,
The choice to never hear your little girl's voice.

So many nights she called out your name,
Then you walked back into her life, without any shame.

You ask a lot of her to be so young,
Yet you give her so much love when wrong is done.

You brighten her day with each little word,
Yet each word is always deeply heard.

Let love strengthen each and every day,
Because your daughter will need it when you are away.

Give her the joy that was not always there
And the knowledge that you will always care.

That little girl's voice will always call your name,
So hold your head up, this will end all shame.

Jeannie Gray Butts

Mary Lee

Mary Lee, you are my moonlight through the black before twilight.
You are my early morning sunlight.
Mary Lee, you're my angel of light.
My never-ending affection of you softens my dark and dismal nights.
You my love, you're my greatest delight. . . .

Bryan T. Moore

Kaleidoscope

Through my kaleidoscope the picture
Is broken and senseless
As it seems to the ordinary seeing
Eyes of man
Each piece seems like a puzzle that
will take a century to fit together
But slowly turn the kaleidoscope and
Behold a clear, distinct and beautiful picture
My kaleidoscope is my magic marble
For it makes sense out of a senseless
Blur
And puts meaning and life into any
Ordinary picture
And thus my broken-up life out of place,
So senseless and incomprehensible
When viewed through the kaleidoscope,
They fall into place and I see nothing . . .
But a wonderful life.

Vivienne Sabrina Oby Ozobialu

Today

What's this world come to?
Hate and lies
Most things we do
God despises
Cruel intentions
Bad feedback
Evil all around us
God please keep me on track

Revenge, oh don't it sound so sweet?
The bible says see that none payback wrong
for wrong
In other words, two wrongs don't make a right
If you do that man, you could end up in afight
This my friends is what is happening
To this world so full of rot and bile
But if you pray and stay true to him
Then he'll watch over you, all the while

Daniel Gallagher

Roll One

in Amsterdam
working women uncross their legs
while homeless mustaches
part the smoke,
and I,
one soul abandoned
on the wayside,
anonymously giggle.
bustling neon chit-chat
chatter
strangers
saunter
slide
through the shadows
and sink away.
drunk with indulgence,
leaning easily against the cobblestone
my tongue slithers through Dutch phrases,

while I roll one.

Ashley Ann Smith

Freedom

Author age 10
In a world where war is all around
There are even countries where freedom is not found
In some foreign lands, there's not one happy day
And in some places, you're not allowed to pray
We live each day without a clue
What does freedom mean to you?

Jillian Kaylene Zaleski

Society's Child

Pity the small child fed words of wisdom
by adults who don't know themselves
what it's all about.
Sleeping with eyes open,
they grow and find a world that thrives
for all the wrong reasons.
They're too much society's child
to bring me around to their way of thinking
because I have found . . .
inspirations that expand my mind
to depths of dimension unknown to those left behind
in the mist of their emotions shaped by life's pantomime.
Living their lives with fears and doubts,
driving them on to avoid
thinking too much of who they are.
They're too much society's child
to bring me around to their way of thinking,
because I have found . . . myself.

Kimberly Mulvaney

Halloween

Written at age nine
Houses, candy, funny clothes,
A big, green witch with a big, long nose.
I have chocolate, sweet tarts, popcorn, too.
I have candy and so do you.
Doorbells ringing all around,
Ooooh, have you ever heard such a funny sound?
Chocolates melting on my tongue,
Oh, what's that? Another ding-dong,
Yahoo, it's Halloween!
Screaming, yelling, giggling, too,
Aaaah, what's that, and who are you?
Goblins, ghosts, skeletons, and all;
I can't believe it's already fall!
Hurray, it's Halloween!
I feel like I'm a queen,
I feel lots of candy in my bag,
What's making my neck itch? It's my costume tag!

Allysa Archondous

my journey

as i wander down this road
the jagged thoughts pass
eclectic reason vents
never to capture the mind's eye
hope fades like the rose
till all has turned
the color of doom
the ancient paths of despair
are trodden upon
this litany of agony reflects
the trials of growth
could i ever finish this palette
my travels are my own
yet the longing to share the burden
grows with each passing step
a lonely man on a lonely journey
through that which causes my misery . . .
my life

Scott Brady Trager

Valentine

My hands are here to hold
And comfort you when it's cold.
They will help you up when you fall,
They're at your beck and call.
All I ask is that you put your hands in mine
And be my Valentine.

Danny Lee Hecht Jr.

My Light

Lying awake on a sleepless night
Basking in the glory of a soft, red light
It shines through your eyes and into my soul
Casting a warm glow over my entire world
Shadows and fears exist no more
What lies before me is an open door
Just take my hand and walk me through
I'll endure each step, so I can be with you
You say I'm an angel sent from above
I think only a heavenly creature is worthy of your love
I heard the sound of your voice, as you uttered my name
And I knew that without you, my life could never be the same
Now I relish the nights and long for the day
Happy and carefree, as fairies at play
All these emotions both tangled and free
Right here in this moment is where I want to be
So, hold me now and release me never
With you in my life . . . I'll find forever

Nerissa Rene Hosein

Give Her Back

Dedicated to Glinda Scott

My heart bleeds to see you lying there
To think that you were so vibrant last night
The Pensacola sun on you face
The Florida breeze at your back
And now the sickness takes over your glow
The light in your eyes
The brightness of your smile
Damn the cancers that have taken you
Forgive me, Father, for the thought
You are my friend, my guide, my mentor
The love of my life, my center
Please, for all the love in the world and in Heaven
And that supplied by God himself
Return to me and to he and to them that need
Place at the feet of man that which has your touch
Place in the hands of man that which holds your love
Come back to him and them and me

D. Loraine Allman

God Took a Great Man

There was a great man laying in a coffin;
people say he died of what we call coughing.
Others say he was God's chosen one;
he did all the work he could have done.
He was always there when you needed him,
but one day God just let his lights go dim.
He always knew, he had a great sister named Sue.
Then there was wonderful Sarah and pretty little Jenny,
who always could afford a penny.
His parents were always there, but God just couldn't bear.
God just took him away one day,
but we will always know he is here to stay.
He will always be in us, no matter how hard we work in the dust.
God took him for something, but we all know it wasn't for nothing.
He was a very special, kindhearted type of guy;
he will always be here, no matter if we told him BYE.
We will love him forever,
and he will never leave us; NEVER.

Christy Sterwerf

Kisses

I asked you what you wanted for your birthday.
You said a kiss.
So in this bag are a dozen kisses.
On each one make a million wishes.
Close your eyes make a wish.
I will give you another kiss.

Kristin Michelle Gibason

The Sun Can Still Shine Through

No matter how down you get,
You can still feel good!
Like when it is raining and pouring,
You don't always need a hood!
'Cause even on rainy days,
The sun can still shine through!
So if you're feeling alone,
Grab some pictures or pick up the phone!
Because, even if there is distance in between,
There are memories to be shared or seen!
'Cause even on rainy days,
The sun can still shine through!
If there is anything you ever need,
I will always be there in your heart!
And if you ever miss me, just search,
You'll find that we are never truly apart!
'Cause even on rainy days,
The sun can still shine through!

Robert Schuster

What I Want

I want to be loved, not for who you think I am,
not what you want it to be, good loving for me.
Real love, with no strings attached,
I want to give you my heart, don't want to take it back.

I've been searching a very long time,
for that, oh, so true love to comfort this heart of mine.
Baby, please don't waste my time,
a woman like you is really hard to find.

I'm telling you, lady,
I'm only human, searching for that possibility
for that genuine someone, with the sincerity,
Someone who is always there to hold me.

Caress me, love me, teach me, and hold me.
Who will shine my feelings,
all the good meaning,
all morning, noon, all season.
I want to be loved.

Chanlah Codrington

Who Am I?

You've shown me a world,
a world I can always feel joy.

You've shown me a life,
a life that was unknowingly mine.
You've shown me love,
a love that surrounds my soul.

You've awakened my confidence,
the confidence that lies deep within.
You've given me your heart,
the heart I hold dear.

You have shared with me your soul,
the soul I found sincere.
Everything I am, Everything I will be,
will be for you

For it was you who made me into who I am
today.

Tina N. Lively

Why?

Why must it be me who is always stepped upon?
Why dost the sun bring this dreadful dawn?
Why must a life be torn apart for the love of such an art?

Why is my mind pounding with thought?
Why is the painting still unbought?
Why is the answer yet untold, for the question isn't too bold?

Athena Jean Hernandez

God's Greatest Gift

To Erin, God's greatest gift
I woke up this morning to a sound
It was the sound of a message waiting
As I reached over to see what it said
I felt a sensation all around me

When I looked, it simply said, "Good morning"
But they were a very special two words
They meant more than anyone else's words
Because they came from God's greatest gift

As I walked home from school
I was thinking of where I'd soon be
Not just another house, but something more
It's the home of God's greatest gift

Someday you, too, will see what I see
You're not just another girl in my life
In fact, the others didn't even start to compare
And it's because you are God's greatest gift

Daniel Allen Grevillius

Seeing What Is Behind

Open your eyes to a world that is blind,
Sacrifice you'll find.
So find out who is to blame for this humanity in shame.
Draw upon yourself a circle,
A circle that will become a miracle;
But make it a different shape, but caution,
Because the mind can rape.

"Communicate, my child," says the constrictive mother,
Yet I alone am unable to grasp its significance.
But significance does not matter,
Let your eyes be your telephone cord
From your mind to the outside world.
A life with a purpose, you're really "on-line"
To the net of beyond.
Advice comes and goes,
But the best, no one shall know.
So, love, do not love what you want,
But love what you have.

Alonso Isaac Hernandez

Hidden Away

I love you so much,
You don't even know
The feelings I'm dying to show.

They're locked up, hidden away,
Much like the sun
On a cloudy day.

The sun is my heart,
The clouds are a wall,
Blocking my feelings from moving at all.

They try to break away, and try to be free,
But there's so many things
Standing in the way of you and me.

There's my heart and my head,
My mom and my dad,
And last, but not least,
There's you.

Harmony Jean Waldron

Love

Love . . .
Like popcorn
Always has a habit of bursting at the wrong time.
It always seems to pop . . .
When the cover's not quite on the top . . .
And I'm not ready for it.

Cynthia R. Moir

I Am

I am a loving person who likes to help people
I wonder why there are fish in the sea
I hear the mute speaking
I see a light at the end of the tunnel
I want to experience the world from another angle
I am a loving person who like to help people
I pretend I'm a bird flying through the sky
I feel the pulse of the unforgiven sinner
I touch moon rocks never touched by the hand of man
I worry when I think of my sister and her broken family
I cry for the ones who don't know Jesus
I am a loving person who likes to help people
I understand that not everyone believes in Christ
I say everyone is a sinner
I dream of freedom for the world
I try to reach out to the unforgiven
I hope I make a difference in somebody's life
I am a loving person who like to help people

Erin Alltop

Moments Anew

What is it I have embraced
All that I knew has flown away
Wondering am I, how far is far
That last embrace
Is this really the day
The time my embracing has turned away
In on me and mine arms so lean
As those days behind the scene
Soft and round were those days
So small, so helpless
Those little birds I grazed
And nightly watched a simple gaze
My heart it is a blaze
With fear and wonder so complex, a maze
I know I was there back then
Holding, holding till when
The time clock ticked, the little birds flew
Away, away to something new

Lorraine Cannatta

Dreaming

Puffy, white clouds;
And castles fair;
Tall, white oaks;
And a large, stone chair
Are all noble symbols
Of the dreams we share.
A phantom, green ship
On a peaceful, blue sea,
A rainbow-painting eagle
Flies the galaxy,
And all the stars twinkle
From the thoughts you send me,
As our souls rise high and mingle in eternity.
Fairies will dance upon crystal atmospheres,
While multicolored leaves sail the air.
Flowers will bloom with colors so fair,
As they smile at the thoughts of the yesteryear.
Do you dream?

Lisa Gladin

New Awakening

May the rays of the new day's sun bring you new hope and joy.
Give you light, love, and comfort at your deepest time of need.
Hug you, hold you, and protect you all throughout your day.
Guide you to inner peace and true happiness.
Lie you down at day's end and rock you to sleep.
Only to awake to a new day's sun.

Gigi Nanette Freeman

Differences

Why am I different, so strange to you?
Why do you tease me, is it fun to do?
'Cause if I'm so different,
Then what do you think you are?
The embodiment of normality?
With no emotional scars.
Because if you are normal,
And if you are cool,
Then what about everyone else in the school?
Are they all "uncool,"
Are they all strange too?
Because if they are then I think that I'm sick of you.
He, she, they, me.
Different then you,
As you can see.
So give up your image,
give up your frame,
Because it is getting so lame.

John Perkins

A Wrinkle in Time—Take a Breath

Everyone's life is just a wrinkle in time.
We
leave our mark in our passing.
With this in mind she sits by the water's edge
as she
ponders the meaning of her wrinkle in time.

Have I done all that I could?
Do I need to do more for everyone?
Are the things that I
have done good enough?
Or can I be better?

My life goes on, as it does for everyone and
should do.
She caresses the water's edge,
the
ripples sending out the meaning of her
wrinkle in time. She sighs. . . .

Kristina Diane Lunsford

Sensual Inhalation

Breathe in, breathe out,
The air is thick about.
Necessity to my soul,
My lungs take you in and hold.
Air that holds purity, air that holds fear,
The anxiousness I possess when drawing you near.
Where do I stand in this battle for my heart?
Am I outnumbered, did I lose before the start?
Colors inside you, so beautiful, give me so much pain,
Worries so in depth cloud my flustered brain.
The lust I held in my spirit left this stain!
Love that seems so lovely causes me to go insane!
It seems I am no longer Abel for this Cain has slain;
Just a game, all in vain, love made to be so plain
I am no longer an angel, a demon I have turned!
Wings clipped by hatred, halo scorched and burned!
My face moist, sweat-beaded; my eyes teary and hot.
Yet I continue to inhale you; breathe in, breathe out.

Angel Pierre

My Heart

My love for you flows freely, like the river to the sea
and like the majestic eagle soaring high above the trees.
My heart is but a butterfly flying on a gentle breeze;
keep it safe and hold it tender when in your hands you seize.
Hold me close, but not too tightly for I must walk on my own;
then when you do recapture me, I surely will be home.

Nancy Teresa Gilbert

Shores

The ocean needs the shore to embrace it
After its tumultuous journey.
Likewise, its depth to gain its strength
And fortitude building wave upon wave
Until the shore calms its fears.
But what if the shore were to disappear?
What then becomes of the tenacious sea?
It will continue its rage
And peace will never come.
The sea will look to the heavens for help,
Calm, and guidance,
But soon will realize that
It was its own tirade
That forced the shore to leave.
For even a seashore requires
Tenderness and care.
Left only with fear and anger
It too departs.

Willa K. Ward

What Is the Truth?

"That is in accordance with the fact or facts."
The formal definition of truth . . . but does it always fit?
To tell your parents the truth is to tell them what you believe.
It may not be exactly what happened,
But as far as you're concerned it, is the truth.
A mother has a dying child, do you tell her that he is dying?
Or do you tell her he is dead, at peace, to ease her agony?
Truth can be as much as one word to a mother
Or a testimony to a grand jury.
It can be the most joyous thing ever said or not.
A baby cries, she's not lying to her mother saying, "I'm hungry."
Truth can be told in so many different ways,
A baby's cry, a silence.
Why is the truth always forced to be told?
If just one white lie was told, it could save a family.
"That is in accordance with the fact or facts."
The formal definition of the truth . . . but does it always fit?
What is the truth?

Andrew Colman

one thousand ill-faded wishes and kisses

sometimes i have
colorful dreams of . . .
foggy alleyways and naked trees who, with red dawn lips
it hurts to smile . . . sometimes
never i fear to tread
in gestation of an apocalypse-torn moon
the heavens yield
for her
parcheesi vixens . . . control your every move
never letting go
we make statements
in moves and gestures
if they were any closer
i may have gotten hurt . . . by understanding
relaxing highways of mine
massage your dreams
always leaving you
wanting more

Ian Morsch

Love

Love is the color of a new spring flower.
Love sounds like waves washing upon a lonely and romantic shore.
It tastes like a kiss.
It smells like something new.
It looks like a newborn child.
Love brings along a feeling of happiness.

Joseph Micheal Faulkner

Michael Is Seven!

SEVEN—What a great age to be . . .
So much to learn, to do, to see!
And here you are, in second grade . . .
Smart as can be . . . you've got it made!
Just pay attention and do your best;
You'll have an A on every test!
But having fun is a part of life—
And days are nice when free of strife.
So have your fun and play baseball;
Relax and read . . . go to the mall!
The week we visited was so much fun!
You kept us busy and on the run.
The hardest part was leaving you,
And now we know what we must do.
This decision we must face
With lots of prayer and God's good grace.
If New York is where you'll stay. . . .
Look for us; we're on our way!

Sherry Jackson

Fathers

I don't know why, and no one else seems to know,
Why little girls need their fathers to help them to grow.
To help them adjust to this ever-changing world,
All you fathers out there take care of your little girl.
I never had my father's love, but I guess that's OK,
I just can't help wondering if I'd had it, where I would be today.
My mother, she loves me, but it just isn't enough,
I need you, Daddy, because I'm just not that tough.
I don't know why you left me, I haven't got a clue,
But know one thing for sure—I really needed you.
I often say that it's just too late,
Because over the years there's been love, fear, and hate.
I sit here today wondering what next to do?
I've just got to find a way to get closer to you.
Finally, I know this isn't all my fault, because
For so many years you were the parent, and I a child to be taught.
All that's the past, and it's gone for good,
We've got to find a way, Dad, to both be understood.

Delecia Page

A Seasoned Fancy

Belonging to a caliginous world,
she wept at the desperation that plagued her.
Sadness and numbness coursing her veins,
freezing her soul.
Her mind crossing the border of solitude, Oh
God . . . oh God, what to do?
At the stem of possibility, her heart pleads
with her thoughts.
Tumultuous and violent thoughts racing and
seizing.
Ultimately, tragically, sadly, she aches for
silence and peace.
An ebb of calmness, means to an end of a life
spent in hurt. A life of being captive to the
evils of her mind.
She wails in pain . . . a monstrous, deafening scream
tearing into her, like a blade. Yet, she goes on
and sleeps to the gentle hum of a spirit fading.

Yvette Maricruz Hernandez

Scarecrow in the Cornfield

Scarecrow in the cornfield always standing there at night
Gives the people walking a deepened sense of fright.
But when all the crows come, he always does his job;
If just one gets close enough, he scares off the whole mob.
So, when you go out walking, don't look to your right side,
For if you happen to see him, you'll turn and run and hide.

Jason Michael Sobota

Missing You

Each day that you are gone, I miss you more;
I wonder how I made it without you,
And you wonder what you are here for?
There is no doubt in my mind,
You were sent to brighten my world;
My promise is to do the same for you.
Move on ahead and don't look back,
Your strength will grow each day;
You'll find peace within your mind
You thought you lost one dismal day.
Each day brings new beginnings,
Don't let yours drift by;
Don't let anything stop you from winning.
The biggest fight of all . . . is life.
The biggest pleasure of all . . . is the love around you.
I am so close to you, my heart will never leave you.
When your days and nights are filled with problems,
Think of me and how much I love you.

Sherene Moore

Who Are You?

The time has arrived at last
When you're approaching me very fast
You are very much alluring
For you I can do everything
I will not bother
If I am hit by other
I don't like when you're swiped
I think the person should be killed
With other you are beset
Everyone wants other to be baffled
They all are using best of their powers
Lest you shall be caught by others
At last I am able to have you
I won't let enemy to get you
Everyone wants you without any fear
What so special about you dear?
No one can dare to touch you at all
As I am the goal keeper and you, my football.

Meenakshi Vaid

Quiet Place

Make thyself a quiet place.
What makes thee worry so?
Dost thou not know I AM LORD of all,
And "all" concerns thee too?
For I know thine heart and feel thy tears,
and I hear thine every prayer.
Didst thou think in thine despair that I had turned away?
Dost thou not know I AM LORD of all,
And "all" concerns thee too?
Dost a father cast away his child if he truly loves his child?
What makes thee think that I thy FATHER would cast away MYchild?
Dost thou not know that I thy FATHER truly loves thee?
Keep thy tiny hand in MINE.
And keep thy thoughts with ME.
For I AM the LORD thy GOD,
I AM a quiet place to be.

Anita P. Slaughter

Within My Heart!

Within My Heart I have found something more precious than gold!
It cannot be bought, stolen or sold,
Sometimes within our dreamers it is foretold.
It is something that shall transcend time till the bitter end.
What, you may ask, is it that may have no end.
It is the LOVE I share from Within My Heart with my best friend!

Scott Alan Murray

Hug Me, Daddy

In loving memory of George Edward Pritchard
Where are you, Daddy?
I need a hug, but I can't find you anywhere.
You left us a month ago.
I need a hug, Daddy.
I search for you in every room, in the yard,
in the stores, even in church, but you are not there.
I cry, because I am so lonely for you, Daddy.
Where are you?
I need a hug, Daddy.
I look into the sky and see all those clouds,
so fluffy and white, and the sky is so blue.
Oh! Daddy, that's where you are, Heaven.
Now I feel your hugs each time I look up.
Thank you, Daddy, for the life you gave me
and for all those hugs.
Hear me now, Daddy, I love you, and I always will.
Don't forget to hug me, Daddy, when I look up.

Dolores Ellen Amolsch

Loving Chance

As I sit here in the silence,
thoughts of you fill my mind . . .
You have been on my mind for sometime;
I wonder if you are the one I was meant to find.
You bring a smile to my face and to my heart.
Sometimes I just don't know where to start.
Being held in your arms when we dance
makes me feel as if we have a chance.
All it took was one fleeting glance.
You are my light when I am feeling down. . . .
You know just how to lift away the frown. . . .
I would go to the ends of this world for you. . . .
For my fears have come true. . . .
I believe I have fallen in love with you.

Teri Ann McKinney

The Hummingbird's Secret

Some people say that the hummingbird hums
Because he doesn't know the words to be sung
Or it's his way of having fun
Other people say that the hummingbird hums
Because some words are just best unspoken
Words like good-bye left his heart broken
For many centuries songwriters, poets, and scholars
Prayed and asked for guidance from above
To describe that which we call love
There is no beginning or an end
The hummingbird's secret is that he knows
Love is an emotion that constantly grows
It's no more a mystery for we already know
There are no words that can describe
Emotional expressions meant to be felt inside
There are no words that man could utter
That's why the hummingbird keeps wings aflutter
The hummingbird's secret is that he knows

Harold Ireland

The Sequoia Tree

I watch over my young, parenting silently
Watching trees tumble and my brothers and sisters topple
I live through violent storms and sunny skies
I tower the forest looking onward and almost touching the heavens
The wind tickles me, and birds use my smooth branches to live
I look on, watching and waiting—waiting for a new day to come

Jonn A. Jackson

New Land

Silence storms through his forehead
Blind sun visions melt to crimson happiness
In the sea of green eyes wide open

Frozen by strange childhood sounds
Whispering echoes from far behind
His steel drum face is paralyzed
Amidst the ants of a crowd
Without refuge, aimless, loud

Yet the flood arrives
And his mind strives
Through fruity water
To toothless laughter

Some wonder hands
Would lead him to
Odd wonderlands
As he dives for the guiding string
To wonder always wandering

Albrecht Barth

I Can't Breathe

Let me up, I can't breathe!
My soul's in isolation and cannot leave.
Boxed up, locked in—I'm really scared.
My focus forced only on you—never shared.
You forbid me to enjoy family and friends.
Is this love? No! Just a route to the end.
Are you so selfish, jealous, and afraid
That I'll lose interest and go away?
Don't you realize what marriage means?
Bringing us all together to make one team.
Instead of pulling us all apart,
Be not the Grinch—expand your heart!
Erase the mistrust in everyone's eyes.
Loving—sharing gives you the greatest prize.
If you refuse this timely advice,
You'll follow the last two and pay the price.
Instead, drop the fear and the NEED for control,
Please allow us to reach the ultimate goal!

Judy Strunk

Red Roses, Red Roses

Red Roses, red roses come over and stay
Make our day and we'll see you all the way,
Although you don't last long
you often brighten our day,
Standing there in water looking so peaceful
Watching your buds open and bloom
seeing you give life to the room,
After closing, then dropping your pedals
they begin to settle,
You make us realize how short life is
and to take it as bliss,
We can go at any given moment
as we know we would be missed
Not knowing when or how
something can pull us away,
Even on a wonderful, brightful day
as you made us feel the first day
when we brought you home to stay.

Christine Sanko

For You

I reach out for you
In the dim light I feel your arms
Enveloping me and pulling me close
I inhale deeply, your scent fills my lungs
It is spaceless here
No world outside me exists
Except for you . . .

Shirley Buchli

Only This

Only This
Enchanted though it is I be,
By thy visage . . . bewitching me,
I know 'tis only this . . . no more,
So you see, that's what the tears art for—
For I think of thee . . . quite truthfully,
In a way suggesting more,
Not merely as someone that I love,
But as someone . . . I adore—
One to whom . . . of heart and soul,
I would . . . so . . . surrender,
But enchanting as such thoughts may be,
They have little hope . . . in reality.
So this is why thou see the tears,
for though I think of thee,
The tears remind me, that in fact,
Ne'er shall they e'er . . . be real.

Rycharde M. Wey

The One for You

A single mom doing the best she can
To raise her family without a man.
There was one who hurt her and messed
With her mind, oh, he must have been so blind.
From the moment I met her,
I couldn't help but see
This beautiful woman made for me.
She goes without, so her family can have.
She washes the clothes and gives
The baths and never once complained,
But not one sees her pain.
She needs someone to hold her tight,
Someone to tell her it will be all right.
Someone who will listen to her
And never let her down,
Someone who will always be true.
Someone who would never make her blue,
Babe, that someone is me, the one for you.

Richard Sanderford

Sunshine

She comes to me constantly
I awake from her glare
She arrives within my eyes with a flare
She wraps her rays upon me romantically
The sunshine and she come to mind instantly
Many days I find my eyes lost in a deep stare
Planetary bodies tell me to beware
She and I are separated by day and night
But our bodies will cross eventually
It is night and I feel isolation
The cool air surrounds my blue physique
Millions of lights try to convince me to become her lover
Without her near me I find seclusion
But forlornness brings forth a search for
Her warm beautiful yellow body
I can't find her, so I will sit in the sky
And hover around until she shines
Then I will know the sun is all mine

Jerome Lawrence

Allow Me

The child within me
screams for forgiveness
to allow the spirit of adventure
to roam the voids of time, space
To relive past enjoyments
to taste the sweet nectar of laughter, love
Am I a part of this child
who seeks truth honestly,
or do I yield to the present now?

Antoinette Shahak

Such Love

I often wonder if we'll know each other
That awesome day when once again we meet.
Will you rush forth in rapt anticipation
Will I fly to your open-armed Retreat?

Or will such things be forfeited in Heaven?
And will no touch of fire be welcomed there?
And will our eyes not be allowed to focus
Upon such depth of love still smoldering there?

Oh, God Divine! Omnipotent, Eternal!
By your design, this love was deigned to be!
How can I ever discipline my spirit
To put aside such love, to set it free?

Yet knowing God is love and total wisdom
I place my trust in His Almighty Plan
And know love will be love, in Earth or Heaven
And God will teach us both to understand.

Edith L. Piret

Provided

I read his book, *The Science of Being*,
I thought to myself, now that has meaning
I gathered up three of my five children quickly
And off we flew to Majorca, Spain, near Italy.

It was there we were given a glorious treasure,
A Mantra of our own, oh, what a pleasure,
To transcend the relative, I have to say,
We all chose a winner that blessed day.

Now we have what it takes to survive
Any negative happening while we're alive.
We transcend twice a day and over time,
We join God our Father, who is also thine.

It's thrilling to know we're welcome in His home.
It's amazing to realize you are never alone.
It's just the greatest joy there is,
To know that not only I, but you, are also His.

Ruth B. Ferguson

Hidden Meanings

Shrouded ideas of freedom from the grip
The grip of evil confusion
Mankind is bound to fall head first
Only to realize that they were warned
Subjected to the ones they raped and scorned

There will be no mercy

Justice has a balance
The scales lean in favor of the despised
The day the proud gets chastised
Revenge for those baptized in the holy hoax
There is an antidote for the poison
The truth will blare
Blare like Bird blowing his sax in defiance
Defiantly awakening to the reality
The reality of being a dead man walking
Meanings are often hidden

Matthew Anderson

I'm Back and Understanding

We were young and didn't know of such things as love.
We never knew we would one day leave each other.
If I would have known I would be out of your life,
then I would have learned about love the day I met you.
But it was too late, and I was gone with the years.
Now I'm back and I want to let you know I loved you,
but my mind just couldn't comprehend.
So here I am, older and filled with experience and ready
to love a man like you. Do you understand?

Precious U. Williams

Father of Mine

Oh! Dearest Father of mine,
The love we share is of a special kind.
From the moment I read the scripts on the cards of long ago,
I knew that my "Father" must have loved me so.
I knew in my heart what I did was not wrong,
The "Love" in those few lines was so strong.
I want you to know how much I do care
For the understanding and kindness you share.
I know that no matter what I've done or do wrong,
You'll always be there with an arm so strong.
You're kind and gentle and have a strong back,
Courage and thoughtfulness you'll never lack.
I hope you can see from these few words,
My "Love" is not like the tiny bird
To come for a while, then fly away.
My "Love" and I are here to stay.

SCAR

Sherry Ryan

Teachers Are So Great

Teachers are great; they teach us to do math and read and write.
Teachers teach us to play right.
Teachers teach us not to fight.
Teachers teach us to do so many things.
Teachers teach our minds to be smart and bright.
Without teachers we wouldn't learn anything.
Our minds wouldn't be smart and bright,
Couldn't add or read and write.
Teachers teach from the heart; they are so great,
Teach us about the present and the past,
Like dinosaurs and fossils and old things like that,
Teach us why the moon is so bright
And how to count bright stars in the night.
Without teachers we couldn't learn to do these things.
They teach us so many things.
Teachers teach from the heart; they are so great!

Edna Mae Goeppinger

Awaiting My Soul's Assignment

While my soul waits, I anticipate the
challenge that lies before me.
While I remain in this life, I throw away
the strife and look forward to a new beginning.
I dwell not on my failures or the past,
I live not for promises that may lie in tomorrows,
I live in the moment and with all of my
being, delve deep to understand it's meaning.
I contemplate what has made this life great,
not allowing my judgement to overtake me.
Eternally grateful for the time that I've
had and for all of my worldly experiences.
I can only pray that soon will come the
day when my soul will go on before me,
I smile at the thought, and know there is
not, one moment that I will regret it.

Joan Esther Kearns

And I Smile

Your name echoes through the recesses of my mind
And I smile

Your voice fills my heart with inexpressible joy
And I smile

Your touch stirs passion's desires within my breast
And I smile

Your love permeates the depths of my soul
And I smile

Cynthia-Joy Webber

My Whole Heart

I held my child close as he was drifting off to sleep,
Rocking him as I sang lullabies.
I whispered, "My whole heart is filled with love for you to keep."
Then quizzically he looked into my eyes.

I smiled at him and wondered what had bid him to awaken
From gentle dreams that drifted toward the dawn.
As if he'd heard my thoughts, he turned to me and said
"You have so many hearts; I have but one."

Taken by surprise I stirred the words within my head.
The prospect of a simple phrase was bleak,
Searching for an answer, where more questions formed instead.
That's when my son again began to speak.

"You gave me one whole heart you filled with love for me alone,
And one each to my sister and my brother.
I know you must have more in there for others you have known.
I guess God knew just how to make a mother."

Sarah A. Taylor

Whatever It Takes

Teardrops are falling, it's been a long day,
Perhaps my memory might bring you back this way.
Long distance calling, just like it's free,
Maybe one little tender word will bring you right back to me.

You're across the ocean, you embrace it all so well;
You hide the most important part, the rest I just can't tell.
Rather than emotion, you laugh at simple lies;
Take heed of Eastern influence, I still see it in your eyes.

That fragrance that you're wearin' escapes me now and then,
But if that's all your wearin' tonight please, dream of me again.
Thanks again for sharin' those tender thoughts of me,
It didn't seem to take that long to bring 'em across the sea.

I hope it only needs to be a letter or a song,
Whatever it takes to bring you home could only be too long.
Missing you is easy, my heart is in your hand,
Bring it back in tender peace and in my arms again.

Anthony D. Broderick

His Final Pace

How can a person die so young?
I ask myself where did he go wrong?
I forlornly wait for the moment to come,
for a person who's dearly loved to be taken away.
Even though he might be gone,
my love for him will always be strong.
Days, months I sit and wait awake for the moment to come,
someday he'll be gone, and I ask myself where did I go wrong?
He'll die young, but my love for him will grow even more strong.
How can I take his fate that I wait to begin and throw it away,
when I go to bed and look to my right I know he'll be in a better
place for this moment I'll be ready to face.
Even though I ask myself was this his final peace?
Then I sit and say someday we'll meet again
and forever will our love will be strong,
I ask myself how can a person die so young?

Olga Rivera

I Miss You

I remember the day we met in June,
How I looked into those deep blue eyes.
When I tried to speak, I just sounded like a buffoon.
So I just stared into her eyes,
And it was as if I could see, past all her secrets and lies.
That day I remember so well,
How I miss it so.
If only that guy had chose
Not to drink and drive.

Adam Rogers

With You at All Times

When you are drowning in your sorrow
Every step of the way, I shall follow
To lift you up by giving you a hand
So you can pull yourself back into this land

When uncertainties of life are casting a shadow in your mind
Answers to questions, I will help you find
I hope you know, you have a friend ready to hear
Waiting for you at all times with an open ear

When every door seems to shut in your face
When of hope you can't find a single trace
Just remember, in this world you are not alone
I am here for you, together we shall wonder about the unknown

When you are smiling or when you are crying
When you make it or when you are trying
When you pass or when you fail
I shall be your bird that will get you out of your own jail

Nayla S. Obeid

Holy Lands Quest

Written for Eric, my lifelong friend
Going to the Holy Lands in my pickup truck
We're going to catch some 'gators if we have any luck
We drive down the road slowly with 'gators on our mind
If we look carefully, they won't be hard to find
We spot some across the way, but pictures are all we take
We also see some big ones sunning by the lake
As we travel further and further down the street
Eric spots some baby 'gators that he would like to meet
Quietly he walks down a path along the land
Hoping that real soon he'll have a 'gator in his hands
As I turn back to get the camera to take pictures of our quest
There Eric stood with a baby 'gator near his chest
Pictures are all we took of that 'gator he caught with ease
We went home with pictures and the alligator was released
So we plan to return to catch one a size much greater
As the old saying goes, "see you later, alligator"

Lawrence Blau

Friendship

Friendship is the most wonderful thing,
The most wonderful thing I have ever seen.
Full of surprises and suspense,
All up-to-date and never past tense.

Friendship is never hard to find
If you're nice, generous, and always kind.
True friendship never ends
As long as you live you'll be forever friends.

If your friendship should suddenly end,
You might not get it back, it will all depend
On how you act and how hard you are trying.
Life is full of pain and full of crying.

But don't worry now, it will all be okay.
Just be nice, don't give it away.
We will all have a friend,
A great friend that will last till the end.

Samantha Lynn Birch

Untitled

I hear God's voice in laughter and in song
I feel God's touch in kindness
And in the gentle breeze
I see God happy in dance and in play
I smell God in the fragrances
That are carried by the wind
I am aware of God's presence everywhere
I see God's face in all creation
I know God is

Angelic Maude Wheatley

Thunderstorms

I sat there and laid in my bed,
while thunderstorms and tornados ran through my head.
I looked out my window and started to cry
when I saw all the things flying by.

I went to get my mom and dad out of their room,
I thought to myself, we have met our doom.
We went through the hall and out the front door,
I said to my family, I don't want to see more.

We went to the storm shelter, and we fled in;
there is nothing in here but cans made of tin.
We waited a minute and a tornado came by,
and that's when my father started to fly.

After the storm was over we stepped outside,
and tears came to my mom's and my eyes.
On that night we watched our father die,
that's what happens when thunderstorms come by.

Eric Keith Johnson

Forevermore

Shh, listen! Can you hear that?
Listen close, "Drip, drip."
What's that noise, you ask?
It's what remains of the heart I once had,
Before he broke it.
He held me close and whispered in my ear,
"I will protect and love you always."
Instead he pushed me away, showing me
What pain and heartache really was.
Listen, it's getting louder! "DRIP, DRIP."
My heart breaks more and the life pours out onto the floor,
While he sits with a smile, waiting for me to walk out the door.
His life will move on
With just the feeling of victory,
For he knows I can never love again.
How can I, for he'll be gone,
And what remains of my heart will be on the floor, forevermore.

Mona Christina Martinez

Fallen

I've fallen for you, hard and true
The things between us I will not say,
Except to my closest friend.
I could have told the person I hate ,
She said that you and her are "Together."
I wanted to ask you out,
hoping it would not end on a sorrowful note.
But the things I did not do I cannot revoke.
But things I did I do not regret.
She said that you hate me.
Is it true?
Or does she lie beneath a protective blanket of lies?
My friend assured me, "None of it is true.
If it is, why does he talk to you from dusk 'til dawn."
I replied, "There is probably nothing better to do."
I have fallen for you,
If you hate me or if you don't, tell me true.

Jacquelin Anne Joslin

The Heart

Lord, allow me to preach
Your word for all to understand
Reach out to every woman
Child, and man . . .
So that each may hear from you
And know from the start
Know in their heart that you meant
For them to hear with the inner and outer ear
The heart

Lorna D. Dorham-Pipkins

My Family Pets

I have a dog and his name is Maxx
He never ever wants to relax.
He's black and white with one big collar,
and when he barks, he makes a holler.

He stretches his body
and his tongue sticks out,
and then he yelps
with one big shout.

My cousin has a dog, and he is brown.
He looks at me with one big frown.
His chain is silver with one big tag,
and when you pull it, he tends to gag.

My grandma has a dog, and he's a poodle,
and his hair is like a fusilli noodle.
He looks just like an Easter bunny,
but when he prances and dances, it looks so funny.

Shannon Catherine Farrell

Undying Love

My undying love for you is a never ending
story where i don't know where to begin
heart felt passion more than just friends
thoughts of you that last forever my
undying love wishes we could always be together.
My undying love is so strong, as my heart
beats each beat carry's my love on. my
undying love for you you will never go wrong.
as i close my eyes i think of you my
undying love , wishing we could be together
forever with our undying love that will last forever.

LaShaun Patrick Cooper

The Flames of the Storm

All across the sky
The flames of the storm burn and die,
And the sunken grey clouds provide
A shadow to the bolts so high.

While all along the sunset ridge
Another day is passing on,
In the eastern plains only hope exists
Of a day born anew.

Only to stop and think of the beauty
Takes a moment away from a long day,
And it shapes a feeling of timeless ages
Of which a small part has been played.

A new breeze blows low and fresh
From the newly dampened eastern plains,
And the arched lights lost in a sky so grey
Give thoughts of rain to a new day.

Thomas Rockwell

The Voice

As I sit here in this crowd,
I hear a voice harsh and loud:
"I know you want to get away from this place
Where you feel you have no face
No voice, no soul
Because the world is bitter and cold."
As the voice got louder it said,
"You can never escape from me . . .
I'm in your head."

Margaret Williams

Enter My Reality

Once you step out of your reality
and into mine,
there is no chance of reentry,
so don't look back.
You have just crossed the threshold
of an undiscovered world,
occupied with twisted thoughts
and demented dreams.
This is my castle,
my safe haven,
locked away from everyone else.
Before opening the door,
remember to wipe your feet
and clear your mind of all you have known.
My palace of deliberation
will teach you the truth,
and show you the way.

Rachel M. Watson

Drifted

Far away, I know I've drifted
Off this Earth and that which inhabits it
Off to another world
A better world
One without complications
One without grief
Without the hassles of reality
Is this paradise?
Or is it another hell still dormant?
Waiting for civilization to come and change it into our world
This paradise, once inhabited, is no longer a paradise
But a mere isle awaiting its destruction
Much like the Earth
Once this paradise is destroyed I drift off again
Onto another paradise
And the process repeats
Far away, I know I've drifted

Tony Divel

A Friend

This poem to you I wrote soon after your painful death.
A friend you were to me
So much a part of life.
I always could depend on you
In fun, despair, or strife.
I helped you out of friendliness,
this none could understand.
Your life was sacred to me
as lending a helping hand.
My thoughts were always with you,
wherever you did go.
Could have been more meaningful
if only I did know.
You were so very ill
those last few months of life,
in vain I hoped and prayed to rid you of the strife.

You were a friend so dear.

Rhonda Maree Wilson

Where Am I?

I am dazed and confused, wandering aimlessly.
I am lost, then found, then lost again.
Where did I start? Where will I end?
Will I ever find my way through this world I am in?
It is like trying to find an exit in a room without doors.
I can run for miles and never move from where I am standing.
Is this just a dream I am having, or is it reality?
If it's reality, who can help me?
And if it's a dream, who will wake me?

William Charles Cagle

Need Someone

Why am I so alone, I feel so incomplete;
What I need is a man to make me feel unique.
I need a man to hold me tight
And kiss me on my cheek,
I need someone to tell me "I love you,"
Just so he could speak.
I don't want someone, who will make me cry
Or make me feel like I want to die.
I want someone just like this,
They always say there is other fish—in the sea of love.
But what I want is something only Heaven can send from above,
I need someone right now before I go berserk!
I really don't want a dumby or a stupid jerk!
If any guy is reading this and think they are this kind,
PLEASE tell me, 'cause I must be very blind!
I need someone right now, at this time;
I must go now, for I have nothing else to rhyme.

Bridget Shelton

The Race

As dawn's early light shines its ray on the track,
all the drivers and crews are getting unpacked;
it's the Daytona 500, the greatest race of the year.
And the ones who have won it hold that memory dear;
there've been many winners to take this great race
with its 200 laps and its blistering pace.
A daring challenge to all in its ranks
with its long, straight always and its high turning banks.
All the drivers know of chances they take,
the risk that's involved with each lap they make.
Only one thing changed at this year's race end,
the sport lost its greatest driver and many's great friend.
He was a legend in his day and always will be,
he will be always missed, that black #three.
On February 18, 2001, the Heavens opened up
to take another son, a husband, a father, a great man, you see,
the Lord said, "Welcome home, Dale Earnhardt, mighty #three."

John Dale III

Rain

The rain continues,
streaking down the windows,
puddles in the courtyard,
rivers in the street.

Hibernating roses begin to sprout
too soon; there may still be a frost.
The grass is tall from so much rain;
the gutter's filled with fallen leaves,
and still it continues to pour
through a cold and damp weekend.
plans for shopping cancelled,
plans for a visit postponed.

The dampness is everywhere, inside and out.
I bundle up in boots and hat and umbrella
to experience the splash,
the fresh scent of an early spring.

Jean Van Tuyle

Life's Cruel

My life burns with an outrage of pain
Pain that has built up like a pressure cooker
Some steam escapes but very few
The rest remains to haunt you
It may be soon, or it may be late
But at one point it has to escape
And when it does, it will be with an outrage of hate
All who cross this path will be my bait
To cast away with a hook in their back of hate

Daniel V. Pittenger

The Rite of Choosing

A path of light opened before my very eyes,
So bright that I dare not venture in,
I saw visions of a beautiful thing,
So lovely that one yearns for eternity.

I sensed a path of darkness to my very right,
Behind me a voice kept urging me, "Hide,"
I saw nothing but never ending darkness,
So dark that it shivers my very soul.

Time and tide waits for no man,
Fearing what I saw was just a mirage, and,
The dark felt so comforting and safe,
A choice must be made at once.

Torn between the choices I have to make,
One of light and the other dark,
I chose the path to my very right,
Only to feel betrayed and regret.

Lim Kok Wei

Pilgrimage

Life is an island floating on dreams,
dreams like an endless sea.
The stars are my guides,
my angels in desperate times.
And somewhere in the distance
I see the lighthouse of hope
in this journey through the heart.
A true pilgrimage this travel is
through vast fields of roses
and roads that seem to lead to nowhere.
When it all becomes too much to deal with,
there I can find the true emotions behind it all.
Fear, anger, and pain; but also sentiment
come from deep within trying to touch my soul.
Then the past meets the present
and it's time to move on to the future
and deal with life, forever floating on my dreams.

Harold Joseph Rosa Herrewegh

Bonnie's Tree

Sunbathed leaves,
A gentle breeze,
Wisps of hair scatter
Falling to the ground.
Another autumn,
We have seen many together.
They talk to me, as if I could hear them.
They know not that
I watch their lives.
Planted melodiously in memories,
In timeless tribute.
Perfumed-stained trunk,
Indelible love, hearts and initials inscribed.
I will tell her story
And theirs,
Long after the fallen leaves and years have
Rolled quietly by.

Rick Alan Harwood

LIFE

LIFE is the greatest thing!
When you hear people say, "That was the greatest thing ever,"
They're WRONG; LIFE is.
When you ask that most important question:
"Why am I here?"
God will answer back:
"Because you are special!"
Answer back to God:
"You're right," and think of life.

Maria Crystle Burhus

More Time

Our friendship was great, you were one of a kind.
You were so perfect, I just wish you had more time.

You are gone now, without a trace.
I never did get to see your face.

Even though you are gone, I know your not that far.
I smell you in the morning dew, I see you in that star.

When I needed you, you were always there.
You helped me through life, and showed that you cared.

So when things go bad, and life is tough, and no one thinks of me,
I close my eyes and think of you, it's an angel that I will see.

The scent of you is everywhere, as if you are still here.
I long to lay beside you now, but can only shed a tear.

God will protect you, and take care of you now,
And when it is my time, I will find you again some how.

Jennene N. Hart

You Are

You are the first star rising on the edge of twilight
The morning glory smile on the glowing face of dawn
A weary traveler's comfort closing eyes to the night
The loving mother's nuzzle to the newborn fawn

You are the wishing child's wonder sent from up above
The fallen feather of an eagle soaring on its way
The laughter in my heart, as I dream of your love
My gaze of admiration when you brighten up my day

You are the ancient, living flame that warms the heart of man
The glimmer of the angel's wing sprawling on the snow
A single ray of guiding light upon this troubled land
A gift of subtle secrets under wrapping and a bow

You are the hidden treasures at the bottom of the sea
A savior cloaked in mystery so few will ever know
Descended of the goddess love come to set me free
As fate has given half the chance, I'll never let you go

Gary Emerson Clarke

Ode to a Beautiful Girl

Another milestone in life, dear birthday girl
Smile evergreen worth a zillion pearl
Younger with each year, you really whirl
Yes, you always put my mind in a perpetual swirl

Work hard, they always say in the IT line
Work smart you say, it is in the mind
What more you need, everything is fine
Where else a more caring person can I find

You are more than a mere lovely face
Pushing through life at a punishing pace
Stop, look, and bestow your profound care
In the new millennium with ease and flair

May the Almighty, His choicest blessings shower
Health, wealth, and desires onwards forever
Upon his pure child, so fair and clever
Eternal happiness, sadness never

Venkateswaran Ramachandran

Love Is to Trust

Here are some things I want to tell you about.
The things I'm going to tell you, there's no need to doubt.
For everything I tell you is sincerely true.
I don't want to be sad and blue.
All I want is true love from you.
For love is to trust and stand by each other.
You have me and I don't want any other.
So give me your love and I will give you mine too.
Truly and forever, I will always love you.

Jamie Rhault

Lord of the Dance

I sit amongst them in a world of darkness with swirling lights
High above stands their lord on a platform erected to the gods
Spinning and preaching their words of praise
They dance around and howl into the night
As if in some kind of trance
and yet as I watch I suddenly feel compelled to join
It is as if the lord on the platform were a wizard
casting a mighty spell on those below him
And I one of them, though not a follower,
cannot resist the call
so I rise and join in the dance.
And as I dance I feel at peace,
the world flashing by in a swirl of colors
The music giving me clarity and putting me into
some kind of trance.
Now I understand what it is like to let go
And why it is that they worship him so.

Robert McGinnis

Don't Cry

Don't cry now, child
Close your eyes
And the pain will go away
Hold your head up
And pretend you're strong enough
To carry the world on your small shoulders
Close your eyes, little one
Dream of your future
Dream of leaving this place
Find yourself there
Don't be afraid, precious one
Someday, always someday
You'll be whole again
Someday, but never today
You'll be strong enough
Keep running, child
Someday you'll find your peace

Laura J. Loveless

Season of Love

I know no sorrow, pain or fear,
When by my side you are standing near
No demon, no evilness, nor unkind thoughts
Do I seek for refuge for which I sought.
Happiness, love, joy, comfort, and peace
Come to me as I understand you.
In your heart are hidden feelings, Give me
your key, I beg you for I am kneeling.
Your love is what I want to share,
Only God knows there cannot be a spare
For He has seen the empty spot in my heart,
and says, "Go in confidence and find that part."
Love so undefining and lasting,
How long must it be until I have found you?
Why waste time looking into the Heavens,
when over the hill and into the valley,
Love is awaiting.

Charlene Curtis-Maki

Tree

The pulsing sunshine moistens my skin and falls,
like a shouted whisper from the sky above.
My feet reach deep into the gritty loam and
draw forth the strength of the earth,
spreading deeper; ever-reaching, ever-hungry.
With my hands, I hold the weight of the wind,
even as I dance to her caressing voice and let
her fingers play her seductive game.
I stand, as I have always stood.

Don P. Harner

Gift from God

It was on a Friday afternoon
In our hearts sorrow loomed

Our mother the artist
Said it was time to part us

We looked to Heaven filled with sorrow
Asking God for support through tomorrow

He sent us an angel in the clouds up above
Letting us know she is ever so loved

I give to you this angel to comfort your heart
All the beautiful colors of her art

When you are sad and can't go on
Look to this angel to know she is not gone

She lives in our hearts and minds
And touches our lives all the time

Linda I. Ellis

My Umbrella in the Rain

I'm happy when you're by my side,
All the bad feelings inside me hide.

You took me from my world of pain,
and helped me through the pouring rain.

The rain that fell when you weren't there,
the rain that I just couldn't bear.

You taught me that it's good to cry,
it helps make the rain puddles dry.

Without you the rain would still fall,
my life would not be happy at all.

I spend my days thinking of when I will meet you,
the one that will make my dreams come true.

The one that I can walk through the rain with, without getting wet,
the one that I haven't yet met.

Kayla Rebecca Vinson

Mistakes

I've made a few mistakes in my life.
I can't help but say I've lived to die.
I smoked, drank, and did bad things.
Thing only good thing I do is sing.
I've stolen, stumbled, and I've drifted off course.
I have never stopped in front of closed doors.
Instead I pressed though without a doubt.
You wouldn't believe how late I stayed out.
I'm getting scared for myself, I wish I had help.
I wish I were able to stay alive.
But now it is my time to die.
If I had a second chance, I would change my life in a single glance.
I wish I could take back the things I've done.
But then again I did have fun.
Good bye cruel world, it's time to leave.
But when I'm gone, please don't weep.
For death is my destiny.

Crystal Dawn Babb

Within the Sea of Tranquility

. . . clothed in a sundress
She walked naked through the field
the virgin, uncut grass
caressed the sides of her legs
as she Aimlessly tried to get there . . .

. . . cloaked in a vail of sadness
with darkness all around
He lay his head within his hands
and waited to be Found. . . .

Stephanie Crain Klemons

My Father's Eyes

My father's eyes were a beautiful blue,
In them I saw a lifetime of wisdom.
I could always pace myself by looking into my father's eyes;
When I pitched a great inning I found pride in my father's eyes;
When I made my goofy faces I found laughter in my father's eyes;
When we had fun together I found joy in my father's eyes;
When I screwed-up I found disappointment in my father's eyes;
When I took responsibility for my mistakes,
I found forgiveness in my father's eyes
When my dad made mistakes I found remorse in his eyes
When we lost grandma Clara I found deep sadness in my father's eyes
When dad looked at my mom I found an unmistakable
sparkle in his eyes
No matter how often I looked into my father's eyes,
no matter what the situation,
I always found love in those beautiful, blue eyes
I'm not sure where to look right now—I miss my father's eyes.

Benjamin Petersheim

Who Am I

I'm who I am, and that's who I'll always be
look into my eyes, and there is nothing more you'll see
I truly believe that in my heart I can be all I can be
but in my mind I am no one until I am me
Reaching for high goals is a big potential, you see
but I'll have to look inside myself to find me before I succeed
I have been told you are just a little girl
you have the rest of your life ahead, you have to see the world
I know that I'm not perfect, and I know I'll never be
and I know that others have failed just like me
but soon they grew stronger and got over the part of failure
That makes me see that I can get over it and have a good future
To end this poem I'll tell you to be who you are
You're always trying to impress someone your mind is
made up of so many parts
but never change for anyone, always be you
I found that out long ago, it's very hard to do

Stacy Ann Nwoko

The Truth Within

The feather floats quietly through my mind
Tickling lost memories that I could not find.
My thoughts are abruptly interrupted,
My solace is soon corrupted.

I am transformed to another time
When life tried in vain to rhyme.
But blackness covered all,
And the feather began to fall.

It plummets to my lonely past
When sadness holds on and firmly lasts.
I feel I can't hold on any longer
Until I find myself getting stronger.

I am now able to face the truth,
Knowing I have the proof
To continue life's story
Without pain and worry.

Marisa Kelley Moore

Why

Why do you depress me so
Why can't I just let you go
I have loved you once, I have loved you twice
But I am the one paying the price

It seems you do not care about how I feel
But do not worry—I think I'll heal

Love takes time, I understand
But just for now will you hold my hand

Claudette M. Desmarais

That Last Good-Bye

The hour of death strikes without warning.
Perchance in sleep, there'll be no morning.
Left unsaid the last good-byes,
when unwarned, your loved one dies.
Reflections crowd your daily life,
of things you should have told your wife.
Alas! Forever they'll remain,
until you reach that last domain.
Penitent and filled with guilt,
you ponder dreams that two had built.
Alone and lonely you become,
that single, desolate, number . . . one.
Time now seems to last forever,
when before it wouldn't . . . ever.
Hours, days, months and weeks,
so much time for one who seeks,
The days gone by, to say "Good-bye."

Lynne Snyder

Dad

I wrote this poem for my dad on the day of his funeral.

Dad, we've come to say good-bye to you,
But we have memories to help us through.
Each day as we continue on,
Memories of a man who was so strong.
You taught us, Dad, with love and laughter,
And encouraged us when there was a dream we were after.
You taught us to work hard and to know right from wrong,
And even shared with us a Korean song.
Your love and commitment to Mom and we seven
Have earned you that rest you deserve now in Heaven.
You fought long and hard this battle with health,
But the Father now gives you your health and your wealth.
We'll miss you, Dad, and it's going to be tough
Not hearing those "I love you's" just before we hang up.
But you've given us hope that when our days are through,
We'll be together again; until then, Dad, WE LOVE YOU!

Michelle L. Qualkenbush

My Little Angel

To my little Amber

I give you my strength when your body is weak.
I give you my voice for you cannot speak.
I give you my legs for yours still rest.
I give you my promise to always do my best.
I give you my eyes for yours cannot see.
I give you my love for you are my baby.
I will dedicate my life and all my love, too,
For you need me now like I have needed you.
You gave me hope when mine was fading,
You taught me patience through months of waiting.
You told me giving up was never a choice,
You spoke in your cry and by the tone of your voice.
You taught me that love was deeper then I knew,
You taught me how to be strong for you.
All we need is to hold out our hand,
And together, my Amber, we will always stand.

Sara L. Guastella

Childhood

I miss my childhood.
When I was a little girl, I was happy and free.
I enjoyed my dolls, toys, and a big world with make of believes.
My life was fun.
This was my precious memories.
When I got older, my world of childhood disappeared.
Now I am an adult.
I wish that I could go back as a child but I can't.
All that I can remember is my childhood.

Nokomis Patterson

The Demons in My Head

They whisper to me at all hours of the day.
They sing songs of death and destruction.
"Take your life with your own two hands."
They say, "Come join us and have some peace.
You'll never find tranquility with the living."
The demons in my head said,
"Close your eyes if you wish,
Rest your body if you can.
We'll always be with you.
We'll cocoon you in a shadow of darkness
And cover you with morbid thoughts and gory dreams."
The demons in my head said,
"Try to live a normal life.
Pray to have a happy thought.
Failure is all you'll ever find,
So come join us—in death you'll find a friend,"
The demons in my head said.

Soumaia Yates

Around Many Times

In the abyss of never ending sound,
The rails stretch once around,
Elevated by magnets' magic hand,
Always rushing to no ones purpose,
I wonder how it all started,
The mighty explosion that tore the chassis,
In the gambling roulettes grip,
And the smoke fizzled to the meager end,
I fought the fiery battles for ages,
It's all inscribed in my watery genome,
I have no power to recite the text,
But it's all printed there in fine print, I know.
The sound rushes all about at the bend,
The metals scratch from the birthing time,
Remembering ages past is so vague,
To the gray matter that passes with time,
Only as printed it will stay to the end.

Acs Saric

My Love

In the moonlight I see his face
Full of calmness, beauty, and grace.
I wait for him, he waits for me;
We are in love, as much as the deep, blue sea.

In dreams I run to him,
In dreams I fly,
In dreams I swim to him,
I see him by and by.

We'll be together forever,
Or so they say.
He loves me and I love him,
This I pray.

He is mine,
And I am his,
I'll be with him through heart, soul, and mind;
And I'll be with him 'til the end of time.

Ashleigh Nicole Behravesh

My Dog Harley

Harley is my favorite dog.
He sits outside in his dog house.
He does not eat a mouse.
When we have leftovers we don't eat,
We give them to Harley, because he likes meat.
When he was a puppy, I was scared of him,
I think that's because he is a vegetarian.
Harley will help you when you are in danger.
When he was little, he laid in a manger.

Allison Inman

Love

Love is tender
Love is kind
Love is loving, pleasant times
With sensitive thoughts
Beyond a dreamer's dream
Sparkling eyes, blissful winds
Charmed for the heart
Kindhearted is he
Compassionate, affectionate, yet also sweet
Fragile strength to overcome
Patient for the other
Understanding the keepsake
But also generous, delicate, with gentle hands
Gleeful moments prance across my mind
With merry days yet to come

A dreamer's dream is never done
Just as his curiosity and love

Kelly Rawhoof

My Hideaway

A cool, cool breeze blows by my head
Whispering soothing words in my ears,
Cleansing my mind.
Tall trees swaying to the wind's soft melody,

Night falls slowly.
The sun lingers in the sky
Radiating an orange glow
And a feeling of peace.

Nature in all its beauty surrounds my being,
Freeing all fears,
Removing numerous doubts.

I have found my hideaway,
A place to be free of me.
Serenity and beauty abound,
My soul is released,
I at last am free.

Glenda Louise Hoagland

A Father's Pain

No one knows a father's pain
Each day he lives he stands in rain
To wonder where his kids might be
The babies he has but does not see
Hey, bad guy; hey, criminal, the system calls
They listen to him, like he speaks to walls
Not worth milk and cookies, not even some honey
All that he's good for is just some money
No walks to the park, no bicycle rides
He sits as the mouse, who always hides
No knees to bandage, no tears to wipe
He sits all alone to smoke his pipe
Perhaps he should die, it's a better excuse
Than to listen to why he is of no use
So, please, remember when you stand in the rain
That somewhere in the world
There's a father in pain

Michael J. Fortsakis

Secret Thoughts

Suddenly, there was you and me
sailing upon the deep blue sea.

We embrace and engage in a long but passionate kiss,
as our hearts pound against each other's chest.

But there are tears falling and a deep pain in my heart
as I awaken to find our travel has led us apart.

Yet the memories linger on in this time of gloom
while the love we shared remains locked in this room.

Bill Edmond Johnson

Yours

During the time we have been apart
I have looked deep within my heart
In search of who I would find there
Is the truth for which I fought

In solitude and silence
I sat within these walls
And asked the Lord for guidance
In finding for whom my heart calls

With each passing day your face I would see
Night after night on my mind you would be
Good night my Love the last words I would say
As I fell asleep at the end of another lonely day

Now my minds question is no longer
I know who my heart always longed for
For my heart foretold my love true
The day I first met you.

Barbara S. Miranda

Noble Retreat

Beyond expectation came a great surprise
Engraved in an invisible driving force
Raging mightily with no point of return
Ne'er before felt, like a flood in a storm.

In the midst of fear, an overpowering warmth
Embraced in the linings of a heart in love
Like a river stream . . . a mountain peak, 'twas a natural mold
It'll live . . . it'll survive . . . only God knows.

Many a time in the life of a woman
Apparelled in distinctly varying styles
Yet leaps painfully to her undestined fate
Succumbs to the dictates of a wrongful love.

Ultimately . . . an escape from the imperfect bondage
Yielding not to her tempting emotion;
Alas! Awakened . . . what an impending failure!
Nobly heartbroken, but a victorious retreat.

Marilyn Uyan

No Going Back

Distanced from my world of safety,
Floating on an open sea;
I look around for familiar faces,
But there to find—only me.

Brothers and sisters no longer touching.
Sons and daughters have gone to shore.
I look around for familiar faces,
There they are found no more.

Once the sun was brightly shining,
And the moon did light the way.
I looked around for familiar faces,
There I saw them every day.

But the bonds of family changes
When the mighty spokes are gone.
Still—I seek familiar faces.
How I long to go home.

Claudette L. Ferguson

It's You!

It's you that makes me feel like this!
I don't know why or how I put up with it!
It's you that makes me so angry inside!
But all it does is sit there and hide.
You blame me for every little thing!
I get so mad I can feel my insides sting.
You make me feel so guilty that I can't even stand you anymore!
Everything you do aggravates me!
So much I don't want to be around you anymore!

Eryn Faille

M.M.

His name is Mickey
Real big eared
Fun for children
Never feared

Oh, Walt Disney
Oh, what luck
To invent this children's wonder
And that Donald Duck

His first cartoon was "Steamboat Willie"
And yes, it was in black and white
There was a bad guy in it though
But Mickey won the fight

In conclusion, Mickey here
Friend to all, not foe
Roaming 'round the TV sets
With his faithful dog, Pluto

Eddie A. Worrilow

Every Time I See You

While I was lying there picturing you
My thoughts were of every time I see you.
My eyes light up when I see you
Your face is so intoxicating
I can't get enough of you.
Every time you touch me
I just can't get enough
I long for more, of your soft gentle touch.
I never want to lose you
I always want to be with you.
Your my dream come true
I'm so glad I found you.
These things will always be true
I always want to be with you.
These thoughts will be in my mind
From now and forever, till the end of time
Every time I see you!!

Tina McBeath

The Strings of Love

The strings of love we learn to tie,
In heart shaped knots, don't say good-bye,
That word so sharp can sever the strings,
The strongest souls will suffer the stings.

Deep true love is a feeling sublime,
To end that love is truly a crime,
A physical love that is driven by lust,
Is simply untrue as it is unjust.

Where a deep true love comes from the heart,
A bond so strong right from the start,
Two minds consumed by just one thought,
So true this love which we both are caught.

Two hearts together beating as one,
Their passion burns as hot as the sun,
The strings of love won't be untied,
They forever in my heart reside.

Paul S. Rhyne

Aura

With the light that shines through my windowpane
I sense Your peacefulness surrounding me
With the hum of the ceiling fan
I hear Your calmness swirling about me
With the touch of my true love's hand
I feel Your strength embracing me
Staring deep into my true love's eyes
I see the love You have sent to me
I am still, and I know that You are God

Angela Chapman

Commitment to the Lord

I wake up in the morning and to God, I say,
Thank you for bringing me through to such a beautiful day.
I am committed to our Lord, because I love Him so much
I know He loves me, and He has such a soft, gentle touch.

I love to give our Lord praise and I worship Him so!
When the Holy Spirit is within, my eyes are all aglow!
God gives us choices that we must make,
And it's up to us not to make a mistake!

When God talks to me in that wee small voice,
I know in my heart that I don't have a choice
But to listen to Him, and agree all the way,
Because I do know I'll be seeing Him one day!

I start my day by praying out loud,
By praying in my room, and not in a crowd.
I read verses in the Bible, and Daily Guide Post, too!
You know God loves all of us . . . yes, me, and also you!

Lois Kowalewski

The Wilderness

Hardly any people live here,
It's like a desert.
It's as if it's trying to push away anyone who comes near it.
This is the wilderness.

It's very quiet,
Like a mute person.
You have the perspective of a deaf person.
This is the wilderness.

What is so sad
Is that in ten years time it will probably be gone
For people to live on.
This is the wilderness.

The sun sets below the horizon
Blazing orange, yellow, and red.
All is still.
This is the wilderness.

Bryan Sipho Martin

Alone I Know

Alone, sitting in my room once again,
I know things will never be the same.
Alone, I hear the sound of madness;
I know that all I'll feel is sadness.

Alone, I wish you were here with me;
I know you're not coming back to me.
Alone, there's nothing here to hide;
I know you're not here by my side.

Alone, I wonder where our love went;
I know the time we had was not well-spent.
Alone, I cover my face;
I know when to give you space.

Alone, I can feel the pain;
I know things will never be the same.
Alone, where I really want to be,
I know that it is best for me.

Annette Tavitian

One's Own Fantasy

Like a fly in a web, I've been stuck to my own decisions
As to beyond the walking point of one's own destination
To breath the air that I breath of my own life's fantasy
for to see what I see beyond an owl's night vision
To go find your true love and then be wakened by a dream
To be able to see wondrous light, only through the bars of a cell
For to be the greatest explorer, yet just a glare on TV.
But when you wake up, you find yourself thinking,
The greatest thing in life is one's own life fantasy.

Joshua Stevan Lawrence

Time Alone

With time alone I sit and stare
Into a window that reflects my thoughts.
It accepts my words and does not wander off
My mind is free to converse anything
Without fear, without guilt;
It reserves all I give and sits
On the memory I build.

With nothing but time I decide
What is important to write;
It waits with steady patience
For a roaring wave or for a calm tide.

What have I achieved
With my time?
No one is here,
I have written my heart
But only the window cares. . . .

William Figueroa

Never through Years

Anyone who sowed their isn't
Anyone's any was all to them
Through bell down years
For the swallow that closes

He the leaves is everything, except one
Anyone thought they started, but were done
Hearts married their everyone's
Broken and never slept their dreams

Fighting through wars of heartbreak
Alas, their world is their hope, their salvation
Wandering midnight stars never meet that beautiful how town
Through years of blue

Seeds up through lead earth
Decaying in hope's sorrow
Ever ending temptation grows
Down years, up years, anyone never change

Katherine Noelle Neurohr

Sun Sets in the Sky

My life is burning out of control
Will you not step in and stop the to and fro
I see the sun as it sets in the sky
Without a wonder why

Let me see into your life
You ask me how to take away your strife
Your work is done but your heart is not
I love you my child because you were not bought

My name is the one you read everywhere
Just let me come in your story to share
Just like the sun sets in the sky
Each night ends your worries and whys

I am hear to listen and to give you love
Like no one else, you turned to me above
Thank you, my child, for listening to me
The Son will rise; wake up, and you will see.

Dorothy Lord-Lloyd

Right or Left?

A poem about the Holocaust
Right or left?
Right or left?
Which one will they choose?
Death by gas, death by night; one shall never see the light.
Right or left?
Right or left?
Which one will they choose?
For one will take the journey with their life that they are to lose.

Alaina Michelle Yates

Innocent

How I long for innocent love.

The love that enters the heart with
No weariness, no caution.

The love that fills the heart with
unbound happiness, complete wholeness.

The love the heart knows
Only once,
Before the break, the excruciating descent,
that shatters it into unrecognizable pieces
of a puzzle that can never be put together
quite right again
Because some piece was misshapen
by the horror of pain.

How I long for that innocent love
Lost.

Beth Johnston

You Have the Strength

Though your world may be dark
You have the power to light it.

Though your world may crumble
You have the strength to build it.

Though through your day you may struggle
You have the strength to make it to tomorrow.

Though doors may close
You have the strength to open them.

Though your hourglass may be running out
You have the strength to flip it.

Though your ship may sink
You have the wind to sail it.

Though you may have hills to climb
You have the strength to make it over mountains.

Lindsey C. Kerwin

Anne, Will, Out . . .

Slowly her gray eyes closed, the flame
behind them waned in the sunshine.

Her grip eased, the voices beckoned her to
release, to let go, to end the struggle.

I stood by, my voice stifled, my urgings go
unheeded, the painful sky ever present, the
calm below ever so close, awash in the sea
of pain, they all muse her end, except me;
the silent one.

Oh! Bard thou advised, no thou commanded us
to "rage against the dying of the light . . ."

Oh! Have we failed? Is the light so bright
we must go or is the dark too warm to stay.

Thee question I ponder . . . does the candle
flicker to an end or snuff itself out?

Joseph Hamilton Barrett

The Great Purification

Teardrops fall like sweet summer rain
Releasing the heart, easing the pain.

Footsteps fade into the dark of night,
Freeing the spirit to swiftly take flight.

Over mountains and meadows where land remains pure,
The essence of a child's love will bring forth a cure.

For it will be they who remain upon this untouched land,
Guided by the power of the Great Spirit's Hand.

Karen A. Proulx

Losing You

Of all the things lost in this world,
losing you has hurt the most.
You fell behind and lost this race,
even though you should have finished first.

You left without a warning,
and you left me all alone.
You left your friends mourning,
and your family's hearts were turned to stone.

"It wasn't his fault," they said,
"He was really depressed."
How can that be, when you knew
you had so many good friends?

Time has passed now;
it will be a year in March.
I still wish I could have stopped you somehow;
then you would be more than just a memory in my heart.

Kristin Marie Scott

My First Love

This poem is for someone I lost a long time ago
I hope you got to read this because
There's something I want you to know
It's been five years now, I don't what to do
I'm sad, I'm lonely, and still trying to replace you
I've tried to move on, there's more fish in the sea
But the problem with that is you were the one for me
Sometimes I wonder if you're enjoying your life
Or maybe you're out there as someone else's wife
Please don't be mad at me for living in the past
It's just that only you have the love that can last
A lifetime or two, if only with you
I'd give anything to see you—you have no clue
Words can't express the way that I feel
The strength from your love is so strong and so real
If I got one more shot to give you my heart
I'll never let go . . . till death do us part

Jerome Robinson Jr.

Wonder

Winter, spring, summer, and fall,
Just like the seasons, everything in this world changes every day.
The days of the week, the months, and even the time changes,
but most of all, people change.
They change their hearts and even their feeling,
everything in the world changes sooner or later.
I don't know why or even where to begin.
Sometimes change can be a good thing,
but in more situations, change can be a very painful
and difficult experience, especially when children are involved.
Love can change to hate and happiness to sadness.
I often wonder why my life has to change so drastically in one year,
I have to look back and wonder where did it all go wrong!
How can I go on and make the changes in my life?
I need it so I can put this past year behind me.
Wonder this, how can I make a gloomy day sunny,
a hopeless day into a hopeful one, wonder this.

Jillyvette Marteina

Ode to Burning of Age

My mother gently guided me from the pain of a hot stove.
She carefully smeared my nose from the searing summer sun.
With a firm pat and a dash of pepper, she scolded my childish rage
And I cried warm tears of childhood pain.

As King Arthur, I long for those heated days of innocence,
Yet they visit me still within the arms that stoke my soul.
With searing words of silence, you pat my heart.
The burning spice of your love rages,
And again I cry warm tears of childhood pain.

Mark Edward Hart

Distant Fire

Would I bite the hand that feeds
To touch the fire that may burn me?
Fear of getting too close.
Should I care to breathe softly, so softly?
Without fire there is no heat, no light
Only shrouding darkness beneath my feet
Fanning desire within . . . burning bright
A distant lantern beckons from across the sea
So far, yet so wide
I sense it coming nearer, holding the key
Searching for my inner journey
A purpose for existing
To feel what I cannot hear
Hear what my eyes yearn to see
Without heartfelt fears
Live through love
Then love shall truly be

Karen M. Fleming

My Special Children

For my SCSDB family
They came to me as babies,
Walking into my heart with ease;
Have grown to teen years,
Lending a lot to my ears.
There were tears of joy,
Tears of success,
Joy of pain in success,
The pain of defeat with smiles of well done!
Ideas beyond belief,
Dreams, the same as you and I.
A vision that they too could reach the sky.
Independent Living is what I teach.
That's what I want them to reach.
With their hands, they do more than I with eyes.
And so they come,
My Special Children!

Sara Jean Brownlee

Why?

Why is life so brutally honest?
Why does everything seem to be forced upon us?

Why does it feel like my life is the worst?
Why does it feel like a horrible curse?

Why must I feel this way?
Why does my heart hurt every day?

Why is my existence a lonely one?
Why do I feel like it's only me, the Earth, and the sun?

Why is my head the only place I can go?
Why is that the only place where there is no sorrow?

Why must I feel sorry for me?
Why can't I just let my feelings go free?

Why am I writing these words here today?
Because it's easier to write than it is to say.

Maxwell Dale Birkholz Jr.

Mystery

Sometimes I just sit back and look up into the mysterious sky
and wonder what it is like to be a bird and fly so high.
And I wonder what lies ahead . . .
dark and deep, the color of lead,
peaceful and as soft as a feather bed,
to fall in love with and then to wed.
Then I realize the answer will never be in my head,
not for years to come,
until after I am dead.

Marybeth Tamborra

In Your Eyes

I see the pain in your eyes.
Is it from hiding your hidden desires?
Is it temptation or contemplation?
Are you hiding the pain, with your smile,
And hoping the pain will go away for awhile.
Are the tears you cry for something you may lose,
Or for something you can't choose?
Are you reaching out,
Or are you in fear and doubt?
Are you afraid it is a sin
Or a heart you just might win?
Are you pretending everything is all right,
And living a constant fight,
And you see no happiness in sight?
Are you following your true heart
Or is everything around you Falling apart?
'Cause I see the pain in your eyes!

Alex J. Dibble Jr.

Silence Embrace?

As my heart weeps and dies,
I read your words and begin to cry.
For your words are soft, but I'm a fool,
for your actions are in spite, so very cruel.

All I can do is sit and stare,
as your song of silence is blown through the air.
I sit in my chair and begin to wonder,
but all I can see is you, singing beyond a silent thunder.

Every time I think of our love,
I vision a beautiful, soft white dove.
This illusion I see is fuzzy and fazed,
this dove I see sets my soul ablaze.

This song of silence I just can't bear,
it has destroyed my heart with a single tear.
Spreading from the heart and into the soul,
it's slowly killing me, the poison is taking its toll.

Michael Joseph Cali

Wanting

I want to love without fear
I want to be able to shed a tear.
I want to do something
without thinking it much.
I want to be able to embrace your touch.
I want to leave normal
and go into the unknown.
I want to try and call you
and not hang up the phone.
I want to be able to crawl up and cry in the arms of a dear friend
and not be afraid of how things will end.
I want to look at people right in the face
and not lie about a past I can't replace.
I want to always do what I feel is right.
I want to realize that my hurt won't disappear overnight.
I want to know that I am not alone and I can strive.
I want to realize that I'll get back on my feet and live my life.

Alessandra Valconi

Show Me the Way, Lord

To St. Luke's Catholic Youth Association, Loitokitok
Show me the way, Lord,
Not to fortune and fame.
Show me the way, Lord,
Not to win laurels for my name.
But show me the way Lord
To spread the great story
For the kingdom the power and the glory are yours,

NOW AND FOREVER!

Simon Njoroge Ngugi

What?

What makes you who you are

You are established from many years of being
what others say you are or what you are born with
The reputation you carry is exactly you or is it you
possibly a contorted you, but nevertheless it is you

Some may say others have no effect on my you
but that very statement shows those others do
It is impossible to say something contrary to that
because others around you are you, too

The very uncertainty of this question for you is you
but you are only you with accordance to others
For you cannot be defined by you
but sculpted by the outside beings other than you
you are what others perceive you as
Which in turn makes you who you think you are dependent
Reason enough to say you are someone else

Benjamin Roy Mudra

My True Hope

You are my shadow in the night,
my sunshine in the morning.
You are my everything so right,
my new day always dawning.

You are my one true hope,
what will I do if you're gone?
You are the one to help me cope,
what will I do when the nights are too long?

You are my window in the storm
when everything is turned upside down.
You are there to keep calm
when you're acting like a circus clown.

You are the one who makes me happy
when I just feel like crying.
You are the one to set me free
when I feel like I'm dying.

Deborah Cushman

The Touch of an Angel

Out of my mind that leads me
Happened I upon an angel to be
Couldn't help notice, as she drifted her way
Touching lives and winning so many souls a day

Little did I know what God had in store
While our paths crossed and our burdens we bore
That this perfect creature would be a beckon
For this lonely heart so ready for love, I reckon

Into the night that greets me
In and out of sleep that should not be
Her tender voice and touch make its way
Tugging at my heart and giving closure to my day

A little more now I know, but God's the one
Who knew before I thought this day done
That His Earth angel tends his wanting sheep
And bring thrones of joy, as I silently sleep

Lewis M. Oakcrum

You're Gone Now

You're gone now and you were here yesterday.
You're gone now and I'm at your funeral not knowing what to say.
You're gone now and all I can do is pray.
You're gone now and my life is falling apart.
You're gone now and I have a shattered heart.
You're gone now and I'm really missing you.
You're gone now and I hope you're missing me too.
You're gone now and the memories I have of you are few.
You're gone now and I hope that I'll once again see you.

Kacianne Sydoney Fowler

Our Father's Eyes

To look into our Father's eyes,
Now at very long last,
To look into our Father's eyes,
Our trials, and tribulations, now past.

To look into our Father's eyes,
What love to behold,
To look into our Father's eyes,
He gave his son, for our sins, we are told.

To look into our Father's eyes,
Oh, what glory will abound,
To look into our Father's eyes,
Satan, no more, to be found.

To look into our Father's eyes,
Along with loved ones gone before,
To look into our Father's eyes,
Rejoicing, forever, more.

Bruce Lane Craig

When Bluebonnets Grew

I wandered outside, in the cold lonely night,
I saw my breath drifting, in the silver moonlight,
My thoughts drifted back to a warm sunny time,
When bluebonnets grew, and there was only you, on my mind. . . .

I remembered that time, as if yesterday,
When the mockingbird sang, and the little fawn played,
And the squirrels scampered through the oaks and the vines,
When bluebonnets grew, and there was only you, on my mind. . . .

I still see you standing, your eyes full of wonder,
At the mysteries of life, of the seasonal splendor,
The honeysuckle dripping its sweet nectar wine,
When bluebonnets grew, and there was only you, on my mind. . . .

And now time has past and my little boy is grown,
Soon you will have a child of your own,
And you'll know a day as special as mine,
When bluebonnets grew, and there was only you, on my mind. . . .

Jay Smith

The Tear

A
Single
Tear drops
From her face
Feeling alone in
This place. The feeling
Subsides. The waves roll in
And the smell of the ocean tickles
My senses. The fish leap, the whale
Swims, the divers dive, the fishers fish
But that solitary tear that fell from
Her face, shows strong emotion from this
Place. As the night rolls around, the
Sun in the sky starts to die. And
The Tear drops and joins so
Many more in the big
Sea of tears . . .

Heather Marie Young

Grace

In a created image, you see a smile
Lost in your own confused spirit
The humbleness you seek in your heart
Preserves your soul from the corrupt world
Powerless boundary incompatible with love
A smile so harmless could be corrupt
When you're in God's presence
Heart, soul, spirit, and smile
Are faith to live a fortunate life

Samuel Edward Broyles

Stop, Look, and Listen

The windswept rain in the dark of night
The eagle's strong, majestic flight
The miracles of sound and sight
Take my breath away

The crashing of the waves to shore
The lightning's flash, the thunder's roar
The rainbow's gift from storms before
Take my breath away

Sunlight dancing on the sand
The beauty of God's open land
Mother Nature's desperate stand
Before the beauty's gone away

Poisoned by the works of man
We must act soon with mighty plan
Protect the Earth, while we still can
Before IT takes our breath away

Christine M. Tozzo

At the Ranch

I can see you standing in the sun.
I see your face and I see your eyes—
And through your eyes
I see your soul.
I know you stop—
To see the sunset on the water.
I know you stop—
To feel the wind and to feel the sunlight on your face.
I know you stop—
To hear the footsteps of phantom creatures.
Unseen beauty—but within your reach.
I know you stop—
By clear running springs
To taste the pureness in this life. I know you stop—
Which is why I stop—
And I see—
A man that is in the heart of me.

Gayle Yarbrough

One Day . . .

One day . . . hidden love will be no more
It will be set free to soar
Love will fly high like a bird in flight
Growing sweeter every day, and stronger every night

One day . . . I will joyfully call you mine
My one true love of all time
The one who touched my very soul
Who pieced me together and made me whole

One day . . . all the shadows will disappear
I will proclaim my love without fear
I will rejoice because you are here
No longer apart from the one I hold dear

One day . . . my love, just wait and see
You and I will become "we"
Our time will come because we are meant to be
Together, in love, eternally . . . one day

Gwen Anderson

Sea to See

Have you ever looked out to sea?
To see all that you could see?
When I look hard and look long,
Sometimes I stop and sing a song.
I sing songs about things I like
Such as swimming, running, and riding a bike.
So the next time you're at the sea
Look real hard and you might see,
Something to bring out you and me!

Christine Marie Gamboa

Life Lost

Life is so many things
It can be wonderful and spiteful
It can be joyful and sad
But at its worst it can be cruel
Becoming an ending well before its time
Without seeing dreams become a reality
Without seeing children grow to have their own
Without a chance to share memories of a time long past
Oftentimes it's a life taken
A life only just beginning its journey
But more often it's a life that has tasted joy
Yet not here long enough to savor it
It is when that life is a part of your own
A soul you share with a mother
The life so precious to me
It will forever live on in my heart
The life that was my BROTHER

Lori Stout

Love We Do Have

Wealth have we none,
That is, in money or possessions.
But we do have wealth in love,
Oh, what a true confession.

Time have we none,
That is, to explore all the world and sail.
But we do have time for one another,
Oh, what a relationship that has entailed.

Sad times have we none,
That is, to make us angry and hate.
But we do have our moments,
Oh, for goodness' sake.

Love we have plenty
That is, to nourish and keep our relationship.
But there are times we fail to show our love,
Oh, that's when we make up with a kiss on the lips.

Rikkita Yvette Hughes

The Courtyards of Quann

When you run around through the woods, the
trees will throw you back into the mind from
which the greatest melodies have touched the
hearts of all the griffins in The Courtyards
of Quann. When the courtyards are aligned,
Quann will show you back into the slowest
part of death, otherwise called life.
If that would really make any sense in the
unprivileged mind, then that mind has been
blessed with the hate from which love has
sucked its last bit of hope. It is that
hate that has been sucked dry to form the
life that has held together the Courtyards
of Quann to form the basic properties of a
guitar string. Once that string is broken
the existence of life has become obsolete for
one more spin of the wheel.

Zanny

Cancer's Cost

It weakened her liver and her colon, too.
She experienced pain that may happen to you.
Kathy was dying from a deadly disease.
Cancer was killing her with the greatest of ease.

She tried to get better, but she found she could not.
We prayed for her, 'cause we loved her a lot.

But soon Kathy died, and it caused us sorrow.
But she will spend her days in Heaven with everlasting tomorrows.

Lauryn Michele Seeds

October Eighth

My heart is in a million pieces
It can't be put back together
I have never felt such pain or cried so much
My love has crushed me

I don't know how to go on
I am so weak
The pain in my chest is so fierce
and it won't go away

Love can bring joy,
but it brings me pain
How can I live without my love?
I don't know how

My feelings will never change
My love is always in my heart
even though it is broken
I love my love

Jacquelyn Michelle Vondrasek

Definition of a Father

What a day that was when you became a father

I looked at you with my little eyes
definitely not with any despise.
I favored your company every day after
and with that came my joy and laughter.
Then suddenly my growth appeared
and boys, money, and cars you feared.
I showed less attachment and you saw
I now wanted to make my own law.
You thought your baby was forever lost
wrapped up in friends and their materialistic cost.
You might not see your baby for days on end
until you find her heart you need to attend.
The tears you then catch one by one
All the pain you say will come undone.
She's still your baby, now do you see
I'm still your baby, it's all just me.

Kautouya Rheanette Dixon

A Father's Love

A tiny child with big brown eyes
reached up for you to your surprise,
and gave to you a baby's trust
that you would smile and pick her up.

As this child grew, she laughed and cried
and fell from grace to rise with pride,
for many things would come and go.
Her father's love would only grow.

This child has now become a mother.
For all of life's joy there is no other.
For every dream that may pass by,
you've helped her spread her wings to fly.

Though it may seem age has no heart,
each day is a blessing, a special part
of a tiny child who still is ready
to hold your hand and call you "Daddy."

Felicia S. Gueterman

Gimp Manifesto

"When my father realized I have no left leg,
he became nauseated and vomited for the shame
of all the gory frailties I limp.
Shame settled for mock, and so he built me a
bunk bed—
bottom-bunkless."
Then your cheeks blushed,

and I wanted to caress your missing limb
and know it, with sincerity.

Eleanor Rose Moonier

Escape of the Mind

Escape the lies and sorrows,
close your eyes . . . go deep within,
to a place where there's no tomorrow
and yesterday has never been.

Create an image with colors so bright,
ride on a beautiful rainbow,
or dance through the starlit night . . .
be on top of the world, never below.

Envision yourself in a place of peace,
where nothing but love exists,
where all creatures live in harmony
and even a rainstorm is only a mist.

Fly with the eagles, play with the bees
dive down a waterfall, dance in the waves,
You can do whatever you please,
just use your mind to find a way to escape.

Evelyne Oriliva Plante

Free Fall

The words you speak sing quietly in my ears,
Softly wrapping my mind in a warm fog,
As I feel the world beneath me gone.

With the cool wind upon my cheek,
I find myself locked in a free fall;
Weightless, unhindered, and totally free.

I stretch my arms wide and shut my eyes,
Allowing the memory of your song to guide me
Through billowing clouds within the deep blue sky.

I release control to your hands alone
Where the way you welcome the words I speak,
Gently coaxes my body with your sincerity.

As the world fast approaches my surreal trip,
Your curiosity cradles my mind, slowing me tenderly,
Leaving me eager once more for your song of free fall.

Kevin M. Bogatitus

My Life

Once I had a dream,
I thought I went down a stream,
Up the hills, and across the sea
With my shadows in front of me.

As I trailed the narrow way,
I focused on the light of day.
The path was rocky and rough,
I climbed and climbed and hung tough.

I met a man, who said hello;
As I reached to touch, I fell below.
My fall was broken with a limb,
And I held on for dear life on a whim.

I was about to give up on everything,
But luck would have it that I grew wings.
It was a dream, like I said,
The only thing is I was dead.

Anthea Marilyn Jeffrey

My Dream

I can dream of an environment that is pollution free
But without help from everyone that can never be
I would like to breathe the fresh, clean air
This can be possible, if we little no more
I can imagine the Earth, if we litter no more
Let's use the trash cans, that's what they are for
I can only hope and dream my whole life through
That others will care as much as I do

Deanna Pronel

The Sunset at School

I see the sunset at the end of the road,
So many colors, like in the rainbow.
No words can explain what I see,
So many memories of you and me.
I wish we could be together while I am here,
But please don't give up on me;
I will be home in three more years.
Do not worry about me finding another;
You are the only one for me.
I am here to make my life better,
And trust me, I will send you letters.
I will miss you one hundred times more,
And trust me, when we see each other, it won't be a bore.
Every time we see each other, it feels like the day we meet,
Don't believe it could be so special? Let's bet!
I remember the cool spring air and the bright colors of the rainbow,
And hopefully we can watch another sunset at the end of the road.

Krystal Beth Worpell

Circles

Beating indiscriminately crude tools form a
circle, it rolls, Earth gives up a secret.
Biting metal downs foliage, ingenuity bending
wood in circles covered with animal skin.
Earth weeps.
Nourished visions cover hide with metal,
Earth shudders. Inspiration drains trees
forming rubber circles. Earth shrieks, a
hollowed globe derived of significance.
Circles abound tirelessly, circles in
circles roar raucously, jostling aimless
rolling circles. Earth turning endlessly.
Revolution clamors from the circles, Earth
stops, slowly drawing the circles within
itself, expanding. Bursts of light spring
forth vanishing scars of fashioned circles.
Earth's laughter girding the universe.

Sandra Jane Axtell

Love

Love, such a simple word
One with so many meanings
One might say
"Being kind is love"
Another might argue
"Love is to show your utmost affection for someone"
And yet another might argue
"Love is all the peaceful things in the world"
Love, it has so many meanings
Will we ever figure out it's real meaning
Well, we already have
Love is what WE feel
Love could be a cloud in the sky
Or a blade of grass on the ground
Love is what it is
What we feel . . .
What we know . . .
Overall, love is love

Rebeccah Anne Maier

River Love

Dedicated to my brother, Brian Clay Holliday, and my cousin, April
Love is like a river forever winding.
You never know the lovers and friends you will be finding
It may be a hard river to row,
But what comes ahead, you will someday know
Rowing can come with ease,
If you make yourself easier to please
Never let the stones keep your oar from pushing you
If you push with ease, you are sure to go through
It is a river of love,
and always try to keep yourself true.

Benjamin Holliday

The Year of 2001

The year of 2001—is a different
Year then the other years
As it started to snow and snow
It never quits—so
Then the strong winds blow the
Snow into drifts that get higher and higher
The weather gets colder and
Colder and then as
Spring comes and we'll get floods
Into the low land and field and
The homes flooded so people will
Have to move out as the
Rivers-Dames and all will flood
Land—the year of 2001 will
Be known as the big flood year,
Of 2001 in South Dakota

Irene Mary Larson

A Poet's Soul

Undefined by most any means
Beloved though by many, it seems

Ballads of the heart
Sung to the rhythm of a poet's soul
Tears brought forth
By the stories he's told

The rhymes he's made
Though they were not great
The rhymes ring true of love and hate
Stanzas and verses you read, as you loll
The many lines defined by a poet's soul

Ageless, as myths and tall tales
He takes you down his many trails
You need not worry where you stroll
When you let your heart follow a poet's soul

Bradley Joseph Niekamp

Lilies

Behold this family of great plants is the lily of the valley
that only you can bring joyfully, for it tells
of this lily lasting throughout time. Its reproduction is
by seeds or its own roots as perennials.
For no toil or hardship is too much, as you watch it grow
from the shade where it dwells.
Basically comparing, are you, the one that sees a pair
of basal, oblong leaves claiming the shells.

Over all flowers have you the right, as speaking
of this lily's singles leafless raceme it foretells.
Overcome are you, as this lily sweeps you off your feet
by the very fragrance as it smells.
Storming in pleasure are you by this lily of the valley
that's handed life of beauty like it yells.
My gleaming is this treasure so placed before you these
lilies—a flower, small, white, and shaped like bells.

Paul Robin

The Empty Heart

An empty heart embraces pain
Trying to fill the hollow place.
The empty place calls for tears falling,
Like rain from a troubled sky.
An empty heart builds a wall,
A fortress to hide behind.
The bitter tears ebb and flow searching
For breaks in the self-made wall.
An empty heart tries to hope,
But somehow blocks the sun.
Darkness falls and engulfs the space . . .
A place for nothing else.

Laura Dodd MarbutM

The Beyond

Nothing in life prepares us for a miracle,
where the beyond we reach for, being really there,
is really astonishing, like a flight of birds
or the opening of a flower
or the speckled foam of seas
not marveled at by those who, knowing what to expect,
expect what is already known
and close their hearts to glimpses of beyond.
Beyond is rushing to the edge to find
more compassion than the ego holds,
more longing than the soul can bear,
more kindness than the world can tolerate.
Beyond is an endlessly radiant garden
planted by one's own hand
with seeds of eternity.

Joseph Satin

Island

If I were a captain, and you were my crew,
we'd sail the whole ocean, the whole ocean blue.
We'd search for an island, an island of new,
an island made just for us two.
The island we'd find would be just the kind
we both have been searching for.
Together we'd live a long life through,
with the one we both adore.
Then one day they'll come a time
that our love would be hard to find,
we'd search the whole island, the whole island through
trying to find where our love went to.
Then a night as we lay on the beach,
staring up as the stars go by,
we'd think of our trip as we sailed on my ship,
and return as passersby. . . .

Vincent Malloy

Brownie

Brownie, a lonely old woman, so fragile and bent
Lived in a white house with large windows and spent
Most of her time looking out in the street
For any kind face that would take time to meet
And chat with her for awhile about this and about that
As she tended her roses and stroked Fluffy, her cat.
She kept mostly to herself, but ventured out for her walks
Taking care of small business, walking south five long blocks.
Then precisely at four, each day of the week
She went into her garden to spend time with the meek—
Those fine feathered friends who flew in just to eat
Dried bread crumbs she saved week after week.
Their chirping and commotion gave Brownie ultimate joy
Fulfilling her happiness, even more than those boys
Who often rode past while she sat in her house
Contemplating her life, her work, and her spouse.

Artha Slangerup Jackson

Catalogue Choice

So many to choose from,
Music that I love.
Jazz and Rhythm and blues
Where's my dancing shoes?
Rachmaninoff music from Heaven above,
Brahms, Beethoven and back.
Chopin, Greg, Vivaldi,
Music to calm and soothe me.
The decision is really hard.
If I could, I'd buy the lot.
Make up your mind, Sylvia, is what I say.
Pick a winner and make my day.

Sylvia Bakes

A Real Man

a real man opens the door for a lady, his lady
a real man is not afraid to cry
he is honest and will put his heart on the line
a real man doesn't tell a lie; a real man is a gentleman
but he also knows when it is time to get down and dirty, too
i step to you, a real man that knows romance is still out there
i am not afraid of true love
my past is my teacher and my teacher is my guide in life
why can't a man tell the truth and be straightforward by nature
i ask you to judge me for who i am
some men are true gentlemen, truth be told
and some of us do still seek out true romance and true love
step to me and don't be scared of a real man
i will treat ladies with respect and see them as gifts from God
i only seek my true Nubian queen in life
please don't be surprised because i am a real man

Victor Simon Rodriguez

Angora Riot

I'm chasing angora across a winter sky.
In the end I'll shiver, and in another minute will bleed.
Steam to water to slush to ice,
Everybody knows it's the elemental way of life.
They're not going to care if it hurts.
Tell it to the trees and those who hug them.
Burn a church and smash a night.
Play marbles with God and hopefully take his good ones.
Randomly, now, kill all logical thought.
The girl bends her head and the dead crow sings.
Your hands are uncontrollable—
that's the way it was meant to be.
Words are weapons, and fire is flight.
What wouldn't we all give
To lose our souls for one night?
Riot.

Meris Carmichael

One Saturday Afternoon

Folding warm laundry, fresh like morning bread,
I find your washed wallet in with the darks—
contorted between jeans and work shirts;
pieces of you spill out of the worn,
smooth leather.
Your time in the work world over,
signified by 20 dollar bills from Mom,
the hard plastic ID (your companion for 30 years)
now missing from its place.
And in a secret pocket, behind lists and receipts
for brushes and paint . . . between thin sheets
of aging, yellow plastic, rectangles of fading color
capture my face.
It is the way you see me: tiny, six years old,
smiling adoringly at her father behind the camera.
Proud to be the daughter of a strong man.

Jennifer Lynn Schuster

Rainy Days

Rainy days;
they make someone feel sad and lonely,
sometimes you sit there, bored and looking out the window,
waiting for your love to come.
You wait and wait but no one comes;
you only hear and see the rain falling to the dark ground.
Suddenly, you see a someone coming out of nowhere then he vanished.
You start to give up hope, but then the knocking at the door
gives you courage to keep hoping for someone to come for you.
You open the door and fall in the arms of a handsome man.
The curtains of sadness finally open and this rainy day
changes into one of the happiest sunny days in your life.

Lisa Carden

Ode to Vincent

Once upon my dear mind
A passionate painter thee will find
In his hands talent has found a place
And a solemn beauty upon his face
Vincent gave me sunset a breathless hue
Using crimson red and china blue
He brushed for me a shooting star
Thus my heart's wish would not be afar
Vincent painted a garden full of thorn
Betraying my inner desire born
He stroked my canvas soul with happiness
Dashing here and there blots of bare griefness
O, dear Vincent, if only thee could see
How obscure thy soul of art has left me
Thou could paint perfectly a pair of doves
Would thee do the same for eternal love?

Mimi Puah

Sobriety

Sobriety often brings peace of mind
after achieved for a period of time.
Like the alcoholic, the family gets sick, too,
and there is absolutely nothing "you" can do.
Once you are sober and join Alcoholics Anonymous,
you may feel that the miracles are phenomenons.
With all the love and sharing,
you will quickly learn to be caring.
The ghosts from your past
will soon be fading fast.
Your children and your wife
will become your friends for life.
These are just a few
of the things to come true.
This precious gift of sobriety
is of the highest propriety.

Kandie Blevins

Earthquake

Silence descends ominous and deadly
stifling the sonorous sounds of a slumbering city.
The silence is but a macabre prelude
to the crescendo of wails soon to deluge.
The tormented Earth heaves and convulses
its painful writhing enforcing racing pulses.
Steel and concrete come crashing down,
creating a cacophony of pulsating sound.
Myriad souls trapped under dusty debris,
from mutilated bodies crying out to be set free.
But once the agonized weeping is stilled,
deathly silence will reign over the killing fields.
In the violent aftermath of the earthquake
there's nobody to keep vigil at this wake.
For in those frozen seconds of time,
Dreams have been fossilized forever.

Amita Mansingh Jadhav

Dotty the Angel

There is an angel in the sky;
We'll never know how high she flies.
Her life was difficult,
hard, and blue until the day that she met you.
You filled her life with happiness,
her days and nights with tenderness.
Though not much time you had together,
her soul and love will follow you ever.
Do not be sad that she is gone;
her love and sweetness will live on
in everything that you shall do,
for she is watching over you!

Brenda K. Leino

Midnight-Desperation

It's midnight, my silence, my time
One love, one death, just mine
Forget, forgive, and let me die
I cannot stand this life
My loved one has gone away
Away and left me alone
I don't need him anymore
An eagle spread its wing
Only one wing, the other one lost
I woke up, and it was midnight
The worst time of all
Midnight is a lonely place, I read somewhere
I see my face in a plane
Why am I crying here
My home is far, far away
Oh, God, just leave me alone, I pray

Galatia Lambrianidou

The Ultrasound

Two eyes, two ears, one mouth, one nose
Two arms, two legs, ten fingers, ten toes
Oh, little one, breath of life to my heart
Perfection I see, as I study each part
And I pray with each passing day for me
To be all things for you that you need me to be
For it seems we're alone, just we two
Daddy has found better things to do
He thinks being with us would be a drag
So he's off in search of a new grab bag
Isn't that what life is like after all
Wandering from store to store at the mall
Looking at all the great things to be bought
What will make me happy is the mind's thought
And in the end, looking back he will see
What could have made him happy was you and me

Eve Keen

Always . . .

Always give your best and your brightest,
And never get one up on who is the rightest.
Believe in yourself, and be pure in heart.
And live and love each day for a start.
Be true to yourself and those around you,
And do not respond to those that hound you.
Wasted anger and energy is not needed,
Rather your attention needs to be heeded,
Where your talents and service can be noted,
And not spend time wallowing in the demoted.
We all have crosses that we have to bear,
And those that don't are not being fair,
To them selves for we all, no matter what we say,
Put on our clothes, exactly the same way.
And at the end of the day, when the lights are out,
Does it really, really matter who wins out?

Mark Willian Schneider

Lost Love

I cannot love you, as I once did.
I am no longer free to see you
Or to speak of you, my dear.
What love was once so strong and sure
Has been condemned to an impenetrable tomb.
Now, feelings of woe do govern me;
And what I once took pleasure in, I must now scorn.
No saving grace amongst the wreckage
Of my lost love can I now find.
Only a sorrowful and empty void is present.
My heart, once full of you, is now drained
And with no hope of satisfaction.

Caroline Shaw McGarry

Give Me a Moment

Give me a moment of your time, an hour,
a day, a minute. I will show you
wonders untold, wonders to behold.
Let me grasp your soul a moment, your
ears, your eyes, your mind. I will show
you life never known, nevermore will
you be alone. Ask me to guide your
spirit free . . . soar the skies . . . sail
the seas . . . above all the Earth . . . your
spirit will climb the heights, we shall
see those untold sights . . . we are one now,
and forever, a lifetime, an eternity,
an eternal age. Together for that
moment, and all of time,
for that moment,
your soul is mine.

Juliet Kruger

Gone Fishin'

There once was a fish in a lake,
And a man who knew how to fish.
The fish was hungry for bait,
The man was hungry for fish.
The fish saw a worm and took a big bite,
The man felt a tug and pulled with his might.
The fish felt a hook jab through his brains,
The man had caught him like a prisoner in chains.
The fish was then pulled up into the air,
The man's stomach growled like a bear.
The fish landed in his lap, flopping around,
The man thought it must weigh 15 pounds.
Just as the fish thought it would die,
The animal rights' activists just happened to stop by.
The fish was set free to end this tale,
And the man ended up in an uptown state jail.

Lucas Devlin Myers

Is There a Word?

Dedicated to Natalie—she opened my heart and my life.
As I wake up I think of only you.
I ask myself what this feeling could be.
The emotion has some familiarity.
Yet the strength of it is entirely new.

You came to me through an unconventional route.
Yet came you did, into my life, my heart.
Now never again do I want us to be apart.
In my mind there will never be any doubt.

I've tried to express to you this feeling,
To find a word to captivate the affection
A word that describes this emotional resurrection.
Is there a word? Or am I only dreaming

I've prayed to God to give me a word from above
But wait! I've found a word. Our word. It's love.

Jeremy Roberts

Life

Where am I without it?
I sit back and think, where am I with it?
Am I in love?
Am I thinking about the future?
What is life?
Is it something you are just living?
Or is it something you are just giving?
Is life like a vacuum
That sucks you up and spits you out?
Is life a blessing?
Or is it a curse?
Could my life be better or worse?

Nicole Jean McShane

Celestial Downfall

Saddened cries of angels,
Simply because they can't reach their misguided souls.
This has temporarily put all missions on hold.
They retrace their steps, to see what possibly went wrong.
The people who didn't want a conscience,
Really didn't want to live long.
Another sad song, or just a mistaken tragic.
They got caught up in lavish,
Or did naive things to get from living average?
The supernatural tried by force
To save and show the passageway.
The opportunity knocked.
Instead of accepting it, they pushed it away.
Atheist or antagonized by what they blindly see.
You can make it successfully
If you let your mind, body, and soul be free.

Mario Lamont Duty

The Making of My Soul

When the wind blows,
Your soul runs through me.
Filling the emptiness within.

When the birds sing,
I hear your voice—in all of its elements—
And I am contented.

When the rain falls,
I can feel your touch—with all its unspoken
meanings—
And I begin to tremble.

When your soul fills me,
When your voice ends my desolation,
When your touch leaves me weak,
When I tear at the sight of your smile,
Then and only then am I whole.

Priscilla Ramirez

I Love You

I love the way you love me
I love the way you hold me
I love the way you taught me to walk
I love the way you encouraged me to talk
I love the way you sent me to school
I love the way you taught me to be calm and cool
I love the way you taught me to learn
I love my grades you made me earn
I love the way you taught me to smile
I love the way you taught me to bear all trials
I love the way you taught me to grow
I love the way you picked me up when I was low
I love the way you smile at me
I love the way you hug me
There's only one more thing left to say
I love you for each and every day

Rida Salman Alvi

Tick-Tock Clock

'Round and 'round
The pieces move,
Signaling time,
Our senses smooth.
Each tick of the tock
Takes away a lifetime.
Each tock of the tick
Commits an unpunishable crime.
As the pieces go full circle,
Our lives slowly pass away.
Each tick, a moment, each tock, a memory,
Until the world starts a new day.

Robby Ray Stepp

Mothers and Fathers

Fathers help make you
Mothers take care of you
Fathers know of you
Mothers hold you
Fathers leave a hole in your heart
Mothers try to fill it
Fathers run away, while
Mothers have no choice but to stay
Fathers love you, but
Mothers show you
Fathers want to be Fathers when they want to be fathers
Mothers cannot be mothers on a whim, you see
Fathers make promises
Mothers keep them
Fathers call you on special days
Mothers remember every day

Hafeezah Jemilla Johnson

My Annoying Mother

My mom is so annoying.
She comes in my room without me knowing.
She stands by my door, howling like a dog.
She grunts and croaks just like a frog.
She comes in my room and takes my stuff,
then I have to go find them, which is really tough!
She is like a kid and a grown-up in one body,
but, oh, can she be naughty!
Everything I do she has to copycat me,
whether I'm reading, writing, or even speaking!
I'm scared of heights, just like her,
which really sucks because I can't go to the stratosphere!
She is so slow getting out of the car,
my dad has to pull her to get her very far!
My mom orders me around, and I do it with a smile,
but inside, I do it with a frown!

Ashley Easley

A Present State of Mind

Kill my soul with a smile.
I won't need it for a while.
Through wit and whim and woe,
I know that my self is the foe.
Rape my soul with a touch.
I don't need it that much.
Through hills and over oceans,
Death is born from my own potion.
Devour my soul with your nails and teeth
That gives you nourishment . . . gives you relief.
I only know ecstasy through suffering.
God put me on the cross for the offering.
Burn my soul with your breath.
I live better through death.
My "friends" sure do hate me.
I don't blame them . . . just look at me.

Brilund Roberts

The Messenger's Path

The skin beneath my feet crackles
As my toes push through the sands beating fist
Three feathered flying friends whisper chatters
As they shatter through the blinking sighs of one sun's kiss
My eyes are pulled into a north wind, by a great hand not of my own
Twisting, I see the day's beauty, as my soul's windows forever close
My skin grows a shadow, as one single unbroken stone
My hand grapples a paper with one tight infinity bone

Though all words have been lost, diminished, severed
My hope carries onward, for an empty throne

The bird's whispers fall into a lion's throat

Jody Robert Pierce

When a Tear Drops

When a tear drops from your eyes
I tender, then render a scream
for your agony and stress inside
When a tear drops from my eyes
you emotionally freeze, realistically see
the hatred released that is a part of me
When a tear drops from my eyes
focus is regained, versatility distilled
everything diminishes that I thought never will
When a tear drops from your eyes
sunshine follows surprisingly plentiful
glorious tomorrow, experience purposeful
When a tear drops from our eyes
goals reached, peaceful and harmonious living
When a tear drops from our eyes
all our struggles are only in our remembrance

Glenn Williams

Medieval Nights

We are foolish kids
Playing queen and king
Thoughts of swords, armor, and shields
Illusions of demons
Dragons, and fairies
Slaying the monsters beneath the sea
Fighting the dark knight to the death
Crossing fiery lakes
Living in a world with wizards
Where magic is all around
Being the prince lifting his princess up to the star-filled sky
Living in a world where only a golden medallion
Will save us from the evil that will end all life
But remember
We are just foolish kids
Playing in the flower garden at night

Michael A. Ciliberto

Montana

Montana, it is a beautiful land.
Montana what a wonderful land,
Have you seen such mountains?
Such beautiful mountains, mountains everywhere.
There is Baldy and Pattsknob and many more.
Living in Montana was a wonderful time,
The best time of my life.
Sometimes I would wonder are there any fountains
On those beautiful mountains?
Montana, what a wonderful place to live.
What a beautiful place to live,
Montana is filled with such friendly faces.
Montana is a wonderful place to ride horses.
Montana, such mountains, such wonderful friends and faces,
Such a wonderful place to be,
And one day I will return to . . . Montana

Rebecca Joyce Hamilton

Hope

When all things have come and gone
Would we have ever known
The kind of hand we had been dealt
Or hoping the lives we touched were felt
We live each day as if it were our last
Hoping soon our sorrows pass
With every day that passes by
It brings another tear to the eye
Being handed another temptation
There will be more trials and tribulations
Even living in a world of sin
We hope to see a day once again

John Gibson

The Final Lap

Dedicated in memory of Dale Earnhardt, the "True King" of Nascar
It was the perfect day to race.
But one not knowing it would be his last.
All the drivers were keeping pace.
The cars approaching fast,
Mike was in first, "Little E" running a close second,
"Big E" in third, and Sterling right behind.
THE FINAL LAP!
Now it was his time to shine.
God only knows what happened then . . .
As Dale went down and Sterling up.
He spun around,
And without a sound
God took him up to where all legends go.
NASCAR died with one lap to go.

Shaun McCray

Left Alone

I was born on an April day, left alone in the hospital till June.
Because my mother didn't want me,
I was an accident, so they say.
Adopted by parents as a trophy, wanted by a
would-be mother, she, placated
by a man who was not to be bothered.
Alone again in a house with relatives and friends,
trouble is none were mine.
Left to find out who I was, and to me that was fine.
For years and years, I searched alone even
when wed, with children at my feet.
I could not be alone and free.
Then I found my love, my life all in one body.
I found out how to be free,
You can be alone and free with a mate who
understands you. Take a tip from me.

Roy W. Schoener

Far beyond the Stars

As you see the dark, glorious night
And see its glow of strong light
The twinkling stars of Heaven above
Show visions of undying love
When the velvet sky breathes down on the earth below
Lines of every raining tear, drop in rows
Death swallows the living fame
Everyone's heart yelling out in aching blame
Little angels riding in magical clouds of roses
Little sparkles on twinkling noses
Shooting arrows reach high above
To the Heavens with messages of heartbroken love
When world meets and reunites with peace
Shouts of joy and praises are released
Will the world come to an end?
No, for its precious smile puts upon new friends.

Andrea Valentina Lopez

Mom

Mom, you've given me all that I'll ever be,
The love that's allowed me to be me.

I know it's impossible to ever repay,
The gift you gave that chilly fall day.

The journey that started so long ago,
I'm so thankful, will you ever know!

The power it takes to let your heart walk away,
Letting me go, come what may.

Thanks so much for allowing me to live,
A gift so precious only you could give.

     Daniel H. Adams

Woven Strings

Passion wove among us, I believe,
is wound around in circles,
in the web of dreams I weave,
The dew that sparkles gently
among my silken strings,
is made with a salted tear or two, which, with
time, amount to . . . within their puddles tiny rings.

Every once in a while,
my web will be threatened by a buzzer by,
that will become entangled in my trap.

Frightened will be that bee or fly that
buzzed and buzzed among my dreams,
and struggled the entanglement in the
passion among my woven strings.

     Melissa Marie Williams

Gameboy vs. Homework

Gameboy's a favorite game of mine,
I like to play it all the time.
homework on the other hand,
Homework I just cannot stand.
I jump into my gameboy land,
put that away comes mom's demand.
"You know that you're supposed to study,
I'll even be your homework buddy!"
So I trudge up to the table,
and open up my book or fable.
But when mom is out of sight,
I go and do, I think it's right.
Suddenly my gameboy flies 'cross the room,
And hits the wall with a great big boom.
"Homework, homework!" she demands,
"Homework has the upper hand!"

     Angela Marie West

In Memory of Michael

For my younger brother, Michael Joe Phillips, who died Dec. 26, 1999
Like seeds dropped in a field to grow for hunger,
We hungered for life—to give us love.
As the rains came and the sun shone,
The seeds grew and filled the plants with fruit—
As a choice made.
The fruits picked—leaning are the plants . . .
Unbalanced, as is life.
Still . . .
It rains, the sun shines, and the violent winds blow.
The fruits fall . . . as does the life of the plants
Into the field from which they came.
I love you, Little Man.
Your brother,
Anthony

     Anthony Scott Phillips

Molly

When placed in my hands I did not know
How fast she would grow
And quickly become my little girl
That she would be the center of my world
Loving and teaching each other well
Bringing me completely under her spell
Never thought I would love her so much
That she would pull me through times that were tough
But none like now since she's gone
And now I feel so alone
Missing and wishing she was here
So that there would be no more tears

     Betty Booker

Together Once Again

In loving memory of Branden Murphy and Brandon Abshire
As we sit and weep, knowing you're both watching over us,
through trial and error only to stand true.

We know you both are there for us
because together again are you.

As the glowing embers fade in the night,
the brightness in you smiles shines bright;
now that you are both gone, you two still live on
in our hearts, and forever in our minds.

And, as your candles have now grown dim,
your lights in Heaven still shine within.

BJ and BM are together once again,
only to watch over us, to be our guardian angels,
so that we will soon be together once again.

     Krystle Patrice Lancaster-Murphy

Happy Birthday, Mom

Today as a man, I reminisce over my years,
And as I realize what I've been through, my eyes fill with tears.
But these tears aren't for sorrow—my eyes wash with joy,
Because I'm thankful for the woman who raised this little boy.
When I didn't know the answers and couldn't understand,
Mom was there with knowledge, to educate her little man.
When my pride was wounded and I didn't know what to do,
Mom was there with comfort to pull me through.
Whenever I was injured and worry wrinkled my brow,
Mom was there to dry my eyes and ease the pain somehow.
When God decided to take my father and we were all alone,
Mom was there to push me forward and tell me I must go on!
Mama, I want to thank you, for your guidance and your love,
For your patience, and your wisdom and your faith in God above.
I want to thank you for your warmth and your chastising right hand,
But most of all I want to thank you for making me a MAN.

     Larry E. Flagg

Questions!

Is it a miracle to have someone like you?
Is it a wish that every lover dreams of?
Is it a chance that only lucky people meet?
Just tell me honestly what, darling, goes on?
From which land have you had come?
From which substance have you been made?
Your silvery forehead is shining bright,
Your golden hair is waving in delight,
Your blue sapphire eyes are telling me a lot
Of dear precious promises since we have met.
Your ivory pure neck is calling my lips
To rest in there in a warm, long kiss.
Your soft, moistened lips are red, like a rose
Covering white pearls in your pretty, dear mouth.
If that wasn't heaven just tell me where
Can I find my paradise, just give me a hand.

     Ahmed Hassanain Abdul Aziz Zedan

Real Me

I'd look you in the eyes,
but I'm too scared of what you might see.
You may think you know me,
but you may never know the true me.
I'm scared you may run in spite of what you see in me.
But if you give me a chance,
I just might give you a chance to know the real me.
So please be patient, wait your turn.
Don't give up on me.
Soon I know I will show you the real me.
If you are true to what you tell me and there have been no lies,
you will get me to take off my mask and see the real me.

Stacy Lynn St. Andrew

Hope for That Cure

The fall of 1993, I had to see a M.D.
I started to get numb; this was not fun.
He gave me a test, and said it was M.S.
You got this disease; it won't be a breeze.
I must confess, I was really a mess.
I wondered what went wrong.
I hope I can be strong.
My life consists of a shot,
And they hurt a lot.
So I'll take that pill
So I won't get ill.
I'll take one day at a time,
And hope I will be fine.
As you can see,
This won't get the best of me.
I live in fear, and hope for that cure.

Jane Krajewski

Change

As I lay upon a barren hill, my eyes wander
across the empty sky.
Everything in this world has changed,
especially you and I.
The simple pleasures of childhood are long
but past behind me.
The visions of bright and carefree days
dwell only in my dreams.
No more is the rose a deliverer of sweet
passion and love.
No more is the angel inside of me that was
sent from above.
Now, I see the truth in all that has existed
in this lonely place.
Now, I see the truth from the lines of sorrow
on your face.

Lauren Cunningham

Life's Game

In your life of mass confusion,
There is nothing but illusions.
Everyone will pay its price,
For to gamble, you must throw the dice.
To get the money, you have to win;
For to lose, you'll roll them again.
It's a vicious circle, this game we play.
Just to survive life day by day,
We go on fighting this circle called life
With your daughters, sons, husbands, and wives.
There is no peace or rest, you see,
This is what living in our world must be.
For each must play to win,
Or never live a life again.
So I say, "I will be a part!
I'll take my chances to lose my heart."

Darlean J. Hall

Angel Wings

When I see my grandmother,
I see a soldier gone into war,
and the war has not yet ended;
a lonely sheep in wide, deserted pastures;
an eagle that isn't afraid to
spread its wings and fly;
a foal that may fall to its knees
every time it stands up,
and isn't afraid to try again;
but I also see an angel,
that has loved me and watched me
all of my life.

Hannah Clare Hudson

Despair

Deep mists hung low, clinging to the valley floor.
I watched her as she stood atop the rocky precipice,
hands clenched into tight fists at her side while she gazed
with teary, swollen eyes, blue and faded—a mirror of her soul.
A small drop ran down her hot cheek and
spattered on the foundation at her feet,
mixing with the wetness of the early rain.
With incredible anguish, she gushed forth,
arms raised, crying and screaming at the
dark, swollen sky, begging it to either
swallow her up or strike her down.
I moved closer, but it was too late.
My last view was of her gliding silently
downward with outstretched arms,
disappearing through the mists
and into the canyon below.

David Naslund

My Mother

This is to tell you of the woman I loved,
She was as sweet as an angel from Heaven above,

She was loving, sweet, gentle and kind,
with never an angry thought on her mind.

Although she toiled and worked hard all day,
No matter when you saw her she was happy and gay.

She could never go directly to sleep,
Until she heard that last pitter of our feet.

When she knew we were all safely at home,
Then no more would she let her mind roam.

Yes she was a wonderful woman and never a bother,

Because she just happened to be that special person,
My MOTHER.

Helen P. Harpster

Kayla

The phone call came, about midnight,
"It's OK, Mom" . . . "She'll be all right."
"It's a girl, Mom" . . . "Pounds? Two or Three."
"She'll be fine, Mom, wait and see."
To the altar of God, I prayed and I cried,
Please, dear Lord, stand by her side.
She's so little, God, I really must go,
I have to see her, I just have to know.
Hold her safely, Lord, in the palm of your hand,
Help her grow, Lord, help her to stand.
Well, Lord . . . You answered . . . My thanks to you I owe,
She's almost eight now, it seems so long ago.
She's strong and healthy, and ever so smart,
She's a pretty little girl, who's won my heart.
How beautiful and precious you have grown,
Kayla, Kayla, granddaughter of my own.

Carol E. Kenyon

Give Thanks

Give thanks for arguments,
for they may bring compromise and knowledge.

Give thanks for annoying people,
for they may teach you patience.

Give thanks for younger and older siblings,
for they may teach you great respect.

Give thanks for other people's rudeness,
for they may teach you manners and kindness.

Give thanks for everything even though you don't like it,
for they all may teach you lessons in life.

Shilo Elizabeth Cushman

So Long!

The sounds of birds attract me no more,
No more since I said goodbye,
We were so much in love before,
Didn't know we were broke till my soul had died.
I'm sorry to hurt your feelings this way,
This is not what I predicted to be,
I guess there will be so many things to say,
When there's nothing to let you see.
Even the rain knows how to stop,
Unlike this cold tears of mine,
I hope you always had the way to cope,
So I'll know you'll be doing just fine,
Will you face this reality of life calmly?
As we kept falling apart lately,
'Cause the chemistry between us has just passed,
And the tragic tale of us will never last. . . .

Harim Izzati Hamdan

Imprisoned

Overwhelmed and confused with no chance of escape
How did I end up here?
Caged like a bird, no freedom in sight
Walls upon walls of confinement.
Fury and rage every time I dream
Followed by depression and sorrow so deep
Only happiness I have is fake
The kind that pleases those around.
Word from the streets brings split second joy
Without touch and smell it only lasts so long.
Surrounded by the disowned, the abused, the crazed.
The animal society could not tame.
Must have been a mistake, wrong environment for me.
Or was I just as bad as the rest?
Did society look at me the way I look at them?
Or am I on the wrong side of the fence?

Brandon Butler

A Sticker in My Boot

Ouch, Ouch I am heard to shout,
I got a sticker in my boot and need to get it out.
It's poking my little toe, you see,
and that little pig's a squealing, "WEE WEE."
I don't know how it got in that boot last night,
it's been in the house, and there
ain't been a sticker bush in sight.
But sure as heck something's a poking
my little toe deep down there,
and all this shouting and jumpin's making my children stare.
As I hop on one foot and pull at my boot,
the little ones shout and begin to hoot.
Their laughs now fill the air,
as I stumble and fall into a chair.
I grab that boot and pull it back off again,
just to see fall out a plastic Army man!

Archie M. Matthews

The Coming One

From the rising of the sun to its going down
You will see signs and wonders all around.
Yes, these are the days of My Glory.
Don't be in a hurry,
Neither do I want you to worry.
Stay in My Spirit.
Make sure you really hear it,
Then with all your heart
Begin to declare it.
My will be done in this Earth:
Father, Spirit, Son,
My will be done.

Artis J. Banghart

The Book of Many Colors

Yellow—
Yellow is a color that is very bright,
Like the moon and the stars that shine out at night.
Yellow is a pencil that is very sharp,
Also a pick that is playing a harp.
Yellow is a butterfly that flies in the spring,
Also a bumblebee that gives you a sting.
Multicolored—
Multicolored things are the greatest.
They are colors of a rainbow up high in the sky,
Hot air balloons that always catch your eye.
The colors are many like crayons for you,
Red, orange, green, yellow, and always blue, too.
So when you look around, always remember
All the wonderful colors we see
From January all the way to December.

Barbara Ellen Fahrenbruch

My Mother

She was my inspiration
She was my guide
She was my mentor
She was my pride

Every time I needed a friend,
She was there

Every time I needed a shoulder to cry on,
She was there

She gave me advice and kept me going on my way

She gave me strength to live each day

I greatly miss my mother dear, though I know she is not far away.

Someday I will see her in Heaven,
And be with my best friend again.

Jennifer Minnick

The Soul's Kiss

In your sleep sometimes I contemplate you,
As the moon illuminates your sorrel skin,
And your sinewy chest tenderly replies
To the rhythm of your delicate breath.

A silhouette of sun-kissed curls
Encircles your refined face,
Which bears a complacent expression,
That narrates dreams of childhood fantasies fulfilled.

I am moved by your harmony
With the serenity of the night,
And aspire to be wed with your illusions.

As my lips gently embrace yours,
I am captivated by your spirit,
And drawn to slumber,
Where we become one.

Terese Ann Revercomb

The Seasons Changed Along with You

The seasons changed from winter to fall.
Like leaves on a tree always will fall.
Like summer breezes turning to winds.
Like little children that followed you in.
The seasons changed along with you.

The seasons changed all year long.
Like me and you off and on.
Love and hate which one is you.
How can I tell when I am going to lose.
The seasons changed along with you.

With you they changed, with them you left
Your spirit of love I so deeply regret.
The times that we had all the happy and sad.
When I look back now it makes me so mad
That you changed with the seasons instead.

Danielle Christine Freitas

Silver Bullet Freedom

Swimming in the moonlight,
Waiting for a soul surprise,
Minds fly high, high over sight,
I'm pinching sores of wasted life.
I need you to shade my eyes from what I see.
What I see doesn't involve what's good,
But what is me.
A silver bullet pierces through my heart,
So what's to be?
I now find out the true meaning of being free.
The struggle for freedom is at our hands,
But all we do is sit and stare.
A woman is raped, a priest is killed,
And suddenly, our freedom disappears.
The rapist walks, the lawyer grins,
Man's fight for freedom is at its end.

Joseph Abraham Kaminski

Venus Intangible

Her eyes, boundless tunnels in which I become lost.
Her lips, instruments which mesmerize me when played.
Her face, I would die for the slightest glimpse, no matter the cost.
Her hair, a river of beauty whose depth I am not afraid.
Her body, a work of art, the only true masterpiece.
Her skin, a soft salvation which only occurs in dreams.
Her hands, gentle creatures which bring only peace.
Her legs, idealistic wonders, just as Heaven's streams.
Her mind, the sole object which can control my being.
Her laugh, the sound of angels strumming their harps of gold.
Her voice, the captivating drug which alters my seeing.
Her smile, the constant warmth which drives away the cold.
Her innocence, that which raises her perfection to another level.
Her kindness, the perfect complement to her caring soul.
Her heart, a pure goodness that could overthrow the Devil.
Her love, without which I could never be whole.

Khalid Aleem Uddin

To Silky, My Best Friend

I brought you home, so small and sweet.
Little black puppy, all over my feet.
Big brown eyes showed so much love.
So proud with your first dove.
I took you with me wherever I went.
Your dedication never bent.

God gave you to me years ago,
A wonderful gift of love and devotion.
I gave you back to God above
To end your suffering, but never my love.
Run the fields, retrieve the ducks,
Painless days of joy with Pup.

Donna Robbins

Grandma

As I sit here and wait, alone by your side,
I pray your eyes open, pray you're alive.
I'm holding your hand, can you hear my voice?
If God's chosen you, he made a bad choice!
I love you, Grandma! Why can't he see?
That by taking you, he's taking me!
You're all that I have, I need you right now,
Going on without you, I just don't know how!
Who will I turn to when I need a friend?
Help me with my troubles? Help me to mend?
I will never forget everything that you've said,
And the stories you read me before going to bed.
But Grandma, don't leave me! Stay with me here.
The pain of you going, that pain I fear.
I need you always, I have from the start.
But if you go, just know you'll be in my heart.

Carlee Ann Potochar

Hey, Mister

Hey, you, yeah, you.
Why don't you treat me fair?
It shouldn't matter
If I am white, brown, black, or red.
Or that we don't have the same texture hair.
You don't even know me
Yet, you try to speak my sound.
Don't you know that it takes
Different shapes, sizes, and shades
To make the world go 'round?
You may have hurt me in the past, mister,
But, I forgive you
Because
Your God is my father
And
I am your sister.

Margaret Elizabeth McRobbie

Trapped

Do not go gently into that good night
But with ranting, kicking—give a good fight
The screaming pain is no violent stranger
To the mind kept in constant danger

Voices louder, demanding, creeping nearer
Blinding pain, escape, flee rises clearer
Stop, hold fast the spark of sanity cries
Expand, surface from the dark recess, rise

Day in, day out the demanding battle rages
Sanity trapped in the dark mind's cages
Refusing to surface, to combat the blinding pain
Fight, rise, surface from the dark to light
Awaken spirit, soul, sanity put up a fight

But do not go gently into that good night
Keep ranting, kicking, give a good fight

Anna R. Haney

The Hand of Pain

I can feel it again, reaching for me,
Trying to snare my soul once again.
To brutally rip at it, and perhaps even to pull it out.
To plead for help I look to the sky, only to be blinded by the sun.
I fear that there is no place to hide from it, it comes from within.
It's hard to breathe.
I can feel the ripping,
The tearing,
The splashing of ice cold blood against my organs.
I . . . I don't know how much longer I can stand it!
Please!
Please, let find the end of this . . . please, let me find salvation.

Brock A. Fields

Something Small

A swirling mist sprang forth to life
Upon the air of morn,
And when the mist was given birth, a miracle was born.
It scattered drops of crystal dew on all that it did touch,
And tiny flowers drank the drink and were filled with life SO much,
That all the meadow and forest grew till it could grow no more.
With lavish greens and vibrant reds and dainty cornflower lace,
They filled the soul with such delight as to brighten every face.
The sky was bright and cheery,
And the earth was rich and brown,
While animals once leery now entered every town.
Butterflies danced upon the breeze and beetles graced the ground.
Pretty wings of hummingbirds and robins everywhere were found.
Dogs sat contentedly in fields of creamy corn,
And all of this took place because
A small mist of dew was born.

Samantha Diane Hester

Daydreamer

When I look out the window
And see a bell tower,
If it can be called a tower;
A shuttered dome above a columned building. . . .
When I look out the window
To see this sight,
I know that I am daydreaming.
I am paying no attention
When I look out the window
To the speaker before me.
A Professor, a Doctor
He is speaking of poetry.
When I look out the window
I am no poet.
I am a Child, a Student
Searching for a place to hide.

Trevor Lance Paradis

Seeking to Sink In

Seek first God's kingdom and He will add the rest of everything you need.
Let me fly away and soar
With the sensation and awareness
Of air lifting me under my wings.
I need to run away aimlessly, sometimes;
And, experience every joy and dismay
In discovering rocks and smooth sands
Beneath me as I move over and around them,
Searching for the place to emerge into
My own ocean.
For, I look towards the truth where there is depth.
Discovering, more, the things I can't see,
Are proving to be more real than me.
Such, is that my spirit is me; and, so,
I am not that which I can see.

Deborah Eileen Sauers

Nana

Her hair was gray, she was old;
She'll love me always, I am told.
Her memory is here for me to love and cherish,
And my love for her will never perish.
I look at her picture and start to cry,
I didn't even have a chance to say good-bye.
Why did this happen? Why now?
What am I going to do without her around?
Someday I know that I will learn
To banish all those tears that hurt and burn.
For there will never ever be another,
As my own sweet, loving great-grandmother!

Tammy Acosta

Vacuum

Lying down in a semi-embryonic mode
Downcast with emotions
Created to convey meanings to my blue mood
My heart is filled with a Huge Vacuum
A vacuum worth filling with your warmth and touch
Touch of redeemable feeling
A feeling of longing
Longing to see you
A sight of ever-anticipated union
Union filled with a long-felt love
A love of everlasting light
A light of endless beam
A beam made to shine forever
Bringing with it a satisfaction
Of a reciprocated and affirmed union
A union consummated in the unending heaven

Yentel Ada Arinze

jazz dipped truth

there was a moment at table
with glasses of wine
poured with jazz
knowing if my pride
wouldn't be swallowed
that the truth would be invited in
no lies to cover up
sincerity
that his truth if wicked with fangs
will be invited to leave
the pride is gulped
i hope he remembers
that night at table
with glasses of wine poured with jazz
as i invited him to leave
that i really wanted to invite him to stay

Hillary Fara Black

Dove

Tiny little precious dove,
God sent you to me, from up above.
Planting you deep inside my womb,
I felt the presence of your love.
I'm caught up in imagination,
of how angles blew their trumpets loud,
as you descended down through generations
to my arms of love.
He gave you wings in order to fly.
You soared from the Heavens,
across his deep blue sky.
I felt your love from beginning to end,
the cycle of life, love, developing within.
Oh, tiny little precious dove,
God sent to me, a gift of love.
You.

Joyce F. Lewis

I Hope

I am a boy.
I am a boy that hopes.
I am a boy that hopes this world will change.
I hope that the people will stop killing
Children and adults who did not do anything.

I hope the drugs and cigarettes will stop
Influencing the children and adults to use them.

I hope we all can change.

I hope.
I hope.
I hope.

Rickey Dale Turner

Emotional Snapshots

The memories of you wash over me like waves
along the shore, one right after another in rapid succession
These emotional snapshots engulf me
giving me just glimpses of you and I
bits and pieces of our life together
as the emotions well up inside me like an angry storm . . .
They are so intense that I cannot even
remember my life without you
and yet I will cherish these emotional snapshots until
they are replaced by the whole memory in time
I pray that the complete memory will bring
the gratitude, love, joy, and peace
like a still lake on a warm, summer's day
When I can recall the memory in its entirety
When I can recall the complete memory with a smile
Then I will know that the healing is complete

Janet K. Estes

The Anne-Marie

The beacon of light circled the sky,
the sound of waves against the shore.
In the dead of night there was a storm,
a forlorn sailboat upon the sea.
The swells crashed over, under, through,
the screams of the crew barely heard.
The boat was tossed and turned about,
Poseidon and his unusual ways.

The boy's father did not return,
concerned and frightened for this, was he.
The boy walked the shore that humid morn,
the sight of a vessel, all too familiar.
The tide had washed in the gnarled wreckage,
the name of the boat, covered in seaweed.
When he read the name, the boy began to weep,
the name of the boat: The Anne-Marie.

Stephen Thomas Britt

À la Belle Etoile

The wind rushes through my hair and clothes,
sending a warm breeze right through me. . . .
The stars twinkle and dance, as though they're
speaking to me. . . .
I stop walking and look at the ground,
the lush, green grass seems to cue me—
I light a smoke and cop a squat.

I sit Indian style leaning back on my arms,
body rooted to the ground. . . .
The clouds cover the moon and it darkens all around . . .
I sit and think in silence.

The night air smells sweet,
the way that lilacs smell . . . it almost smells,
like a fresh rainstorm might break,
maybe not, I can't tell.

Catherine Leigh Collingsworth

Random Waters

Openly feeling the storm
Whirlwinds of emotion touch my being
Lying next to your aroma is my tonic
Gusts of desire surge my veins
Softly touching
Gently kissing
Feeling your craving
I answer your wishes gracefully and forcefully
Filling the waters with a crashing tide
Sailing with all sails
Floating in the void
So glad we met tonight

Clyde Baldo

When Abandoned by All Else

For Sara
My eyes never see yours cry
but when I look into them I see the darkest of clouds
filled with all your longings and sorrow
these clouds hide behind the most brilliant sparkle
in fear of burdening it your eyelids protect
the world from the storm brewing within
Sensing a similar longing,
my heart wandered too close
and although my chest now burns from the
strike of lightning
the thunderous beat within is of the same storm
So when your clouds reach the end of their capacity
I'll be there,
not huddled under cover,
but standing in the rain.

Chris Gordon Acosta

Griffin Silver

*"Where do you go when you feel this way?
When there's years to go and they started today?"*

Tears fall
and ink runs
from his pen
symbolizing:
the day it went away,
the week they'll never forget,
the month they'll wish they could,
the life they'll never share.
So her tears
fall
and his ink
runs
and time moves on,
uncaring.

Michael Sanchez

impoverished

social apprehension
we seek our fortunes, we choose our metaphors
and for a time we are content
by are own effeteness to hit bottom
if only to satisfy our interest in sacrifice
outside looking in
it's not safe to be accountable
but either to manipulate or play dead
like sheep or as rats
all with the same conclusion
to keep you is no benefit
to destroy you is no loss
below the screams of the high-pitched crowds
hear your voice ringing
above the shallow and righteous hymns
raise your song and scream

Abby Normal

Best Friends

Someone to look upon in anger or fear
Always there to remind you that they care
And light the way through dangers that come with dares
To tag along with and turn somber to fun
Never disregarding or forgetting the love
That you two have chosen to be best buds
They're there to go shopping and share good hugs
Through the bad times that develop
And the good time that have come
But you'll never know
When it is your time to go
Moving away to find another friend to play

Crystal Lee Boone

Love

If love is suicide,
then I am dead.
Wandering through the afterlife,
looking for a love that's been lost.
If love is a rose,
I bleed from the thorns.
They pierce my flesh,
as you pierce my heart.
If love is Heaven,
I am a fallen angel.
Looking for a saint
whose love can save my lonely soul.
For you, I will let the thorns pierce the flesh.
I will commit the suicide that is love.
I will fall from Heaven.
Just promise me you'll be there to catch me.

Beth Anne Aylward

My Love

The stars in the heavens are shining bright,
Spreading the Earth with a misty light.
The night owl hoots aloud his eery pleas,
While a cool, gentle wind murmurs in the trees.
I lay here tonight and look up above,
And think to myself of the one that I love.
She's gentle and kind, loving and sweet;
Of one like her, history will never repeat.
They say love is blind, I don't know it's true;
But I know in my heart no one else will do.
Then I pray to the Lord on high up above
To bring me together with the one I love.
Yes, faith and love are gifts to be treasured,
The bounties they bring beyond being measured.
And so may it be till the end of time,
That we may enjoy a love forever sublime.

Morris Jerry Vivian

Awakening

Come my friends—run among forests and streams.
Come my brothers and sisters,
So that we may sup together.
Let us dance like wild spirits,
Beat drums, and howl at the endless night;
Let us breathe life into each other.
Jump up and SHOUT! Lead and make way.
Awaken; tell the world your truth,
Give them your way and I will herald the day
For the universe shall answer tenfold.
Cry—cry out to the Heavens and weep with joy,
Know with all of your heart that you are God.
Create—for this is the greatest joy of being.
Come, let fall those sheaths, so ye may see.
Radiate love in all of its abundance.
Embrace and witness the birth of your self.

Ryan Lee Stillwell

To Laurel

To be alone, or to have a friend.
Could be the beginning, or the end.

A friend must have a heart that is true.
And, so for my friend, I choose you.

You're warm and sincere.
A friend I could love.

To you I'd give the Heavens above.
The warm sunshine, the sky that is blue.

These are the things I would give to you.

I thank GOD for our friendship.

Dorothy A. Rossitz

The Dream

I chase the dream or . . .
Does it chase me?
The basis for my deepest core,
And my unclear identity.
The dream has all the elements . . .
Beginning, middle, and end;
Alas, there is no making sense of it,
My life, I thus, defend.
A birth, a time, a season to be mine . . .
Is just drawing so near,
Time is only a thought, a prayer, a dream . . .
I have no more to fear.
And when the dream ceases to be, and all
Angelic hosts are seen . . .
Life will ever be so sweet—
A dream, no more, to me!

Cathy Lynn Chase

Letter to Father

Dad,
So many nights ago I cried,
Feeling only the sorrow from your tongue.
The things you say and the things you do
Combust all that is good.

You stand over me, watching me sob
As if taking pride in your actions of evil.
The months and years of sadness
Have drained completely my supply,
And now, tonight, I cannot cry.

You have ruined sadness for me, Dad.
All things that should make my heart fall,
Simply make me shrug.
In my mind, now, you have died,
And now, tonight, I will not cry.

Andrew Virgin

The Little Girl I Knew

The times were new she was the first baby born,
She'd sleep through the night even during a thunderstorm.
When she could walk she was a busy bee,
She would hug and kiss everyone and especially me.
She'd ride on my shoulders and I'd sing her a song,
I'd show her the right ways to keep her from doing the wrong.
I put in a pool and taught her to swim,
At night I would carry her to bed and tuck her in.
As she got older this is sad but true,
Finding time for special things together is getting hard to do.
Hormones take over and the love for Dad fades away,
As younger men come into the picture to stay.
Memories of the past put tears on my face,
As birthdays pass by blowing out candles on all those cakes.
Through out all these years every day she grew,
Into a special lady from the little girl I once knew. . . .

Michael William Wessling Sr.

One Wish

If I could make one wish, I'd wish for you to love me
If I could make one wish, I'd wish for our love to be
If I could make one wish, I'd wish for us to be together
If I could make one wish, our love would last forever
If I could make one wish, you would love me more
If I could make one wish, more than anyone else before
If I could make one wish, to you I'd be like Heaven to touch
If I could make one wish, you'd want to hold me so much
If I could make one wish, you'd want me more than anything
If I could make one wish, to you I'd mean everything
But just one wish wouldn't make all this come true
I'd make a thousand wishes just to be with you

Jenna Lea Combs

Wedding Day

On this blessed day we will make a vow
Never to purposely hurt one another
Your hands in mine, I look into your eyes
The snow is falling outside
On this quiet winter's day

Never has such beauty been in my sight
I promise to hold you the rest of my life
To search the world over
Finally finding my true soul partner
Happiness is with you

As we say our vows, a tear will appear
For in my mind I see the life we'll share
And while our children play I'll be saying
How much I am still in love with you
More and more each day

Stephen Douglas Bearden

God's Diva

Look at God's Diva with her hands held high
praising the Lord with gleam in her eyes,
Hallelujah! Praise the Lord! she says for
all to hear, for she loves the Lord and has no fear.

That's right, uh huh! For she has been there
and done that, but now she is saved,
ministering now to others, so they, too, might find their way.

Just wait, be patient, and you shall see, they will come
to touch her Holy hands, some will need her listening ear;
others will come, drop to their knees, in need of prayer.

For God's Diva has been blessed and not for
the song she sings, but for the faith she
has kept and the praises she brings forth
upon those who are willing to listen and
believe, her trials and tribulations are her testimony.

Lena Cecile Dodley

Fly Away

If I could fly like an eagle
To be free from all my pain
I would fly so far away and know one would know
I would find a place to mend my heart to dry my tears
For life would be no more.

Lingering memories of days gone by.
Your gentle touch and embracing hugs
Forever gone like a cold winter wind.
For why did you set me free
With a broken and aching heart?

Would you miss me?
Even if it were for a little awhile.
I doubt you would even know I was gone.
The days would pass and the years would come and go
Then one day maybe I would forget who you are.

Terri E. Leavitt

How?

Dear Montel,
How can we heal this broken world
Full of broken boys and broken girls?
How can we begin to cure?
How can we begin to heal?
How can we be sure of anything
When we're not even sure how we feel?
How can we make a stand
When it seems we're asleep at the wheel?
People, we need to wake up before it's too late!
Otherwise, will there ever be a cure for hate?
I fear not, not at this rate!

Judy Leolich

The Way It Ended Up with Us

Once upon a midsummer day,
there you were, standing all alone,
walking beautifully in my way.
My heart grew with love, and could've flown away,
I had to take the chance,
and so I did, and now I'm with you,
but what seemed like a quick glance,
you were gone and off to a far away place,
and even though it seemed to be forever,
till you came back to see me and be in my arms,
what seemed like a lifetime, was better than ever.
It was like a shocking alarm to see you back,
but there you were so beautifully standing,
wanting to be held in my arms once again,
and on that day, tears were shed,
and hearts were won back.

Dirk Dean Barry

As You Lie Sleeping

I watch you as you're sleeping,
and a smile plays across my lips.
I kiss you on your forehead,
and caress your face with my fingertips.
So overwhelmed with love for you,
as you lie there with your dreams.
While the moon shines through the window,
sprinkling your face with all its beams.
So content with you lying next to me,
I time my breath with yours.
And lay my head upon the chest
of the one whom I adore.
And then I listen to your heart,
slowly and sleepily beating.
And I let you go and close my eyes,
and lie beside you, sleeping.

Amanda Erin Kibben

The Spirit of Number Three

Dedicated to family, friends, and also the fans of a legend
There was a man named Earnhardt,
Who raced until the end.
He had a car that refused to bend.
The race was fast,
And we thought he wouldn't last.
But he surprised us all, when he stepped onto the gas.
His life was fulfilled,
Even the crowds were thrilled.
But the end was near,
And he drove into a steer.
God came down to bless his son
For a well done job he had done.
So in memory we say
That the number three is here to stay.

Anthony Scott Peters

A Daughter's Return

The wind is whistling through the trees,
and the birds are singing again;
The sun is shining, and the streams are flowing,
mother nature is my friend.
The once weeping flowers stand tall,
and the sky as blue as the sea;
The eyes are blue, the hair is blond,
and she's beautiful naturally.
The minds are thinking more clearly now,
I think that we have learned;
The life is much more beautiful now,
because she has returned.

Gregory Val Atherton

Before It Rained

The holidays are so hard. I hate being alone.
How many times I've wanted to call you on the phone.
I tell myself to just forget everything and go on.
But I can't seem to let go
and I feel like my life is gone.
I wish the rain had never came.
I wish we wouldn't have been put through all that pain.
But when it starts to get cold,
I start remembering when we met.
And when it starts to rain,
It's so hard for me to forget.
I'll always feel this stabbing pain.
It's driving me insane.
And I miss you.
Just remember me the way I was
before it rained.

Rhonda Mae Miller

Marry Heaven

Dream a little dream for me.
Tell me all that you see
At the end of the night,
While I'm holding you tight.
Tell me all your thoughts and fears.
Let me kiss away your tears
One be one,
Until they're gone.
I've been dreaming of the day,
The day your daddy gives you away.
You're walking down the aisle,
Smiling your sweet smile.
Something old, something new,
Something borrowed, and something blue . . .
Oh, baby,
You know I do.

Paul Douglas Twilley Jr.

Cemetery Town

I laid fresh flowers on Mary's grave on
the hill above our town.
Her address now is C street in Cemetery Town.
The neighborhood is peaceful here,
no arguments resound.
All earthly issues quietly rest in Cemetery Town.
I pass the graves of others of more or less renown.
The souls of most have surely risen;
some must have sped straight down.
A history of the town is here carved out in lonely stone.
Some simple, some are lavish,
some forgotten and unknown.
For all that lie here, rich or poor, the bird of time has flown.
A wind flows through the sighing pines.
My flowers fade and brown.
There's a whisper of eternity in Cemetery Town.

Thomas R. Varnell

Dear Mama

If I could tell you everything I'm sorry for,
the letter would never end.
If I could tell you everything I'm blessed with,
I would just say "you."
If the world was coming to an end,
I would rather have it come to an end with you.
If I was on my deathbed,
I would be just fine, as long as you were by my side.
If I didn't have any friends to tell my deep dark secrets to,
that's all right, I got you!
But in the end I know you'll be there for me.
So Dear Mama, I love you!

Shawna Marie Shakespeare

Best Friends?

Wind.
Noise.
Speed.
Separation.
What had happened to us?
To me?
To her?
How long had it been since we'd spoken?
An hour?
A day?
A week?
A month.
And best friends?
No words spoken, not even a glance.
Had we really grown that far apart?
The question is, were we ever really that close?

Emily Pearl Gordon

Rain of God's Love

Rain flowing from the skies,
flowing like tears from the corner of my eyes.
Why would tears fall from the sky?
Could it be your children, Lord, we make you cry?
Is that why rain is flowing from the sky?
Could it be that the rain is not the Lord's sorrow,
but instead our pain the Lord has borrowed?
Could it be that the Lord has turned our pain into a gift,
That our spirits need more lift?
Rains flowing from the sky, nourishing his Earth,
bringing forth new life, like our mother giving birth.
Rains come to bring us strife,
NO! I cry rain comes to bring us life.
Come, Rain!
Flow through the air like the wings of a dove,
bringing us remembrance of God's love.

Joshua James Rouleau

Our Climb

As you place your hand in mine,
We shall start our mountain climb.
We can't afford to stop and watch,
For we must head straight for the top.
We tire, we weaken, we almost retreat;
But can afford an entire defeat?
Our feet feel heavy and we want to drop,
But with each step forward we see the top.
Constantly upward, striving to and fro;
Now, only a short way left to go.
Our journey decreasing,
Our strength increasing,
Rapidly running up we go.
Now, looking down, for we have stopped.
Together with love,
We have reached the top.

Gloria Bryant Evans

Evyn

This poem is for Evyn.
She is as sweet as an angel in Heaven.
She has long hair,
She doesn't really have any care.
Her tan skin is fair,
She is as soft and cuddly as a teddy bear.
Her dad's name is Tony,
All she wants for her birthday is a pony!
She likes to learn and play,
She likes to play all day.
This poem is for Evyn,
Someday she'll remember this in Heaven.

Caitlin Marie Moseley

Spring Flowers

Waving in the morning breeze,
colors glowing as the sun shines,
sitting down under trees,
there are many, many kinds.
The flowers are painted by God,
growing in the flower bed.
The dandelion is goldenrod,
and the prickly rose is red.
The bee searches for pollen,
before it is too late.
The flower petals are falling,
and flies off with his mate.
The smell is full of wonder,
the feel is like a kitten.
The sight is as strong as thunder,
the sound is a visual of this poem I have just written.

Nate Christopher Hall

Bahia Kino

Dead fish island, Pelakus
yielding rotting carcass
and childish adventure.

Poor?
If I could be so poor in spirit
to have only a dirt floor to grow upon
with bare feet.

Did you eat any sweet bread
baked like a fevered baby's bottom?

Do you know Sonoria, the diver
who fed us fish and squid and tequila
until we became the dancing women with the town whore?
The sawed-off shotgun wreaked havoc
on our dance; he took her.
After all, we were Americans.

Tammy Francis

I Picture

When I picture 1940, everyone poses
for me as though I had the one
camera in the world. I cannot distract them
from their studied, ghoulish jolliness.
My grandmother is posing, yelling "Smile,"
and my grandfather is horsing around
with a tire, making his biceps big. I
can't know the past because the past
keeps arranging itself before my lens. People
call out "Here" and "Over here," striking
their prewar, rural, easygoing stances.
That night, when I try again, everyone
is indoors in parlors reading quietly.
A woman rocking in and out of lamplight
studies me. The neighbor's
middle child died this afternoon.

Felicia Y. Tabiti

Spirit Horses

I love the spirit horses
Warring through the Heavens,
Soaring in the distance, noble as
marble chess pieces.
Beautiful and very regal, bursting out of the air.
The time between Heaven and Earth,
Going here and going there.
On those spirit horses my soul wants to roam.
Imagine your spirit horses
Bowing down to God's throne.
In his celestial city which passage
and place is unknown.
I would love for the spirit horses,
To take me to my previous home.

Michelle Burrow

Beautiful Butterfly

Beautiful butterfly lead me to your peaceful place.
Where everything's in bloom.
Take me far from this place.
Far into the fields away from the world.
Far from sadness where you feel no harm.
Where I can forget my thoughts and get lost in my dreams.
I want to hear nothing but the winds
Whistling through the trees.
See nothing but elegant colors around
I want to smell the earth around me.
I want to feel the sand between my toes.
And go swimming with the fish in the beautiful oceans.
I want to touch the clouds soar
Through the stars, and up to the Heavens.

Ashley Baillio

Dandelions

We pick all the dandelions;
Nice lawns don't grow them.
Stuck inside glass vases
Behind rose-littered curtains,
They have their place.

I asked Mama, "Where do they come from,
Those noisy sunbursts that we kill?"
She said, "Don't think it's killing.
They're only dandelions,
And this season is for real people."

After that, I stopped giving names
To the ones I tied around my neck
In chains and kissed before they withered,
But I kept skipping the small ones
Just starting, with buds tightly shut.

Kristine Lamey

Sharable One Bedroom, Full Bath, Eat-In Kitchen

Sunny One Bedroom
"It's cooler in there,"
our secret code to spend our summers not leaving that room;
the light defies me each morning as I try to sleep,
restless, defined by half-waking dreams
of my guilt and other self-loathing;
it's no longer an active room

Hardwood Floors
Over there is where we'll put the bookshelf,
near our first swimming, explosive kiss,
where you peeled off the last note I ever wrote you,
taped to said bookshelf, my Pez collection looking on,
saying "I won't trade self-respect for love,"
stating "Slip the key under the door when you leave."

Amelia K. V. Hennighausen

Siriusly

In a dream, or maybe not
Orion stalks me, hard and hot
I shrink in shadows, splash through streams
Still he comes, his dagger gleams

I'm not sure why, but on a whim
I wheel around—now I hunt him
His stride is long, my burden light
We cross the sky in just one night
Colleen McLelland

You Are Like

You are like the sunrise,
Rising to brighten everyone's day.

You are like the sunset,
Setting slowly to make sure everyone's okay

You are like diamonds,
Always glowing with pride.

You are like a nurse,
Always helping someone, always by their side.

You are like time,
Not rushing, but always getting the day through.

You are like love,
And that is why I love you.
Amanda Jo Shirley

My Grandma Lived Her Life

My grandma lived her life near the rail yard:
By night, a world of bright screeches
And dark bumps,
Of noisy couplings
And haunting wails and whistles.
Peering out a window,
A dreamy child could see
Penitent workers waving stygian lamps of oil
To hasten hoppers of black coal from the underworld.
By day, a brighter place,
But dark,
Stained by industry.
Grandma planted roses in the black dirt,
And they stood guard along the picket fence.
She planted tulips in the black dirt,
And they marched valiantly along in unswerving lines.
She planted daffodils and crocuses in the black dirt,
And they sang in triumph.
Grandpop claimed she could make things grow on a metal drum.
David Earl Athey

Love's Critic

I am a critic of love
If I can't see the emotion, it's not there
I don't believe that there is one divine
person for each soul,
But only a dream of one which we live off
until we die
There is no such thing as an emotion that
causes you whiplash,
But only insecure hormones
"Once Upon a Time's" are a poor, lonely
woman's fantasy on her take of love
"Happily Ever After's" are hypocritical,
just like when a man tells a woman she is
the only one for him
And this is written from the heart of a
love wounded soul . . .
that will never be healed
So . . .
Once upon a time, I never fell in love.
Bristol LeeAnne Finch

Life Incomplete

Dedicated to Yvonne Yip Yok Lian
Every day I wonder
What woman would I meet.
I chance upon a wanderer
Who would my life complete.
But alas, she's only an e-Forum wanderer,
And my life's incomplete!
Richard Chew

Hope for a Cure

We all hope for a cure,
Everyone prays, hoping each day.
We wait, unsure,
We pray.

Sends us a cure
We loved Ms. Barnes in fifth grade.
We're sure,
What a difference she's made.

We hope MS will soon go away,
For we wish it will leave us free.
In the future we will see.

As we sit month after month waiting to hear,
"We found the cure, Sherry, my dear!"
Angela Cheatham

The Abyss

Lost in the abyss of his unyielding love,
Drawn into the cavernous depths of his love,
Surrounded and comforted by his matchless love,
Who is he?
My husband

Tender and true I will always be,
Faithful and cheerful I will endeavor to be,
Provider and soul mate e'er in times of strife,
Who am I?
His ever loving wife

Thoughtful and pure, may our love evermore,
Be found entwined through countless time
Lost in the abyss of an unyielding love
Maryline David

Caring Mother

You're such a caring mother
You're always there for me
Whenever I have a problem
You listen patiently

You've been there all my life
Seen me grow up so fast
You don't know how hard it is
Now I'm doing many things I haven't in the past

Mom, I apologize for everything I put you through
You've always been here for me and I'm here for you, too
Sorry for the times I've let you down
I know you want to see a smile, not a frown
Thanks for every story you've read
Every night that you tucked me in bed
And the movies that we have watched
While the popcorn popped
You're the one who made me laugh
Who put a smile on my face
We played many games
And no one will ever take your place
I wish your mom was still alive
To see how great you are
She taught you all you need to know
That's why you are the way you are
Mary Carnevale

Growing Up

My children are grown, I feel so wary,
But life must go on, it's time to be merry!
Children are a blessing, they grow up so fast,
learning life's lessons, on their own at last!
So many times, I've heard each one remark,
When I grow up, I'll be happy as a lark!
Learn as you go, don't call on me,
I've done my part, at last I am free.
Now I am learning, I'll not be a quitter,
Grandchildren are coming, I'll be a babysitter!

Lula McCage

Owed to Mom

It's hard to say good-bye after all these years,
And to look and leave without showing tears.
The lady who always took time to give aid,
One of the most caring persons God ever made.
For her children she was always there for us,
From the time we were born through the time we rode a bus.
All of her children are grown and live one place or another,
But even as adults, she will always be our mother.
As the population of Earth has one less than before,
The Lord has increased the number in Heaven by one more.

Darrell Jenkins

Eternity

Lovely shadows soft and blue,
cast your spell upon this place
where all dwell within.
For in the winters of our lives,
we are gently undressed,
as the days of our youth unfold.
Regretting all the tomorrows that are gone
and all the yesterdays that will never be.
For there lies in the future
the reflection of time
that once held the balance of yesterday's dreams.
Dissolving and floating endlessly,
like the whisper of love that lingers
only for the breath of time.
Lovely shadows soft and blue,
cast your spell upon this place
where all dwell within.
For here, and here alone,
our souls entwine through time,
through endless time, through eternity.

Violet Zigler

Knowing Happiness

I have experienced happiness in diverse ways
From the earliest of my memories, through to the present day.
Each of us has different needs for satisfying that comforting feeling,
But my first experience was in a rented
house that was small and low of ceiling.
The only money available within that
domicile was spent on clothes and food.
But my parents myself and siblings were a very happy brood.
Every moment in those early years
until I left that loved abode
Was where my understanding of respect
and the seeds of love were sown.
So I have never considered material things
as a requirement for a happy life
because the greatest examples of being without them
were my mum and dad, a Loving man and wife.

Sidney M. Wiffen

Never Really Ends

Conclusion—where it never really ends.

In schools they taught us a lot of things,
Except how to live!

At work, we manage a lot of things,
Except our own lives!

This concludes where it never really ends.

Cheah Cheng Teik

Loneliness Leaves

He comes to me in the darkness and stillness,
His dark eyes flicker with sparks of brilliant light.
His touch is strong, yet filled with tenderness,
I know this night will hold all that is right.
His hands are strong, yet soft and gentle,
Able to warm my soul deep within its recesses.
When his lips touch mine, they are like lighting,
Yet tender as the wings of butterfly kisses.
He remains here with me in this moment unending,
Our souls are filled with radiant feelings of joy.
The love we share witnesses our hearts transcending,
These earthly chains and shackles our love hath defeated.

Charlotte Stanley Cook

Velvet Rose

I touched a velvet rose today,
Dark crimson, perfect in every way.

Feeling sentimental, it brought back to mind
One March early morning, when I heard a new born baby cry.

Skin like velvet and perfect, with eyes
So blue, they light up the morning sky

I held her in my arms, touched her tiny fingers.
She stirred a deep love with in my heart today still lingers

She is all grown up now, not much has changed
Her skin is like velvet, and perfect she remains.

Carmene Daniel

More Than Conquerors

There is power within us all
That makes us more than conquerors.
It is not something that you can see, touch or smell,
But it is an immovable force that resides all around us.
It is the one constant in the universe
That can withstand the annals of time.
Through this symbolic force we share a common bond,
And we are unique, interchangeable parts
That work together to serve the collective.
Indeed, there is an indelible force in the universe
That predestinated us from the beginning of time.
It is a force that makes us more than just conquerors.

Ronald K. Hicks

Blue Sky

Today I can see the blue Sky
The sky that I have seen all my life
The sky that I have been seeing from my window

When I first saw the sky
I thought that I was dreaming
But no, that was the beauty that I had seen before
That was the beauty that I had been admiring

One day I will be able to see again
One day I will have seen the sky with a passion
One day I will have been staring at the sky for so long
That I will be blind again

Pedro Joel Silva

Nothing Changes

The leaves take off in the gentle breeze,
Happy to see the daylight.
The sun rose high in the blue, blue sky;
The hottest day came into sight.
Because that breeze had deceived us all,
We now wait for the rain to fall.
Nothing changes.

Helen Down

A New Best Friend

I cry now for things I have done,
friends that are lost, of races not won.

The things I have done, I still wonder why,
why have I done this to make myself cry?

This is my life I've torn all apart.
Oh, what I wouldn't give to go back to start.

What I wouldn't give to start over again,
to start all over from beginning to end.

Please give me one more chance to try it again,
just one more chance to be your best friend.

Victor H. Ferrebee

Shadow of the Past

Was it a dream . . .
Was I awake or asleep . . .
As I think back to nights past
That dreamy shape in my door . . . past
Standing. Gazing. Through my door . . . past
That shadowy figure that resembles mine
Could it be. Was it to be. It had to be.
That shadowy figure standing in my door . . . past. Gazing at me.
What could he be thinking about . . .
Standing there not saying a word
Could he be. Does he know. He must have . . .
poor old Dad.

Donald James Boyd

Life Is a Gift

Life is a gift
received the day we are born.
Many think our days are a test;
but the only test is the gifts received,
whether used or discarded in scorn.

Beautiful are our sunsets, beaches and mountains;
poetry, music, and sparkling waterfall fountains.

To appreciate all these beautiful and wondrous things in life,
one needs only to retain the given gift of life.

So when you are down and depressed in thinking life is a test;
look to it as a gift, and you'll figure out all the rest.

Elizabeth Anne Hall

ponder

is God really there
do we really care
if seeing is believing
then no one would care
what is the reason, should I dare ask
or even pursue the age-old question
of many a soul before me in the dark about
what may be
perhaps the answer is simple
and simple rings true
perhaps the reason you're here is
because he believes in you

Karen Marie Williams

My Life

If you look in my life, you see what I see.
A empty heart with pain and grief.
A confused child with nothing to believe.
Wanting to have bigger and better opportunity, but can't.
Depending on my uncles and aunts
To help but nothing change.
I'm back where I started—alone, empty-hearted, and confused.

Starr Keisha Calahan

Blurred Intentions

It is so hard to catch my breath
My heart beats yet is completely broken
I hope you are pleased with what you have done
Now as I speed away through flashing yellow lights
I think about how I am going to overcome this
You are my first love and don't even realize it
The damage you caused cannot be undone
Your thoughtless words are spoken without regret
I tremble because now I am without
It terrifies me to think there is a very small possibility of
rejoining our two hearts
So that they may beat synchronized and steadily together.

Elizabeth Faye Miller

A Presence

For Paul—I love you always.
I find strength in his eyes
Happiness in his smile
Security in his voice

But when the night comes
I look at him, and there is a presence

With his eyes, as black as coal
His smile greedy for my soul
And a laugh that makes the room turn cold

Yes, there is a presence
The presence of the unknown

Tammy Lee Leduc

journey towards eternity

i opened my eyes into a world unknown
where there were moments to cherish and moments to mourn
time and again i stumbled in my journey towards eternity
since life holds no guarantees or certainties
i came across people celebrating moments of joy
yet there were others who were helpless in hands of nature as a toy
there were moments when i felt overwhelmed with grief
yet there were others when i breathed a sigh of relief
even now in my journey towards ultimate destination
i am in awe and utter fascination
about the marvels of nature so diverse
the endless paths which man has to traverse

Farah Khizar

The Words I Speak

Lies, cheating, gangs, sex, hate. . .
These are the subjects of the songs we listen to.
The words we repeat.
The beats we dance to.

Have you ever stopped to listen, to understand?
The creators say it means nothing personal.
Does it?
Maybe not to them.
To some it does.

Suicide, shootings, depression, anger, rape, withdrawal . . .
These are the things words can create.

Danielle Antoinette Foster

Heavy Rain

As you walk through the road of life
you'll see that there is
heavy rain upon your shoulders
That heavy rain never goes away
it evaporates and pours back on you
Heavy rain is unavoidable
That heavy rain cannot get to you if you carry an umbrella

Ian Burgess Corneille

Self

Sometimes I feel my thoughts are locked in cages
so, I let my mind free on loose leaf pages
thinking of high costs and even lower wages
I can see why some turn to glocks and gauges
but I don't want my soul lost to Satan
Steady, hoping God hears my nightly prayers
I want to share my views, but I'm kind of scared of stages
I guess I just need to let go and forget the haters
if you're in my line of sight, know you're in grave danger
My mouth is a gun and my thoughts fill up the chamber
I don't discriminate, whether you're a friend or a stranger
I unload on you, and your mind becomes greater

Daniel Velarde

The Reoccurring Smile

Like the dark, cold, rainy day,
when it seems nothing could get better,
you look outside, and get depressed,
while the ground keeps getting wetter.
But what is always forgotten about the rain,
is that there is a rainbow on the other side.
When the sun breaks through, and relieves our pain,
our depression begins to hide.
So when you have those dreary days,
and your happiness is in denial,
remember what will happen soon:
the rainbow will bring back your smile.

Steven Diego Kent

Reasons

The reason I love you is not your hair,
Even though it flows freely and fair.
It's not your eyes so beautiful and deep,
No I can see those even in my sleep.
It's not your figure even though it's good,
I know that's why a lot of fellows would.
It's not your kids even though they're great,
No that's not the reason I want you for a mate.
It's not because you're sweet and kind,
Even though those things always come to mind.
All these things are good and true,
But the reason I love you is because you're are you.

Mirth L. Traster

My Heartbeat Finally Came

The body is an empty shell and my life was just the same,
until September the 6th of '94 when my heartbeat finally came .
I've lived 29 years of emptiness, harshness and in vain
not knowing unconditional love until September 6th of '94
when my soul was filled with love, and my heartbeat finally came.
God has given us gifts like the animals and the lands,
but the greatest gift he could have given me
was on September 6th, '94 when I held it in my hands .
Nothing in this world can take its place, not money, glory or fame,
because on September 6th, '94 my heartbeat finally came.
Since that day in '94 my life has not been the same,
for God has given me a heartbeat, and Jonah is his name.

Albert Linwood Brinson Jr.

Recognition

As the gypsy moon nestled into the depth of night
The mournful cry of a lone coyote
Penetrated the darkness with a primal scream
And the terrified heart awoke in chilling pain
Feeling the knife of inconsolable grief
As it ripped through the universe
And pierced the very soul of existence

Jan Waddell

To Love Again

It seemed to me that Love was gone, a very distant thing.
I never thought I'd meet someone for whom my heart would sing.
I knew when I first met you, beyond the shadow of a doubt,
If in my hart Love remained, that you could bring it out.
In your eyes I saw a flame, such warmth within your smile.
And when you spoke, my heart stood still, but only for awhile.
And now I know that Love exists, my life seems so complete.
In this world I've known few things that ever seemed so sweet.
I long to hold you in my arms, to kiss your precious face.
And keep that loving heart of yours deep in my embrace.
Of pain you need not worry, no fear shall I let in.
For I never thought it possible to fall in Love Again. . . .

Pamela M. Mintz

My Grandma's Tears

My Grandma's tears are the rain
and my Grandpa's laughter is the thunder.
My Dad's happiness is the lightning in the rain,
and my Mom's smiles are the tornado's wind.
My aunt and uncle are the hurricane
that blows through the bay.
My sisters are the typhoon
every other day.
My cousins are the earthquake at dawn.
And me?
I'm all of those,
All of those together.

Jennifer Lynn Porath

Dreams

Isn't it funny what a dream can do,
It can make almost anything true.
If you are young, you may dream you are old.
Are you bashful, then you may dream you are bold.
Have you lost the one you love most of all,
Well, in a dream there is lots to recall.
If your happiness is a thing of the past,
In a dream, this happiness may last and last.
It makes no difference what you do.
Dreams are made by you and you and you.
'Cause isn't it funny what a dream can do
For just last night I dreamed of you.

Rita Jane Bailey

Good-Bye

Down by the ocean,
feeling the breeze.
The warm sand,
that tickles my knees.
How I miss her so very much,
her happy eyes, her gentle touch.
The sun shines as bright as her face,
her soft smile as soft as lace.
Tears slowly absorb into the sand,
I see us together hand in hand.
She is with God now in Heaven in the sky,
it's not fair, I didn't get to say good-bye.

Jaime Lea Birk

Moments

It was cloudy, cold, and gray
As there I stood
Watching over the lashing waves.
The birds flew from rock to rock
Undisturbed by other members of the flock.
Is Death like this—
The cold, the gray?

Sharon Ann Walls

Elegantly Wasted

It's more your taste I think about
My thirst insatiable
The bittersweet smoothness coating my tongue
Once you've filled me, my thoughts become incoherent
The air gets thin
The light gets dim
My sight is clouded with forbidden images
Of your smooth, rich texture
And your distinct aftertaste
It is an addictive intoxication
It is a sensual inebriation
I am elegantly wasted on your love

Yindra Toi Cotman

Love Is

Love has no boundaries, it condescends
Love is wise and sometimes hard to comprehend
With much patience, love endures and many times stands alone
Love is kind, gentle, and speaks with a soft tone
Love is like the calm that comes after the storm
Love takes hate and makes it conform
Love is peaceful and never keeps company with confusion
Love is truthful and never a delusion
Love is more than a mere emotion
Love is faith and real devotion
Love is something we are commanded to give
Love is what we are to be and live

Mary Louise Gibson

The Big Open Sky

Up in the big open sky,
Where birds and airplanes fly.
If I keep on going up,
Soon I'll find God with his cup.
If I wait long enough,
I'll be with God hand in hand cuffed.
Have I thought about coming down,
Yes I have thought about coming home and to town.
Though I'm stuck up in the clouds,
Never coming down back in the world that is loud.
Up in the big open sky,
Sorry that's where I'll die.

Meredith Kay Scherer

Raindrops of Love

Raindrops of love.
I can feel it in the air.
Walking hand in hand with the one you love.
Exchanging gifts and making plans
For an enchanted evening of love.
Valentine's Day comes once a year.
Your love, your valentine, your dear.
Make it an everyday thing.
Every day of the year.
For true love is not a one day thing.
It's something you should enjoy every day of the year.
Sweet raindrops of love are here.

Eugene Wynn Brown

Heartbeat

Lost hope I regained instantly in one heartbeat.
My faith I lost in mankind came alive in one heartbeat.
The human race took on a new face in one heartbeat.
The joy that was faded became unjaded in one heartbeat.
The peace I ignored was restored in one heartbeat.
The miracle I found in one ultrasound
gave meaning to my existence in one heartbeat.

Denise Majors-Moore

Friends

Friends are forever,
forever by your side.
Friends are for keeps,
keeping you in their memory.
Friends are there,
there when you need them.
Friends are upset,
upset when you leave them.
Never leave your friend behind and they will never leave you.
Lose one friend,
lose all friends,
lose yourself.

Shelby True Rader

To the Mothers

A mother is a person always there,
Letting you know she will always care.
A shoulder to cry on in times that are sad,
A force of discipline when you are bad.
With tenderness to show you her love,
And the happiness from clouds above.
She is also there to be your friend,
With loving care until the end.
When she passes, we all do see
What life without will have to be.
So remember your mother with each passing day,
Showing her you care in every possible way.

Keith Richard Neidig

Silly

Silly kids, silly life
A hurting pain, a bloody knife
A wrong made right, a fleeting light
A blue tear shed, a hunger fed
A silver glint of blood red tint
An escaping smile, a taste of vile
Sun shining bright, a crazy sight
Road made grey, but turned red
Chances are final bed
Scary dreams that turn real
Cold surroundings that turn teal
Colors change before my eyes, put an end to my life of silly lies

Ashley Marie McKeever

Expression

The sky has not one star
as beautiful as the one in your eyes.
The sun shines not
as near as your smile.
The river does not flow
as lovely as your hair,
nor is silk as soft as your skin.
Blessed am I to have such a luxury
to have a child with so many qualities.
There is one thing that I haven't mentioned—
that is the warmth in your soul
and its expression.

Loretta Martinez

Miss You When You're Far and Love You When You're Near

I miss you when you're far, and love you when you're near.
I think of you for hours, wishing you were here.
My love for you has deepened; there is no turning back.
I fear to live without you, my life would fade to black.
I hope you understand me, I hope my words were clear.
I'll miss you when you're far and love you when you're near.

Rachel Lyda Caravetta

Frustrating Thoughts

People only know sin and pain
but don't know how to weep
Even though the evening is long
and frustrating child sleep
Don't let money take your soul
But let love make you whole
People, let the soul shine for everyone to see
That beauty lies within you, like a fresh apple tree
Let's minimize the violence and stop behaving like tyrants
Love our children, it takes a village to raise child
One day that seed will grow to be successful
and make that village proud

Charles Lamont Jones

The Knife

The pain he felt was great
His wounded heart just couldn't take
He fell to the floor
As his shallow breaths became no more
Lights flashed and sirens sounded
As a dozen cop cars surrounded

At the end of the day
They suspected no foul play
They said he was just sick of all life's toil
So he shuffled off his mortal coil
He had picked up his knife
And fatally ended his life

Amy Jo Thackston

True Love

What true love brings is the sorrow of blue
In my mind, all I can think of is you
The rejections I received are like a dart
Sharp and pointy, stabbing through my heart
Being rejected by the one you want to see
Then it makes you wonder, how can it be
Was this never meant to be
Will I once again hear the words
"We'll be friends only"
I seen you once, I wish to see you again
Even if it is just for one glance
But now, how can it be, if I can't even get that one chance

Dac Quay Su

waves on the sand

a swish of wind
the taunt of the past
a feel of pain and love from old times past
the ground falls
the trees swish
a swimming sting of love and bliss
a mountain of cries
armies of hate
a songbird sings of a new kind of taste
whatever you wish, whatever you dream
anything's possible in this weary land
it's just another wave on the sand

Samantha Nichole Fullerton

Untouchable

The moon's untouchable beauty
brings happiness to everyone, everywhere.
It brings hope that the one you love is
watching the moon, thinking of you. You
look at it and see a face with no worries,
no cares; it is just a face looking back. The
beauty alone brings tears to your eyes,
and the untouchable is touching your lips.

Pamela Matlock

To the Love of My Eternity

To the love of my eternity,
You have brought much joy and happiness.
You have beauty inside and out.
Your kindness shows what is truly in your heart.
Your playfulness is a welcome distraction from the mundane day.
I wish I could convey all the reasons why I love you,
But it would take forever to do that.
May the happiness continue in our lives together,
May the honeymoon never end.
You are my true and everlasting love.

Ron L. Hill Jr.

Love

Love doesn't last forever,
no matter what anyone says.
All of the feelings you're feeling
can just be inside your head.
Love hurts and you will most likely cry.
Even though you think you're in love,
your relationship could just be based on lies.
No matter what you think,
almost every relationship dies and almost everyone cries.
So if you ever get hurt, remember this . . .
Love is something some people can't resist,
but to me, Love just doesn't exist.

Katherine Marie Mahady

clockwork

standing in the shower at two a.m.
all of the lights turned off
loving the water drumming off of my shoulders
like your fingertips   like your words
curling perfectly around my skin
water building me up again
forming and shaping me into the woman i was
my body swaying with the moon's undying pull
as the tide comes in again
clockwork

the cold tile offers up shadows of the sea
for me

Leigh Katherine Schnell

Grief

As tears roll down my cheeks, no control do
I have—my emotion is so deep.
But I must have strength to carry the burden of my grief.
The watching and the waiting in our home
Where death is knocking, knocking at our door.
I must be strong and not give up—I must
Have faith in our good Lord,
Who cares for each and all upon this Earth.
The day is near when I will be left all alone,
Alone with only memories of good days that are no more.
I must be brave, I must not cry,
I must pray each and every day for the dear one,
Who is near death.

Marjorie H. Boring

Twilight

As the foreground colors turn black,
And the background sky turns bright, I sit and ponder.
Memories, light, reflections, sounds of the night.
Birds go to bed while bats come out to dance.
Crickets play their tune,
Hoping to find romance.
Light fading fast now,
Darkness envelopes.
Stars start their evening show,
With distance so overwhelming
The speck that is me must know.
What is this thing called life?
Who is the source of the moon's glow?

Mark E. Clowser

My Daddy

On June 8th 1992, the Lord had a purpose to call you.
I didn't have the power to keep you here,
I'm afraid of loosing and live in fear.
A Father's love is more precious than gold,
In my eyes you would never grow old.
I never thought you would ever leave me,
But God had a place for you to be.
The journey you took was way too far,
I can't drive to see you in my car.
No one knows what they're got till it's gone,
The doors are shut and not one light is on.
I will never forget the tear in your eyes,
My heart was broken when I said "good-bye."

Sherry Foster

Impressions of My Friend

Silly little simpleton, you chatter with your hands,
As you skip across life's troubles in bare feet.
Looking to the left of you, while talking to the right,
And not knowing how they sound when your words meet.

Climbing up the stairs of life, you often stub your toe
On a misplaced star or some forgotten wish.
Or you fall into a lake of thoughts that try to pull you down,
And while learning how to swim, become a fish.

You drink the water of life too fast and strangle on a song,
As the strings that bind your heart begin to fray.
You jump into the world of love to chase your heart it seems,
As you catch up with yourself along the way.

Joan Ellis Anderson

Till the Last Star Fades Away

Can trees grow where there is no soil?
Can flowers bloom without the sun?
How can I go on without my Mom?

Do kittens chase balls of string?
Do birds sing up in the trees?
Were her last words calling for me?

Do curtains blow in the breeze?
Do dirty dishes pile up high?
Thinking of my Mom makes me cry.

Just tell me where you are going.
Just tell me if you are at peace.
Tell me can I visit and will the pain cease.

I have to let you go Mom.
I have to say goodbye.
Have to keep moving forward, or at least try.

No matter where you are Mom.
No matter what comes my way.
I will love you forever and a day Mom.
Till the last star fades away.

Sara-Lee Giumelli

Ode to Love

I thought my heart was that of stone
Until now I know, I'm alone
Every night there is a tear
Gallons more throughout the year
Your face in pictures always seems to remind
How you always were so kind
One more night, one more day
Now I know you've passed away

Sally L. Nolan

The Belly Dancer

Colors fly, coins jingle
Zil and zagharet trill and chime
We dance on, we dance as one
We dance for our sisters, we dance for ourselves
Joy, laughter, pain, and despair, birth and death
We dance
We turn the wheel with our flying feet
We dance

Aynne Price Morison

No News

It's really too bad about your condition.
An arm that can't write, my what an affliction!
Fingers can't dial, yes, it's very pathetic.
You have my compassion, I am sympathetic.
I hope this ailment isn't contagious.
But of course, that is outrageous.
Oh, dear! Oh, me! Alas! Egad!
My arm feels s—

Doris Gill

Lost and Unseen

Quick steps, moving fast.
Slipping and tripping, blindly reaching for the past.
All has turned to nothingness,
leaving shreds of emotion for the keeping.
Staring into the darkness,
lost and unseen.
Reaching for the sane, yet grasping the crazed.
Letting illusions take control of the fantasies untold.

Jessie Danielle Mechem

Unstable Suns We Are

Unstable suns we are
Giving light in varied measures
On this cloudy Earth that strips us bare
Devoid of all, not even our minute treasures

While time works our bellows
We gather faggots into the fires
Creating moons out of our desires
Moons forged with varied blows

Iziegbe Idemudia

Self-Worth?

What is it that defines one's own worth?
Is it something inherited upon his birth?
Do we earn it through great deeds,
Or just by faith and our creed?
Is it in the stars, written by fate,
Or is it God who determines who's great?
Is it the price we pay for what we have gotten,
Or just to simply not be forgotten?
I think it is not determined by man, God, or the stars above,
But just from the joy of spreading one's love.

James Kristoffer Taulbee

The Rains

The monsoon is here.
The singing winds herald the rains,
sating the parched grounds,
fulfilling verdant dreams.
Laden boats will carry, once again,
cargoes of life
on swollen breasts of lactating streams.
Dark pathos of the sky is pierced
by fiery arrows of cognitive lightning.
Rivulets down my windowsills
flow to the sea.
The heavens weep.

You arrive
with the softly falling tear drops
to meet me in the deep.
Mahfooz Rahman

Mom and Dad

In memory of my beloved mom and dad, Thelma and Joseph A. Taylor
We have left this world of sorrow,
Full of heartache, strife, and sin,
To enter a world with Jesus,
Where our new life will begin.

We hope all the loved ones left behind us,
Will not grieve forever more,
For they know where they can find us,
Here on God's celestial shore.

When we walk through those gates of glory,
Our lost loved ones we will find!
And we'll smile from Heaven on you,
For we know, the rest are not far behind!
Walton M. Taylor

Awake

Day and night I dream.
I dream of a world of shadows
Shadows masking the face of reality.
Costumed in their abundant fallacies
Embodied in the illusion of importance.
Desiring the chimerical happiness
Found only in the surreal mentality of
Morpheus.
I search relentlessly for this unattainable
Utopia.
I wish to live eternally in its virtual coma.
Forever dreaming
What it could have been
What it has become
What it is.
Ann Caps

My Valentine Poem for Roderick

I Love you every day
and in every way.
You are the only Dad, I wish I had.

Every day I remember you
and your eyes of blue.
Every day I think of you, and all your charms,
And how it felt when you held me in your arms.

I still see you in my thoughts and dreams,
Sometimes I think it seems
Nothing is fair.
Most of all I wonder if you care?

And if you do, then why can't you come back and say,
"It's me and I'm here to stay."
I miss the very Best Dad, I ever had.
Ariel Gustanski

Tell Me Why

I'm sitting here trying to remember
all the good times we've had together.
It seems to me we had so much in common.
So why did you have to go and leave me?
Please, tell me why.
Well, yesterday I needed you by my side,
but you weren't there for me.
You said that if I needed you, you'd always be there for me.
Please, tell me why.
I had a dream last night,
and you were there dancing and having a good time.
You said that you loved us all,
then said, "Good night, my daughter," and left again.
But you never told me why you left us in so much pain and sorrow.
So, please tell me. Why did you leave us?
Cynthia A. Dowling

Nightmare

I feel the worst has come upon me.
An inescapable feeling of doom
overcomes me.
I have lost all hope.
No longer do my days lead me toward my goal,
but take me further and further from it.
The darkness covers me,
like a blanket of uncertainty.
Helplessness leads the way
with her head held high,
her cloak I cling to subserviently.
The harsh winds howl in the night,
like messengers of despair.
Can I turn out this grim reaper,
or am I lost forever?
Toni Christine Farley

Where I'm From

I am from broken dreams
and rotting souls.
I am from losing a father to too many drinks
and too little time.
I am from a childhood left abruptly
but not forgotten.
I am from too much given love
and not enough return.
Too much pain
and too little smiles.
I am from almost unreachable goals.
Too much perseverance
and too little inspiration.
I am from a broken heart
mended only with scotch tape.
Ashley Powers

Delight Myself in the Lord!

I delight to do your will, oh, Lord.
Please give me the desires of my
Heart. My desire is to be real close
To you . . . From your word I'll never depart!
Help me to always trust you, through my
Anxieties and afflictions. Be merciful
To me, Lord, and take away my addictions.
I am trusting, Lord . . . in you right now. . . .
Take away the sins that hurt me . . .
Let me not be put to shame . . .
Shine your light brightly around me!
Hide me in the shelter of your presence,
Lord! To be strong in you and always have
Hope! May I be like a beautiful growing
Tree . . . a strong and beautiful oak!
Adele Jo Jack

Stay Silent

Don't tell me the sun will not shine.
Don't tell me that she is not fine.

Don't tell me that she is upset.
Don't tell me this is as good as it will get.

Don't tell me that this is my friend.
Don't tell me this is how her life will end.

Don't tell me the last thing that she said.
Don't tell me how they found her dead.

But most of all, don't tell me that this is really real.
Don't tell me you know exactly how I feel.

Because you don't.
You never will.
Tell me the sun will rise again.

Sakana Kawaii

The Rain

The rain went pitter-patter on the window sill
The boy looks out in dismay
The wind rages against the tree
A dog howls
The lighting crashes against the tree
The tree splits in two
The thunder sounds like drums bashing together
The lights flicker on and off
The boy's mother is down stairs lighting candles
The rain will show no mercy for anything
The wind will range on
The lighting will clash
The thunder will bang
The boy will look out the window with dismay
The neighbor next door is playing in the rain

Amber Manda Moore

Prayer

What is a prayer?
Is it talking?
Or then can it be a groaning
When all words seem to fail?

Is it in times of blessing, or
Must it only be in tribulation and stress?

Regardless of the intention,
Know this, dear reader—that our God, Jesus Christ
Is greater than any problem,
Than any ailment.

He cares so much that He died for us—you and I,
and it is a small portion of His care that
we hope and pray
He is showing you through His grace.

Pamela Hee

Perfect Love

Somewhere out there I know it exists,
the perfect love simply can't be a myth.
The kind that warms your heart,
like the sunshine in June
and is always on your mind, like a catchy tune.
It can make you smile when there is no one around,
and your lips even forget how to frown.
Secure, safe, and wanted is the way you feel,
and sometimes you pinch yourself to make sure it's real.
So far my heart has been left empty-handed,
but my search for love I will not abandon.
Until my heart finds this place where love does abide;
I will endure, my sadness I will hide.
For I know that it truly does exist,
the perfect love simply can't be a myth.

Sharon LeAnn Reece

Loving You

For Betty Borde

Love is full of joy and sharing,
Always wanting and caring.
Let me help you through your troubled times,
'Cause I'll need your help through mine.

Let me share all that's in your life,
Let me share it as man and wife.

It's for your love I long to stay,
Without it, Dear, I'll go away.

But for now I feel your love,
And for that I thank God above.

I just hope your feelings will last,
I don't want our love to be a thing of the past.

Gary L. Borde

The Encounter

A bald man and a hare did meet
Upon a sweltering summer street
Where said the balder of the two,
"I am more wise than you.

For you will find no head of hair
Residing on my shoulders where
There sits instead a head quite smooth
That lets the winds, the heat remove."

At which point did the hair bristle
Upon the hare, who said,
"This all is nonsense and I am quite sure
A head of hair would be the cure

So anger caused by jealousy
Would not fall on poor harried me."

James K. Bashkin

Memories

Rage, silence, wrath, low self-esteem
Do these words define the adult in me
Shallow, meek, stubborn, distraught
Losing all faith in what I've been taught
No one educated me on pain, loss, and sorrow
No one told me as a child I wasn't promised tomorrow
Rejected, hurt, alone, confused
Betrayed by human nature
The feeling of used
Walk with me down memory's path
I promise you won't find too many great laughs
My memories are distraught and never taught
Momma never told me of a past that will destroy my future
If she couldn't teach me
I wish she had found a tutor

Shameka L. Sawyer

Who Am I?

Look at me closely, what do you see?
Is there anything different from anyone else in me?
Does the fatigue in my eyes and the smudges on my face
Tell you I've just come from a terrible place?
Where ashes are still smoldering,
Smoke continues to rise,
There is pain for innocent people, I don't bother to disguise.
I'm dedicated to saving other peoples' things.
And, my friend, let me tell you, I'm not out to gain.
I don't get paid for this deed that I do,
But it makes my day knowing I've saved a life or two
From losing their home and all that they love,
And maybe being sent to Heaven above.
I want you to know I'll do all that I can,
Because I'm so proud to be—a volunteer fireman.

Tim Edward Smart Jr.

Time . . .

Time, it passes,
And days go on,
Yet sometimes you feel you'll never see the dawn.
It's always darkest before the light;
Why can't anyone see your plight?
Where's the silver lining?
That always seems so far.
It's like you're wishing on the farthest star:
You know that star,
It always seems so bright,
But then you notice it doesn't look quite right.
You finally realize it's not what you see
It's that one and only thing you always hoped it would be
Oh, Heavenly Father, please hold me tight;
Please ease my pain If only for tonight.

Lela Waggoner

What the Future Holds

We are never sure what tomorrow may bring
Many of us act as if it will always be here
We step on the toes of our sisters and brothers
Just reaching for that allusive brass ring
Try slowing down and holding someone near
You will realize that this feeling is like no other

This day will not happen twice
Don't waste it by reaching for things
Reach out with your heart to everyone
Take time to do one thing nice
Teach someone to sing
Remember as the day is done

Give Thanks for this once in a lifetime moment
Because you can never be sure what the future holds

D. J. Acrey

And It Makes It Hard to Think

And to think I did it all for you
but I did, and it makes it hard to think.
It was you who made me feel.
In your voice, I found truth.
In your eyes, I found hope,
and in your kiss, I found it all.
If only you knew how much you mean
but if only you felt the same.
What else is there for me to do?
I think of nothing else but you.
I no longer have my hope.
I no longer have my truth.
I have lost it all.
And to think I did it all for you
but I did, and it makes it hard to think.

Ashley Elizabeth Simmons

Let Me Know

Get the key!
Open it up!
Let them all know
what's deep inside
my heart.
My feelings are here,
my ideas never shown,
bottled up inside me and left unknown.
Tell me what you think of it.
Tell me if you care.
I have emotions deep inside.
I won't just leave them
anywhere.
Get the key!
Because without it, you'll never know what I don't show.

Stephanie Jeanette Mannion

My Search for Me

Running fraily on an endless search
for what I have forgotten
I now wonder what all this sad time has bought . . .
and why I even continue my search.
Is it because I let the emptiness consume me
or because the darkness I've found is all that's left to be. . . .
Or maybe because in the hollow center
of the exhausted me is a little bit
of determination and hope.
Perhaps darkness has clouded but not overcome.
Maybe I can ignore the pain in my heart,
or the scars of your words,
or the tears I cry for you . . .
because in this endless search for nothing
I have found a new beginning, I have found myself.

Alison Renae Clark

Broken Glass

I am like broken glass thrown into the sea
Repeatedly found and forgotten,
Until one person sees its perfection.
You are like the ocean to me,
Smoothing my rough edges.
I am that glass; broken and thrown away.
You are that one person
Picking up the pieces.
Shards of my youth
Are softened over time by your charm.
The glass cracks again (inevitably).
As tenacious as the sea
Washing its sharp pieces
Of a broken heart,
You are my sea.

Illaina Walters

Shackles to Wings

What may turn your mind
So sharply that you cry to me?
Unhappily weeping, please smile again.
I see you're hurting.
Your heart is ripping and so is mine.
You are me and I am helpless.
I want to take it away,
Melt these rocks into gold
And turn these shackles into wings,
But I am a helpless child and I am sorry.
What can I do to satiate
The need that you are craving?
Please tell, I will do anything.
Smile, my blessed angel,
For you are loved.

Shannon Marie Brooks

Emptiness

We were so happy together,
our lives were full of love.
I thought it would last forever.
Now, emptiness. You're gone, it's over.
I want to cry, I need to cry.
Emotions, where are they?
I feel so alone, so utterly alone.
My life is full of emptiness.
I try to keep a smile on my face.
I work the day away,
but when it is time for sleep, there is none.
No matter how hard I try.
No sleep, No tears, No happiness.
What is it that fills my life now?
Emptiness.

Bobbi Jo Christiansen

Gram

Gram, before you left you said these last words,
To always be good and always be strong.
One evening all was silent—nothing heard,
To Heaven you traveled where you belong.

I miss your giggle, I miss your smile,
You left me too soon; I needed you still.
I saw love in your eyes all the while,
Nine grand kids whose hearts your love did so feel.

I get so lonely, but not like Grandpa,
He lights a candle and visits you often.
"No loneliness!" That ought to be a law,
He feels you; his loneliness will soften.

So my feelings for you are not a sham,
I miss you so much and I love you, Gram.

Cathy Charmaine Devers

Hair

I'm a hair in your food.
Stringy, tangled, scratchy in your mouth.
Eat me . . . for you can't see me.
Take a bite
Chew, chew like a train.
You won't notice me until your mouth
sends a message to your brain . . .
an impulse to spit,
or when dinning with the president to
SWALLOW, SWALLOW.
You can feel me on the back of your tongue
and down the rear end of your throat,
clinching onto my disguise—
the food.
I'm a hair in your stomach.

Mikey Pat Mignogna

A Friend I Never Knew

In dedication to Justin Van de Berg
Today my brother is sad
I don't know why but yet I see him cry
Everyone around feels bad
I feel out of place for I am still glad
I walk down the street and see the blood and broken glass
My brother whispered to me . . . "He was in my class."
I think to myself . . . He never had the chance to live
He never had the time to give
He didn't even have the time to say his good-byes . . .
So as I watch I know why everyone cries
I start to shed my tears
Because I realize, it doesn't matter how many years
We live . . . They can be so very few
And now I know . . . This was my friend I never knew.

Jolene Lynne Winterfeld

Strong

As I walked throughout the midnight air,
I looked over and noticed you weren't there
At first I thought it was a bad dream,
but I missed the face I once had seen
Then a pain shot through my heart,
I couldn't believe that we were apart
I thought of memories when we were a pair
and remembered the times I knew you'd be there
I always loved to hear you speak,
for I knew your words were always so meek
You'd always said you'd stay with me,
through good and bad whatever trouble would be
I can't wait until I see you,
for that day I will long
But until then I promise to you I will stay strong

Erin Rachel Detherage

Depends on the Day . . .

I see the light . . . it's so far away.
So very bright, but sometimes grey.
Even at times my vision will fade,
My ray of light simply goes away.
It's funny how the tones change.
I guess it just "depends on the day."
Sometimes I'm happy, sometimes I'm sad.
Sometimes I wish this depression, I never had.
You can only relate by experience.
To understand it can only be heaven-sent.
I'll live with it now and accept my challenge.
Become a survivor, that's who I am.
Until that day I'll fight my whole way,
And then taste victory.
I guess it just "depends on the day."

Tracy Louise Jacobsen

Loss of Someone Special

Though my eyes fill with tears
And my chest fills with pain,
I search for you through every dream.
Though your voice will never call my name,
I listen for it just the same.
I have missed you these past years.
Even though I write these words for you,
Your ears will never hear.
I want you,
Oh, so near.
But now I have lonely tears.
I hope wherever you are
Is really as nice as the say.
I wish sometimes I could be going that way,
But it's too far away.

Danny James Helms

Dreams

I dream of things that are far away,
I dream of things that I want today.
If there weren't any dreams,
then what would we do to occupy our mind
the whole night through?
I dream of things that I could have,
though sometimes I dream of things that are bad.
Is a dream something that may come true?
Or is it an illusion your mind sends you through?
Now, some dreams are good and some even bad,
and there are sometimes dreams that make you feel sad.
Now, of all the dreams that I have had,
I remember the ones that made me laugh.
So, may all of your dreams in life come true,
and may all of them be nice to you.

Barbara D. Salinas

Walk of Life

As I walk through life,
I wonder why, as I look
around, we have to die.
Our father in Heaven we are taught to love.
The greatest father of all, he lives above.
Our short time here on this great Earth,
lets us prove we have earned a berth.
To be with him in the clouds above,
we have to prove if he is the one we love.
So, while you live with your family here,
make sure you love them for your time is near.
Kindness, compassion, loving care
will surely help us all get there
to be with our father, as you will see,
to live with him for eternity.

Robert E. Brill III

In Love with Him

I swore to myself
it wouldn't happen again.
I vowed to myself
that this was the end.
The end of this longing,
this yearning so strong.
I said I was over you,
but oh, was I wrong.
Now here it is
and not too much later.
My love for you
is now even greater.
I spend all my time just thinkin' of you.
I am in love with you,
and there's nothing I can do.

Cassandra L. Hardy

You

It's been almost eight years now, we've been friends.
We have grown up in two different worlds.
Yet similarities, to us, won't end.
And when we get it right, it comes uncurled.

I'd love to come and visit now that you're gone.
Being away, sad to see you go.
Some don't know what they've got, time just goes on.
But I knew! That's why I miss you so.

It's like a plane with no where to land.
The jokes, the movies, they have left with you.
I feel so helpless, buried in the sand.
And I bet you're feeling the same way too.

But don't worry, Best friends forever!
That bond we have, no one could sever.

Teryn Ashleigh Peterson

Personality

Can you believe where I am today?
When I saw you, you just blew me away.
I know all the girls like you, but it's not the same.
I like you 'cause you're smart.
I like you 'cause you're funny.
It's not your looks, it's what's behind them.
It's not your talent that I see, it's your personality.
I can love you better than they can.
'Cause I have what it takes to be yours.
Do you know how you make me feel inside when you're near me?
I only wish you could see me the way that I see you.
So will you try to notice what I love about you?
I like you 'cause you're there when I need you.
I like you 'cause you listen to me.
But what I love most about you is your personality!

Brandy Lee Clayton

Gold

A body, a person, a soul.
Manifest in his spirit a whole.
His will made of gold;
He's too late! It's been sold.
For him, no recovery is in sight.
The cold, dark metal whispers, "Doom."
Death arrives with a swift, resounding BOOM!
Then there's blood on the wall,
Someone else takes the fall
For mistakes that the murderer has made.
In the cold, in the dark; in a cell.
He looks down at his life (like a well).
Then they take him away,
It's the end of his day.
Never again to feel the joy of human touch.

Chad I. Drake

Fancy Dancer

You whirled and twirled to the beat of the drum.

The beat got faster, and you were quicker,
a flash of blinding color.

You danced and pranced to the song
that seemed to last forever.

Like diamonds, my heart broke into tiny, little pieces.

As I realized who you were with,
my emotions got twisted, and I was drowning.

Was anything ever real, except the pain that I feel in my heart,

Now that you are gone?
We both didn't say a word,
just turned and walked away.

Carolyn M. New Holy

I Wake Up in the Morning . . .

I wake up in the morning,
Wondering what the day will bring to me.
Maybe it will bring happiness,
Or maybe it will bring sadness.
Maybe it will bring new love,
Or maybe it'll bring everlasting heartbreak.
I wake up in the morning,
And I think of my past and my future,
About the good times, and also the bad.
I wonder peacefully, how will this day go?
I wake up in the morning,
And I know not a thing. . .
Except for this one thing:
I know only that no matter what happens today
I am, and will remain, the same me forever!

Gillian Blair Goodhue

In Love

I love you!
And I thank God for you.
I thank Him for every minute
He gives me to breathe,
And every day
I'm able to live,
And give,
The wonderful love
That comes from above.
I thank Him for the time we've spent
Although it went
By too fast,
But there is more to last.
I'm looking forward to the time we'll have together
And may it be, in God's will, forever.

Peggy Wohlgemuth

My Stinky Shoes

My shoes are made all of pebbles and stones,
pebbles and stones that are all my own.
I feel they are pains I'll never forget.
They bite and they scratch and will not let
me rest my weary mind, body, or soul.
But no one else wants them, I already know.

I've begged others to wear them for just a mile,
to let me be at ease, to rest for a while.
"Please, take my stinky shoes," I implore,
"for these burdens and strains I can't take anymore."

But no one listens, and no one cares,
so I trudge on alone through the toils and snares.
My shoes hurt me like nobody knows.
But they are much better than most, I suppose.

Debbie Sue Pelc

A Cold Love

As I walk through the cold bleak valley
I think of you
the day I lost you
the day my life fell apart.
As I walk through this cold bleak valley
I see you
I see you calling me.
I run through the thick ice
I approach you,
you start to disappear
all that it was, was a big oak
my heart shattered I fell into a deep hole.
I felt my life flash right in front of me
but strangely I only see you, my love
the last image before my death was the day we first meet.

Walter Johnathan Mushi

Life

Life is a journey
Full of many seasons.
Times to experience, to learn, to grow.
Times to remember, times to forget.
Times to hold on, times to let go.
Full of questions—who will be there?
What will happen? When will I know? Where will I go?
I believe if I knew all the answers,
I wouldn't need faith in a greater power.
How lonely the journey would be.
I believe there is a greater power to guide, protect,
And come along on the journey.
I call the power God.
If all the people, places, and things change, I will journey on.
My God is always with me.

Susan Gayle Garrison

Purple Sunrise

I would fight the world today,
If I could go back when
We had seen a purple sunrise
Across the whole horizon.
Our lips would touch with elegance
Together, passion guaranteed.
Like the cloudless sky and purple haze,
It's AMAZING what you had done to me
Under purple skies with blues, pink, and crimson hues.
Your hands in mine, I pull you close,
And witness heaven with you.
I would fight the world today,
If I could go back when,
'Cause I'd do everything I could
To only feel that way again.

Glen F. Seabaugh

Bestefar

Dear Lord, You are my savior
the one and only, the true.

I'm kneeling and praying on this very night
Please! Please don't let Bestefar give up without a fight.

We love him so greatly;
I know you do too.

He's here with us now, though
I know he'll soon be with you.

If you must take him I'll understand,
for I know I'll be with him, once my hourglass is out of sand.

Though I'll miss him greatly,
his presence will be clear. For he is my Hero,
and his love is always near.

Troy Matthew Koren

Strings

God gives us strings to hold on to.
They stop us from falling,
They stop us from fear,
And when one of them snaps the ground grows so near.
You try not to fall,
You try not to scare,
But when your hanging from strings sometimes they tare.
As I hold on to the few I have, I thank them for being there.
You hold me up cause you are the strings God gave me,
So please do not falter,
'Cause if you break who will save me from falling?
I have three strings left,
And just as long as you stay in twine,
Holding on by a couple of strings isn't always enough,
But as one of them is you I will be fine.

Thomas Gary Emch

Poem 58

I loved you from afar . . .
My heart knew we were . . .
suppose to be together . . .
however my head was saying forget it..
Our love was ill-fated from the minute we met . . .
Until we part . . .
We know we connect on a certain level..
Yet how we can make our love become one . . .
Puzzled the two of us . . .
Others told us to forget it . . .
but we won't listen to them . . .
How I long for . . .
the day we can let our love take flight . . .
Until then my love for you will be in . . .
my dreams forevermore. . . .

Christine Pilar Guerrero

The Compassionate Jesus

Pain, pain, go away;
    over me, you have no more sway.
I know your footstep, I know your name;
    whenever you come, it's always the same.
The grief-stricken heart is no stranger
    to me,
I've walked alongside him
    when I should have said, "flee."

The crushes of life weigh
    upon many and most, and
    pain comes to all when we
    become its host.
So, recognize pain, but diffuse its power
    by inviting Jesus to walk alongside you
    every hour.

Joan S. Sluss

I Have Found New Hope Today

Today, I will no longer believe that I am
Hopelessly out of control with my bad habits,
Because I will take control of myself.

Today, I will no longer believe that I cannot
Achieve my goals, because I will keep trying till I succeed.

Today, I will no longer believe the negative
Remarks that people make about me, because
Their opinion of me, is not the one I have of myself.

Even with all my flaws, there is no one like me.
I am not a carbon copy of anyone else.
I am an original masterpiece, who is still in the potter's hand.

Today is a new day, and who knows which flaw
God will perfect today.

Lena Bothwell

Forbidden Love

Why is it that the love that is so strong
and intense is a forbidden love?
Both knowing that our hearts belong to
no other but the two of us.
Both knowing that we can never really taste
nor have what we both really hunger and desire.
The burning and yearning that is felt between us two.
Never being able to feel the warmth of our bodies intertwine.
Not being able to awaken in the way late
hours starring into each other eyes.
Finally knowing the pain that would be
caused if we were to ever cross that line.
A Forbidden Love, a love so strong, but yet not in our grasp.
The pain that remains, to know that your one and only love
can and never will be your very own.

Monica Denise Bonner

Beware

A Shakespearean Sonnet

Beware the man who falls in love too deep,
For poison leaks, as deeper sinks the heart.
Through veins into his mind this poison seeps
And eats away and tears his mind apart.
And evermore a piece of him is lost,
Never to be found or brought back again;
Yet to him this is just a minor cost
To pay for such a never-ending pain.
Still, mention nothing of his lack of pride,
Your words would stand as but a wasted breath;
For in his eyes he sees himself inside,
As without her, there would be nothing left.
So, other paths you should begin to stray,
If you find yourself trailing 'hind his way.

Richard Robert Drews

A Simple Promise

I feel your gentle touch
And I'm subdued by your love
The love that burns the desires of foretold
Everlasting, I will not withhold

I gaze upon your tender lips
The grace, which within me dwells
And conjures the strength of the unforetold
For within my heart, your magic I hold

I tend
I love
My grace
My desire
Supremacy exists within our bond
For there is no extent to this burning fire

David Josiah Wing

Where Shall I Be?

We are here and then we're gone,
Some are short and some are long.
Some are up and some are down,
Some are smiles and some are frowns;
And some are always somewhere in between.
Some are white and some are black,
Some on their way some coming back;
And we wonder where we'd really like to be.
Some are happy some content,
Some are straight, and some are bent.
Some go north and some go south
Where it may rain or have a drought.
Where shall we go? Where have we been?
Are you an enemy or a friend?
Where shall I be when comes the end?

Ellon Ham

A Spark

A sliver of desire captures the imagination,
it dances like a leaf in the wind.
Will it be realized or denied?
A little trust is placed as delicately,
as a lily sits on the pad.
Will it flourish or wither?
A tiny hope ignites the heart,
while its future existence relies on fuel.
Will it grow or diminish?
A simple, unadorned kindness is
left, as a unanimous gift.
Will it increase or disappear?
A spark of happiness: a smile
dresses up a solitary face.
Will it end there or spread like fire?

Denise Lee Phillips

Desolate Musings

Black branches extend into gray clouds
Piercing melancholy skies, like
Savage spikes of dark demons.
Cruel winds whip through trees
Stirring up decaying leaves,
Crinkled and brown.
Depression and despair seep into
Despondent varmints that scuttle around
In their own discourse.
A whisper of winsomeness is seen in
One bright-hued tree still clinging to
Innocent ignorance of the coming bleakness.
This frozen hell keeps our thoughts
On sickness and solitude, killing our
Fragile philosophy of sunshine.

Jennifer Nora Wilson

Confused

Fascinated by the air's breath on me
I inhale life and exhale frost
representing lost creation and ideas unformed
We always find a way to fall
My heart leaps to my throat
I become confused, frantic, embarrassed
Maybe it represents lost creation and
the love of Earth
Forgotten anxiety
No job too big, no pocket too empty
Love is breathing around me
No person can move me to feel that
Everyone helps you feel regret
Their lives lived through your lack
The frozen air and pain give you life

Brian Patrick McMahon

Dusk

It was dusk in early July
The fourth to be exact
We were walking slowly and silently along the beach
When he turned to me
I saw the reflection of all the stars dancing wildly in his eyes
He looked down and softly took and kissed my hand
When our lips met
I felt as if fireworks were going off inside of me
Then when I opened my eyes
I saw the fireworks going off across the lake
He held me in his arms
And we just watched in wonder and silence
Of how beautiful and wonderful it had turned out to be
Then I slowly closed my eyes,
And drifted off into a peaceful sleep

Andra M. Barry

Bill

Little boy, I miss you with your smile and winning ways.
The frogs and jackknife in your pocket have been set aside for other days.
I miss your friends and muddy tracks that followed you it seems.
I miss these things, the only way is to remember them in my dreams.
I will love you always.

    Mary Jarvis

Going Home

"I'll be going home tomorrow," the bellhop looked surprised,
"Where will you go at your age, what is it, eighty five?"
"My father's coming for me," I saw his altered stance,
As he gave the man beside him, the "He's lost it," kind of glance.
"I've sorted all my life's things through, there was so much I had to do,
I've put my house in order with a very fine toothed comb."
They found him the next morning, he had indeed gone home.

    Margaret Roberts

What I Know

I know there is a God
He loves me and He loves you
I know He's always there for me
And I hope that you do to

I know He sent His son to die
To save us from our sins
And open up the gate to Heaven
So as to let us in

I know He lives forever
He loves forever too
He loves me unconditionally
No matter what I say, think, or do

I know He has a plan for me
And be it whatever it may
I need the faith of the mustard seed
To move the mountains in my way

Now you know what I know
It's all here in these lines
Believing in the "foolishness of God"
Will surely save our lives

    Carrie Jean Bray

Supreme Court Judges

One heathen woman did succeed to stop the prayers in public schools.
Supreme Court judges failed to see that prayers in schools were moral tools,
Which shaped our students' growing minds and taught the values of mankind.
Without the moral discipline, our students' values fell behind.

Religious people seek God's guidance to uphold integrity.
And people who believe in God are blessed with righteous dignity.
In God we trust is wisely printed on our money as our creed.
Good moral values are essential for our nation to succeed.

Most honest people have respect for any nationality.
With noble values, men promote good friendship and prosperity.
Supreme Court judges were appointed to uphold the righteous cause,
But they upheld the plaintiff's plea and overlooked religious laws.

Since prayers were stopped in public schools, we've seen some students go astray.
Their moral values have been dropped, and some have killed the savage way.
The richest country in the world is failing to control its schools.
The atheists have won in court; some students now use deadly tools.

Hard drugs and AIDS destroy young lives; the tragedies are hard to bear.
Oh, what a shame! Who is to blame? The highest court ruled out school prayer.
Supreme Court Judges should have left the prayer and Bill of Rights intact.
We ought to find a remedy and stop this antisocial act.

    Albert Schmidt

Copy Act

To hide who you are from me?
Rip your essence from my soul.
Not to leave a trail to follow?
Do not enter.
I copy you to me,
and when I lose you,
There I find you.
Cry on my shoulder?
I wish my shirt never dry.
To forget you?
I would have to die.
The act of copying you
to this soul of mine
is a necessity to existence.
Leave you?
I cannot.
I have copied you to my soul,
and when I lose you,
there you are again.

    Nicole Renee Greeley

My Baby Sister

She's full of fun
She's full of tricks,
My baby sister
Is now "66."

She is no different
On that you can bet,
Than the "Cutie" she was
The first day we met.

She was a great playmate
All through the years,
She never fussed
Nor shed many tears.

She went a long way
To make happy our days,
I'll always remember
Her some funny ways.

Yes, she's a honey
Yes, she's a twister,
Yes, she is still
"My baby sister."

    Anna Durant

Life's Treasures

I stand with regret
As life's chances
Passed upon me
Never to be touched

I stand with sorrow
As my heart
Has never felt the passion of love

I stand with pain as my soul
Has never felt the warmth of happiness

I stand with hopelessness
As my mind
Has been empty with no loving memory

For these were the feelings
Through life I have endured
As for now I see

The ship of chance
I set sail for a journey

To find the priceless treasure in life
For I let the winds of fate
Send me on my way

    Michael A. McCaughrean

The Black Man's Wings

There is such a thing as a black man's wings.
They make their appearance through visions and dreams.
A black man who didn't know anything,
He looked out of an empty shell and wrote these words, "I can excel."
One thing he had to do was lift his head to see his way through.
This made him happy, and then it was said
There is such a thing as a black man's wings.

Munday Bosha Smith

Cloud

Wonderful is this fruit tree, so ready to share and quite
With kindness expressed by her loving joy did I write;
For the Lord so uses this fruit tree to always stand for what is right,
As his living testimony before this world in his might.

To have this wonderful lady always there and so polite
With character so expressed by her from his glorious light;
For the Lord has placed this caring lady before all in his sight
With his loving grace to share, by choice, so placed by his delight.

Paul Robin

Leaving the Laughter Behind

That day is long gone but not in my mind
All the folks were so kind
There were times when I was sad
Even short periods of me being mad
Your death brought a lot of people together
And we shared all the things about you that matter
There was laughter and crying that day
My pain was in shock so in my heart it stayed
I remember the day we all sat under the tent
I couldn't understand when I started to wiggle
Until at that moment I heard your sweet giggle
There's not a day that goes by, that I wish you were still at my side
Your memory is like the splashes of the ocean tide
God left me with such a beautiful sign
Because he left your laughter behind
And when your laughter I will hear
I always, will know in my heart you're near
Thank you God now I know I will be fine
Because you left Troy's laughter behind

Darlene Null Nichols

Contentment

I had overeaten.
So I reached inside myself and pulled
Up whatever could be pulled up
With what strength I could muster up.
I labored long and hard and
Brought forth snowcapped mountains
And the tallest pines with cones intact
And sparkling stars draped with clouds
And songbirds with half-sung melodies
Resting on their beaks and butterflies
With magnificent wings, extended
And poised for flight, and rainbows
Capturing the essence of promises.
I wept, not due to any emptiness,
But due to the incredible beauty
Of the lone rose that rested
Just out of my reach so that it
Remained in my innermost parts.
I was spent but at peace.

Mary Scott

Dear God

Who am I?
I am poor.
I have nothing.

Who am I?
I am weak.
There is no strength within me.

Who am I?
I am dull.
My knowledge is lacking.

Who am I?
I am inarticulate.
I cannot speak with power.

Who am I?

I am your servant.
You are my knowledge.
You are my strength.
You are my speech.
You are my riches.

Without You I am nothing.
With you I want for nothing.

Joshua Paul Batchelor

A Mother Defined

From her womb an into this world
I came out uncurled
Loved and cared for by another
Who said to be a mother
You had to have conceived

In my heart she has a place
My love she can always embrace
Though I came not from her
The love we share
No one will ever know

My scraped knees she has healed
My runny nose she has cleaned
My broken heart she has consoled
My whole life she has guided
Naturally she belongs to the motherhood

So, tell me again
Who said to be a mother
You had to have conceived
Born to one
But loved by another
To the world she is my father's wife
To me she is my mother

Aminata M. Kamara

I Am Like a Star

I am like a star on a summer's night
longing to be wished on.
So apparently beautiful and bright on the
outside, but so scared inside.
Thriving and burning to change a life, to
make a difference;
all while trying not to burn myself out.
As the night comes to an end,
another day of my life has passed.
Did I miss out?
Scared to lose, scared of failing;
did I live it to the fullest?
'Cause if not,
tomorrow will be a much brighter night.

Richard Wayne Henegar

Friend

A friend is someone who is very special to you
A friend is someone to laugh at your jokes
A friend is a gift from God
A friend is someone you can trust
A friend is someone that never hides something from you
A friend is someone who tells you the truth
A friend is your friend because of who you are, not what you try to be
A friend is someone who isn't afraid to say they are your friend
A friend is someone who helps you when you need help
A friend is someone who won't keep anything away from you
A friend is . . . a true gift

Cara Marie Fetzer

Night Breezes

Fade away, night breezes, blowing into looking glass.
Shed the coolness upon the bones caving in from strain.
Drift over minds and seas, blow away, night breezes, far away from me.
Tangle dismay up in my hair and wrap flowers 'round my fingertips.
Let splendor linger on my lip.
The taste tingles the flesh I nibble on from shaken nerves.
Run away, night breezes, spindle about her untamed leg.
Does the reflection resemble uniqueness?
Does it pay for my unsettled view?
Slip away, night breezes, don't look around your wings.
Drift over storms and tears, fly away, night breezes, far away from me.

Megan McCluskey Boling

Diner Party

Tobacco smoke in the air, and regardless of how many times she has
seen wet cloth sweep absently over the counter, caked grease
everywhere else. The radio might be spilling easy listening, pop,
but it slips below the diner chatter before she can grasp it, for
her, childhood hero Natalie Wood still is slipping below the
waterline. Sitting at end of counter across from dirty aluminum ice
cream machine that captures, she all sanguine makeup and dirty silver
hair, her almost favorably. Wash from heat lamps and nearby kitchen
blunts January's cold. Beef patties sizzle richly on a skillet nearby;
out of sight. Waiting, as every day, for coffee in a worn brown mug
that may never come, a husband in worn brown skin that may never come,
a son . . . she wonders if by now her own flesh is too dry to sizzle
richly on diner skillets.

Ryan A. Hagen

Night

Now not a soul can I see
In the large garden after spree.
Gone are all human noises!
High above in the space marquee,
The naughty stars wink at me.

Kwok Yuk Yau

Lady from Leeds

There was an old lady from Leeds,
Who swallowed a packet of seeds.
Then she said, "Pardon,"
Then blew to garden.
And now in her garden grow weeds.

Corrie Weber

Why Has the World Turned Around on Me?

Why has the world turned around on me?
Could it be . . .

Just another day,
Another way of life?

I guess it's just a phase,
But will it ever go away.

Nothing is the same,
Everything has changed;

My mind, body, and soul!

Everything goes wrong,
It seems just like a song
That keeps playing only for me.

This is not a song
Or a play story;
This is my life,
An actual story.

People say, life goes on,
But does it really?
What really goes on?
My sad memory. . . .

Nancy Shwaiki

On the Wings of the Angels

On the Wings of the Angels,
Lord, You carry me home—
up the great, golden stairway
to the foot of God's throne.
You clothe me in linens
that are whiter than snow—
You restore and renew me—
as You welcome me home.

And the blessing continues, Lord,
I feel so secure—
no more pain, no more suffering—
only peace that endures.
I can see all my loved ones
that preceded me here—
this is just the beginning—
no more reason to fear.

And to all of my loved ones
that I left behind—
you'll be joining me one day—
all in God's time.
Yes, I know you're heartbroken—
but that won't last too long.
Just remember the good times,
for you must carry on.

Francine D. Dispenza

Laughter

Laughter is the smell of a sweet red rose.
Laughter is the taste of a ripe, tangy orange.
Laughter is the brightness of the yellow sun.
Laughter is the smell of fresh cut green grass.
Laughter is the sound of a little chirping blue jay.
Laughter is the sound you hear while running
through a field of indigo flowers.
Laughter is the sight of violet hues in a sunset.
Laughter is the colors of a bright, glistening rainbow across the sky.
Laughter means so many different things.
What does Laughter mean to you?

Christopher Michael Sanchez

Who's Free?

Being bored it struck me odd, let's take a walk.
My life partner always quiet, doesn't talk.

Down on the street, a loud noise, confusion ensued.
Laying on the ground, something in my shoe, like glue.

Helped in a vehicle, truck or van I think.
Smelling of blood, heart racing to the brink.

We arrived in seconds, as a bird in flight.
Being helped hearing, one hell of a night.

Put in a steel chair, wheels, shaking, my insides shuttered.
As the ride came to a halt, clearly, "Oh, my God, murdered?"

Feeling a touch, the voice softly relented, "Sorry about your friend.
It was too late, used every means, fought right to the end."

As a stake driven through a heart, gasping, "Thanks, you're so kind."
For my partner's very special, and I am blind.

Bill Allen Taylor

Hope

When I was a child I wondered and used to say,
The moon above like a ripe fruit would drop one day.
Before anyone found the yellow fruit on the ground,
I'd pick it up close to my bosom and dance around.

As I grew up year after year I came to realize
That the moon never would drop nor become ripe.
Also, I knew I would never have it all to myself,
And I cherished the moon all along, tranquil and relaxed.

When I found my love with a devotion so deep and strong,
Not an iota of doubt that to my bosom he'd one day belong.
Basked in the esteem and inspiration of my love a'plenty,
I cherished my love with all my heart, tenderly and affectionately.

Sometime during the rains I lost my love I'd vow,
Lonely and forlorn, upset, mindless and restless up till now.
Friends and relatives, monasteries and shrines I unwittingly trotted
in and out,
Day after day, month after month, year after year, year in and year out.

Like the moon never close to my bosom as my own,
The same with my love for reasons not known or very well-known.
Or, I might have my love time and again in lengthy Samsara all the way,
A plausible hope or a wishful thinking I dare not at all venture to say.

Sein Sein

Your Flame

This Flame,
it burns like red hot coal,
shining brightly in your soul.
Be not afraid of what lies near,
your flame could lighten someone's fear.

James Joseph Woody

Little Girl

Little girl, so young, so true.
So much to learn, so don't be blue.
You're young, you're pretty.
Be happy, be free.
'Cause I'm your Mama, so listen to me.

Donna L. Rohrbaugh

Waiting

I'm watching the clock,
waiting.
I watch the second hand
push the minute hand
around the face
that seems to smile,
enjoying the agony it creates.

Dixie R. Ganshert

Gold

Like summer
like your halo is all of the time
You don't know you don't know
I'm a gilded 14 karat
plated solid
Gold
Liar.

Emily Schmitt

Butterfly

colors of perfection,
leads to a magical interpretation
and creates a wake of musical splendor,
the Butterfly,
ah . . .
how she inspires this love
so tender.

Dixie Rivas Pattison

See Only Me

Lock me in your eyes. See only me.
Baby you know it was meant to be.

You're the center of my celebration
Baby you're cause for my admiration

Lock me in your eyes. See only me.
Tell me, sweetie, what it takes to be free.

Regina Trantham Sheehan

Intimidator

Dark day February 18
Guarding like a lion guards its young
Bang slammed in to the wall
How a sword stabs into human flesh
Crash on the last lap
The scene was pretty horrifying
Never again will there be another

Michael Anthony Smith

Have You Seen the Rainbow?

It seems so wonderful to have eyes to see,
to have a warm heart to give . . . one's love so freely.

The skies of Heaven have blessed us with the warm rays of the sun,
"I jester to say, a gust of wind, heavy rays, it's time for me to have fun."

The glimmer of light has reflected off the lovely lady's skin,
the beauty of luster, I felt that she had a warm heart within.
Such beauty, I'm convinced she can be a lovely friend.
I'll love to be her friend someday.

The hectic wind shows mercy, as it swirls her lovely dress
and her lovely hair. "What I'll give" to help the lady in distress.
The wind swirled around without care to the beautiful lady standing there,
she was just standing there.

There was a loud cloudburst, and lightning that surrounded the square.
The smell of fresh dew, the fresh smell of rain was in the air.

I asked the angel, could she see the rainbow that's far off in the hill,
with an array of colors so fascinating it gave me thrills.
The glamorous rainbow and all its color,
was like a field of flowers, just meant for two lovers.
A beautiful lady and I, running for shelter, "became great lovers."

Charles Copeland Jr.

Of Thought and Time

"I hate you" are words of such ugly thought,
as they go through the body and mind.
Leaving no room for reasoning to be sought,
they are so unkind.

Years have passed, and a few times have I heard
that demeaning phrase, those piercing words.
No one deserves to hear them, whether it be family, friend, or foe.
The heart-wrenching grief they cause, the sadness, and the woe.

From the window across the room, shines in a brand new day,
a shining, reflecting off cat's furry coats, who are busy at play.
Thoughts of forgiveness, sharing, and joy are needed to be said,
before it is time to sleep, before we go to bed.

Should ever those words of injustice and impure thought abound,
I shall not utter one sound.
Instead in comfort and calm will be said,
"Sweet dreams, princess, I forgive you, and I love you, now go to bed."

"I love you" are such wonderful words, and is such a lovely thought,
as they go through the body and mind.
They leave room for reasoning and for more words to be sought.
They are so kind.

Charles Robert Nooney

It's All My Fault

I'm sorry, and you haven't the slightest clue
I'm sorry for being in love with you

I didn't mean to hurt you, I knew what I was doing was wrong
I never wanted to hurt you, I'm sorry, it's all my fault

It's all my fault
I'll never let you down again
It's all my fault
I've ruined it all before it even began
It's all my fault
Maybe things will all work out in the end
It's all my fault
I'll make you feel like this never again

I'm sorry, and there's nothing that I can do
I'm sorry 'cause I'm so in love with you

I'm sorry because I hurt you; I'm sorry, I'm who's wrong
I'm never going to hurt you again; forgive me, it's all my fault

And another sleepless night, thinking of you
Only this time I've done something wrong, and I don't know what to do
Yet another hopeless dream that I'm holding you
I just want to know that you would want to be with me

Kenji Petrucci

Her Dad's Dream

SPLEEN,
YOU fight for what you want.
YOU stand for what you believe.
YOU believe in what you know.
And when you feel you can't move . . .
I'LL pick you up and bring you home.

JaMese Morris Black

Terror (A Godzilla Tribute)

As people cried and sparks fired
Buildings crumbled and fire transpired
Explosions emitted
S.O.S. calls transmitted
I gazed up towards the sky gleamed
And I screamed

A. Paul Melin

Wrinkles

These crevices on my face
waterways of my tears
lines that were a once tight complexion
multiply with every sagacious smile
distinguishing marks
joyous in their rough texture

Graham Baechler

All These Years

After all these years
And all the fun that we could have had
Isn't it so sad
That we were far apart
Yet close to heart
For all these years

Kimberly Ann Lee

The Never-Ending Race

In remembrance of Dale Earnhardt Sr.
Dale was born for a reason.
That reason was to race for us.
He left the world last Sunday
In a big cloud of dust.
He is in Heaven now
To race the "never-ending race."

Brian Greene

Tissue

A tissue can be . . .
a child's project,
like a parachute or ghost;
a person's comforter,
like something to wipe up tears;
a decorative napkin
with all the different styles and colors.

Patti Ann Lyons

Love Within

Is love understanding or caring?
is love happiness or sadness?
is love war or peace?
is love forgiveness?
Love is all of the above, but more true,
love is within.

Mark H Verbeeren

Our Ever-Shrinking World

In a world so fast-paced and ever-shrinking,
Conversation between two is limited and so is individual thinking.
You can be in a crowd-filled room and still feel alone,
Where words of friendliness and a smile are replaced with feelings of stone.
When people talk of the "good old days," it's hard to relate
To the time when bad luck was not man-made, but by fate;
When poor taste was a flash of the leg or the edge of a slip;
When disrespect to a parent got you a sore behind or worse, a fat lip;
When "gay" meant happy and men and women didn't dress the same;
There were no drive-by shootings or a murder because of a name;
When your first goal as a child was to reach the age of sixteen;
When honor, trust, and love were more than words;
And children were heard and not seen.
A time when having a belief in something meant life was real;
The family unit was alive and the house a home, and not just a meal;
Love between two people was more than just sex, it was a start
Of a full-time commitment and sharing of a heart;
When having children was a reason for joy and not self-doubt;
To love and trust your spouse and not worry if they went out.
Yes, this shrinking world has touched everything and everyone in a small way,
And I'm a dinosaur, for I believe you love one person forever and a day.

David A. Komorowski

Me, We, Us, You

Who are you to ask me who I am?
Who are we to look for the answers to life's query?
What is the question that we all forget, previous to meeting the answer?
What should I do when faced with all I need to know
about me, we, us, you and what is right?
In this moment, all time is still and motionless
with only one satisfactory path.
My chosen path feels good and scary.
Is this the way I should look forward, with eyes wide open
and meet the day with a new face,
or just never trust in all I think I know again?
But with this way of thinking,
can I ever be happy with me, we, us, and you?
Where is my little voice that keeps me from going mad?
Where is the voice that gives me guidance to help with my choices?
It is the voice that shows me the truth.
It is the voice I never listen to until it's too late.
I feel that I will do what's right and I do know that I can feel for others,
no matter what I may say to others.
But I will never show all of me to anyone again
unless I hear my little voice, and it says, share with her.
So till then, I will be thinking of me, we, us, you.

Aaron Michael Merritt

Echo: An Ode to All Women

Let the shackles of womankind
Fall
Upon the ears
Of all.

Helped a man—
A deceitful man.
Voice lost
Bouncing off
Fading out
Into the darkness.

Loved a man—
A conceitful man.
Lost body
My body.
Lost soul—
Soul.

Pined away
Within the rock.
Reiterating whatever I'm told.

Patricia Ferraiuolo

Smile

When all around the sky is grey
Just pause, reflect awhile,
For nothing drives the clouds away
Like sunshine from a smile.

Mary A. Dunnell

Toast

May your marriage be
Healthy, happy, and wealthy.
With faith, trust, and love,
It will be all of the above.

Alice Plimpton Enos

simply in love

soft scented jasmine smells
silky smooth supple skin
angelic songs sung sweetly
savor every succulent kiss

Michael Osakowicz

Together As One

Together as one, we dance
to the music of our heartbeats;
dancing the song of life forever,
spinning and turning, never-ending,
the melody of love, so sweet.

Bonny Rigley

Who I Am

Sitting in a classroom
frustrated, confused, annoyed;
I am alone, flawed, different.
Call the doctor: questions, testing.
I'm not flawed, I'm learning disabled.
I'm not alone; there are others
I am different, for I see the world
with a new perspective.

Ingrid Amtmann Schultz

Until I Met You

I thought I would never be content,
Until I met you.
I always wondered what true love meant.
Until I met you.
Time drags on and on
Until I can kiss you.
I'll think about you from dusk to dawn
Until I can have you.
I had never wanted someone so badly
Until I met you.

Diana Vergara

Eternity

To see
To want
To meet
To touch
To know
To love
To want again
Brief seconds last forever
We are timeless
We have been

Charles Joseph Slavis Jr.

The City

The city is a magical place, the sights, the sounds, the human race.
But amidst all the beauty there, there is darkness and pain,
Does anyone care?
The faces you see on the street—they smile, laugh, they even greet.
Now look deep in their souls, beyond the happiness,
There's nothing but holes.
Hearts that once did truly ring are empty, cold; they no longer sing.
If you look you'll surely see, the pain, the sorrow.
Is this the way it should be?
Children's eyes should glimmer, but for them life could be no dimmer.
Tell me where are their clothes, their food, and homes?
This is not the life they chose.
The children have no food to eat; garbage is their Christmas treat.
For these are the faces of the homeless, the forgotten—it's true.
Their lives should not be hopeless.
A child is such a gift of life, a joy, a treasure. Why live in strife?
Who are we to let this happen. People talk, mouths keep flapping.
No one helps or does a thing so these voices can once again sing.
For these are the faces of homeless, the forgotten—it's true.
Their lives should not be hopeless!

    Marie L. Rabolt

Heart Break

If my tears are enough to make you cry
And my joy enough to brighten you
why don't you come back
It's been . . . since you flew
the minutes have become hours
turned days, weeks, months have
become years and yet, still no sign
You'll have to swim to catch me
My endless tears have pooled our romantic garden
and stilled life in all the plants we lovingly grew
The chickadee sings your loneliness to me
and the stars at night, refuse to shine
The Sun, only tells me much more
Noon time is no consolation
It seems to me, as if the moon delights in torturing me
with your nocturnal escapades.
In my anarchy, I can turn but only to God
Who keeps telling me
There is no joy like love
  . . . No joy like love . . . joy like love . . . like love . . . love

    Klorkor Okai

Friends

It is my wish to be your friend,
To make each day a tasteful blend
Of life's delights and simple pleasures.
To be your friend would be my treasure.
So think of me as I will you
And drop a line, one or two.
Go enjoy and have some fun
But don't forget where the trip begun.

    Patricia Stonecypher

Love

Love is Happiness
Love is Joy
Love is Doing what you need to do
Love is Enjoying what you do
Love is Understanding
Love is Respect and Compromising
Love is being Together
Love is Forever

    Linda Caracol

Sleigh Bells

There are no bells in all the world
So sweet as sleigh bells over snow.
The horses arch their necks to hear
That pretty music as they go.
If it is dark, you cannot see
The horses curveting and prancing,
But you would know to hear the bells
That those who shook them must be
dancing.

    Tenna Kull

Just for You

There are those who say
Our time has passed for love
That we should wait on death
And pray we go above.

But my mind still burns with passion
My heart still beats strong and true
And I refuse to believe that
Since I have met someone like you.

    Bob Willis

Me

I used to dream
of being myself
and you and you
and everyone else

I used to dream
of knowing everything
that will be, that is,
that ever has been

I used to dream
of being in love
like a sky-high eagle,
like a pure white dove

I used to dream
of my beautiful wife
of being her soul mate
and being her life

Now I dream
of how she did lift
me up into Heaven
to realize my gift
Me

    Edwin Zhang

I Have a Dream, Too

Here is the one thing I dream of in my life
that I want to happen when I grow up.

That thing is to become known everywhere,
To be someone that everyone in need can rely on.
To be someone that can always be a help in
the future to many people,
Like a person who gives charity,
or someone who goes around helping people
make tough decisions in life.
All I know is that whatever that thing is,
someday, I will be known to all.
To all, I will be someone.
And not just someone,
but a good friend.

    Victoria Antoinette Esquivel

Bill

Close your eyes and think of us, walking on the sand
The sky is clear the moon is out, we're walking hand in hand
A warm summer wind gently blows your hair, I feel so close to you
The feelings that I feel inside, I wish you only knew

Close your eyes and picture me, as you wish that I would be
A dark knight that's fighting for, your love and destiny
Imagine me as someone who would fulfill your fantasies
Because it's you and only you, who's a dream come true to me

Close your eyes and think of you, through someone else's mind
And this is how you'll understand, why I feel your sublime
Your eyes, your smile, you're beautiful, and I knew that from the start
You'd be the only one for me, I love you with all my heart

Michael Russum

My Friend

Did you ever fall in love with a guy but he didn't love you?
Did you ever feel like crying, but what good would it do?
Did you ever look into his eyes and say a little prayer?
Did you ever look into his hands and wish yours were there?

Did you ever see him dancing with the lights down low?
Did you ever whisper, God I love him, but never let him know?
Although falling in love causes broken hearts, it happens every day.

You wonder where he is at night.
You wonder if he's true.
You're one moment happy, the next, sad and blue.

Love is fine, but it hurts so much, the price you pay is so high.
If I had to choose between love and death, I think I'd rather die.
So when I say don't fall in love, you'll be hurt before you're through.

You see, my friend, I ought to know—I fell in love with you.
I LOVE YOU.

Sharon Rae Welch

My Knitted Afghan of Many Colors

Have you ever wondered what you can do with your extra yarn?
You get so much through the years, you swear you need a barn.
I had so much from this project and that, I didn't know what to do.
Then my sister-in-law brought me a book, and asked me to try it, too.

Each page had a different pattern to knit, and so I went to work.
Knit one, purl two, pass the knit stitch over; I wasn't a jerk.
The left over yarn from projects I'd made all could tell a story,
Soon turned into a heirloom, a story to my glory.

A cable here, a twist there, and then the basket weave I did.
I purled and I knitted until all the extra yarn boxes I did rid.
I edged each block in black to make them all stand out.
Now I have a lot of stories to tell my grandchildren about.

My Aunt gave me the pattern for the knitted lace border on the sides,
It set it off just right and adds just the right touch, who decides.
The 100 blocks make it a little big for an Afghan,
But it will fit on a queen or king, and for that I'm a big fan.

Debra Marie Jensen

Life Unfolding

One day we came to life,
Then we lived our life.
When we were troubled by life,
We looked onward through life.
When we where happy with life,
We looked in the past of our life.
Then we truly loved life.
Just don't let yourself overcome life.

Jason Swanson

Future Baby

Babies are so fun to have
so have one now and you'll be glad.
Babies are so nice and sweet
with tiny hands and tiny feet.
Bottles, Blankets, Bibs, and toys
will it be a girl or boy?
After having so much fun
why not have another one?

Melissa Ann Lawrence

Forgiveness

Sometimes I wonder
What I should have done
To make the anger go away,
And just have fun.
Many years . . . many tears have past
Since it had all begun.
I wonder, now, what will we do
And where our lives will run.

Wayne Kusnery

Separated Now

Dream to believe
Believe to dream
I've seen the tear
That tore the seam
A bitter heart
That broke the team
Relentless grief
You can't redeem

Renée Magritte Floyd

Life's Seasons

My life is like a tornado,
like thunder when I cry.
If snowflakes were my happiness,
then winter would fly by.

If our souls could shine,
and tell all that we feel . . .
then mirrors would be windows
for our souls to heal.

Kristina Canu

Will You Be My Eternal Love?

Will you be my winter whisper,
My spring rose,
My summer cry,
My fall diamond,
'Til death do us part?

Please be my shining diamond,
My red rose,
My gentle whisper,
My delirious cry,
Not for just the moment, but for eternity.

Angela Jo Smith

Sent by Grace

I know it seems rushed, but you mean so much.
From the moment I saw your face, I knew you were sent by grace.
Not a day goes by when thinking of you doesn't give me a natural high.
So, I give this phrase to you, please, baby, please,
Love me as much as I love you.
Sent by grace with that angel face,
Here to remove my pain and show me what I have to gain;
I was lost, then I was found.
You have my heart in your hands, show me your plans.
When you hold me in your arms, I'm free from all the world's harm.
When I gaze in to your eyes, I get lost looking for a way out,
Only to get lost again.

John Edward De Los Santos

Sunrise

The most beautiful part of the day
is at sunrise when the sun's rays first come
over the horizon of the Earth.
Everything is so new, the dew on the grass,
the chill in the air, and the dreams in our hearts.
This is also the time when things look the best to us.
Whether it is the sun glistening over the newly fallen snow,
or if it's the sun shining upon the birds, as they bask in the warmth.
Seeing this beauty it is hard not to put your best foot forward.
It inspires you to enlighten the lives of others.
Therefore we have to go forward with an open heart
and keep your true friends close to you.
But keep a warm smile on you lips to invite new friends in.

Rob Lee Canann

My Friend, the Garbage Man

We have the nicest garbage man.
He empties out the garbage can.
He's just as nice as he can be.
Why, he often stops and talks with me.
My mother doesn't like his smell . . .
But then she doesn't know him well.

James Lloyd Phillips

Dreamer

As I lay in my bed,
thinking and thinking,
I finally fall asleep,
I ride horses, fly, I win prizes,
In a dream I am the ruler, the winner
Only me and my mind.

Cheryl Ann Lounsbury

A Flame Burning Within

Softly your eyes I do see.
Gently they do burn for me.
Gracefully do you walk.
Softly do I talk.
Brightly the smile on your face.
Knowingly I have fallen from grace.

Laura Ann Sismondo

Family Treasure

My family is my treasure
All of whom to bring me pleasure

If one can only measure
The joy of family leisure

Your family will be your treasure

Vincent Franco

Tracks in the Sand

Sneaky snakes in the sand
Plan to eat what they can.
Right, left they slither
It's time for prey to quiver.
Near the weeds of young and prime
Good night was said one last time.

James Adam Hebb

Going Nowhere

You must go there
To be everywhere
To go everywhere
You find nowhere
To reach nowhere
You are there anywhere

Douglas Michael Harrison Jr.

Ode to Lovers

Blue skies and sunshine:
A forest of trees all are pine:
Warm night and a bottle of wine:
To have to drink while we dine:
Two lovers sitting on the sand:
Listening to the local band:
Evening time has come and gone:
Lets sing the rainy day song:
Because blue skies and sunshine are gone.

Carol Jean Keeler

The Traveler

I am not a person, I am the air you breathe, the wind that
passes beneath your nose, that smell is unexplainable only
to know, if you are one.
My nights come sudden, my mornings come intrinsic without form.
time is the maker only to know when?
My adventures are repeats from when they use to be unexplained.
My mind is undefinable and only knows form the history of its making.
People I study to find answers,
and to only be more different then I already am.
I seem to move form place to place not but my choice but by
the spirit inside that awaits and cries.
Happiness is something I feel when my imagination creates my
next day and future, it only comes from things that trigger
my deepest emotions and my dreams that are real,
from I the creator of it.
I am indomitable yet there's a book that explains there
only one that is, and that is isn't me.
I am the traveler can you comprehend he that is?

Cameron Thomas

Seashore De-Lights

Here in the midst of a neon-window this water
shines with bright, metallic glare.
I'm taking in the therapeutic, relaxing smells of the ocean breeze
that lives here and early day smells of fresh fried dough,
hot-buttered popcorn, and creamy coconut suntan oil.
A secret place, out of the way, unlike no other.
I can hear the faint music in the near distance
serenading me to stay.
Even though I'm just passing through—my villa is just over the hill not faraway.
I know I'm blessed to be able to enjoy all of this!
The moon at peak can be seen from my back patio.
I delight in the sounds of the waves crashing against palm trees and rocks.
Here I can collect my thoughts and keep them.
I sit in constant admiration at the silhouette of the nearby,
busy, night-lit city still at work.
Its bright neon-casino lights and sounds aren't far.
Life is best here—by this small, steamy, heated eruption of water!
Total power of peace and love can be yours here so easily.

Lana Marie Onassis

The Witches!

There was an old house that belonged to an old witch;
She had three daughters, but didn't know which was which.
The house had four bedrooms, one for each witch;
And another for the maid, who was also a witch.
Whenever they did something, they used a little magic;
This way they lost their cat, which was really tragic.
They all had black cloaks and a black, pointed hat;
And whenever they held a party, the chief guest was a bat.
They always keep doing silly, magical things;
And then jump and shout whenever the door bell rings.
Although they didn't have that many guests;
Still they kept sandwiches made of birds' nests.
This made the birds angry and they got crosser and crosser;
So they turned the witches' house into a flying saucer.
Now the witches are trying to get their old house back;
Still they cannot find a way, so they're planning to attack.
Now each day the witch learns the names of each of her daughter witch;
Because she still can't really remember which witch is which!

Nashwa Jamil Rathore

You Run

You listen, but you never hear
You worry, but you never care
You look, but you never see
You run away from me
It's your eyes that I can't ever read
Vast and deep as an ocean sea
You talk to anyone about anything
But you run away from me

Allyson Jayne Adame

My Love Poem to My Wife

As I look over the morning dew
I find myself thinking of only you
How wonderful it is to know
Of all the love that to me you do show
Through the years of each new day
My love for you will never stray
For the love with you that I do enjoy
Should be just like a brand new toy
I thank God for you all my life
For you are there through joy and strife

Coley Padgett

Blessings from Above

Dedicated to Tanya, Frey, Nord, and Mikey
The more good you do . . .
The more Angels you attract
To bring you blessings from above.

These Angels have in their possession,
All that you could ever desire,
And they are just watching
To see you release of what you have,
To replace them with your desires.

Marcia A. Linton

What to Do with You

What am I to do with you, me
You keep causing me trouble
You just keep dragging me
Deeper, deeper down
Every time I'm just fine, floating along

We can't keep going through this
These unexpected visits
When my friends come around
Because we look exactly the same
And it's driving them crazy

Tremain White

Tip of My Tongue

Standing before you
faltered by a glance
my mind sputters Neruda
toward the tip of my tongue
clocks fall from my heart
spilling into the sea
leaders of the revolution
rising up
and spitting from their graves
wagging tongues of
abstract eulogies
and liquid seductions
quoting Lorca
and tango dancing Burmese whores
who sang beneath rusted castanets
that only the bold
forget to survive.

Shelly A. Parsons

Wake Up!

Wake up!
Are you asleep?

Your human form as precious as a jewel.

Wasted,
Having to see your body and its beautiful attraction.
I fell in love with it.
Wake up!

Have you not come to your senses yet?
Are you not ashamed of yourself? You have diamonds, jewels, and pearls
Why do you waste it out of your ignorance? Wake up!

Wasted, every breath of your life.
You lied, spoke truth, your life wasted—wake up!

Sheyzlin Karim Hirji

The Real Reality

We live an empty minded society
Not from a real reality
Always changing policy
From a changed world masterminding role model
We always accuse the accused and never the innocent
We always believe the victim and never the criminal who did it
Just 'cause they had a couple of felonies or two
What makes them different from people like you?
Have you ever thought that maybe the criminal was the victim?
The accused was the innocent?
Who could they turn to if y'all were the one with hatred on the brain?
If y'all were the ones hurting?
Bring the pain
It's a shame

Shannon Leigh Gibson

Girl Blankets

we play in girl blankets
we romp under a fort of we care not
and when we laugh, we laugh for the world
that they detest our tented glee
i curl up next to her
and sleep a sleep of a thousand nights
in her warmth i glow—a new woman
and when the sun rises, staggered
filtered through the dusty green blinds
hung crooked like her smile
she tells me good morning
and chitchat and what not
through her banter i hear her heart
my ear to her soft skin
in the nook of her breasts
beating out the night before
our toes chasing each other
under our girl blankets
where we wish and hope and love
that this morning is every morning

Melissa Stephanie Tata

XtremeDaPoet

Peers are lead a different way
In truth they are looking for God
They search in all the wrong places
He's in sex, 'cause I make love
He's in crime, Jesus understands what I'm
going through
He sees my doubt, why have you forsaken me
But what you truly find is sin
You kill your bodies and others around you
And who are you?
The lost child of God
Searching but cannot see
Your eyes are blind, because you don't use
your heart and mind to see
Am I crazy to have a vision?
Or am I crazy because I don't
Keep me this way, dreaming today
Gone tomorrow, everlasting days
Where should I be?
Holy father stay with me

Stephen D. Green

I Am Me

Me.
I am me.
What to do
When they cannot see.
See what I feel,
See what I think.
Judge me not
For I am me.
And only me
Is what I'll be.
I know it's hard
To not care
About the clothes,
About the hair.
But it's worth it
For I know
Without the stuff,
I'll still be me.
I am me
And only me.
Me.

Stephanie Toro

When Love Begins to Die

When love begins to die
I die a little, too
Our love grew together
Now, I'm a part of you

You began to pull away
How could I survive
You're breaking all the cords
That kept me so alive

When I know it's over
I'll no longer be
Every time I lose
I lose a part of me

You say take another chance
Find a love that's new
I used up all my chances
When I fell in love with you

So much in love with you I am
My life is in your hands
If your fingers let it slip
I'll fall when it lands

Ernie Jones

Dear Brother

Dedicated to my brother, Douglas W. Rayburn (5/3/65 -4/24/00)

I sit and I wonder
Sometimes all day long,
The unanswered questions;
what I did wrong
Answers will not come,
This I do know,
But I keep on asking
And feeling so low
I hope you know
How much I cared,
The memories, the laughter
The childhood we shared
These are the things
I will always hold dear
I think of them,
And I feel you near
Just know that I love you
And I'll see you someday,
When my time is through here
And I'm on my way

Susan M. Trovato

This One Girl

To Nikki and the lifelong struggle to beat anorexia—I love you.

I know this one girl better than anyone—parents, siblings, friends.
If they only knew what I do. They'd see her in a different light.
This one girl she is so popular. Good grades. Friends. She has it all.
This one girl has it all together.
Life planned out, everything in check
This one girl is so lucky. This one girl—is she really?
She is so happy. That's why she cries herself to sleep at night.
In her eyes, she isn't good enough.
She has no friends. She has nothing.
Her togetherness, a jigsaw puzzle strewn on the floor.
Everything said is taken to heart. Jokes. Sarcasm.
Only thing not absorbed is the truth.
This one girl is so troubled.
Held prisoner in a mind of doubt and insecurity.
What powers that mind possesses.
Only to be locked up with doubt.
I'm willing to sacrifice and be there for her.
So maybe one day I can find the key.
To kill the doubt and set this one girl free.

Jared Allen Hartford

A Journey

The night's affectionate air breathes gently through my skin.
My body, my soul; securely warm.
I sit high above the congested city, wondering how I got this far.
The twisting and turning roads that I have encountered.
I endure each one with a hard swallow.
Who am I, what have I become?
Expectations that I carry, like chains tightly wrapped around my frail existence.
Each link made for what people want and what I desire for myself.
An innocent dove, so delicate.
Trapped in a dispassionate, lonely cage.
Desperately seeking to be released.
But the time; the time was never right, never safe. I turn to you God!
The smile on your face shines with brilliance.
The child inside me; she is timid and shy, all the most frightened.
Like the girl she is; she blushes and laughs gayly.
Holding your hand that is so soft to the touch, embracing thee.
Waiting for the dear moment when the sun rises
And kisses the horizon with a sweet whisper.
Hello . . . It is the beginning of a new day.
And the angelic dove, so vibrant and indestructible,
Expands her precious wings to take for her deliverance.

Heather Ann Hill

Sailor's Lust

I flirt and frolic with the thought
Of riding on the wind
Her warm caresses touching me
Embraced as I begin

A journey into ecstasy
Her touch excites my sails
I am enthralled and drawn to push
Her passion raised to gales

As deeper, I press deeper
Than I have ever been
Press for all that's possible
Tack flutter, press again

And sometimes turn and run before
In tranquil motion towards the shore
Enjoy the peaceful lull until
I seek once more the passioned thrill

Of tightened sheets and powered thrust
Into the wind . . .
A sailor's lust . . .

Ned Cray

Seasons

A Spring breeze
a Winter freeze
the summers sun is
brighter than the
Falls yellow leaves!
Fresh flowers
flowing waters
sparkling seas
blowing breeze.
Seasons come
and seasons go
but I must say
mine is here to stay!

Katie Jo Wheeler

As Fast As My Heart Beats

As fast as my heart beats.
As fast as my heart speaks.
My love for you, will always be.

No matter how much
I try to fight.
This love inside
will not run and hide.

As fast as my heart beats.
As fast as my words are spoken.
The vows from my heart to you
will never be broken.

How must I live
knowing you don't feel this way.
My heart is weakened
from begging your love to stay.

But your part of me
and your love is what I need.
So if your love comes back
this love inside of me, you will see.

As fast as my heart beats.

Terry Leo Falkenstein

Happy Birthday

Today is your special day
See how you've grown
Back then you're still in my womb
A small angel waiting to be born

I sang to you songs of joy
Songs of love I hardly knew
I hummed them just for you
Lullabies as you closed your eyes

Catching your breath
As I gently blew that tiny nose
Air full of affection
See how my reflection

Look at you now, my dear
Can you still remember
The songs I used to sing
Caressing your inner being

Now that you've grown
Each birthday, a bit of good-bye
Each passing year, a kiss of adieu
How I wish you're still my little you

Yousuf Ronilo Panes Ocate

A Man with a Big Heart

A man with a big heart,
You loved us all from the start.
That's the way I looked at you,
A man with a dream for all of us, too.
But when the day came,
All I could think of God made some cruel game
To take you away from me.
I want you back I'll beg and I'll plead;
I didn't get to tell you how much I love you
And how my heart feels torn in two.
I can sit here all day and remember a lot of good times we had,
But knowing it's over makes me mad.
Maybe someday I'll come to grips,
But for know I feel stripped.
So, if you're in Heaven, which I know you are,
I'll look for the brightest star,
Because I know that's where you'll be
Looking down and being proud of me.
So, it's hard to part,
But, Dad, please, remember this, to me you're a man with the biggest heart.

Tina Lynn Miller

Father

Woke up this morning I thought I heard father call my name
I was still on the plane. Father, memories from the past fill my head;
All too soon tears fall from my eyes.
I reached my hometown glad to be home.
My letter I send to you, father, at my sister's post office address—
Will it reach you, or will she throw it away?

A choice we had to make; you could stay in a rat-infested place.
You left with her the next day; was I forgotten from your weary mind?
I wish you, father, sunny days ahead, perhaps some rain to water the grass,
So beautiful green along with good health and good cheer.
Father, let your weary mind soak up the new memories you acquired each day;
Hear those birds at the window's ledge welcoming the new day out there in the
west. Father, do you wonder wither I come again, or was this my last. . . .

I put my arms around you, and I kissed your cheek as said good-bye.
With her anger, I left that very night.
Father, I miss you, the letters, but most of all the phone calls we shared
Is she good to you? Do you get along? Will you let me know where you're
living? Maybe a telephone number so I can call you. I blunder these
questions in my mind. Father, life settles; a new day begins; you shall abide
your days with a smile. . . .

Marie Baun

It Will Be

Third of a trilogy to all who believe in peace
Strength from LOVE.
Boundless Space.
Hand in hand, Every Race.
Galaxies by Wonder explore,
come spread The NEWS,
WAR NO MORE.

Blending in the night.
Catch the SONG that rides on the wing.
Sing it LOUD sing it STRONG,
PEACE—
behold all things are
RIGHT.

The Universe will sing our SONG.
And ALL will know they can
bring forth a Thought and a SONG
that will
BE—
Even longer than MAN.

Margaret Ann Portwine

A Poem

If I tell you of my poem
Will you tell me who will care
'Cause who is going to read them all
When no one else is here

You put down your thoughts and words
For everyone to see
But no one seems to comprehend
They'll never know of me

We plod and toil through our lives
But tell me what we gain
'Cause in the end we're all just dust
Death's the answer to the pain

Write two words that sound alike
Let the rhythm ebb and flow
You have control, unlike life
You can move it fast or slow

For the masses I don't write
Myself's why I bore a poem
'Cause who is going to read them all
When Death takes us to our home

Bret Reardon

A Place All Her Own

Once upon a starry night
A child and her dream took flight
Across the sky they drove
To a place all her own.

"Good-bye, Grandma," she called
As her dream carried her away—
To a place she knew well
A place all her own.

Beautiful ballerinas
Greeted her upon graceful toes
Dancing upon clouds of gold
In the place all her own.

Bluebirds sang her favorite song,
Her grandmother's song,
And hot cookies were always there
In the place all her own.

But soon the night was done,
And the time came to return home
From the place
That was all her own.

Alison Faith Benson

Why?

One day love will find me, one day I'll look it in the eyes.
Oh, how many questions I will have to ask.
I'll sit for hours and listen to its reply of why it
often touched me, just to simply pass by.

I'll ask it why my heart was always full, and why so many
times my heart grew empty giving more than it received.
In our long conversation, I would hold love hostage there.
I would beg for answers of why it didn't care.

I'll wait on pins and needles for love's reasoning why
and when the restlessness of love's impending flight,
I'll grab on tight and not let go until the perils of my life explained.

I'll plead my case from deep within, I'll make my trials known.
I'll make love vow that now found
and its secrets shown it will not leave me alone.

Casharion Kirk

The Search

A young man eager to be rich someday
Was told of a lost city of gold,
So he set out for the Sahara Desert,
Where nature favors no man.
Finding the city was now his life
For it would take him 47 years.
When he had arrived in the location told to him,
There was no city of gold, but another older man,
With a lost expression on his face.
"Why have you come to the Sahara desert?" the old man said.
"I am in search of the lost city of gold." the man replied.
"I'm sorry to say but there is no city of gold out here," said the old man.
The once young man,
Eager to be rich someday, died
Making nothing of his life.

Adam John-Olaf Karlsgodt

Little Joe

Watching the tide roll in and out on the beach at Flora-bam.
My mind went back to another beach, another place and time.
When little Joe stopped a while to rest and watch the ocean spray.
That faithful day a riptide carried little Joe away.
His daddy passed away and little Joe was left alone.
He never understood the dad he had until he was gone.
The hurt and disappointment he carried deep inside.
He always wore a smile but deep down inside he cried.
Life was hard for Joe, but he found the strength to stand.
In his wallet was found a worn copy of footprints in the sand.
He found the strength he needed in the promise of that great man.
Now he'll walk the beaches with his father hand in hand.
And he'll walk and talk with the man who left his footprints in the sand.
The man who carried him when alone he couldn't stand.
And there left just one set of footprints in the sand.

Albert Brown

The Only Thing We Need

I wish I had wings, so I could fly. I would fly away up in the sky.
Then I could see what no man can beyond the crystal sea.
I would fly even higher in the sky, so I could see
The thing that is so desperately in need
And ask him to come down to me.
We need you by our side to help us to decide.
That what we need is more of you to see.
You are the only one who has wings.
So, please, come down to me, so I can see
Your wonderful face and everyone else can see
How beautiful you are to me.
You can save us all from our sins and help us all to forgive.
You are the one that gave us all our lives to live.
So, I just want to thank you, Lord, for being the only one I can see.
I want to only go home with thee.

Delores Jean Moses

Loss of a Hero: Dale Earnhardt

Your talent so incredible,
not many could deny.
So often starting in the back,
still passing the others by.
Many people followed you,
while some would rather not.
Regardless, what they spoke of you,
they all knew you were hot.
I dreamed to one day meet you;
now that can never be.
So much more than my hero;
you were a friend to me.
Black Sunday fell upon us;
it left me in a trance.
I wish that fate had granted you
just another chance.
It's comforting how all your fans
are showing so much love.
We know you're racing angels now
in Heaven up above.

Lavonne Joyce Crews

Careless Driving

The wind in your hair,
But you just don't care,
You're going real fast
And don't stop to rest.

The world blends together
And you go on forever.
You don't want to stop,
Even if there is a cop.

All the feelings inside
Twirl around as you ride.
Your heart pumps much faster,
And you feel like a caster.

By now, you feel sick;
You feel like a wick.
The sight of the sun
Can turn you on.

You finally quit,
Stop, and have a fit.
You don't know where you are,
But you're sure it is far.

Narine S. Asriyan

Time

Time is a thing that we must follow.
Be on time and be a good fellow.
Inside and out, time is hollow.
Sometimes time can make you bellow.

Watch the clock and time stands still.
You then can see what time will tell.
Time is something hard to kill.
Sitting in class, you wait for the bell.

Time is of the essence, you will see.
The time for now is half past three.
Time can change very quickly.
Time will fly for you and me.

Time to get up real early.
Now it's time to get a little dirty.
Be on time, at nine-thirty.
Hope that time is forever sturdy.

The time has come to end this poem.
Safe to sleep in my very own home.
Time stands still, all alone.
Time for now shall never be known.

Jason Lee Donahue

The Love That Never Came

I watched the horizon for a sign of your car,
a note, or a message or a letter from a far.
I waited and waited, until I couldn't anymore;
I wanted to cry out and run out that door!
But one thing kept me back, one thing kept me strong,
it was the strength of your heart that I've loved for so long.
Each day grew grim in waiting for you,
each day I knew that you probably wouldn't, too.
I wish I could take back all those wasted years,
waiting and waiting with wiping back the tears.
My life was never really the same,
ever since I started waiting, waiting for the love that never came. . . .

Sorah Shin

A True Mother

She adopted two children with backgrounds hardly known;
she adopted two children and raised them as her own.
With extreme love and care, she attended their wants and needs;
with extreme love and care, she planted these wondrous seeds.
With sacrifices of her own, she put her two girls first,
for they were God's gift sent to her from Heaven to Earth;
for they were worth every tear she shed and every prayer she said
in the want of children to fulfill the longing in her heart,
with love for them never to depart.
And with her guidance, two fine young women emerged
and are now grown with families of their own.
And this love and unselfish legacy from her to them is shown,
and this love and unselfish legacy from her to them is sown.
She adopted two children with backgrounds hardly known;
she adopted two children, raised them as her own,
and no one could even tell that they were not part of her very own bone.

Ruth Goldfarb

Things That Stacey and Julie Have Taught Me!

Love comes in small packages.
It's okay to be myself.
The size of the gift doesn't matter . . . it's the thought that counts.
Not to scare the waiters at Pizza Planet.
Let Julie dress me up for church.
It's okay to cry when you need to.
The Bible is the best book of all time.
Always remember that God comes first!
It's okay to laugh at myself.
Not to go bowling with Stacey, she's good.
Never play spoons with them, they'll win.
That I am special in my own way.
Keep waving at people in the car when they give you a mean look.
To share my happiness with the people around me.
And I love you two for that!
You guys are my best friends and I love you!

Jamie Dale Kiser

Eternal Bond for Life

Out of the Heavens above you came into my world.
Rainbows of bright colored ribbons around my heart you curled.
Two hearts intertwined, eternally bonded as one.
A life force warm and golden as the sun.
The eternal true love we grace each other with is rare.
The past pain and sorrows vaporized into mist as if they were never there.
Like a flower that blossoms its pedals so soft, stem so strong.
Yet hear my words, cries God above, the flower is dead in body alone 'tis true.
But the flower will live again to rise to the sun and catch the morning dew.
For within the flower I placed a seed; the seed is bonded to the soil.
As with the flower my children you too have a seed; 'tis your Soul you see.
And like the flower, my gift to you is life for all eternity.
So Robert, my love, together our hearts and soul are joined as one.
And just as the flower and Earth are bound together my love, our journey has just begun.
For together the bright rainbow-colored ribbons, God sent you down to give to me.
Have we woven around our hearts and souls, you joined to me and me to thee.

Jacqueline Lee Soucy

House in the Clearing

As I gaze out my window
and gaze 'round the yard,
I see that "house in the clearing"
standing and staring so hard.

The people inside it are laughing
at all the good times they have had.
That little house in the clearing
where nothing ever is sad.

The children are laughing and romping,
as baby gurgles with glee.
That little house in the clearing,
Oh, if it only belonged to me!

The children have left now,
The parents are gone.
The little house in the clearing
stands in sorrow without song.
Someday, I'm going back to that house
where sorrow clings all around.
That little house in the clearing
where I was brought up safe and sound.

Carol Ann Thies

The Pigeon

The pigeon is a silly thing
Around his leg he wears a ring.
He flies from here to who knows where,
Having only one big care.

This care, of course, is big to him,
But to his owner, it's just a whim.
For if he doesn't make the run,
He simply sends another one.

Jane K. Booth

An Angel's Touch

An Angel touched my hand today
and helped me make it through.
He showed me how to laugh
at a time when I was blue.

An Angel touched my heart
and showed me that he cared
and held me in his loving arms;
I felt so protected there.

An Angel touched my soul
without saying a word
and showed me how to live again,
flying free as the bird.

For all my friends are angels
whether on Earth or up above,
And each has taught me lessons
in how to live and love.

For everyone who's touched my life
I feel such abounding love,
For you have made me who I am
With God's help from above.

Jolynne L. D'Anthony

A Sleek Black Cat

A sleek black cat walked on thy grave—
'Twas on last afternoon.
I knelt to pet the sable beast
It hissed—did not meow.

It took its little furry paw
And scratched across thy name.
Its nails dug deep into the rock
And tore apart the words.

Thy name faded behind his claw—
It withered like a flower.
I scarce can tell what state it was
When I left it alone.

I chased the beast across the road
For it hurt thy memory
That I had kept of thy dear life:
'Tis gone—I cannot see.

And with thy mem'ry washed away
And thy name removed from stone,
Thy soul walks aimlessly around
Thy life was never known.
          James Jerald Day

a prism of thoughts

the ocean of time splashes
over the cliffs of life,
the river of dreams runs
through the forest of mind,
the stream of agonies flows
through the meanders of pain,
the spring of youth arises
from the source of innocence.
          Kausar Saad

Blinded

How could I have been so blind as to think
that I had found a love to outmatch all others.
A love to last a lifetime and beyond.
I was as blind as the ancient prophets were,
But unlike them, I could not tell what was lying ahead of me.
Who could have known of the heartache
and pain that I was to be feeling now.
Why couldn't it have lasted like we both
told each other constantly it would.
Yes, we both had our mysteries about us,
and we both had our secrets, but love is supposed
to be the strongest force in the whole world.
Why do I still love this creature
that can't even stand to look me in the eyes?
We were supposed to be the one for each other.
Not the one to be fighting and doubting our love.
You always told me that you wanted me to "take you to the stars."
I would have given the stars to this creature that so loved me before.
But, I was blinded by false force of that love,
And now I am still blinded and do not want to open my eyes again.
          Brentston Daniel Sharp

The Perfect Lie

I don't ever think of you,
you're not inside my head;
my hands don't tremble
when you're near,
and I'm not happy in our bed.

Your eyes don't remind me
of a beautiful, blue sky,
your lips aren't sweet,
your body not perfect,
for you I would never die.

I understand you perfectly,
so I don't ever try;
it doesn't bother me at all,
when I see you cry.

So now you know
how much I care,
I love to say good-bye.
And if you need me
I won't be there,
"remember" it's all a lie.
          Dwayne Charles Wilson

Solitude

I gave myself a tea party
This afternoon at 3:00.
'Twas very small, three guests in all,
I, myself, and me.
Myself ate up the sandwiches,
While I drank all the tea.
'Twas also I who ate the pie,
And passed the cake to me.
          Charlotte Bernadette Noronha

The Vision

Endless are the dreams we see
Each night as we rest.
And some, I lay and ponder thee
Always wishing you my best.

I picture you asleep in bed,
A sweet smile on your face.
I gently kiss your forehead
And leave one last embrace.

I look towards you and wonder,
In this dreamy vision of mine,
Could you too be in wonder
Of me in a vision of thine?

But alas, the morn has come,
And to you I must bid adieu,
And I walk restless toward my home,
Through green grass and dew.

For in forever rest and peace,
I know I bring you sorrow.
But haunting your dreams is a release,
Until our next tomorrow.
          Victoria Nicole Gallagher

Desire

Lord, I've never asked you for a sign.
Nor have I begged to see your face.
The only plea you hear from me
Is "Keep me in a state of grace."

Lord, I've been like Cain and Esau,
And I've been like Jezebel.
I've been where great evils flourish.
I've been the woman at the well.

Just as sure as I was evil,
My sins are gone without a trace.
And yet each day it is a struggle
To maintain a state of grace.

Lord, you know my heart is willing.
Though I limp, I'm in the race.
On my lips these words are forming,
"Just keep me in a state of grace."

Let no sin lay undiscovered
Or unconfessed. Unmask my face.
No word or deed or idle thought, Lord,
To drive me from a state of grace.

Maggie Boltz

My Flower

You are my flower
I am your stem
you reach the stars
only if I am there to hold you
You keep my dreams high
I keep us safely grounded
together we strive
apart we die

Curtiss Ketter

Ready

Tonight's flight is a glisty go
For who knows how far it will show.

People are running to and fro.
How confused, just like a stow.

The emptiness of feeling inside.
What must I do?
Should I get on this ride?

Zona Monique Dargan

The Cherubs in the Sky

Dear Marie, I only know you by your name,
But as kindred spirits I feel the same.
For at five months old in my womb my son died,
The shock and sorrow hit me, as I cried and cried.
For as I bled, the reason doctors did not know;
Blood tests were given, my pregnancy did not show.

As in a hospital bed I lie, I felt deep sorrow and shame.
For the death of my baby son, there was only me to blame.
Now looking out the window, I saw a holy bush;
Upon the branch of this leafy tree, sat a singing thrush.
I could not believe my eyes, as I saw Jesus standing there;
The words of comfort came to me, as I turned my mind to prayer.

So never be alone again in this time of deep sorrow,
As The Lord, The Son, The Holy Ghost will get you through tomorrow
For your daughter is now safely playing in The Garden of Eden,
Looking down, telling you, this happened for a reason.
My thoughts are with you in every way, especially at night when I pray
For Jesus for your needs to tend, and hope to you his love he will send.

Eunice Ray

Why?

Dedicated to my family and friends
Why does love have to be so confusing?
One day you're happy,
The next day you're sad.
What is LOVE?
Does it have a meaning?
Is it just a strong feeling?
Is love something you can pass up?
How do you know if it's true?
I've got a friend who's being abused.
He said he loved her,
And she had to choose
Between him and her friends.
And she chose him.
He beats her and cheats on her.
She needs to get a clue.
She says she's in love,
But does love do this?
Why does love have to be so painful?
And just to think,
It all started with a kiss.

Heather Miller

May Age Invoke Me Gracefully

A tribute to my mother, Aracely G. Lopez
May age invoke me gracefully
and I not rage her course.
May silver strands root up on me
and I not fight their force.
May I abandon youth's demise
for more prudent pursuits.
May I reflect on others' eyes
dear wisdom's attributes.
May I look on forgivingly
to every friend and foe.
May I love others boundlessly
and reap the love I sow.
May good faith keep me focused
and endow my soul with might.
May I always lead a righteous life
that keeps me free from plight.
Can I surrender vanity for all
I'll come to know?
May age invoke me gracefully—
I'm ready to let go.

Anna Elisa Lopez

Reflections

Gentle raindrops
beat the ground
Pools of memories
producing mystic sound

Events of years past
now only ripples of time
Foggy illusions
an aging sign

Reflections of generations gone
We all get older we just live on

Unseen pathways
guide the way
Miracle of birth
dying the next day

Feelings emerge
emotions race
Time catches up
the lines that crack your face

Reflections of generations gone
We all get older we just live on

Shawn L. Deets

Along the Way

If I had to choose between them I would not know what to do.
The choice appears so simple, but hard to really do.
One way is life's true journey, the other seems like death.
But I would rather live with all I can than to feel sincere regret.
Time will keep on going, for it really has no end.
Yet my heart would cease its beating, the world would all seem dead.
The past is all behind us now, while the present comes to end.
The future takes and holds us, posing to be our friend.
I look into a mirror and see my life pass by.
I find true love and happiness, but not all the reasons why.
I ponder all the questions of why or where and when.
It is here I finally realize that on fate we must depend.
There really are no answers, to questions without end.
Life's river keeps on flowing, to round another bend.
We have to let go of our possessions and let them run their course.
We too are on a journey, not knowing its real source.
Hold on to what you believe in and make best with what you have.
Your time may soon be over, so realize what you hold at hand.

James William Asmus

best friends forever

i always thought you'd be around
safe and carefree in our hometown
we were best friends as friends should be
my buddy, darren lopez, and me
as i sit here wondering, trying not to cry
why did the coolest guy i ever knew had to die
i never thought you'd leave so soon
like how you said you wanted to live on the moon
you said you'd leave without a care in the world
and take me with you when i was a little girl
but now i am grown up, and i wish you were here
i miss you telling me secrets softly in my ear
i miss you so much, and i am sorry you're gone
i remember how our phone calls lasted so long
at nights i cry, thinking i put you down
when your funeral was going on, while i was out of town
you were the guy that would make me laugh through all kinds of weather
that's why i pray you'll know we'll always be BEST FRIENDS FOREVER

Kassie Kay Sneller

The Dead

TRUST is for the denied
denying reality
the truth
no one is there

FAITH is for the sinners
hoping to be saved

LOVE is for the weak
depending on lust

GOD is for the untouched soul
Believing in fear

DREAMS are for the lost
hoping and believing

Life is for the unlucky
reality is pain

METAPHORS are for the unhappy
the hated
the sinners
the "DEAD"

Giselle Lynette Pace

Echoes

Echoes of laughter,
Echoes of song,
Echoes of heartbeats,
Which now are gone.

A family lived here,
Children so small.
Now, you can't see
They were here at all.

Echoes of first words,
Echoes so sweet,
Echoes of warm hands,
And tiny feet . . .

Echoes of laughter,
Echoes of smiles;
Now, there's just freeway
For miles and miles.

But on a still night
Eastbound you'll hear
Echoes of laughter,
Echoes of tears.

Amelia Hawkins

Reflections

I am a simple girl
One who rides the waves of black
Twisting and turning
Never looking back.

I am a complex girl
Looking for a sign
Deciphering my limits
Claiming what is mine.

To those of you who tread
The same land as I
Live each moment
As if tomorrow we could die.

Wearing these masks
Never did one of us good
Be a stronger soul
Haven't you always wish you could?

I am a simple girl
Modern and precise
I look back at my reflection
And take my own advice.

Angela Michelle Buckman

Heaven Just Could Not Wait

Mommy, why do you cry?
Daddy, why do you weep?
The angels up here
Are so loving and sweet.
What a beautiful place,
No sadness or fears.
And whatever you ask,
God always hears.

His love surrounds me,
I am not alone.
I am comforted and loved,
I am happy at home.

I'm very close by,
And in your hearts I will stay.
I'm not really gone,
I'm just a heartbeat away.
The angels were singing,
As they opened the gates.
As you see, for me,
Heaven just could not wait.

Gina F. Archibald

afterglow

blood seeping—pain easing
reality severed
crimson ecstasy
slowly dripping
dripping
a repetitive whisper—final song
slightest grin
terminal gaze
tears held back—an angel cries
razor friend
beginning
now
the end
savior's bend
your smile—last thought
shadow closes in
obscurity
from my wrist
dripping dripping

Craig John Reuterm

revelation, 8-12-98

sitting on my stool here at the
gas station, staring at all the
sweating gallons of milk in the
cooler,
thinking:
we are just like them.
we're squeezed out of mama,
we exist,
we go bad.

Andre Villanueva

Reunited

Bodies bumping
Hearts thumping
Breathing patterns escalate
Hands wandering
Minds pondering
Wishing to relate
Emotions bursting
Mouths thirsting
To envelop each other with passion
When a love that was depleted
Is again completed
With such intense aggression

Aeron Marie Collins

The Faith to Leap (Excerpt)

Christmas and New Year's
And St. Valentine's went
I didn't open cards
Or letters that were sent
No gifts did I buy,
Or happy holidays said I
All I wanted to do
Sadly
Was just get high

For the God I called Crack
I hailed on high
My praise was to a deadly
Cold
Harsh
Lie

Mark K. Horton

Killing Love

Darkness falls as evil calls.
Curtains close on evil flows.

No eyes to see what it might be.
No questions asked it starts its task.

Strangling out all the passion.
Drinking blood smooth as satin.

It can taste their fear.
They know the end is near.

Now you cry and watch love die.

Julia Ann Crawford

Cobblestones

Look down, down at the cobblestones
What do you see, see when you look
Do you see the pain, the suffering,
the people?
Up here where I am
I can see, see all that's going on
It's not a pretty picture.
Young girls selling themselves to
young boys so wasted that
neither of them know what the hell
they are doing
The parents are all drunk and beating
the s*** out of each other
The teenagers are all driving fast cars
Drinking Bud
and telling lies about how cool
their parents are.
Look down, down at the cobblestones
What do you see, see when you look
Look at the Cobblestones.

Cindi Laws Vinson

A Simple Dress

Allow me to wear a simple dress
with pearls that drape so low;
dance with me barefoot in the sand,
as we feel the full moon's glow.

Allow my silky breast to lay
upon your mouth so near;
falling into the purest sand,
our bodies disappear.

Take your arms and wrap me tight,
look in each other's eyes;
and as we fade into the night,
we hear the sea winds cry.

I want to love you, as you wish.
My desire is your command.
So, I will wear that simple dress
with pearls that drape so low,
as we feel the full moon's glow.

Sharon Diane Sigal

The Venetian Rose

They met in a foreign land.
He loved all the parts of her completely.
The child who laughs and plays and hates to be alone.
The eyes that shine and shed big love crumbs in a yawn.
The quick, bold laugh and slow, sad tears.
The rhythm of her dancing soul.
Yes, one of his dearest haunts.
The open end of a proud groove. That, too. . .
The smile shared in private suites on the house.
The heart of a lady's love. Big as the moon.
The blinding luminance of Love's reflection.
The silent joy of winter midnight spoons.
The "Hold me, I'm so cold . . ."
The love of her clan. Dark as the secrets of the sea.
The troubling sense of time—so quickly passing.
The poetess she always is. The woman she has become.
All these he loved then and loves still.
Then and even still. . . .

Rafael Orozco

Good-Bye

You're not making this easy on me.
You said you'd do this
And you said you'd do that;
What the hell happened?
You look into my eyes and I lose strength,
It can't be that way.
Without my strength I'm no one;
I refuse to be no one.
If that's who you want me to be,
Then I can't be with you.
This is hard for me to say,
But this is the way it has to be.
Good-bye then;
Don't write, don't call.
I need to be me,
And I can't be me with you.

Carolyn Ann Theriault

Soul Fire

The sunlight glimmering on your skin,
I run my tongue up your back.
Shivers of passion rock your body,
The sweet taste of honey
running down your skin.
I chase this with my tongue,
driving you wild,
hearing you call out to me.
The delay, the waiting,
only makes it sweeter.
The ache deeper, more intense.
The knowing of the past
fueling the fires in our souls.
We so know how to love each other.
The heavens are watching
the ultimate ending
and the fire that consumes both of us.
Exploding the rapid beating of your heart
over mine,
Forever bound, forever together once again.

Myst Marie Foster

Goose Shoes

Seven times, twice removed,
monkey spitting, feces eater,
spiders craving lust, magicians brewing dust,
horses, cats, frogs, and me.

Locus day, enjoy life,
penetrate conceptual,
aggravate periodically,
march twice, smoke a cigarette.

Don't forget bobsleds and trains,
coasters for the lizards, rakes for the deer,
and a shovel for the woman,
and get beer, lots of beer.

Zachary Mead Lawrence

The Point to Die Is Death

What's the point to death until you die?
I am asking you, you held the gun,
you pulled the trigger, you left me.
Falling from heaven down to hell,
you screwed me over.
The dark thunderous clouds float
above the grave
and sins release upon Earth
from your heart.
The tears race down
until forming a river.
Yeah right! You're not worth it,
you made me hate you,
you made me have no faith,
you made me hate the world.
A black hole inside is all that I am now.
Until you rot away
and your grave stone decays,
then don't ask me why.
What's the point to death until you die?

Erika Lynn Staples

Why Did I Get Pregnant?

Why did I get pregnant just to be the victim?
They took one child from me.
They didn't bother to ask if she was mine.
They went against all odds—wouldn't even set her fine.
Why did I get pregnant just to know
people in high places hated her so?
I tried to raise her best as I could;
they say I didn't do a damn thing and she's no good.
Why did I get pregnant just for them to take her life
when all they can show is violations of their own laws
and tainted all of her constitutional rights?
Why did I get pregnant for it to be
a day of hell for my kid and me?
If they feel that she shouldn't be,
then why did God made her happy and free?
To bring down judgment on someone else
only shows lacking judgment—for upholding yourself.
Why did I get pregnant? Can't you see?
God gave me that child—she lived in me.

Roszalia E. Smith

Stolen

I was pure, white as snow, smooth as
glass, innocent, not knowing what he
could do to me.
I caught a glimpse of him way down the street.
He was walking briskly
but nothing seemed unusual to me.
Into my path he crossed and then it began.
I was snatched, slapped, thrown around.
Afraid I was, but I dared not make a sound.
I was degraded, stripped
half naked of my clothes and my pride.
Whoever passed would see terror in my eyes,
but no one passed and it went on forever.
The pain and agony was unbearable;
every thrust became harder and more violent.
I couldn't understand
why it happened to me.
Seconds felt like minutes
and minutes felt like eternity.
And just when I thought I'd die,
it exploded.
The intruder lifted himself off of me
and ran away like the thief he was.

Candice Marie Freeman

If I Wanted To

If I wanted to
I could bend steel with my sex
And move canyons if necessary
I could run 'cross country in no time flat
(and my hair would still be perfect)
I could wear red, velvet g-strings
And lacy, white Wonderbras
And smell like perfume all the time
Maybe even record my dreams in black and white and metallic blue
Or put on a Broadway show
God, if I wanted to
I could let you go

Cherie Rita Melancon

Yearnings of a Corporate American

I yearn somehow for simpler times,
For men of peace, for church bell chimes,
For corner stores, for penny candy,
For kids in "Keds," for neighbors handy,
For jobs in town and men in suits,
For milk delivered on the routes,
For babies born and raised at home,
For big-*ssed cars with room to roam.
But Monday snarls,
NASDAQ awakes,
The Big Board yawns,
So much at stake.
With suit and pumps
I hit the door,
I yearn somehow now, never more.

Deb Durkin

Mild

Mildly healthy, mildly sane
Mildly hungry, mildly in pain
Mild interest, mild drive
Mildly feeling, mildly alive

Sit in the bed, stand in the hall
Walk outside to lean on a wall
Weather is mild, sky is clear
Light conversation, while sipping light beer

Half empty, half full
Tried to cut a hole, but the knife was dull
Sort of hurt myself, kind of killed my child
Goes down easy, when it's mild

Max Goggans

Julie, You Can Smell Cyanide

Like the grace of God,
a weapon against weapons,
an aversion to death—
the scent of survival
brings bitter almonds to mulled wine.
Like every chair becomes electrified in your presence,
and every gun becomes a gun,
the trash rot is underlaid by the exotic, the tang of poison.
Like the spice that tints the dregs of morning coffee
and evening milk—
the taste of a warning,
the sky turning gray,
the smell of it everywhere,
the bodies shot three times
fading to snow on your lawn.
Still, you sliver almonds for Christmas cake,
crying a little when the knife slips, and when it doesn't.
For your secret, you would cross the street without looking,
because there are other means of murder
not sensed, unknown.

Jocelyn Gillece

Hush Now

Hush now don't cry
Just close your eyes and say good-bye
To a world that's no longer your friend
To a family with too many problems to mend
But don't worry about them they wouldn't understand
All you needed was someone to hold your hand
To tell you everything will be all right
So you could sleep peacefully through the night
But nobody was ever around
To so much as utter a sound
So across your soft skin the blade glides
And down your arm the warm blood slides
Now for a short time your soul's free to go
Away from the pain it shouldn't know
But this is only a dream soon you'll awake
To a chaotic world full of people so fake
Hush now don't cry
Close your eyes and say good-bye

Nicole Amber Reyes

(J.A.B.W) Just Another Black Witch

Whose defecated words becomes less of importance,
which what is less is far from ignorance.
And, extracted physical living from own kind,
has got you in a holy state that might shine.
Plain rhymes seems wack to self, if it hasn't dealt a pretty portrait to thine ears.
Who tears through thy fears, as love brings upon tears,
and pleasure seems to be trapped within the hottest volcano with much mass.
Place on mask, to be heroine like She-Ra with a deadly task.
What's your meaning we asked life,
the being told us, "I slice you with a knife,
so you realize the strife you must fight."
Flash back on bended knee as we see Yeshua (Jesus)
he be the seed of this, blessed tears pours down like pure bliss.
Us, sinners who practices righteousness, us women on top of it.
Whom fights because of truth and steady the call it religious.
It's amazing how humans view this belief as another leaf upon a tree,
so chop down the whole tree to see that one belief perish just like we.
Ashes to ashes, dust to dust, so you see.
So you see that there are many trees that live on, carry on that one belief.
And as we look through the barrow of a black hole.
We steady twirl thine double-edged sword, upon a treble clef made of soul.

Monique Allen

That's Life

I think about my ill fated past, immortal man can't understand.
And what's next, it seems like my future is damned.
I think of buried friends, a past I need to bury.
I see a blurry end, but do I need to worry?
It's always pain on this level, no good gained on this level.
Love, hate, are you controlled by angels or devils?
Confused, big Q's (questions) with no answers in my mind,
makes me think and after every blink I'm looking for signs.
Shocked I'm still here after all lost at all costs.
Love and friends lost, some switch sides and double-cross,
came across big decisions, it's hard to decide.
It's like death was on my left and life was on my right.
Everything from life to singing are thinning, the devil's grinning,
but God's winning, though we were sinning from the beginning.
But still, am I blessed? I won't rest.
At least not till I'm deceased and got this stress off my damn chest.
Why do we react only after the fact, then realize
the wrong we did? Evil in our eyes
separate the truth and lies till I die.
Does hate leave with our tears or is love lost when we cry?

Shane Hiroshi Hironaka

morning sun

we are ugly laying in the morning light,
the magic of last night's darkness
now just dried alcohol and sex sweat.
i can see the dark circles beneath your eyes
sitting naked before me, knees bent, legs spread,
your tangled hair falling to your lips.

we were beautiful last night, dressed and primed,
dancing and elegant, smart and witty, stealing
flesh beneath the table and in the crowds.
we closed the club, drove to my place, lit candles
and incense, undressed before the flames,
made love on top of the sheets.

we wake beneath each other, tangled, tired, hung over.
in the morning light we are just naked and ugly.
we are ourselves and we are unsure.
such an honest beauty grows from the morning sun.
i may just love you.

Kip Silverman

Tight and Shiny

It is all reduced to the surface
only then, or now, or maybe tonight
he will want to touch
only my new red shirt of fabric
that pulls between my breasts
but my thighs are bare
freshly exfoliated but still loose and dull
only tight and shiny when covered
neatly in red or black
but I like pink
or neutral gray like steam
or scars or unwanted things
that casually surface
under the stretching thread
I scream
relatively soft and muddled
clogged in pores no longer clean

Jennifer Ann Shonk

The Last Night

White skin on white sheets . . .
(There is a point where nothing can remain)
Red hair on red blood . . .
(And each visit only leaves a stain)
Flowing out, mingling with tears . . .
(A scar that never heals)
Arms at odd angles . . .
(Hidden away, but constantly revealed)
Like broken wings . . .
(In gestures, in slips of words)
Tiny cuts innumerable . . .
(Fragments of a story that should not be heard)
Bruises blue and brown . . .
(Cannot be told, Should not have been)
Smelling of smoke and sex . . .
(Things that can only be whispered sin)
And all the things that shall remain secret . . .

Matthew Alvin Smith

Crack!

It's funny how you look back at a cat
who burst on the scene and didn't care about
race, color, or creed.
He has killed people and destroyed dreams,
and I thought he couldn't mess with me,
until he crept through the back door
and attacked my family.
He took us under siege and
now we can hardly breathe.
So beware of this cat,
who can become a monkey on your back,
and all I can tell you is . . .
DAMN! CRACK!

Demetrious A. Brown

The Daffodil

I saw a lonely daffodil way up upon a hill.
I saw a lonely daffodil so quiet and so still.
But then the wind began to blow, the flower began to sway.
I saw the lonely daffodil leaning toward my way.

Phillip D. White

Be Free

Devil in me, be free,
to ride the old and free the bold.
Let me go! Forget it now, for they are dead and gone.
Let me go, for I am lost and alone! Be free!

Theresa A. Moulders

A Flower

A flower with golden petals as whisky wind goes by,
and as it gets cold nearby,
then the petals may fall off the homes they used to have,
but then the years go so fast, it is hard to ever tell.

Megan K. Haugh

Crashing Waves

The foamy, turquoise waves crash on the sand,
The bright sun shines down upon me;
I look across the sparkling ocean,
But land I cannot see.

The air smells of salty fish,
The birds sing songs of joy,
The cool breeze dances all around,
I hear the laughing girls and boys.

Christi Lyn Bruckschen

Exist to Me

An unknown time, to an unknown place,
from an unknown name that belongs to an unknown face.
From unknown reality that I created,
the figment of my imagination, that which loves me completely.
You exist in my soul as a constant yearning.
You exist in my mind as that which cannot be forgotten.
You exist in my heart as beholder of my love,
yet in my life, you exist not.

Daryl Thomson

I Was Here . . .

Like I was here once before . . .
Like I knew you and . . . even more . . .
I saw this river once in a time
And same this forest stayed in my mind . . .
I heard your voice, I touched your hand
But when and where—I don't understand . . .
Maybe I dreamed of it . . . or . . . it was true
Same smell in the air, same sky, and . . . you . . .

Jackie Z. Mitrovic

My Husband

To some he was a hero, father, son, and friend.
To others he was uncle; a tall, quite gentle man.
To 14 he was Poppie with lovin,' carin' hands
With just a touch of temper to show us where he stands.
A workin' man, truck driver, whose loads where there on time.
To others he was a brother, who would always give a helping hand..
So help us, Lord, today for we don't quite understand.
For, you see, he was our world; this tall, quite gentle man.

Shirley LaComb

The End

The lighting shimmers through the sky.
You look at my cold eyes as I look beyond you.
Feel the memories come back: walks in the park,
candle light moments take you away.
You take your necklace back, my skin is so cold,
The wind starts to blow as the snow begins to fall.
They lower my casket into the snow.
I said I would love you till I die and this is the day I
Stop loving you.
I kept my word . . . Did you?

Melissa K. Dorough-Calhoun

Change Is Coming

I have dreamed many dream
most of them seem unreal
but one thing is for sure
If I sit at the table with my God
my meal shall be of such a feast
never seen before.
I have prayed often enough but yet I search for that ultimate touch.
The touch of my Lord holding me close
when I receive this
have I surpassed enough

Monica Raymo Ladet

Again

We kept going, when we shouldn't have even
Started
To fall in love the first time I talked to
You
And I are too far apart in
Age
Doesn't matter later, but it does
Now
We have to be apart, but only God knows if it will happen
Again

Stephen Christopher Schiavo

Memories

Unable to sleep and all alone in my bed,
Flashbacks of the past make me live in dread.
Down my cheek, I can feel a cold lonely tear,
But is it through the pain, torture, or fear?
All I want is for all this grief to end;
Though, can a broken soul really mend?
If only someone could take away my pain
So that I could learn to trust again.
He raped me of my mind, soul, and my innocence was lost;
Why couldn't it be him instead of me who paid the cost?

Jennifer Jane Barnes

Opposite Ends

From opposite ends of the Earth we came twindling
our bags our treasures our laughter our hearts.
From opposite ends of the city we came from
different points where we once stood so near,
Yet so far apart.
From opposite ends of a lifetime
we came and found a breath of magic hovering over us.
From opposite ends of a kiss
we came to hold each other tight below a starry sky.
From opposite ends of a heart
we smile, two lives have blended into one,
with more opposites yet to approach.
But simply together laughing, beginning anew
the beautiful man that you are and I.

Lisa Flynn

The Stranger

One night, while I was walking, I saw a man that glowed.
I knew Him not, but as we passed, He gave a sweet "Hello."
I felt a warmth inside me, an urge to follow Him.
I watched Him, as He raised the dead and healed the lame man's limb.
I thought, "Who is this stranger, whose powers are unreal?"
As I looked up, He called to me and asked that I might feel.
He showed to me His hands with wounds that should not be.
I knew Him now, and with great love He said, "Come, follow me."

Jeni Jones

Friend

Friend . . .
They are always there to be with you,
They remain always by your side.
And whenever you are on a journey,
They are there to join you for the ride.
They remain loyal at all times,
They are people that you could trust.
They are people you feel comfortable with,
So to care for them is a must.
They are God's gift from Heaven
Sent here to give you peace.
They settle down your attitude
And put your problems at ease.
They are part of your family,
They're with you till' the end.
So never doubt the power
Of this person we call "friend."

Paul Edward Vallade Jr.

The Cathedral (in Mind's Eye)

Its pillars reach up toward Heaven
Like the limbs of a giant redwood,
Straight and sturdy, yet aged.
Its high arches seem to beckon, "Come in."
Through the tiny, winking windows
The morning sunlight streams down
And rests on the floor with an icy stillness,
As a pond frozen by winter wind
In the midst of a quiet forgotten forest.

It seems almost an eternity
Walking down its never-ending, hollow halls
Hearing the echo of footsteps—
Your own footsteps on the marble floor.
There is nothing but stillness; yet,
A kind of ethereal mood that creeps into a man's soul . . .
A reverence for an ancient citadel
Left by centuries, to look to the future, alone. . . .

Barbara J. Hix

The Calling

The darker the world may become
The greater the light in them will grow
They shall become a great nation of people
Able to endure a long storm

The new age shall open up to them
Feeling the burning fire of truth
They shall enter into a brotherhood
And the shadows of the evening shall fade

Their generosity shall cover the Earth
And they shall hold within their hearts
Gentle whispers, but out of their mouths
Shall come a thunder heard by deaf ears

They shall be called from every country
And background and from all religions
They will cover the Earth
And warm others with eternal truth

Eugene W.

A Day's Wait

Every day I wait for you to come home,
Day after day I wish you were by my side.
Days go by that I never see you,
Then I only wish for you and me to stay together.

When I come home and you are not here,
I wait for you to come.
When you get here, I am already in bed.
Oh, how I only wish you could be here.

Casey L. Williams

Reality of Luck

Does thou knowest what luck is to man?
Is he playing in on each and every hand?
Like children playing with the beach sands,
Forever building castles throughout the lands.

Or is he found in the destiny of greeting spring?
Passing time idling by, as the robin sings.
The seeds sprout forth awaiting what may bring.
Are treasures gained a significant thing?

Is he the dawning to which you await to come?
For in his grasp, tightens deaths total sum.
Echoing in the valley, like distant drums.
To pass this mark; and continue with defiant income.

Tis is luck, dear reader and nothing more.
To live vigorously beyond each slamming door.
'Til peace comes; the Earth is your covering floor.
'Tis luck, dear readers to adore!

Michael James Blaylock

Understanding

Sometimes I long for it, that thing
that I can't see,
speaking quietly like a shadow which really
cannot be.

No one knows what I know and I must
keep it like a part of me,
hidden in darkness but not in the dark
for in light I can see.

Not like the others yet so wanting to be,
not normal so it says,
the world, a question, waiting to be
answered by my eyes.

Unlocking secrets with the soul and
heart, no mind can see,
closing doors waiting to be opened
by me.

Kimberly A. Addington

Earth Woman

The spring sun shines down to warm her soul.
Winter was hard and long.
She closes her eyes and tips her head
To accept its healing rays, like a soothing song.

Her hair is long and flowing,
More streaks of gray than the spring before
Glint in the ever-stronger God's light—
Testimony of life's trek to that faraway shore.

Her face is a witness to the onward marching of Time,
Wrinkles attest to the changing of the seasons.
Her heart is bruised and sore
From the passing of life and love, death and passions.

Rejoice! Winter is over—spring has brought the healing sun.
Her frozen heart is melting; rejuvenated and once more enthralled.
A gentle smile curves her mouth, as the winter pain is washed away.
The sun's love has revived the Earth Mother in us all.

Linda L. Roberts

Open Your Eyes

Darkness arrives, as the sun goes down,
I search and search, but nothing is found.
The wind she blows, yet I don't see
a person, an animal, or even a tree.
Why am I searching so hard to see?
Have I been so blind, is this my fee?
For lots is out there, if one can imagine;
give it a chance, it's more than you can fathom!

Patricia Lynne Lee

Beyond the Past

As I sit here, to gather my thoughts
alone; yet feeling so near,
I dream of you becoming my wife
a future of joy; not tear.

Your past I hope you never forget
for memories are yours for life.
Some happy to tell to your children yet born
others that cut like a knife.

I've come to add; not to erase
your life that's cherished within.
The love I have to share with you
cannot be written in pen.

Come with me, through life hand in hand
believing our love is our fate,
not just for now; forever more
even when past Heaven's gate.

Michael Douglas Perez

Untitled

I open your heart
It's a story of love
All gone in a moment yesterday
And today, I want to return to pursue you

I need what you give to me
I need to see you one more day
I only think of you
Only you

You no longer believe in love
It's only a diversion
Everything close to you is not real
And I feel like running to your arms

As time passes
What has remained
Are you forgetting me
While I obsess living for you

Kerry Leigh Kelly

A Quiet Thought

I love to sit alone and think
To talk to I, myself, and me.
A soft breeze to cool my face,
A quiet seat in a quiet place.

People try to distract my mind,
When I sit in plain sight.
Away I escape with a book,
Never turning for a second look.

My ponderings come out clear
In the dark, when no one is near.
Some days I long for a moment of peace,
A second of reflection to slow the pace.

Take a look around,
Turn a frown upside down.
Pick from a lot
A single, quiet thought.

Ali Renee Treloar

What Happened

I use to be your safe haven,
A soft place to rest your head,
And now I feel like nobody
With millions of tears I've shed.
I don't know why you've stopped believing.
You've let others destroy our soul.
I never thought the day would come
When you're right here, and I'm alone.

Melissa Stant-Pacheco

Mother of Mine

Mother of mine, your so precious to me,
you're the best of the best,
no other mother could be.

When I hold you in my arms,
there's a warm feeling there,
and nowadays, that's very rare.

Our relationship just grows and grows.
God is so good, our hearts desires
he really knows.

If ever in your life you need a helping hand,
my dear mother,
beside you is where I'll always stand.

Take care of yourself; this you must do for me.
Hold your head up high, and proud,
'cause a family we'll always be.

Christa S. Mode

A Mother's Trust

Focusing eyes, searching face
Tiny fingers envelop mine
Whispering breath
Trust.

Sleeping sounds, tender touch
Soft skin, smooth
Silently speaking
Trust.

Inhalers, midnight coughs
911, hearing the tiny drum of the beating heart
Mommy's here, it is okay
Trust.

Angels touch tiny soul
Hold tightly in my arms
Hearing the voice of God
Trust.

Natalie Cassanja Robinson

Untitled Soul

Waters of fire the sea churns gold
Dreams of the past, my soul foretold
Laughing in silence at your ignorant face
I know the truth of time and space

Running in the garden of midnight's full moon
Love evades me, it says too soon
Tapestries of stars and a canvas sky
Capturing nature for my eye

I feel the touch of Night's caress
Inside my soul it loves to rest
Unspeakable words of truth and heart
I rest my wings to play this part

My true self unconcealed to you
You love to kiss the depths of blue
Know the truth as I depart
My spirit lives inside your heart

Natalie Louise James

Husband

You are my love, my best friend, my ambition for the future
You are the ship when the waters of life go raging
You are the sails that protect me
Your love reminds me of a delicate rose
Your ability to be yourself allows me to be myself
You help me to smile no matter what cards are dealt our way
I love you for so many responses you help me to achieve
Thanks for being in my life when I've needed you the most

Marlena Renee Hutchinson

Absolution

I wish I would have been there
To watch you like a movie,
Knowing you would be safe.

I wanted to have been there
To feel the very fear that you felt.
Giving the nonbelievers the chance
To watch us like a movie
Not knowing if they, themselves, were safe.

I should have been there
To help you, when you needed help most,
To guide you when you were lost,
And to be a friend when no one else would.

But I wasn't there
To watch you like that movie,
Knowing you were going to be safe.
God was!

Paula Rogers

Crystal Ball

Shadows of a crystal ball float in the air.
Our future is gone, nothing can be repaired.
Just yesterday we appeared to be in love,
now the hate is so thick . . . said to taint a dove.
What do you do when the love is gone,
when the threads of our love have all come undone?
The sphere said that the end was near,
but I denied the truth. . . .
We should have lived in fear.
We were provided the proof. . . .
Your rage became too wild.
You smashed the future ball,
you didn't like what you saw.
Denial creates such a cold stare.
We know that all is not fair,
said to be too much to bear.
Shadows of a crystal ball hover in the air.

Tyniesha R. Maynard

Despair

As I sit watching the notes on the board
I think of what I am missing
There is love in the world, love others hoard
And for me, none can be found

I sit in my seat, thinking on this
Despair wells up in my heart
I feel it building, a great hole in my soul
A hole that will never depart

I look around me seeing happy couples
Holding and laughing and kissing
I sit, and I come quite nearly to tears
When I think of what I am missing

If only there were someone in my life
Someone to hold on to, to laugh with, to love
I wouldn't be like this with a hole in my heart
A hole there is nothing above

Ben M. Kephart

The Little Boy in Khaki Pants

The little boy in khaki pants,
is standing by the tree.
The little boy in khaki pants,
keeps smilin' over at me.
The little boy in khaki pants adorns a smile 'cross his face,
because the little boy in khaki pants,
wears his own fashion taste.

Ali DeGray

April Fools on Beale Street

His cheeks looking like ripe plums,
A thick black man plays his saxophone
On a spring midnight at the Rum Boogie Cafe.
Patrons dance around a wooden stage
To a rousing version of "Mustang Sally."
Scurrying bar maids jot down drink orders,
Passing a table where a lone man sits.
He sips from a bottle, writing on a napkin
To someone who isn't going to show up.
A woman trying to look younger than she is,
Throws her hips to the beat of a distant song
Which is telling Sally to "slow the mustang down."
A 23-year-old boy smiles at the woman,
And for but a second, she feels pretty enough.
Drinks and soul draw more to the floor
As the wallflowers hide in the shadows,
Each just hoping to be noticed.

Brian Bartalos

The World Beneath

To Mr. Reynolds who has helped me to become a poet
Walking through the crowded street,
turning to view your disturbed face,
I see tears streaming downward,
and realize that rushing you to view my world
through my senses, causes your mind
to experience things undesirable:

hearing the cries of misery,
seeing the world in revealed form,
feeling the pain of society,
tasting the ignorance impounded upon our "gentle souls,"
smelling disaster burn away at the love that never existed.

I am sorry for you; I have removed
your glasses far too quickly.
Uncomfortable, isn't it?
Welcome to my mind.

Ben Tanzer

The Dream

Lately I have been dreaming of you and me,
How can it be?
We danced all through the night,
Under the full moon so bright.
The moon light reflected off your smile,
It made me want to hold you for a while.
When you looked into my eyes,
It made me feel so alive.
The smell of your cologne made me so high,
It made me never want to say good-bye.
I put my head gently on your shoulder,
But then it suddenly got colder.
The warmth of your arms disappeared,
That is what I feared.
As I look all around for you,
I realized it wasn't at all true.
Even if the dream was real,
You wouldn't feel what I feel!

Jamie Elaine Rose

New Beginnings

I looked, but you were gone.
Gone forever it seemed,
Like the ashes from the love letters you wrote.
Your words didn't hang in the air
Or stick in my memory.
It felt good
To know that you had finally left my life,
So I could claim it back.
A wave of peacefulness enveloped me
And pushed me towards a new day.

Eva D. Rhines

You've Changed My Life

You've changed my life in so many ways
If only I could show
And give to you the happiness that I have come to know
As long as you will let me, for you I will be there
And give to you a love that only two can share
So today I give to you my heart, so gentle and so kind
For the love you've given me, one I thought I'd never find
A life and love now filled with hope, grows stronger day by day
The future is so bright now, with your love to light my way.
You've changed my life in so many ways
With the little things you've done
I ask you now to take my hand, as our walk has just begun

Brian Alley-Freeman

Grandpa, May You Rest in Peace

In memory of my loving grandfather
Your last breath at the break of dawn
It's been three days since you've been gone
Time has gone so very fast
I wish we were still living in the past

To hold your hand and feel your touch
God I miss you oh so much
The days are long and empty
Without you here I can't see clearly

In my mind I see your face
And long to give you one last embrace
The times we shared I will remember
My love for you will last forever

I hope you're happy up there in Heaven
And you get to meet your unforgotten family
But every night upon my knees
I pray to God you rest in peace

Diana Rae Turner

Well, That's Happiness

Sometimes I'm reminded of how lucky I am,
and sometimes I'm reminded of how
little we are honest with ourselves
and each other
What a romantic thought—each other
It's so nice to feel like someone loves you,
like someone cares
I was always the one who cared too much
and the other person never cared enough
That seems to have passed, dissipated
somehow, maybe that is why I'm
reminded of how lucky I am
Because now I feel as if I'm loved and accepted,
something we all search for,
something I suppose I have now
at least from myself
I feel as though I accept myself, I love myself
And that isn't luck, that's happiness

Layle Odette McFatridge

A Best Friend

A best friend lifts you up
When you feel down but a
best friend needn't always be around.
And if you need them, it's always clear
They'll be there shortly, and be sincere.
Just to listen or hold your hand,
They always seem to understand.

A best friend can be a kindred spirit
and some of their greatness you can inherit.
A best friend when they leave will give you a hug,
and believe me, that's the most potent drug.
So when you think your life's at an end
Stop! And Think! Then call a best friend.

Betty W. Heisey

Dreams

My dreams seem to flicker and fly away,
As I begin a brand new day,
And thoughts buried deep appear misty and dim,
As draining sleep fades my image of them.

Some days they color my thoughts with a glimpse
Of a long-gone, long-forgotten event;
And I ponder the purpose, the meaning of it all,
As they flutter and dance just beyond recall.

Yet my conscious mind ever nips at this glimpse,
As it slips ever deeper to subconscious depths;
But as time weaves its way, I slumber deep
To virtual reality in the corridors of sleep.

Jacqueline Lawrence Keller

A Place to Live—a Place to Love

The world is an adventurous place
To love one day and hate the next
The sky is blue and then it's gray
A reflection of our moods they say
With strength and weakness we live our lives
To ride with happiness or fall with strife
To pick ourselves up and to try again
To overcome sorrow and to soar in faith
That we can make it a nicer place
And live our lives in the fullest way
So that we can look for a better day
And see the good as well as the bad
And make it the best we ever had

Winifred H. Boyles

The Memory

silence.
Your world has ended
the battle continues.
Eighteen—your duty—to leave
family, home, and country for
Hate, Jungle, Napalm.
Your only solace,
a close friend who accompanies you.
It was any day. It was every day.
M-16's Jungle, Rot, Fear.
Ten feet ahead of you
your friend trods on Silent Death.
Landmine.
silence.
You return to family, home, and country to be
spat upon.
Your friend—his dog tags—all that returns.
Thirty-five years later
Your eyes harbor the silence of that
any day, every day.

Christina M. Cody

Keep a Watch

Keep a watch on your words, my darling,
For words are wonderful things:
They are sweet like bees' fresh honey;
Like the bees they have terrible stings.
They can bless like the warm, glad sunshine,
And brighten a lonely life;
They can cut in the strife of anger
Like an open two-edged knife.

Sue Krivka

Grandmother

When I was three, my grandmother died
and left me no choice but to cry.
When my tears dried, I wondered why?
Why did she die, then I thought wow, my grandmother died;
the one I loved for three years, she died.
She left me all by myself thinking why?
Why did she die, then I thought
she left me to sigh and to make my tears dry!

Courtney Lynn Hebert

God Bless Christmas

God bless Christmas, a happy time of year,
and bless the little children as you're lending them your ear.
Yes, Christmas is a happy time when folks begin to love,
and children ask of Santa what comes from up above.

We want you to be happy with what we try to do,
and maybe it's the only time that some folks think of you.
Please bless our little efforts to show you that we care,
and help us to remember to keep it through the year.

Look out for those who carelessly forget what it is for;
please help them each and everyone to find the open door.
As we give our gifts of love to sister and to brother,
we ask that you will smile upon and bless us one another.

Gloria Scott King

To Calvin

Barbed-wire wraps halfway around my arm
And, somewhere I want to be, the other half
Can be found on yours
I imagine us, 80 years old, sitting on the
Front porch of a nice house,
Drinking imported, Mexican beer
And scaring little kids
While a greatly appreciated, old woman
Bakes chocolate chip cookies in some new,
Over-advanced stove that
None but us can figure out,
And while we reminisce about geometry class
And laundry jobs and California
And thousands of pages yet to be written,
I finally feel that I may die happy,
But it is then I will realize that
We are invincible and cannot actually die

Ryan Matthew Kitchell

Thank You for Being My Mother

You brought me into this world.
You taught me to stand on my own two feet.
You were hard on me when I needed it,
Which made me the person I am today.
But when I was young, I didn't understand.
But since I am older, I do understand.
SO, THANK YOU FOR BEING MY MOTHER.

Janice Anita Dean

Unseen

Unbending darkness swallows my every breath,
Suffocating my reasoning and heightening my imagination.
A feeling of euphoria, as in accepting death,
Neither reason arranged, nor explanation;
I am trapped in my own hallucination.
The fear inside me rises, as the world falls away;
Voices inside me calling, begging me to stay.

Lauren Noelle Valadez

Happiness

You are the one that gives me hope for the day.
You are the one that helps me enjoy good times.
You cheer me up when bad times are near.
You are there for me when saying
good-bye seems like the toughest thing to do.
You share the good times of life with me,
yet I do not know who you are.

Willem Johannes Ellis

My Secret Place

There's a secret place I like to go
Everyone is there, but their faces don't show
If you get inside, you can't get out
There's nobody there to hear you scream or shout
Let me in, get me out, I can't do more than twist and shout
I lost my soul without a trace
Found it again in my secret place

Wade Charles Erdahl

My Sister

My sister has gone to Heaven, where she will forever stay.
And among the clouds with angels, she is at play.
I shall miss her deeply; there shall always be tears.
In my empty silent dwelling, I know she well always be there.
Twenty years have come and gone, her memory is still clear.
How I still miss her, and wish she was here.
So again it's a silent good night and a soft whisper, I love you.

Cindy Lee Thompson

Only One Man

Only one man can raise the dead,
and only one man can feed the unfed.

Only one man can calm the sea,
and the only one man to walk upon it was he.

Only one man can heal the sick,
and only one man can see a sinful trick.

Only one man can rise to Heaven,
and only one man ate of the unleavened.

Only one man would do this for us,
and that one man would be Jesus,
the Son of God.
The End

Cory Cannon

You

I look at you
Awash in moonlight
Your chest gently heaving
As your breath blows a great weight off my shoulders

  David Jeremy Wadler

Just Fall in Love

You are my love, the one that I cherish,
Without you in my life all my dreams would perish.
Stand by me, I stand proud before you,
I promise to forever be true and blue.
You are the one that I want, the one that I need,
Without you in my life, my heart would bleed.
Without you in my world, my heart would die.
How many mountains do I have to climb
To prove that you are my guiding light?
Till my last dying day, it's for your love I fight.
I will be your man and your soul provider,
Your lover, your fighter, your days get brighter.
You are the one, the shoulder that I lean upon.
I live my life every day with the goals that we dream on.
You are to me sunshine on a rainy day,
Hold me, mold me in love we play.
And in the end, we will stand as one together.
Stand amiss in memory bliss, now come and give me a kiss.

  Keith John Peraino

Time to Pray

The time has come to get down on my knees
Facing the one who created me.
He knew me first.
I had to learn
God lives forever,
No need to be concerned.
I lived my life
The way I thought it should be,
Pushing Jesus far from me.
He stayed silently beside me,
While I selfishly ignored
What he did for me.
In all the world
The time is now
To let Jesus be silent no more.
I prayed Heavenly Father, God above,
Come into my life, things began to change,
I began to love.

  Shannon Gaye Blevins

Consequences

I stood on the edge of today
And watched
As tomorrow came and went
And suddenly I realized
As I walked away
That life was the mere existence
Of the choices we made yesterday.
What I am . . . what I do . . . where I end
All nothing more than a choice.
Sometimes in a moment's notice,
Sometimes with a lifetime
Of thought . . . all the same
The choice is where I came to be
And all the other choices ahead
Will come
And once again
Make me, break me, love me, hate me
Take me to the final end.

  Cheryl Gambrell Bailey

Flight

I have broken the confining bonds of Earth
and have climbed so high above
to soar the skies the eagles soar
and glide on the winds thereof.
I have roamed the boundaries of the Heavens
and have entered a realm of awe.
I have traveled amidst the wings of flame
and ridden in the hand of God.

  Diane Kathleen Hauer

Me and You

Even though we aren't together,
I wish I was with you right now forever.
I know you had to make you decision.
I wasn't good enough for your attention.
We had our good times
and even our bad.
My love for you is deeper than the deepest sea,
but I can't go that far.

  Julia Lindsay Richardson

Please, Don't Leave

The little girl sat looking at the man
He was packing up everything, even the pots and pans
The little girl looked so sad
The man tried to hold up and be glad
The little girl said sadly, "Please, don't go"
The man looked down and walked away very slow
The little girl started to cry
But the man never looked back, never said bye

  Amber Danielle Vance

Farewell

A leaf floats gently from the tree
To settle on the ground

A tear slowly slides down my cheek

Other leaves will follow with the blowing breeze
Along with my tears

Until the final leaf falls to rest among the others
Gathered over the years

  Melody Dotson

Runner's Life

Very dedicated to the team
an easy life as it may seem . . .
Strength and endurance may seem to be all you need,
Not true . . . You need the power to succeed.
A runner's life may seem to be easy,
but a runner must believe to succeed . . .
For a runner to be #1,
they must believe and have much fun.

  Heather Ann Masusock

Pure Elves

Northern lights glimmer as pure elves enter the ice palace.
Snow flakes fall as if they were visitors.
Snow freezes the beauty of your furnishings to a solid bed.
That you would sleep on, songs dance in your head, soon you dream.
Spring is the time to have playful joy, to hunt, your wolves' feast.
Bearclaw hunts alone, clothes of white rabbit.
Fiery Warrior gives to whom is in the most need.
Winter, time to hibernate, to dream, your tree den a place to sleep.

  Christen Scott Rubio

On Father's Day

The flower that flowers
I give you as we part,
For you it is my love,
For me it is my memories of you.
Thou shall not be forgotten, nor disgraced,
Nor dishonored, nor disrespected.

So I shall be remaining to love you,
honor you, and respect you till thou is passed on to a better world.

Suzanne Marie Cuellar

Lizee's Poem

Although I travel across the miles
There's still one thing that makes me smile
For when my trip is through
I'll always come home to you
You're in my heart and in my mind
We share a love that's hard to find
The days go by; some cloudy, some blue
I only long to be with you

Bradley Yasika

My Guardian Angel

Dear Angel, ever at my side, how lovely you must be.
To leave your home in Heaven, to guard a child like me.
When I'm far away from home or maybe hard at play,
I know you will protect me from harm along the way.
Your beautiful and shining face, I see not—though you're near.
The sweetness of your lovely voice, I don't always hear.
When I pray, you're praying too. Your prayer is just for me.
But when I sleep you never do. You're watching over me.

Chreé Mychell Steed

The Best Friend

There's a young woman and Shannon is her name
Instead of trying to be someone else, she just stays the same
She's always there to pick you up and help you when you fall
And whenever you have a problem, all you have to do is call
Through rain, shine, sleet, or snow she will always be there
No matter what the situation, you really know she does care
My best friend is Shannon Coyle, and she means so much to me
She's like the sister I never had and I hope she'll always be

Jenny Ruth Wilson

Night

The night is but a shadow of the day.
Within its depths, no answers will you find,
But all her lies are exposed.
You awake not out of fear, but of the dread
Of the morrow coming.
The sounds of the night are only the echoes
Of your dreams not yet real . . . but always
To be believed in.

Joan Cristene Kleinmeier

Tiresome

Homework, homework, and more homework;
It just keeps coming faster than a speeding bullet.
Do I do it all?
Yes.
Do I like doing it?
Sure, because every assignment that
I get is a little grain of
Knowledge that I gain.

Guadalupe Gallardo

Change

Totally fictional—any resemblance to real events is your fault.
I call you at your home.
You're on the machine, just as you were
A year before.
I arrive at your front step.
You don't answer the door, just as you didn't
A few months before.
I go downstairs, there you are on the couch,
Just as you were the night before.
I look out the sliding glass door, and
I see the way the morning sunlight hits the
Cold, concrete floor.

Then I drift into a memory . . .
Of you sitting at a windowsill
Looking at the empty street below.
This memory so very old and from so long ago;
Slowly I fade back, and
I am torn.
Because it is then that I realize,
Things cannot be as they were before.

Tristan Ramos

Soul Mates

Love at first sight, is it true?
Can you trust me? Can I trust you?
My feelings are deep, I cannot confess.
A simple "I love you" would never express.

A burning touch, a lingering kiss,
The feel of your arms around me,
An electrifying caress;
My body grows hot, but it is just physical.

My mind is constantly being stunned.
One person with one soul mate,
Is it fate for that soul mate to be found?

Can love surpass an old lover's wounds?
Yearning, hoping, asking, wanting
A passionate lover with open, loving arms;
A lover who needs someone, too!

Old scars, new bruises, and obstacles to overcome
Communication, participation, admiration;
Shoulders to lean on for years to come,
A soul mate made for a special someone.

Mary Elizabeth Stephens

Always Pretty, Always Beautiful

She was a Lady in all ways.
She was a wonderful Mother in more ways.
When she was with her family she glowed,
and her love flowed continually.

My Mother was pretty, she was beautiful.
Her love for life, and the love she shared.
Friends and Family knew how wonderful,
and everlasting her love was and is.

During her last year of life,
With cancer eating and devastating her body,
Her smiles, and love, was her beauty.

If you have a friend or family member,
Let them know how beautiful.
How pretty, and wonderful they have been,
in your life.
Let them know that their love is for always.

My Mother, Always Pretty, Always Beautiful.
Her love and smiles will never fade.
Never grow dim, and never cease to have been.

Michele R. Schmitt

Promised Dance

Looking back, I can remember
the smiling eyes, the witty humor;
A hesitant glance needs no response
as I escape beyond the crowd.
I find a man with charm and grace
providing lasting warmth, a sincere embrace.

Passing from his mouth to mine,
he shares a smile, a wicked delight.
We keep a distance, a fair disguise.
A dance begins; we are alone,
Caught in the moment, all to ourselves.
Time is endless; a question unfolds,

Wandering through the darkness;
he approaches me with a kiss.
No words are exchanged; no words are needed.
I continue my journey, lightly brushing my lips.

An enchanted evening with no regrets
remains with me today and always.
The stopping of a stranger did embark
a journey of love and everlasting hope.

Michele L. McMullen

My Special Friend

To my little brother, Noah, who is autistic
He doesn't talk so clearly,
he loves me oh so dearly.
He is not a normal boy,
he could care less about his toys.
He doesn't have any friends,
his care for his family will never end.
He does not socialize well,
he sits by himself and will never tell.
He is not stupid,
he is almost as loveable as cupid.
His disability is not his fault,
when it happened his life came to a halt.
He will definitely be hard to teach,
and maybe even harder to reach.
I will always stop and give him a hug,
it doesn't matter that he may act like a bug.
He is the cutest boy I've ever seen,
I don't think he will ever be mean.
He will always be my special friend,
his love and kindness will never end.

Bethany Hope Trojan

Remember Me . . .

I have not died a final death,
But started a new life.
I may not be here with you,
But I am in your hearts.
Though I admit death is sad,
And life is hard without me,
Please move on because I love you,
And not because I'm gone.

Remember the times we've spent together,
And all the fun we've had.
For I am happy now in Heaven,
Resting with my dad.

Love and laughter we have shared,
Should fill your hearts with joy,
Until the day that God should call
For you to come and join.

Remember me as time goes on,
For I do truly love you.
And remember God is with me,
So I am not alone.

Bobbie Lee Coontz

Regret

Why do we suppose there is always time, time to dream to wait
Time to let things fall into place; time is relevant
There's never enough time where love struggles to exist
To break the bonds of happiness, time is what we'll miss
Dreams lay squandered, never realized
No time to exist
Misinterpretation is the endlessness of regret's abyss
So we ponder with reflection the moments hours, time has drifted by
We sort and categorize the memories to answer the question, why?
Still the question is the mystery, born too blind to see
Life in the here and now is what you make it
Dreams, simply a moment of faith away from reality
There never seems to be enough time when
we learn our spirits can soar and fly
It is in that time, that moment too late, we close our eyes to die
In that very moment of all knowledge we realize
Not enough time was given to say hello,
too much spent on our good-byes
The answer to all the mystery may be found in the question and yet
Never to have open our eyes to the light of truth
That sums up and defines the meaning of regret

Derrick James Calloway

Poetry

Your dreams, thoughts, ambitions and feelings.

The essence of love from the pen to the page.

The exciting rivalry of fact and fiction,
This is poetry.

Foresight or prophecy you may call it
I describe it as, one allowing their mind to
Explore the possibilities of greatness.

Happiness, joy, pain, eagerness, having a
Slight hint of confusion, but at some point
Turns into understanding.

Hidden messages closed to the naked eye.

But through full mental focus, the mysteries
Of ones centrifugal and cerebral fantasies
Come alive.

This is poetry and its qualities, some of
What it can do. But when it all boils down,
It's nothing more than that which lives inside of
Me as well as you.

Christopher Michael Jackson

Ghost Monkey

They never found her body here
They never found her body there
They never saw what really happened
so how can I go on living
with a smile on my sunken face
with another gone from the human race
Tell me how . . .

Another girl gone from this world today
They never really cared about her then
so, why should anyone care about her now
So, how can I go on in this world
when I saw all the liquid blood
and her lying dead in the filthy mud

I won't take the blame anymore
because I was as innocent as she was
No, I won't do it anymore
You can't pull this on me
Where they took her body, I'll never know
that's the way we'll end this horrific show
So, go ask my Ghost Monkey, ask his secret

Mo Singh Anand

Days of Your Dreaming

Childhood blissfulness, no adult sarcasm.
Daydreaming desires of fun and greatness, never prejudice.
Beautiful butterflies in reach—like a peach for the picking.
A ripe treat, like the love so sweet.
Coming without barriers to enslave, control or precipitate hate.
Each day a rebirth, welcoming a new sun passing again this day.
Fanning fires of unadulterated optimism. Disposing of barriers.
Ready for new frontiers.
Each second—a day. Every day—a year, seeing the horizon so clear.
Stars bless this masterpiece yet to create.

But beautiful hands grow taller and longer.
And precious childhood days are getting shorter.
And fading into the ether.

Hold tight to those days of your dreaming, and those beatitudes.
However heavy the fight, remember the Sun of your first sight.
Bright and boundless, as your soul, still unashamed and bottomless.
'Cause once you pass that border, only older you become.
And heavy will be your heart, and harder and harder to jump start.
So remember the stars in the skies, and the twinkle in your eyes.
and you'll know today's sunrise—will last forever. . . .

Troy Thomas Head

seeing you

seeing you standing there
seeing you touch her hair
you've moved on
but i feel the same
even though i pretend i'm through

what happened to our love
i miss those happy days
now we don't even talk
and it's killing me

we aren't even friends
so what is this girl supposed to do?
stand here seeing you with another?
please say it's a bad dream
and that i'm going to wake up soon
say it's not true

i guess i've got to move on because
you're not through with her
and in this life there are no second chances
so i'll say good-bye to you
and hopefully find another true romance

Lindsey Davis

Windows of Happiness

Life through a blurry window,
stained and smeared by the mishaps and
misfortunes of your life.

The rosiness of the outside world often
washed away by the rain.
The perceived picture from the inside
washed away by the tears.

On either side of this invisible barrier
where life is seen, and the changes are witnessed;
it is washed clean on both sides
for the cycle to repeat itself.

Each time I look out of the window,
a caption of life taking place is evident.
Happiness, joy, laughter; all washed away
by the tears of sadness.

Through the windows of happiness, life goes on:

until one day the window is broken.

Life is gone.

Parzeda Marlene Ross

The Promise of May

For Dad
As the child grows,
the apples fall
shedding seeds of life
on the freshly cut grass
under mounds of brown
that her father told her to
rake away, but she never did . . .
and he didn't care.

And they sat together
under the tree eating apples,
shiny red with the skins still on,
and they planted the seeds in the earth by
Mother's garden full of blossoms.

Laura Jeanne Talbott

The Grief of Death

Why must you leave and go,
for surely I can't contain this great sorrow.
I know your spirit is with me,
but without the presence of your body, it's overwhelmingly.
I can never sever the emotion of grief,
It's like something that's been taken from you like a thief.
For we all must experience this,
death is something we cannot miss.

Before this time comes we should make our peace,
death is something that will not cease.
We all have a picture of how it may be,
but we don't know actually.
Death carries a burden of grief,
to some it is a sign of relief.

Roselyn Ann Pierre

It Ain't Easy Being Married!

We haven't got much money
We drive an older car
We still call each other "Honey"
We still make each other laugh (he's funny!)
We fought small battles, but never a war
We tried and erred
We always shared
It was easy—we cared.
What's best about our marriage is not hard to put in words.
We simply listen to each other's thoughts.
We're each other's better half.
We're what "together" really means
We are a team.
Hey! It's <u>easy</u> being married!

Carol Zic

Mother

Have you ever set back and asked yourself, "What is a Mother?"
If you were to look in the dictionary you can find a basic
definition, but a mother is greater than any Webster's
definition. A mother is a woman of many talents. She is a
friend, family leader and counselor, a spiritual director,
a doctor and nurse, a referee, and don't forget a sparring
partner too. She is loyal, caring, giving, trust worthy,
gentle, understanding, and very determined. As you think,
many other talents may come to mind but, there is one thing
that she gives fully and freely and that's "Unconditional Love."
As I look over my life, I could not ask for a better
woman to be my MOTHER but you!!

Love,
Your Daughter

Marla Jordan

Bonded for Life

Bonded for life to a white man and his wife,
Lived on a plantation all my life, too.
Ain't never been no further than two miles up,
Ain't never seen a ocean that's blue.
Bonded to the person next to me by chains,
Bonded to the person next to him by blood.
Can't say that I have feelings for anyone of them,
That whip then took all my love.
I had many siblings to love, or so I was told.
But I never loved anyone, my heart was too cold.
It was hardened by the whip upon my bare black back,
By the humiliation, the suffering, I always wanted to fight back.
Bonded for life by papers, words and unknown facts.
Taken from my home and forced to work from the sweat upon my back.

Channon Devane' Morrell

Life Is Hard

Life is something that no one seems to understand.
When times get hard there is nothing that can take away the pain.
Life is hard.
When trouble comes the way of the righteous beholder
He is not spared.
Life is hard.
Not spared from trouble's wrath.
Not spared from the hatred of others.
Life is hard,
But when life gets hard, never get discouraged,
But keep your eyes on the rising sun,
For a new day will begin when times are the hardest.
So keep your faith and do not give up.
When life is hard.

Henry Graylin Robinson

Remember God?

Today in the world things aren't what they seem
To some it's real, to some it's a dream
Things have changed, and the world's going bad
It's not what God intended, and I imagine him sad
Why can't things be like the master planned
Instead of the opposite and the word of God banned
Can you, yourself, imagine the pain
Of hanging on a cross in front of others in shame
Especially his own mother, who watched nearby
Having no choice but to watch her son die
He hung up there in the burning heat
With a crown of thorns on his head and nails in his feet
As tears rolled down his bloodstained face
Jesus died for us by his wonderful grace

Rachael LeAnna Slayback

The Stranger

When gazing eyes should fall this way
They'll see a man who's lived a brighter day.

His head hangs low and his skies are black,
Remembering a love that won't come back.

Fearing the debt that must now be paid,
Feeling the pain of mistakes he's made,

He's been told time will ease his pain,
But on his soul there's a stain

For every useless tear he shed
Over a love already dead.

I hope you're kind to the man you see
For after all, this man is me.

Bryan Eugene Cyrus

Lighthouse Mother

There she is standing so bright and tall
through the summer, winter, even the fall.
She watches over the placid or angry seas
like a queen bee watches her swarm of bees.
She guides ships and sailors safely to shore
She keeps you from sinking to the ocean floor
Her smile is cheerful, warm, and bright,
it's a smile you can see miles away at night.
Her spirit seems to fade during the day,
but at night you can tell it never went away.
She is protector of the sea,
she is a warning to you and me.
So when you see her be kind to one another,
be like her, be like Lighthouse Mother.

Hailey Wainwright

Right before Valentine's Day

You broke my heart; I fell apart
Right before Valentine's Day
I thought you loved me, would never leave me
Right before Valentine's Day
In my heart, you were the one who made me feel safe and warm
Right before Valentine's Day
I see other lovers pledging to one another
Right before Valentine's Day
How could you just run, saying good-bye to no one
Right before Valentine's Day
As hard as it is, I'll guess I'll live
Right before Valentine's Day
I'll never give it all, set myself up for a fall
Right before Valentine's Day

Ruth A. Gant

Reality

I have waited so long for someone like you
I cannot believe you are in my life.

Now it seems I may have to give up what I have had with you.
It hurts to think that but I know it can become a reality.

I will hold you in my heart always
I will remember everything we shared
I will cherish the "us" that was
I will pray that we can become one again

May your journey be safe and may you remember
that I am holding a special place in my heart for you!

I LOVE YOU!

Marion Frances Arnold

Time Standing Still

Dawn is near, the sounds of life are once again heard.
Crickets' music of the night are replaced by the chirps of a bird.
The smell of morning breakfast makes its way to my room.
As does the smell of roses that are now in bloom.
I rise, look out the window and realize just how quickly time flies.
Just how many moments are really cherished before one dies?
I quickly get dressed and take a walk to a stream.
A place untouched by human hands, mystical and serene.
I look at this work of wonder where time stands still . . .
To a moment so beautiful, you have to ask, "Is it real?"
If only the world would stop for just a minute or two . . .
Just take time to notice that the sky is really blue.
If I was magic and had one wish I could fulfill . . .
I would let the people of the world see time standing still.

Sherri Hollinshead

What Else Is There to Do

I walk past the pain of your unloving arms.
Your hands, covered in thorns, lead me into
the passion that has now become my existence.
I can't turn away from your blinding light.
I struggle against reason, letting emotions blur my way.
Understanding has vanished, only to be
replaced by an aching heart, by fleeting
moments of uncontrollable desire.
What else is there to do when a single stare
makes your blood boil away into insanity?
What else is there to do when you are
trapped on a one-way road to unhappiness?
What else is there to do when there is
nothing left to say but good-bye?

Kayzim Yadira Suarez

Angels

Coming down from Heaven above,
Angels surround you with wings of love.
Guiding you through the night
And waking you with Heaven's light.

This bright and beautiful light
Shines on an angel's face,
As they come down from Heaven's grace.

This sweet and tender grace helps
You on your way, as you walk your
Path to Heaven.

The path of Heaven is blistering with gold,
Because, so many people with angels
Walk this road.

Renea Leanne Tackett

What We Share

Though we do not share a home
Do not be sad or angry
Each night, as the day fades away
Look for my smile in the moon.
I will do the same, and
This we will share instead.

Though we do not share each day
Of our bloated lives
Do not question the reasons for this.
At midday's time
Raise your face to the sun and close your eyes.
Feel the warmth of our touching faces.
I will do the same, and
This we will share instead.

Jeromy Pinkham

Missing You

As morning breaks, I open my eyes;
I'm missing you, I breathe a sigh.
I yearn for your touch, the caress of your hand.
I'm missing you, this we both understand.
A kiss from your lips, I fantasize;
I'm missing you, in your hand my fate lies.
To hear you laugh or say I love you,
I'm missing you, my day starts in blue.
So many things I feel the need to convey;
I'm missing you, so goes my day.
As the day passes, many thoughts come to mind;
I'm missing you, will you ever be mine?
The nearness of you, the thrill of your touch,
I'm missing you, I love you so much.

Sharon Kay Merrill

When Dona Comes This Way

It seems eons and one long-lasting kiss
Since Dona left me standing in the rain
With "good luck" eyes for one I knew I'd miss;
With words "I love you" pulsing from my brain.
Oh, no! She never knew that faceless pain
That peered so shy out from a sad heart breaking.
When all her friends hurrayed her off to fame,
She could not know that one stood there forsaken.
I heard this morning of a plane she's taken,
Returning home to celebrate success;
How can she quell this flame that she's awakened
In one who stands to win her smile at best
When Dona comes this way and sees my tears,
As she parades through crowds of shouts and cheers.

Jerry Gorham

Stages of Human Life

Childhood is the thread of inquisitiveness
when we ask, when, what, where, and how?
Adolescence will be entangled in the web of
acquiring knowledge and thirst for experiencing it.
Youth is full of fulfilling our ambitions
And aiming to acquire it, when we may fall
or rise according to our own deeds.
Old age comes to us as a condolence when
we know what we are and what actually
we could have done.
But, alas, by that time, He who gave us the place to breathe
takes it back.
Oh, God, you are really a wonderful person
whom we will never see, but experience only.

Subbaraman Ramakrishnan Avittathoor

Daddy

Daddy, can you hear me when I say that I love you?
Daddy, do you watch me and everything I do?
Daddy, can you see me when I stand above your grave?
Daddy, do you still remember all the memories that I save?
Daddy, can you feel it when your pictures I kiss?
Daddy, do you see how much of you I miss?
Your laugh, your hugs, and face that I remember very well.
Daddy, I know now that you are my guardian angel.
Daddy, I'm your little girl, and I hope I make you proud.
And I hope you hear every thought that I don't say out loud.
One day I will see my Daddy's face again.
I only wish that I knew when.
So, Daddy, hear every time I say that I love you.
And, Daddy, watch over me and everything that I do.

Jenna Dawn Mosher

Tears

Dedicated to Christopher—rest in peace
You told me time and time again not to grieve
for it was your time
Every time I see your face, I think back to
when life was happy, no tears were discovered
Now that your face has erased,
those tears are remembered
Once in a while that happiness comes again
and I am filled with remembered joy
you placed with our friendship we shared
Then I come to the end of our joy when those
tears are remembered, because you were wanted
from the Heavens above
Chris, we all miss you

Crystal Dawn Neumann

One More Day

As I walk along the street side,
I realize that I have gone one more day
One more day with a home,
One more day with a family.

As I lay down to sleep,
I remember that today I have grown older
That I have grown wiser,
And I am more loveable than ever.

As I go on,
Loving myself more and more,
Praying to enlighten me,
I remember that it is just another day,
One more day that everyone has to face.

Katelyn Jade Dillon

Our Brightest Star

Joy fills your soul when you get to see her,
Every day and night.
She is the sweetest little angel who was ever brought into sight.
She'll make you smile and feel good inside,
If only you could have seen her.
'Cause now she lives in Heaven above,
And in all the hearts who loved her.
So if you see a bright shining star
Understand that it's her,
Shining for her mommy and daddy
Who miss her all the time.
Little Miss Jessica Summer who was lost so young,
Will ever remain in all our hearts and minds.
Never feel sad, just remember she's that bright shining star.

Charlotte Renee Stumpff

I Only Wish

How can someone I don't know make me so mad?
I only wish that you could have been there.
All night long I ponder, where is my dad?
I lie in pain, wishing you could be here.
Only my mom is here to comfort me,
Just because you hide away from my life.
To be there with you, I wish I could be.
You will spend time with your kids and your wife.
Do you hate me, tell me, what did I do?
Harsh pain to deal with at such a young age.
Why me, what did I do to feel this blue?
Did you plan this, or even was it staged?
Do I have half-brothers and sisters, too?
I only wish that soon I could meet you.

Theresa Anne Boyle

Love

Love makes you smile,
Love makes you cry.
It makes you feel all tingly inside.
You love me, and I love you.
We hold hands, but you quickly pull away.
What is it?
What have I done?
Then you come up to me and break my heart!
Our love is over,
Just like our friendship.
All I want to do is cry all night.
I told you
It takes an eternity to forget someone,
But all you say is good-bye, good-bye.

Ania Agnieszka Korowajski

Untitled

I have died
And travelled to the stars
I am the stars
I know why the moon glows at night
And why the sun beams warmth on us during the day
I have seen the terrors of daily pain
And the glories of your heart
And I have been to Heaven
The pureness of truth has been revealed to me
I feel the breath inside you
Your blood pulsing though your veins
And taste the food you eat
I feel the swell of your belly
And the life inside you
I know the love between us
And I am reborn

Jackie Bishop

Daddy

Angels are like going to peaceful places, the ocean, to be exact,
bringing peace and harmony wherever they show up at.
Angels are like your best friends,
even if you can't actually see them, or they exist,
only in your heart, your mind,
they have a special spirit that will never die.
My special angel has a heart that is so strong,
someone I can always turn to and lean on.
My angel is with me always,
I feel her here beside me each and every day,
at work sleep, or play
I can't imagine where I would be today,
without my special angel to guide me and help me through each day.
Thanks Daddy!

Lucinda Lee Tinsley

Not Today!

Oh! Look at all the fish!
Oh, God please grant our wish . . .
We told him not to go near the water,
but I guess he didn't obey his father.
We pulled him out as quick as we could!
His lips are blue! That can't be good!
Now let's start CPR,
the hospital isn't very far!
The doctors have him now, he'll be fine
What? A coma! Mason, give us a sign!
Oh, my God he's awake!
We'll never again make that mistake!
Oh, my sweetheart, how I love you so. . . .
Now I think it's time we go!

Amber Nicole Dunlap

Ungrateful

You think I'm ungrateful
When you try to give me everything in the world
And I act as though I don't want it
It's not that I'm ungrateful
It's just that I don't expect it
When we were all alone
You, a young, single mother with two children
Working three jobs to get food and pay the rent
All you gave me was love
That's all I'll ever need
I love you so much
And hate to see you cry
But without you in my world
I know I would die

Cortney Ann Keller

Love's Touch

Show your feelings, act them out.
Show me words are not what you're about.
For you can say many words and not mean one.
In one touch our conversation can be done.
Each kiss, each look, each single touch,
Silently you can say so very much.
I love you is only three words to be said.
Why let that express all that's in your head.
There is an energy that can only be felt.
It's love's touch that makes you melt.
Don't talk with words from your lips.
Let your love come from your fingertips.
Use your mouth only for the sweetest kiss.
Hold me and send me into eternal bliss.

Reba Moran

Memories

So faint, so far, the days gone by.
Visions past come to the inner eye.
Life's heartaches and sorrows
So remembered in our tomorrows.
Sadness, alas, of many a kind,
Happy thoughts also come to mind.
Fondly remembered, a dear, little lady,
So caring and loving her ways with a baby.
Bedtime so sweet, walks hand in hand,
Many tales so true from across the land.
Growing years full of encouragement
Brought forth a future of great contentment.
Always there to help along the way,
My granny I will miss forever a day.

Myrtle Snidal

Split

Which way to go, man never knows,
They split their group and go both ways,
And with it splits their lives.
The road continues to split and split,
And soon they're all alone.
Soon they come upon another split and know not what to do,
There's but one of them, two ways to go.
Lonely, soon, do they become,
Seeing the error of their ways.
They start to wander aimlessly.
And so we live out our useless lives,
Trying to find a purpose,
Before the unknown road ahead,
Starts to split again.

Alex Tome

Try to Please So Many People

Each and every day I try to please so many people
I try to please my mother
But she always seems to find a flaw
So I am not perfect, but why not try?
I try to please my stepfather
This cannot be done
Just because I am not like his daughter
I try to please my husband
But nothing is ever good enough
There's always something more I could have done
Out of all the people I try to please
I always forget the most important person of all
This person is
Me

Mindy Cahhal

Life

"Why?" we ask whenever things are bad.
Confusion in our hearts makes us sad.
"Where?" we ask when we are lost.
Excitement in our mind makes us pay a cost.

There is hope if you reach out.
There are answers if you search.

We have fears and feel no one cares.
Someone is out there who is willing to care.

Don't give up.
Push on through.
Fight to be a better person and you will find the hero in you

For all of our children.

Nina Samaroo

I Just Know

My darling Rhonda, from the moment we met
I could see us together until life's sunset

Your heart, smile, eyes, and caring ways
Touch me deeply and always brighten my days

There's so much more I admire and compliment
That's why I believe you are heaven-sent

The miles I travel between us can take more than just a short time
But they give me the ability to reflect and to rhyme

As I think of each moment, I can't help but sigh
I never want or need to stop and wonder why

I just know in my heart that these feelings are true
I want, I desire, and I dearly love you

Carl W. Scott

Friends

What is there in a person that makes a special friend?
Why does one sometimes go out of his way?
Where is the fine connection, the line that's sometimes crossed?.
When someone special gives another all.
Giving all to one entirely, and never question why.
Always being there in times of friendships need.
Never asking any favor or seeking some fine edge.
Simply being there for someone is their deed
How wonderful the knowledge in knowing day to day,
That someone near and dear to you is there.
Always faithful is their mission,
At all times their aim to please,
Ever present, always with you,
Your life throughout to share

Robert J. McGilvray

Dreamer

As I lie here in the darkness,
I think of you as I fall asleep.
I can feel your sweet kisses,
your tender touch,
and loving embrace.
Together forever is what we will be.
Exchanging the words, I love you
Lying in each other's arms all through the night.
I awake to birds, chirping us a beautiful song.
I roll over to see your smiling face,
but it is not there.
It was all a wonderful dream
to hold me until I see you again.
The joy of being a Dreamer.

Denise Christine Plonski

Employment of Hell

There is so much hate and jealousy in the place I work.
There is no talking or laughing 'cause the supervisor's jerk.
The place is like a prison of hell.
There is no one you can trust or tell.
Once you get in, it's hard to get out.
They snag you with the pay that puts you in doubt.
The supervisors are wardens who make their rounds.
Just waiting for someone to step out of bounds.
When they catch you, just keep cool.
Remember where you are and what they can do.
They think they are humans .
When in fact they are really demons.
The place of employment is a living hell.
This is how I see it to tell.

Sherri L. Kellogg

Sonnet to Mara (Minus Shakespeare's 130)

She sings of fire's rhythm to the night
Born unto the night she knows her timing
And at her place of refuge does invite
Walk through forest with the moonlight shining
Upon her beauty and her knowing eyes
Into a state of sensuality
The witchcraft twists a dream unto our lives
I start to question our reality
The time that flows is now just finally ours
By this girl I must concede to never break
The dreamy state cast down from all the stars
Unto her artful spells I must partake
For Venus holds our magic and does let
Our love and music flow immaculate

Matthew Michael Gangi

Becoming One

We were sitting there all alone,
talking, telling each other our dreams, our fears,
and what we want in our future.
It was a beautiful night,
the sky was twinkling with stars,
the air fresh as can be, sitting there on the pier.
The night was ours, it was pure ecstasy.
Two people in love sharing their most intimate thoughts.
Two people becoming one.
We kissed and made passionate love,
but it was more than sex.
It was a commitment to each other.
Two lovers sharing a night,
becoming one!

Brittni Kovach

Advice Untaken

Although friends tried to warn me,
My stubborn ears denied the verity.
I couldn't believe the betrayer be,
He tore my heart with no fragility.
Even though time will generate healing,
My ripped heart is encircled behind bars.

My mother was always good with the dealing,
She opposed drinking and driving any cars.
Hearing preaching in the back of my mind,
I now know attention should be paid.
Why couldn't I have avoided this bind?
There was a much wiser choice to be made.
Now we must learn from these flaws mistaken,
Steered if we heed the advice untaken.

Caitlin Elizabeth Murray

I Remember

I remember the look in your eyes when I first touched your face
I remember the strength in you to me in your warm embrace

I remember hot spiced up chili on a cloudy, cool, rainy day
I remember staying up all night and then sleeping all day

I remember long conversations through modern device
I remember the sweet way you played piano precise

I remember making love with you, actually being one
I remember dreaming with you the very same vision

I remember the 20 times a day you would say "I love you"
I remember calling you crazy and you saying "Crazy about you"

I remember your gifts both great and small
I remember our love, I remember it all

Zerlinda Kay Chavers

Desert Storm

Out in the desert, feeling all alone,
boy how I wish that I were back home.
Receiving lots of hugs and kisses from my twin sister.
Instead of sitting here all hot, and getting blistered.

Here I am fighting for my country.
It seems like it's been unendlessly.
Oh, will I ever live to see my friends and family.

Saddam Hussein is a crazy man,
but I will bring him down for I know I can.

When I feel like I am on my last limb,
I see my twin sister's face, it takes
me to the highest mountain of all
for that's what holds me so I won't fall.

Victoria A. Cole

Sonnet 52

The twisting and anguish
You cause by simply whispering my name,
The hope of you ever coming seems to languish;
Why must you play this cruel, cruel game?
You have stolen my heart,
And you carelessly threaten me with your power;
Then you paint yourself in such an arrogant art,
As you gaze into my eyes, I cower.
What can follow this?
What else of mine can you steal?
Will it be a gentle kiss?
Do you even consider how I feel?
I don't know what else to say,
Just leave me alone, stay away.

Katie Elizabeth Jones

Learning to Let Go

The frustrations of life find a way to
tangle my mind and distract my soul.
I've wandered all over the world—in my mind
and yet I sit in the same old place, day after day.
The challenges force me to scream for help—
out there, yet no one answers back.
I get mad, angry,
and I'm still wandering in the same place. . . .

Today my thoughts bring me to the past of yesterday.
All I know is, I can't go on this way and things must change.
The wonderment I found
from traveling all over the world in my mind
is whispering,
let go, just, let it go.

Renee Mitchell

Nostalgia

Driving slowly past the place I once called home
Memories rush upon me
A tidal wave of tears

Driving slowly past the place I once called home
The movie of my childhood
Making mud pies
Catching fireflies
Playing pretend
Remembrance of times now lost but never forgotten

Driving slowly past the place I once called home
Must leave the past behind
Moving on is what I must do
But I am left still wondering why

Kelly Jeanne Bundy

Ebony

My name is a whispering breeze
Sailing through the night.
My hands are like angel wings always in flight.
My eyes are like big, bright stars shimmering in the sky.
I'm Ebony.
Look at me! See me fly?
My heart holds simple peacefulness,
I'll bless you with a grin.
No matter who you are up here,
You'll always fit in.
Should you ever need me,
Just look among the stars.
I live in the heavens,
And I brighten all that's dark.

Carmella Ebony Roberson

Casey

As I laid in bed I heard my son giggle.
Five minutes later he did not even wiggle.
The fear was sudden that illness was here.
A trip to the doctor brought on the tears.
I asked God to give his pain to me,
Because innocent and blameless was he.
My worst fear of my life was losing my son.
Prayers to my God assured me the fight would be won.
As I sat holding him in the hospital room,
I could see all the lives that were affected with gloom.
Eighteen days later, he was smiling at me.
The meningitis was gone and all could see
That God answered my prayers and gave me back my son,
Because the fight for Casey had finally been won

Kerry L. Lane

The Touch of Your Love

The touch of your love, like a feather on skin,
reminds me of moments of places we've been.

This touch, like a wave, flows over my heart
crashing and reeling, while we are apart.

Your touch has the power of souls
intertwined in passion with only each other in mind.

The touch of your love comes quietly at night
with heavenly dreams fading gently at light.

Like a flower to sunlight, I am drawn to this touch,
craving warmth from your body, your kisses and such.
The touch of your love, a gift without measure,
something received to forever treasure.

Janet M. Couch

Everlasting Love

I sit here thinking of our past,
Wondering the exact reasons why we didn't last.
Did I want too much
From a guy who isn't made of such?
If only you knew
Just how much I miss you.
I'll do whatever it takes,
Like our first date by the lake.
I remember every time we were together so well,
And now without you I'm going through hell.
I want to be with you.
We make the perfect two.
Please look deep down and see,
That this isn't the way it's supposed to be.

Kelly Ann Skilondz

Memories

I hear your voice and it moves my soul,
I feel your touch and it enlightens me,
I smell your cologne and it fills me,
What do I do without you,
Oh, you bring me strength,
You bring me hope,
And I'll never ever let you go,
So smile those smiles,
And cry those tears,
Remember you were there throughout the years,
I'm still here fighting the war,
I'll be up there soon to help you more,
So fasten your seat belt 'cause I'm coming up there ,
So no more tears unless I'm there!

Lauren Elizabeth Raft

God's Love

Today as I knelt in prayer,
To place on God my every care.
I thanked Him for His great love,
And for His blessings from above.
I thanked Him for His precious Son,
He gave us hope when there was none.
I could feel His presence there,
It was His love that lifted my despair.
Tears of joy ran down my face,
I'm filled with peace by His saving grace
Thank you God for your love so true,
I give my heart and soul to you.
You are as close as a whispered prayer,
Yes I know you are always there.

Virginia Ruth Thornton

Journey through Life

Man has his unseen friend, like a twin,
All that he has, was, or ever will be.
Places they can go and live again,
Through thick or thin, no matter the degree.
Always there, like an eagle's wings,
A bond that can never be broken.
You two, a pair of crimson kings;
You never stray, no matter what's spoken.
When it's all over and you start to decay,
You remember summers shared and summers lost.
You remember how the wind made the water spray,
But still you never cared how much it cost.
While your skin sheds and starts to spread,
Now it's all over, and you're glad you're dead.

Nathan Alan Palmer

All Summer in a Day

I hear the dogs yelping as I sit and sleep.
For today is the day for summer and to catch up on sleep.
We have been let out of prison
and we have a few months of freedom,
before we are caught and put back behind doors.

We run, jump, and play with our voices ringing with laughter.
Our break is now coming to a close
and we feel like a disaster.
We wish summer could last a whole lot longer.

We now walk back with our faces full of fear and dread.
Will I get the witch or the one that makes me laugh?
It usually turns out swell, but for now we look back
and think how summer only felt like a day.

Jennifer Marie Cox

Dream or Reality

Dreams—are they real? Do they really come true?
Are you real? Or are you another unrealistic dream, too?
Are you really beside me? In real arms do I weep?
Or are you only here when I close my eyes and sleep?
It's so hard to tell—is it a dream or is it reality . . .
Will I awaken in an empty room with only me?
In a vision . . . on the beach, walking hand-in-hand,
Together we lay in the peachy sand.
Watching the water . . . which is so deeply blue,
You look into my eyes and say "I love you."
Together we share a chocolate ice cream
And listen to the sound of the running stream.
So, again, I ask myself if you are really here,
Or will I wake up to a room with nobody there?

Danyah Levia Young

Heaven through Hell

On my way to Heaven,
I've had to travel through the pits of Hell.
I pity all those who still live in that house.
Yet in some way, I pity Satan himself.
He's so cold, so frozen from the outside world,
An ex-socialite, if you will.
The exact opposite of love, feeling, and remorse;
So abrasive, so self-centered.
Hard as a stone, cold as ice; killing.
Damaging to one's social life.
But in the end, I rose victoriously
From the chains of Hell into the bright light of love,
And the feeling of being wanted,
Thus leaving Satan to Hell's destiny.

Bradlee S. Conner

Breath of Fresh Air

The scent of passion fills the air.
You take it in, but do you dare?
Your mind starts drifting through wonderful places
The past is gone and so are the faces.
Thrills and wonders engulf your being.
Do you believe what you're really seeing?
I dive into your eyes of crystal blue
The sun's reflection an awesome hue.
I thought these feelings were gone forever
Sent off to a place of never-never.
You've added light to a dimming soul
And brought me life, to make me whole.
I will move gently, easy and true,

Because the best thing in life is knowing you!

Bruce Todd LeGrande

Just Be

Foggy mystical lakes and crisp mountain air
Evokes the dreamer in me. I want to be there.
The water glistens and sparkles like glass in motion.
Why am I so drawn there? Always searching for a solution.
A giant mirror in effect reflecting the trees and the sky.
Connect now with the energy of the powerful eagles as they dive.
The waves incessantly lapping against the boats and the shore.
Their power and the energy are within me. I want to know more.
What shall I dream about? What shall I do now?
The tree of life now before me; adventures call out, "How?"
The path now the past and new crossroads are before me.
What or whom shall I choose? Only to adore thee.
Lovely experiences of today; awesome tomorrows we see.
Joyous adventures which I choose, only to just be.

Tommye Henderson

Always for You

I will be your soul mate
forever and ever
to cherish for as long as we live
be by your side at the time of need.

I will love you
as much as I can
kiss you when you are down
and be your lover as long as you are to me.

You mean more to me than life itself
I will take your tears away when they come
I will come for you when in trouble
I will risk my life
Always for you.

Eric Charles Green

Sacrifice

Happy is he who never felt loss.
What is loss?
To no longer cherish another,
To be denied . . .
Is love what makes you alive?
Then I have always been dead.
Does life have no meaning without someone to love?
Love is only for the weak;
Those, who are stricken with love will feel the pain,
Those, who are strong have callused themselves,
Realized the repercussions.
An open heart will be filled with torment.
The strong are oblique,
We have not the need for tears.

Joshua J. Crain

Tiger, Stranger

In the grass a stranger lurks, dark and bright.
Loud roar and humble purr, these are his voice,
Lonesome by design not by a made choice,
The passion in him burns, fire in the night.
Filled with words that speak out about the plight
Of wind and storm against the steady noise
Of countless tiny wars, he keeps his poise,
And with aid of stars and moon, takes flight.
OH! Stranger, lurking lonesome, dark, and bright,
Speak out loudly, and dissipate the fear
Of ignorance, and the sanguine stain it leaves.
OH! Tiger, burning fire of the night,
Proclaimer of birth and of dying tear,
Savor life once, before its flavor leaves.

Charles Edward Jolliffe

One Summer's Eve

The sun descends and zephyrs conceive;
a gentle curiosity one pure summer's eve.

Within such grayness, shadows may deceive,
but colors invade this blind summer's eve.

Her free spirit plays, so he cannot grieve;
his spirit follows hers this free summer's eve.

One lasting touch, your lips mine receive;
the perfect kiss one perfect summer's eve.

Eyes are opened and hearts believe
that love is found this sweet summer's eve.

The moon descends and zephyrs leave;
a beautiful beginning one ended summer's eve.

Alisha Rae Blanton

New Light

His slow and tender kisses
Planted in the hollow of my collar
His warm and gentle hands
Around my waist
I am lost with him forever

No longer do I see sorrow
Loneliness, no longer my friend
He bathes me with his love
Never feeling so pure

As when the richness of the yellows and reds
Change slowly to violets and blues
And still we sit alone
I am lost with him forever

Jonay Tanisha Santoro

Relax

Relax, that's what I have to do
When dancing close to you.
I find there's more than dancing on my mind,
Because you are so divine.
Relax, I've got to stay in line,
Until your love is mine.
Relax, until the dance is through,
For I enjoy being this close to you.
As my temperature goes higher,
I begin to thrill and tremble with desire.
I part my lips to take your kiss of fire,
Oh, stop me please, before I start to cry.
Relax, that's what I have to do
When I'm dancing close to you.

William A. Banks Jr.

Psalm 151

Treat me like you do, more than ever now.
Who, what, when, where, why, and how?

I was committed more, more than ever before.
Your words of wisdom beat down on the shore.

Heaven's harness holds me near;
Such a loud voice, so much to fear.

Gracious, giving, loving; yet pain.
I wash my hands, yet there's still a stain.

I try not to stumble, but I still fall.
Someone is screaming; don't answer the call.

You do not want to hear what will be said,
As you're laid down in your eternal bed.

John Fredrick Clark

Untitled

I listen to the story that Rosie told well,

Of a walk through her own personal hell.

"Sixteen years" she said, "since I drank my last drink.
Today is one more behind me and tomorrow isn't yet.
I'm sorry for the yesterdays, for I wasted each one,
I didn't like who I was but I like who I've become.
There's no turning back the pages, only those left I can right."

She slowly walked away and I saw all her regrets.
So I softly bowed my head for Rosie's days left,
then I whispered, "May God travel with you,

May you find the inner strength,
and may you always have one more day of peace."

Barbara Carlene McDuffie

I Am

I am but one:

one, who lives and dies the next day
one, who forgets to laugh when I pray
one, who suffers, when the day is all through
and one, who wishes the sky was still blue

one, who has patience with everyone but me
one, who longs for my spirit to be free
one, who thinks I'm a caboose and I can
one, who thinks that I can't and I'm damned

one, who rejoices when the day is anew
one, who respects the Old Lady with the broom
one, who can't think of anything to say
one, who believes that my life starts today

Douglas E. Crane

A Good Friend

You are an angel in disguise
At least in each of our own eyes.

You're always there through good and bad
No matter if it is happy or it is sad.

It could be a wedding or a funeral too
We just turn around and we'll always see you!

I hope you know how much this does mean
To know that on your shoulder we can always lean.

I hope in the future we can do the same
Whenever you need us just call our name.

Remember this and at life's end
You'll always be our good, good friend!

Maxine M. Dalland

You

I saw the terror and the tears,
I feel your sorrow, I know your fears.
This life will bleed all that you earn,
With it you take only what you learn.
And what you learn may be a lie—
Instead of laughing, you have to cry.
In days like these, there is no rest;
Everything you're told you second guess.
How can trust become what's needed?
You won't listen, I begged and pleaded.
Forget the story you were told,
Look to the bright side and grab a'hold.
Slipping away, how should I feel,
When I realize too late this world is real?

Ben Bernard Johnson

Life

We rush through life, then at end, we grieve
Sorrows overcomes us as the end we see
No more tomorrow will there be
As we say good-bye to life and leave.
How we search to be immortal and find
That time is not in our hands alone,
But instead it's placed in God's, our way to be shown.
Only one life can we live, for each day is timed,
But there must be a way
Somehow I know it's there to be found
Yet time and again, it's overlooked when searched around
Then a voice spoke to me and said one day,
Through our lives memories we attain,
And with our memories, our lives forever remain.

Heather Amanda Lisenby

Catharsis

Sometimes I just want to stick my head
Out the window of my stuffy sixth-floor apartment
And scream at the top of my lungs,
"Please, just shut up!"
Over and over and over again until
It echoes—bounces
(just shut up!)
Off of buildings through all five boroughs
(shut up!)
And everyone stops and looks up
(up!)
And I pull my head back inside and pack my bags and leave—
But I can't do that.
I still have 11 months left on my lease.

Kevin M. Lappin

Fishing with W. B. Yeats

We found the oxbow quiet. Rod and reel
at our sides, our shadows followed tall behind.
The sun hesitated at the horizon,
impatient of our arrival. Far off,

the reeds sang of gods. I sat calm and still,
watching the skillfully worn hands and the
downturn of the old man's wrist with the hope
that a fish might rise. The red hat shadowed

his freckled face and his eyes, which shimmered
still as the line went taut and the surface
of the ink water rippled where a fish
would soon emerge to our imaginations.

I have never since found dawn as cold and passionate.

Zach L. Duffy

Long Awaited Moment

She lay in lake shallows,
drifting glances at the stars
like holes poked in the universe's flesh,
bleeding streams of light onto the Earth.
Her head rested on lake slime,
her face above the water,
and minnows brushed across her arms, her stomach,
and tickled at her shins.
She watched silent winds comb Cypress branches
or wrinkle the surface of the lake
as they sucked its warmth,
stored from the faded summer sun.
And the water rippled up her body
and lapped against her ears.

Benjamin Holliday Wardell

GOD Smiles

Look at the trees swaying at me,
Look at the stars twinkling afar,
Look at the ocean with all its motion,
Look at the ground life stirring all around,
Look at the mother giving birth to another,
Look at the moon shining so bright into the night,
Look at me underneath this tree;
GOD is surely smiling at me.

Elana Carol Henderson

Dedicated to My Best Friend Who Died

On August 16th, 2000, we lost a great friend,
We never expected that this would be the end.
I still remember all the things that we've done.
But here we go one last time to say you have WON!
We all remember the times that we have spent knowing you.
But now with you being gone we are experiencing something new.
We loved you dearly with all of our hearts,
And we never thought that you would go so soon.
We have gone through so much pain but your heart will always stay,
But we never got the chance to say, "Remember us this way."

Tiffany Renee Reed

Japanese Signs

I watch
as you scribble Japanese signs
on paper and doodle in your mind.
Your lip is bitten, held tight
by dead English poets and your grocery list.
You glance up
and ponder the meaning.
Your eyes caress,
as you stare into memories
of a life you once had.

Your freckles dance when you smile—
I shatter from the glow.
A soft layer exposed in conversation—
you wish your soul were harder.

We're just theory before reality
that will never be.

David Michael Taylor

Shape-Shifting

For Hope
Otherworldly talk of spirits and shamans always turns
To shape-shifting. And I wonder,
How is it man
Can shift shapes?
Woman
Is the quintessential shape-
Shifter. Shifting, morphing,
Swelling for 280 days into
Two in one body,
Until time stops, stands
Still,
As the heavens roll
Earth's core down around
Itself and
Squeeze
One from two.
Woman shaped, shifted, transformed
Into God,
Birthing life itself,
Wet and fresh and whole.

Heather McCarron Allard

Gone, but Not Forgotten

Gone, but not forgotten, with you he'll always be
Kept forever in your heart, a treasured memory
Taken from the family; the circle incomplete
A void left in your world; your spirit in defeat
How will you go on? How will you survive?
Remember that although he's gone, you are still alive
He knows that you must go on; you have to live your life
Getting past the sorrow, working through the strife
To that end I offer you a helpful, caring ear
A hand to hold in yours, a shoulder for your tears
The wound to your soul I cannot heal, nor will I even try
Often times we need to be sad, often times to cry
And when those times are over, when those times are done
Then comes the time to remember the laughter and the fun
Remember his loving manner; remember his caring way
Remember the way he held you and kept your fears at bay
Remember him as your father and keep him in your heart
For of the person you've become he surely is a part
As of now, he is God's creature, an angel in Heaven above
Gone, but not forgotten, he continues to give you love

Andrew Ramirez

And When the Wind Begins to Blow

When the wind begins to blow across my body,
skin, and throat
and when the rain begins to fall gently
upon my face,
I stand in wonder thinking of that perfect
time and place
of when the wind brought us together,
in that wonderful summer weather.
And the rain it felt so cool to drench my skin
standing there with you.
For the wind and rain are who we are,
while standing as an evening star.
The sun shall show the future to me,
for I know we are meant to be.
So come on, wind, begin to blow,
take me to the place I want to go.
Clear my mind, pick up my thoughts,
take the agony along.
Come on, rain, wash over me, cleanse me,
so that I may be.

Tammy May Parsons

Climbing the Stairs of Prayers

Sometimes happy
Sometimes sad and blue
Sometimes troubled and confused
Sometimes just me
Saying my prayers tonight, under the moonlight
And the starry night—behold! What a beautiful sight!
I'm climbing the stairs of prayers tonight
I'm walking up by Jesus's starlight
I have climbed these stairs of prayers before,
Left my troubles at Jesus's door
Some big, some small, some prayers answered,
Some prayers not at all
As I climb these stairs of prayers, Jesus, tonight I pray
"Would you please help me to understand me?"
I'll try to listen carefully when you answer me
Sometimes happy
Sometimes sad and blue
Sometimes troubled and confused
Sometimes just me tonight in prayers I'm asking Jesus
"Would you please help me to understand me?"

Sylvia Loucks

The Gift

Christmas, Christmas,
The most wonderful time of the year,
With gifts, and presents, and trees
All full of cheer!
Sure, the trees are lit brightly,
And the gifts make you want to shout,
But is that what Christmas
Is really all about?
Do you know why we get presents
On Christmas day?
You probably don't know,
So I'll tell you if I may.
Long, long ago, God sent Jesus to Earth
To be born in a manger..
That gift would grow up and live
In a world full of non-Christian strangers.
He did that and much more, just because He loves us.
So remember this, oh, you must!
When you open your presents on Christmas Day,
Don't forget they represent Jesus in a special way.

Kaycee Elizabeth Garringer

The Daddy I Loved (But Never Knew)

I loved you, Daddy,
I hope you see;
When I could see you, I was scared,
I hadn't seen you since I was three.
I was afraid you'd be disappointed in how I
Had turned out,
But I always loved you, Daddy.
Now when I'm ready to see you,
You're not here anymore,
You said good-bye.
The Daddy I loved, I didn't know,
But when I heard what happened, it hurt.
They told me you put a gun to your head and
Said good-bye,
But they didn't tell me if you were cremated
Or buried in the dirt.
Now you're in Heaven
Watching me from above;
I just wanted you to know,
You're the Daddy I loved!

Stephanie Renée Beck

Whimsical Climbs

Climbing the wintering trees
I wonder, who is she
Shooting for the sky, reaching
Slipping on the trials of life
Swiping my net of desire
Missing, but am not dissuaded
Spotting the glistening hope, I strive
In sight is a beauty unmatched by the dawn of spring
Pure, as the silhouette of a morning's shadow
Casting strength, compassion on the land
Sounds a note, a reason, a calling
A rare vision unmatched by serenity
I continue on my quest
Sudden, as a whispered breeze
Falls a shining ladder of purpose
The trials of time beaten, I climb
And she sits, like a diamond princess
My goals and wishes realized, wondrous
To feel her soft touch, just now
Fulfillment, feeling, unguarded love on high

Nicholas Lawrence Moser

Let Peace Reign—
Are We Our Brother's Keeper or Usurper?

Let there be peace on increase
Let human hatred cease
Let there be love, which never decrease
And man to man brothers be
Though difference of color race and creed
That each country helps to let peace breed.

Build for progress our nations exaltation
Build like ants in united consolidation,
And selflessness be a part of the foundation;
Condemn outrageousness and provocation,
Let the weapons of mass destruction their silence keep,
And the "Spirit of God," we all reap.

Materials and power spoil the show
As some think it the better way to go;
Let togetherness disregarding strength
Have peace and love at full length;
Let quality of life be real
And substantial for the benefit of all to reveal.

Cyril L. Goffe

Do You Want Me?

Please tell me why because I need to understand.
Why look for another love when you could be my man?
I spend so much time with you on my mind.
I wonder if I could be your miracle?
How could you throw a miracle away
Knowing nothing could ever take its place?
All we have to do is treat each other right
And give each other a little space.
I fight the urge of picking up the phone to see if you're okay.
I'd rather be with you than anyone else at any time or place.
When I'm with you I can't wait another minute.
I'll love you all season knowing love has no limit.
Don't go! I'll do what I have to do to make you come back to me.
I need a gentleman, a man with sensitivity.
Baby, I'm ready to give you a piece of my love.
I'll always defend you; how can you hurt the one you love?
I just want to hold you and kiss you looking into your eyes.
Giving you a passionate chill that rushes up your spine.
Come to me here and now; let's not wait for tomorrow.
Share your mind and time with me and let love follow.

Mollie Hibbler

The Sky and the Sea

I am the sky and you are the sea.
Night and day we're a world away
I watch you as you watch me
You seem so near some may say
The birds fly so high and free with me
While the whales swim free to your depths
The clouds give life to my heights
But what makes you so beautiful?
Darkness meets light at the break of dawn
Sun and rain kiss with a rainbow
Where will our elements meet
The distance is so infinite
I can see no walls in between
Only horizon from within
Though we are in parallel
Feels like we're always together
I am the sky and you are the sea
The sky of hopes and the sea of dreams
If time is the road to get to you
Then I shall wait like unweary stream

Jason Velasquez and Lucille Tuason

I Am Woman

I am woman, hear me roar.
I am one you won't ignore.
My voice will echo deep in your ear
And make you think again with fear.
Because I will not be used,
Nor the one to be abused.
If duty calls, I will fight
For everything with all my might.
I am one of a kind.
I voice my opinion and speak my mind.
I can do all things you won't believe.
With God, I can achieve.
When I speak, I will be heard.
Listen to each sentence and every word.
For every woman, I will stand tall,
And be the voice for all.
I am strong, brave, courageous, and proud.
I am smart, bold, beautiful, and loud.
I am woman, hear me roar.
I am one you won't ignore.

Faith Butts

Over the Rainbow

A childhood summer playing Rainbow Brite with my cousins
We spent that summer playing in Grandma's basement.
Every day we traveled over the rainbow
To an invisible world that only we could see.
When Andy would come, we let him in.
He thought we were stupid,
He said we were dumb.
Then Murky killed Reb Butler and we went as normal.
I had so much fun that summer,
Even though they said I was too old.
You had so much fun that summer,
Even though you were too young.
You didn't understand anything I told you,
All the stories and ideas.
I didn't understand anything you told me,
All your protests and excuses.
We were in two different worlds,
But we had so much fun that summer playing in Grandma's
basement.
In the world of colors and gloom.
Over the rainbow lies our world, the world of Rainbow Brite.

Sandra Tuttle

Darkness Abode

I wander forever within the dark
Time is but a word;
I am lost with no place to turn,
I am but a little bird.
Surrounded by perpetual twilight,
I search and search and search;
Searching for a symbol of hope,
Searching for the Earth.
Yet I do not find what I am searching for
Or any hope at all,
I find but constant darkness
Surrounded by endless wall.
I have no will left to use
Or any strength to see,
I am weak and tired and useless now,
I have not even a pint of glee.
So I stand and wait in sorrow,
Until the time has come
For me to wake from this dream
And find where I am from.

Warren Wong

Concession

Admirable intention in public relations,
Smart officials in seaman nations,
Especially discharged to generalizations,
Are marshalled imputed insinuations,
Started, to rock the very foundations,
Demanding internal investigations,
Likely a loss to bar generations.
('Cause half the cost of looking lost,
Amounted on the whole,
Will find the box at Pentecost,
A quarter bit and sold).
But if it's lent and not present, hold ajar a door,
Spring airs admit much room to vent, than justifying more.
So to feat ahead my right left eye,
Though management, blew dusk red sky,
And tried appointed to commit background,
Too pride recorded, too stick rewound,
No slide applied could hide that sound,
That die avoided to mess around,
"I'm bound to a party."

Geoffrey Mitchell

Why Do Angels Cry?

I see tears fall from your face:
What makes an angel like you cry?
I hate seeing an angel as beautiful as you cry.
In all of this human race,
I have never seen a more beautiful face.
But to see tears of sadness fall from your face—
It pains me to see you cry in this place.
The place in my heart you make as bright as a summer day,
But when I see your tears that place is dark
Like the midnight sky with not a single star.
I just hope that those tears don't leave an emotion scar
I hope later down the road we might have a spark
Because I will not let your tears fall
From an Angel as beautiful as you
There is no way I would ever make you blue
Because the beauty I see in you is mightier than all
There is no reason for Angel's tears to fall
If I had an Angel as beautiful as you
She would never have a reason to be blue
Why do Angels cry?

Dustin Tolliver

True Friendship

What is true friendship to me
It is sacrificing my everything
My heart, my soul, all of me
To give to that someone who is suffering.

I've only had a few friends so far
But I deeply thank them all
I cannot visit, because I haven't a car
But I can go make a phone call

My dear friends, I will never forget you
Even though we are miles apart
You have kept me from feeling blue
And I've placed you in a special part of my heart

The memories of you will last forever
I will never forget what you did for me
You stood by my side and left me never
You saved my life and set me free

Yes, you have been the world to me
Let me be the same for thee

Mike Burnside

Are You My Friend?

When first I stumbled along the path
falling as I feared I'd reached my end,
your gentle kind way of lifting me
begged the question, "Are you my friend?"
Adversity was my companion.
The weight of its load caused me to bend.
You stood by me shouldering the weight.
I asked in wonder, "Are you my friend?"
I wandered into a fearful place
and an exit did not itself lend.
Suddenly, you took me to safety.
Gratefully I asked, "Are you my friend?"
Your face had many shapes and colors
that disguised the message which you send.
Thus, it clouded my understanding
causing me to ask, "Are you my friend?"
Finally, I've come to understand
and knowledge aids my thoughts to amend.
Though you come in varied disguises,
Humanity, you're my friend.

Paul Arnett

The Greatest Play

Open chords relent sounds to stray
their nervous echoes
haunt this hall
been haunting me for much too long
The solemn drift
of wasting soldiers
their armor knows no rest
pray to keep their rusted medallions
plead to intermission give
nothing less a more trivial part of play
So as the silken drapes collapse
sick and marvelled applauding stands
War's casualty blinds and paves
another prisoner of the play
walking off this stage to grave
So come and watch us rave
It reels you mad and gay
When we are deity's dolls with hearts
and all the world their stage
(please, no more encore . . . encore . . .)

Hannah J. Koh

The Dreamers

Total strangers, or so it seems
Yet a connection exists,
neither can deny
Kindred souls they seem to be
each dreaming of another day.
He dreams of a past, she of a future.
She knows where he's at,
she's been there too.
He needs time, she'll patiently wait.
She longs for his arms to hold her tight
to take her through the long, dark night.
Yet he's so far away, his words her only
comfort until the morning light.
She tries do deny her feelings,
to bury them deep inside.
She feels his confusion, nothing makes sense.
She'll be his friend, and share his pain.
How can they be so close,
yet be so far apart?
Will their dreams ever be the same?

Patricia Lynn Skinner

Prepared

There comes a time when you least expect it
You're faced with sudden change
Though unprepared you move along
Feelings must rearrange
You may take a long walk by the ocean
Breathe some fresh air, while feeling the sun
Smile kindly at each passing stranger
Admiring all of the work God has done
Then all of the sudden you realize
Clear as the waves on the breakers ahead
God knew of these changes long ago
As well as the tears we would shed
His gentleness lives within each of us
He forgives us for every mistake
Only asking of us to believe
Extending loving hands for us to take
So knowing this—what does it tell you
All answers are right in your heart
Not unprepared we move along
Prepared by him right from the start

    Cherie Ann Hoagland

World of Silence

Let me be free from this unknown silence.
Let me be free from all this violence.
Let me go; let me run.
Let me cry; let me burn.
All the patience I have within me,
all the endurance I have left,
is starting to fade away
like the light of a setting sun.
Let me be the way I am.
Let me be the way I stand.
Please, let me stay within me,
please let me shun.
Let me be free from this unbearable stress;
let me be away from all this mess.
Let me stay in my own world of fantasy;
let me stay in my own world of fallacy.
Let it be the way it is;
let it be the way it exists.
Let it stay; let it rule.
Let it be my own world of silence.

    Zehra Kazilbash

Airborne

Nikki at nineteen months

She comes on a cloud like a bird
chipper
light enough to fly
the memory of song and rhyme in her throat
of Mother Goose wandering
over landscapes of jungle and farm.

She comes on a whirl of joy
like a celebrant feasting on colors
numbers
shapes
tasting pages of paper
and earth.

She comes on a dream
like a star twinkling
like the shifting of wind on wings
looping
spinning
nesting.

    Margaret Elizabeth Irvin

The Missing Person

Sittin' in my room thinking of you
Makes me want to cry
But when I'm around you
I'm breathless
I miss you holding me in your arms
I miss you when you breathe in my ears
I wish I was still with you,
Because I hate not hearing your voice
I love hearing your heartbeat,
I just wish I could hear more
I always think of the time when we were together
And I always wonder why you left me
I wish I could of got one chance
To fall asleep with you next to me in your arms
I miss hearing you play your guitar
But I wish I could still hear it
I miss kissing you every day
But I don't get that chance anymore
I wish I knew why you broke up with me
Because I thought you cared about me

    Jennifer Kelso

Winter Weather

In winter, (my) moods soar and dive,
    As weather affects disposition's wiles.
With intermittent rain and snow,
    Winter can't make up its mind, although
Like any matter, it changes its state
    From heavy drops to lightest flake.
Rain falls in heavy lines,
    While snow drifts without reason or rhyme.
Directions change until it seems
    That snow falls in whirlwind streams.
Snow so thick, it obliterates
    The ground, some trees, and school yard gates.
Even smoke, that from chimneys swirled
    Is dissipated in a snowflaked world.
From finest powder to largest flakes,
    It blows and drifts, as it makes
Its way from snow clouds, heavy there
    To a moving mist all through the air.
So let it fall and magnify
    The beauty of a winter's sky.

    Dolly Johnston Crossley

Happy Mother's Day

There was this boy, who loved girl this girl;
She loved him, like he was her world.
They loved each other with all their heart,
But her mother wanted to keep them apart.
She never wanted her daughter to have anyone else,
She wanted her daughter to be by herself.
So, she tried everything to break the two,
But the boyfriend said, "There was nothing she could do."
He told the girl that he would not leave,
And in him she could believe.
Months passed and he held on strong,
But his strength soon faded and was gone.
The girlfriend cried asking "Why must you go away?"
He told her, "I've tried my best, but I just cannot stay."
The girl was hurt, heart broken by the two.
She hurt so bad she didn't know what to do.
But in July of that year, her pain would be put away.
Because that was the month of her mother's wedding day.
And when the preacher asked, "Why these two should not be wed?"
The girl stood up and shot herself in the head.

    William Moreland Jr.

A Father's Love

From little steps to little hugs,
that's a fathers love.
From all the questions that you ask,
it seems to come from above.
Through each year I hold you near
in hopes you will always be mine.
Through the thick and thin of time,
I know you will be just fine.
For today I saw the little girl
grow up into a beautiful woman.
For today I am a humble old man,
who was among the stars of heaven.
This is just a father's love
from a dad to his daughter.
As I walk proudly with you down the aisle,
and let another man love you at the alter;
I will always love you, no matter where you
go or what the cost,
because today I shed just one tear for the
little girl I lost.

Wayne Errickson

My Family

Now I am fourteen.
And I am a high school student.
The time when I was a little baby
Has slipped away like an arrow.
"Don't come to my room!"
I often shout.
I hate when my family
Comes into my room.
I don't know why, just don't like . . .
"You are not perfect either,"
I often retort to my parents.
I know it isn't a good thing, but
I hate when my parents teach me,
As if they know all things about me.
Some people say,
"It's your age!" however,
Even though I easily get angry at my family
And my ego and thought grow,
My mind will never change
That I love my family.

Jangwoo Kim

My Many Lives

I seem to have had several lives;
And each, though gone, still survives.
I see the child, awkward, shy;
And all those scenes go passing by!
They haunt me with such keen precision,
Filling heart, as much as vision.
I only just recall, and then
I am that little girl again.
That daughter, sister, student, friend;
A new me starts where old ones end.
Young wife, new mother, new time, new place;
Life rushes by at rapid pace.
At every turn, as in a fable,
Each life brings a brand new label.
Single mom, professional,
They join the long processional.
In memory of my pasts gone by,
I smile, and then I heave a sigh.
Retiree, Grandma, each new day
Brings a brand new life my way.

Annette R. Smith

Shining Star

As in yesterday
You're still far away
Running around
all over town
Saying you need me.
You're just a friend
You've always been there through thick and thin
And that's the way that it goes
And that's what everybody knows
Is that the way that you want it to be?
You've been around
You've been up and you've been down
And I'm just a little girl
From a different world
Could you take me that far
Will you be mine
A different day and a different time
It's not so hard to try
Once you realize
You're still my shining star!

Carey Martin

Waiting

Paralyzed from waist to toes, from toes to waist,
as I sit,
wait,
watch,
for that someone to come for me.
Waiting, as the bloody tears just drip from my body.
Waiting
patiently
for someone special.
I sit here as the tears just drip off from my eyes
and beyond my
cheeks.
From my cheeks to my heart,
there is where my tears
must
part.
Watching the people go by and stare,
I just wish someone
was
there.

Rachel Rebecca Jackson

The Love I Can't Feel

To Melissa Roskowski, my true love
To breathe your hair
And kiss your mouth
To hold your hand
Then living an eternity without
To press my hand against your face
And say I'm in love with you
A feeling my kind cannot experience
I'm the only one that believe it's true
I miss you, now that you're gone
And still I will not leave
You still are everything
You were the greatest thing in life to me
I know you can't see me, but I'm there
I've got my arm around you to breathe my air
And when you cry your tears from your eyes
I feel your pain at its peak
When you say never to see you again
I disappear and can't experience the pain
I know you want me to show myself again

Derek Daisey

Stolen Innocence

My years of childhood innocence are gone
But the troubled child deep within goes on
A life of nightmares, both night and day
Triggered just by what someone might say
A kind deed or gentle touch
Doesn't seem like so much
To make a person feel this way
But for me I must keep them at bay
For the hurt I carry deep inside
Comes from knowing I live with his lie
Not in word, so much as in his deed
For the darkness that hurts me is like a growing weed
No matter how good or how nice
A heart full of dark lies turns you to ice
And only the one drug into their fixation
Can understand the guilt and self-incrimination
To have someone of your own flesh and blood
Touch and use you . . . makes you feel like crud
Only the lost little girl, who could love and admire
The man who continually hurt her, she once called father

MaryAnn DeCarlo

This Is Not Good-Bye

I came in to say good-bye this morning, Mom,
but you were already gone.
I looked for you out the window,
to the end of the driveway and beyond.
Now I'm making you a card in class today, Mom,
as I sit alone at my desk.
The silence is broken at the sound of a blast
and I am moved by a bullet in my chest.
Never did I think today would be my last.
Now I'm just lying here staring,
as my blood continues streaming.
All noise is muffled now,
even frantic screaming
and distant sirens blaring.
I am still lying here; Mommy, hold me.
Hold me please.
Now I know it's time for me to die,
but, Mommy, please don't cry.
We'll see each other again someday,
so this is not good-bye.

Adam James Hedglin

Math Starvation

Starved of loneliness, sitting in a dark dusky gray room,
Feeling angry, sad
But yet feeling quite hungry—
Hungry for attention,
Listening and still listening
But all I can hear is silence,
Only a gentle whisper of a hum,
In my head is little voices laughing,
Making me feel horrible.
All I can smell is my own dripping sweat,
All I could see is the heat waves of my body.
I feel my pencil in my hand,
Grabbing it with stress,
And suddenly I find it all chewed up,
Then I gaze at it,
And thought it was a twig.
Sitting in a dark room completely solo,
Thinking hard about the math problem set before me.
Then I was saved by my teacher.
She said, "Alexis, detention!" You can finish this tomorrow.

Alexis James Sotelo

The Forest of Youth

Ye who wanders through the Earth,
Dine to cheer and drink to mirth,
Content you are with a den in the ground,
Not troubling humans with the softest sound.
But small one I wish to see you today,
Don't hide your festive forgotten way,
I'm shivering old struck with the chill,
Others before me have taken to ill.
I'll freeze in this forest dim and cold,
Dancing shadows under a moon so old,
Where are you oh dear little tiny one,
Hear my cries for age has won.
Then it rained one fairy dust drop,
And I was young in an elven cave shop,
Old weathered skin melted far away,
Now I was a child destined to play.
Those wee folk gave me the greatest gift of all,
The gift to be young and the gift to be small,
They saved me from death that very cold night,
May I always see elves and shine in their light.

Bonnie Jean Gutsch

The Morning Commute

Rushing to get there on time
To find a parking space that I can call mine
I race from the car to the light rail stop
And as I get my ticket, I smile at the cop
All that rushing, now to wait
Waiting for the light rail to reach the gate
I hear it whistle as it moves down the rails
Time to get on when the bell wails
The train glides smoothly around the curve
Then it wobbles and begins to swerve
Over the bay and into the city
Camden Yards always looks so pretty
Next stop—Convention Center
Most get off and few enter
Rushing to cross the street
The red light we have to beat
The city is bustling
And the commuters are hustling
All to start another day
All trying to make that elusive city pay

Sharon Kellogg

Untitled

The blank white canvas . . .
First drop of color . . .
A new dream . . .
A new meaning emerges . . .
Strokes through time create a new emergent
With acquired qualities to turn real.
A haze descends
I'm unable to read through
New qualities get etched on it.
With only remnants of the past visible,
Patterns generate . . .
Though I hardly stroke the canvas.
I'm left with the generated emergent . . .
An emergent which leads me
which absorbs me
I become part of it . . .
Now trying to add my own strokes to this pattern,
To recreate . . .
To add a touch of my own . . .
To make it mine.

Arthi Amaran

Broken

Love—so grand and precious.
Once you have captured it, you try to cage it.
You put all your strength into it to keep it.
But as time goes by, you begin to neglect it.
Take it for granted.
Then you lose it.
Not sure when it exactly left.
When you stopped trying.
This fragile thing
Left broken on the floor.
Stomped on.
The tiny pieces scattered on the floor like a broken glass.
You try so delicately to pick up every shattered piece.
No matter how hard you try to glue it back.
There is always a few fragments left behind.
You treasure this glued-back piece of glass.
But it's never the same.
The cracks and missing fragments only
remind you of what you did.
You dropped it.

Rebecca Faucher

Where Has She Gone?

I still have a daughter, I guess?
She is the one who made this big mess!
I lost her 'bout a week ago
under clothes and junk, I'm not sure I know.
There's crumbs and dishes and leftover pizza,
an old love letter that says let me kiss ya!
I opened the closet, now I'm under a heap
of books, and shoes, and a stuffed parakeet!
I should hang a sign that says condemned . . .
and a warning before someone else walks in.
There's blankets and covers and a little blue tee
all on the bed where normally her body would be . . .
I stepped on an earring and tripped over a hanger,
now I'm searching for a rope in which to dangle her!
There's tons of makeup in all colors and shades
and a curling iron in her roller blades.
There's all kinds of trinkets on top of her dresser,
I don't think this room could get any messier!
She's my daughter, and I do love her so . . .
but still I am left wondering, just where did she go!

Terri Harrison

Side by Side

Side by side we share the sky,
And light the night just you and I.
We share our secrets, we share our fears,
We show joy with laughter and woe with tears.
You're always there for me and I for you,
No matter what our bond holds true.
Always together we balance out,
A perfect match, I have no doubt.
You stole my heart and set it free,
And opened my eyes to help me see.
You've touched my soul and forthwith I say,
"Lord keep us close," for this I pray.
So here we are, a pair of stars,
Side by side, the night is ours.
Together we stand, bright, strong and tall,
Holding on so one won't fall.
And if one does, then together we go,
To streak the sky with a shimmering glow.
So sad it is, we both may die,
But side by side, true friends shall lie.

Jubilee Ann Paige

I Find Comfort

You are my bright shining star
that lights up my world,
the light that has not grown dim,
but increased as each day unfurls.
I am always so glad
when you are here;
the time we share
I hold so dear.
We talk of each day's plans,
discuss the work, relive the fun;
you always encourage and cheer
my hopes and dreams that are to come.
I don't know how you do it,
but you always make me smile;
no matter what my mood,
you have me smiling in a while.
Our friendship is like the bright shining sun;
I feel the warmth that radiates from it:
no cloud will dull, no storm will damp;
I find comfort in your companionship.

Dianne Gayle Allen

Angels Are Watching

There are angels up above,
watching over you and me.
They're always there when you need someone,
even if you can't always see.
In a cabin high in the sky,
smiling down on all.
There are the ones who embrace your heart,
when it begins to fall.
These angels were taken away,
not too very long ago.
Even though I share the pain,
their memories have touched us so.
God took them up around 4:00,
as smoke filled the air,
but our dear friends felt no pain,
they knew God, our father, did care.
So whenever you feel scared and alone,
or ever mad or sad,
just remember these angels words,
"We'll cherish the good times we had."

Lynnie A. Carl

Imagine

Love is a figment of imagination . . .
Imagine what could be done with it.
Imagine . . . holding the hand of a child,
feeling the innocence.
Imagine . . . helping a friend in need,
sensing happiness inside.
Imagine . . . morning after a rain,
breathing freshness, purity in the air.
Imagine . . . giving a smile to a stranger,
glimpsing hope flicker in the eyes.
Imagine . . . sparing time for your family,
watching the bond grow stronger.
Imagine . . . a cool breeze on your face,
sand in your feet, peace.
Imagine . . . a mountain at dawn's light,
the presence of majesty.
Imagine . . . giving a hug to someone,
a gift of caring and sharing.
The power of imagination—could it start a revolution of love?
Do you imagine?

Sherry Courtright

A Friend

You were my friend, best friend, I suppose.
The only person I would defend.
About all my secrets, you're the only one who knows.
Then you met her. She didn't like me too well.
She's cold inside—brrrr!
Way too cold to live in hell!
Then she met others.
She dumped you like you dumped me.
Eventually, everyone goes home and cries to their mothers.
She's going out with your ex-boyfriend, Lee.
She's hanging out with all your friends.
And where does that leave you and me?
Her heart never mends;
I don't even think she has one!
From all of the heartbreaks everyone has given me,
My heart weighs a ton.
Don't you see? All this pain is unbearable.
Sometimes it hurts so much; I wish this was the end.
Life without people is terrible,
'Cause all anybody ever needs is a FRIEND.

Hallye Rae (Flores) Nanamkin

Forever

You have left, but I know you're still here,
Concerned when I'm in trouble or fear.
Everywhere I'll take you along,
'cause you'll forever be in my heart.
Years will go by,
And time will fly,
But I'll always remember,
'Cause you'll forever be in my heart.
You'd cheer me up when I had a frown,
And you never ever let me down.
I'll remember all these things,
'Cause you'll forever be in my heart.
I know you will be happy where you are,
Even if it's so far.
I'll cherish all the times we've had,
'Cause you'll forever be in my heart.
We will all greatly miss you,
But there's nothing that we can do,
Except think about and love you always,
'Cause you'll forever be in my heart.

Danielle Jean Saltalamachia

The Ghost of Memphis

They say on a moonlit August night
You can hear his voice in the summer wind
You can see his face in a candle flame
While a silky breeze softly whispers his name
And a red, red rose proclaims the love
And the loss of the Ghost of Memphis.

He came on the scene when the world was a-dreamin,'
And nations were heavy with hearts that were schemin,'
Poor boy, poor boy, lonely crooner, magic mystery man,
See the trembling silhouette the blazing backlights span,
Hypnotic steel blue eyes and sweat a-streamin' down,
Where in the world did you come from, and Lord, where are you now?

We see him brother, lover, friend,
Bedecked in cape and jewels grand,
Dropping kisses upon children playing in a cloud.
And we see his face in a candle flame
While a silky breeze softly whispers his name
And a red, red rose proclaims the love
And the loss of the Ghost of Memphis.

Sandra Mackey

Artistic Wizardry

Many folks now-a-days always seem not amazed,
Tell me, has it changed? For I cannot explain,
Arthur was a King and had with him Merlin.
Now Merlin with a wand, cast a spell, command.
No one really knew the mystery that he knew,
I like one have come keying on the keyboard.
Keys that come alive, appearing on the screen;
If I switched it off, nothing you would see.
Did it with a mouse, a pointer, a virtual wand;
I key it in my room, it's gone like that, yahoo!
Dragons still exist, firewalls that restrict,
I got no crystal ball, hey! This is a desktop.
What is called a spell, data saved and read?
Where is the cauldron? Where are the demons?
A virus for the other, a network and a server,
The mix of all proportions, Apple, any others?
Really I am wiz' encountering deadly twists!
Servers up and down, witches at www dot com?
Funny, how all fits. Oops, that computer glitch!
Artistic Wizardry—that is all it will ever be.

Gboyega O. Sanni

Michael

A sparkling glance
A smiling face
These are the memories I won't erase
Your soft touch
Your warm glow
I never thought it would be you to go
Your rosy lips
Your tender kiss
These are all things I'm going to miss
I wonder if you're listening
If you can see my tears
You knew everything about me
Like my hopes and fears
But on that Tuesday morning
My worst fear came true
I lost someone very close to me . . . I lost you
But Michael, if you can hear me
There's just one more thing I have to say
That I'll always love you
And that will never change

Angela Meredith Cox

Dead

What is this Lembasts?
Annoying and aggressive feeling that I had.
It took away pride, peace, dignity and self-esteem.
It had become an important part of my life.
There is no fear of darkness
No fear of death
No fear of jail
Such an overwhelming thing in my life.
It kills the brain of common sense
It takes away responsibility, compassion and understanding.
It leaves no time for self examination
There is no longer time for development
No one cared
The affect of a torn world, has caused a reaction.
Down with the sin sick soul.
No longer wanted in society
They have no origin
We are society making, now denounce.
We are dead from a White Monster
Her name is Cocaine.

Eloise Bins

January First

My mother shook me awake on the cold, dark, first day of January.
The first day of 1994.
The first day that my life was changed.
Her face was saddened, and wet with tears.
I took her trembling hand while she lead me to my awaiting family.
I felt the softness of the old, worn-out rug under my feet,
There, in my living room.
I saw the cold, limp body that once was my father,
Propped up on a soft, white pillow on the rented hospital bed.
Slowly, I walked to the bed.
My family watching, waiting for me to break down at anytime.
I was strong.
For the moment.
I carefully reached for his hand,
He's so cold.
"Some one get him another blanket, he's cold!" I screamed.
"Sweetheart, he's gone. He can't feel anything."
I looked into my father's light, lifeless eyes.
Willing to say good-bye,
I reached out, and shut them.

Kelsie Massengill

Mother, I Don't Remember You

I remember when I was little in the small town where I lived
There was a church with a bell; ding, dong
Each day it called the people to go and pray
Mother, I Don't Remember You . . .
On a cold day in September,
I was only two, too little to remember
You received a call from God, telling you it was time to go
You left me for a long journey, and you never returned
Mother, I Don't Remember You . . .
Why was God so mean and greedy, snatching you away from me
Every day, I sat with tears in my eyes
Each night I cried myself to sleep
I dreamed you'd take me in your arms and
Keep me warm with the heat of your heart
Mother, I Don't Remember You . . .
Even though I've grown old, I still miss you the most
You left me with nothing to remember you
Only a picture on the wall that I cherish the most
It has no life, no love or memories of moments spent together, but
Mother, I Still Love You. . . .

Michelina Ferro

I Was There

I was there in Africa when we were kings and queens,
Families and food, lives filled with hopes and dreams.
I was there when Europeans first came to take us,
put us in ropes and chains, slaves they wanted to make us.
I was there when they put us to work in the fields,
picking cotton till the skin on our fingers started to peel.
I was there during the civil war—lynchings and more,
afterwards Jim Crow crept through the back door.
I was there when Rosa Parks wouldn't give up her seat.
I was there when Malcolm and Martin made their first speech.
I was there when Jackie Robinson started to play.
I was there when the Oscar was won by Sydney Portier.
I was there in the room when Stevie Wonder was born.
I was there when Marvin Gaye asked "What's Goin' On."
I was there when Spike Lee directed his first joint.
I was there when Michael Jordan scored 63 points.
I was there when hip-hop developed from words and beats.
I was there when our music dominated the streets.
I was there when our culture influenced the time.
I'll be there when the next generation is better than mine.

Sterling Brent Warren

Thankful Friend

I know you and you know me.
When I look at you, a special friend is what I see.
Whenever I am feeling blue,
Your smile gives life a different hue.
You always listen to what others have to say,
Just to help brighten their day.
I have never met someone so warmhearted.
Because of it, many a friendship started.
On the road of life, different paths we walk.
But still with you it is always a joy to talk.
On me, I will always let you lean.
A shared moment so much will mean.
Maybe someday, we will even share an umbrella in the rain.
I just hope that friends we will always remain.
I hope the distance never becomes too far,
So I never forget what a special friend you are.
I have never had many a real friend,
The true ones will be there in the end.
So I say thank you for being a friend so true.
Thank you for just being you.

Thomas Andrew Latona

PerfectHalo17

Break these bars, let me out of this cage.
Why do I feel this way at my age?
I feel like such an outcast,
a stray.
When I get back in,
I'll find a way
to make them like me again
to make him like me again.
And when he does,
I'll tell him how it's been
living without him.
Not that he was ever mine,
because I just thought
I'd give it time.
Time was not the thing, it seems
to help the wounds
come clean.
Single now and single then—
with time, my patience wears thin.
Will he ever look at me again?

Megan M. Landes

Footprints

By the silent roar of a clear, windy shore
Beneath new, ancient light from suns at twilight
I lift an oar from the small rock floor
O, what a fine sight is the heavens tonight
And the small sand grains mirror stars far above
As my sole footprints follow me on the beach
I roam in gloom, like stars sure enough
Ahead I spy a lonely boat within reach
I'm caught in a space trance with an upward glance
Held witness to star dust's earthly, fiery end
Proof painted on black canvas expanse
All that's created must surely follow trend
With the sound of the sea gently lapping wood
I'm beckoned towards that small, wooden vessel
A rocking cradle to soothe my mood
And carry me where footprints will not settle
The tide gently washes my footprints away
I've become lost at sea, ever free to flow
And old suns lasting prints forever will stay
As the dawn's new glow fades old sun's ancient show

Scott Joseph Maley

Delusions

Running through the forest of fear
searching for help,
and all you can hear
is all the hurt, all the pain,
all the loss, and not a gain.
Swimming through the illusions of the mind,
frantically looking,
and not a friend you'll find,
hurting, screaming,
praying you're dreaming,
trying to find your way through,
hoping someone will help you.
Laying down, crying,
giving up, dying.
This is the maze of the mind,
the way out,
very few ever find.
Welcome to the world of fear,
the stages of depression,
all begin here.

Jennifer Jade Hamilton

The Flamenco Guitar

Like a Spanish Flamenco Guitar
Playing softly in the night
Your love tenderly comes to me

When I can't hear your voice
And when your words no longer speak to me
The cold gray dawn
Of a blustery winter's day
Will fill my cold and empty world

Why has fate dealt me such a painful blow?
Why has Lady Luck turned her back on me?
My eyes are dry
Yet my heart weeps
Like a summer willow tree

Lying silently in my bed
In a dark and hollow room
I strum the strings
I softly sing
The words of a melody
That never shall be sung

Ignacio Nick Garcia Jr.

I'm Scared

Oh, yeah.
I've been through hitting and screaming,
Moments of hatred, belittling, and seething.
I've been through a younger sister kicking,
An older brother hitting.
I've been through a mom and a dad
Not working out what they had.
Me sitting alone,
Wondering alone,
Beginning to see things only alone.
Oh, yeah.
I have been alone and hiding,
But nothing has matched you and your riding.
I don't know if I should let myself love you,
"Leave me alone!" you cry out of the blue.
I know you have love for me in your heart,
Time you spent will not allow you to part.
Never have I felt so exposed to anyone.
Love is hope with each rising sun,
But I'm so scared.

Amy Beth Netzel

me and my unborn

mother and daughter, the best of friends
upon my pregnancy is where it ends
how could she betray me so
i must move on, but i can't let go
from noon to night, we shopped the malls
hanging cheap decorations on our walls
this is the night that i choose to die
me and my unborn, side by side
the same mother that laughed and told jokes
despises my pregnancy and clutches my throat
i was kicked in the stomach and labeled a slut
nursing my wounds, as i tried to get up
pain screams out from the depths of my soul
banging my head against the toilet bowl
i was betrayed, so i must betray
as i take both of these battered lives away
me and my baby will leave this Earth
in hopes that we will experience rebirth
maybe then we can smile, as we wave bye-bye
me and my unborn, side by side

Kevin Ray Cormier

Sweet Tenderness

Every tender moment we spend . . .
Last in my mind, beyond the days end . . .
In my lasting memory of you . . .
So does my heart lend . . .
You in my mind and heart . . .
Where my love for you blends . . .
Me with you now . . .
And the feelings it sends . . .
With loves hot embrace . . .
We see it, in the eyes of a smiling face . . .
Passionate touching takes us . . .
To a higher place . . .
As emotions and desire in the flesh . . .
Do they race . . .
It's the love making on our tender lips
That we taste . . .
Pleasing one another, In a sweet loving pace . . .
With peace, contentment, and grace . . .
We long for these moments . . .
For no time shall we waste!

John Joseph Baker Jr.

A Warning to the "Next Generation"

I will tell you this,
And I'll tell it now.
This generation tries and tries,
But it doesn't know how.
The diseases are bad,
No cures for the worst.
People want to help,
But it seems that we are cursed.
The violence is horrible, adults tell us,
"Stop, it's the wrong thing to do"
But we won't stop,
Because they do it, too!
Take heed of this warning,
People, you're our only hope.
We can't take anymore,
We just can't cope.
Can't you see the "Next Generation" after you leave?
If things don't change,
It will be filled with
hate, hunger, greed, and disease.

Deirdre Evans

Dear Lord

In memory of Donald Sullenger
Today I write to you with my heart full of sorrow,
For I was told my son has no more tomorrows.
Tell me O' Lord how do I let go of this young man?
How do I relinquish him to your loving hands?
Do I try to be brave and let him quietly slip away?
Or do I shout and scream and beg him to stay?
The memories come back to comfort me,
his struggles and accomplishments I still can see.
A proud young man who went his own way.
He lived his life from day to day.
I guess that's how I'll make my way,
taking it day by day.
Comforted by a shy quiet smile.

Rebecka Lynn Sullenger

Mission Statement

Our mission here is very clear;
Look at these people, they live in fear.
To serve and protect against all nations,
Even under the NATO sanctions.
Satan is at work all over this land,
God has sent us to lend a helping hand.
Some of us man checkpoints, some on the gates,
Others sit in the TOC, while we all wait.
Waiting to see what the next event will be,
And how it will affect guys like you and me.
After seven months of this stuff,
We will say we've had enough.
The next guys will come down,
We'll let them have their round.
We will return back to our station
In another country, another nation.
Back to our families and our homes,
All of which have always known
To serve and protect was our mission here,
All of it now seems very clear.

Scott Ricky

Masked Angels

We all have desires, fires burning inside us
Wanting to reach out, labelling ourselves as "humans."
Humans with passions, are we all humans?
Are there angels among us?
Can we ever tell who is who?
They don't have wings, no haloes either.
But I bet they are the ones with kind souls,
Always in the right place and right time,
Saving lives, changing our future,
Bringing people together, creating miracles.
Do they really know what they are?
Or just do what their hearts say?
Not even thinking about risking their own life
Or dying saving others.
They just act, that act of kindness.
I believe they are here in our lives
Around us, maybe even our friends.
Or even ourselves that we think we know.
You'll never know until it's over,
We may all be Masked Angels.

Patricia Christine Rupert

Apple Seeds

Nariman, my daughter, my heart, has strong fear
To be the gloomy cave of forgetting near
To be like neighbors in nearby building, living
No one remembers, neither their names, nor their games
As if they are in nearby building not existing

Daughter, sow apple seeds in the island!
Even if you are in the evening leaving the island
Your children, village children will play under apple trees
Your grandchildren will enjoy the apple pies
Bee will be happy with apple honey
Wise men will admire the beauty of apple trees

Their happiness will clean your soul and heart
To be smelling like angel heart
Will save you from the gloomy cave of forgetting
During your stay in the island and outside the island of life
Since you, a tiny fragrance of eternity, will be breathing

Dear Father, give me a piece of time, give me
To find apple seeds, good deeds, for you and for me
To sow them in the island, everywhere in the Island of life

Khalid Abu Al-Sand

Death of a Wild Duck

Heavily the unbelieving wings
Beat air that will not hold him up.
The shock of something that burst within him keeps his eye
On the receding, decimated flock
Slowly reforming in a wavering v.
He longs to join them, but the rocking marsh
Is rising fast and fills him with confusion.
Feathers and water clash, the landing harsh,
But reeds support him.
In a wild illusion it is the wind; he sees the painted land
And ruffled lakes beneath him as he flies,
Churning the mud; this isn't as he planned.
He turns his iridescent head to see
And stares amazed at such an awkward angle
Of the once tireless feathered things
Amid the reeds and salty mud a tangle.
Gently the retriever lifts the bird,
But mark, the buckshot did not make him die.
It was the sudden knowledge of his kind
That never could his wings surprise the sky.

Frances Puckett Wilbur

Heroes

With this ring, I thee wed
Those words were spoken that day
Forty years after they were said
You've honored those words all the way
Though the times weren't always easy
And the days weren't always bright
Just having you as our parents
We knew you would make things all right
The heartaches we've had can't be counted
All families have had their share
But remembering the blessings we've gathered
All those heartaches don't even compare
Though parts of our childhood grew cloudy
And life seemed at times out of place
The one constant we could always count on
Was the love displayed on your face
Heroes are only in comics
Or some Saturday morning cartoon show
But you're our heroes, Mom and Dad
And we love you more than you'll ever know

Steven Michael Culver

Obsessive Love

My heart is paralysed,
Encrusted by your love.
I feel smothered . . . restless, bothered
By your undivided attention.
I need some space
To grow, to breathe, to create.
You stifle me. . . .
Encapsulated by your obsession
That I am yours to own,
My heart and soul under your control.
You're killing me . . . though softly.
Release your loving arms,
Let my soul fly free again;
So my heart can sing
With correct refrain,
The melodies of life I used to know.
It was nice at first . . .
Your candy lips with sugary outbursts,
Like frosting on cake . . . but
Becomes hard after the due date.

Rosmi Binte Mori

Mountain with Snow

Mighty moguls on a mountain majestic and high
Carving your bumps, never asking why
The meaning of life is simple and clear here
Skiing and living life moment to moment
Marvelous mountain where peoples'
Lack of compassion doesn't bring a tear
Where the cold air is cleansing
And heightened emotions evaporate
In the effervescence of snow
Glistening under a warm sun
Adventuring down through your glades
The smell of pine, the beauty of birch
Acceptance-forgetting lost loves,
Fair-weather friends, and false family members
Magnificent mountain, where happiness halos—
Solace, run after run
Perspectives change, paradigms shift
Coming together again
Slope side, outside, nature and man are one
Mountain with snow, humbling and homecoming

T. Michael McClain

The Sea of My Mind

As I lay on a cushion of soft, white sand
And stare at the gentle glow of the moon,
I hear the waves crashing onto the beach
In a melodious, hypnotic tune.
I long to feel the water wash over my body
I think, as I lay along the shoreline;
So I get up and stare at the rolling waves,
And I know that it is time.
I go out to where the water meets my
Shoulders and wait for the perfect wake,
And just before the swell meets up with me
A deep breath and leap I take.
Again and again I ride on top of the water,
But then I realize something it lacks;
So, I decide to swim out into the ocean
And never ever come back.
So, I become one with the sea creatures,
Knowing they will never leave me behind.
"You'll never see me again," I say to life on the shore,
As I swim away in the sea of my mind.

Laura Anne Penley

Really Miss You

The rock upon the wave falls slow when the
time comes I'll finally see you go.
The waves a child lost in games with your
face inside of every picture frame.
You see the moon and fear the most.
Identities for like a ghost that frights me
to know you'll go.
I really miss you
The waves that beat upon the shore left me
feeling stranded out the door.
The child's left to stare alone at
photographs he sees and loves to hold.
Far from gone but far from sane in
everything you try to gain and still it
frightens me to see you go.
I really miss
'Cause I'm the child and it frightens me to
know you'll go.
I really miss you.
I really miss you.

Jason Michael Hawn

Black Rose

Death knocked upon my door
He said he came for me just once more
He gave me a red rose
And said only you'll know
The secret that I bestow
The rose was new
For it never bloomed
I put it in a vase
And poured water over it, just in case
As the water touched the rose
It opened up just like so
Then it turned black
I thought it was something that I had lacked
After that it turned to ash
And looked as though it had gotten smashed
Then death appeared in front of me
And said that this is meant to be
You live, you die
And that's no lie
So, now take my hand, it's your final time

Wanda Ann Morris

The Soccer Player

It happens every year
In the spring and in the fall;
It's such a passion of his—
'Tis the season for soccer ball
He'll arrive in great anticipation
He'll dress in the parking lot—
First, his pants, then his shirt,
Next, the shin guards and then the socks.
But this player is always watched
By those on and off the field
Amazed at what he'll do next
With him, one can never tell.
They'll marvel as they observe.
His strategy is frightening.
But even more mind-boggling—
His speed is like lightning
Aches and pains may come his way
He'll shake 'em off for sure
He'll rest a spell and get revived
And go right back for more.

Shelia L. Jones

I Will Survive (The Holocaust)

I will follow the orders
I won't cross over the borders
I will remember your name AND your number
I will not ask questions and try to cumber
Because . . . I must survive
I can't stand to look at my face
I keep staring into space
Thinking of this horrid place
I ask you, will we win this scary race
Will we all . . . survive
I never thought it possible
For me to have such misery
Just take a minute of your time
And look at your surroundings
Can we ALL . . . survive
I told myself, I won't give up
I told myself, I won't mess up
I will make sure I do not die
And I will never say good-bye
Because . . . I WILL survive

Lia Demchenko

Thank You, CP

To Catherine—I'm going to miss you!
I can't believe I may have only one more year with you!
I'm again getting scared, what will I do?
You've been a great Teacher and the Best of Friends!
You've helped me so much through thick and through thin.
I've learned so much from you, just not yet enough.
You've even guided me through personal stuff.
I know I'm learning lots and I'm getting older.
But, now who will I have to look over my shoulder.
I used to say "I'm scared" a really, really lot.
But since you've been my teacher, it's something I've fought.
I can't really say "Thank You" enough.
For everything you've done for me, even the simplest stuff.
When you tell us, you're now going to go.
I'll be the first one to say "Please, NO!"
I love my job, I really do.
It's just never going to be the same without you!
You've had faith in me, that others, maybe couldn't see.
I "Thank You" CP for the person you are,
and the friend you always will be!

Kelli D. Simmons

Friends

Lie together, together as one,
Nothing is something as long as were together.
Love comes faithfully to ones who love,
But if you won't forget me,
I won't you.
If you listen to the wind,
I know that you could hear
one little voice of joy
singing, do not fear, friends are here.
If you need a hand to help you,
Love, life, fantasy, I will be here for you,
Because we are friends,
and I have meant for you to see
How much you mean to me.
I think of you as my sibling,
as one of my family,
as part of me.
You see, I care,
You are friends,
Lie down together, together as always.

Jamie Lee Beene

Get Scared

All this time I stand and wait
I get scared
It's getting late

Start to cry I think I'm wrong
I get scared
I'm not being strong

How would I be if I wasn't me
I get scared
I can't see

Don't let that guard down and start to cry
I get scared
I don't know why

Why do you look at me in the face and lie
I get scared
I don't want to say good-bye

Sitting here looking at you, you look so shy
I get scared
As I watch you die

Valeria Priscilla Bacajol

Dad

I'm lost, scared, don't know what to do.
You say you love me, your love is true.
You've lied and lied and still persist,
After thirteen years you should've quit.
Why can't you love me for who I am?
Instead you only love Ronda, Barbara, and Pam.
Dad, I've tried through thick and thin.
I don't know how to make you love me again.
Remember when we would ride horses together,
We used to be a team, the best ever!
Why did you tell me never to come back
When you said that I didn't give any flack?
You might not know, but I cried and cried.
It ruined my Christmas, but that's a surprise!
You know you hurt Mom, you know you hurt me.
Who will be next on our family tree?
I miss you, Dad, can't you see?
But we can't go back to how it used to be.
I love you, Dad, maybe one day you'll love me.
Sorry if this hurt you, but you need to see.

Ashleigh Lauren Limbaugh

At Last

He felt old and weak and tired,
As he doggedly rode through the night.
After a battle in a perilous mire,
He strove to the east, to the light.
Coming back to whom his heart belonged,
Valiantly trodding with a blanket and sword.
Ever onward to the haven they called a pond,
Never stopping or slowing; a man of his word.
His eyes started sparklin' in the sun's glare,
He was nearing the end of his quest.
And he knew that by noonday he would be there,
His stout heart beat apace 'neath his breast.
At last to the pond he mused in his mind
To my love and life quiet and serene.
He knew when he got there whom he would find,
The woman he considered his queen!
He went through the grove that led to the pond,
As she rose from her place on the grass.
At last the two lovers were where the belong
Together, forever . . . at last.

Monday van Camp

Walking Is Talking with Your Feet

Are you hiding your walk or do you flaunt it
like a fool. Your feet will hurt in the end
because words can be so cruel. What attitude
people have as they put one-foot in front of
the other. One word is so alone until it is
followed by another. Your walk is not
complete until your destination is reached.
If your sentence isn't structured right you
will not have a speech. For those who walk
too loud, you'll have to slow it down. Your
great escape is not to fake, but strive to
walk around. Your walk is stronger than your
talk and talking isn't easy. Walking gets
you somewhere else and looks a little
cheesy. A walk on the beach is more than a
walk. The further you walk the more likely
you'll talk, and the more you talk the
further you'll walk. So treat your walk to a
talk and find out what your walk is saying.
Don't let me get started on Communication vs. Transportation.

Steve Christopher Keckeissen

Love?

When I saw you
For the first time,
I knew I loved you,
But I was too young
To know what love was.

As we grew up,
The love I had for you
Grew stronger and stronger,

Until that day came,
The day,
I wouldn't see you again.

We gave our hugs
And said our good-byes.

I cried endless nights,
Trying not to believe that you were really gone.

We never stayed in touch,
Then I realized that
The love I had for you was gone.

Trista Jane Myers

True Courage

I lie here in this dirty trench as bullets fly overhead.
I wish I were home in my nice warm bed.
This all seems like such a bad dream.
The bombs and grenades light the sky with a yellowish gleam.
You're so composed, with not one shake of fear,
But in your eyes, I think I see a tear.
As we return to camp, men dead, lives gone,
I think I hear voices as the sky nears dawn.
We look around and the Charlie are nowhere in sight,
But something about this place just does not seem right.
As a grenade flies toward us, we all run away.
My foot gets caught. Will God let me stay?
You smother it with your body and save my life,
But lose your chance to ever again see your beautiful wife.
I watch in amazement as for me you fall.
Me, a man you hardly knew at all.
I saw real strength in you right from the start.
I will be sure to give your family the Purple Heart.
One day I will be able to share with my kids
That I once knew a man who showed me what true courage is.

Nicole C. Bouchard

For His Sake

If I had a son with eyes of brown,
or light and down and he looked like you,
would I know and feel and teach and do
the fantasies which do not come true,
for his sake?
If I might see and I might hear
the wrongs I've done throughout the year,
would my mind with muddled thoughts surmise
the things one step beyond my eyes,
and show and make me wise for his sake?
I will teach my son with eyes of brown
or light and down and dew,
the fantasies which do not come true,
and give him wisdom to follow through
with those that do.
I will tell of the wrong without the tear
that will carry through to another year,
and take his eyes one step beyond,
and show and make him wise, less guise,
for his sake, but, for you.

Rheta T. Lane

The Gatlinburg Experience

You can't say that you haven't heard,
Not after being in Gatlinburg.
You can't say that you didn't know,
Not after seeing all that crystal white snow.
You can't say—can He be there?
Not after seeing chunks of water frozen in mid air.
You can't say—can He be real?
With over forty-plus black folks being still.
Elevations of over two thousand feet;
Still at your window, a tree you meet.
As the sun comes up over the mountain top
And the blue misty clouds just seem to drop.
Winding roads and houses hanging off a hill,
And you still want to know if He is real?
We can't even be in a rush
As we watch the Master Painter take His brush.
With each color scheme, with each shade,
We know that this is what the Master has made.
Oh, you can't say that you haven't heard
Not after being in Gatlinburg.

Dr. Dovie Wesley Gray

The Bouquet

The flowers burst forth in a delightful frenzy
draping a stark expanse with ravishing beauty.
Riotously I reeled in a dizzy
spell, steadied and clasped serenity.
The rest of the world faded in a mist
as the flowers continued their sway and dance.
My senses enraptured with its radiating kiss
of intoxicating fragrance.
Drawn to touch I drew close
to their buds on slender filaments erect.
Colored roses filled the rows
with prickly thorns poised to inject.
The pretty petals blushed with dew
cupped in a diffused calyx intricately layered.
Perked up with confidence anew,
my plucky desire instantly seared.
Mentally gathering every shade,
I placed them astride sprig and spray
and in an imaginary vase were laid
to often recall a memorable bouquet.

Seneca Bernadette Rodricks

I See You . . .

Always leaving something behind,
Could it be that it is unimportant,
Or is it that YOUR life is full?

Someone, someday will see how significant things are,
A penny is a wonderful find. . . .
Look into a well and notice
A rich man will throw a penny,
Yet a man with nothing will throw his silver hopes.

Someone, someday will see how significant things are,
A smile from a stranger . . .
Leaves you with a treasure of your own,
A contagious fortune that spreads like wildfire.

Someone, someday will see how significant things are,
To us a day gone wrong is a day cherished
By a person with a limit on life. . . .

I see what is left behind,
And I treasure the day I find the worth
Of what YOU leave behind. . . .

Veronica Maria Diaz

Cage of Love

Chain of love is what unites us both,
your heart is secluded in a golden cage,
idle and concealed.

My love vagabonds through the free air
in a melancholic and intimate rhythm.

You're like a prisoner between grates,
and I, a vagrant desiring
passion, seduction, and corporeal fire.

Your love is blind, but mine
is a lit candle like a full moon at dusk.

The monotony of the starry night
will erupt the lewdness of our love.
When that cage opens, we will break the
silence of our oath and make of our
dulce vita a dream.

Among murmurs both will devote our soul,
making a solo palpitation, and when I
enter your cage we'll make a legend of love.

Banesa Maldonado

Love Is Like the Seed of a Rose

Love is like the seed of a rose
That is planted with the most delicate care
With the hope that someday that seed
A beautiful rose will bare.
One spring afternoon, to his surprise
His rose had finally bloomed.
It was like looking at the stars,
And as if God had brought him the moon.
On a very busy day
The gardener forgot one simple thing:
That the rose needed his attention
And for just himself to bring.
Wanting to retrieve what was lost,
He reached to grab it, and said,
Don't leave me now! I'm sorry.
But his fingers had been pinched, and bled.
A cold wave ran through his body
He stood up quickly and he said . . .
I rather not turn back now
Because I know the rose is dead!

Janice M. Lopez

Sixteen

Sixteen and all alone,
I have no place to call my home.
Wandering the streets, aimlessly,
Not enough money for a bite to eat;
Digging through the trash, trying to ease the pain
From hunger; hurt; cold, beating rain.
I want to cry, but the tears won't come.
My body's cold, and my heart is numb.
No mother's love, no father's home;
I have no place to call my own.
The homeless shelter is full tonight,
Beneath the bridge will be all right.
Huddled up, trying to keep warm;
A cardboard box, shelter from the storm.
Alone and scared, I try to sleep.
I pray to God my soul he'll keep.
I do not know what tomorrow brings,
Maybe, a promise of happier things.
Another night, another box,
Another bridge, another thought.

Barbara Lee Bailey

Locomotive

Lying among the uncertain shadows
While the
    piercing
Shout of the fortified
Entity shatters still night and power of
Endless strength ROARS through silent light,
    images of
Tranquility and the
Serenity of sweet-smelling streams of
Impenetrable meadows invade the
Disturbed pleasantness of previous time.
Soon
    the Devil-of-the-Night
Has become impregnated by the enclosing of
Mind artillery which destroys every
Element of the despised screams which
    haunt the
    unexpected
And susceptible individual,
Only to arise and fight again.

Derek Paul Claxton

Love Me, Love You Not

When you love me, or love me not
Please do not forget this thought.
We were two, but one to me
Why's this hard for you to see?
You said you loved me, which was a lie
And broke my heart, you let it die.
Now I sit and wait each day
For you to come to me and say,
"I loved you then, I love you now,
And for this, I'll say my vow.
You're my one and only love
My heart, my soul, which I'm made of.
Till the day death do us part,
You will always be in my heart."
These words, I don't know if they're true.
I'll just put my trust in you.
So when you love me, or love me not
Please do not forget this thought.
We were one, but now we're two
Because I said good-bye to you.

Marissa Wagner

A Vision of Love

A vision of love was shown by one man,
while he hung in my place,
and took the nails in his hands.
Nails that were waiting,
and prepared just for me.
He took them with no questions,
as if it was meant to be.
Love was the reason,
He hung on my cross.
Love was the reason,
He didn't see it as loss.
For as a father loves a child,
is how He loves us indeed.
For as a shepherd loves his sheep,
that's where His heart is—do you see?
Now close your eyes,
and I ask what now do you see?
Is it a vision of God on a cross for you and me?
Accepting Jesus and all that He's done
is receiving a gift like a father gives his son.

Carin Lynn Wilson

Picnic at Flamingo Park

At Flamingo Park, life was beautiful.
It was summertime.
In the afternoon, I walked
through the paths
And watched nature display her green art.

I looked at the trees, beautiful flowers,
the green grass.
Nature in her art had created newborn flowers,
again having on their petals the freshness
of an infant.

The leaves of trees, trembling to the effect
of zephyr winds, fell to the ground.
Birds migrating and the melodies they sang
made everyone joyful. We listened.

After some reflections and meditations,
the realization came that Flamingo Park
was the best place to be.
Each family took their picnic baskets and blankets
And started home.

Jean P. Saintsurin

As I Await Your Call

As I await your call
I'm obsessed with the thought of saying something to you
that would make all the difference in the world to you.
I could tell you how striking you are to me,
But I'm thinking that those words have rung like
Church Bells on Sunday Morning.
I could tell you
That I think you have the most exquisite structure I have ever seen
But I'm thinking, somewhere along the line, someone
have already softly whispered those words in the wind.
I could tell you
That I think about you when you're nowhere near,
But I'm thinking, since I've gotten to know your heart
Your silhouette is always around.
So as I await your call
And I contemplate in my mind what I could say to you
So that your smile glistens in the sky.
All that I could come up with
Is that I'm glad you have walked into my life
To be Anything, To be Nothing, but Everything to me.

Karen Marie Coleman

Stars

You always smiled
in a way I could call my own.
You had a twinkle in your eyes
where only I could see the stars.
You have a touch
my sheath from the storm.
Your voice, tempting, yet innocent
seemed only fit to call my name.

Fearful of a flower
that would bring eternal beauty to my life.
I silenced your voice,
Shunned your touch.
The selfishness of my actions.

You always smiled,
but not for me anymore.
Your touch reaches out for another
and I am left all alone.

Although sometimes,
I can still see the stars.

Cindy M. Gurecki

How Do I Write a Letter to My Wife?

Just how do I write a letter to my wife?
A letter that explains all can be right.
Knowing all is not well, within my sight.

Then how do I write a letter to my wife?
Taking time to start on this very day.
Expressing in her heart, a special way.

And how do I write a letter to my wife?
The words that I know show what I may say.
The words that I know show love every day.

Just how do I write a letter to my wife?
A letter that explains all can be right.
Knowing all is not well, within my sight.

Then how do I write a letter to my wife?
Showing and telling her that I do care.
Whether it's on a whim or through a prayer.

Now how do I write a letter to my wife?
A letter filled with love by grace above.
A letter filled with the magic of our love.

William Lee Arrington

My Life

This is my life
No one can take it away
You better stay to yourself
'Cause I don't need anyone's help
I can manage alone
I choose to go alone
I want to be isolated
Ain't no one got a feeling that's related
'Cause this is all me
Can't you see
You don't got anything to do with who I am
I'm a man and I'm standing on my own feet
You can't match my glare
You can't match my thought
You think you're like me
No way you can be
Try and walk in my lair
Try and stare into the darkness
You can't so don't try
This is my life so let me be

Frankie Matthew Coronado

Beyond Rage

A fire burning in the heart,
Poisoning the mind and soul,
Acting as a lethal dart,
Targeting its one main goal.
Hormones are raging to maximum extent,
Figures all are blurred;
The things that are felt are beyond resent,
Roaring now is the cat that once purred.
Calming-impossible, thinking-improbable,
A scream splits you, as Hell tears you.
You pound with fists of wet cement
And stomp with feet of stone,
Things are flying, being broken, and bent;
Warning: you've entered the danger zone.
A flash, a whirl—faces are seen,
Pause; think—what's happened to you?
Caution: your body is running on low,
You're starting to feel the pain;
Hormones are now beginning to slow,
And once again you're tame.

Taryn Elizabeth Jones

Yet a Woman?

Something inside me fiercely burning,
Is it something I know or secretly yearning?
An emotion, a passion, a stifled dream;
A feeling expressed, now gone downstream?
A lump that's just waiting to nurture and grow;
Am I exhilarated and happy
Or really down low?
Do I know what awaits me—do I really care?
Should I sit down and decide, or do I dare?
Do I wear a funny mask to hide my fear?
Shall I toast with champagne, or cry in my beer?
What am I searching for, what do I need?
What direction am I going,
And where will it lead?
Have I sought the right values
And weighed the right things?
Have I interpreted correctly the lines on the faces I've seen?
Should I have been this or attempted that?
Am I yet a woman,
Or still a spoiled brat?

Martha McKee Koletar

Another Day in Hell

Tonight I'm standing at the end of the world,
Just standing on a mountain of dreams!
Why is life so bitter and relentless?
It never turns out the way it seems!
You fall in love with all your heart,
A memory is all that you get to keep!
You wake up to a whole new day,
Losing them always when you sleep!
One of these days I'll be flying away
From the prison walls of my mind!
Maybe someday I'll be thought all this
Without seeking what I wish to find.
Today was an endless day of hell.
What's the point of carrying on now?
Where can I go to escape all this?
Looking back, I can do it somehow!
Today I fell down so far and hard,
I was just climbing on a rainbow.
The pain is so close to my heart,
All this suffering you'll never really know!

William Joseph Sinclair

Children

Look at their laughter . . .
Look at their smiles . . .
Look at what they are becoming with love and support
From the ones that love them.

Now . . .

Look at their tears . . .
Look at their fears . . .
Look at their hearts broken and shattered.
A child such as this will not become much.
They are lost.

It is our love and support that keeps them alive . . .
Keeps them full of hope . . .
Keeps the wanting to strive and become better.

Do not hit . . .
Do not beat . . .
Do not scream . . .
Just love, cherish, and respect the children.
And you will be rewarded beyond your wildest dreams.

Kelly Michelle Hinman

Various Shades of Blue

It's a paradox
of tears falling from smiling lips
when no one knows
changing like the moon yet growing with every heartbeat
It's the same breathing stage
with new props so far gone past people's eyes
A concept that selfish minds can't understand
that I live every day without doubts of clouded judgement
and feelings rearranged
Maybe it's a contradiction against the world
to sing without reward
when it all breaks down
But could anyone feel so lucky to simply share the same stare
Could they see a life beyond their own
where human nature means nothing
Don't ask me why I give it all for nothing
I see in various shades of blue
and my petals feel only her
bittersweet beyond this presence like no one knows
Maybe it's better this way

Matt David Jonsdotter

Heart's Lament

From filth and guilt, I have risen
Cruel words with thunderous impact
You turned into a half beast, unrecognizable
Did I really deserve a beating?
You are an enigma, a cherubic pitbull
Ugly words . . . could be therapeutic!
Embalmed thoughts of you
Preserved in a glass case
I closed my teary eyes, whispered your name
But then again, you were dead
De-intoxicate, I'm trying
Maniacal desire to belong, I'm fighting
Like a wounded animal seeking shelter
Redemption too for those violated
No more river of tears!
I learned from the Master
Chase . . . and then kill
Stone cold, unfeeling and Machiavellian
Tell me, do you have a black heart?
I have yet to conquer. . . .

Maria Europa

Take My Hand

Trust in me and take my hand
Believe in me and make a stand
Don't be afraid I am your friend
I'll lead you safely to the end
Of your troubles to a fresh new start
In my life you'll always be a part
No one could turn back the time we spent
Or the love and trust we meant
Don't let life pass you by in your sleep
Keep the promises you meant to keep
A drug life just ain't going to last
Soon this will all be in the past
Then your new life can begin
That's when you'll start each day with a grin
In your future I can see
You being happy with your own family
It takes time but you'll get through
Don't give up, I'll always believe in you
You can do it I know you can
All you have to do is take my hand

Linda G. Moreno

Joe

When the snow drops I think of Joe.
With his big smile
And the way he would act like a child.
You're so special
I wish I could hug you or simply
kiss your cheeks.
It all happen in a sudden rush.
Everyone was struck.
I felt as if I got crushed.
I wish you were still here
so you could heal
the pain I go through
When I don't have you near.
I'm happy you don't have to go through pain,
but now I can't see your face.
It was a pleasure to hear your voice
Now there is silence
Except when it snows.
All I wish is to see your face please!
Until then I hope you rest in peace.

Celia Antonia Alvarez

I Remember Mama

The smell is sweet like baby powder,
as she plays out by the flowers,
I remember you, Mama.
Your touch was warm and oh, so tender,
and I bet you think I don't remember,
but I remember you, Mama.
Even though I was two years old,
and you left me alone and cold,
I remember you, Mama.
Grandma says that you'll be back,
and with all my heart I hold to that,
I remember you, Mama.
When you see me you won't believe,
all the things that I've achieved,
My world is good with lots of love,
with Heavenly things from God above,
All the things a child would need,
and I know that I'll succeed,
growing, playing, learning, and asking please,
remember me, Mama.

Debra Fern Herrera

The Battle

Through the mist strode the gallant legion
Battle-ready, conquering the large region
The dawn sun shone on the opposing castle
And in the dawn, it looked quite impassable
The legion rode up and drew their swords
And the battle bugle blew some chords
The catapults fired unto the wall
Yet only small chunks did fall
The defenders peppered the legion with arrows
But they were nervous down to their marrow
The attackers sent their charge
But took a terrible toll of large
The defenders started gaining morale
And took their horses out of their corral
Charge they did
And into the enemy they came at the mid
The attackers fled, their shining helms gleaming in the sun
And of their dead, there was a ton
Never again was the castle in grave trouble
Nor even reduced to lowly rubble

David Joseph Rogg

All Alone Where No One Can Hear

Today, the man I call father, will come home.
He'll be on his best until we're alone.
Then he'll come towards me
With a smile I so much hate.
He will put his force upon me
Until my bare skin meets his taste.
Then once again he'll steal my innocence
And leave me with my loss.
I will feel cold and dirty,
And the feeling can't be washed.
My mother would protect me,
But she knows nothing more
Then a perfect angel daughter
And a lover she adores.
So again, tonight, to the bedroom I so fear,
All alone where no one can hear.
My pain will last until someone comes home,
But they have been told, I need to be alone.
My heart will break, as I hear the words,
Again father has raped me without remorse.

Aschlee Jean Drescher

Inner Hell

Inner EVIL hides inside
Soon awakes opening its fiery eyes
Looking to INHABIT its host
To TEAR them DOWN
An EMOTIONAL HOLOCAUST
Was it just a slumber
Or a warring FIEND my soul to blunder
Taking all I have left
KILL, PILLAGE, and RAPE my hopes
Till there's NOTHING LEFT but an EMPTY shell
Destined to live ALONE, Destined to HELL
But would that be worse than WHAT I FEEL now
This INNER EVIL
a PERSONAL HELL
all these DEMONS running through my head
Causing me to wish for DEATH
How easy to GIVE IN
How easy NOT to LIVE
To LEAVE THIS all BEHIND
In a kind of HELLISH BLISS

Elizabeh Maretta Putney

Always with You

Do not look down at my grave and cry,
rather look upward to the sky;
through your tears—in a cloud you see,
a bird or a rose my Spirit will be.
I am always with you.
If you just need to talk or to share a fear,
I am always with you, I will always hear
your laughter, your sadness, your every care.
Be happy and hopeful as you can be
and know you can always talk to me.
I will never leave you, so never fear;
I am always with you, always near.
Remember all the good times we've had;
celebrate my life, it wasn't so bad.
Laugh, be happy, smile, cherish the
times we had for awhile.
Never forget when you're feeling blue,
you can call on me, I'm always with YOU.
You're forever in my heart,
"Old Horse"/Gramma/Meema/Mom

Elsie Mason-Lee Davis

Summer Storm

Summer's sunrise, warming rays
Translucent forests, fog lays cold
Accentuated layered purple haze
Below bright puffs of cotton gold
Billowing silver lines high clouds
Toward skyward, reaching anvil tops
As an obscure painting in black enshrouds
A freshening breeze lays down the crops
Clover aroma of new-mowed grain appears
With large drops of rain, but few in number
Fall as crystal percussion musical spheres
That play in tune with distant thunder
A menacing, rolling cloud approaches
Harmonics of rain and sound and light
The music of the spheres encroaches
As cymbals clang with primordial fright
Ebbing now to a distant drum roll
A lattice work of flickering light
There's a freshness to the air and soul
From rainbow arch to pristine night

Robert Byczynski

Lenny

Through the storms and rain
You were there to ease the pain
The stains of tears, your shoulder does hold
Forever grateful this story untold
The joy you brought was one never felt before
Inside and out your beauty is what I adore

Never have I felt the deepness of your love
A love that goes with so much more than words
Love of the spirit and definitely the soul
How special in the sight of God one must be
To be given a gift for all the world to see
One can never express the true feelings felt
For what is to come of such a thing

Maybe one day you will express yourself to me
To say all those things longing to be said and heard
To just take a chance and let God control the rest
For you will never know if your feelings you don't express
So give it a shot, there's nothing to lose
But a life of everlasting joy to gain

Sherika N. Hatcher

Fulfillment

I am in pain but with every contraction,
I know that the time is nearing
when I will hear my baby's first cry.
I welcome each contraction and when it is over,
I forget all that I have gone through
as I hold my beloved close to me,
as I feel his breath on my cheek,
as I feel his fingers exploring my face.

It is over and I know
I will never forget this moment
for it is now that I truly feel
the joy of motherhood,
the joy of having delivered what
God planned and what we made together.

Thank you Lord,
for making this great moment.
Thank you that I too can know this great joy.
Thank you for your infinite love.
Thank you Lord and guide me.

Marie-Louise Bugeja

Sitting in the Sunset Alone

Hairs on end by the warmth of the sun.
Feelings of peace when the day is done.
Hearing the waves crash ashore.
Makes me hope there is something more.
Almost like wishing the ocean breeze,
Would carry away my soul.
As if my being was in a state of null.

Searching for substance in an empty life,
The kind you might feel in your heart,
When you meet your future wife.
Extending out for this chance of bliss,
Afraid inside that it may never exist.

Of happiness that radiates from within,
Holding hands and walking,
Along a beach that never ends.
Looking for a love,
That you can call your own.
In order to keep me,
From sitting in the sunset alone.

Gerald Daniel Colpitts

A Mother's Broken Heart

Who knows the fear in a mother's heart
when her darling child says "Mom, I'm leaving
home. There's things to do and things to see
and school and home, they're not for me."
God loves her too, He'll not let her go.
That was months ago. He'll bring her back,
His glory to show; that too was months ago.
Now she knows she'll not be back and she
recalls a day a long ways back when she'd
said "God, she's yours you know, this baby
girl that I love so."
Now in the lonely hours of the night she
lays awake and contemplates, God's still on
His throne and He still loves my girl, He'll
not leave her alone or give her to fate, but
He in His wisdom knows best what she needs.
 but "Oh, God, what about me?
Things have become so confused and I find
I don't know so much about you. Or . . . wait . . .
could it be, this is one less step between you and me?"

Shirley Ann Flanigan

The Play

The scope of the stage on which we play
(as well as the part we must portray)
might well cause an actor some dismay,
but each role must be filled anyway.
The curtain's open; the stage is set.
Enter a child who has no regrets.
The scenes go forth from morning 'til night.
The young man heaves sighs of his delight.
A middle-aged man, seen in Act II,
knows life must end for me and for you.
Learning to cope, each scene fades away,
as he faces life from day to day.
The last act begins much like the first;
the old man suspects it could be worse.
He draws forth his sword with a great curse;
his last energy seen in one burst!
Celebrate life, the curtain is high.
Remember, my friend, you, too, will die.
And so now down the curtain must fall;
the end of the play comes to us all.

Rene Sue Schnake

Hidden Child

Inside is a hidden child
Scared and afraid
Cowering in a corner
Hidden for so many years
Hidden for so long she's been forgotten
Scarred for life
Hidden due to a trauma
A trauma she will not share
she's tied down by the trauma
Afraid to get close to anyone
Afraid to share
A child so little she couldn't defend herself
She could not then and still cannot
So weak and frail
She's afraid to get close to anyone
Afraid to show her face
Afraid of the hurt and the pain
This little girl is love
Yet never will she love
This child is hidden inside me

Phyllis E. Sinkler

Along the Path

Into this world we come alone
And the journey we have, none but our own
Yet along the path, if true
Others will cross; of those, some do
Even follow along for a time
Not always obvious reason or rhyme
And though at these moments we feel
That our journeys shared are real
And our solitude has come to an end
All must realize maybe here, or next bend
That those paths may separate again
Till fellow travelers none remain
Of those lives we knew and shared
And whose hearts we lifted and bared
No longer part of our continuing trail
Left behind as memory and tale
From one life and to another move
Our soul locked tight in its groove
Forever growing, hopefully fair and wise
Till one day when our spirits rise

Roger A. Joslin

A Depressive's Prayer

Dear Heavenly Father;
I pray that you will be with me as I try to start this day
I hardly have the energy to get out of this bed
I don't want to do anything at all
There are mouths to feed, dishes to wash,
 laundry pilling up to the ceiling
Please help me do some of the day's chores
I should go to work but I am calling in again
I keep crying off and on, not really knowing why
I hate myself and my life
I wish for a way out of this pain
Lord stay close beside me today
I really need your help to make it through
Let me feel your warm presence that I may feel warm too
Surround me with your angels so that I will be safe
Even from myself
Show me the way out of this lonely darkness
Help me and the ones I love to understand this illness
Help me find a way to manage it and find peace
I need to know there a better days to come. . . .

Jency O'Neal

Fathers

Fathers are very special
in every way.
Sometimes you think they are not,
until they fade away.
When they're here,
you're not with them.
When they're gone,
you wish you were with them.
My father was special
in every way.
I never really realized it,
until he faded away.
Away from my life,
away from my home;
but away from my heart,
he'll never roam.
So, when they're alive,
just remember they're special in every way.
And spend more time with them,
before they fade away.

Jaime JoAnna Archer

Where Does

Where does love go once it's lost
Can it ever again be found
Or does it become like an elusive treasure
Hidden just beneath the ground
Where does the pain come from
That replaces that love you lost
Does it go away or stay forever as punishment
For losing that love you lost
Where do people go
When they say they've grown apart
Can they ever be stitched back together
Or does the scar left behind fully harden their heart
Where is this wonderful god
Of whom I've heard so many boast
It seems he's never around
Just when you think you'd need him the most
These are just some of the questions
To which the answers will never be found
They will stay like that elusive treasure
Hidden just beneath the ground

Jack E. Downey

The Wall

He just stands there . . . I am like a wall,
Wrapped around him—tightly to let no one in.
He is mine, and none is able to get to him.
But there are people, those with ladders,
Who with little effort,
They may not move me, but still can reach him.
More people come, chip at me, the wall,
Or knock me down.
Penetrating my every existence . . .
I turn to dust and blow away with the wind.
I am still there, but forgotten.
He has forgotten who I am,
And what I used to mean to him.
I am no obstacle for them.
They no longer have use for me,
But what I have gained.
Little by little,
I am wasted, torn down, obviated.
Here I fall, where I used to tower.
I was nothing but a wall.

Angel Anna-Marie Harvey

A Farewell

I did not know you well
Which is a shame
Because your fate proved
That we were the same
We have lived throughout life
With heavy loads of pain
Where inside our minds
We see gray clouds and rain
For you there was a point
Where the pain became too great
Which made you take your life
In hopes of reaching Heaven's gate
Although I am just like you
I somehow carry on
I do not want to give up
So, I try to remain strong
I completely understand
Why you thought suicide was right
May your tortured soul finally be at peace
Farewell, my friend, and good night

Daniel Allen Farnow

The Dance

Up and down the scales of imagination.
Tap, tap, dancing on the keys of the piano.
A cascading waterfall of music
comes from within.
A river of emotion flows
through sunlit fields and majestic mountains,
rising up through the clouds
to dance upon the very stars themselves.
Pushing though gray deserts of despair,
and black nights of tears
the lilting melody is quiet but still strains
toward the ever present light ahead.
Dancing to a yet unknown tune,
beyond the stars and into the heavens.
Tap, tap to the flowing stream of sound
always up and down, sometimes around
but forever moving forward
'til the dancer is but a dream no longer seen
and the notes linger hauntingly in the air
played by an artist that is no longer there.

Kasie Elaine Veen

Our Infinite Persistence in Impossibility

I can barely breathe in an empty crowd.
Have we been listening?
There is the absolute possibility of
intrigue and awe,
But I am too human to grasp such far-off
bounds of knowledge.
No need to be solicited for emotions that
don't exist, fail to emerge.
The implications involved in the
vulnerability of space
are only necessary to facilitate life—
In this house of mirth and blight
we can only stand to swallow our faith,
our hope, and everything in between.
The warmth of enriched souls seeps through
the aura of blunder and dearth.
Who do we turn to in dire despair?
Rejoice in pain, embrace the end.
Judgment is ultimately inevitable, dear friend. . . .
we remain puppets to the masters we call Fear and Glory.

Jessica Kim

My Sister, My Friend

Our hearts, our souls entwined,
similarities striking as if one mind.
Within my heart and soul you can be found,
look into my eyes, you'll know, I need not utter one sound.
No distance, no time, this love it cannot touch,
words unsaid, not to worry, they're known, I love you this much.
My heart is bursting to say these words,
missed chances, times scarce for such things to be heard.
They can turn on a dime these lives we lead,
missed chances, just gone, no getting them back, why plead.
My words today are to let you know,
of all the missed chances that I'velet go.
Chances to tell you what's inside of my heart,
and that even in death our souls shall not part.
So today please know, my sister, my friend,
that without you in my heart my life would surely end.
So before one more day passed, not a single one,
I must say, without you, what would I have done.

Jamie A. Dolson

Lucky

"Shoo! Go on home," I said
To a scared, little kitty;
But taking one look at his pleading face,
Immediately came a feeling of pity.
Looking for help, I went and called
Some friends on the telephone,
When one said she knew someone
Who would give him a very good home.
Several weeks later something happened,
While taking a walk with my dog.
We discovered the same little kitten
Hiding behind a log.
"I'm going to keep him," I declared,
"He's 'Lucky,' what a good name."
From that day forward and forever more,
My life has not been the same.
Reflecting one day, years later,
I said to "Lucky," my pal,
"We've shared it all; laughter and tears,
I am the LUCKY one now!"

Dorothy J. Anderson

The Choice

There comes a time
When you have got to make a move
And you know leavin' is the only thing to do
So pack it in, you have got to tell him
It's good-bye, the man has you in ruins

What can be wrong with a choice you can make
When you know it's hurt so very long
On the flip side, it's a better life
It's your choice, the only one that's right

Just walk away, if you can, my friend
Don't be afraid, don't be afraid of the plan
You're better off without that man
And I bet you, I bet you,
You will shake my hand

Listen to me, I won't steer you wrong
'Cause I been there, done that,
A long time ago
It's worth the risk, just give it your all
Use your faith, your hope, and your love

　　　Lyndia T. Day

Forbidden

He stands there.
His sexuality imminently lingering.
Her heart skips a beat, but she turns away.
His soft voice forces her to turn around.
Mischievous eyes lock with terrified eyes.
"Stay," he says gently.
Nothing else exists.
"Stay," rings sweetly in her ears.
Nothing else, no one else matters.
Their fingertips touch.
Electricity runs through their bodies.
A soft cry is muffled by a tender kiss.
It is wrong, yet it is so very right.
"Forget about me," she whispers.
Her fingers trail down his arm to his hand.
Finding the painful intrusion on his finger.
Tears fall from sad eyes.
"You ask me to do the impossible."
Tell me.
Where does one learn how to not remember?

　　　Barbara Ann Knicely

Society

They judge me as if I'm a prize to be won
But what do they really know about me
Can they honestly say that they know who I am
What I enjoy, what I love, what I want, what I need
The nerve of these people, what do they know
They don't know me, they cannot relate
The actions that I take are for me, not them
The things that I do are for only my fate
So what if I don't have the best job in the world
So what if I have big dreams of my own
I always thought that this was a good thing
But obviously I'm wrong, as these people have shown
Why can't they all just leave me alone
Why can't they all understand who I am
By now you're probably wondering who they are
You're in suspicion, so I'll go out on a limb
They judge us all by what we do every day
They all think they know what we should be
They are made of many, but have only one name
The name that they go by is simply, Society!

　　　Derrick Weaver

The Sun, Mother, and Father

The Sun peeked over the mountain
and looked about the world
then shivered in sheer sadness
and talked to the Earth.
"What have they done to the world
once beautiful and bright?
They don't seem to care enough
to put up a simple fight."
Mother Nature replied in her sad and
mournful way, "They have brought me to my
knees, but there is nothing I can say
that will make them change their ways
and live a few old happy days."
Then Father Sky added his thoughts.
"They have so very many faults.
The air is dirty, life is tough,
and things are getting fairly rough.
I guess we'll have to let them be.
And what will happen to the Earth?
I guess we'll have to wait and see."

　　　Kristin Marie Waltersdorff

From the Heart

Do you wonder how people can live
In a world where no one will give?
Why doesn't anyone care,
Unless to them it's not fair?
We hide our fear, our unrighteous acts;
Even though everyone knows the facts.
We put on masks to hide our face,
For all we have to show is disgrace.
We try to cover our sins and mistakes,
But we need to open our eyes to become awake.
We curl up in corners to sit and forget
Our wrongdoings with thoughtless wit.
We cheat and lie to be the best,
Trying to beat all the rest.
When we finally reach the top, our dream;
Everything seems to split down the seams.
All because we cheated and lied,
We now have an empty space inside.
To fill that space inside we need to restart,
Learning all over again now from the heart.

　　　Amy Lynn Lomas

Down Time

I want you to need me, I need you to want me
I want to be with you, I want you to be with me
I ask myself why I feel this way
I begin to wonder, and my feelings stray
Still in doubt and no answer can be found
I turn to thoughts, but my energy is down
You want me to do this for you
You need me to do that for you
You want to be alone right now
You act this way, and then wonder how
You ask me why I feel this way
You begin to wonder, and my feelings stray
Still in doubt and no answer can be found
You turn to your thoughts, but your energy is down
So, tell me what to do, tell it to me plain
Tell me the truth, because lies end up in pain
Be direct, be clear, be honest, be cool
Follow your heart and obey the rules
Still in doubt and no answer can be found
We turn to our thoughts, but our energy is down

　　　RJ Armstead

Time, Past, Future, and Life

The past is the window into the future.
The past holds the key to the future.
The past brings the events of the present.
The past is to some degree defined.
The past defines the present and future.
The present is the past of the future.
Time is endless.
Beginning of Time is of debate.
End of Time is debated.
Time is debated without end.
Time heals.
Time kills.
Time creates.
Time destroys.
Time can slow in brief moment.
Time can speed by in long spans.
Life is passage of Time.
Time passes in Life.
Life must end, but Time goes on.
As so it must, life goes on.

Yung Joon Robinson

To Be a Child Again

Did you, as a child, ever call a star yours
And watch in disbelief as it grew brighter
And suddenly disappeared in fiery death?
Or have a balloon gently brush a bush
And be heartbroken as it burst?
But children grow up
And their problems follow suit.
Now it's a wish that is exploded, burst.
The hands are cut off, brutally,
And they weep drops of red, mourning their loss,
But the heart and voice continue;
Until the heart, too, is destroyed,
Taking with it the voice, unable to survive alone,
The quasi-corpse is left.
It might as well be dead, for without
A means of expression,
It is nothing but walking, breathing Death,
Unable to live, unwilling to die.
Oh, to be a child again with no more problems
Than an extinct star and a burst balloon.

Renee Relyea Vorbach

the pain of a thirteen-year-old girl

as i am crying
i ask myself why
everyone is lying
why can't i just die
i never wanted this
don't believe what they say
all the bad memories i can list
please, make them go away
no matter how hard i try
i feel this loneliness inside
i've tried so hard not to cry
but the pain is so alive
sometimes i think
why me, why
will i ever take off this mask i hide behind
and show how i really feel inside
i'm asking now
although not aloud
please, show me how
i can fix the problems i have found

Amanda Marie Mazzocchi

This World Built for Two

In this world built for two,
You make my life seem so unblue.
On this Earth we stand apart,
Miles between us and nowhere to start.
Objects stand in our path,
Love between us never laughs.
A fork in your road, which path to take?
No one knows whose heart will break.
People pass by, they sit and stare.
Do any of them know if we really care?
Now time has passed, we've been through so much.
I shutter to think of life without your touch.
So many times I've thought of you
Sitting with me watching the view.
Out on the shore, sitting in the sand,
We listened to the ocean's band.
As the days roll on and time flies by,
I sit and wonder why I cry.
Just to hear your voice or to see your face
Makes me want to be in your embrace.

Alana Francesca Trombetta

My Dearest Friend

Written for Erin Donahue

My friend is as close to me as a bumblebee,
Who is sitting on me waiting to sting.

The hands that reach out to people in need,
In pain, or need someone to talk to.

The heart that cares
And forgives me for my wrong.

The eyes that stare deep to judge
Thy person.

A friend you are for now and forever.

You were there when I needed
Someone to comfort me.

Now I know,
You are that special someone,
My best friend.
What shall I ever do,
If our friendship crumbled?

Felecia Elizabeth LaQuire

And I Pray

The skies got dark and I pray,
the rain began, I prayed harder.
My boat began to sink, the increasing
weight of the water was too much.
Lord, I wonder if you could hear my call.
The sea became rough and I began to
lose faith, but I prayed, nothing else to do.
The boat rocked and rocked
approaching the water fall.
I closed my eyes to enter the dark world. . . .
But there he was when I least expected.
At the bottom to lay me down, safely.
Yes, he was there and I prayed.
How could I have give up so quickly?
Without a struggle, there is no victory
With no challenge, face it when it comes.
I can see the clear skies now . . .
And I pray, in the distance rain is a drizzle
The water is calm and still, I must get
there, yes I prayed.

Jacqueline Margaret Anthony

The Gift

We are born and given this life as a gift.
With open arms, we do not resist.
Seeing this world with eyes of wonder,
We are overcome and surrounded by its thunder.
As we continue down life's road, we grow older.
The luster of life gets a little colder.
The gift of love becomes the test.
For the value of sunshine, rain, and flowers become less.
With misgivings and lies that work the trust,
The light dims, hope fades, and dreams turn to rust.
We must find the fire of our soul and correct the wrong
To find the gift and renew its sweet song.
We do not want to be remembered for the sorrow,
Not for the wasted time that we borrow.
Light the soul on fire, until it's burning with desire.
We can light the match that will inspire,
Then we will be born and given this life as a gift.
With open hearts, we will not resist.
For the gift is love.
It will continue and cannot be stopped from coming from above.

Roy J. Cunningham

The Curve of the Moon

When night unfolds its deep fabric
This sky becomes a dress I wore when I
Was just a child: my garment's pure blue hue
Sapphire of twilight slipping into indigo night
We wear together the delicate brooch
Of silver-white moon rind

Woman and daughter, I wonder: Would you seek
Shelter there inside the moon's sickle curve
Within its thin but waxing rocking chair
Silver sleigh of snow in the vast blue field
Of my dress, a healing place where
The echoes of day cannot follow?

I'll give you the moon from my garment
And fit it with comfortable things:
Deepest sleep and endless peace; a blanket, too
So you, weary woman and child
Might rock together in solitude, safely
Cradled in the curve of the moon
Wrapped in my blue-hued dress

Ronda Kay Broatch

Foreigner? (Drive II)

Missouri hills
reaching up to the sky
winding roads heading upwards
a natural high, yearning to fly
An illusion of my senses
that I don't care to comprehend
Just turn the radio on
let them soothe me
As I downshift up this peak
to crest and up shift and coast to the next
I find Ian's place
where doctors and lawyers aren't
From the radio a lady tells me,
"nowhere to run to . . . nowhere to hide"
And with a shift from fourth to fifth
and a drop from a cliff those words died
Here are peace, contentment, joy, and beauty
lovely colors accented by slight guitar riffs
Amidst a blue background see the hawk dive
bringing me the joy of being alive

Alestair Thomspon

The Real Paula

My former baby-sitter of fudge-roll fingers
and caramel calves,
An always out-of-breath artist who couldn't
walk without wheezing—
The house she shared with her mother
was filled with clay and a kiln.
There she caressed the clay
and left the world that laughed
at her divine obesity.
(She didn't have a single ridge or corner
on her body and gracefully wobbled
as she walked.)
Her heart gave up on her
long ago—but I remember
an egg-white ivory sculpture
of hers, titled "The Real Paula"
A Venus-like woman shedding a cocoon of fat,
revealing a butterfly's body,
leaving a caterpillar's corpse.
She lives again, weightless as air.

Trey Teufel

Fade

Tonight, sun sipping down blind venom,
I released that old vinegar bottle
from its crystal shelf. I poured us in,
one at a time so we couldn't spill tonight,
distilled all the faces
into a bitter mantra, and
collapsed into a snub glass.
I iced them slowly tonight;
I blew the dust, pressed play,
and bathed the room in particulate
blue. I sat down to condense,
and then I absorbed tonight.
On the bare corner of floor
I sat rocking, singing
over those four smiling words;
they glow in my throat tonight.
I'm giving up on you finally,
holding myself, as a baby.
Tomorrow I'm going to be
puffy-eyed and pure.

Sean Robert Brennan

Pins and Points

Ripped from the loose tapestry of the night,
the sky, like a sieve, showing only pinpoints;
Missing, like pages in the phone book
torn loose by forgetful men without time;
The cover, worked like leather with care,
so much detail in every doodle made on it;
The spiral from the classified ads you took
to sell your grandmother's jewelry
pulled away, like taffy in the fall,
butter and sugar, saucepan and water boil.
Hard crack is a stage we all create some time;
candy is like life—never perfect, but good.
Tugged and discarded, like a bobby pin
holds for a while, has a purpose and point,
much like a needle without an eye, blind,
but the pin isn't for beauty itself.
It only shapes the beauty it touches,
like a whisper on the lips of anyone
who realizes life is made of sieves and stars,
phonebooks and candy, pins and points.

Kristin Michelle Punke

Three Square

It's an eighth of a mile to the Miller's
weeping willow. Our ten-year-old
limit. We had a blacker-than-a-furnace
dinner bell that would call
above the rattle of October winds.
Three-quarters to the Redmons' and the
twins' party every July 27th, past the western
edge of their drive, hanging out, pulling apart
and tasting the honeysuckle that grew on the southeast
side of their house. And there were our mothers.
With flower-bed dresses tugging at the breeze,
their laughter riding between whispers.
One and a half or so to the Jamisons' reservoir,
rectangular and buzzing. Its oxidized copper
made it greener than pictures of the Pacific, but weaker.
Holding up a corner of sky and failing under
the four-pronged dimple of water spiders.
300 paces to their green maze of corn and
Afghan rows a shoulder's width apart.
Shadows lifting a languid sun to sleep.

Grant Matthew Rost

My Church

Sitting bareback on a copper-spotted majesty
of equine spirit amidst a lonely open meadow,
we are surrounded for miles by tree lines of
various levels turning a palette of golds,
oranges, and reds. Wild turkeys pass us by; a
young buck studies us a moment and then
chooses to graze. The geese honk good-byes
as they travel in pattern, following warmer
air in southern skies. The crisp wind blows
colors in circles around us, whispering that
frost is coming. . . . The sky above is a deep,
inviting blue with sleepy, thick, white clouds
slowly moving across to somewhere else . . .
the rhythmic sound of teeth crunching on the
last few blades of sweetness, before it
succumbs to the decay of winter. I am—as I
look to the sky—at peace. God is all
around me. I am comforted by all his
creations, for I know that anything that is
good . . . is God. This is my church.

Christianna Elizabeth Capra

Arena

she said every man is
a forgotten stone
lost for the pleasure of invention
no direction to take
just the utopia of a north
and a bunch of stars
for a finest decoration
she had a good taste
for creation
a perfect sense of limits
stones travel through sand
and become rootless
how can a desert survive if positions change
she really knew well her story
rocks dream to walk
longing for miles to conquer
wanting so bad the blinding sand
inside the strong shapes
of the timeless
arena

Christian Jean Abes

Nature's Masterpiece

Fair morning was awakened
By a blue bird's twill
And every note was encoded
By the robins on the hill
Roses nodded their unison approval in silent
By unfolding their petals before the song was done
The hollyhocks and heather bathed in the morning dew
While bashful, little violets blushed in shades of blue
Every morning paints a picture of God's unending love
Every picture is a memory in His gallery above

Gloria R. Lowther

Why Is This for Me?

Nailed to a tree,
All of this for me.
He died for my sins, and so that I could live;
All of this he decided to give.
I know I'm not worthy, but he made it so;
I cannot wait to see his Heavenly glow.
When I'm sad I go to him,
Jesus Christ, the one who knew no sin.
When I get to Heaven, I'll be filled with glee;
But can't help but to think, why all of this for me?

Cortney Nicole Mlsna

Being Myself

Looking in the mirror, I do not see
Who I am, myself staring back at me
I created this sham, this farce of a life
In order to deal with daily strife
I hate this person, what they have become
I want them to die, their life to be done
I am so full of anger, I think I may bust
If I could just put it on the shelf to collect dust
Returning back to the mirror from the shelf
I see what I like, I see myself

Francis William Andrews

Close to You

I lie beside you you close your eyes.
I sit and stare and I'm hypnotized.
I must be one of the luckiest guys.
This is more than a feeling
I get when I'm close to you.
I'm lost and don't know what to do.
Then I look at you it all seems so clear,
I just can't believe I'm here
I want to be close to you.
Do you want to be close to me?

Cosper Waring Callan

A Tale of Tears

I feel bad as you sit there and say
That your family of love is starting to sway
I cannot believe that this is true
Or that this much pain can be happening to you
A tale of tears as you sit there and cry
You weep and weep till you've run dry
I feel my friendship is not enough
And my sisterhood has grown tough
I hope that can help through trough these days
I love you my friend in so many ways.

Jennifer Lynne Karpinski

A Prayer for Michael

As I look down at your precious smile;
I can't help but wonder all the while
how your mother, the woman that gave you life,
cares more about a high from a pipe
than about you or your sisters; it's sad as can be.
How she can be this way, I'll never see.
Another thing that I find truly sad,
is you'll go your whole life not knowing your dad.
Just remember one thing that'll always be true—
the rest of your family will always be there for you.

Jerry A. Vanderwoude

The Quiet in You

When you smile, I understand what you are saying.
When you laugh, your words are loud and clear.
Your eyes speak louder than words ever could.
They speak your wants and desires.
When you touch me, I know how much you love me.
The gentleness of your soul is overpowering.
It inspires me to be more than I am.
Even in your quietness I know how much you love and care for me.
I only hope that even though I don't tell you enough;
In my quietness you know I love you.

Ron Kenneth Hysell

Mystery

There is a fullness to life that cannot be explained
Many have tried and tried
There isn't a word, one word to describe it
Many picture so, but yet it is not
Because life is an indescribable
It is not one of the mysteries, but
It is The Great Mystery
Always to be unexplained when thought to be predictable
One of those immaterial materials
That always makes you wonder

Hayne Kim

Different Time

When we met, you were so nice,
But that was when I thought it had a price.
Now, as time goes by, I learn you're a simple truth,
Nothing to hide behind and no secrets to keep silent.
Only precise truth and gallant words left to take up your time.
A different world filled with new hope . . . and love.
Thoughts surrounded by a sweet mist,
Clouds gently filled with private hope of even better days;
Quickly my dreams have come close

ALL BECAUSE OF YOU.

Cassandra Eileen Gonzales

The Night of Demon Dreams

The midnight smeared on my muddy face,
as I knelt silently against the crooked oak tree.
I sat as branch and bark played evil music to my willing ear.
The demons heard, and soon I was not so alone.
My terrified hair wrapped briskly on my frigid cheeks,
as bony elbow rested on bonier knee.
I crawled quickly back into my shell—
shell of bone and flesh and rotted blood.
This is where I live. This is where I hide
from the evil demons of society's hypocritical standards.

Heather Renee Cowles

Love

Oh, love! what art thou, love? The ace of hearts,
Trumping Earth's kings and queens, and all its suits
A player, masquerading many parts
In life's odd carnival; a boy that shoots,
From ladies' eyes, such mortal wounds darts;
A gardener, pulling heart's ease up by the roots;
The Puck of passion-party false-part real—
A marriageable maiden's "beau ideal?"

Rebecca Lucinda Felts

Pain

The laughs and jokes I hear,
The snickers and cracks I deal with,
The pressure, the pain,
The feeling I know I won't be the same.
I try to ignore it, but I can't.
I try to escape it, but I can't.
I try, I try, and I try, but I can't
Find a way to evade the pain I get every day.

Jesse Segal Wides

A Mother's Hope

Another chapter in my daughter's life.
She chose to get married to become his wife.
He says he loves her. I know she loves him.
They'll say their vows and commit from within.
Am I losing a daughter or gaining a son?
I really don't know him, but I hope he'll be one!
If he protects her and loves her as a good husband should—
if he shares trust and understanding
and does the best that he could—
to keep her happy, secure, and be very much able
to provide some comfort and put food on the table.
If he's open-minded and is willing to share
his inner most feelings with his wife who cares.
If he respects her true feelings for her family and friends—
there are so many "if's," it just never ends!
When a child grows up, it's hard to accept.
But we have our memories, so with love and respect—
I say good-bye "to my child, my gift from above.
"Hello" to a grown woman, still a product of love.

Debbie Greig

My Only Gift

All I can give you is
This "moment in time"
To really be with you
And love you and honor you.
I will never be able to give it to you again;
Time . . . passes away, never to return for us.

All I can give you is
This "moment in time"
It may seem small
But it is a gift that only I can give
Filled with my love for you.
True . . . tomorrow may never come for us to share.

All I can give you is
This "moment in time"
To be with you now,
Touching love, touching God,
Connecting with you—you alone.
Time . . . the essence of my being—my only gift.

Thomas T. Tanemori

Justin of NSYNC

Love the little things you do
Your eyes are a beautiful baby blue
Inspire to live
Before you, I felt I had nothing to give
All I felt was pain and sorrow
Now I can't wait to see what will happen tomorrow
Lost on words, but with you near, I don't need them
Because on my face, it's easy to say how I feel
Thanks, Justin, for keeping it real

Randi Lynn Evans

Back in the Old Days

Out in Wyoming, back in the old days,
They rode horses right down the street.
Those days, women rode sideways.
I'd love to go back, that would be neat.

Out in Wyoming, back in the old days,
Even their houses were strange.
The way they rode horses, I'm still amazed
All day and all night on the range.

Everything they did amazes me
Working and driving the stock.
What I would give for one chance to see,
Oh! I wish I could turn back the clock!

Samantha Rochelle Shepherd

A Familiar Friend

It is rather sad
Already to have an intense hate for the next fifty years
Based only upon evidence from the past twenty-five
Or even just from the past one.

To think that a choice made
When too young to make it
Can sour two lives
And to feel so helpless to be anything but miserable.

And it is sad
To welcome as an old friend the bitterness that eats at you
Because sometimes you think it is all you have known
And, at least, it is familiar.

Christopher Jersan

For My Dutch Nanny

Beside the window where you sewed all day,
you brushed my hair before I left for school.
I remember that day you let me stay home, sick.
You danced as I watched from the stool, in awe.
You baked my favorite apple strudel.
I dreamt of getting lost in the batter
as you folded it with the wooden ladle,
the eggs and milk soaking up the sugar.

The aroma of spices still lingers,
although I can no longer see your face.
I can only imagine your fingers
kneading the dough as I beg for a taste
of the pastry you made from memory,
unaware then you would one day leave me.

Christiane Jane Huntley

Here Are the Unbreathing

Here are the unbreathing, the white faces,
Their actions spoken for by sword,
The cloven helm, the rusty halberk.

Here lie the unbreathing, the white faces,
Their blood not yet dry among the sand,
Both sides lost before they began.

There lie the unbreathing, the white faces,
Dead and buried in the caves of the minds,
Basking in the midday sun.

Somewhere behind. The undreaming. The forgotten faces.
There dreams tossed and torn along the way,
Their hopes, their lives, their fate.

Ahmed El-Khuffash

Grandpa's Battle

Dedicated to my grandpa who continues to fight cancer
You are my true hero I said
As helpless thoughts filled my head
I whispered Gramps I love you
He replied Rippie I love you too
After an embrace he was out the door
I wondered would I see him anymore
His body was shaky and weak
To any outsider his future seemed bleak
I was uncertain how the cards would be dealt
My broken heart was all I felt
Every night I cry as I pray
Asking God to take the cancer away

Tara Ann Barnow

Happy Cow Disease

Cow,
Mad Cow,
I understand your pain.
You don't like to be a cheeseburger,
You prefer to be grazing the plain.
Unfortunate T-bone,
Unfortunate flank,
Some kids may tip you over,
But it's only a prank.
This Mad Cow disease is a terrible scare,
We wish you would stop.
Or we'll start raising Bears,
Please, be a Happy Cow. . . .

Vance Fisher

The Tree

A tree stands tall, swaying in the wind
Never letting on the pains within
It grows and grows, reaching for the sky
Never once stops to ask why
But if the tree could speak, I believe it would say
You are killing our world in the worst kind of way
You cut us down and push us aside
When all we want is to be free and alive
We have many talents people fail to see
We create the air for you humans to breathe
So stop destroying our kind, you'll begin to see
The world is a beautiful place
On great part of the trees

Thomas Jeffery Pentecost

The Storm

Sometime life is like wading through a storm,
you often wonder when will the next one form.
When a storm comes up and darkness covers the land,
there's no need to worry, you are in God's hands.

When lightning strikes close to you
the Lord is saying give it all to Him and He will see you through.
When thunder roars loud and about
that's God's angels letting out a big shout.

When rain starts falling and it starts to flood,
just remember you are covered with God's blood.
When the sun comes out and it's shining bright,
that's God's way of saying it's all going to be all right.
Wanda L. Yarbrough

Dream

An individual's dream is a creative thought
That occurs within one's mind
You can make things happen
Or disappear
It's your many wants combined

You can look to the future
Or bring back the past
And make right what was wrong
If alone in reality
With no true friends
In your dreams you can belong

Dream. . . .
Cheryl De Loyola Gepalaga

Sunset

For Paige
Thinking of your face, picturing you in all I see
Feeling your warmth slowly fading away from me
Staring at the setting sun so distant and far-off
Missing your angelic touch, so caring and so soft
Remembering your eyes, seeing my torch fall
Is it better to have loved and lost than never loved at all?
The last streak of sunlight, a warm and golden cane
The one thing you never did was bring me any pain
The sun is dropping fast but, I beg, before you go
I want to give you a few last things—my mind, my heart, my soul
The bright has disappeared at last, darkness wipes away my light
Without you looking over my world, my life turns into night

Trevor Thompson

Someday in a Dream

To my husband, for loving me
Someday in a dream I'll meet my love,
And I'll have something to hope in—
That he'll come to me with love in his heart
While the gates of Heaven all open.
Someday in a dream I'll see his face,
And I'll know that he's right for me.
He'll open his arms and hold me tight,
And the love I've awaited will be.
Someday I will really live my dream;
Our vows will last all life long.
Our love will go on 'til the stars cease to shine;
Then I won't need to dream in a song.
Carmella Rita Maffia

Answer My Prayer

The blowing winds, darling, are close to my side,
Never too far, and yet always astray.

I speak your name aloud with soft, whispering lust,
Imploring your heart and soul to hear me pray.

But you are not here.
And I am not there.

The blowing winds ever so close to my side,
Wishing and hopeful one day you will appear.

Come to me, darling.
Perhaps you are near?

Forever wishing and hopeful you will answer my prayer.
Patricia Grace Joyce

Evergreen

The evergreen whispers softly, so not a word
is heard.
It lends its soft branch out to help a
weary bird.
It sways in the wind looking as soft as
velvet fur. When I'm sad, I just look at
it, for this tree's the only cure.

I wonder what it's thinking, this beautiful
friend of mine.
Since it lasts through winter's harshness,
it must be a sign—
That when I'm gone, it will stay here
for the next generation to find.
Brooke N. Goerman

Sarah

It started with a dance
and a soft touch.
As I lay in your arms,
I have never felt safer.
Voice of an angel,
touch of a dove,
the smell of a winter garden in full bloom—
it must have been fate, because
of the beat of a heart at a rapid pace.
I love who you are,
I love who you're not.
You are just you,
and I love that.
Jared Spencer Kohl

Fixing the Faucet

We swore to fix the faucet while Mom was gone away.
We conjured our rusty tools, and sat down to save the day!
But then the spout popped out, followed by the drain.
Dad bellowed, "Come on, girl, we've still got our brains!"
So we found the chain saw, and quickly made our marks.
The room was filled with roaring, and boy, did it throw sparks!
Dad pulled the up the pipes, and then got out the glue.
We were brave and we trudged on, like knights tried and true.
When Mom returned she would she be proud.
(The fire alarm was oh, so loud!)
But the firefighters came and saved our house by noon.
Maybe we knew less about plumbing than we thought we knew.
And maybe we'll read the directions before we start so soon.
Jolie Glaser

Have You Got the Vision?

Have you got the vision?
There's a million and one dreams
but have you got the vision?
Many are called but few are chosen,
but have you got the vision
to have the courage and the faith to do the impossible?
Have you got the vision to let God be your eyes?
Have you got the vision to soar like an eagle?
Have you got the vision to stand alone for what is right?
Have you got the vision to fight for your destiny?
Have you got the vision to listen to God and obey?
No matter what
have you got the vision?

Kalimah Muhammad

Tide of Emotions

With a wave of emotion
Like the wave of the sea,
The strangest feeling comes over me.

Your touch gives me shivers
That tingle my skin,
Like the pebbles and sand, one ends and begins.

The joy I have with you
Is the highest obtained,
Like the swells on the sea when a storm is inflamed.

My feelings for you
Will never stray,
And like the tides of the sea will eternally stay.

Lucinda Crima

A Daughter's Prayer

I pray the Lord will watch over
my mother every passing day.
And with the touch of his hand,
keep her safe from harm.

Because she always has a smile on her face.
And she will walk with so much grace.

She has more patience than I ever
could ever have.

I always thought she was a god sent to me,
because she love my hurts away.
And when I was bad,
she'd scold me in her own way.

Dorothy L. Rafferty

To Say . . .

There is so much to say
But I cannot find the words
I could talk for hours
Still not to describe how much I love you
You have done so much for me
And what have I done for you
You are my pillow
You are my teacher
You are my bodyguard
And more
But most of all you are the one and only
The all powerful and knowing
Daddy

Jacqueline M. Beard

Loss of a Baby Boy

In loving memory of Zack Strauss
'Tis late at night,
All the world's in fright.
The death of a baby boy,
The loss of a mother's most precious joy.
A life that's been forsaken,
His soul has now been taken.
A pool of hearts left broken,
A million words left unspoken.
The Heavens above you shall see,
Angels on high now watch over thee.
Rest in peace, my darling son,
Your life in eternity has just begun.

Amanda Jean Kidd

Beauty in Confusion

Contemplating the creation of such a woman,
Can only begin to continually confuse me.
How did she come to be,
Such a force of emotion and tranquility?

Will I ever know the sacrifices made
To create such a woman for all to enjoy?
How will I ever appreciate
This woman, who is more than priceless to imitate?

For if I could only hope
For a blessing in the flesh as this,
Then I would know to never hesitate
When being approached by total bliss.

E. Davis II

Definition Beauty

You're as beautiful as night
As beautiful, as a full moon's glow
Your skin is a milk chocolate cream
I like to smother you all over me
Your voice is so quiet and sweet
Just hearing you speak
Makes me weak
You have a smile
That could cover a thousand miles
You are definitely a work of art
Something that was developed through the years
Just looking at you
Brings me to tears

Maurice Franklin II

With Love

Girlie,
I love you like a sister, more than just a friend.
You always have a shoulder for me to cry on
And an attentive ear to lend.
When life gets rough and everyone else is gone,
Just know I'll always be there for you.
No matter what, just call.
I know as a friend, you'll always be true,
Even if we've had a huge squall.
You know in my heart, there's always
Going to be a special spot for you.
With love,
Your best friend forever

Amanda Carol Beyer

Trust in Me

I'll be there, trusting in you,
Wanting you to trust in me.

I'll be there when you finally fall
To catch you and clean you off.
"Face the fight tomorrow," I'll say,
While helping you back on your horse.

"Keep high with all your might,
Strike hard with my heart as your strength."

I'll be there, trusting in you.
Wanting you to trust in me.
There to be your companion
Through all the obstacles of life.

Nicholas Steven Schrader

Rain, Oh, Rain

Rain, oh, rain, why don't you fall?
Let Mother Nature's children rise.
Wash all the sins of man
And let the rebirth of sanity thrive.

Rain, oh, rain, why don't you fall?
Nourish the Lord's land's thirst.
Bring lovers together embracing,
As the raindrops seem to fall.

Rain, oh, rain, why don't you fall?
Listening to your voice through the meadows,
As you sing a song of purity,
That makes nature's will stand tall.

Sara Takieddin

From the Stars

There was once a single shooting star,
It was never destined to go very far.
But fate was there in the sky,
And another star came to fly.

Never destined to die that night,
Only to live for the fight.
Life is a battle that is fought in loves,
The stars burned out and formed two doves.

The doves flew to the edge of existence,
Fighting all this world's cold resistance.
And like all living things they died,
But in their love a new star has flied.

Joseph Alvarado

after good-bye

i almost called you yesterday.
got as far as the phone in the hallway
before stopping again.
day before, i made it to my car;
but after nearly half an hour of trying,
i gave up on the idea of dropping by.
really, what can you say after good-bye?
it's not that i'm afraid of what you might say;
rather, that we'll have nothing to say.
the scar hurts less than the opened wound,
or the memory of the pain.
the comfort of your voice might stay with me a day,
the pain through eternity.

K. Z. Salmons

Rotations

I kiss Mother Earth.
She whispers to me the secrets of her rotation.
All day I walk in mindless circles,
Never realizing my true rotation.

A man mumbles insensibly.
His calculations come in endless rotations.

Water and hair spin down the drain,
My eyes follow the rotation.

At the rotation of the wheel,
I feel my life slipping back into nothingness.
All the trees are dead, but like me,
They will all be back in their own rotations.

John Edward Orman

Gracing the Heavens

A tribute to Bob Baldschun
You left so many of us behind.
A father figure to most,
A friend to all.
Your teachings taught us the wonders of piano.
Your kind voice coaxing us to strive for the best.
Second best wasn't good enough for you,
And after a while, we all felt the same.
For all of us you left too soon,
But you had to go when the Lord called you.
You have left us with a precious gift,
One we'll never forget.
Now you are gracing the Heavens with your glorious music.

Jennifer Ann Cost

Broken Friendship

I can still remember when we were still friends
We used to have some fun and talk about things
Used to care for each other in times of problems
And to always laugh together about almost everything

All those beautiful things were unmercifully broken
Just because of a very selfish and unconditional love
We already forgot those murky and dark, but happy days
And started looking forward to the enlightened future

I hope you could and would have a very satisfying life
Without even having any pinch of worthless problems
Wishing you wouldn't remember our happiest days
The darkest part of our lives—our broken friendship

Parida Bianca Matuloy Dolor

Unseen, Unheard

The screen goes on, a name appears
And words are typed and sent.
We speak of life, of dreams and fears.
We laugh, we cry, we vent.

And over miles the feelings fly
By touching once on "send."
Careening through a cyber-sky
And landing on a friend.

Someone who touched your heart with words,
Evoking love anew,
And though unseen, untouched, unheard,
Is now a part of you.

Joseph L. Arotin

Godot

Well, I got a dog named Godot;
He's a good dog and I love him so.
Oh, Godot, Godot, Godot, don't ya know I love you so.
I give him a bath to wash his fleas,
He's under the car and into the grease.
Oh, Godot, Godot, Godot, don't ya know I love you so.
When strangers come around these parts,
Godot will bark and bark and bark.
He ain't afraid of nothin,' 'cept the dark.
Oh, Godot, Godot, Godot, don't ya know I love you so.
Well, he might eat dirt and he might eat sand,
But he's my dog and I'm his woman.
Oh, Godot, Godot, Godot, don't ya know I love you so.

Nancy Moore

Me in the Mirror

When people are around, I am me,
Just plain me.
But when no one is looking,
I dance and I sing.
No one can see me, but I dance like the rain.
No one can hear me, but I sing like the wind.
No one can feel me, but I am as soft as silk.
No one can smell me, but my fragrance is as
Pleasing as that of a field of daffodils.
No one knows what I do when they're not looking.
But I dance like the rain
And I sing like the wind,
All as beautiful as a rainbow.

Noel Ruth Leon

Snowy Sunrise

The candle light danced on the painted walls,
Music echoed softly off the corners of the room.
They didn't even notice when the snow began to fall
Or when the morning sunlight slowly began to loom.

The only thing they saw was deep in each other's eyes,
Their hands clasped together never to let go.
But soon it would be time to say their good-byes,
He would tell her this once how he loved her so.

She then walked downstairs and out the back door;
Quietly, so quietly, because no one could know.
Not a sound would she make as her feet touched the floor.
She would now be alone to walk in the snow.

Mandy Lynn Power

Throb of My Miss

Today, I miss . . .
I don't know what is the cause,
In the moment of clock already cracked
To bring throb of my miss.
Your voice . . . one of I miss,
Your sight . . . brings a love.
I'm really miss you . . .
In the moment you aren't present this time.
What?
My heart is dream,
Falling in love, which never happened.
Now all of this just a time can change,
And your love would answer all of this.

Maria Magdalena

White Fantasy

Unicorns dancing over clouds white as snow,
fairies surround you with a breathtaking glow;
a white shiny gown and hair like the sun,
this is the place where I come undone.

The fairies' laugh is like a high pitched chime,
money is nothing and neither is time.
The waterfall glistens and drops down on me,
I'm growing too fond of this sweet fantasy.

Isolation is peaceful for your spirit within,
love cannot hurt you and neither can sin.
Though I dream of this place, as sweet as it may seem,
this place that I see is only a dream.

Alicia Leigh Willis

From Where You Stand

From where you stand you can't tell
the dark side, which takes just one yell.
You see the smiles and the singing,
but not the frowns and the screaming.
You see the friends and the games,
but not the loser and the pain.
You see the sparkle in the eye,
but not the tear in the sky.
You hear the problems, but not the real,
because you can't handle them.
From where you stand,
you will never know
the dark side.

Krystal Calderon

Grandmom

Grandmom taught me how to walk
From her words I learned to talk.
She taught me how to play each day
and live my life in a righteous way.

My Grandmom is really neat.
I love most of the foods she cooks to eat
She yells at me when I leave the meat.

With out Grandmom where would I be?
somewhere standing on a lonely street.
Thank God my Grandmom is really neat
I love her, I love her, this I can repeat.
My Grandmom is really neat.

Dante Lamar Brownlee

The Sound of Love

If you listen, you'll hear secrets
Whispered softly from above.
These secrets are not ordinary,
These secrets are called love.

These secrets are the softest kind,
They'll impress you by their grace.
You least expect them to come,
Then they'll gently caress your face.

So, when beautifully whispered secrets are what you hear,
And your heart starts to beat fast,
Someone special is coming near . . .
The one you love—at last.

Johna Serenity Vandyke

Sing to Me

There must be a way to reach you;
there has to be a way to touch you.

I want a way to know you,
I need a way to show you
All of this beautiful love I have for you.

All your songs, how they've calmed my storm . . .
I yearn,
I wait
to see your eyes shine in sync with my smile . . .

Sing to me, oh, sing to me . . .
I don't want to be without you anymore . . .
You take the terror from my world with your song and smile.

Allison Polkinghorn

Me

I am surrounded by my kind, they help me play the game.
Sometimes I let them take the lead, to help me find my name.
And then I stumble and I fall, they keep on running fast.
Until I cannot reach them, now I'm behind at last.
Then one bright day I see a light, I wonder now and then.
Will I ever find out, could this be my kin?
Then as I go on wondering, about this light I see.
I really try to find out, what has been bothering me.
Now if I try to find too fast, I'll never reach the light.
But if I take my time at last, things always turn out right.
And so by going step by step, and missing none you see.
I find myself through all there is, and know that light is ME.

Shirley Carolyn Blair

Who Wants 'Em

Catlings, catlings, who loves 'em
Turtsies, turtsies, who loves 'em
Batlings, batlings, who loves 'em
We do, we do
Yell the catlings
We do, we do
Yell the turtsies
We do, we do
Yell the batlings
Catlings, batlings, turtsies, dogsies, ratlings . . .
Doesn't matter
Who you are
Someone will love you

Alyssa Rochelle Pratt

Unglued

Softer than this, I wonder.
Broken are the wings that held me,
and I have fallen . . .
If shame had a face would it look like mine?
Would it have my name?
The pain screams like the Styx
might sound on crossing.
The tiny German with metal boots
stomps around my head.
The migraine pulling away the
adherence of my resolve.
Softer than this, I wonder.
Will death be as soft as life?

Ryan Daniel Thomas

Plunge

She falls rapidly
into her symmetrical pit of despair.
As gravity begins to suck her descent,
she looks towards the stars.
The downward spiral becomes a distant memory,
A mere mirage, floating away
with the rigid springtime air.
The candlelit sky reminds her heart
it once felt whole.
Each glimmer seems to get smaller,
and then fade completely.
Until no longer is she falling,
but suspended in the night for always.

Lauren Nicole Gunsel

Mikey

He sits alone at his computer,
Wrapping his mind around the laptop
and fully immersing himself in writing.
It is of the past he thinks.
It is of the girl he loves.
It is the story for which he obsesses . . .
All else is nothing, there is only the screen in front of him.
His emotions flowing freely to the electronic void.
Inspiration hits—
He hammers at the keys relentlessly,
chasing the illusive thread.
He titles his masterpiece, types the last letter.

And says "Hardcore."

Kart I. Neuharth

Like an Ocean

Like an ocean,
Wide with wonder,
Hidden treasures deep down under.
Tears flow over ocean walls,
Sometimes can't contain it all.
Strong with emotion, raging waves,
Amazing calm, moments away.
Reaching out, open and inviting,
Sometimes scary, a little exciting.
The beauty of an ocean, is the calm we see,
Giving to others graciously,
But the wonder of it all sets it apart,
Just like the treasures of a woman's heart.

Rhonda D. Aulds

Little Angel

My little angel from above,
Daddy and I made you in love . . .
And from the moment I knew of you,
I was filled with such happiness and joy.
I can't stop thinking about the day I will first meet . . .
My little girl, my little boy.
You consume my thoughts, and all of my dreams,
I cannot begin to explain what you mean to me.
When you are born into this world,
I will hold you in my arms . . .
My little boy, my little girl,
And tell you how much I love you.
My little angel, how I love you.

Katherine Noel Rich

Artificial Friends

Then I closed my eyes and saw the emptiness
around me and inside of you.

The vast darkness crept upon us, like a thief
in the night, it stole your heart and robbed
me of my mind.

A great wall of nothing between us
surrounds me.

Then it crumbles down on top of me, but you still stand,
alone in a world of statues
that you have all become.

I will not die, and I will not be turned to stone.

Rebecca Sue Nix

A Champion

As your mom dances in the wind
Bows down and sings a hymn
As she praises the one and only treasure found in Him (God)

As your heart continues to mend
Let the love of God, a friend
God's love forever He will send
Always there to help you mend

So that through the sorrow His love can shine
Becoming brighter and brighter, one of a kind
As His arms embrace
His wings encase
Remember your mom has finished the race

Diane Phillips

Not by Your Lonesome

Everyone needs someone,
not just to call them a friend,
whose job is to support their heart,
but not completely mend.
That job can only be completed when the hurt
realizes that relief comes from God.
That is when the pain begins to end.
Everyone needs to know that
someone out there really cares,
but if they don't care about themselves
and realize that that is what really counts,
finding true love from someone else will be
as a good as a tree that will never bear.

Sophia Morisseau

Pamela Christine Finch

Little bird at twilight you come
flying home to me, to rest your little
birdy bones just close enough to see.
I wonder what you do all day, away
in another place. Are there baby birds
in a nest somewhere, is it away to them you chase?
Stay a little longer for I miss you
when you roam or bring your family back
with you and make this place their home.
I have given you a name you know,
though its sound might make you flinch.
I christen you from this day on as
Pamela Christine Finch.

Kathryn Everett Singleton

Love

Love doesn't come entirely from the mind,
Nor does it entirely come from the heart;
But it comes mostly from knowing and respecting each other,
As well as growing spiritually together.

Love can appear in many different forms.
People can love others as family or friend,
And even out of respect for a position.

People sometimes have different meanings for love.
Some think that love deals with physical affection,
And others think that it has to do with the spirit within.

Love is nothing but a giant mystery;
A mystery, which may never be solved the same for everyone.

Leslie Alan Koonce

Open Doors

As long as the doors are open,
you will always be in my heart,
As long as these doors are open,
we will never be apart.

As long as these doors are open,
we can tell our secrets true,
As long as these doors are open,
I can say how much I love you.

But if these doors shall close,
the love between us must not end,
Because no matter if these doors are not open,
you're still my dearest friend.

Mandie Nicole Nelson

Smiling Eyes

She bursts into the room
Like Ten Thousand Supernovas,

Spirits brightened by her Brilliance

Energy

Enthusiasm

and . . .

A certain sense of
Virtuousness.

How could anybody *NOT* notice
The Girl with the Smiling Eyes?

Gifford H. Teeple

The Poetry of Life

Underneath the blankets of melting snow
Are several seedlings starting to grow.
They tough through the crust of Earth's topping.
Sunshine and warmth seduces them from stopping.

Their progress continues quite uninterrupted
Continuing upward, seldom corrupted.
Never knowing that life's cycle is succeeding.
That becoming a plant is nature's repeating.

We too push on through our drifts ensuing.
We step ahead intent on improving.
Our temporary time to try out our vine
Of life with meaning and sense and rhyme.

Eleanor Kalman

Walk Me to the Bend

Anguish laden, I tread the bouldered path laid at my feet.
Stepping from the womb, separation complete,
Truculent forces straightway claw my being.
Fearful, I seek relief. My up-stretched arms a plea.
A Divine Invasion of my soul is launched.
The Infinite Pursuer thirsts for the fray.
Strife wages on through golden lock till grey.
Nature divides Red Sea-like,
Heaven and Earth vie for my allegiance.
Both entice, both glitter. A leviathan quandary.
I am at the bend. I choose.
Tears dilute with joy as Golgotha begets lilies.
I touch the Hand of God.

Bob J. Snyder

Crying Eyes

On the Holocaust

Screams are like hollow prayers that the whole world can hear
Silence is like a million voices screaming in your ear
Eyes are like empty buckets that were never filled with sand
Tears are like a storm whose raindrops never land
Dreams are now vision of the day that it will end
Hope is a message that a survivor dreams to send
Safeness is the feeling only a rescuer can bring
Joy is the emotion only birds can sing
Laughter is the medicine only a rescuer can provide
Freedom is the echo we hear from the world's chimes
Reminding us how people like this will forever change our lives
It's amazing how something so terrible could happen in so little time

Serene Ann Virtue

Purple

Purple runs and jumps.
It tastes as cool as shimmering spring grapes.
It wanders everywhere, singing its joy and triumph.
If you could feel it,
it would be soft and warm,
like never ending peace.
If purple could talk, what would it say?
It would probably say it is here to stay.
It would smell of wildflowers, hornbills, and jelly.
Purple would be the secret of colors, hiding till called upon.
Purple is a one of a kind; radiant, bouncy, joyous color.
Purple is as loving as a mother's gentle touch.
Does anybody dream of purple?

Jennifer Echo Harris

Vietnam

I watch my brother load the bus
He waved from the window above
I cried knowing he might die
On an unknown shore far from our love

Would I ever see him again?
How many years would pass before we embrace?
Could anyone understand our pain?
No one had anything to say; we needed grace

Riots on the campuses
Professors abandoning their classes
Smoking pot became the norm
Everyone acting like asses

Nancy Elizabeth Smalley

I Miss You

I sit staring into nothingness
realizing just how bad I miss you.
Visions of your face dance on the surface
of my every thought, of you . . .
you, I miss you.
That sweet intoxicating smell of you,
has wrapped itself around my senses
refusing to let me go . . . as if I would
want to be free of you. . . .
Your voice echoes in my head, conjuring up
glorious promises . . .
Something to look forward to while missing you.

Wanda Denise Mcphee

Glances

Eyes
more importantly your eyes
dark, lipped pools
reflections of your soul
sharp, piercing, penetrating,
and yet soft, soothing, welcoming

I get lost in their depths
I touch your pain, your desire
souls connecting, embracing, intertwining
I'm impaled by the sharpness,
stung by what is there
Hurt, yet the pain does not last
Then you blink

Heidi Ann Walcutt

Great Dad!

Dad
Dad the helper
Dad the Dad
Helped us through the good and bad
Loved him so, but we had to let go
We love him and he loves us
He used to drive a bus
He was nice and did not like to fight
But one day he passed away
I have to admit that day was a terrible day
But we still love you, Dad, we love you a lot
And don't worry, Dad, we will keep you in our hearts
Dad

Kenny J. Janson

My Friends

For Jenny Hartwell, Margo Thomas, and Tabitha Fiorello
My friends are fantastic!
No, they're not plastic,
My best friends are Tab, Margo, and Jenny,
They shine in my heart like a new penny . . .
No there's not many,
But they mean plenty . . .
They're there for me,
I'm there for them . . .
They care for me,
I care for them . . .
Better than all the rest,
Simply the best.

Tricia Carr

Nothing

Nothing is nothing to man or to beast,
for nothing can't surely exist;
for nothing ain't nothing, the more or the least,
if so, then please publish a list.

For nothing is nothing, be it con or pro,
for nothing is nothing at best;
yet, man has a habit of thinking it so,
making something of nothing his quest.

For nothing's a word, which we use to refer
to something which never has been;
a good word to use when one's mind is a blur,
hence, making what's not, known to men.

April Gower Rhodes

A Friend Like You

Written for my three best friends
I now know the true meaning of friendship,
It means a shoulder to lean or cry on
And to experience new things together.
The days I've cried,
The days I felt angry,
And the days I was sad,
You were always there for me.
When you walked into my life teaching me new things,
My life truly changed to the better.
I don't even know how to start thanking you,
But I do know that I know what friendship is . . .
It's a friend like you!

Yukari Holton

Daddy

I cry a tear, for every fear
misbegotten and forgotten
for every breath I take for tears I cannot shake.
It is your fault I'm locked in this vault
the silence here is bringing back my fear
every step I take, every rule I break
every night is darker than the last
it's happening so fast
I turned and you were gone far away, my happiness it would not stay
now your back wondering what to say, and still I sit sad to this day
you can't change my past, this will be the last
you want back in hopping I would forget your sin
never again will you be let back in.

Becky Michelle Leahew

You

You are the true meaning of what a life of
love should be based on.

You know how to show your love undying.

You know how to make me feel very much like
a woman.

You know how to hang the stars in the skies
and set the moon a blaze.

If there ever was a position for this to
be thought as a class then there would be
no better chosen than you.

Making you a class above the rest.

Tamarun Paullette Jones

A Perfect Day

I dedicate this poem to my husband, James Chase
Fourth of July has come around.
Oh, but I wish for Christmas.
A day on the beach, fireworks and flags.
But still I wish for Christmas.
Sand in your toes, sun on your face;
But none of this compares
For the warmth you feel at Christmas time
And someone with which to share.

So, when you see the fireworks
Think of me and say,
If only this were Christmas,
What a perfect day.

Sarah Louise Chase

He Runs

He is an exact copy of his father
Strong and forceful, shining in the sun
Running headlong into adventure . . .
Dirt flying as he tears through the fields
Then, silence as he stands with his
Nostrils in the air.

He catches a familiar scent and comes flying
Back with the anticipation of arms thrown
wide and a peppermint in my pocket.

Silvery white with his neck arched so
Beautifully . . . A gift from my husband
My horse, my friend, my Karbon Kopy.

Dorinda Lou Robinson

Ask Why

On my knees, with the wind at my back
and the sun on my face,
as I look up to the sky and
the tears fall from my eyes,
I wonder why mankind as taken the love
that God has given use for free.
As man kind kills with no tears of regret,
we have become no better
than the snake in the tall grass,
waiting to kill its pray.
So take a good look at your heart and ask, why?
As a baby is born, a cry sounds out
and with sadness, I ask, why?

Steve Moore

All You Need

I give and I give,
but I rarely get back.
I gave my phone,
but I didn't get anything back.
I gave my bike,
but I didn't get anything back.
I gave my car,
but I didn't get anything back.
I gave my house,
but I still didn't get anything back.
When I thought there was nothing else to give,
I gave my love,
and I got everything I wanted.

Francisco Javier Escalante

Arbor Day

Planting trees and watching them growing
Is like, so beautiful, a waterfall flowing
They cover the clouds that look like wool
These trees, so beautiful

Arbor Day comes in spring
When the flowers bloom and the rivers sing
The barren trees of winter are gone
And the mother deer has had its fawn

The summer breeze will come so soon
And the leaves of green are in full bloom
So don't be sad when the trees start changing
It's just God's way of rearranging

      M. Daniel Scarbrough

God's Love Will Abide!

As I walk alone in this field of dreams,
I wander aimlessly. Or so it seems.

I search for truth to see me through.
Some glimmer of light of what I should do.

I come to a brook and sit on a stone,
and it seems to me I am sitting alone.

Then a voice speaks to me "Do not despair
for you are my child and I am always there."

It is then that I realized God is
by my side and I know through it all,
His love will abide.

      Leslie Coates

When I . . .

When I was young, I'd sit and dream
I'd walk the hills and wade the stream
Playing with puppies and kittens, I'd be
Content in a world that set me free

When I was young, laughter was easy
I'd walk with friends that flirtatiously please me
Playing with images my mind only knew
Content with the touch of the wind, as it blew

When I was young, I never grew old
I'd walk with the knowledge of stories untold
Playing with memories never been made
Content with my youth, if only it stayed

      Cherie Dotson

The Abyss

As I stare into the abyss,
I try to figure out
Where the warm is coming from;
Is it coming from the fact that I am alone?

Wonderful yet scary,
There is so much yet to learn from it,
Yet I will never know its secrets,
As I stare into the abyss.

Maybe if I learn where it comes from,
I can learn its future
And where I'm going,
As I stare into the abyss.

      Melissa Ann Jacobs

No Longer I

Yelling, screams flowing through my head.
When will it stop?
I lay awake in my bed wondering.
Why do I have to listen?
Writing to my rescue and the comfort of my yearbook.
Now . . .
No longer I listen.
No longer I look.
No longer I love.
No longer I cry.
No longer I am happy.
I have lived my life to the extreme.
I am neutral, now and forever in eternal sleep.

      Sara Jin Correll

Why'd You Do It?

We were once best friends
That came to a quick end
When you got in the car
And you didn't get far
You had too much to drink
It all happened in a blink
I raced down the road
When I saw your car explode
I asked myself how could this be
Why couldn't it be me
You had so many things you wanted to do
Our kids were going to grow up together like me and you
All this because you wouldn't let me take you home.

      Melissa Marie Haslett

Ode to Me

To be or not to be;
God asks this every day.
Will I look to Him? Will I obey Him? Or just go on my way?
I know He loves me, I know He cares;
So, why am I afraid?
Why can't I release the world?
It is the thing which betrayed.
God only wants my love and my life;
After all He gave His Son.
Do I love Him that much?
Oh, I don't know, that's a big, big thought.
Well, on second thought, that's why Jesus died;
My sins He bought.

      Dorothy Ann Lester

Thinking of You

It was a year ago today.
That God snuck in and stole you away.
We think of you each and every day,
and in our hearts is where you will stay.
Every day we miss you more and more.
Hoping and praying
you'll walk through the door.
We are oh, so very sad,
that you left us behind, Dad!
So till that day we meet again.
I know God keeps you next to him.
So when I pass away and die,
God will take me to you in the sky.

      Deena G. Bear

Caught between Two Worlds

This is where I am, caught between two worlds?
I've lived a thousand lifetimes now,
All brightly woven, spiraling swirls.
You would think that I'd know how.
This is how it goes, not a simple dissertation in prose!
Some vestiges of a vibrant green,
A soul searching, a coming clean?
An expansive sky of azure blue—so very, very much to do.
A shimmering pot of shiny gold and aspects of patience unfold.
A deep, dark and muddled maroon—maybe memories of a distant moon?

A wave of daffodils, bright lemon yellow,
An illusive, undulating state of mellow.
An angry ocean of bloody red, loudly lamenting our loyal dead?
A rippled pier of brown and rust, a higher, wiser avenue to trust.
A flowing stream of aquamarine—the prettiest thing I've ever seen!
This is where I am, caught between two worlds.
I've lived a thousand lifetimes now,
All brightly woven, spiraling swirls.
Yes, I am beginning to remember how!

Leslie Jo Cheshire

38 Degrees

sun rises—molten heat
sweatin' already and it's only 6:18 a.m.
the air is humid—asleep or
suspended between worlds
the loud rattle of the fan is irritating
but it's that or slowly melt
that would be a sight . . .
brown chocolate thick melting in the heat
spreading viscous
too hot to think
watching in fascination as her
brown skin glistens with
sweat
pooling between her breasts
slowly
trickling
down
her smooth brown belly
collecting in her navel

Junie Desil

The Lightning's Lesson

I've likened the soul to a lightning strike
scorching the fecund earth below.
A potential difference between earth and sky
then the incarnation.
Like water seeking the course
of least resistance—we're here.
The ground absorbs and dissipates the charge
sooner than later,
ashes to ashes dust to dust.
The question perhaps is then
(as the spark leaves its dying trail
in the earth scorched no sooner from its arriving)
will the soul leave a pathway
for what must come next
but cannot—
were it not for this brief
flowering,
a showering of sparks
signifying our life?

William Kallfelz

Never Out Loud

He always rubbed off on me . . .
His mannerisms, his sense of humor . . .
His scent . . .
Sunlight made his eyes glow . . .
(Who thought brown would be such a pretty color?)
I loved him even then . . .
Thought about him every second . . .
Saw his face every time I shut my eyes . . .
Blinking . . .
The way he was to me, the way he has always been . . .
The way his gentle arms wrapped around me . . .
(I never wanted to let go)
He doesn't know that I think these things . . .
There are no words available . . .
(I am a conscious effort maker)
I can't help what I feel . . .
And I am rambling . . .
For the boy
Who doesn't love me back. . . .

Alissa Ann Cameron

Soulbound

Born into a heart of soul,
carried aloof by a pair of wings,
we spread them wide, so they sing,
of life to death, our last goal.

We root the stem of our heart,
in our beliefs, fragile and small,
from those blossom ourselves apart,
true in a dizzy appearance we dwell,
blooming in a heart shaped tulip.

Our grown souls sway between,
in between our reckless wings,
tearing wherever the wind blows,
the path we imagine, to which we cling.

From twilight dusk till shady dawn,
across playful life through vaining death,
we try to remember over and again,
who we resemble, which flower we grew
to become ourselves.

Jens Nedal

The Bard's Tale of Darkness

Beware, Beware the darkness . . .
For in the darkness of the night,
Red eyes glow bright,
Fear of nightmare take a shadowy plight.
Legends of beasts and monsters to come,
For blood they hunt from many or one.
Never again see the light of day,
As Evil stalks its virgin prey.
Yet, from near or far,
Come an adventuring fool,
Enter thee for a deadly duel.
Armed by weapon or by faith,
Courage found or speedy fate.
Monsters live for real or not,
The mind does quiver in its thought.
Steady ye stand in fear of the beast,
Unknowing in the darkness, it still sees its feast.
For this we find another death,
Torn . . . Shattered . . . and without Breath. . . .

David W. Hepp

No One Decides These Things

Once, when she was four years old,
she took the hand of her father
and stepped over the puddles left
in the potholes from the rainstorm.

One puddle was underneath an exhaust pipe.
It shone with oily colors: swirls of red, yellow, green.

"Daddy, I see a dead rainbow."

Her father clutched his heart
because it was such a beautiful thing
for her to say.

The years have gone fast.

Here she is now,
thirty-one years old, trying
to breath new life into a dead bird,
mouth to beak,
with her own small son watching
very carefully.

Jessica Anthony

To Imagine a Perfect Person

I thank God for being a sovereign God.
To imagine a perfect person and compare them to me
Would only lead me to wonder why God created me?
Why he made me to be not perfect,
But as human as man can be.
If God created me to be perfect, I would have no needs.
No need to learn about God.
No need to call upon the name of the Lord for help.
No need to depend on Him to guide me to the light.
No need for trials and tribulations that shows me my strength,
As I walk not by sight.
No need for setting goals to be as Holy as He.
No need for Him to teach me to love my enemies.
No need for faith to work with during my day.
No need to pray to ask for forgiveness when I go astray.
All these needs make me human
For all these needs make me, me.
So instead of God creating this perfect person,
He created ME.

LaDonya Trinise Posey

My Heart Is So Weak

My Heart is so weak.
That I can't even speak.

He makes me cry,
But I don't know why.

Why doesn't he love me,
is what I don't see.

He has deeply broken my heart,
Why do we have to be apart?

If I send him hugs and kisses,
Is that what he wishes?

He's like a dream come true,
but why am I so blue?

Us together,
Will be never.

I think all day, and I pray
that he will love me one of these days . . .

Cassie Lynn Justice

Cursed

A breath,
A heartbeat,
The soft whisper of unspoken words.
Caressing one another without even a touch.
Knowing each other intimately,
Being as one,
Knowing each other's most treasured secrets,
A caring that can never be explained,
A love that has crossed the ages.
The full circle, never broken,
Always ending the same,
Only to start over again.
The love never dies,
Even after the people have moved on.
The soul cannot rest till all has been completed.
So until then, they are doomed to return,
To start the cycle again.
Until they have found the love they deserve,
For they are cursed with love.

Stephen Lawson

Serenade of Darkness

Caught up in the Devil's dance,
Every curve, every movement,
In perfect sync with its solemn tune.
My body sways back and forth,
Like a tree trapped in the wind.
Every note that spills forth
Is a little part of my soul,
Finding freedom in the stars.

Devil's little angels,
All in a circle, hold hands and dance.
Dance with me under the moon.
Leap, spin, flail your arms in the air,
Become a wild mass of chalk white limbs.
Green, blue, brown, and gray eyes come alive with an eerie glow.
Chant the words over and over again,
Until you can't get them out of your head.
Dance and sing until the sun rises in the East.
Then it will be the end of our dreary tune,
Our serenade of darkness. . . .

Caitlin A. Lyons

As You Go

The angel came down and brought you a child.
We were so happy it made us smile.

Because you loved your child so good,
Your feelings about leaving are understood.

You're going from us will be a great loss.
My! I'm glad I got to be your "boss."

Easy to work with and ready to please,
Doing all your duties with all ease.

Friendly, kind, and considerate too,
No way to express how we feel about you.

Gifted and talented, you gave us your best,
While wanting to be with your child was your greatest test.

Now the decision is made to put your child first;
That makes our heart so full it almost bursts.

May the path you take be in God's plan,
And I know he will hold your hand.

Jewel Virginia Norris

By Day or Night

When there is light, it's day.
Where there is darkness, it's night.
When I'm with my guy, I'm so gay.
But when he barks, it's such a fright.
In the eve of falling leaves.
We go boating among the open seas.
A little one brings me his silent cries.
He just gives me a laughter of sighs.
When it rains, it seems to flood.
When it dries up it becomes mud.
In the morning black birds sings.
In the day, all hopes they will bring.
In the eve, he comes home.
At night, he likes to roam.
What is a girl to do, when she feels blue.
For she knows, what he'll do.
In the day or night, if her dreams come true.
She'll be gone from this feeling of the
Truth.

Susan B. Duet

This Race

My heart is troubled, and
I don't know why;
sometimes I feel I want to die.
My mind is weary, my eyes are teary,
my whole world seems dreary.
I cry out for help!
For someone to hear, for someone to love,
someone to be near, for someone
who knows my dreams,
as well as my fears of dying.
At an early age, sometimes I feel caged,
like a bird that wants to fly free,
to go and discover the real me.
Today seems no better than yesterday,
but why do I constantly feel this way?
My heart seems troubled, but I don't know why;
sometimes I feel it's time to die.
But if indeed my time has come,
I've truly enjoyed this race I've run.

Christopher J. Holmes

Friendship Love

To a dear friend, you have touched me so;
your unconditional friendship,
your caring soul.
You have been sent,
like an angel above.
You give new meaning to
Friendship Love.
Your caring, kindness and ability to share,
your faith and love lets me know you care.
You never judge. You lend an ear;
when I cry, you also tear.
The feeling of comfort and
warmth you give,
always willing to forget and forgive.
We share our thoughts and bare our souls.
We share our laughter and our woes.
Not many are blessed with a friend so true.
I am grateful to God,
I found Friendship Love in you.

Joanne Derchi

Challenge

Oh, my darlin',
Is life and our happiness
yet so hateful to you?
Do you mourn, yet so quiet
long for a new challenge;
life is but a challenge
and a possible new beginning.
You once had nothing but
a new beginning
coming into a strange land
with nothing.
Now half a lifetime has been fulfilled
with growing, loving, and raising yet another
unfulfilled life.
Is it so bad to move on,
to fulfill yet another dream or challenge?
Life is all but too short to pass up.
So let us grow old together in the
land of yet another challenge.

Brenda Biesinger

Nothing to Lose

I used to sit lonely, aching inside where I hurt,
Thinking "if only," wishing I knew what was wrong,
No one to comfort me, no one to say, "I love you."
You opened my eyes, babe; in front of me, I found you;
You are the light to lead me to my greatest fortune,
The cure to all heartache, the love to end my hate;
So now I have you in my life.
I will proceed forward,
And with you by my side, there is only one way I can go.
Holding your hand, we will climb the highest mountain,
Knowing we will keep each other safe.
I will always be with you, no matter what the case;
I don't care what I've left behind me,
For I know I have nothing to lose.

I got nothing to lose;
It's now time to follow my heart.
You are now here;
Forget my past,
For you will show me the way.

Dean Stephen Roberts

A World of Confusion

Life would be simple if we all truly lived by the same set of rules.
But we don't.

We live in a world where one person's love is another man's hate.
A world filled with so many types of religions.
Yet we are all just one nation under one GOD.
We all share the same faiths.
People go to church and pray for the same things.
Yet they call each other by different names.
There are those of us who believe in GOD and have faith.
But choose not to go to church to pray.
Does that make us fake?
I think not.
They say GOD is always listening to what we have to say.
If you think about it, he hears every prayer we make.
Whether we pray in church, our home, or even on the bathroom throne.
He hears us and loves us just the same.
People are unique, and they express all things in their own way.
GOD knows this, he wanted us this way.
He wanted us to be exactly what we are: human.

Kimberly J. Brown

My Fireman's Mistress

She selects the location; he hastens to her call.
She breathes a smoldering breath; he rushes to quench her passion.
She throws sweltering, fiery kisses and strokes his sweating brow.
Temperatures rise and rage way out of control.
In smoky embraces, she holds my man and laughs with a crackle.
He willingly plays her game without remorse, regret, or shame.
All their energy spent and their strength depleted,
he returns to me weary and worn—her appetite appeased.
With joy, relief, and pride, I welcome him home again.
She entices him over and over again with the promise
of passion reserved only for a fireman's need.
Let the mistress beware, his interest is that of a double blade ax.
His overwhelming concern is how fast he can put her out.
He renders her cold and dead in her path of mortal destruction.
What drives him from my arms into her flaming embrace?
'Tis far and beyond my reason, accept it be God's calling.
I always fear, despise, and dread my fireman's mistress.
Yet because of her, I love and admire him the more.

Sharon Denise Hunsicker

The Glass Ceiling

Ladies,
If the glass ceiling's in your way,
Climb the crystal staircase,
And make it a window in your floor.

Ladies,
Don't use the glass ceiling as your excuse.
You're not porcelain dolls.
It won't break you to crash through it.

Ladies,
Knock on the glass ceiling
To make sure it's really there
Before you come back wielding sledgehammers.

Ladies,
If you do have to shatter the glass ceiling,
Bring a dustpan and broom,
And be kind enough to clean up the mess.

No one wants to walk on broken glass.

Amanda Mary Doran

The Friend I Always Needed and Sister I've Always Wanted!

Like the friend I always needed to dry my flowing tears,
The sister I always wanted to help me overcome my fears;
You have faith in me at times when no other soul could
When my life is filled with bad, you seem to always find the good.
I love you in a way that words could never describe,
How do I let you know this way I feel inside;
I need for you to know these feelings that I've felt,
These feelings which will not be felt by anybody else.
We have this love for each other in a sisterly, friendly way,
This love and care you have for me I have no idea how to repay.
To imagine life without you, there would be no reason for living at all,
For no one will be there to pick me up when I trip and fall.
Without you in my life, no love like this would exist,
This friendship I have with you is something I will never be able to resist.
So here you have it, my sister, my guider, my best friend,
Here's to the love and friendship I know will never end!

Meg Adams

Sometimes

Sometimes I wake up in the dark or in the light of dawn
Sometimes I lie in bed and stare up at the empty ceiling
It reminds me of me, I feel useless, so I make some coffee
I am sad, so I write in an old notebook and dream of day
It's all right sometimes and unbearable other times
I like it when the weather is cold, and I go numb
Sometimes I remember being not so alone and cold
Sometimes people pass by my window during the day
When I don't feel so damaged, I sometimes see them
Sometimes I run outside when the wind blows
It makes me feel like I'm open, like I'm still alive
That and waking up on the floor of the bathroom
With slits and scratches up and down my arms
Sometimes the only way I know I'm alive is through pain
Sometimes I shut the blinds when the sun comes in
Then I sit in my chair, here in the dark, and I think
About society and what it does to people like me
Sometimes I wish I was in outer space, drifting away
Toward a black hole, ready to be erased into oblivion

Chris Prowant

True Love

When I heard the sad news of your passing by,
I knew that instant that I wanted to cry.
All of these emotions went through me fast,
As I thought of all the memories from the past.
Each time that I think of you,
I know that you are thinking of me, too.
I felt so wasted of everything
And what we both went through.
Nothing mattered to me,
Except that I had you.
I wonder what I am supposed to do,
Life isn't worth living without you.
Even though you have gone,
Your memory still lives on.
I know someday we will meet again
In Heaven up above.
But till then,
Please, remember,
It is you that I truly love.

Alana Renee Ford

So Willing to Die

Day by day,
Hour by hour,
Minute by minute,
Second by second
I am losing part of her.

Her life is coming to an end.
Some say it's not fair, some ask why.

An explanation awaits us all because she is so willing to die.

The angels call down from up above and ask her to go play.
She wants to be pain-free, no more sadness;
She doesn't want to stay.

I try to understand, I try to be okay.
However, the tears are unstoppable
I've cried myself a stream, a river, and then a lake.
She is still with me by my side, but leaving with little time.
Who knows when, who knows why
But she is so willing to die.

Bekah Lee McKinney

Maybe Someday

I want a life with a good man,
One who is kind and gentle.
But who will respect who I am,
Maybe Someday.

I don't want to be rejected anymore,
I've been used and abused enough.
My emotions feel like they've been cut and tore,
Maybe Someday.

A life with a man I can truly love,
A real family atmosphere.
Someone to be comfortable with,
Snug as a glove,
Maybe Someday.

There must be a man for me somewhere,
I wish he were here.
Sometimes I feel he is nowhere, oh well,
Maybe somewhere,
Maybe Someday.

Belenda Jo Gill

Silence

I sit here, staring into nothing;
The thoughts race through my head.
What is truth? What is life?
The words flow through me onto the screen.
Dark thoughts begin to take over.
What does it all mean?
Am I so different from everyone else?
Why does this happen to me?
Is this what drives men to insanity?
What's that? I hear screaming.
Maybe it's just my imagination.
My hands covered in blood.
My face, it's wet. It must be tears.
But grown men don't cry.
The room begins to spin.
Shadows surround me. Laughing and pointing.
They rip every fiber from my soul.
A life not appreciated; dreams unfulfilled.
What have I done? There is silence now.

Gary Gorneault

With a Heavy Heart

With a heavy heart, I tell you this
When I was with you, it was total bliss

With a heavy heart, I let you know
All my feelings that I never let show

With a heavy heart, I hope and pray
That you will come back to me someday

With a heavy heart, I found someone to care
And now I look around . . . lost . . . everywhere

With a heavy heart, you will find
Another heart for you, but not mine

With a heavy heart, I will explain just one thing
I gave up my safety for a single feeling

With a heavy heart, I try not to cry
As now I must say, "Good-bye"

It is with a heavy heart, that I now say
I will remember those moments every single day

Andrew Mangan

Forever Friends

Two little girls so full of life,
dreaming of the future and becoming wives.
Teenage years bring boyfriends and tears,
now looking forward there are only fears.
Feeling awkward and beginning to blossom,
braces are gone and life now races.
Then time seems endless and yesterday so far away.
Memories to laugh at but no time to play.
A fork in the road you must choose your way.
One becomes a wife the other loses life.
Time freezes and life becomes a picture book,
frames in time you pull up and look.
Moments remembered and never forgot,
but time still ticks forward on the clock.
Memories held throughout the years,
but now remembered without the tears.
Death is someday faced by all.
So laugh, dance, love, and live each day
as though it were your last while you're at this wonderful ball.

Clarice Eleene Larson

Eve

I have seen you, Eve,
sitting under a cherry tree.
I have seen you, Eve,
so young and naive.
You were gazing at the water
with your big blue eyes;
You were staring at the river,
reading between its lines.
When the sun came upon you
out of the blue,
You were frightened to know
It revealed your own soul.
When the ground beneath your feet
was burning with desire,
The rain and heat gave you their answers.
But was it an answer to you, too?
So fresh, wild, innocent, and new,
Or was It your own salvation,
setting free your true creation?

Tali Reuveni

Maybe

What's that you say? Maybe.
I think that's what I heard.
If you were a friend,
you'd say yes.

What's that you say?
You're not.
I think that's what I heard.
Then I'm not yours either.

What's that you say? You're sorry?
I think that's what I heard.
So am I.

What's that you say? Good-bye.
I think that's what I heard.
But our time was so limited.

I am sorry for the fights.
We've been friends forever is what we are.

Good-bye. I'll see ya, well, later.

Lauren Elise Davis

Nature's Gift to an Urban Girl

One fine day
When the weather was gay,
I went to the beach.
A sight beyond reach
I did see,
It was like nectar to a bumblebee.

The shells that were washed to the shore
Were more precious than any ore.
The waves that lurched up and down
Were more valuable than a king's crown.
The palm trees that swayed to the breeze
Were more musical than piano keys.

The feel of the sand in my hair,
The whisper of the wind in my ear,
The sun's light on my face
Enriched my life with God's grace,
Changed my figure of an urban girl
To one with the beauty of an oyster's pearl.

Niti Nandwani

Simplicity

The sea of grass caresses me as I lay upon it,
With my hair fluttering in the wind.

The air of unanimity, it smell so sweet,
With the cloudless dark blue sky of glimmering stars,
And the giant luminous white pearl reflecting upon the still waters,
As it gradually rises to relinquish the duty of lighting the way
For the lustrous yellow lamp with no switch.

The tree nearby lets loose an assortment of cherry blossoms,
That land in the water to drift silently and leisurely,
Interrupting the mirror image of the moon as it wanders on through.

The setting was so perfect,
As if a painter plastered it in this place,
And yet in this world, it happens so often,
So I wonder,
Why does it create such an enchanting and precious scene?
How is it so unadorned and yet have more than a thousand words
to describe it?
Such simplicity.

Ricci Marlo Yuhico

Christmas

'Twas the night before Christmas
and all through the house,
there I was, as quiet as a mouse,
looking to see if a good boy you had been
and leave a surprise, some toys, maybe a pen.
Then I saw all those thoughts that dance through your head.
No! It's not toys I will leave, but kisses instead.
I see by your dreams that you're too old for toys.
You have passed the age of being a boy.
It's not visions of sugar plums, or angels with wings,
but luscious girls and grown-up things.
'Twas then I decided, without any doubt,
without this desire, you surely would pout.
A fantasy dream, or sweet memories,
so I leave you with thoughts that only will please.
And when you awake, you'll remember not this,
but with a smile on your face, and the feeling of bliss.
Should I leave you that kiss, or leave you that toy?
I'll leave you your dream, your heart filled with joy.

Charlotte Carter

Transition

You're growing up
Forging your own path, your own identity
Leaving childhood behind.

You found a soul mate,
who makes you laugh and dream,
who makes you question your goals.

We're questioning too,
whether we taught you all you need to know
for this new adventure.

We're unsure as to our role now
You so grown up, we suddenly old,
in-laws-to-be.

We love you
and we have faith in your ability
to find your future.

You will always be a part of us
and we will always be your rock.

Susan M. Gessford

Kingdom

It was just us in our kingdom.
A simple courtyard of cool green grass
encircled by cream colored concrete that was
toasted warm in the afternoon sun
and chilled in the pale indigo evenings.
In our kingdom,
We were superheroes with beach towel
capes and pine cone grenades . . .
We were princesses with clover crowns
and 25 cent lip gloss . . .
Sometimes, we would sit barefoot in the dewy
summer grass and watch, with popsicles bleeding
their sugary nectar over our scraped
knuckles, as shades of evening rolled over
the oranges yellows and purples of a fading sunset.
We were all alone then.
Just me and my friends, all alone, in our own kingdom.

Micayla Naomi Nelson

Overcast Mirror

Overcast mirror covered with mist,
Mist—I can hardly see my face.
Faces I can see, but distorted, distorted faces irritate me.
I have tried to clean, but in vain.
Vainness it might be, but not hopelessness
Hope is the key to happiness,
Happiness which shall be mine, mine as long there is hope.
Hope which will create a way, a way out of this dark night.
Dark nights always have bright days ahead.
Ahead I know, there shall be gleaming sun.
All this will take time,
Time as requisites by misty mirror to elucidate.
Elucidate to show me brightness,
Brightness I deserve after such a long journey.
Journeys like these are always long,
Long enough for people to despair.
Despairing kills the soul.
Soul death—wanders one off from one's destiny,
Destiny which each one has to fulfill.

Zoona Zoka

A New Lullaby

I think I'll try a new lullaby.
Floating up high, up high in the sky.
Passing the stars that twinkle my eye.
One last deep breath and last blissful sigh.
My heavy eyes close, they're needed no more.
Seeing visions of worlds never seen before.
A glimpse of heaven, it must be, I'm sure.
It's hard to decipher these sights I adore.

I think I'll try a new lullaby.
Floating up high, up high in the sky.
You can come, too, if you give it a try.
Welcome the freedom your heart can't deny.
Floating up high, up high in the sky.
We're floating so high in this new lullaby.

The spectrum of colors I see with delight.
And the shapes that are forming overload my mind's sight.
Time's obsolete when you get to this height.
You can span three forevers in the space of one night.

Jimmie Ray Whittaker

Once for Me

Maybe I'll never be able to touch you again,
touch what we had,
but you were there
once for me.
I can still feel your skin,
taste your lips,
hear you breathe,
see the eyes that penetrated mine.
Maybe I'll never have that again,
but you were there
once for me.
I still have the imprint on my cheek from where you
carefully wiped away my tears.
Your arms are still there,
wrapped closely around me.
I'll never have that again,
but being able to have those things
just once,
meant the world to me.

Angela E. Fenn

I Should Have Painted the Road Grey

I should have painted the road grey
all those saints you told me would be there
I would not have wanted so much
had the road and doorway
been not so colorful
as your empty promises
of rainbow-moistened eyes
and rivers of sun-soaked clover
and naked souls that blend with the trees
I searched so long
to see these things
And had the road
been painted grey
I might have seen
the contrast
of a tear to the desert
and a song to an echoing vacuum
But instead you adorned my pain with hope
of long-stemmed roses feasting on a pebble

Lawrence Larry Termo

Unseen Bliss

Optimistic, open palm;
Single-handed sighs;
Tenterhooked-heart;
Glassy, glazed eyes . . .

Sweet summer breeze,
Autumn turning leaves,
Windy winter sneeze,
Colorful spring trees;
She has spoken,
There's a quiver in my knees.

Countless nights and endless days,
I've searched for treasure among the maze.
Empty discoveries have sunk the heart,
Then a vision begins to start.
The mighty trees part their ways,
And there you stand with a starlight gaze.
Rugged terrain is soon to follow,
But all is worth it to end my sorrow.

Richard Furman Thomas

Love

Love can mean so many things.
It can be
the most complicated word in the world,
and other times
it's as simple as black and white.
Sometimes it's used where it doesn't belong,
and other times it's never used at all.
Where love leads to
or where it ends,
we can never predict.
Love can be a drug, an addiction,
a happiness beyond your belief.
Love can hurt as well.
The reality is
words can never explain love,
but your heart can.
Just close your eyes and feel it . . .
if it's there,
you'll know.

Adoracion Radan Diaz

You

Freedom—always free . . .
Birds are flying, flowers are growing
Something different every day
Life can be really good
But only if you know how to choose your move
Choice in life is free
If you really want to learn
Then you'll feel the freedom in your skin
Always have to do with you
Don't forget to make your dreams come true
As long as you learn yourself
You'll see . . . this is what's all about
Learn to like you . . . learn to encourage you . . .
Learn to please just you . . .
Selfish you'll probably think
Who knows, maybe it is
But close your eyes and think
Why you do the things you do
Because mainly that pleases YOU

Kiki Hatzidimitriou

No Smile Today

No smile today.
Words spoken only a day ago
echo within the ear.
Rain drones down, God's tears, they cleanse.
Alone, heart warmed,
A touch, a lasting imprint.
Soul cold and hardened by this
Mechanized world, yet
Brought two a moment of brief lasting eternity.
Emulating transition.
Confusion, a state of mind.
Sorting through a verbal scar left behind.
Challenges naught a question of life
but a question of choices.
Fate deals a mean hand.
Heart talks, brain questions, warmed and alone.
Down drones the rain, echoes in the ear.
Yesterday words were spoken.
No smile today.

Cameron Scott MacDonald

Long Way Down

Looking down over the cliff
Deep within the ocean's mist
Clean, crisp air
With silent waves
Not so tall
Palms sweaty
I stood there
Above it all
Jumping forward
Falling eternally
Towards the sky
Only two thoughts came to mind
This is a long drop
And I wish I could fly
After one hundred and twenty feet, I'm still alive
Amazed and embraced
By soothing peace and motionless space
It's not hard to understand
Why my friends and I come to this place

Breeze Roznowski

Memories of One

Four years past now, since I have last seen
my small sister lying in her crib,
breaths small and short. A small whine echoes
through the room, Time to tube feed.
Feed machine uncontrollably beeps, long
silent now
Her skin soft just as her hair,
She is pain to the eyes to be seen this way.
Her lips soft to kiss good night.
Now a pleasure to the eyes all made up with make up.
And wearing the last outfit she will ever
wear, a long flowing baptism gown.
She is now resting in her coffin,
With hands clenching emptiness.
Memories are still held of her, still
missing her,
but eventually we will all see her again.
Hoping the last memories of her will not be
folded up and put away like her crib.

Phil John Gruver

One Minute

One minute, I think I'm in love or have a crush,
and the next minute, I don't.
One minute, I think I know things I'm going to
buy in the future, and the next minute, I don't.
One minute, I think I know what kind of house
I'm going to get when I'm older, and the next minute I don't.
One minute, I think I know what's going to become
of my talents, and the next minute, I don't.
One minute, I think I know how much money I'm
going to have and what I'm going to do with it,
and the next minute, I don't.
One minute, I think I know if I'm going to get
married or not, and the next minute, I don't.
One minute, I think I know if I'm going to have
children or not, and the next minute, I don't.
One minute, I think I know what's going to become
of my family, and the next minute, I don't
So, what is going to become of my life?
One minute, I know, and the next minute, I don't.

Keara Lynn Derr

No Peace of Mind

Sometimes it's hard to find
anything to ease your mind.
You look, you listen, you try to feel
what's there for you and if it's real.
There may be many options at this time,
but which one of them will be fine?
You try to choose the one that's best,
while you're contemplating the rest.
The one you choose may not work out;
but there are many, so don't you gloat.
You sit, you stand, you look for that thing
knowing the great joy it will bring.
How will you get it? Where will it be?
Would you find it under a tree?
Is it sports? Is it music?
Why is it so hard to choose it?
You're getting frustrated now, it's too hard.
You've reached the end of the rope;
it wasn't long enough, so you lost hope.

Craig J. Johnson

Beauty Unseen

Cast my body to the wolves
Their hunger desires me more than I
I need not be saved, so please don't try
Let the dogs tear my flesh
The earth take my blood
The sun dry my bones
Do not cry for me, not one tear
I feel no pain, I know not fear
This is simply my body
It contains my mind and soul
My body is nothing without it I'm still whole
My eyes may be pretty to see
But I don't need them to BE
My skin is clean and clear
But I don't need it to be here
I wish you could see only my soul
And not care about my body as a whole
I am me
And it's all I'll ever be

Torie Aleece Kimmel

Our Time

I've been sitting all alone
for the past 12 months.
Looking for a girl and it really sucks
Trying to find that girl I know,
then I finally find her . . .
You're the one I've been looking for
all this time.
You're the one I need,
till the end of time.
You're the one I want; girl, it's our time!
She wants to go with me,
but she can't.
She has a friend that
won't let us dance.
You're the one I've been looking for
all this time.
You're the one I need,
till the end of time.
You're the one I want; girl, it's our time!

David Brandon Tollison

Miss You, Love You, Need You, Want You!

Dedicated to Itamar, who lives so far away
Missing you means living on a bridge.
On a bridge of hope and waiting
to finally see you again . . .

Loving you means flying in heaven,
floating on the clouds so soft and white.

Needing you means living . . .
For to live, I need the air . . . you are my air.

Wanting you means being ready to give up everything.
And just for being able to spend one second with you!

I want to cross this bridge as fast as possible.
I want to float on these clouds forever.
I want to breath my air forever.
I want to give up everything for you forever . . .

I miss you, I love you, I need you, I want you . . .

Forever!

Jardena Tamar Lande

Wonderful Parallel

Somewhere in space
Between you and me,
Across the pallid, white fabric
Blackened with eclipsing regret—
We'll walk together,
Mirror reflections of a future
Not meant to be.
Ghostly silhouettes,
Skipping through the pale haze.
Young children laughing
In the wake of innocence,
Singed to ashes and scattered
By the aching breeze.
Salt and pepper snow
Waltz together, a slow spiral
Swirling around lifeless sculptures,
Frozen in time's fractured crystal.

Every crossroad only meets a short time;
All paths not parallel, fade away.

Anthony Westenkirchner

The Voyage of Christopher Columbus

Christopher Columbus sailed from Spain,
a straight route to India to show the Queen.
"The world's round," others said "It's flat;"
but him being the Captain, he said, "We'll see about that."
With Nina, Pinta and Santa Maria at sea,
October 12, 1492 will go down in history.
The direct route
didn't really work out;
scared of falling off the Earth
or in some sea monster's mouth.
Then the lookout shouted, "LAND HO!"
The entire crew smiled.
Chris said, "The West Indies, San Salvador,
Let's explore this new isle."
This was truly a sight rarely to be seen,
but now it was time to report to the Queen.
He made more voyages, searching for land.
This is Christopher Columbus,
an extraordinary man.

Nicole Joanne Watts

Rain

As I await it so patiently
For it is so hot,
And as clouds gather . . .

My hopes rise, and I cannot contain my glee
For ever so hopefully
The rain has come to take away the pain.
I cannot wait, I cannot say,
I wish it had come yesterday.

But I don't have time, even for regrets,
They're nothing of over which to fret.
Because, as it rains upon the world,
All is washed away,
And everything is new and fresh.

And as it rains, I think,
All my past has gone away.
Everything is once again new.
If only, if only this feeling, new feeling,
Could stay.

Jacob Lee Veltkamp

Long-Lost Love

As my eyes open
From the lonely night of sleep,
I realize I'm falling,
And I'm in too deep.
I just can't let go,
No matter how hard I try.
Just thinking of our memories,
I can only lie down and cry.
I miss you so much,
Regardless of how little it seems.
Just one touch of your lips
Can fulfill hundreds of dreams.
When you need me at all, I will always be there.
Just close your eyes briefly,
And say this little prayer.
My father, my all,
From the heavens above,
Please bring him back to me,
My friend, my hope, my one true love. . . .

Sean R. Joiner

The Struggle of a Woman

Born of a woman, you are her pride or scorn
You grow up yearning for love and attention
A simple hug, a kiss, or a smile
Really makes all your struggles worthwhile
Struggling hard to get an education
To be a value to your nation
Then came a hand that seems so gentle and kind
You open your heart and end up being mangled
Fear and rejection can make or break you
Where do you turn, who do you trust
Where is your mother when you are in the dust
No matter the hurt; love and respect is due
Up goes the shield of protection
Down goes self-esteem and confidence
The thought of dying crept in your mind
Then the soft voice said, "I LOVE YOU"
Tearfully smiling, you hugged your child
Thankful that there is still hope
You have the strength to be able to cope

Pauline Ethilda Hamilton

When I Was Young . . .

When I was young, I was thought to be older
than I was, it was very sad 'cause I was
restricted from saying and doing things
other children my age said and did.
When I was six, they expected me to act like
a sixteen year old. I was supposed to be
bold, was shouted at when I caught a cold,
But I was never ever as precious as gold.
Was it my fault that I was more observant?
That's the way I was born, that's the way I
was meant to be, why couldn't they see?
The truth was there, it lay right in me.
Now I am sixteen, thought to be twenty six.
Unfortunately those dreadful years haven't
passed, they still last. It doesn't make a
difference anymore, I had to bear what I bore.
I now know how to fend for myself, my parents
taught me, I now hold the key, and I put an
end to my misery!

Alison Anne Rita Aranha

Stay

some love stays and some love fades
it's the never-ending story of love these days
but I don't want this love to be the same
I want to put all else to shame
every day we are together I love you more
every look in your eyes makes me feel so sure
I pray our love never dies
I hope this is how our future lies
we can get through whatever
as long as we're together
so you stay with me and I'll stay with you
and I promise no matter what
we will always make it through
'cause without you there is no me
without me there is no you
as long as we remember those three words
and never let the meaning fade
never let it go away
together forever is how we shall stay

Sarah Marie Giacopuzzi

Black

Blackness,
The color of death.
It mourns the souls of the living,
And comforts the dead.
Scares society,
And creates individuality.
Darkness is the only place we can be ourselves.
No critics, or standards,
Only you.
Black causes fear in strange places,
But brings relaxation in our own beds.
How can a light change make the population quiver?
A color bring criticism.
Superstitions run wild in black.
The fact is this:
It is only a light change,
A color, and a superstition,
A figment of your imagination.
Black is anything you want, or wish it to be.

Jill Kristine Young

The Silencer

I do not sleep, I do not eat.
Human necessities, I do not meet.

I see your every move, yet I am blind,
My very name numbs your mind.

I don in black, yet with white angel's wings I keep.
Because of me, millions weep.

I bring mercy; I bring fear.
I bring the entire world to tears.

I am here, I am there,
I am simply everywhere.

I relish the shadows, darkness is my light.
But regardless of what time it be, I strike in both day and night.

Can you guess who I am? Or what?
There's no denying it, no if, and, or but.

I am the Silencer; Death is whom you have met.
But don't worry; I'm not here to take you . . . yet.

Gabriela Ramirez

Without You

I'd do anything
To bring you back to me
my baby my inspiration has left my life
tried my best to be nonchalant about it
but that day you left I broke down within
didn't know how to deal
you'll be remembered
In my heart my mind my soul
I'll never let go This is for you
for everything you do the inspiration
that keeps me going
my life flowing this is for you
In my dreams In my prayer
I know your there I know you care
But without you
I don't know what to do
who to turn to where to guide my life
how to get through
without you

Ashley N. Stanley

At the End of the Rainbow

Two birds flying in the evening sun,
Their plumage flashing in the glow of sunset.
A rainbow rises from the lake,
The hope for a new love
Rising from the heart . . .

The years of pain and childhood torture
At time filling my soul,
Clouding the memory and
Racking the heart . . . And yet
He is beside me, he understands my heart. . . .
His family gone in the fires of hate . . .

As the birds above the lake,
Soaring to infinity in the heavens above,
These two hearts touch in gentle love,
Deep as the sea, filling the soul with hope,
The rainbow's promise of
Love for all eternity and
Hope at the end of the rainbow.

Janetta J. Rosenberg

Frustration

I feel frustrated
When I know that you're there
But somehow you won't show yourself to me
I know that you know who I am
So why won't you come forward?
I am frustrated
That every night I wish for you
And yet you won't appear
I wish I had a genie
So I could snap my fingers
And then you would be there
I'm so frustrated
Wanting, needing
Knowing that you're there
But yet you won't show yourself
I need you
Don't you understand?
You can't leave me like this
I'm so frustrated

Lindsey Caryn Woolf

In Front of the Mirror

In front of the mirror . . .
I'm looking at my reflection
And it stares back at me.
It copies my every move
And every tiniest expression.
"I am your master," I say.
My reflection just smiles . . .
As if it's saying:
"Do you really believe that,
You silly little creature?
Who is more fragile, you or me?"
"I can break you in a thousand pieces," I shout.
It replies "I will come back again and again.
But if somebody breaks you,
No way can you be put together!"
In front of the mirror . . .
I am afraid to step away
And break this precious link
To a "mirror me."

Svetlana Gurevich

Marine

Trustworthy and strong,
thoughtful and kind,
courageous and steadfast
is the mind set of the Marine.
Yet he believes in his task;
sets forth to succeed without delay,
for his mission is of freedom and
security of a nation of nations.
Yet he is scorned for his diligence
to duty and commitment to country.
Why? Due to ignorance of a society and
fear of retaliation by the oppressors,
we, the nation, ridicule those who fight
so faithfully for us who cannot.
So remember the tears, the bloodshed, and
the relentless, faithful loved ones who fought for us to live free.
The Marine does daily.
So shall we!
Semper Fi!

Cathy Riley

The Light of Day, Mr. Tyler Ray

Today is the day that the heavens above
Carry away Tyler Ray from this Earth.
As beams of bright light shine on his face.
They lift him up to welcome his birth.
I don't understand; I can't see why
You had to leave in such a hurry.
So innocent with a child's precious touch
All along you were OK and we were with worry.
It's been over a year now, yet is seems like yesterday,
You were right beside us, laughing and playing with care.
There's not a day that goes by without thinking
That one day we'll wake up and you will be there.
The stars are the kisses you've given to us.
The moon is your soul, everyone can see.
The sun, your smile, has given us strength, love, and courage.
While raindrops for your tears come falling down on thee.
We want you to know that you'll always be in our hearts.
You're our angel looking on us with pride,
For one of these days, we'll be right by your side.

Tiffany D. Gonzalez

That Day

The trees swayed a dance of mockery that day.
Their rhythm merely reminding me of the
vibrance I have lost.

The birds soared to new heights in the sky—
with pride that would surely be unmatched,
telling me of the hollowness
that every new experience would bring.

The sun rose and shone brightly on the
horizon—taunting me with the promise of
eternal light in which to see my wounds.
The wind blew a sweet and bitter breeze
that glided across my skin like a gentle lover,
showing me the emptiness of another's touch.

I woke, an unsuspecting child
with bright and grand expectations
and the hope of a passionate future.
I slept, a broken soul with dashed dreams
and a new view of the uselessness of it all.

Lisa Marie Salvatore

Poet's Words

Poets of the past
Delicate words ringing throughout the years
Great minds and beauty spirits last
Mind and talent of a generation down
Useless words piling up into a meaning mound
Free of soul, free of heart
Give the beauty to their part
Play the role of the foe
Words unheard wanting for the voice
People already made the choice
Not to read the poet's skills
Not of force, but own free will
Poet's flow of intricate words
Dumfounded at the sound
Intelligent residents come to a halt
'Twas not the poet's fault
That the words of his mind
In their gallery of design
Should leave the "intelligent" so far behind

Julie Mandolin Long

Purple Dragon Dreams

In my dreams, I see him so clear
His outstretched wings
His fire-burning eyes
His thundering bolt
His breath of fire

I think sometimes I can hear his heart pounding in the sky
Like the sound of thunder
I can feel the burst of air his wings make
Like the wind so strong
I can see his fire-burning eyes
Like the sun so bright
I can feel his breath of fire
Like the heat from the sun

I think I might have seen him in everything around
In the sun
In the thunder
In the wind
If you look hard enough, you might even catch a glimpse

Nicole J. Akins

I Am Alone in the Darkness

I have a secret that no one knows,
That I know I must find. . . .
I am alone in the darkness,
The power is too strong;
I know that I am to suffer
Forever long. . . .
I am alone in the darkness,
Tears fall;
I will regret my treachery,
If I can at all.
I am alone in the darkness,
All is gone to sorrow;
I think if I can
Wait until tomorrow.
I am alone in the darkness,
But if I wait
My friendship,
My trait . . .
Will be lost forever, because . . . I am alone in the darkness.

Cind Colleen Jasmin

Happy Birthday to My Tree and Me!

When I was one, we had lots of fun!
On my birthday, Grandma gave me a maple tree,
And wished Happy Birthday to me!
As I got two feet tall, the tree was right behind me,
As I got three feet tall, the tree was taller than me!
We grew together each and every inch,
Each year my tree and me grow just a pinch!
April 18th, that's the day,
We both grow the same way!
This red maple has plenty of red,
It lives in a rock bed!
I like to call this tree the rainbow tree,
This tree has the most colorful leaves of any tree!
Green in the spring, red in the summer,
Purple in the fall, and pink in the winter, then loses its leaves,
Until next year on April 18th,
When we celebrate our 11th year together!
Happy Birthday to my tree and me!
"Thank you, Grandma, for my Birthday tree!"

Stacey Nichole Scarrozzo

My Best Friend, the Love of My Life

There was a time when I thought we were just friends,
But something changed . . .
The wheel spun a different way.
You looked at me and in your eyes I saw
a different scene.
You smiled . . .
my hand, a gentle touch it gave . . .
fingers, lifting your chin . . . lips, flawlessly placed.
There was a time when I thought we were just friends,
until a kiss took place.
We walk to a tree, a stream nearby,
flowing so gently under a clear, blue sky.
We sit there together and talk for a while,
then you look at me with that beautiful smile.
You look into my eyes and our lips meet.
You smell so good, you taste so sweet.
I lay you back on the warm, soft grass.
Our passion takes over, our love, at last.
Exhale, exhale, exhale.

Khalil Brian Zaghian

I Know Me

I know what I can do and to what lengths
I know my weak points as well as my strengths

Because I know this and it is never too late
I will apply the right action to determine my fate

Failure is definitely nothing I fear
'Cause I know that path keeps success far from here

The opposition all around me will not get in my way
My concern will be on the steps that I'll be taking that day

I know I'll have a clear focus along on this ride
It will be on those I live, serve and work beside

I know that the situations, people and things that I need
Will come to me as I focus at an alarming rate of speed

This mission gives me vision and puts lots of wind in my sail
It gives me daily passion to take the steps to ensure I prevail

I must remember to keep balance if success is to be
But I do not see a problem because—I know me

Tim A. Clark

Just One

I sit out staring into space
Desperately awaiting your warm embrace
I listen to your voice embedded in the wind
And remember the day when you were just a friend
The days of insecurities and fears
When each day ended with tears
You brought new hope in this heart of mine
When our romance started one place one time
And now it seems like forever has taken part
This week seems like years we've been apart
So I close my eyes and see your face
As I do so my heart begins to race
I can feel my lips pressed against yours
I hear your mom telling us its time to do chores
I hear your brothers battling again
Just because one can't see a friend
But nothing destroys this thought of you
Because your in a place in my heart set not for just few
Just one

Thomas Harold Hamm Jr.

A Child's Hope

A country traumatized by Mother Nature
Overlooking the needs of the living!
No respecter of persons, no warning of timing,
The Earth shakes, rumbles and cracks,
As it swallows what life it holds.
A surprise to much of the people's demise!
A child crawls out of a shattered home,
Her sad, brown eyes gaze through all the rubble.
Such unfamiliar sights and sounds,
She hears the cry of despair.
Minutes and hours pass, she sits and waits
Her brown skin covered with dust,
So hungry, so thirsty, so lonely.
Her exhausted body slumbers into a deep sleep
A tap on her shoulder awoke her.
She looks up silently to see a smiling face,
"You are one of the lucky ones to survive this earthquake!"
She waited and then asked . . .
"Sir, what is an earthquake?"

Lorrie Gawryla

To Tom with Love

To my brother, Tom
Your name was Tom, we loved you so,
But how we hated to see you go.
And now you're gone, we're all so sad,
We all wish God hadn't done what He had.
In the hospital, every night and day,
A preacher came, to help us pray.
Our prayers were answered a many of times,
But our last prayer, didn't make it in time.
When you died, the smile on your face,
Looked as if you were saying,
"I'm happy to leave this place.
To leave this place, to the Heavens above,
To look down upon the ones I love.
My friends, my relatives, my two brothers,
My sisters, my girlfriend,
But especially, my mother.
I've left to live up above, but still,
I'll look down, upon the ones I love."

Patricia E. Leone

Good-Bye

I am a women burdened with a heavy heart—
My heart cries what my eyes dare not reveal;
My lovers I must cease.
My morality bids them a hasty and painful release.
A forbidden touch to say good-bye
Would bring my flesh some peace.

To know what is right is often a hex.
My conscience doesn't sleep,
My mind becomes an enemy.
Stimulated conversations, grasping at visions
That you know you cannot keep
Your reason searches—

Forbidden phrases and feelings aroused;
Lovers to play—I cannot keep,
My husband has come home.
Toys to place in the closet,
Loves to bury deep.
I treasure you and wish that just one kiss I could keep.

Sheryl Ann Watts

God Answers

don't ever let anyone tell u that God
doesn't answer your prayers
it may not be when u want 2 know, but
it always comes just when u need 2 know
so many times i can remember when
i asked if certain ones in my life
were the ones sent 4 me, or maybe i just
hoped it was so, and i lacked the courage
2 ask the question 4 fear that the answer would be "no"
and it would have been, each and every time
only becuz i had not yet learned 2 luv
God first and best, be4 any man on His Earth
so when i realized, i asked 2 be fixed,
and from that moment, there was no more
confusion about who comes first
and there is no more asking, "is he the one?"
"or is he?" becuz i'm shown constantly
what's in store, and i'm pretty sure i know
that "the one" has now come

Erika Michelle Bryant

Aaron

Aaron, so small and cute, is the sun in my life.
His smile warms my heart, his giggle is
contagious without him I am unstable.

He came to me from Heaven above, full of love
and happiness I adore. My little grandson,
Aaron, who could ask for anything more?

I am lost without him and look forward
to the next time I see him. He is the
sunshine of my life and the hero in my house.

Aaron is the small but precious reward for
having children who have gone elsewhere
to live. I truly enjoy being the grandmother of the house.

Love to Aaron my special reward and hope
someday he too will feel I was special in his life.

Liz Jane Wilder

Love Gone Bad

Sometimes love just keeps pounding on this door,
Door to my heart and soul.
I wish I could stop it from spinning out of control,
but it just won't ever give up.
Tell me—where were you when I needed you?
When did you ever help me?
You have become my greatest fear.
Look at you, you crying loser,
you have hurt me again. . . .
How could you use me?
After all we've been through, you did it again.
I guess you feel you must,
Ashes to ashes . . . dust to dust.
Every time you think of me,
remember you threw away the key.
I've said good-bye to you and our past.
I'm sure you've found someone new to use and throw away.
So don't bother with me again,
I know better than to stay!

Megan Marie Greenstreet

Blind Hannah

Blind Hannah sits upon the bed
Vacant eyes wide, staring
Knows not the color of his shoes
Or unwashed socks he's wearing
And if you'll listen, he'll tell you
He's no longer caring, he's no longer caring
Blind Hannah's voice booms down the hall
In this house of worn out men
And he'll tell you 'bout the better days
And how it was back then
How he went to sea when but a lad
Saw all the beautiful sights
Until a shot in a Shanghai bar
Turned Hannah's day to night
Blind Hannah sits upon the bed
Blind old eyes wide, staring
And the bugs run up and down the wall
But he's no longer caring
Hannah's no longer caring

Kenneth Ray Boles

Lost in a World of Daydreams

Whenever I'm with someone and it's quiet,
Except the loud people around me,
Suddenly I feel like I've gone
deep inside my other thoughts,
But everything is still like it is.
The people around me are talking,
I'm still talking,
Yet, I feel like I'm not even there,
or I stare blankly at everything,
But I understand, talk, and answer.
Then when I snap out of it
And realize what just went on,
It feels like I was in a trance,
Like my mind was gone.
Yet it was still there,
Still telling my mouth what to say next.
But that is something that mankind doesn't know about.
Like many things are,
Everyone is just lost. . . . lost in a world of daydreams.

Stephanie Anne Dutton

Too Young

In the library all is quiet,
till two teens create a riot.
Hate is in their eyes,
their revenge will be when someone dies.
Cassie says yes,
but was that choice best?
She lies shot in the head,
yet her spirit isn't dead.
A teacher tries to save others;
please, dear God, don't let them kill another.
When it's over, 15 are no more.
They will no longer kiss their mommies and
daddies when they walk through the door.
The whole nation is in disbelief.
When will there be relief?
When they are laid to rest,
will come the real test.
All the people will break down and cry,
for they were all too young to die.

Natasha Lynne Hunt

If I Could Switch Places with My Parents

If I could switch places with my parents,
I'd make 'em do all the things they make me do.
Clean the floors, vacuum, and sweep the driveway, too.
I'd make 'em do everything, as far as it goes.
Take out the trash, wash the dishes, clean their room.
If they are bad, they're at their doom.
If only I could switch places with my parents,
I'd make 'em shovel snow a mile high,
Scrub the basement floor, by and by.
And plus they'd have to go to school.
They wouldn't have time to go to the pool.
They couldn't go out and play,
They'd have to work, even on a gorgeous day.
And when they're tired of cleaning up,
I'd say, "Stop whining like a pup!"
They'd clean up the dog's poop,
Scrub clean the front stoop,
Shake out the rugs, rid the attic of bugs,
If only I could switch places with my parents.

Teresa L. Sanders

Longing

I long to fall in love,
To be carried away by your touch,
To melt when you kiss my lips.
I long for you to take my heart, treat it well,
Don't leave it neglected and abandoned.
Help me grow,
Help me to understand you,
Love me for me.
Remember that I also have flaws,
And love them, too.
Teach me how to show my feelings.
Show me things I've never seen,
Tell me words I've never heard,
Touch me in ways I've never been touched,
And give me passion I've never had.
Oh, how I long to fall in love.
Carry me away from here with your angel's wings,
Take me to a place where we can be together,
Forever, in love.

Celina Dawn Sansone

What's in a Winner?

Winners take chances.
Like everyone else, they fear failing,
But they refuse to let fear control them.
Winners don't give up.
When life gets rough, they hang in
Until the going gets better.
Winners are flexible.
They realize there is more than one way
And are willing to try others.
Winners know they are not perfect.
They respect their weaknesses
While making the most of their strengths.
Winners fall but they don't stay down.
They stubbornly refuse to let a fall
Keep them from climbing.
Winners don't blame fate for their failures,
Nor luck for their successes.
Winners accept responsibility for their lives.
Winners make the world a better place to live.

    Mike Stanley Mendoza

Peace in the Storm

As the harsh winds blow, violently
bending the tops of the tallest trees
and battering the smaller one in all
its fury, I look out at the blackened sky.
I can see the (enormous) clouds rolling in.
I can hear the crash of the thunder
as the storm quickly roars
to where I am . . . it's going to be a bad
one, I thought to myself.

Yet through the raging storm,
I feel peace in my heart.
Because the one who controls the wind,
the rain, holds me safely in His hand.
He whispers to my heart,
"Fear not, I will never leave thee nor
forsake thee."
Lord, lift me up and let me stand in the
hollow of thy hand. Keep me safe till
the storm passes by.

    Juanita Plaster Roland

That Night

Iridescent moon, glistening over the water.
As I gaze into your eyes the hours are getting
Shorter.
Caressing your tender body, holding on so tight,
I didn't know what to expect, when we embarked upon
That night.
The whisper of your voice put a tickle upon my ear.
When I looked into your eyes I knew there was
Nothing to fear.
Thought my heart would leave in flight; knew the
Words you said were just right.
Only if you were in sight, could you understand
That night.
As we let our love come together, yours tickled
Me like a feather.
All the thoughts I had through the years left
Explicit thoughts in full gear.
Thank you, for being so polite, while giving me
Pleasure, that night.

    Takisha Rochelle Mellion

Final Days of My Father

I recall how he marched off to work with his lunch box in his hand,
How he stood over me and my brothers and
sisters barking suggestions and commands.
Telling us the right things to do at certain times in our lives,
Hoping at some point we would mature and take his advice.
As the years went by his advice turned silent,
His health became an issue, his body dormant.
Always the provider, adviser, and witty old man,
Now I live knowing the call will come soon—
that I cannot stand.
The sparkle and glimmer long gone from his eye,
Will always be there for me because I never can say good bye.

    Sandra April Jones

Seasons of Friendship

In cool winter, I like to go on the farm
Where I walk with my sisters
To the big barn.
We'd eat good green apples together,
As the blue sky went dark.
We talked of spring days, following butterflies
That flew in the fields,
And picking wildflowers.
In warm summer, they told of happy times
That went by so fast
And swimming in the water hole.
Of colorful fall with moonlight down
Upon the shimmering pond,
The stars, they glowed for us.
Nature's music was magic for me;
It brought joy to my heart.
I saw silent snowflakes bounce around treetops,
Night came. We started for home . . .
Love grows, and you are true friends.

    Jeannine Rucker

Unspoken Words

There are times that you look at me,
And I don't know what to say;
There are times that I look at you
Knowing exactly what to say.
These are the times
That the unspoken words mean the most.

It's best to remain unspoken,
How you can look at someone
And everything is said.
It is hard for me to say what I want to say,
Words that can best be said in writing
I can't even do that.

The more I like you,
The less I can say.
The unspoken words are understood the most.
We both know what they are, can't force it.
What I feel inside
Will be understood, but remain untold.

    Sharad Agrawal

Letter to My Goddaughter

This morning a new baby entered this world
And to our surprise it was a baby girl
A daddy's girl she surely will be
A brown-eyed girl now, but we will see
With tears in my eyes
I wish we were there to see our first girl with curly, blond hair
Mommy is tired
Because sleep she's had none
The first of many sleepless nights to come
We are all proud of your mommy and daddy
I know I am
Hopefully you won't make a habit of
Showing up at 3:17 AM
A lifetime of trials and tests of fate
I am sure daddy's already thought about your first date
As our families both lie awake in our beds
It is about you, Brittany Elizabeth, we have in our heads
We wish the best for you, as a precious eight lb. three oz. baby
And for mommy and daddy who will help make you a young,
beautiful lady

Brian John McGlone

Never-Lasting Love

Just when you're feeling safe and secure,
You'll find yourself alone, meek, and demure.
If you're basing your happiness and life on a man,
It'll soon come to an end, and you won't understand.
If you give him your everything, your heart, and your soul;
You'll be left all alone with the pain taking its toll.
You think it'll last forever,
And you'll always be together.
You feel like your love is enough to survive,
Then you'll have your hopes and dreams dashed.
And you'll soon realize,
Maybe love wasn't meant to last.
And you'll find yourself seeing your life as the past.
When there's so much good going on,
The bad will take over, and it'll be really strong.
You'll lose everything before you'll start to gain,
And you'll go through so many emotions, but mostly pain.
It really hurts to lose the one that you love,
But you can't place anyone higher than the one up above.

Tammy M. Benavidez

Her Face

I see her face.
Yet it has no shape.
She watches me, her eyes unseeing.
They're vacant and hopeless.
There is a sadness around her that is heavy.
I see her stance.
It is not tall and proud, but small and frightened.
She carries a world of someone else's making on her shoulders.
She has no expression on her face.
She is void of any emotion she may have felt as a child.
She has no color to her cheeks.
That proof of her existence is gone with everything else.
She has been beaten down by life.
Reshaped into something more accepted
and yet so lifeless and without spirit.
They have destroyed her dreams,
killed her hope, and broken her spirit.

I see this in her face,
When I look in the mirror.

Christina Kathleen Giese

Six by Four Feet

The Overcast shields the sun
Appropriate for the mood
A family mourns over the hole
six by four feet.

The family in disarray
over the fall of the family leader
a man, though old, still strong
before the death on the job
For on the cutting of his final tree
the tree gave out and fell upon he.
DOA, they told his wife
Grandma, now only devastation in her life.

As I stand before the mourning mass
Still too young to understand what's past
The man back east I never knew
The man only seen twice before
The man I mourn too, for it's the least I could do
The man in the hole six by four feet.

Michael Ryan Nierstedt

The Summer Breeze

I can feel it,
Warm and fresh.
The summer breeze is not at rest.
The trees are full of iridescent beauty,
And animals, butterflies, and bees are out again.
The colors, purple, blue, pink, and gold,
shine all over in patterns that unfold.
The tulips, marigolds, and wild flowers are out and spread,
The smell of pie and warm bread.
These are the things that all make spring.
This summer breeze will always change.
Life in the summer is lemonade and tea,
and long walks in the park, just like spring.
Summer is special and full of light,
While spring is just rain, rain, rain.
Spring is compared to flowers in May,
Summer is compared to sunny days.
Why compare the two? Why do these things?
Why can't summer and spring be the same?

Phaedra Dionna Williams

Here in Dodridge

You know, it will be different when we see each other again
Things change in weeks
in days
in hours
in minutes
in movies
in books
in music
And you'll change
And I'll change
And there won't be anymore electricity between us
No more light
The urge in urgency is back
to change this boredom
To not sit
not drink
not smoke
the brains out of my head
to help forget I miss you

Katie Marie Rodgers

Love Long Gone

We met so many years ago;
I remember now, I loved you so.
We parted, we went different ways,
Not knowing we would meet again someday.
You touch me, as you walk by;
The feel of that touch I cannot describe.
I know you want me, and I want you.
But time is gone, it would never do.
You have yours, and I have mine.
But you still make my light shine.
They can't see what we feel,
Not knowing ourselves if it's for real.
And once in awhile, I'll relive it in a song.
The memory of time soars, like a bird.
But loving each other now would be unheard;
You go your way, I'll go mine,
Remaining friends throughout time.
Wondering if ever what would become,
If we had loved all those years long gone.

Claudine Mosshart

To My Love: You Are . . .

You are my special star in the sky,
you are that last ray of hope,
that twinkle in my eye.
You are the best that's in me,
that hidden beauty that lies so deep.
You are the opening where stream turns to sea.
You are the shoulder on which I cry.
You are to me
that glimmer of faith that gets me by.
You are the originality that started it all.
You keep my balance,
never letting me fall,
You know my faults, inside and out.
You are that special feeling
that my heart never doubts.
You are the one my heart will long for
until the end of time,
you are my fuel and my fire,
my free verse and my rhyme.

Nicole Christine Shipman

Blue Hour

A cold darkness fell
in the morning stillness
at 23 Fitzroy Road.
A killing fume
drifting Sylvia into slumber,
sometime after that blue hour;
the blend of darkness and silence
before dawn breaks.
While the babies slept,
her lungs ceased breathing oxygen,
her literary genius left us wanting more,
while her children were abandoned,
like she so often felt.
Her daddy, her husband,
we've read about them in her literary gems
that pique our interest,
our wanton fascination with life and death
that touches the soul
of every true artist.

Christine Nanfra Coil

Lordess of the Porch

Watching her jump off the porch
into the great green unknown
takes me back to when I used to do the same.

The porch and I were younger then.
Dad poured the cement,
not letting me put my hand prints
in the steps.
I tried to add some of myself to my porch
when his back was turned away.
He saw what I did and smoothed it out;
mad as hell, he chased me away.

The porch and I have both grown old,
the top step crumbled away.
Now there's a new kid on the porch.
I heard my granddaughter say,
"You need permission from me
to sit down here.
I am the lordess of this porch!"

Nada Lynn Anderson

Making Do

Who can forget the ripple of disgust
that twisted the piano tuner's lip
on viewing the repair some former owner
(oh, no, not us) had made with a bootlace?
It did the job, holding the pedal up,
but who could fault his scandalized recoil?
By now we ought to be familiar with
that look of flouted, outraged expertise
surveying the offense of ignorant
contrivances, cheap shortcuts, slovenly
expedients only a manic devotee
of puttering could approve or even think of.
Just so, when we moved in, the electrician
stared at the spider web of circuitry
some tinkering precursor hooked on wiring
trellised the basement with. And the house painter
almost swallowed his cigarette when he saw
the alligatoring my hapless, hand-done
sanding had left sitting on the clapboards.

Omar Isidro Torres Garcia

Napoleon

She asked me for a secret;
like eight-year-olds with handshakes and
passwords through door seams,
she craved the words
without sound, asked permission to know
the Rosetta of my thoughts beneath granite
and carefully spliced air,
and I don't know what to say.
Why is she so hungry for silence, why won't
she trust the fragile vibrations of voice
wet with air?
To hold inside my mouth the awareness of
time, to conceive the raw blood
of human threads, to wrap our arms together
at the vein
and spend a gasp of time
with bleached airwaves,
but I hold my eyes down and whisper beneath
my tongue; I don't believe in silence.

Alissa Joy Walter

To Infinity and Beyond

The first time I saw you,
I knew you were the one for me.
The years we spent together were
the best that could be.
Then it came to an end, and we had to part.
We parted as friends,
but our love still remained in our hearts.
That is one thing that can't be taken away.
We are soul mates
from now until the end of days.

Kimberly Renee Holeman

Questions

The what if, the how, the what now, why, and when
Have come around to visit me, once more and again.
I sometimes find them quite frightful,
But the doors they open much too delightful
To try and stop, or lay down and drop.

And if you find you've asked the right one,
You're sure to find that the journey has already begun.
And when you find the answer to be "what now?"
You'll find the rest at the end, somehow,
And then return to the top.

Elizabeth Ann Nalepa

Beauty Is in the Eyes of the Beholder

A child walks aimlessly
Through the grass covered field
Enjoying the beauty that's highly concealed
His imagination wanders
As he lies on the ground
He listens quite eagerly to hear every sound
He chases a butterfly deep in his mind,
But in reality he can't
You see this child is blind
Beauty is in the eye of the beholder

Thomas Ace Hallowell

Modern Divinity

Marlon Brando could eat two entire chickens
at one sitting, but I cannot take in
two hours of pixels in transformation
wherein the man who made the method gold
speaks plain-like and mumbles a grated whisper.

No, he is not a god per se, but we
will always hold him to the waterfront
by his unkempt intensity (token
to a black, gray, and white motion picture)
that will perhaps exist longer than we.

Some have said that God dies when forgotten.
The Catholic crucifix should be commended;
the reformists didn't like to see him dead
and preferred the golden-globed depiction:
a risen, triumphant, unable-to-be-defeated god.

Maybe if we could hear him cry aloud
the death scream, not a stagnant whisper,
with the pain of our pain,
Marlon Brando
would die.

Sara LeeAnne Snyder

My Zachariah

Dedicated to Zachariah T. Hall
His words are simply music.

Gently flowing through my body,
Their truth primes me to reality.
Drawing laughter from my lips,
Their wit stimulates my mind.
Gracefully captivating my heart,
Their tenderness comforts my soul.

My world is simply him.

Baring the thoughts in his mind,
He awakens me to controversy.
Letting me see through his eyes,
He compels me to care about me.
Revealing the depth to his heart,
He entrusts me with his being.

I love my Zachariah more than simple words can describe.

Beth A. Mikulka

I Still Wonder (By Your Sisi) Chasity Chavis

I still wonder what you would look like today.
That is what I say every day.
I still wonder if you remember me.
I wish we could be together watching TV
I still wonder how you would be doing in school.
I wish we could swim together in a pool.
I still wonder what it would be like to
touch your hand again, but I just keep
wondering over and over again.
I still wonder if you're having fun,
because I know your time on Earth is done.
I still wonder if after all that sickness you are all right
but now I know you don't have to put up a fight.
I still wonder if you can hear me say, have a
Happy Birthday, Brent!!!

Chasity Nichole Chavis

Dreams

A world away, far from pain.
Nothing to lose, nothing to gain,
Anything can happen, anything can go wrong.
It's never determined, never long.
Flashes in your mind, flashes fly by.
There is laughter and tears, people die;
Up in the air, below the ground,
Pictures fly past, floating around,
Weightless, heavy. Laugh, weep.
Anything can happen as you sleep.
Chasing, run fast, beating, tears;
These meeting your worst fears.
Lovers kissing, passionate, love making;
This vision invigorating to your senses, breathtaking.
Senseless, painless, falling, flying;
In each glance people are living and dying.
Sunlight, darkness, chained, free;
Just to be left . . . just to be.

Brandi Gewin

The Balance of War

The smell of blood, the stench of fear,
bodies lay impaled on spears.
In their eyes the glow is gone,
back to God from which it spawned.
Proud and tall the victors stood,
and from this pride would bring more blood.
For with this win brings power and lust,
and to increase this power is a must.
Power and pride corrupt the soul,
to obtain more is their only goal.
Evil spawns from this hate
that sends many men to meet their fate.
In the end faith decrease
that good will bring them to their knees.
Evil loses and is gone,
but still the battle rages on.
Together bound by cosmic thread;
without them both, we are dead.

William Joshua Shields

My Mistake

Was it my mistake I let you go?
Was it my mistake I will never know
Racing down a darkened corridor
Running from the only thing that's pure
When we were together everything was all right
When we were apart all we did was fight
But the answers always came to diffuse our gloom
except this one last time couldn't save us from doom
I often still think of what could have been
But wonder if my actions would have burned me like sin
When will this pain ever go away?
Was it my mistake I never let you stay?
But now you're gone and there's nothing I can do
And this sharp pain reminds me it's true
I drop to the ground and begin to crawl over the rain-soaked leaves
My face buries itself in my dirty hands as my inner soul grieves
Must this confusion be the cause of my grace to fall
as I desperately crawl somewhere yet nowhere at all?

Justin A. Fisher

One Sweet Dream

It was a cold, wintry night
Not a soul was in sight
The cold air outside gave a heavy chill
The world inside was silent and still
In my own dreamy world, I looked out at the sky
Smiling at myself, I asked myself why
Perhaps it was the deadly darkness
Which, as creepy as it could be, gave out a sense of brightness
Or maybe it was the forever moon
Which sang in silence a beautiful tune
It could have been the electrifying stars
Fighting with each other, like racers with cars
Or maybe it was just the unknown mystery
Of what was really up there and its history
Whatever the reason, whatever it could be
The world up there was a dream for me
What was truly up there, I really did not care
As long as my dream was still there

Era Singh

Lost

How many times have I spoken to thee?
How many a night could I not see?
You were there watching over me.
Time is very precious my dear, but it is mostly death I fear.
A frozen breath chills down my spine, I was losing what was mine.
I lay in bed, listening to the clock chime.
I knew you were there, I could hear you breathing,
Your smiles through my memory, seething.
How could I not see you were slowly leaving?
Pain was cold and hard to my heart strings,
It's as if your touch was left upon my things.
My heart cries as the nightingale sings.
My breath is cold to the night sky,
I have no more tears left to cry.
I sense you all around the room,
It's sad and cold, like a tomb.
Now you withered away like a dying creature.
As I wept those painful tears, innocence lost.

Bianca Haeck

Thoughts

Breathless in anticipation,
in regards to the art of communication.
Wakeless hours spent
with someone who is heaven-sent,
who is a treasure of joy and intrigue,
and is pristine in the highest degree.
Melancholy feelings are swept
with sound of her sweet and beautiful voice.
It's a shock with her unlikely choice
in giving thoughts to me.
Her delicate soft eyes with a whisk of sleep,
that they embolden such a creep.
Her gaze which is so pure,
pierces the coldest heart like a cure.
Her shiny smile melts to the bone,
it corrupts the most devote drone.
These are just a few aspects which speak beauty's voice.
The thoughts given carry this voice to me.

Paul S. Smith

Heartbreaker II

I see your pretty, glittering face
upon my window at the base.
I wish upon a star so bright
that I can have you one more night.
Your face glows with light,
when I close my eyes tight.
I see you in my mirror,
when I brush my teeth.
I have dreams where I wake up crying in the night,
where I see you far out of sight.
Where you yelled I was yours,
I want to see you for 1 night, 1 second if you may.
Please, come running back to me,
and I will come running back to you.
I want you to feel the way I do,
so you know what I go through.
This poem is just for you, did you read it?
Now do you feel the way I do?

Heather Eliene Hartman

One Breath

So unbelievable is this living land,
Solely created by his holy hand.
So perfectly set against the Heavenly wind,
It's almost impossible to hold it all in.
Even the darkness of pain cannot hide
Earth's immortality when you feel it inside.
So within the shadows of your life
Breathe in and say, "Let there be light."
Just look at what was given to you;
The purest of pure, the truest of true.
With the crash of the seas against the sand,
So grand is the simplest creation of man.
Divinely cast upon the mystic stars,
He embodies all things from near to far.
Allow his essence to surround the soul.
Feel pure life in your heart taking hold.
Powerful even in the eyes of death,
And thus feel the world in a single breath.

       Elizabeth Marie Nemia

Goddess

I saw the night over the horizon
I felt the ocean mist spray life onto my face
I could not see anything before me
And yet felt safe where I was
I go into the future unknowing of assurance or certainty
I feel awkward yet brave
I have lost much, but have gained my courage
But only to go forward, not to go back
I lose myself in the wonder of my memories
I forget myself in the promise of my future
I have been to hell
Yet I have seen the face of God in many
I have known despair and witnessed cruelty
I am helpless, yet powerful enough to fight life's treacheries
I watch and hope of a future where I am a
Goddess of my own choosing
Owning the belief that I have created myself
For the benefit of my future

       Jennifer Kelly

Move On

I thought that you were it.
I thought that you were the one,
I never thought that this day would ever come.

How do I move on?
How do I forget?
How do I regret the day that we have met?

Please, help me realize that you're not the one.
Please, help realize that I need to move on.
Please, tell me that it's over.
Please, tell me that it's gone.
Please, tell me it'll never happen,
So I can actually move on.

The pain I feel is much too strong,
So you must really tell me to move on!
And if you tell me to move on,
Maybe then I will actually realize
That what we had is gone.

       Natalie Alkanovich

The Good Old Days

The days of quiet and calm
have been replaced by an early dawn.
The rush to meet life's demands
has really, kind of, sort of gotten out of hand.
As people scurry and hurry around,
they have forgotten where true happiness can be found.
It can be found in a friend's eyes
and in an elderly parent's sighs.
As people take the time to care
and love and share,
the true meaning of life begins to thrive
and people begin to be glad to be alive.
Families begin to come together,
to enjoy, visit, and, oh, yes, for laughter.
Have we, in our rush for success,
sacrificed any hope for happiness?
Oh, how I long for the bright, sunny rays
of the Good Old Days. . . .

       Renee Knobloch Richardson

My Hero

My hero isn't a superstar
He isn't an athlete
And he's not a comic strip
He's a real guy.
He doesn't exactly lead the perfect life
But he's got two cute kids and a very helpful wife.
My hero just recently entered my routine.
He came on such short notice
But he took a ragtag group of kids
And taught them what to do.
My hero helped us out, not even knowing us.
My hero is just an ordinary man
But an extraordinary teacher in a very long line of boring ones.
My hero was my Freshman year band director.
My hero is Mr. Scott Dodson, who always had his office door open
And was always there when someone needed help.
Whether it was with school or home
To my hero—thank you.

       Misty Dawn Kenly

Lonely

Lonely is a feeling I try so hard to hide.
I have no one to call "best friend" and walk by my side.
I prefer it that way. So nobody feels my pain.
I've nothing to lose and nothing to gain.
Some days I wish I could turn my life around,
instead of picking up the pieces on my filthy ground.
I've disgusted myself in so many ways.
I'm diminished inside by living in this haze.
When the sun comes out, I go in;
no one can see me for they'll know my every sin
The shame I bear keeps me dead inside,
I prefer to cover myself and forever I'll hide.
Hope is a word I will investigate for I'm not
sure of its true meaning or if I can relate.
Faith is a goal for me to have for now . . .
I'll enter it in my soul, someway, somehow.
For now, to survive . . . is all that I care
for loneliness . . . is the feeling I bear.

       Kathlene M. Cain

My Doll

To my dearest Apoopan,
who always thought I could do it!
A soft comforting arm
for me hold
when I am lost
That's what he is
be it day or night!
He always gives me a warm shoulder
for my burdened head to rest.
Late at night, when I cry,
he lies beside me . . .
His lifeless warmth
always finds its way to my heart.
Never he complains of my tears,
which stain his old jacket!
Then, when I am dancing with joy,
he stares passionately . . . asking,
"Will you need me again?"
But then I always tell him,
"You must be here always . . .
for I am just a living being!"

Sreevalsan Sasikumar Syama

Oh, Where Could That Gorgeous Sun Be?

Dedicated to those beautiful days out in the sun!
Oh, where,
Oh, where could the sun be?
So bright and beautiful,
shining your light upon me.
Can you come out?
Can you come play?
Can you bring happiness to my day?
I want to see the flowers,
beautiful as can be,
gleaming under your light of energy.
I want to pass people on the street,
watching their smiles,
as big as can be.
People laughing and having fun,
playing underneath the wonderful sun.
So please tell me,
Oh, where,
Oh, where could that gorgeous sun be?

Valdon Jeff Thompson

A New Beginning

When I looked into your eyes,
It was there I saw
All you had to offer
And knew that I would soon want it all.

The first kiss we shared
Meant more than you know,
Bringing back feelings
I thought I'd never again show.

Filling me with emotion
And touching my heart,
You gave me hope
From the very start.

Your hand in mine
And mine in yours
Allows me to feel
So safe and so secure.

I can only hope now
That this will be
A brand new beginning
For both you and me.

Elizabeth Ann Zavala

A Soldier's Fear

As my thoughts are sinking,
the life I had before
keeps me constantly thinking
of the things I adore,
leaving an endless aching.

My heart is cold as ice,
I am amongst the brave;
we fight only to entice,
bringing me closer to my grave.
What an ironic sacrifice.

My life in persistent danger,
I must fight to survive;
but I live in anger
in order to stay alive
from an unwelcome stranger.

Dressed in combat gear,
always training for war,
it is then that I fear
as a soldier, we will score,
but for now, I shall persevere.

Celeste Adele Heyer

Maybe I'll See You in a Dream

Though we're not together
And we haven't been for awhile
I sit here and wonder
What happened to the time
As it slipped through our fingers
We watched it go
Thinking we could go back
Or at least have some more

You're a bright shining star
That illuminates the dark
Lighting a pathway
For us to follow
Through our own sorrow
And cries of grief
You tell us to be strong
Your spirit is finally free
And I know we'll meet once again
Away from the pressure and the pain
But until then I'll wait patiently
And maybe I'll see you in a dream

Laura Renee Kuhn

The Coming Reunion

There's a morning that is coming
When that shout shall break the blue;
When our loved ones that are sleeping
Will rise up with me and you.

When together there in Glory
When around that blessed One,
When our trials on Earth are over,
And our sorrows all are done.

I will look to see my Savior,
See those marks in hands and feet;
I can't wait that glorious morning,
When my Savior I will meet.

Then I'll take a look around me
And I'll see my loved ones there.
What a joyful glad reunion,
When we meet them in the air.

But I wait with hope most precious,
With a tear that fills mine eye;
And I cry, "O, come Lord Jesus,
Haste that meeting in the sky."

David Netti

Universe of Love

The whole sky,
brightened by a small star,
This whole world
is passing by.
I think of us
While I think of you;
This must be love,
the one I feel for you.

Marco Stafrace

Instant Winner?

You click it seven times
Boxes are checked and windows pop up
Name, e-mail address, and interests
Entered into rectangles
More e-mail sent your way
Every day the same
Why do you do it?
Because you are a Winner!

Kismette Momo Cone

Just Right

Like the smell just after rain
Or dew at early morn,
My love for you my darlin'
Is perfect, never worn.

It's like the sparkle in the snow,
Like glitter at its best.
Just like a shower after play
Or like the sweetest rest.

It's like the sunshine after rain
Or thunder with its roar.
It's a drink of water
But satisfies me more.

It's like the flowers in the spring
With fragrances so bold.
It's the strength of armor,
Or price of purest gold.

It's like the bud before the bloom
A full moon late at night.
As long as I have you my love
My life will be just right.

Sharon Lee Theis

Choose

To miss out on something
Could be what you regret
You may want the chance to get it back
A chance you might not get

A chance that comes once in a lifetime
Might live up to its name
It could be gone forever
Your chance might come back to maim

Yet there are some things
Again you'll get the chance
To make your choice
To fall back or advance

It's unperceived on what life's based
It could be your choice
Based from your ability
To stand and sound your voice

So be very careful
Try not to make mistakes
To make or destroy your life
A choice is all it takes

Brett Allen Cagg

Hypocrites

They tell me to speak my mind,
then berate me and my opinions.
They tell me to be myself,
then ban who is the real me.
They tell me they will be there,
then shy away when I need them.
They tell me to play nice,
but they don't.

Susan Leigh Atkeson

Only a Dream

I felt the beauty of your love
as the breeze blew in the spring
I tasted pureness from above
my heart began to sing
If only what I feel and taste
were things from on this Earth
And not the fleeting thoughts of mine
to which my dreams give birth

Grace Christine Pittman

A Poem for God

My mom—she's gone,
How can this be?
The pain—so intense,
How could this happen to me?

I cry and it hurts.
She would not want this for me.
My son—he needs her.
He needs a Grandma, you see.

I awake and I front this fake smile.
I am fine, doing okay.
Time will make this better,
That's what they all say.

At home, I shed my mask.
I cry and I cry,
When will it get better?
Why did my mom have to die?

I need my mom,
Can't you see?
Please, send her back.
Please, send her back to me.

Tiffany Rene Hanrahan

Patchouli

Reeking breeze brings to me
The TV war again
Soldiers falling, falling
I knew them then.

Where was the love in
Where was the peace march
Where was I
When they died.

Connected by music
Connected by dope
Connected
I watched them die.

We all grew up
We all sold out
We all moved on
And there they lie.

So, I'll drink a beer
To TJ, to Jack, to Gil
And know that for some
War never dies.

K. Stuebing

Love

Love can light a darkened alley,
feed an African tribe,
it can save an unborn baby,
bring peace to front lines,
it can put a smile
on a child's dirty face,
it can build homes for the homeless,
and cure all loneliness.
You can go to ends the world
and see all that you can see,
but nothing is quite as lovely as love.

Anuj Chatterjee

Playboy

He was out on the town
Dispensing wit with a flair,
Debonair.
Devil may care.

Everyone envied him,
Handsome and tall,
Never suspecting a problem at all.

His best friends didn't know,
It was *peace of mind* he was after.

But I did.
I found his pain.
It was hidden in his laughter.

Ann Kingston

Sleeping with Sadness

I sleep with sadness
like I would a blanket,
all tangled up in the sheets
that I have been thrashing
at all night long
because of nightmares,
wishful thinking,
and the noise of grinding teeth
while I sleep,
while I live for that matter,
and I keep piling on more blankets
to try to stay warm,
but the blankets accumulate,
like my sadness,
and somehow
I have to wake up
and throw all those blankets
onto the floor.

Sara Maye Hanscome

Forever in Love

I live my life to love you.
You are my world, my dreams.
Loving you is what I do,
when your smile reflects moonbeams.

I was born to hug and kiss you.
My heart is in your hands.
Your love is strong and true.
We're bound by gold bands.

You took me as I was,
I never thought a man could.
You say you love me "just because"
and adore me you always would.

We'll spend our lives together,
'til death do us part.
All life's storms we'll weather,
never ever to fall apart.

Lydia Rose Murray

Forgiving Friends

You are my best friend,
You always will be.
Yet, sometimes I get mad at you,
And you get mad at me.
A lot of times, I just don't understand.
Sometimes I'm not sure what I should do.
But remember always.
I will always forgive you.

Katie Elizabeth Brown

Our Relationship

Ever since last year
I've waited for this to happen again.
I will always love you.
A part of my heart
Will remain with you
And I will have a part of yours.
You were my friend first
And I hope that will remain.
I need someone to talk to
About things going on in my life.
Please don't not be my friend.
I couldn't stand it
If you walked out of my life completely.
I've had a broken heart before.
I don't think I could stand it again.
How many times can one's heart break
And still mend?

Janet Hofmann

My Dreams

Sometimes I lie in bed at night
With dreams of what might be
Then there comes the morning light
And no more do I see.

My hopes and plans are in my dreams
They're wondrous and they're grand
But somehow when the great sun beams
They wash away like sand.

What happens when the sun does rise?
Why do they fade away?
Am I looking through with dreamy eyes
For those unattainable days?

So are those dreams within my reach
And I'm too blind to see?
Because grains of sand do form a beach
To be what I may be.

Sherry L. Wilson

Invisible Angel

I have walked with an angel,
Who suffers with every step.
He walks upon the Earth
Unaware of his divinity.
Marred in his mind,
Shunned by the pretenders,
Who everyone believes.
Tortured by his goodness
He struggles,
And suffers,
And screams.
And am I the only one,
Who can see his wings?
Maybe we all have wings,
And once in our lives
If we are blessed,
We will see one fleeting glimpse
Of one who will fly.

Jennifer Scuderi

The Power of Control

You drink life from my bottle—
Does it taste sweet or sour?
You leave me with only a drop—
Does it fill you or leave you empty?
You crush my bottle with your hands—
Does it make you feel in control?
You throw my bottle away—
Are you happy you are rid of me?

Kristen Kae Parman

Ode to Glen Ellen Cannon

Gallant Warrior, here you rest
Far from din and battle's quest.
Tales you hold of actions bold
By the boys that now lie cold.

In my youth I sat astride,
Spurring at your iron hide;
Bare feet bruising, but no mind;
Valley of the moon was kind.

How I've changed, but you're the same
Thanks to General Wagner's fame,
And Glen Ellen's spunky grew,
Who, with chains, stood guard for you.

Through the years, I've often thought
Irony that can't be bought.
There you pose, with steady aim,
Treating tourists like fair game.

Donald R. Oswald

Posting

Love's waiting here
That's what the sign says
Did I mentioned is it waiting for you?
Or did I forget to add?

These words make it clear
That more than ever
Love is waiting to pay
A price to feel blue
Or to live a life that's renew

So for these words
I'm posting
Hoping for something
That will transcend
More than any typesetter or pen
Can comprehend

Timothy Reeves

My Love

Love,
now that you're here,
I'm afraid you'll disappear.
Love,
love that is true,
and it's all because of you.
Love,
when you're with me,
it's like I'm in a dream.
Love,
you're on my mind,
love that I thought I'd never find.
Love, you are "My Love,"
sent from the Heavens up above.
Love,
when you love me,
I'm as happy as I could be.
Love, I will love you, for eternity.

Renee Rae Small

A Summer's Eve

My heart is like a rushing stream
amid the moonlight eve.
My love is overflowing
with an awe that can't conceive.

Bring forth the youth of feelings
from the depths of the unknown,
and I will show you just how much,
of me that you now own!

Irene A. Young

Fear

Fleeing like a thief
In the night,
Stealing nothing
Other than my soul,
My life.
How guilty I feel
When I have nothing
Left to give.
Fear has captured my
Carefree soul
And bound it evermore.
Fear has threatened my selfsame being,
So that I no longer trust that of me
That once was so giving, so free.
Fear has now cleaved my tongue,
That once spoke of love,
That once sung.

Jeannette Hinton Dorsey

Bare Your Blue Burden

Think of me while you sweat
That hot desert stretched out whole
I'm sorry it is not born of passion
Am I really what you wanted
Am I really who you wanted
And yet you are not here to say

Did you bear your blue burden
In order to lure me in

Am I merely an acceptance
Of something you felt unobtainable

What do you dream of more
Colors of orange and navy hue
Or burgundy warmth within you deep
Am I really what you wanted
Am I really who you wanted
And yet you are not here to say

Glenna J. Baldwin

A Flower Like Me . . .

One leaf dies
Another is born.
One tree grows
Another will survive.
One flower quits
Another will try.
And only God knows why?
One leaf falls
Another will soar.
One tree grows fruit
Another grows acorns.
One flower blooms
Another will say
Only one God knows
Who lives in Heaven above
And only one God could
Really and Truly LOVE

A flower like me!

Shannon Crouse

Stars

A crystal broken,
Way up high;
Of glory, a token
In the sky.

Sugar illuminated in the night,
There for all mortals to see;
Shining divinely, strong, and bright.
White fire arranged randomly.

Christopher James Thornton

Fear

I have a fear
Of losing control,
To fall asleep,
To be all alone.

I have a fear
I cannot explain
So I look to myself
To seek out that pain.

Christopher David Tice

March Promises

The sky is dark,
Winds do blow,
Snow is falling,
'Tis time to grow.

Love is waiting,
Soon shall it be,
Spring is coming,
My love to see.

Patiently I wait,
The time has come;
I say, "LET GO,"
THY WILL BE DONE!

Lorraine Hudson

The Moss

It is the coat of the living,
And the blanket of the dead.
It is the carpet of the wood
Covering trees and gravestones,
And perching tiptoe upon
The rounded stones of the brook.
To press of palm
It is a sponge—a balm
To overheated skin—while to the thumb
And finger gently grappling, it becomes
So many coolly pricking spikes;
The carpet for the living
That's woven from the dead.

Eric E. Hamilton

Only Yesterday

Retracing memory's footsteps
with only the horizon
keeping fading shadows beyond the surf.

Timeless sand
giving birth to silent shape,
receding tide my only welcome.

Dying crown of orange,
keeping pain's company
for returned alone have I.

Tapestry of salt and foam
unwoven, and yet renewed
saddened by your journey for but one.

Lancelot Elarionoff Jr.

Praise the Lord!

Dear God walks beside me,
And holds my hand each day
Without his strong support
I could often lose my way
He never fails to guide me
Should the need to call on Him arise
He gives me comfort, courage, and hope
He lifts my spirit high!
Oh, God! How great thou art!
Dear God, you are the greatest!
There are no substitutes.
Praise the Lord!
Hallelujah!

Catherine Beck

Good 'n' Plenty

Sucking on romances like candy,
I consume them,
pink and white
and sugarcoated,
as though they will never end.
But when I bite down
expecting some final sweetness,
I taste the core
of bitter, black licorice.
And spitting them out,
one after another,
I don't know why I take
any more into my mouth;
they all have licorice centers.

Ronald Swofford Arendas

You Are Joy

A tribute to Malcolm X
You don't look like a white man

And your beautiful smile
and presence burns
a spirit of truth in mankind

You overcame their hate
and their lies

by understanding
that a reflection
of what it is
and how they are
makes them not be
that way anymore

Wenfred Walker

Rock

Alone.
I stand against battering,
holding an unprotected arm
against bruising
harsh words, sticks,
stones, self-lack,
debris
from all parts of our world,
caught up and hurled at me
by the current.
Each one etching ache.
Give in.
No.
Waters rush over me,
beside me,
engulfing my mind.
But I stand firm,
no longer rough,
smoothed by the debris that beat upon me.

Andrea D. Lund

The View on TV

Women of intellectual different
backgrounds spark
a fire of knowledge and interest

Linda Bartlett

A Present

A present
wrapped in linen
clothed with
generosity
Its ribbons are sacred
possessing inner beauty
with lilies that
are ivory and no longer
white, because of
her frailty
Her bones was seasoned
and broken, bearing harm
to her soul
but
the center is heart-shaped
filled with diamonds
Many scars
yet many facets
It is beautiful

Kathleen Kane

Forsaken

I sit alone
In this god-forsaken world
Staring in fear
As the dark room begins to twirl
I know not what to do
Or how to stop the spinning
Like runaway baseball
Inning after inning

My heart
I feel it crushing
Held so deep within my breast
The blood begins its steady gushing
My soul is filled with its unrest

As waves that crash along the shore
The searing pain
It rolls upon me
And I fear again
My heart shall beat no more

B. N. Fields

A Mother's Love

To my baby I must say
I love when you move from inside of me.
I love when you kick
from the outside; I can see.
To my baby I must say
I love knowing you're growing
each day as I do.
I love the feeling you bring over me:
unconditional love so rare and true.
To my baby I must say
I love the beating of our hearts,
synchronized and in time.
I love knowing you can hear me
as I say to you this rhyme.
To my baby I must say
I love you now;
I love that we are together,
For you are a part of me,
for now and forever.

Tom Sawyer

Love

Love is gentle, love is kind
Love is peaceful in my mind
Love is where I like to be
I want to stay with someone who loves me

Ashley Kay Harshbarger

Sand and Sea

You are the sea,
I am the sand.
You can move me with a touch.
You can drown me with a smile.
Your sparkling eyes,
like shimmering sunlight on the waves,
can gaze into the depths of my soul.
The sea is so strong,
so silent, so serene.
The sand is so easily moved,
shifted by the tide,
shaped and formed
by the fingers of the mighty sea.
And yet, it is the sand
that surrounds the sea,
holding it gently,
enfolded with love.
I love you, little one. . . .

Jason Christopher Synodis

Dark Angel

Into a lonely, black, and empty space
Falls an angel with a tear-streaked face
Her heart knows not which way to turn
Her wings are charred, her fingers burn
The black fire blazes bright with heat
Her face is sad, her heart once sweet
Now lies lonely, black and burned
The life she knew now has turned
She spreads her wings and tries to fly
Only to fall from the deep black sky
All around her the darkness falls
On hands and knees to nowhere she crawls
She reaches out again into the night
But broken wings can bring no flight
The black fire burns her hands and feet
To what dark end will this angel meet
A dismal grave doth lie ahead
Where innocence dies and pain is fed

Andrea Nichole Burns

A Starlit Night

Have you ever looked in to a
Starlit night.
Your eye's wide open.
The reflection of the bright starlight.
You gaze into the dark night
with eyes bright with starlight.
Can a person go on with the
Light from a star
To look so far into the dark sky?
With light that surrounds you to
Keep you warm at night?
To sing a warm song, to keep
A sad heart, from coming apart?
To no one's eyes that have
Seen so much,
To let the starlight into one's
Life will bring happiness.
So, one will glow as bright as the stars
In dark night, with all the other stars,
That glow so bright at night.

Michael Lauterio

Underneath It All

Underneath exterior,
Underneath clothes,
Underneath my words,
A special heart still grows.

I might not be a queen.
My looks might not be the best.
My words might not always be kind,
But I am as good as the rest.

If you look underneath it all,
You will find out it is true—
You will see my beauty inside
And understand me too.

Michelle Keep

Not from Here

We are not from here
We came from another
Place and time

Our home is long since gone
This is our home now
And yet it is as if only
A moment has gone by

Oh, to be home again
If only for a moment
Yet never to return

We are not from here
But here we will stay

Dove Head

Are You There?

Are you there?
A look of pure gold,
A feeling only I can see,
A judgement untold;
Why can't I just be
A flower that won't bloom,
A love that can't stay?
Feeling of loneliness . . .
Run far away.
A beautiful song resigns,
The name of it unknown;
I now know why my flower
Just can't see to grow.
The peace of not knowing,
The silence of despair,
A sorrowful look toward heaven;
But all I see is air.

Christina J. Pryor

The Racehorse

How happy is the racehorse,
to run along its race;
for it knows not of win or lose
though win its saving grace.

How happy is the racehorse,
to run around a track;
it matters not of running fast,
or beating the others back.

No longer happy is this racehorse,
to run around a ring;
for now its spirit can only fly,
like bird with broken wing.

And taken back to stable,
to sit and wait and wonder;
of what joy, oh! What glorious days,
had waited for it yonder.

Nicholas A. Pizzi

Always Stay Strong

"Always stay strong"
You always told me
That whatever I do
"Always stay strong"
In everything I did
I was successful
Because I
Always stayed strong
I know things aren't
Going too well for you
Right now
So I want to tell you
"Always stay strong"

Britney Renee Robinson

Music

At first there is quiet
Then the ballerina moves
As she goes
Her body goes
In graceful movements
The room
So empty but then
The ballerina
Dances to an empty audience
And when she finishes
She hears the bravos
See the roses fly down
Then it ends.

Mary Catherine Edwards

To My Love

Dragons flew through electric mists,
They crossed my soul and opened doors.
They brought the light into my life
'Cause they bound my heart to yours.

"If you're true to one another,
The love will feel divine!"
That was what the dragons said
And bound your heart to mine.

I feel your warmth so close to me
Even though you're miles away. . . .
I see you whole within my dreams
And know it will be real someday.

And even though we're miles apart
I hope you feel my beating heart.
I know my love will shine on you
And may one day our dream come true!

Alina Rubina Tomescu

Tomorrow

Soon today shall be gone.
It will simply fade away
To make room for tomorrow,
The sweeter, brighter day.

We shall see the brightest sunshine
That we have never seen before.
And we will cherish its memories
From now to evermore.

We shall hear the sweetest songs
That the birds could ever sing.
The good news of tomorrow
From mountain tops shall ring.

Tomorrow shall be happy
And lively and gay;
For as you shall see,
There will be no today!

Marcia Elaine Young

A Red, Red Rose

Thou art a red, red rose
Without any thorn
Like a newborn
Full of affection, but silent
Like breeze in twilight
And as a shiny star at night
Thy eyes say everything about thy heart
But thy lip closed as bloom
And there is only sound of boom
There is only a dream that smile
In thy feature, as sunset
Because of life, as a bet
Thou think to lose in this lottery

Nader Naderi

Inaudible

Tortured, twisted, out of shape,
the body folds in such disgrace
The mouth stretched wide,
the stomach wretched

Crumbling, falling, to the knees
the breath expelled
so deeply till suffocations warning cry
brings an inhale just in time

It comes and goes throughout the night
the silent cry becomes a roar . . .
At last it's spent and brings relief
sweet sleep for now my Inner Child.

Kathleen Elizabeth Holdaway

A Teardrop Falls

A teardrop falls
A mother cries
No one hears
All but lies

Coming far
And coming near
No one listens
Hard to hear

A scope is focused
On a tree
Where the teardrop
Fell for thee

A light grows dim
Upon a limb
A teardrop falls
Once again

Janean Michael Earley

Distance

Distance is many times like a force
Driving two apart . . .
Although you can't see it,
you can feel it in your heart.
Distance causes things to change,
and what was once right seems wrong.
It blows everything out of proportion
For it takes over, robust and strong.
Distance brings forth darkness,
hate, confusion, and dismay . . .
It is so controlling,
and it won't go away.
Distance embeds itself,
deep down in the vicinity of the heart;
To move it, you have to face reality,
and you have to make a start.
Distance . . .

Andrea Faith Hinson

The Decision

The decision could be,
The best or the worst,
Overconfidence,
In reality is lost.

Could it be the end,
Of a satisfactory definite,
And the start,
Of an overwhelming possibility.

Conformity screams for definites,
But happiness,
Happiness breathes,
Ambition for a greater purpose.

Ruth Hannah Dack

Simple Joy

From one I asked a hug,
From another I asked a smile,
From a third I was given both,
Haven't had that in a while.

Each of these acts,
As simple as they are,
Can bring so much joy,
Even to those who seem far.

Happiness may be to each his own,
Yet there is something we share;
The simplest things can mean the most,
In times of grief or despair.

Jacqueline Wilson

secrets

one flickering candle
lights the watch tower in my mind
and i rest peacefully
with the sounds of life
trickling rivers through my ears.
a natural rhythm etched
deep in my brain
reverberates softly
in my warm, dusky cave.
all the secrets of every world
are known to man
in the moments between
life and sleep,
amorphous in form,
unidentifiable to any sense,
just leaving you filled with
the warmth of knowing.

Tina Lore Stolz

Explanation, Please

How do you
Describe a feeling
That is completely
Indescribable?

How do you
Speak words
That really shouldn't
Be spoken?

How do you
Control an anger
That flashes
At a moment's notice?

How do you
Understand
What is going on
in your mind?

Mandy Janney

Christmas Given

Christmas tidings for Christ was born,
Now 'tis the season His name adorned,
Some behold Him, some untrue,
For we decide this life anew.
In a manger lay His bed,
Stars a'glitter upon His head,
Just a world, His Father's love,
Forgiving freedom, wreath of love.
Angels whisper, silent night,
Wise men traveled, by God's light,
To offer love, in a world with none,
And now we hold, His work undone.
Alas, the wreath that suffered Him,
Has now become goodwill to men.

Amy Jeanette Jones

Lot's Wife

Amidst euphoric dreams,
In a drunken stupor,
Petals of turquoise fall
From the eyes of the
Black Madonna.

Repentance is not necessary.
Nor a kerchief to hide her
grief stricken face.

No communion for the past,
No confession for the present,
Only to turn back now
Would transform her into
A showering pillar of salt.

Scott Kulowitch

The Kiss I Miss

Time can be such a precious thing,
No one knows what tomorrow brings.
One thing I rather missed,
From your lips that one sweet kiss.
Some days turn to nights,
Though we've had many fights.
There was always that one sweet kiss,
The one now I surely do miss.
My heart begins to pound,
My legs wobble on this shaky ground.
A tear starts down my face,
As I begin to state my case.
All I need and truly miss,
From your lips that one sweet kiss.

Johnnie Cornwell

When We're Apart

Love
separation hurts,
your touches and warm embraces
the shine in your eyes and laughter
the jokes and anger we once shared
missed like the moonless night
when birds stop singing
the seas never waves and clouds cold.
Love
when will we ever meet again
to mend the patches and tears
to whisper the sweet song again.
Deep inside the cold eternity
lay the body and soul
in deep sleep and endless peace
share our prayers of devotion.
Love
How I ever missed you.

Norisah Hashim

Confusion

So much pain and suffering,
Nothing ever ending it.
Life always so depressing
With each waking day.
Suicide may be the answer,
But I don't know
If I want to go out that way.
I just want someone
That understands me,
That doesn't judge me
For what I've done,
For what I've said,
But loves me
For who I am now.

Rosalie Peck

Thinking of You

Thinking of you
every day and night,
crossing my mind,
and undermining the might.
I want to hold you
and to hug you,
also keep you by my side.
Your beauty has captured my attention
and captured my thoughts.
And of all the things
that you may have caught.
There's one thing left for me to do,
and that's for me
to give my heart to you.

Charles R. Heisinger Jr.

Creature of Magic

She sits there all calm,
Breaking with the light of dawn,
Sparkling with beauty,
Guarding her duty
With the move of her head
And her wings that do spread.
She casts out her magic
And throws out her light,
Giving those who are blind
The vision of God's sight.
The magic is grand
With glory and prayer;
Those who know this creature,
As the angel up there.

Paul Fioroni

Take Me Home

Time and time again, I wonder
where you've been. It's getting
dark and I'm all alone. Won't
you please come take me home?
My soul cries out to you,
it's bitter with regret.
My heart is full of pain
and sorrow, over things I
can't forget.
I played the game the best
I could. I thought I did it
right. Only now, do I see your
mercy and grace in the light.
Dear God, please come and take
me home. How long must I
continue to beg and plead?
Surely you must know there is
nothing of me left to bleed.

Dee J. Ryan

roger

1, 2, 3, roger is the one for me,
roger is for me and not for laramie.

i wish he went to my school,
that would be so cool.

he is my heart and soul,
you know that is my goal.

i dream about him at night,
he is always in the spotlight.

i love when talk to him on the phone,
i really wish he had a clone.

1, 2, 3, roger is the one for me,
not for laramie.

Leah Jeanette Thomas

Hummingbird

Hummingbird
fluttering effortlessly,
seemingly searching
for what lies beyond the nectar.
What secrets do you keep
beneath your sweet, short wings?
When you sleep
do you dream of iridescent petals
and the smell of the air,
pure, pleasantly pungent,
subtly changing
from bud to blossoming bud?
Your life for mine,
so short, salubrious, simple.

Abbe Louise Lyle

Roses

Don't bring Roses when I'm dead.
Bring them to me big and red.
Bring them to me when I can see
them in their bloom and full of life.
Just don't bring me reds.
Open your mind
and bring all kinds of whites, yellows,
and ones I haven't seen before.
God has given us such a beautiful Earth,
plant my roses in my home.
One day when you have your home
and I can't see you every day,
I can see my roses
and I will think of you.

Deborah Odette Salazar

This Something Special

Something is always with me,
even when you're not here.
Something is always with me
with hopes that you were near.
It's with me everywhere I am
and everywhere I've been.
This something is always with me,
although it can't be seen.
This something that is with me
is found inside my heart.
It's something that feels so strong,
it's been there from the start.
This something is so special,
it means everything to me.
This something is so perfect,
it's like the stars above.
Shining, twinkling, lighting my way,
this something is your love.

Johanna Binstead

Home

While driving down the street, I see
A tired, old house in front of me
The paint is chipped
The shingles gone
There's big dirt patches
In what once was lawn
It looks so bad
The neighbors frown
The big, old fence
Is falling down
It makes me cry
It makes me moan
This is the castle
I once called home

Carole Lindsay

One of a Kind

To a lady with a beautiful warm smile
That can brighten your day
Or light up a room.

To a lady with an amazing magnetic
Personality which shows because she is
Loved by many.

To a lady with an enormous big heart
Because she is caring, sincere with her
Feelings, and has a lot of love to give.

To a lady with a heart of gold, so
Priceless, yet so pure.

To a lady who is truly one of a kind.

Joselito Damian

The Sacrifice

Tear Thy heart out
from mine flesh and cage

Behold and
Feast thine eyes
upon the beating mass

Peel away gothic walls
and gorge thine spirit on
unvanquished flesh

In this offering
I must accept that
I may forever walk this Earth
a ghost in winter
next to death

Michael Raymond Thyfault

Lost (A Child's Wish)

You criticize
You put down
Ridicule
And call a clown

Never once thinking
That this was once you

You change your ways
Just to please another
We see you for who you are
For you are our brother

We see you
We miss you
We hear you
But we aren't heard

Please, come back to us
The way that you were

Anthony Grzeskowiak

A Lifetime of Love

You nurtured us and helped us to grow
then sent us on our way

We've come together this afternoon
to honor you on this day

With memories of days gone by
your special little gifts

Sunday drives and camping
and all those wonderful trips

And now, our families enjoy
many of these same things

While you enjoy the peace and serenity
a lifetime of love brings

Sherry A. Gillespie

Morbid Lifespan

The sky is dark as night
The ground soaked in blood
I open my eyes
Blood dripping from my hands
Cursed this life that I was blessed
Deep in the bowls of my empty soul
I lie hidden where your eyes can't see
No one knows what's wrong
In the bottomless empty soul of mine
I sit as tears paint my face
Dripping down to never splash the ground
You will not find nor will you see
What you don't know
I lie hidden deep within.

Luke S. Bergsten

In Loving Memory

Now that we're apart
And I am feeling all alone,
I close my eyes and think of
All the happiness we've known . . .
I think of how your loving smile
Was such a precious sight,
And how your arms around me
Felt so comforting and right.
How you made so much in life
Seem wonderful and new . . .
And somehow, I feel better,
Because I clearly see
Within my heart,
You're always here with me.

Donna L. Savoie

Be Assured

For Bill
If you could see
within my
heart
you would see the prayer
that's there
One that brings you
peace of heart
a mind that's bright and clear
That even though this day holds
thoughts
of someone lost to you
I pray that you will know
and feel
his presence with you still
in memories that you both have
shared
you'll always find him there

Lynda Diane Thomas

Overwrought Shortcoming

No one seems to care if I feel sad
they just care when I do bad
All these weird emotions
I've got locked in my heart
maybe I should have let them out
from the very start
I can't run to anyone, 'cause
they're too busy
They better drop what they're doing
'cause my brain is gettin' dizzy
I need comfort now before these
feelings just end
What I need now is a
true best friend

Angela Heidi Grimm

Complete

What breeds my hurried search;
of a love unacquired by time.

What rushes my demands for her;
as decay decreases my mind.

Whose soul will fulfill my heart;
as we hold each in the night.

Whose love will warm my thoughts;
as we hold each other tight.

Why must life make wait;
for this moment to rise to keep.

I can only begin to find her;
as my weakened soul begins its sleep.

Gregory Dwayne Estes

Merlin

O, Merlin, in your crystal cave
Deep in the diamond of the day,
Will there ever be a singer
Whose music will smooth away
The furrow drawn by Adam's finger
Across the meadow and the wave?
Or a runner who will outrun
Man's long shadow driving on,
Burst through the gates of time,
And drink the water from the shrine?
Will your sorcery ever show
The sleeping bride shut in her bower,
The day wreathed in its mound of snow,
And time locked in your tower?

Jessica Lynn Maturo

Freedom

Don't do this.
You can't do that.
Don't sit.
No standing.
Don't walk.
Walk.
I just love my freedom.
I live in the land of the tree.

No smoking.
Smoking only.
Don't run.
Don't skate.
Don't have a same sex mate.
Yeah, people! I just love my Freedom
I live in the land of the free.

Now all I need is to feel free.
Now all I want is a taste of Freedom.

Ron J. Witherspoon

Love?

Love is great;
love is true.
But not the love I gave to you.

It's just not right;
we just don't fit.
Maybe now it's time to quit.

We went the height;
We took the fall.
Guess it wasn't love at all.

Maybe soon love won't defeat me.
As for now, what's love?
Beats me. . . .

Danielle Wust

Friends Are Like Flowers

Friends are like flowers
touching in the wind
Friends are like flowers
Separated by small hands
Friends are like flowers
who disappear in time
Friends are like flowers
whose memories bloom again in our minds
It is with this thought
that I am at Peace
for one day soon
We will stand side by side
again as friends

Gwenda Jo Barnes

In Difference

What of this different love I hear
Where two of the same bodies share
Where two so physically alike
Would dare to share each others night
Would care to share each others day
To live their life and love their way

What of this common love I hear
Where two of different bodies share
Where two so physically apart
Would dare to share each others hearts
Would care to share each others day
To live their life and love their way
For all who live in love must share
So there can be know difference here

Rhonda Mae Schuster

Non-Negotiables

I cry the river flowing
To the core of my Mother Earth.
The waves are clashing
Against banks of slimed stones,
Sinking, toxemic, splashing
Through the jeweled keeper's coat.
Many red rivers meeting
Water kites of flowerless trees
And empty nests hanging
Over the fire of hearts.
Clouded minds, raving
Are burning the air dark,
Melting the flesh, dusting,
Cooling the cores fast.
Howling dogs are longing
For muted birds' wind-song.
Ravers beckon the criers, wanting,
Taunting to beat the time gong
To blow the past and now, spinning
To change a fate for golden coins.

Helena Sosin

Fireflies

Fireflies come out at dark
across the street in the park.
I take a jar to put them in,
and then I let them out again.

Tianne LaChelle Pettis

For Michael

As the soft, cool breeze
Finds its way through the branches
Of the trees,
I see the leaves fall,
As the breeze blows softly
Across my neck.

The breeze feels almost as though
It is your hands,
Your fingers
Running through my hair,
Your breath blowing against my neck.

I get a chill,
Just thinking of you,
And an overwhelming feeling
Of love and warmth.
And I know you will be there.

I love you.

Amanda René Smith

How Long ?

How long must it last or endure
this pain in my heart,
where do I find a cure?
Lord knows I've searched
my mind without end,
I've looked in secret places,
queried all my friends.
I went to see the Doctor,
asked him for advise.
He shook his head, looked away,
Sixty Dollars was his price.
Now I feel, I can grasp,
when they say you'll know.
How the answers will come to you,
and the way that you should go.
Yes, it all seems so simple
the response that comes my way . . .
now will someone kindly tell me
when the pain will go away!

Ray Miller

My Sunshine

I watch him as he sleeps.
I wonder what he thinks.
I wonder if he knows that
he is my light at the
end of the tunnel,
my pot of gold at the
end of the rainbow,
my silver lining behind the clouds . . .
He opens his eyes—
what is wrong, he makes right.
What is bad, he makes good.
I need him.
I need to feel him,
to know that he is there.
I take one look into his eyes,
as he reaches out to take my hand;
and I know that all
will soon be well.
I wonder if he knows. . . .

Melissa Birdsong

Clouds

Clouds are like love in a way;
they drift in and out of our lives,
and yet we cannot live without them,
even when the skies are grey.
Natalie Maya Fischer

Hiding

All alone again . . .
shivering in the cold.
Too many times in life
I'm left in the dark.
Without knowledge of love,
Without a heart to hold as my own,
Without the warmth of another,
Without an embrace of a lover. . . .
So, here I am,
sitting in a damp room,
holding my knees to my chest,
hoping THIS embrace will fill me . . .
keeping myself warm.
Maybe I'm too scared of love
or maybe I'm searching too hard . . .
either way, I'm here:
huddling in the corner
Hiding from something. . . .
Nicole Tai

The Voices

Don't listen to them,
those voices will drive you mad.
But who do you listen to?
They both sound right,
but only one can be.
But still,
those little voices keep screaming.
One on one side,
one on the other.
Some call it a conscience,
others say it's just you,
the evil side.
But it still comes down to it,
who's right and who's wrong.
But that just cannot be,
a right and a wrong.
It's all in your head.
Piece it together,
if you can.
Brett Griffith

Lauren

Her soul escaped earthbound chains
On the gilded wings of an angel
A wintry tempest
Blown in by the heavens
To freeze the rivers of pain
Etched by tears
On the faces of those
Who longed for her
To stay
We had loved her in a renaissance
Of garland
Echoed by phantom refrains
Inspired by the grandeur of
A benevolent sunset
Encouraged by
Druid soothsayers yet
Each day dancing more dangerously near
To a time when she
Would have to leave
Cheryl Hitter

Forgetful

Traces of you
evanesce,
and you linger
like an old taste.
Callous and hourly,
the ancient idea of you
makes me smile,
the residue of laughter
on my still lips.
And I can't remember
why I walked away.
Margaret Alexander Li

The Piper by the Sea

The Piper by the Sea
Marches on the rocks,
Music haunting—stirring,
Free as the sea.
Waves and notes meld—
One eerie sound of times
Long past and ne'er forgotten.
Tells a story—
Of ones come and gone,
Their marks left
On the Piper by the Sea.
Barb Rees

Smile

Sue and her brother
looked at one another,
And thought to themselves,
what can I do to show I love you?
Sue gave a smile, and he smiled back,
and then they knew.
For the smile was one of loving,
not the one of a kind of hating.
So when you give a smile, remember,
you'll get back the kind you give.
Smile, God loves you.
Buelah I. Belch

Pegasus

Perfect creature
Pure like the moon's light
Shimmering, pale, gay, magical
Powerful wings
To take her anywhere
Near or far
Long, muscular legs
Pumping, even as she flies
Majestic, flowing mane
And tail dancing lightheartedly behind
Perfect creature
Ashley Lynnette Van Erem

Breakfast in Bed

daily—I grind
the coffee fresh
brewed,
bacon. Syrup and
eggs somersault. into
amber Depression, glassware
and a bedside
tray
Where orange-juice and
ketchup collide.

kiss.
Sarah Cook

The Seraph

Spawned from my blood that curdles hot,
the fury of the coarse touch
the fingers from which I furiously ran,
the lips from which I bit in vain.
Spawned from the netted trawl
that snapped unwillingly.
And I stare now
at its golden hair and
cobalt eyes.
I am condemned to love this seraph.
This . . . devil's spawn.
Riya Sen

Arms of Love

"I want a divorce," I heard myself say.
My heart was ripping apart.
Swallowing was becoming difficult.
He simply said, "Okay."
That night as I tried to fall asleep,
Tears were gushing from my eyes
Sobbing hard—thunder from my soul.
"Please God, send an Angel to help me."
Just then, the door creaked open.
Arms of love held me tight.
I surrendered to slumber.
Brenda G. Autry

Thinking of You, Mom

I was thinking of you today,
A month ago, a day ago, and always,
How you smiled and hug me,
How you disciplined me,
I wish you were here,
But I know in my heart you are near,
Heaven which is your new home,
Sitting by the masters throne,
Looking down on me,
Thinking the same memories as me.
I love you mom, always.
Vanessa Yvonne Schroeder

Why?

Why did I love you?
Why did I care?
It was your voice, your eyes,
your touch.
What did you feel?
Was it the same?
Deep in my heart you will
always be there.
No longer together, moving
farther apart, but you will
always have a piece of my heart.
Stacie Renee Trail

My True Self

To myself and the friends who are curious
I pour my heart into all of my poems
hoping someone will care
There is never anybody around though
to know that I have been there
I always am depressed
but no one knows
because I act
I have not shown anyone my true self
for fear of getting hurt
Jessica Kathryn Powell

Thunder

Thundering hooves . . .

straining muscles
hot flesh on flesh
One with the beast
slow, rhythmic nature dance

Fence in sight
tension building
Take flight . . . flying . . . soaring
landing . . . dust flying.

Thundering hooves. . . .

Rhonda Jo Fisher

Somewhere over the Sky

I am thinking of you, hoping that you
Are all right. The stars shine with their
Glitter over the sky to light up the
Sky for me to see my way to your heart.
Somewhere over the sky I see you
Standing there with your arms waiting
For me to show up. As I watch the stars
Shine so beautiful over the sky. I
Can't stop thinking of you. So I send
You my love with the stars somewhere
Over the sky

Martha Cruz

Cousins' Weekend

Ten hearts bonding, by calm waters,
Picture books of sons and daughters.
Laughter pierces every heart
As each person does their part.

Quiet walks around the lake;
Precious memories here, we make.
Mending fences, sharing dreams;
Spirits soaring, mid the streams.

A quiet smile, a soothing touch;
This cousins' weekend brought us much!

Cynthia Louise Lapierre

Self-Image

I am a fish swimming in a river
The wind blowing across a field
of flowers
The snow falling on a small town
The mountain raising high above
the clouds
The rain gently falling on your
head
The ocean running beneath the
earth
I am a child of nature

Omar I. Campanioni

Missing You!

I once said I love you,
so many years ago.
A love that grew within myself
and never letting go.
Never knowing what become of me,
I threw that love away.
Thinking only of my fantasies,
our loving grew astray.
Now, years go by, I realize
love only fades
and never dies.

Debbie A. Cieslik

Water Droplets

Water dripping down my face
when you make me feel disgrace
Sad, salty, and slow
is how my eyes let them go

If only all you could know
how you have hurt me so
You have spun a web of sadness
and through it shines no gladness

For what you did I cannot forgive
not now, not ever, I must just live

Zachary Roy Blankenship

Success

What good seed can be sown
What great harvest fills the barn
A grain of thought
Buds of sweat
And the will to succeed
Buried in the soil of good intent
Invested in moments of time
Under the strain of patience
One waits for the first rains
To come with the divine bliss:
S U C C E S S !

Kwasi Siaw-Lattey

Love

Love:
Love is true,
Love is blind,
Love is for ever,
Love is kind,
Love is for you,
Love is for me,
for me someday,
maybe not today
but hopefully the
next day.

Becky Lynn Joyce

The Fear of Failure

To try
And in so, give each ounce
Of sweat up
All in vain
Where it leaves pain
To distill
In a worthlessness state
Of insecurities
Overwhelmed and
Feeling deprived
Of your own beauty

Victoria Rose Smith

Lonely Boat

To the one I might love someday
Love is like an ocean current
It can take you many places
Far out to sea or in close to shore
You never know where you're going
When you figure out where you are
It's such a beautiful sight
Right now I'm a lonely boat
Drifting at sea, not knowing
where I'll end up or where I'll
Settle down and stop

Thomas Brewster McIvor

Wind

Is it ever not windy
Wind this, wind that
It's always windy
It doesn't help to live in wind city
No matter what season the wind blows
Why, oh, why does it blow
Who knows, only God knows
Why the wind blows

Cliff Ball

Silence

The sound of silence
Is deafening to me
I can stand it no more
Darkness conquers me
And I am no longer human
I leap into the air
And my wings take flight
I try to scream in terror
But an evil laugh rolls off my lips
I try to go home
But end up in a dark cave
The darkness envelops me
And I feel at peace
For the first time in my life

Kristina Miyo Lear

The Curse of Life

I feel like my soul
Is going to explode.
All that spirals through my head
Over and over—
Until it disappears into dark emptiness.
What is there to do?
Silence the voices with drugs,
Stop the world in my sleep,
Whither away into
Nothingness?
Sometimes I wish I could close my eyes—
Erase everything;
But even if I went blind,
I would still have the pictures
Of yesterday
Flashing in my mind.
It's impossible to get away.
How could you ever escape yourself?
Life is but a curse.

Erin Dee Moran

Miss Kitty, What Do You Say?

I've got a date
With a pretty, young thing.
She makes my head light
And my heart wants to sing.
I know you've been thinkin'
'Bout us every day.
Fate's at work,
'Cause I'm the same way.
A life together,
I've made it my quest
to prove to you
I'm doing my best.
To my friends,
I've come to surprise;
and to win your heart,
means I take first prize.
So, Miss Kitty, what do you say?
Will you fall in love
With this cowboy today?

Randy Leon Miller

Ecstasy

Two hearts pass in the night,
their eyes glimmer with delight.
Not knowing what will happen,
their bodies flush with passion.
Red lips and wondering eyes,
how your time together flies.
A tight embrace and a longing kiss,
a thing you never want to miss.

Lora L. Kostelecky

If I Were to Tell You

If I were to tell you
You would laugh
If I were to tell you
You wouldn't believe me

If I were to tell you
Nothing would be the same
If I were to tell you
I would be the one to blame

If I were to tell you
You might say oh
If I were to tell you
You might say no
But that is if I were to tell you

Faith Lowell Doherty

Love Set Me Free

Can you see me?
Through the deepest oceans
I feel your touch.
Through my darkest forests
Cold and damp with many years rain,
You see me.
Naked and cold,
Bruised and old,
A prisoner of my soul.
Come through my deepest forest,
Walk my desert of tears,
Ocean of fears,
Touch my life and bring me light.
The mirror in my heart . . .
I see you through the other side.
Break the glass,
You lift me out.
One look at my soul,
You see me, I am free.

Anna Susan Duncan

Who Is He?

He's older then I, but he still sees me.
He's gentler then I,
But his words still pierce me.
His heart is pure, but misguided;
His love is given yet often misused.
His face can shine like the heavens,
yet frown like doom and gloom.
His humor light and tasteful,
Yet his heart is like an empty room.
His past shows signs of pain,
Yet his life has much to gain.
His path lay straight before him,
Yet courage drenched by his rain.
I search for ways to tell him
just how much he's loved,
But God's plan can look so grim
When his rain doesn't come from above.
In my world, there can be no other,
for you see this soul is my brother.

Irene M. Schneider

Being Avoided

Sometimes I am
Sometimes I'm not
Usually by some certain one
He has made a crushing blow
Right in my chest
I used to be his best
Now I am just one of the rest

Debra Lynne Uresti

The Dove

My love for you is so amazing,
Yet dwindling like a flower.
I need for you to pick me up,
And give me endless power.

You'll always be here in my heart,
Continuously, until we part.
I'll need you always by my side,
To love, to hold, until I die.

Every time I lay eyes on you,
I wish upon a star
That one day you will love me too,
And that this day is not far.

My love for you is like a dove,
Soaring through the air.
Just because you may not know it,
Doesn't mean it's not there.

Leonard N. Telesca

Me and a Shaggy-Coated Zebra

To ride on a shaggy-coated zebra
Over the plain of Madagascar
To gallop and trot
To a jungle of vines
To rest at the pool all afternoon
In the shadow of a misty
Waterfall
To ride a shaggy zebra
That is my dream

To ride on a shaggy-coated zebra
Over the grassy plain
To clippity-clop, clippity-clop
To the jungle so green
To dream by a pool all afternoon
In the ghostly shadow of a
Waterfall
To ride a shaggy-coated zebra
That is my dream

Justin Aaron Weakly

Angel Face

Do you believe in angels?
Do you think they're out there?
They are standing in your presence,
Do you have to see to believe?
Don't worry, there's proof.
Every morning you wake up,
The moment you look in the mirror
The face you see in the reflection,
That's the face of an angel.
You have the hope . . . the help.
You need the faith and the love.
You ask to forgive and for guidance.
When you see that angel face,
Look inside your soul,
Look deep,
And you'll believe.

So, ask me if I believe, absolutely.
I know there are angels . . . I am one.

Erin Nicole Borowiak

Cold

I massage your tiredness away
My fingers penetrate, feeling
Through to your soul
Your bones crack and twitch
Your skin leathery to my touch
Your flesh grows warmer
And warmer and warmer
But still you do not feel
The fire in me

Hadeel Essam Shaikh

Together

The sun was bright and shining
That day when we first met,
Every cloud had a silver lining,
And my heart, you did get.

You had my love from the start,
I knew my goal in life
To be with you and never part
Through happiness and strife.

We were meant for each other—
Our love will light the way,
As hand in hand we walk together,
Looking forward to each new day.

Each passing day my love grows stronger
With sweet memories from the past;
May our good life go on longer,
And our love through eternity last.

Freda Mae Forester

Flower Child

Daughters are like a rose
God created for you to love
From their head to toes
They're a blessing from above

Little buds growing fast
Cherish them one and all
Memories that will last
Summer, spring, or fall

For your rose has grown
As beautiful as can be
Now she's leaving home
You must set her free

In a vase of this world
You had her for a while
A blessing your baby girl
Your little flower child

Pearl Phyllis Giordano

The Shroud

Wispy clouds
Hover over the crystal blue
Enveloping all
With a misty haze

Kayakers row in perfect unison
A lone sole floats quietly by
Tanning bodies loll
Receiving the sun's slanting rays

Steady waves crash
Against a silty shore
Beating, beating
A timeless symphony

Still overhead
Surveying all
Always floating
The shroud

Kenneth Wayne Grant

mountain of knowledge

knowledge is power,
so learn all you can.
forget about nothing,
and learn the whole land
from the stars in the sky
to the beach and its sand.
and then on top of a mountain
of knowledge is where you will
stand. . . .

Dan William Vierra

My Existence Is . . .

A votive twist
attracts your attention—
Food descends from
the heavens—I'm
voracious, so I
devour—You stare
at me with
your simper—I'm
famished, so I
consume—You tap
on the glass,
like a bedlamite—
I'm ravenous, so
I feast—A votive
twist bores you—
I glide through
the water spectatorless

Scott H. Zucker

Reflections

I look into the mirror,
But I see to my surprise
A whole different person,
Looking deep into my eyes.

The carefree little girl
I saw when I was four to five
Has now become a young woman,
Fighting to survive.

It's really sort of scary
That time has gone so fast.
For what then I called "present"
Has now become the "past."

I look into the mirror,
And the face looking back at me
Is that of a young lady
Where a little girl used to be.

Kym Allaire Montijo

If You Were Mine

If you were mine, I'd hold you
   and never let you go.
And whisper softly in your ear
   how much I love you so.

If you were mine, I'd kiss you
   and hold you tenderly.
Protect you from the outside world,
   make you happy as can be.

If you were mine, I'd miss you
   for when we were apart,
And count the days of longing
   to mend my broken heart.

If you were mine, and most of all,
   I'll always be there for you.
Just tell me your desires,
   and I'll make them all come true.

Ballen F. Perez

Emotions

Why can't I get the words out
To express the way I feel?
Bottled up deep inside me,
My emotions run rampant.
The last time I remember
When I truly spoke my mind
Was when my life was normal.
Now, in the midst of chaos,
My feelings all shut down.

Nicholas Cole Cooper

Mesmerized

I decline to mention my name.
I refuse to answer to your call.
Mesmerized by the ticking clock,
I am forgetting reality.

I hate who I have become.
I am forgetting who I once was.
Mesmerized by the passing of time,
I lose all sense of humanity.

I am neglected by those I care for.
I am forgotten by those I love.
Mesmerized by the turning globe,
I am never reminded of sensibility.

I am abused by my surroundings.
I am tortured by my insecurities.
Mesmerized by the orbiting sun,
I am forgotten by all things remember.

Christina Blanco

Mother . . . My Friend

Mother is a special word
You say most every day,
I cannot say that special word
'Cause mine has gone away.

Mary Hall was your name
I was your only girl,
I miss you more than anything
You were my whole wide world.

God has got you with Him,
You died that rainy day.
I hope that you'll be happy,
With God I know you'll stay.

We were more than family
From start until the end,
We were more than family
You were . . . my best friend.

Teresa Ann Conaway

I'll Love You Forever

If we ever part,
leave an open space in your heart.
And if you ever cry,
let me kiss your tears dry.

It rained the other day,
it gave me nothing to say.
But much to think of,
mostly your love.

Sometimes when I'm doing something,
I'm not concentrating.
I'm really thinking about you,
some don't know what I do.

The truth of it all is,
my love is endless.
When we're old and nearing death,
we've accomplished much.

Christina Dianne Cota

Lady-Girl

Lovely, little lady-girl
Quite the woman, you are
All grown
Yet still not your own
Where you must have been
More important
Where will you be
Lovely, little lady-girl
Hiding inside of me

Diane Gaye Evjene

Lost in Dementia

My wife, my wife, my love, my life,
is gone, I know not where.
She's lost, no matter how I yearn,
beyond my love and care.

She's locked her secret world inside,
someplace beyond retrieve.
I know she's very lonely there,
and sad, I must believe.

My wife, my wife, my love, my life,
has left me in despair.
To think that she cannot return,
is more than I can bear.

When soon death comes to take my bride,
I think I, too, shall leave,
and join her on the other side,
no more my heart to grieve.

Paul Adrian Feldmann

Untitled

So many things
Are so unclear to me,
Sometimes I wonder
can I even see.

Have I just been blinded
By the pain I feel inside,
How could I give up
When i haven't had to try.

It all just came so natural,
Kind of a no holds barred
We were who we were
And now we're who we are.

Does this all make sense
That I highly doubt,
But I know you are someone
I can't be without. . . .

Raymond Anthony Daily

My Life

I have no friends,
I have no life.
20 million emotions
Dripping on my knife.

Nobody past away,
No one almost died.
It's just my life feeding
On what I have to decide.

I have plenty of worries,
I have plenty of fear.
All I see is a mess
When I look into the mirror.

I wish I could be normal,
I wish I could be strong.
But all the pain inside me
Tells me that I am wrong.

Trisha Ann Pratt

Reminiscences

Those days, when love was
full of romanticism, passion,
desire, and a little bit of madness.
You took time to write a love note,
to buy a chocolate, a candy, a flower
a balloon; whatever, but a detail.
That feeling, that heartbeat, that tear.
I missed so much those days,
my days.

David J. Galban

Inside Myself

A darkness falls around me
My soul collapses
My heart disintegrates
There are no more colors or lights
No laughter, joy, or dreams
Only pain
I grasp at hands trying to pull me out
But I can't hold on tight
The darkness imprisons me
I need to find a way out
Fighting, struggling
I will emerge
Like a butterfly from a chrysalis
Brilliant colors
And take flight
New life
Free to start anew

Rosemary Dunlap

Lost

Unhealable wounds,
Bleeding and bruised.
A soul lost in torment—
Scared and confused.

Memories surround her,
Adrift in an ocean.
Heaving her constantly,
Drowned in emotion.

Blinded and tangled
And lost in the reeds.
Lonely, depleted
Of her loving needs.

The love she required,
Was not to be found
In mountainous heights,
Or upon this Earth's ground.

Lynda M. Cope

The Seeker

I am the seeker in my life,
my mind is rife with wondering
the fallow fields of seasons gone,
not knowing quite where I belong.

Fears become reality
when first we fail to perceive,
our mixed emotions held in fright
or not seen in the proper light.

To learn life's lessons we must search
inside ourselves for all our worth,
to question this is not a sin,
just a place where we begin.

The seeker stands alone and scared
looking at the soul just bared;
but if we're brave and look again,
we see inside ourselves a friend.

Bette Sartore

Untitled

Falling down to the bottom
Sadly scraping the outside
shadowing leaves seem to
Caress the fallen soul
But turning and spinning
Smashing everything in
View . . . the ground cries
in laughter
waiting for it

Lisa Marie Shearer

Remember

Why do you say the things you say,
And do what you always do?
You know your son loves you,
But your daughter loves you, too.

It's always you and him
And never you and me.
It's always you and him, Daddy,
How can I make you see?

You never took me to the park
And pushed me on the swings.
You never took me anywhere to show me
All these things.

I love you Daddy, and I always will.
You know your son loves you,
But remember, please remember,
Your daughter loves you, too.

Michelle Smith

My Son, Dan

Next to his grave I kneel in prayer,
My son's body is resting there;
I ask for strength that I may bear
And courage to face each day.

His life on Earth was brief in years,
He lived each day without a fear;
How could he know his end was near
When he left that fateful day?

He took with him part of my soul,
His sweet memory I have and hold;
He left his many dreams untold
When he died that fateful day.

Now that Heaven is his home,
Let us on Earth be not alone;
Lift me up and remove the stone
And free me to face each day.

JoHanna M. Jensen

Life Is a Funny Thing

Life is a funny thing.
One day you're living your dreams,
and the next you're crying streams.
Life goes on with or without you.
Just don't be afraid to live.
Dreams come and go, just like love.
Faith keeps us going.
Life is a funny thing.
You don't know where you are going
or how to get there,
but eventually we find our way.
The road might be short or long
with the certain guarantee of bumps
along the way.
Life is a funny thing.
Don't plan too far ahead,
just take it from day to day.

Sheryl Lee Nazarenus

My Thoughts

You can Love . . .
But not to be loved back
is the worst feeling possible
one would rather die
than not to be loved
so love someone
and you shall receive love in return
just someone to love
that's all anyone really needs

Samantha Rae Haller

Painted Dreams

As a rose blooms in May,
Snow falls in December;
Leaves tumble down in autumn,
Helping you remember.

It requires a paintbrush,
But more importantly an artist,
To paint your dreams;
Maybe you'll be the smartest.

Maybe you'll make decisions,
No one else can make,
Maybe for your voice
The Grammy you will take.

So pick up the paintbrush,
And begin so faint,
A second coat comes later,
But don't forget your dreams to paint.

Amanda Nicole Richardson

Life's Journey

Is this the one I want to be
to hurry along unsteadily?
I am falling in a turbulent sea
of life's unresolved uncertainties.

But why must I go on like this
as a wanderer in a hazy mist?
Not knowing if I am here or there.
To be left out is what I fear.

What is the greatest danger there;
is it life's unrelenting thoroughfare?
Then I must move along that path
that I have carved out from the start.

Then why am I so afraid
to go and come in this cavalcade?
The life and love that will be found
is in all of life's music and a song.

Joan Yvonne Pedro

Voices

Entering softly into dreams
The muse befriends its host,
And blindly leading conscious thought
To realms of waiting ghosts.

In sweetened tongues they touch a nerve
To snare entangled souls,
Despoiling latent thoughts of being
Contriving toward their goals.

Remanded to another time
The guilty past is staid,
And in the place of heart and reason
Life's course is led astray.

On silken wind the voices strum
A counsel to willing ears,
Promise of hope for good or not
To guide man's coming years.

Edward Bonadio

Untitled

I haven't taken a breath
since we last spoke,
and suffocating never felt so good,
but I can't live like this,
between moments,
between spasms of you,
and all the exhaustion of need.
I've thought to call,
but I've never been one
to press buttons
or you.

Becky Ann Martin

The Silent Rose

A gentle wind blows softly through,
as the others are chose,
but know one seemed to notice
that remaining silent rose.

It was not an unsightly flower,
but so beautiful throughout.
It's just no one seemed to care
what it was all about.

Silence is our true captor,
but like that little flower,
we would cry out for rescue,
but we just don't have the power.

So if you should notice a silent rose,
please don't pass by.
Because slowly our petals fall
and we would surely die.

Sherry J. Petrik-Scheuerer

Gift

Oh! What a pleasant morning. . .

Bright ray of cheer
Radiant sky of vigor

Melodious lorikeets to ardor
Mother Nature to shelter

Daring peaks
Rippling rivers

Nurturing trees
Unrelenting bees

Blossom of elegance
Breeze of efflorescence

Makes my being wealthier
Thank you GOD for a precious gift
Called as LIFE!

Sanjay K. Rode

Because of You

Thinking of the road ahead
I lay awake at night.
What to make of things I've said
In case the end's in sight.

Have I been fair, and just to all
And helped to make folks smile?
Have I answered to their call
And lived a life worthwhile?

The sleep avoids my state of mind,
Stirring thoughts turned off and on.
Answers I can't seem to find,
Thinking of the day I'm gone.

Morning takes the evening's place,
Sunlight burns the misty dew.
I turn to see your precious face,
And all is well, because of you.

Dennis Daniel Corcoran

Triumph

The spring flower blossomed,
Unaware of the advancing hand
that would soon pluck it.
It shone in all its glory,
Pure, Innocent, Serene,
Ignorant of its ephemeral existence,
It spread its fragrance,
The bee sucked its nectar,
The wind scattered its pollen,
The menacing hand plucked it;
But
The seeds of its future generation
HAD BEEN SOWN.

Prashant Kumar

Spring

Spring is in the air.
The weather is warm
And birds fly high in the sky

The sun is shining
Flowers bloom everywhere
While bunnies hop right by

Playing outside oh what fun
In the pool the water is warm
And the smell of flowers is oh so sweet

The trees give shade
While the sun shines bright
And little baby birds "tweet"

Oh, what fun I have in spring.

Jena Boen

Guided by Prayer

*Thank you, God, for keeping me cancer-
free for the past two years.*
Every time I close my eyes
I go to the Lord in prayer.
I thank Him for the life I've had
If tomorrow is not there.

He held me close and surrounded me
With all the love He has.
He told me that He'd carry me
If things start looking bad.

So now when I get nervous
Or just a little scared,
I know the Lord is here with me
Just guided by my prayers.

Mary Lorentz

If Only I Could

If only I could make you see
how much I love you, then maybe
our relationship would be better.

If only I could let you see
me when I hurt, or when I
need someone to hold me,

But yet I still hide my pain,
my fear, my hurt, and my sorrow
I hide all of this from you.

I know I should tell you because
you might understand, but then
again I seem to not be able to.

If only I could tell you these
things then it would be okay, but
then again if only you would ask.

Lacey Nichole Diggs

Exist or Exit

Pry into the soul,
search the mind,
wish for safe ground,
reach out in hope,
grope for light.

Live the enigma
in wondrous doubt,
never asking
the unfathomable
question: *why?*

Elizabeth Xavier Ferreira

My Brother

He is like a lion; brave and strong.
With his loyalty he can do no wrong.
My brother is very important to me.
He has been by my side constantly.
He took care of me all my life,
Even though we got into a lot of fights.
Through dust and mud,
Sweat and blood,
I love my brother with all my heart
And hope we never fall apart.

Gino Francesco Montessi

One

Somewhere out of sight,
Hidden from the light,
Someone waits for me.

One day I did find,
A hand that fit in mine,
That touch that set me free.

And from that moment on,
My life sings all love songs
To the one, I now belong.

Now deep within each night,
Where, once darkness lived, now light
Is shining back at me.

And all the empty days
Softly fade away,
Tomorrow's all we see.

No matter what may come
With the sad times and the fun,
The two of us stand as one.

Kathryn E. Winkels

The Last Good-Bye

The hate within me
Grows and grows.
No one knows
The pain I know.
The loneliness
That is me
Is a cage.
I can't be free.
The sadness that
Just never ends,
Cannot be helped
By loyal friends.
There's been a longing
For so long.
Everything I do
Seems wrong.
My death wish
Is a simple thing.
Think of me with love,
And sing.

Bonnie Celesse McMaken

Rain

Rain rain go away,
come back in May.

For then I'll be by the bay,
waiting for the day.

I wish you'd say you'll stay away
until it's May.

But if you won't stay out of my way,
for now I'm going out to play
until its May.

Alysa Soppelsa

The Puzzle

*I am only 11 years old
and I have many poems! Check them out!*
We put together the pieces
Of a puzzle so great
A puzzle of many dreams
Of problems and debates
Of miracles so large
Cutting into the world, like knives
And this very large puzzle
Is the story of our lives

Caitlin Colleen McIlwee

Why?

Why do I have to be perfect?
What if I go wrong?
Why do I have to live up to my sisters?
What if I am small?
Why do I have to be smart?
What if I am dumb?
Why does my room have to be clean?
What if it's a dump?
Why am I too young to date?
What if I "go out?"
Why do I have to suffer
When you are so stressed out?
Why do I have to make the right choices?
What if I make the wrong one?
Why do I have to make my own money?
What if I make none?
Why do I have to be so nice?
What if I am mean?
Why do I have to go through this?
Because I am a teen.

Jennifer Nicole Sparks

How Can We Grow As One?

How can we grow as one,
in a world so full of
vain, self-serving people?
When no one can grasp the
concept of "love thy neighbor."
Where Mother Earth is being
killed slowly by her children,
draining her of her life force,
like a slow growing cancer.
How can we grow as one
when we refuse to care for
new life, when destroying the
old pillars that stand high,
when self-righteous people
fight wars without questioning the why,
these times are full of stress.
Maybe one day when the dawn
of humanity draws near,
we will finally learn
the value of growing as one.

Melea Black Maltba

Deserted Places

Empty buildings all around,
Dirt instead of grass upon the ground.
Going down the stretch of sidewalk,
No one there in which to talk.
Tree limbs standing tall, yet bare;
All you can do is stare.
Roads are long and cold,
No one to reach out to hold.
There isn't any room
For love to grow and bloom.
Broken hearts that show a trace
Of being just one more deserted place.

Linda L. Jett

Golden Sunset

Living past the shore
where strangers go.
Watching the sunset
turn to gold.
As the crashing waves
turn the wind cold,

I see the stars,
memories of what
has just been done,
keep the sunlight warm
and on the run.

Listen to the waves
crashing cold,
watching the sunset
turn to gold.

Michael O. Semeniuk

Love Lost

I lost a friend today
I thought I would be fine
But I wanted to see more of her
I wanted a little more time
You see, she was always happy
Full of love and oh, so sweet
Always busy into things
Then quiet, not a peep
Greeting hello in the mornings
And good night when it's time for bed
Never wanting anything
Just a pat upon the head
My friend was especially happy
When we would go for a jog
I will miss her deeply
For my friend, she was my dog

Elizabeth Weir

When Is It Time?

When is it time
for the snow to come
falling down,
to hide me like it does the ground?

When is it time
for the wind to come and blow,
to carry me high and low?

When is it time
for the rain to come and ruin
a sunny day,
to quickly melt me away?

When is it time
for the moon to come
crashing on my bed,
to stop all these thoughts in my head?

Samantha Moutsos

My Family

As long as we are family
I'd like you all to know
More love lies deep within me
Perhaps than I can show.
You may not ever understand
How much you mean to me
You've made me feel so grand
And very proud to be—
Proud to start my day with you
If only for a chat
Tomorrow I'll be seeing you
And you can count on that

David L. Whittaker

Time Forever, Forever Time

Time, has it slipped away
Have I just passed it by
Timeless, eternity
Lacking boundaries, unbound
Time, it just is
Eternity ceases time
Time ceases forever
Boundaries unbound
Time, beginning, time end
Time front, time back
Beginning ceases, end unbound
Eternity ceases time
Bound eternity, time
Unbound time, eternity
Time forever, forever time
Eternity ceases time

Steve Dupere

Silent Killer

I watched while you slowly
took pieces of my friend.
Looking while you made
her weaker and weaker.
I stood by while you robbed
us of years of memories.
You left me helpless
while you took brightness and life
and replaced it with fear and pain!
You kept growing
paying no attention to anyone's prayers.
I stood by with pain in my heart
and tears spilling from my eyes
while you grew.
Then you silently took
all signs of life!

Lenora Allen

A Memory Away

The moment I left,
I never felt such heartache.
Though my new life was beginning,
it seemed my heart, continued to break.
Then my mind would wonder,
into a happier day,
and I suddenly realized,
you're just a memory away.
Though the miles between us are many,
and the times together are few;
to ease your lonely heart,
I will always send to you:
My love forever,
and the thought of you each day.
Because you're always in my heart,
and just a memory away.

Cynthia L. Rudder

My Brother, George

Did anyone know my brother?
I'm sure he knew some of you.
He took me everywhere with him,
even to and from school.
He did a little drinking
and he did a little drugs.
I really tried to stop him.
But I guess it took more than hugs.
My brother is gone forever now,
and as I look up in the sky . . .
I holler, "George, I love and miss you;
Why did you have to die?"

David Matthew O'Bannon

Wish Comes True

I wish for nothing,
just a cure for misery
that allows me not to sing
in my world of fantasy.
How can it be?
Can it be just like this,
must change everything that I see,
turn it into the world of bliss.
Help me, those from the outer-world
who live freely, in serenity.
Let me out of this hellish hole;
send me to my destiny.
So please, I beg the man above,
let me wish for you,
may my problems be solved
and granted, that my wish comes true.

Wan Nurliyana Wan Ramli

Journey

Ripples in your laughter,
Rhymes in your murmur,
On and on I hear;
In and out I shiver,
Keep on your bliss, I wish.

Tides vary in your ripples;
Tunes vary in your rhymes.
On and off you sigh;
Up and down you heave,
Hold on your strength, I wish.

No ripples without tides,
No rhymes without tunes,
On and on life goes;
By and by life reels,
Never changes the Law of Nature.

Benny Thomas Unithomman
Parambil

Binding Friendship

Friendship is the tie that binds,
A narrow road that curves and winds.
You see someone and pick them out.
They'll be your friend without a doubt.
Friends are such amazing creatures
Who help make trouble for your teachers.
They're also warm and so sincere,
And when they're needed they'll be near.
There's no better person than a friend
Who stays with you until the end.
You talk and share your secret thoughts,
And you bet, there are lots.
So find a friend if you're alone.
Talk to each other on the phone.
When you get blue just call to them,
And you'll both be happy to the end.

Stephanie DePoma

Home

Home is like a peaceful dome,
as beautiful as ancient Rome.
A wondrous place with all our desires,
after a day where we can all retire.
With lovely flowers blooming,
grown from years of grooming.
It may not be apples to one's eyes,
but to me it's paradise.
Home, a tremendous place,
with rooms like a maze.
Everything should be clean and green,
for people to admire what is seen.

Poet Jun Hao Wong

just like me

mossy green the sun forgot
stuffy air sometimes too hot
morsels left on a plate to rot
just like me, too much like me
heaping pile of dirty clothes
scattered papers lay in droves
a journal out opened, exposed
just like me, too much like me
shades drawn block all light
the walls know not of day or night
thin door locked up tight
just like me, too much like me
mirror shows a sad expression
icy surface mocks the vision
the stranger holds a deep confession
just like me, too much like me

Jaime Bourgeois

Life Is Full of Changes

Life is full of changes
from the beginning to the end,
Life is full of changes
and how they all start to blend.
Life is full of changes
from the playpen to college,
Life is full of changes
as we absorb all kinds of knowledge.
Life is full of changes
from diapers to jeans,
Life is full of changes
from Waldorf to Queens.
But change is good,
you will enjoy it!
Just learn to flow
with it, don't avoid it!

Nicole DiMauro

Alone in Sorrow

That breaking noise you hear
Is the sound of my heart
For I have been a fool
And let it get ripped apart
I no longer have my girlfriend
A woman to call my own
There is no one but me to blame
For I have reaped what I have sown
Remember when I tell you
Open up yourself to her
Be sure to give all that you have
And the love will always endure
I failed to do these things I've said
And I let her slip away
But know this, baby, I think of you
Every single day

Russell Roberts

Lost

A tempest rages in my soul;
My heart's a leaden weight.
I live each day in darkness,
Filled with misery and hate.
My mind's in constant turmoil,
Filled with hopelessness and pain.
Emotions that I've known so long
Still burn brightly in my brain.
This life has been a living hell;
Please, Lord, just let it cease,
So that I may finally come to You
And taste eternal peace.

William James McQuaid

Your Love Is . . .

Your love is what I feel
As I kiss you on your lips.
Your love is the way your hands feel
As you place them on your hips.
Your love is how our hearts beat
As we hold each other tight.
Your love is what I long for
Every day and night.
Your love is what you show me
By holding me in your arms.
Your love is also protection
As you keep me safe from harm.
Your love is so many things,
And true love is eternity.
True love is what I promised you,
As you have done for me.

Mai T. Nguyen

Good Child

I learn lot of things in school
and new ones every day,
I think the names of some of them
are very hard to say.
Writing is an easy thing,
but if I'm using ink,
I'll remember not to make a blot
distinction's hard, I think.
If people say sums are hard,
I don't agree . . .
for you know your tables
it's as plain as A-B-C.
Reading is best of all
for reading is like a key
that opens many, many doors,
it opens books for me!

Bakhtawer Khan

Daddy

His hands are calloused and work-worn
His hair is grayish black
He's built a home for eight
With very little pay
His voice is gruff and hard sometimes
But it's mellowed by his smile
I hope someday he'll know from me
His efforts were worthwhile
No one else can ever share
The special place he holds
Deep down within my heart
My love for him unfolds
I hope I can repay him
For all the things he's done
I haven't much to give him
But he will always have my love

Ruth Elizabeth Boyle

At the End of All Our Strivings

All of life is a vain show
We clamor for plum roles
We suffer for the clamoring
And at the end of all our strivings
We know not why the suffering
Until the final curtain falls
And when life's movie is over
Who shall be sorry for us
With all the trophies we collected
Standing staid and silent in a corner
Can death celebrate us

Bee Hua Kang

Daydreaming

I watch the American eagle
So high up in the sky.
I know that someday
I'll fly that high.
I know I will make it
Someway, somehow.
Someday . . . I'll be there, too.
Even if it isn't now.
I'm being patient
And working so hard
To obtain those dreams
That aren't so far.
I'm going to soar like that eagle
And have all those things
That appear now
To be only dreams.

Cynthia Ann Hawkins

A Northwest Evening

The azure sky is shimmery
with red and golden rays
as the Celestial sun is hovering
in a slow-motion haze
With crystallized peaks sparkling
in the ebbing evening light
heavenly scents of evergreen
hang suspended in the air
Evening shades are slithering
through forest hills and glens
Fowls and insects join
in their final serenade
Harmony is everywhere in the
oncoming sun-drenched shadows
and the whispering silent wind
accompanies the closing of the day

Bernice A. Sharp

Unless There Is Gravity

Unless there is gravity
we might never know
the allurement of one
galaxy for another, the
planets for their sun,
the moon for its Earth
or even my wife and I
here on this verandah
watching the night sky
just as it is now for each
April. And even more,
our daughter behind us
in the house, her first
child pressing downward
almost ready to enter the
same universe we live in.

Guy B. Stiles

50th Anniversary

Fifty years has gone by fast,
You're living proof marriage can last.

You were married in '51
Life together had just begun.

The Vazquez family was not done
along came a daughter then a son.

Life together was pretty great
you both picked the perfect mate.

Aren't you glad you didn't miss
fifty years of wedded bliss?

Gail A. Line

Transition

When you are gone
I am a lonely child in winter.
Everything is gray and
I am insecure, frightened
and afraid.

Anticipation of your arrival
Turns everything yellow and green,
Warm and Spring.
I glow with warmth and
Tingle with excitement.

You walk in the door
And my world becomes
Alive and bright.
Suddenly, it's the Fourth of July
and I am a WOMAN.

Lorelei Lawrence Kerr

The Abyss

I walk a fine line
A tenuous hold
Above the abyss
Of hells untold
Together we journey
The path of life
With its conflict
Struggle and strife
Living each moment
Instead of each day
Helps me to balance
This is my way
So maybe someday
I'll capture my soul
That the abyss
So long ago stole

Karen Joy Shipley

Taboo

A word so often used
—but never defined
So often uttered
—but rarely understood
So often revealed
—but seldom seen
Such a powerful word
—love is all these things.
A feeling so anxiously awaited
—yet so quickly rejected
So easily awarded
—but more easily discarded
Much too elusive
—yet too easy to lose
Love is the prize
—we neglect to choose.

Donnell M. Carr

Wandering Thoughts

Thoughts that will not concentrate
Hold tight to any one thing
Aimlessly go so many ways
And when an idea they bring
Off they go a different direction
Hopelessly astray, we can but dismay
Oh, to hold a single thought's attention
Ponder its essence savor its meaning
Yet again this thought is gone
We are left lost and seeming
Stunned and confused a pawn of the id
Sometimes our own mind can be so unkind

Gary Robert Pellam

Precious

The days have come and gone
Since love was within my reach
The warm touch and tender kisses
Are no longer a part of my nights
Lovers come and go
But it's still not the same
You are the one that held me so tight
And covered me with love
We were as strong
As the tallest mountain range
Wonder whatever happened
To turn us so cold
The future has to hold something
Precious for me
But sometimes I wonder
Will it ever compare?

Melody R. Branham

Seasons of Despair

Raindrops running down my window,
A mirror to my face.
Chilling breezes escort leaves
To their final resting place.
A gray sky chokes the summer sun,
The branches can't claw through.
And the antique visage of decay
Supplants the viral new.
The living green of land's fur
Gives way to brown release.
All the hope and peace retreats
On the backs of departing geese.
Rain takes potshots at the ground
Leaving marks, like a man's life.
Have you ever stopped to realize
How fleeting are joy and strife?

Roger Lee Fahnestock

Wingless Flight

Eyes bright
Breath sweet
Nose soft
Coat sleek
Heart brave
Step light
Grace moves in
Wingless flight

Arching neck
Pounding hooves
Streaming tail
Flowing mane
Rushing breath
Reaching stride
Power drives
Spirit reigns

LaDonna M. English

Whom Do I Love?

Just keep thinking
Whom do I love?
Not just the ever so
We marry
More of best
Not contrary
Talkative to you and me
So I'm glad
We all may see
How could we misremember
All we do is just keep thinking
Whom do I love?

Joy Renee Araujo

Living in My Head

Today the sun shines
Tomorrow the rain blinds
Bright is the sky
Black are the clouds
When will it all end
This pain in my head
Like knives striking through
To cut my brain into two
Day is like night
Night is like day
Confusion filters throughout the hours
Pain lingers, even if I shower
When will it all end
This pain in my head
Like knives striking through
To cut my brain in two

Denise Elaine Hynes

Always Close at Heart

When I was still in diapers
My grandmother gave it to me
All soft and new and colorful.

It stayed with me
Through crib and toddling years
Never leaving my little hand.

It went with me everywhere
Through all those first sleep-overs
Always hidden in my suitcase
Away from everyone's laughter.

As I grew older so did it
And now full of holes and tattered
My blanket lays alone, folded and safe
In a box in my room
Where only my memories touch it. . . .

Caitlin Nichole Rodriguez

The River of Hope

The rain falls down.
Just a trickle at first.
Then a downpour.
Forming a stream.
One stream joins another
Combining its strength.
Turbulent flows eddy
In a journey unseen.
From the first trickle of rain
To the torrent you now see,
This river was formed
With a known destiny.
No matter what obstacles
In its path may lay,
Get enough drops of water together
And they will clear the way.

Sharon Belinda Sucillon

Removed

Scared, lost, upset
I sit alone
Searching, searching
Answers yet to be found
Is this the way it is meant to be
Me alone, you so happy?
Burning tears stream
Helping nothing
Eyes red with loss of hope
Mind exhausted from stress
I sit alone
Searching, Searching. . . .

Amber Danielle Quinn

Young Girl

Don't read this and
look at me.
Don't read this and
smile softly.
Don't listen to this and
wonder if this is jazz.
Don't look around
before you scratch your behind.
Don't worry about your weight
when you eat that piece of cake.
Don't speed up when you're
already late.
This time your youth reveals
the moment of truth.
So clap your hands with me
and dance.

Robert Lugo Martinez

this dream i will regret

a pleasured scent moved through fast
but how long did the moment last
what kind of spell did it cast
pleasant images of my past
in this dream i did fall
as she beckoned with a call
as i lay beneath the sky
dream about angels that do not fly
dream about rain that does not wet
this dream i will regret
for she is here with a smile
toward her arms i move with style
here, magic i will find
a magic that will endure my time
no matter how heavenly it will get
this dream i will regret

Van Uch

Wishing

As I look up at the stars
I wonder who you are
I see you every day
as we go our separate ways
I wonder if you care
about the moments that we shared
If given a chance
our love could enhance
I find peace in you
and all that you do
Maybe someday
you'll look my way
Then I will find
some peace of mind
to share our lives together
always and forever

Rachael J. Roman

Moment of Passion

I wasn't supposed to be alive.
Just because she "loved" him so much,
There was a moment of passion.
They weren't even married.
She was leaving,
She wanted something,
Something that was his
For her to keep.
So they shared a moment of passion.
Now she will have him forever,
Him and I.
I was made during
Their moment of passion.

Gisela Sahagun

Let It Flow

Like a sparkling bubbling brook,
Let it flow.
Softly, gently, ever so slowly
Flowing on and on.

Like a roaring gushing river,
Let it flow.
Flowing swiftly onwards,
To the great expanding ocean,
Flowing on.

Like the mighty dashing ocean,
Let it flow.
Like the weaves that hit the shoreline,
Let it flow.
Just let peace flow.

Joyce Lydia Graham

The Photograph

In faded, brown paper
is a memory
captured in time
in awe of her beauty
The long, silky hair
as black as raven
falls along her neck
like the finest satin
The eyes that glow
like two precious pearls
shine with love so pure
and true
The gentle smile remains
a mystery
But to a lover's heart is
a safe kept treasury

Christine Amango Driesbaugh

Just One Kiss

Just one kiss,
happened so fast.
Just one kiss,
maybe the last.
Just one kiss,
meaning so much.
Just one kiss,
your lips to touch.
Just one kiss,
makes 101 dreams.
Just one kiss,
meant more that it seems.
Just one kiss,
only to reminisce.
Just one kiss,
one more to miss.

Demetrius Anthony Spriggs

Headache and French

Thoughtless words fall onto the ground
They smash into millions of pieces
As I watch in boredom
Everything is blurred and useless
I'm so very tired
I honestly don't know anything anymore
My head is turning into broken pieces
Like the words along the floor
The time seems to stop
Will I ever leave this place

Ashley M. Wildes

Satan Whispers

Satan Whispers in my ear.
he Tells his Lies—
with Truth so clear.

he stands upon my
Shoulder—Here.
his Truthful Lies
Call reason near . . .
(But not too close)

The Battle rages
Onward still
Who?
will at last
inform my Will.

David Ray Parker

God's Garden

God looked around His garden
and found an empty place.
He then looked down upon the Earth
and saw your tired face.
He put His arms around you
and lifted you to rest.
God's garden must be beautiful . . .
He always takes the best.
He knew that you would never get
well on Earth again.
He saw the road was getting tough
and the hills were too hard to climb.
So He closed your weary eyelids
and whispered "Peace Be Thine."
It broke our hearts to lose you,
But you did not go alone,
For part of us went with you
the day He called you home.

Daniel Michael Bozurich

Reading the News

Meanwhile in the real world
the shy child
senses the impermanence
of the new insecurity.
One wants to stay
in the still murky
ambiguous flow
of isolation.
The unparalleled magic
of physical separation.
Ghosts lurk everywhere
playing to the extremes
the unclean inferior
dynamics of memories.
Something remains sacred
in the bobbing
and weaving
of the soul.

Melissa Ciccone

The Room

I wish there was a room;
a room where I could hide.
hide from all the maliciousness
and cruelty outside.
A room where there is peace
and joy and happiness inside.
Oh, I wish, I wish I find that room
before my soul completely dies.
In this big, bad, sad world,
I feel so all alone.
The only thing that gets me through
is the hope of finding that room.

Nathalie Wilson

Sweetums . . .

What you mean to me
Is way more than you see
I love you so much
I just melt with your touch
I smile when I meet you
But frown when I have to leave you
At first you led me astray
Now I think you're here to stay
The way you kiss . . .
It's with such sweetness
When I am in your arms
I feel away from all harms
You own my heart
I hope we never part

Melissa Joyce Hodges

Alone

The snowflakes glistened
brighter than a thousand gemstones.
A single path of footprints
were all that disturbed the white
blanket of snow.
The cool, crisp air was almost
as breathtaking as the scenery.
A hush crept its way among
the small gathering of people.
They were gathered for the
love of family.
A low moan made its way
through the crowd.
I was lonely, which brought
my family together.
I was lonely, which put me
in the casket they were sobbing over.

Jayce Lyn Krentz

The Cherokee

Freedom I do not see,
when soldiers come to our land.
Fear and hatred in their eyes,
as they come to kill us.

Our arrows are nothing,
compared to their guns.
Their soldiers are stronger than ours.
Our confidence is growing weaker.

No more hunting with the men,
when a feast is near.
No more laughing children I see,
only blood and sadness everywhere.

No matter how strong they are,
and even if they kill us all.
Our spirits shall linger,
in the land we always loved.

Shama Ahmad

Angel Sent

I sent this little angel to
stand by you in my place.

When she sees your need of
a prayer she'll call to God's face.

And when you're feeling better
I thank God and His grace. Amen

Brenda M. Lewis

Honor and Pride

Dedicated to my daughter,
Cynthia (Perry) Dixon
What does it mean—how to learn?
A chance to give, a will to earn?
Stand erect, give out a grin,
do your best to be a friend.
Keep your promise, hold true the oath.
To God and Country, your faith in both.
We need not brag, nor will we boast
To things we do or love the most.
We're Girl Scouts now, to lead the way.
A light to lead and never stray.

James R. Perry

Powerless

Like all the power
Behind the tide of the ocean
You have taken my heart
Giving you complete devotion
Straight out of a dream
You have come to me
Leaving me defenseless
This is what love is supposed to be
Take me by the hand
Walk through life with me
In to the world only we understand
Together, forever we are free

Kristina Thompson

The Wind in Your Hair

Do not cry, my love, my children dear.
What is it that you fear?
I no longer feel any pain.
I am the sweet summer rain.
So don't shed another tear.
I am the wind in your hair.
Please don't feel any sorrow for me.
Remember my soul is finally free.
I have not left without a trace.
I am the smile upon your face.
Do not cry, my love, my children dear.
I am the wind in your hair.

Julie Ann Rodriguez

Forever This Way

This love is on
and as we go on
from this day on
our love will grow on and on
And I'll never do you wrong
for this love is strong, so hold on
You're in for a experience of love
you'd never felt before
I'll always stay true to you
to you I love and with you
I'll stay forever this way
till our death day

Jessica Lehman

Don't Worry

Have you ever had a bad day
That turned into a bad week
That turned into a bad month
That then turned into a bad year
Don't worry, we all have them
You're not being left out AT ALL
DON'T WORRY, IT WILL WORK OUT

Melissa Kari Slaughter

Reflections

Here I sit,
Beneath the midnight sky.
The noise of daylight, faded
Into the quiet of the night.
Stars twinkling above
And thoughts of you
Racing through my mind.
So many questions;
So little time.
To hear your voice brings a peace
To the depths of my soul.
A peace to know you're still alive.

Katherine R. Mendes

Bartra

Reaching into shore
Broken waves leave their mark
Snaillike on the sand
Out again they roll
To where they were conceived
Recreating more

We are born
We live
We die
Our stamp
On all
We touch

Michael Smyth

For Someone Special

The little things
are most worthwhile.
A friendly talk,
a happy smile.
The willingness
to always share
another's thoughts,
another's cares.
Through sometimes
they may seem quite small,
these little things
mean most of all.

Shelby M. Saunders

Salvation Plan

"This is the end of it all,"
A phrase I heard him call.
"The covenant I set is now
Completed. You ask me how?
I sent my Son to die for you.
He came and lived sinless to
Be a sacrifice. The debt
You could not pay, He stepped
From Heaven to pay."   Now, all
That you need to do is call
On His wonderful name,
And His salvation claim.

Levi Samuel Johnston

Patches of Blue

I came out here on my own free will
To stand knee-deep in mud
My clothes are soaked and body cold
Looking up with mouth open wide
Only to drown in this unfamiliar place
Staring into dark grey
Looking for patches of blue

Stephen C. Ballenger

The Hunger

Eyes closed, passion rising,
Excitement returns, desire burns,
Buried forever with each
Passing moment that we are
Alone together.
Silently breathing, softly whispering,
Sweet nothings and every things,
Surrounded by pleasure, giving
Deeper, faster, stronger,
Beautiful release, hanging on
Soaring, floating, wanting more,
Wanting you.

Stephen J. Reinheckel

Dreams

Buy me a river,
buy me a boat,
build me a tree house
and milk me a goat.
Bake me a bacon,
catch me a thief,
tell me a lie
and make me believe.
I dream of the ocean,
I dream of the sea,
I dream of a lotion
with Vitamin D. . . .

Marlene Winter

Reflections

Look into the mirror,
tell me, what do you see?
Is it your reflection
or the reflection of me
staring back at you
like a thief in the night?
Is it a comforting feeling
or is it a scary sight?
Do you see just yourself
or am I there, too?
Is it the reflection of both of us,
or just the reflection of you?

Susan Jean Stiles

My Love for You

My love for you will be the
sun shining in the mornings

My love for you will be the
moonlit nights

My love for you will
never stop glowing

My love is only for you
and it will always
shine bright

MY LOVE FOR YOU

Nancy L. Steffler

Books

Books, books, everywhere,
People act like they don't care!

They get mistreated, worn and taped,
Beaten, bruised, bent out of shape . . .

Written in and poor ripped pages . . .
PEOPLE SHOULD BE KEPT IN
CAGES!!!!!!

Ashley Noel Whitney

On Marriage

Marriage is a union
between a husband and wife.
Two hearts bonded together
amidst harmony and strife.
Two very different people
linked in many different ways.
Agree, and promise one another
to love and learn each day.
Contentment comes with growing . . .
just as patience comes in time.
And the beauty of a marriage
is like a ribbon that stays tied!

Pamela Ann Fraser

Heartbreak

Do not sit there, smug in victory
smiling, eyes open in gloating.
It does not fit you.
I played the fool, but I myself
find victory and sit in contemplation.
I did it again.
After every rain, there is a rainbow—
when will it stop raining?
Hate. Cold. Black and white.
Love. All colors.
The canvas smeared in tears,
a mess.

Hope Irene Bellamy

Stars

In the sky
Under the moon
Beyond the Earth
After the sunlight
Across the darkness
Like a lamp
Upon a wish it stares
Into a shadow wishing
Since no one stares back
After the last wish
Within the darkness
Is a lost soul

Candi Nicole Hornbeck

Sunset

To Kirsten Giles
The sunset is a place for me.
The sun is all that I can see.

It is a place where I can sit.
A place where I can ponder.

This beautiful sun I see
Is not too far away.

I am hot.
Wait—no, I'm not!

I love MY sunset.

Justin Donovan Odell Kindrix

unforgettable you

you are so unforgettable
my dear, sweet unobtainable
you are so dear to me
so much so you'll never see
you haunt my dreams
and there it seems
you reach for me
and i reach for you

Libby Marie Hogle

The Clear Cut

It spills
down—
slowly
but steadily,
I inhale as its negativity surrounds me.
I watch as it spills down,
my wrist, now becoming clearer.
The air, now becoming sharper.
I can breathe,
because at last
I am freed.

Anita Mills Burt

This Conversation

I can't stand this conversation
I dislike all the hesitation
As danger creeps across my nation
Why so much abomination
Can't get a good education
I think about the devastation
What I need is relaxation
I need not any confrontation
I would like some appreciation
I want my emancipation
Maybe more participation
Is what we need to end this conversation

Lisanne Olivia Magnus

Where Is the Truth?

In the dark of morning
In the silence of night
Looking
Searching
It's nowhere in sight

Keep walking, trudging through
Getting closer to the other side
Creeping
Peeking
Still it seems to hide

Where is the truth?

Carrie R. Reel

Poetry

An item to write with,
and item to write on,
and words that flow from within . . .

A man or a woman,
a boy or a girl,
a thought, a reflection, and then . . .

Poetry flows like music
to every listening heart,
speaking a language
that wouldn't be spoken,
if the poets did not do their part.

Rose Ellen Slater

Strings

A person, not a puppet, am I.
You pull my strings,
You make me dance.
You pull my strings,
You make me laugh.
You pull my strings,
You make me cry.
A person, not a puppet, am I.

Melanie Kay Daugherty

Peas

I am picking peas
off my kitchen floor
for the tenth time today.
I hear small feet approaching.
I lie in ambush.
Peering around the corner,
I spy Joe Michael
slouched against the kitchen wall,
the Fridge door swung wide,
his eyes closed, mouth open,
peas dripping from his little fist.

Diane R. Dahlin

I Can't Look Away

You know it must be right
'Cause it feels like paradise
But I can't look away

I hear my name's been called
But I don't want to fall
And I can't look away

So, you've lived your life alone
You only know what you've been shown
But I can't look away
Look away
No, I can't look away

Corey M. Acord

Friends for Life

Friends may come and
Friends may go
But I guess I'll always know
Of all the times that you were there
Held my hand, when I was scared
You always knew when I was mad
And made me laugh, when I was sad
You gave me strength, when no one cared
Now it's my turn and I want to share
The feelings of love you gave to me
And the knowledge that we'll always be
Friends for life and eternity

Stefany M. Quinn

Dreams

In my whole life I never once dreamed
about the too sweet confection of a
scalloped-edged, melt-in-your-mouth,
wedding-cake dress.
Instead I floated though a fantasy of
barefoot linen;
we would invite your friend the ocean
and my friend the wind
and, with fingers tightly tangled,
raise our cheeks for the
congratulatory kiss from
both of the guests.

Kat Bayley

Friends Forever

All things come at a certain time
As you'll find in this little rhyme
You wear your shoes, until you grow
You wear your mittens, when it snows
You clean your room, when it's a mess
You try to relax, when you have stress
You use a tissue, when you sneeze
You take a deep breath, when you wheeze
You wear shorts, when you're hot
You wear a coat, when you're not
You laugh out loud, when you hear a joke
You feel refreshed, when you have a Coke
You eat broccoli, yuck, never
But your friends, you keep forever

Kristen Louise Eichorn

Serenity

Washed over by thoughts,
By pain,
By happiness,
By love,
By hate.
Emotions encircle me,
Reminiscing each experience.
Pain,
Happiness,
Love,
And hatred.
All existing simultaneously,
In me,
In serenity.

Alison Wong

Never Give Up

When I didn't make
the basketball team,
Daddy said, "Don't give up."
When I got bad grades,
Daddy said, "Don't give up."
When I couldn't
play the piano,
Daddy said, "Don't give up."
When I couldn't get into the college
that Daddy went to,
Daddy said, "Don't give up."
And now I sit in the waiting room
of the hospital,
knowing that
I won't give up on him,
just like he never gave up on me.

Jessie Leigh Raiford

Blues

His hair is greasy
and black;
slanted over his forehead,
it makes a piano.
And I listen.

He doesn't measure his music,
just opens his mouth
and lets
left-handed blues spill
all over the concrete,
slipping, scratching, sinking
his woes into my pockets.
Peddling poverty for pennies.

I scrape together a few wooden smiles
and toss them in to his guitar case.

Natalie Jovon Graham

Perishment

My greatest fear
A little girl
Innocent in her years
Sheltered in her hopes and dreams
Used by the world
Walking a road that only circles
It's so easy to stand still and not walk
But this is her destiny
Unsure of herself, she makes it true
Making others happy
Never listening to her soul
She is killing herself
Smothered in her unheard screams
This little girl . . .
Inside a forgotten woman

Natalie Jane Parria

Food for Thoughts

Food is something
My body needs to survive,
Not something to take
the place of something
missing in my life.
To answer all my
needs with a bite or two
of this or that
is why I am starting
to change the rules.
I've grown tired of being fat.
So now today when
I feel the urge to eat
I'll stop and ask myself
Why? And is this something I really need?

Linda Odom

Right Now

Right now I am dead.
I am cold everywhere
Shallow breaths I take
Barely at all do I breathe
Shaking all the time
Silence all around me
No music, no phone, only,
Only the noise of my thoughts
Pounding away at the only thing
The only thing I have left,
My sanity.
The silence of my life . . .
Dying away.
I want to be dead
No longer alive.

Jennifer Rose Novak

When People Die

Written at age 11
When people die, it is real sad.
Some people cry, some people get mad.

When my pal, Joe died,
I cried and cried and cried.

We didn't have him for that long;
When he died, I thought it was wrong.

When Joe had died, it was unfair;
But I knew he was floating in thin air.

He's now in Heaven, now, that I know;
So, I have to be good before I go.

I'll meet him in Heaven when I die,
And then I will not cry and cry!

Nickolas Johnson

Tumor

Bang! Lightening bolts.
Flash! It spreads.
Her time? What time?
She's been robbed.
Her ambitions, hopes, dreams—
They mean nothing now.
Why? Why? Why?
Her ultimate question,
It shall remain unanswered.

She lies steady, steady, steadier.
Confusion rests in uttered words,
"Why me?"

She lies pale, pale, paler,
Motionless

Kristen Archdeacon

Two a.m.

red lips in sunshine gleam, not touch
brown eyes in dreams awake, not see
touch of skin, I slow . . . so soft

my dessert queen, I wish, I sin
condemned, accused of none, I'm none!

Legions brought by Rome, by me
oh, mighty gods, I pray, not be!

Damned the day I met such love,
pain of mountain tails do throb,
can I? I shall, I can't, I try
oh, why, do I, and I and I?

Worlds I built, now lost, I rest . . .

alone

Yaniv Leven

Heart Constellation

bubbling emotions spills over
from raw unconscious dreams
to my vivid conscious reality;
thoughts flow into
smooth curves of inspiration
and a new perspective
is alive with a gush of power,
true feeling;
steam rises in the heat
of my pure emotion
as the reign of entrapment
cools my desires;
washed from memory is that
from my cosmic mind
not captured on paper

Felicia Ann Riedel

Relief

I seek relief from this numbness
that settled long ago in my heart.
Although through the flesh,
for a few seconds a fire burns,
I have been down a path
that is full of turns,
unexpected obstacles
made me lift my head
to look ahead. . . .

I want to feel
when the rain soaks my skin,
when your hand reaches for me,
when your breath draws my own
to know that eternity
is within me. . . .

Dominique Remy Root

Sweet Melody

So soft and luscious
So strong and powerful
So frail and exposed
Yet faint and desperate
Calling out to me
The raindrops in a storm
That humming bittersweet serenity
My savior
So clear
So warm
It was he; his voice
So pleasing to my ears
That sweet, sweet melody
His voice
My cure

Toni Qiu

Connection

There is awareness
And hesitation.
A look, a smile, a touch.
Words come from your mouth that were
My thoughts moments before.
I feel: You speak.
I feel: You touch.
I feel: You are here.
We are here now—this moment.
You are here, I am here. We are here.
A look, a smile, a touch.
Hesitation. Awareness. We are one.
Here.
Now.
This Moment.

Glenda M. Wood

In Memory of My Father

Though your face I cannot touch
Your smile I cannot see
I know you're in my heart
Standing here with me.

You meant so much to me
And you shielded me from pain
But losing you, I lost myself
It's a horrible strain.

I know in my heart
You're with those you love
Your soul climbed to Heaven
In the image of a dove.

I love and miss you, Dad.
Until we meet again.

Beth Seddon

My Cyber-Buddy

You are out there,
Not just in my imagination
But a buddy,
Who by clever navigation exists
Through bytes and bits
In cyberspace.
So near, and yet so far.
I wonder if we only are
Linked like phantoms,
With cyber lace
Spun so fine,
Like the will-o'-the-wisp,
Do you really exist?
Or were you never mine,
My Phantom Buddy?

Trudie Dingwall

My Friend

There is a friend I know
Who never lets her feelings show
Though her losses are there
And leave her bare
She'll never lets them show
She hides her pain with ease
And thinks nobody sees
The unshed tears
Of painful years
Of which she tries to flee
And so, my friend, good-bye
I will always wonder why
You hid your tears
For all these years
And then you had to die

Mary Darlene Womble

Hard to Accept

As I sit here thinking of you
I truly feel how much I love you
And how much it hurts to know
That I have lost you . . .

I try to act like I don't care
But this pain in my heart
I cannot bear
It makes it hard for me to hide
This feeling of sorrow and emptiness
That I keep inside . . .

No matter where I go
Or whatever I do
It's so hard for me to accept
That I have lost you . . .

Joyce Ann De Guzman

Winter Calls

And so the seasons sing,
as I see with the eye
a new birth, a new fling
and hear its music beyond the sky.
Winter sings, as fall sighs for rest;
the words are silent, but I hear.
As fall departs, it's for its best
for joy has awakened, as winter is near.
Winter calls! Winter calls!
The sweet sound takes my breath,
as the love of nature falls.
In season, there is rest
for there is no death.
And so the seasons sing,
a new birth; a new fling.

Elizabeth Todd Stubbs

now you come

now you come to see me
now you need to cry
now you just sit and stare
wondering if i'll die
now what will you say
now what will you do
take my hand, wish me the best
yeah, that will do
my time has come
i shed no tears
it's clear to me
who really cares
you who love me know who you are
those of you who might miss me
just waited in the car. . . .

Daniel A. Parris

To Be Thy Valentine: (Italian Sonnet)

I fancy the magic in your eyes,
And court that thy heart truly speaks.
Of unmasked candor my soul doth seek,
To know the depths in thy heart I lie.
And win the thoughts of pure delight,
When muse you in the winds,
To know the day replete with friend,
Of lustrous golden light.
To hold that moment in rapture fine,
And bind of me to thee,
I trade my heart and all therein,
To be thy valentine.
And beg the winds to set we free,
For love of two true friends.

Luster Lewis

Domingo

Market Benches. . . .
I must have been lost.

As though tracing the past
was too far to walk now.
And every stolen moment
had finally reached me here.

Standing. . . .

Dispelled by wit alone. . . .

Witnessing the fruits of true labor
through all those forsaken pretences.

And stealing a season,

to skip it along. . . .

Michael John Wiley

Teardrops

Are you familiar
to the sound of teardrops
as they hit your pillow case?

No one around to notice
tears rolling down
your face.

But you wake up every
morning not telling
a soul.

Because then they'd know
your secret

You're empty

You're not whole.

Yvonne M. Darro

I've Seen

I've lived for many years,
seen and done as many things!
I've laughed many laughs,
and cried as many tears.
I've seen the miracles of man,
and watched his failures, too!
I've seen babies born,
and watched many men die.
I've seen seconds turn to years,
and time is always just the same.
I've seen my life in the flutter
of a wing;
I've seen Death!
Now I'll see the darkness and the light
I've never seen!

Ollie C. Burroughs

Great-Grandpa

Like a man of countless wisdom
You would play the game
Moving the pieces on the board
With a plan already in hand
And as I try to counter
You would only smile with pride
For while I never could beat you
I was determined to try
For you were my hero
And the game was my test
And now that your gone it's not the same
The game has lost its meaning
And the test has died away
But you will always be my hero
And the game will forever be ours

Michael Lynn Davidson Jr.

Dream

At night I lie
Hoping that you were mine
In your arms is where I wish to be
Staying so close and tender
If only you wanted the same
Then this wouldn't be a dream
I care for you so much
You just don't know
If only I could say
What was in my heart
But it's so hard and difficult
If you felt the same
It would be so much easier
But until that day comes
I can only dream

Catrina Lynn Gould

It Didn't Mean Anything to You!

I gave it away,
It didn't mean anything.
I believed what you said,
It didn't mean anything.
You took if from me,
It didn't mean anything.
You lied to me so many times,
It didn't mean anything.
You took advantage of me,
It didn't mean anything.
I let you have a piece of me,
It didn't mean anything.

But it did mean something to me!

Jamie Lynn Routhier

I Wish My Eyes Were Cameras

*Inspired by and written
for the love of my life, Kate West*
I wish my eyes were cameras
For I could capture an eternity
  Of moments when I see her
And take in her unguarded beauty

I would capture those moments
When she doesn't know I'm looking
  When she is simply being herself
Radiant with an indescribable glow

I would take the film of my mind
And put the pictures in an album
  A photo album of the soul
And keep forever those treasured moments

Jeffery David Douglas

Above

In my early age
My innocent stage
I was marked by you
From an onlooking view
Foreseeing my nature
My patterns of blood
My time spent on you
My time spent on love
My time spent below
My time spent above

Sebastian Edward Gough Sharp

Long Lasting

*Dedicated to my beloved sister
and her boyfriend*
Oceans are deep
Clouds are high
Puddles are shallow
Mountains are graceful
Valleys are flat
Deserts never die
Love is forever
Like you and I

Samantha Lynn Shevlin

Beautiful Day

A day as beautiful as this one you wish
You could stay outside all day
As the beautiful bird sings you wish
The sound could stay with you forever
As the beautiful wind blows against
Your beautiful skin you wish it
Would stay cool all day
Today is beautiful but is it going to be
Tomorrow, I wish for every day to be
Like this one I mean Beautiful

Samantha K. Morris

Clear in Thought, Clear in Sound

The day I learned my "R" sounds
I was very proud, you see,
For everyone could be understood
Except for little me.

Now I can say
"Such a pretty feather"
As plain as
Can be.

Pamela Michelle Perry

AIDS

It's hard to understand,
it affects women and men.
It's not just a homosexual disease,
you can think that if you please.
I do understand
that by God's hand,
someday there will be a cure.
I know that for sure.
It may not happen in your life.
It hurts like a knife,
cutting through my heart
that so many depart
from the world from this disease.
The people suffering need a cure, please!

Erika Lynn Nahinurk

The Only One

before you, there was no life.
until the day you became my wife.
The sorrow and pain I knew before.
has gone away and is no more.
you make me smile, you make me sing.
with all the joy in life you bring.
in your love I am born again.
in all the love, you choose to send.
I am your's forever more,
because you are the only one I adore.

Steven William McDonald

Clouds

In a bed of clouds I'd like to lay
Having played hard all day
With fluffy pillows for my tired head
And wispy wallows for my bed
The moon and the stars will help me see
That beneath me is the glittering sea
A whale will breach high in the sky
While dolphins sing a lullaby
In a bed of clouds I'd like to lay
Having played hard all day

Kelly Catherine Elena Berg

Dear Cupid

Dear Cupid, I ask of thee
One small favor desperately;
There is a man who completes my heart.
He's handsome, charming, and very smart.
He makes me laugh, he makes me smile;
I'd like to keep him around a while.
Make him love me, make him see
What life with me can really be.
Shoot an arrow through his heart,
So that we may never be apart.

Teresa Jean Osowski

Where Were You?

When we needed guidance
Where were you?
When we needed encouragement
Where were you?
When we needed advice
Where were you?
When we needed a father
Where were you?
When you're old and lonely, you'll ask,
Where are my children?

Jennifer L. Rathjen

Questions without Answers

She thinks he doesn't love her
She thinks he doesn't care
No matter how she dresses
Or the way she does her hair

Her love for him is strong
And nothing has gone wrong
For her love he does not know
And for him anywhere she would go

She loves him dearly
And for her not just anything will do
Yes, of course she loves him
But the real question is:
Does he love her too?

Lynndzey Nicole Chelf

The Roots

The leaves on the tree
are what you only see
instead of the roots that make it grow

It is like pain deep inside
that I always seem to hide
to make sure that no one will know

So, I go on with a smile
throwing the "hurt" in a pile
that I carry with me wherever I go

I just pretend it isn't there
and that I don't really care
and hope the truth does not show

Leslie Gay Gould

Capital Fear

Grey voices grow slowly between trees,
Seeing sparks of humming light
Illuminate the nightly breeze
Of whispering woods.

So gentle hoot and croak
Can drift between the root
Of oak and poplar tree that
Darkness' sea disturbs no call.

From nightfall till the crack of dawn
I'm handled like a pawn and lack
The strength to stand more noises,
Yet grey voices grow slowly between trees.

Eric Braaksma

My Outgoing Colleague and Friend

Always calm and never cold,
Moving at a steady pace
Though not, too, that age-old.

His table is tidy;
The floor is clean;
The wall looks artistic,
And the space is green.
With a beautiful mind
That he has got,
We cannot forget,
And we shall not.

Khoandkar Hannan

What Is on Your Mind

They say, God, that You have spoken
Your intentions are in the signs
No one can doubt these sacred words
I hear these whispers all the time

Still, there are those of us who wonder
What is really on Your mind

How can I question the wisdom of
Those who came before me
All the answers written in the sand
Buried in the sea

True believers would not dare to
Look into Your eyes
Or ponder what is surely meant to be

Still, I cannot help but wonder
If I have privy to Your thoughts
How is my ability so divine

I think I'll wait until You show me
What is on Your mind

Deidre Jefferson King

Good Ol' #3

Dale was a Great Man,
As wise as He could be.
He taught Me about the race,
and led Us to VICTORY.
His Heart was made of GOLD,
You know He gave Us everything,
How were We to know,
He'd be racing for the KING.
Oh, how I wish Everyone could see,
how His life now lives in
LITTLE E.
Dale raced that ROD, GOOD OL' #3
and DALE WAS A GREAT MAN TO ME!

Robin Michelle Steele

In the Night

I saw a shooting star one night,
Falling so beautiful in the night sky.
I wished this wish, you see,
For you to always be with me.

Full was the moon one night,
Who cast her light on me.
I had this dream, you see,
That you were there with me.

Beautiful was the night,
Whose eerie light surrounded us,
While you held me tight,
Promising to always love me.

Shawna Heckaman

He's Gone

Those words are so hard to say
As I wander through each dreary day
The time it passes so very slow
How to get through this, I do not know
Just memories of days gone by
As I sit alone and cry
Is there only thoughts of undone dreams
Nothing left, or so it seems
My eyes, they fill with lonely tears
My mind, it races with unknown fears
I pray for strength to go on
For in spirit he's here
Not really gone

Kathy E. Brucker

Danger

Four more years
And a heart that seers
You looked at me
And you heard my silent plea
Now I'm walking away
Trying not to say
"I forgive you
I still love you
Why did you push me away"
That day I cried
Wishing you hadn't lied
The next morning
My heart was beating
Because I saw you there
The smell of roses in the air
You knelt at my feet
Said, "Will you marry me"
And I knew I was in danger
Of losing the love
Of my life

Kasy Wilson

Sit Here Thinking

I sit here thinking
Thinking about all that has happened.
I don't know what to do.
You toyed with my mind.
You lead me on.
What shall I do?
Should I follow?
Keep my hopes up?
Keep hoping that day will come,
The day when we can be together.
Should I? Or not?
What should I do?
I contemplate it all,
All as I sit here thinking.

Amanda Jo Hermansson

Tomorrow

Perhaps I will call you "tomorrow."
For when I see your smile,
your piercing eyes,
I become curious as to what lies ahead.
With the stealth of dawn you
crept into my soul revealing yourself
as the new day bringing light into a
spirit long held in darkness.
So in appreciation,
as a gift on the wind,
I shall give you a name.
"Tomorrow"
Perhaps I will call you tomorrow.
For "Tomorrow" is my future.

Corey (Ngozi) La'Thair Miller

Child's Play

The child spins, twirls, and dances,
The child sings, hums, and laughs,
The child skips, walks, and runs,
The child enhances her bright beauty
In the falling rain.

And as the rain begins to fade,
Her mother comes out to play.

She spins, twirls, and dances,
She sings, hums, and laughs,
She skips, walks, and runs,
She enhances her bright beauty
With her child
In the setting sun.

Cassiann M. Procenko

As School's End Nears

One month left,
Promises to be kept.
As school's end nears,
So begin all of our fears.

We remember our best friend
On whom we depend.
As everyone departs,
We are left with broken hearts.

As high school nears,
The greater our fears.
We search again
For a new best friend.

One month till,
Promises still.
As the school year nears,
The greatest our fears.

Catlyn Marie Portwine

. . . And Then, a Tear Falls!

My days are filled with memories,
My nights are filled with dreams,
As onward, over the sea of life,
I drift with changing stream.

And oft, I pass, While drifting
by ports that beckon me;
and wonder, would I heed their call
had I never cared for thee?

And so this world seems empty,
and sweet content has gone,
since our paths crossed on youthful seas
and you sailed on—alone.

Ethel M. Halstead

Missing You

The heat that escapes your body
rules my emotions.
The steam dances around my heart.
The song of your voice traps
a thought in my head,
taking me back to when the world
was ours.
Remember the trees,
a rush of wind,
the two of us in harmony
with the river.
We were connected.
I was close to you.
You loved me.

Corina Idalia Rudat

Reverie

Daydreaming . . .
the possibilities,
the wonders,
the blessings.

Solitude . . .
divine freedom,
time to reconcile
our tethered spirits.

Together . . .
they allow the merge
of heart
and mind
and soul.

Madison Mae Ballard

To You

When I'm with you, I lose myself
When I'm alone, I find myself
Wanting to be lost again

And you're the one I choose myself
When I'm lonely sitting by myself
Waiting to get lost again

Maybe it's unnatural
But maybe it's supposed to be
Maybe it's the same unnamed power
That enables once-blind men to see

When I'm with you, I lose myself
When I'm alone, I find myself
Wishing I was lost again

Christopher J. Engle

Farewell

As my love walks away
I watch her go
I feel her go
I can't bare to let her go
I can still smell her
I can taste her on my lips
I can feel her hair between my fingers
I can indulge in her touch
She walks away
To never look back
She's getting further
And I can't stop her
I put on a fake smile
As I wave my hand
My heart is breaking
Right where I stand
I continue my life
I pretend all is well
I am lying to myself
As I bid farewell

Patrick Amgar

Flowers

Flowers can be blossoming bubbles
forming in the dew. Just one ray
of sunlight can shine in the
afternoon and be so lonely yet
still be smiling. That one ray
of sunlight can make the flowers
dance and sing and smile upon you.
One flower can be all the colors
of the rainbow and become the key
to the secret world of creations.
A flower can mean love or hate,
friendship or war. A flower can
be the symbol of the world and
still be kissing the bees and
butterflies in the park. A flower
is a sign of a new relationship
if given at the right time or a
slap in the face of rejection.
Flowers are blossoming bubbles
that show the world.

Danielle Rettino

Judicial System

Must I spend the rest of my life
swimming in this desolate sea of strife?
How dearly must I pay;
what thorny, rocky way
must I tread?
Must youthful mistakes be read
ALOUD
to a hostile, curious crowd?
The woman is always to blame,
the man can make any claim. . . .
Pain and destruction abound,
inquisitive faces are all around.
That sombre court
where so many futile battles are fought;
those judges, who seem "all" to know—
the "Law" gives them power to act so.
It's my life they are deciding,
taking away, and dividing. . . .
Do they care it's a life destroyed?
No matter, the "LAW" must be deployed.

Lillian Davis

Love Nets

For your love I searched afar,
Under each cloud, behind each star.
I looked and looked to no avail.
Would I ever find you, or would I fail?
Someone said, "Try the Nets!
You'll find love there, I'll bet!"
"Are you sure?" I said, "How can that be?
There isn't any love for me!"
The love I'd found so many times,
wasn't always sweet, wasn't always kind.
In my mind I'd given up.
How could they help me, this Love Net?
How would they know? What would I get?
What kind of people write these ads?
Oh, God! I'm writing them, too? Egads!
I yearned for love sweet and true,
And it seemed so did you.
You answered my ad from afar.
I found that love under the cloud,
Behind the star!

Linda Jane Stokes

Like a Little Bird

Like a little bird
Fly high in the sky
Over the seas
At day light and at nights
In fall and in winter
In snowy days and pouring nights
Like a little bird
Fly high in the sky
I'm looking for love
That is so hard to find
Like a little bird
Fly high in the sky
In the dark forest
And no empty nest to find
In the heat of the summer
And no place to hide
Like a little bird
Fly high in the sky
I'm looking for love
That is so hard to find

Yanir Pesok

Touch

I've licked the lips of loneliness
Which left a sour taste.
I've held the hand of hopelessness
Which was not a happy place.
I've rubbed the arm of anxiety
And knelt beside the pain.
I've even touched the tenderness
I only wish to gain.
I've often felt complete fear
Of everything around.
I've often gotten all mixed up
With the surrounding crowd.
I've tried to tackle all my terrors
That live deep down within.
I've even prayed for perfectness
Although I often sin.
I've given up in the past before
And let my enemy win.
I'll keep on smiling to beat him
And hope it doesn't happen again.

Lori Alaina Andersen

The Nightmare of You

I watch your skeleton mind
waiting to string your answers together
in order to come to a conclusion of the
nonsense you speak of
you refuse to speak of the
buried fog
the cardboard fight was unclear
the ghost choked
REMORSEFULLY
as it invaded the field
the sky collapsed
as the
stars dreamed of sin,
the rain
repeated the past and future
as the heaven
rejected their
secrets
but nothing was more frightening than
when the dandelions lost their beauty!

Philicia L. Harris

Waiting for the Ghost

I turn off the light
and the world becomes a scary place.
I call, but you are not here.
I scream, but you can't hear.

I walk around disabled,
hearing the ghost in my mind.
I know it's him,
but I know I'm crazy.

I'm feeling your emotions,
and you are so scared.
I want to reassure you,
but distance rips me from your arms.

I sit; I wait; I watch,
anticipating the 10:10 connection.
It passes. I am scared.

I lie; I think; I dream.
A tear rolls down my cheek,
and I'm drawn into the lair of sleep.

Debbie Neill

God

Gazing out the window,
Just seeing all those stars.
Gazing out the window
At Jupiter and Mars.
While gazing out the window,
And seeing all that snow
I know that God is with me.
He always is, you know?
You may not think He's with you,
But you must learn to trust Him.
After you know what He's done for you,
Your heart He's sure to win.
He's coming again soon,
And when He comes you'll know,
Because you who belive in Him
To His eternal kingdom you'll go.
Gazing out the window,
Just knowing God is there.
Gazing out the window
And at the atmosphere.

Shelley Anne Collins

Sea of Turmoil

Lost in a Sea of Turmoil
My heart cries out in pain.
My soul is saddened and
Upheaval rules constant.

Tossed about in the storm,
My body is battered and bruised.
Is there no relief, O, Lord?
Will I always remain at the
Edge of hysteria and confusion?
Will I ever be calm of spirit
And have peace of mind?

Calm me in the rough seas of life.
Bring me out into the rays of
Warm and glorious sunshine.
Be ever constant in my life.

Still the turmoil of life
Rages deep within me,
Always knowing that with You
Beside me all things are possible.

Deborah K. Joseph

A Crow Named Hope

I was given orders to write a poem
this cold winter's day.
So help me I did not
know what to say.
I sat and thought,
and looked and listened,
trying to find some
inspiring words to help
someone through the day.
My hope was gone with
the winter blues, when
I heard a crow call to
say, "It isn't true.
Your winter days will
soon be through.
I call to bring you cheer
and remind you that the
Earth's long sleep will soon
be through, and everything
around you will be new."

Bertha M. Iles

The Rose

I watch a rose so beautiful
in the deepest shade of red.
As the wind blows upon it,
soft and delicate petals it sheds.
With each new gust of wind,
the petals fall to the ground.
I begin to wonder if the beauty
of the red rose will ever be found.
With another gust of wind,
the last, red petal falls.
Now it's just a stem,
it doesn't appear to be a rose at all.
The beauty on the outside
has vanished before my eyes.
But the true beauty was hidden
by the petals as a disguise.
Its strength and dignity,
the pride and hope it gives.
Without the deep, red petals
the true beauty still lives.

Samantha Jean Bailey

Lingua Enlightenment

For a moment will you but consider
The motive for indulging in anguish?
Humankind subliminally inclined
To endure eternal condemnation
Feebly attempts defense a time or two
But ultimately finds it easier
To bear indignity rather than duel.
What seizes the spirit's sustentation
So stealthily that it forgets to thrive?
Mankind solicits victimization
When it concurs with being brutalized
By the vociferousness of rancor
Until the soul splinters into something
Modeling eradication of self.
Man need only develop expression
To defend who he dreams he is—will be—
Scant only the self-edification
To distinguish salvageability
In a dominion yet unrecognized
As a dwelling that wants to embrace him.

Toni Rogers

What Does That Mean?

Every day I don't see you,
I'm missing you.
Every time I see you,
I want to grab you and kiss you.
What does that mean?
I care a lot about you
and would do anything for you.
I don't want anyone to hurt you,
I would never hurt you.
What does that mean?
I daydream about you
and can't stop thinking about you.
What does that mean?
I want to be with you
and do different things with you.
What does that mean?
I'm falling in love with you,
and, baby, I don't know how to tell you.
What should I do, baby?
Tell me what this means to you.

Lacy Elizabeth Meredith

Born Free

Oh! Mister Dictator
What makes you feel as a donor?
A donor of my freedom
While I have my Kingdom,
A Kingdom of my mind,
Unlimited mental world.
Where I put you down the earth,
Where I declare my own truth.
Outside, in the world we share,
You may have the power
To make a barrier,
To put me in danger.
But not to let me free,
Telling that's your charity.
Who else is giving me?
I'm born to be free.
Ever since my first breath,
It is there to my death.
In my mind,
Unlimited mental world.

Solomon Shumiye Mekonnen

'Twas Nothing Left to Change

Mom, I've known you quite a while,
Just over eighteen years.
If there's one thing that I've learned,
It's you stand out among your peers.
I know that while you love me,
Raising me was quite a chore,
But you never ditched your duties,
A "mother" to the core.
In the past, you feel you may
Have made some bad decisions;
But as far as raising kids go,
You're a woman among women.
Out of all the females there,
God chose you to carry me;
Because only YOU could make me
What he wanted me to be.
You were the right one for the job,
Hand-picked by destiny;
In and out, without a doubt,
The perfect mom for me.

Ian Albert Young

Dream

Thoughts of Barbara
Without reason she rolls over;
I sleep.
I have been summoned.
Her workday is over;
Her legs slide over mine,
Silky, freshly shaven,
She is waiting for me,
She is anticipating me,
She is hungry.
I can stop the hunger,
Bodies wrapped as one,
One heart,
One soul,
Love pouring out of every opening.
Her head rests on the pillow;
She drifts to sleep.
I whisper,
"Good night, my love.
Dream a good dream."

Joe E. Crosby III

Infidelity vs. Faithful Living (An Acrostic)

Intense
Nights
Frequent
Indulgences
Deliberate
Ecstasy
Lovers
Intwined
Tormenting
Yourselves

Fortunate
Are
Individuals
That
Have
Found
Unpenetrable
Love

Angela Marabeth Sechrist

Hope

MS, he said, the words like stone
The tests were in and done,
Emotions dulled by all we heard
No where for me to run.
The information we received
Was sketchy at the best,
But research on the net and books
Did give my mind some rest.
My life, it passed before me
I thought of all I had,
Then I gave my soul a search
And knew it wasn't bad.
I have my aches, I have my pains
And walking isn't good,
But here I go again today
I show up where I should.
Every day is special
I cherish every one,
I spread some love and cheer each day
To each and everyone.

Elsa E. Scribner

As I Am Looking at Your Face

As I am looking at your face
I am facing your grace
As I am looking at your nose
I am sensing the rose
As I am looking at your eyes
I am seeing through the ice
As I am looking at your hair
I am sailing in the air
As I am looking at your ear
I am hearing no fear
As I am looking at your skin

I am feeling the scene
As I am looking at your lips
I am kissing the eclipse
As I am looking at your face
I am looking at the grace
Of the rose that neither
The ice nor the air
Put the fear of time
In the scene of the eclipse

Diego Marcelo Salmon

A New Beginning

Today I feel like a new person,
just awakening from a dream
and suddenly discovering that
life is not as it once seemed.
I'd lost myself to darkness,
couldn't find a safe way out,
until I reached within my soul
and learned what I was all about.
How exciting is this journey
to a place of warmth and light,
for I've left the past behind me
and just carry what feels right.
I look forward to tomorrow
for the first time in my life,
and can see the world in new ways,
calm and peaceful without strife.
I am thankful for the presence
of my wonderful new friend
who's taught me how to love myself,
and to find rainbows with no end.

Gail S. Bicknell

Mom of a Million

You're a Mom of a Million,
This is so true.
In fact, I can't think of a reason
not to love you.
I would trade a million dollars,
and a diamond or two
Just to have a Mom who supports me,
like you do.
I count on you
to pick me up when I fall.
And when I look back upon it,
I'll know it was worth it all.
When tears are shed,
it helps to know you're here.
Mother, to me,
you'll always be dear.
God bless you this season
with all that is such.
I'm overjoyed to have a mommy
who loves me so much.

Samantha Butler

I Found Me

I have traveled life's path:
day by day,
month to month,
year in—year out.
Time my nemesis
Moving along:
endless roads,
stretched across countless miles,
wandering relentlessly.
Destination unknown
Seeking:
my youthful dreams,
my other self,
my lost destiny.
Eyes closed
Suddenly:
I stopped.
Turned.
Opened my eyes.
And there you were

Stephanie Rebecca Hammond

Martin Luther King—Be Brave

Wise men never stop learning,
The foolish never start.
They dismiss me, black, and claim I have
No brain, no soul, or heart.
Yet through these hours of darkness,
In my quest for civil rights,
A ray of hope is born,
And I continue my racial fight.
My social dream is simple.
The cause inside me burns
For all men to rise together,
And sit on equal terms.
I get down on my knees,
And I begin to pray,
That when I go stand again,
The world will hear me say,
We may fight and plea for freedom,
But as men, we can't forget.
Allow not the sun to go down on anger,
For it will rise again on regret.

Briony Sue Douglas

Harvest Basket

This poem is a harvest basket
Woven of autumn reeds on
Staves of wisdom saved
From the long, sweet growing season.
In my basket, I can gather
Diamonds scattered on the ocean,
Berries red among the twigs,
Flags by breezes set in motion,
Songs that raise their praise to Heaven,
Secret longings of the heart,
Sadness soothed by gratitude,
Loves like little works of art.
A poem is a worthy basket
In which to gather all the all
That we know cannot be carried
With us beyond the final fall.
Perhaps my grandchildren will find it
In a book, long tucked away,
And carry it along with them
To gather flowers in one day.

Meredith Hulse

Good-Byes

Good-bye, sweetheart!
No, not "Good-bye!"
For that sends you to God
With a "God be with ye!"
And I am not yet ready
To send you into God's world
Without me.

Rather, I say, "Fare thee well,"
As you leave for a short while.
And upon your return,
I shall be waiting here;
Lonely and longing for you!

Every second a day,
And every day an eternity.
But you will,
You must return to me,
For I need you here
With me to be whole again.
And God must wait.

John Alexander McAllister

My Search

I often search in the depths of my mind
Lost in a place only I can find
In a world of subconscious thought
Lie the answers I have sought
And hunt, as I may for these lost ideas
They are held back and cannot come clear
In search of what, I do not know
I am certain I will find it though
Could this all be a mere illusion
At the center of my confusion
But no, this delusion cannot be
I am certain, though I cannot see
I peak and peer without success
For the source of my distress
Past my ideals, I duck and weave
Beyond what I love and believe
Without the sight of a solution
Without view of any conclusion
Another hopeless search complete
Still nothing has become of me

Kevyn Casey Byrnes Peter Connor

Seasons

In the spring, the flowers
Burst forth in grand array.
Life has a new beginning
To view most every day.
Summer days are lazy;
The sun is warm and strong.
Creatures come to gather
Food for winter long.
With fall comes excitement,
For time is running out.
The days are getting shorter;
There is a chill throughout.
With winter comes the raining
And all the stormy blast.
All nature now is resting,
Blooming, working's past.
In the spring the flowers
Burst forth in grand array.
Life has a new beginning
To view most every day.

Connie A. Roy

Wedding Whisper

It started with a whisper,
taken by surprise.
Never thought of finding comfort,
in someone else's eyes.
Someone to tell a story,
on a stormy winter night.
Someone to walk the beach with,
with the sunlight shining bright.
I don't have all the answers,
for the questions on your mind.
But a whisper like a marriage,
can last someone's life time.
With your family right behind you,
and your future straight ahead.
The wedding bells stopped ringing,
and the vows have all been said.
This journey of a lifetime,
holding true through thick and thin.
With faith in one another,
and a new life to begin.

Dennis Albert Nahal

It Could Happen to You

It happens all the time,
just not to me and you;
someone dies in an accident,
you think it through and through.
He shouldn't have been drinking,
now his friend is dead;
he let some things get to him,
they went straight to his head.
It still hasn't hit him,
what happened on that night;
but now he has to live with this
for the rest of his life.
The boy is helpless now,
he's six feet underground;
the driver stood there silent,
he doesn't make a sound.
Maybe it will teach him
when he gets the beer they gave;
drinking and driving isn't cool,
it could send you to your grave.

Jason Michael Politis

Love of My Life

Love of my mind,
Beauty in my eyes,
Love of my heart,
Angel in disguise.
Your touch, so tender,
Your lips, so warm,
I'll always remember,
Being in your arms.
Never say never,
When it comes to me and you,
Love goes on forever,
Deep down you know that, too.
Walking in the darkness,
Breathing without you,
Living in this madness,
Don't know what to do.
I love you with all my heart,
You're the love of my soul,
Can't stand to be apart,
From the one who makes me whole.

Jacqueline Anneisa Rayman

A Mother in Heaven

There's a garden in Heaven
where mothers go
to watch their children
on the Earth below.
They shed their tears
with joy and pain
for all the years
they can't regain.
Even when the sorrow is deep
a promise from Jesus is theirs to keep.
A day will come for all to see
a gift of hope for you and me.
Once again your eyes will meet
mother and daughter on a garden seat.
You'll laugh and cry and sing a song,
for it's with your Mom that you belong.
Until that day
look up and smile
because Mom is watching
all the while.

Robert Thomas Force

My Frenemy

"Is this the thanks I get
For all the things I have done?"
For all the things but they are none
And all the advice you have said
Is like a ticking of a clock
Is like the nagging of a child
That makes you twitch
then drives you wild
Days go by with all its problems
Your advice becomes fanatic
Then I think it's criticizing
Which makes me know that you're pathetic
Your a freak with all its nature
you might even be a creature
And maybe a creature would be too kind
to be thinking with your mind
You have no mind I am sure
But you will always put me down
Your like a ticking of a clock
Tick tock

Shamma Bin Ghannam

The Dark Dream

I dreamt once of a barren place,
No plants or creatures grow.
This once exquisite planet,
Now covered in ashen snow.
The people of this terrible place?
Nothing but rotting bones.
Buildings, well where they used to be,
Are nothing but charred stones.
No children's laughter graces the skies,
No longer can we see the sun.
The terror we will unleash
Has already begun.
The ground is now a barren waste,
The desolate Earth cries out in pain.
The men before refused to hear,
Now what is there to gain?
The end of all things has been set,
Ironically planted like a seed.
All love for our fellow man
Destroyed by petty greed.

David Kristian Ham

Little Kittie

Little kittie in my house,
Little kittie chasing a mouse.
Little kittie in a tree,
Little kittie on my knee.
Little kittie in my head,
Little kittie on my bed.
Little kittie climbing stairs,
Little kittie says her prayers.
Little kittie has big, round eyes,
Little kittie likes to spy.
Little kittie having fun,
Little kittie in the sun.
Little kittie playing around,
Little kittie fell down.
Little kittie has a scratching post,
Little kittie likes to boast.
Little kittie loving me,
Little kittie stung by a bee.
Little kittie in my cart,
Little kittie in my heart.

Malisa Renée Manning

Oh, Gentle Wings

On gentle wings some will fly
Others shall wonder why
They to cannot soar or fly
Let me soar on gentle wings
Above the Earth and through the sky
When time on Earth is ending
Some will shout and cry
Oh, those gentle wings
Those wings that will let me fly
Let me soar to the sky
Through the clouds
Unto paradise
While others still wonder why
They watch, while others fly
They stand and watch
Shout and cry
Why they, too, cannot soar or fly
A chance was given all to fly
Some chose to stand and die
Unto the flames that cry

Betty Jean Conley

Me

Me is a person I don't understand
Me is part of my family and friends
Me is not a part of boys, or is Me and
    she just doesn't know it.
Is Me even good enough for boys?
Is it the clothes we wear?
Is it our appearance?
Are those the things people look for?
Fat, skinny, blond hair, brown hair
That doesn't matter!
But people still look for those kinds
    of things.
Me tries to change her personality to be
    like everyone else.
Me is okay at sports, okay at school
Just because she is okay, does that
    mean Me is stupid?
Is this how it's supposed to be?
Is this what life's going to be?
Should Me change for everyone else?

Christine Cestaro

End of the Road

When I come to the end of the road
It's always the same
Standing and looking
In Jesus' name
God's word is the promise
So don't be afraid
He will lead you and guide you
Through all sorrow or shame
He will bring you to joy
He will teach you to laugh
So don't worry, little child
He will rescue you at last
We never know why
Just try to obey
He sees all we do
For He is the way
I hope you are encouraged
On which way to go
Look to His word
Then surely you will know

Linna Z. Bowman

Gloria's Poem

We wonder what cancer is
and what it even does.
But we do know that it hurts
the ones that we love.
Sometimes you may have surgery,
maybe big or small.
And then there is the question
did they get it all?
It can be anywhere from
your head to your feet;
but with God by your side
it is something you can beat.
I thank God every day for you
being there for me.
Please, let me repay you
in your time of need.
So, Nanny, the next time
you have your fears,
call me and I will
wipe away your tears. . . .

Amanda Gail Swift

Desperate Plunder

I'd like to see you
—you could not bare
I'd understand you
—how could you dare
I'd like to help you
—you don't know how
There's always something
—for me, not now
I'd like to listen
—and I'd just sigh
I'd reach out to you
—I've heard that lie
Just let me help you
—there's nothing wrong
I see the pain now
—it's just a song
A song of sorrow, a song of hurt
a song of hearts thrown in the dirt
A fear of pain, a fear of sorrow
a fear to face the next tomorrow

Justyna Kinga Macharzewska

Every Minute

Every minute,
Every hour
I wait for you
To come to me.
Every minute,
Every hour
I want to see you,
I want to be with you.
Every minute,
Every hour
You don't know how much I miss you
And need you.
Every minute,
Every hour
I need you in my life.
Please, come back to me
Before I break down and cry.
Every minute,
Every hour
I wait for you to come back.

Stacey Ann Del Sontro

The Stillness

Where has all the laughter gone?
The days of sunshine and joy.
Endless moments of frolic
And hours of carefree play.
Where has all the laughter gone?
The face with the smiling eyes.
A heart filled with love and devotion
Arms of strength and protection.
Where has all the laughter gone?
The parties, the fun, and the games
Phone ringing and cars stopping,
Birthday cakes, presents, and singing.
The laughter has turned to sorrow.
The days are gloomy and dark. . . .
Moments stretch on in silence,
And the hours creep endlessly by.
The laughter is replaced by tears.
The face no longer has eyes.
The heart is no longer beating,
And the arms forever stilled.

Patsy Jean Alford

What Is a Dream?

What is a dream?
A dream is a place
where you can fly.

What is a dream?
A dream is a place
where you can be anything.

What is a dream?
A dream is a place
where there is no impossible.

What is a dream?
A dream is a place
where there is peace.

What is a dream?
A dream is a place
where nothing is imperfect.

What is a dream?
A dream is a place
where there is heaven.

Kathryn Dawn Smart

Almost Always Never

I don't know if I love you,
But there's definitely something there.
I notice everything you do,
But tell you I wouldn't dare.
I couldn't ask you now
If you feel the same way
Because I couldn't see how
You could ever love me anyway.
But I can still dream
of you all the time.
As pathetic as I may seem,
I can still hope you'll be mine.
And I can still wish
Upon a shooting star
That I'll receive your kiss
And we can stay where we are.
But nothing is forever;
This we both know.
And it's almost always never
That as one we will go.

Tori Angelica Farias

Calling Me

I hear you calling me,
Calling my name.
I hear you calling me,
Back from this shame.
Call me to where I belong,
I need you near me,
It's been far too long.
Open my eyes wide so I can see.
Place your hand in mine Lord,
I don't want to fight alone.
Come Lord, be my sword,
Come fill my heart with song.
I will sing out praise to you,
For this you deserve.
Show me who I am Lord,
Show me who I am.
Come and do your wonderful deeds.
Come and show me the way.
Come and work within me.
Come to me today.

Julie Maree Bailey

To the Garden

To the garden—we run
to just be, to forget the pain
that life will deal.
To try and forget, that tomorrow
may change all that we love and know.
My heart breaks,
as we walk to different benches
we sit, we look, we know—
but still, we do not move closer,
we just be.
So long, I have wanted to just be,
but not now, now I want to hold you
and make things right.
That I cannot do, so I will look away
and wait for you have my heart—
and there it will stay. . . .
When and if you need to be held
or can hold me, I will be here
still waiting in the garden you created
and brought to my life. . . .

Ginger Ann Budnick

not

i wish there was such a thing
called
true love,
i wish there was the
perfect man.
i wish there was a
world full of peace,
i wish everything was actually free.
i wish there was such
a thing as you and me,
but of course these things
are way beyond me.
and there are things you
cannot do, say, teach,
hear, believe, or have control of,
but there could always
be a little hope.
but those who don't care,
just simply say,
i really hope not!

C. M. M.

Treasure of Love

Today I found a treasure,
I didn't know was lost.
Its contents couldn't measure
the love that my heart sought.
Just a box of old papers
that no one else did want.
When my fingers touched them,
my soul, they did taunt.
On paper old and brittle,
I read the words of history.
How my daddy had labored
now it was no longer a mystery.
I read how he had toiled,
how he had borrowed to buy,
so he could tend the soil
for food for me to buy.
The treasure that I found
was not gems, silver, nor gold.
Its lid was like a mound, you see,
there was more love than it could hold.

Laura R. Swinson

A Pillow and a Blanket

I do not want a mansion-house
That towers in the sky,
To walk the streets of gold by day
And worship God by night;
Rather, a pillow and a blanket, Lord.
No crown of jewels for me,
I'd lay at Your feet and stare at You
For all eternity.
I wouldn't care if I ever got
The slightest look or glance.
My heart would leap if You happened to
Look down at me by chance.
I'd sit and watch as angels sang,
As the elders cast their crowns.
I'd watch in awe as seraphim
Proclaimed His great renown.
Never again to cry or hurt,
From the sky His praises ring.
There I'd sit by the loving side
Of my Abba, my Master, my King.

Allison Elizabeth Ferrell

Myself

I'm a book not written to be read
May my pages be skimmed
Reading according to the reader
Many meanings to each set of words
Depth of the meaning
According to the reader
Intent placed upon by the reader
My pages form a book
The reader to be selected
Yes, you can scan
I am a reference not open to everyone
Rare book collection, maybe
Words when read, message received
But referenced by the reader
The depth and the meaning . . .
Between the words and throughout
To read me well—is to understand me
To comprehend me is to have permission
To read the truth in my words
Rarely given. . . .

Graham Leonard Ellison

Someday

Someday on this beach
I'll walk no more,
I'll be walking with my Savior
On Heaven's bright shore.
I won't hear the birds, nor
The waves of this sea;
I'll hear sweet angels singing
Glory to Thee.
I won't feel this breeze,
As it blows on my face;
But I'll feel the peace of
God's wonderful grace.
I won't have to search
For what this walk can bring,
I'll be with God's angels
Helping them to sing.
So, try not be sad
For I know I'll still love;
I'll be living with Jesus and
My Father above.

Debbie J. Jones

After All, He Lived It

No need to fly
to the Smithsonian Museum
for a lesson on cars,
just go and see him.
He'd draw you a picture,
explain the mechanics,
tell you how to improve it,
and some of his antics.
After all, he lived it!
Taught English and math
by professors and tutors.
He spoke well, read a lot,
and questioned computers.
He'd tell you, "They don't have all
the bugs out yet,"
and, "It's built by man,
lest we forget."
He just didn't need
all the archives held in it.
After all, he lived it.

Charles Brevard Duke

Dad

You'll never know the way I feel
the hurt and pain inside,
Many things we've been through
I hate the love I must hide
Perhaps you don't believe this, dad,
perhaps you may not care
That my love for you is very deep
and my love for you is rare.
Although we have our differences,
I pray you love true.
My heart feels sick when I think
of living my life without you.
If we only could forget the past,
the anger we both hold inside.
Because I'm still your middle son,
and this you can't deny.
So, Dad, I give you this promise today,
my life will start anew.
Look at me now in a different way,
and I'll prove my love for you.

Richard Alan Sicard

Jesus

To look above,
staring at your eyes,
the scars I see,
from the sacrifice.
I cannot imagine
the immensity of the pain,
as each peg was hit
and punctured a vein.
The blood that dripped,
richer than wine,
that cleanses and forgives
the sins of mine.
Much you have done for me,
with no way to repay,
continue to thank you I shall,
every time I kneel and pray.
In my heart you will remain,
'til the day I die.
To the Heavens I shall go,
and be along your very side.

Kenneth Alexander Blandon

Just Another Day

Here I sit alone
Yet another day
Dreaming of a man
To come take me away.
Away to a place that only
Exists in fairy-tales
Where you hear "happy ever after"
Not relationships that fail.
But in reality
It is too good to be true
An "everlasting love"
May last a week or two.
One day I hope to find true love
For this I cannot wait
Should I go searching for this love?
Should I leave it up to fate?
So I will sit alone
Yet another day
Dreaming of a man
To come take me away.

Jennifer Dawn Luna

My Wonderful Husband

We met one night
Just out of the blue
And right away
I fell in love with you
You're everything I wanted
And so much more
I'm excited about life
And what it has in store
You help make all
My dreams come true
You always cheer me up
When I'm feeling blue
We have many years ahead
Full of happiness and love
I've found my true destiny
Thanks to someone above
You are my husband
My lover and my best friend
As long as you're in my life
My happiness will never end

Jennifer Anne Leasure

In Morning

In morning I rise
I wash and climb into baggy jeans
and toss a loose T-shirt
over my head
It catches one ear
I look at the reflection of
my little struggle
to pull it on
to start the day
I laugh at myself
the mirror laughs back
I sip lukewarm coffee
while I sit at the kitchen table
glance at the morning paper
Read that someone got
Shot
last night at the mini-mart
I recognize the name
The cold coffee splatters the tile
In mourning I rise

Karen E. Siragusa

Rose Marie

Your name you have given me,
Which I cherish as dear,
In my heart held forever,
Keeping you ever so near.
You have filled my brief lifetime
With your wisdom and love,
Talks and walks and knowledge
That could only come from above.
You have returned to the ancestors
Where peace and love eternally last,
The place we have come from
And to which we all one day pass.
I thank you for sharing
This Earth-walk with me
For your example has shown me
All that I would like to be.
In dreams and visions
Will you appear to me
Sharing yourself as always
So my Grandmother I will always see.

White Owl

Take Me Back

I ask of those I meet each day
To take me back to yesterday
To times before when I was young
with hopes as bright as the morning sun
I asked the wind if it could please
take me back to infancy
The wind replied it had no time
to help me in this quest of mine
So I asked the brook to fill my dream
take me back to be a teen
The babbling brook was quite aghast
as how to breach the years that passed
I wondered if the highway knew
the way to take me back to youth
To the highway's deep regret
the route it took was firmly set
I began to sense reality
some dreams I have can never be
If in those dreams I continue to ask
will someone please take me back

Donald Leroy Scalf

Backdoor

Interpret a thought
So all we may see
Despite the perception
A free thinker sees
Ambiguity to some
Is adventure, not cost
A road less traveled
Is security lost
Rationality is warranted
To perpetrate a reason
While most lie in limbo
To discover their feelings
Perhaps certain views
Are better addressed
By anonymous few
Who choose to express
Look as you may
It's just human nature
But no solace is found
From words on a paper

R. J. Savitski

Distant Love

I was walking the path,
which my life was leading,
and distantly I saw your face.

I never knew that one day
I would be speeding
to reach you at your place.

Faster and faster,
step by step
trying to touch your hand.

But the harder I try
and the closer I get,
the further away you stand.

I tried calling
out your name,
my pleas too small to see.

I only hope that one day
when you feel love is near
you'll turn around and see me.

Linda M. Rene

Nuclear Poison

I've been cut in half
And it's killing me
Watching you not realizing
The destruction
The blast radius of your
Emotional bombs
Consumes me
They don't understand
Me not understanding you
How it's eating me slowly
Like a disease
Destroying the vital components
Gnawing like a worm
At the lining of my weak composure
It's only a matter of time
Before it breaks through
Spills over
So that everyone knows
And sees
The death of me

Ruth Moore

Catharsis

Hands bound
Head against a wall
While the relentless pounding
Of fist to stone
Echoes the prisoner within
These hollow walls
Encompassing a dark vault
Created as sanctuary
From the impending flood
Trapped in the spoon whirlpool
Drawing in upon itself
Churning up sediment
Of battles forfeited
Though never forgotten
The sentry incapacitated
As a procession of conjured evils
Invades the tomb
Flinch realization
As time, the inevitable
Sets the prisoner free

Robin Michelle Mendoza

Lost Love

Star dust falling from the sky
Sprinkling lightly in her eyes.
Pools of blue, painful tears,
Distorted visions in the mirror,
Candles blowing in the wind,
Broken hearts find no end,
Shadows dancing on the wall,
Lonely spirits at the ball . . .
Haunting memories soon escape
Dreams that seem to take their shape.
Flowers wilt upon the vine,
Grapes ripen into wine.
Drunk with sorrow, mindless blues;
Very old and yet still new.
Sobbings of forgotten love,
Silent echoes from above.
Eternal souls search for peace.
Blind darkness never cease.
Loneliness is all around.
Silence is the only sound.

Benny E. Fain

To My Love

What little time I've known you,
We've had our highs and lows;
And where our paths will lead us,
The future only knows.
I'd like to take a moment
To tell you that I care;
I hope our love is endless,
I think we're quite a pair.
I love how your eyes shine at me,
Like stars up in the sky;
You're physical and emotional,
You must be the perfect guy.
I know how much you love me,
You show me many ways;
You're caring, kind, considerate,
I see it every day.
I just had to say this,
I had to let you know;
I will love you forever,
Your one and only, Jo.

Jo Tynon

Colors

A splash of red, a tinge of blue,
What's a boy to do?
I'm seeing these colors run together
on a page
I am amazed.

Color me midnight,
Color me crimson.
Make my palate safe and sweet.

Color me amber,
Color me turquoise,
The kind I'll never meet.

See me as silver,
See me as gold,
A tale that may never be told.

Make sure they never touch,
And don't ask too much.
For, if careful we're not,

The colors will run.

Steven L. Hoadley

Maps of Silence

Don't deny it, you remember—
familiar feel of my hand, your hand,
then you shouting back.
You taught me the road not to travel,
the path not to take, showed me
bruises and scars left season
after shifting season.
On my body you traced territories,
pounding until my heart stopped beating.
What map is there for women's silence?
What direction is there to get away?
For the images sunk into my soul
lost the things you'd not tell me—
you taught me the road not to travel,
the path not to take.
When you fired, I felt the pain
moving in two directions, like love.
And when I left you,
there was still a thin strip of me
clinging to the eye, swelling shut.

Melissa Jo Glover

Dreams of Flying

Sometimes at night,
I dream you as you never were.
I fight demons for you,
I seduce angels that have your face.
I presume to call you by your name
in the tone and timbre
that isn't just friendship,
and I hold inside my thoughts
the things I want to say to you
and speak instead with my hands.
(Your mind might not know it,
but your skin understands.)
And I ache and ache and ache for you,
and you never even seem to notice.
Even though I know you know,
and knowing is what keeps me running
from day to day
and always looking forward
hoping that this time
I'll learn to fly.

B. C. Dawson

Nothing Is Fair

Nothing is fair
No one said it was
I learn that more
all the time
Fighting and violence
don't make it any better
Fight for what is right
but there is a better way
So, put the guns and bombs away
everyone has the right
to stay and learn
that nothing's easy
and nothing is fair
Behind the color
behind the uniform
behind the facade
you might find
someone
that feels the same
MORE VOICES THE BETTER

Nadine Marie Noghabaie

The Bond of Love!

The very first time my eyes beheld you
My heart skipped a beat
Or it per-adventure added extra beats
And, as you parted your succulent lips
To spell out the normal salutation
I heard a sweet, rich, and melodic music
Like a mighty, peaceful river
As I tried to talk back
The air around us became charged
And seconds later
I felt a lightning kind of shock wave
Hitting from the bowels of my stomach
This instantly sent droplets of water
Trickling down to all my flesh
Causing eccentric sensations to all
Open-ended nerves in my body
The next time I saw those "eyes"
I felt such a pull, which led to a tag
Then a tough bond
That nothing could even try to break

Peter Ndumbi Njoroge

Soccer

I love the game.
I've seen you on the field,
You always yield.
You don't play your best,
You always rest.
When you do, you hear a loud boo.
You've lost the game.
You must feel so lame.
Unlike you,
I don't smell like a shoe.
When I'm on the field,
I never yield,
I play my best,
And never rest.
I say a little prayer
as the ball soars through the air.
I think I hear
A really loud cheer.
I've won the game,
And earned all the fame.

Megan McKeel Sample

For Brian

How could I know the day we met
I'd love you like no other yet.
You made me laugh, you made me smile,
You stayed on my mind a while.
The night you called is when I knew
Forever your love would be true.
We talked all night and all night long
You told me nothing could go wrong.
And since that night, when I lie down,
I think about my little clown.
The man who sees me when I'm sad
And always tries to make me glad.
And every time you see me frown
You make me turn it upside down.
I can't forget the day we kissed,
A feeling my whole life, I missed.
I know it can't be hard to see
That you and I were meant to be.
'Cause ever since the day we met
I've loved you like no other yet.

Aleida Beaton

The Diamond That Is My Spirit

My spirit illuminates.
A precious diamond
Shining beneath a
Mountain of coals
You'll be amazed by its
Beauty
Inspired by its
Luminosity
Touched by its
Grace
Amidst its
Flaws
It grows
Stronger
With life's
Blessings
Brighter
With God's
Love.

Rana Terrell Cocklin

forest

the secret is kept
by those who discover it
or fail to do so

God is a secret
we keep from ourselves, because
we need this secret

to believe in it
like shaded trees awaiting
unformed rain dropping

predetermined to
find fast-budding leaves through roots
blind to their origin

content with themselves
or asking who begat the rain
their own mystery

asked and understood
as well as our secret that
we need we keep God

Tyson Avram Oberndorfer

Destiny Warrior

I'm a destiny warrior,
Like Joan of Arc,
Repelling all forces of the dark!
Living for God
And all I can be
In the face of adversity!
I fight the mission
That will set me free.
I'm a destiny warrior
And I do believe . . .
Good battles bad
In a world so dark,
A world so sad,
A world apart.
Destiny leads me
To fight for God!
Three loud cheers and I applaud!
Angels surround me from above
To conquer all evil
In the name of LOVE!

Tobi J. Lang

Kristen

O, how deeply I fell for thee.
In my dreams you are all I see.
My angel, pull me near.
When I am with you all is clear.
O, my love, my shining star,
Am I to you so far
Away from what you desire?
O, my angel, tell me this,
Why do you withhold your kiss?
Please hear my cry.
Ahh, but why do I try?
Good-bye and adieu,
But I will always be here for you.

Antonio Nicola DiSalvo-Black

Destiny Unknown

Given of such reasons . . .
A steady stream; quiet.
In the bursts of fullness,
Emitting of light, explosions of joy!

A place of calm surrender—
Bodies unaware.
Ethereal in height,
Textured and dense.

Alas! Destiny unknown,
Stars of infinity
Shine at will
With intensity independent.

Lori Wewers

Eye of the Mind

As I see you
Through the eye of the mind,
I wonder, do you wonder
How close will this mind gets?

They of whom I know in the soul,
A thought as if they might know
Between right and a lesser wrong.

We talk throughout life,
No lip, nor movement in speech.
I believe, they believe, you believe,
Eye of the mind,
It has a soul.

Clem L. Cheathem

Going and Returning

How do I get to where I am going,
is it very far?
How long do I've to keep on running,
following the North Star?

Why am I leaving anyway,
did I do something wrong?
I guess I'll miss my family,
for them how I will long.

But why do I keep on running,
all I do is roam.
So I think I will turn around,
and start my journey home.

Sierra Rose Seward

Light

Rumble
Down from the heavens,
Ethereal light . . .

Rumble
From the clouds,
Yellow flash . . .

Rumble
Flaming grass,
Blinding rays . . .

Rumble
Falling lines,
Florescent sparks. . . .

Anil Amin

Unforeseen Promises

What dreams are made of
Illusions of the heart
So it ignites your soul
As it slowly draws you in
Rewarding then destroying
Unforeseen promises
Jumping into the change
Not seeing the drowning rains
Consumed and swept away
Unforeseen promises
With every breath your truth entails
Glances and gestures also sell
Unforeseen promises

Anthony Wayne Wilkerson

The Secret Gaze

Every day, she gazes at him
Lovingly.
Probably wanting him to
Embrace her.
She stares silently,
For it's her secret.
No one must know,
But we do,
We just let the
Secret play its part,
Without interruption.
Because she lets us do
Our own gazing.

Ashleigh Nicole Whitby

Dusk

Falling behind the darkness,
Once warm and full of light,
The sun sets and the nightmare begins:
Cold and despair fall from the heavens.

Dancing souls, light and cheer
Drift into the curse bounded by evil.
One more day the world sleeps,
Blinded misfortune violates the land.

Questions of wonder to rise again
Everlasting reminders of the past.
Hands clasp and reach toward the sky
Blessed be and surpass the night fall.

Tricia Lynn Forney

New Love

Why Is It So Hard
To Conquer My Fears
To Tell You The Truth
From My Heart To Your Ears

Although Our Hearts Are Close
I Still Feel A Small Distance
Or Am I Just Scared
Creating A Resistance

I Am Not Asking For Promises
Just A Friendship That Is True
Because This Is The Love
That I Feel For You

Danielle Dawn Schmidtm

Waiting

I wait for love to come each day
By one young man that lights my way.
Although this guy that I love most
Doesn't want to walk that coast.

I dream each night of this guy only,
But when I wake I'm back to lonely.
I dream he holds me in his arms
And makes me smile with all his charms.

A day will come when this dreams fact,
We'll bind our love with one small pact.
But until then, I'll wait for love
And answers from my God above.

Lindsey Nicole Starwalt

Daughter

You are the dawn, you are the light,
A dew drop glistening and bright.
You are the air, so fresh and clear,
You are a new day—young and pure.

You are the summer rain, warm and mild,
A rippling brook—running wild.
You are a harvest—fragrance of hay,
You are a sunset, the ending of day.

You are a meadow—green and flowing,
You are wings—gliding and soaring.
You are flowers—growing so rare,
You are Life . . . beyond compare!

Yolanda Van Hooser

Wake-Up Call

Bowing our heads, we ask for grace
Holding it high, we forget to praise
On bended knees, we cry for help
Standing tall, we take full control.

Man, oh man, where is your wisdom
Exalting self instead of God
With blinded eyes and hardened heart
You condemned yourself to eternal death.

There is still time for reconciliation
Accept Jesus Christ as your salvation
For no other name in all creation
Can truly save you from sure damnation.

Ma. Sofia Corral Claridad

Beer Can Parade

Lost the love of my life last night
In my dreams, she'll always stay
The more I think about it
I sort of wish that I was gay

Beer can parade
Waiting for that major change
Another beer can parade
Somehow things just stay the same

As I sit here all alone
I've come to realize I let her go
But all I do is wish away
As my senses slowly fade

Eric Wallace Heyen

For Spinnen

Deep inside, her paw print is
Pressed into my heart
A fragile spot, that if touched,
Would surely fall apart.

Don't scorn my loving memories
Else they'll flow as rivers of tears
For my fearless, gentle girl
Who kept me warm all those years.

Some days can be hard,
Often wishing I could just give up.
But still I feel she'll again be with me
In the body of a playful Pup.

Gay Elizabeth Brent

Always Greater

Greater than I
Are those who see
The love You've given
So graciously

Greater than I
Are those who feel
Your power within them
And the way You heal

Greater than I
Because I'm not great
That's why I need You
Help me open the gate.

Jashana Cheree Copeman

What It Takes

It took quite a while
to give up my heart
I was very scared
to show the darkest part

My feelings are real
though some are just brief
A few steps in my shoes
then he would see

Emotional equilibrium
is the goal after all
I only need one thing from him
he only has to give his all

Samantha C. Mullins

Golden Roses

There once was a time when the rose
Held by a fair maiden was gold,
Like the ring of a finger not of nose
Gold too valuable to be sold.

But in these times of profit and haste
Occurred a depression so deep,
Assets become liabilities to waste
a rose is worth naught to keep.

By the jagged thorns of a restless man
Till destruction of garden complete,
Barren land no flowers stand
For the next man she may meet.

Ben Donald Lilburn

Best Friends

You make me laugh
You make me cry
I love you
But I wonder why

You say we're best friends
Nothing more, nothing less
But you liking my best friend
Puts our relationship to the test

My true feelings
You can never know
And on a date
We will never go

Kelli Michelle Murphy

Pronghorn on the Highway

Creature stark
Whose haven is unsheltered plain,
Rifles' bark
Compels your flight to man again.

Silhouette
Bred half of Earth and half of sky,
Hear you yet
The whanging lead that passed you by?

Present here
In whining wheels another bane . . .
Death to fear . . .
Unmeant, but sure as bullet's pain.

Jean Boardman Murdock

Pick Me up, Lord

I lift my arms up to the sky
and say, "Lord pick me up,"
and with a smile upon his face
he says, "Drink from my cup."

"I want to touch your body Lord."
He says, "Come, eat my bread.
I died upon a cross for you,
I died so you'd be fed."

"Each time you eat my bread,
each time you drink my cup,
my arms are reaching down for you,
and my love will lift you up."

Cindy Jo Van Wyk

These Golden Years

Does arthritis bother you?
Are there wrinkles in your skin?
Are the age spots showing though
where no blemish has ever been?

Do you think on years ahead
wondering how much time there will be?
Do you suddenly realize
that life is vanity?

I have hope good news for you
for nothing is like it seems.
What matters most is just right now;
enjoy the sunshine's beams.

John Evering Marshall

You

With my eyes, I see,
And with my heart, I love.
With the sense of touch, I feel,
And with my soul, I soar.

By your side forevermore,
And hand in hand we hold.
Eyes to eyes, we know the thought,
And feel the feel of love.

This is written for you alone,
For heart to heart,
And hand to hand,
Our souls touch.

Kendra Jean Kenne

Shadow Walker

I feel like I'm living in your shadow
Always stuck behind.
Never getting to be seen for what I am,
Feeling like a waste of time.
No one ever says a thing to me
All the attention goes straight to you
And then you ask me what my problem is?
Truthfully, my problem is you.
I can no longer reach to your standards
And be all you want me to be
From this moment on
I can do nothing more
Than be me.

Jackie Adele Wilding

The Rose

What is it about the
rose,
That endears it to the
betrothed?

Perhaps its color of a
fresh cut wound.
Or maybe its scent on a
summer afternoon.

Could it be the petals, so
soft and smooth?
How deceiving they are, hiding
thorns so crude. . . .

Hannah May Christina Mullenix

Doesn't Matter

Perhaps it's time go,
Perhaps it's time to stay.

Perhaps you'll change your mind,
Perhaps you'll want to play.

Perhaps you need to sleep,
Perhaps you need to weep.

No matter what you decide,
Perhaps you'll realize

It doesn't matter much what you do!
'Cause just around the corner,
Perhaps is watching you.

Ronna E. Paige

The Greatest Sorrow

The greatest Sorrow has
Come here—at last
Though I knew It was
Coming, I was not prepared

It hit me hard
But touched me lightly
I have never met
Something quit like this before

I have danced with it a time or two
In the dark corners of one's mind
And in my mind, she lingers
Watching me abide

Wendy Lee Lyerla

trash

yellow plastic gloves
snapped to
prevent more tiny scrolls
from tallying on
to the forgotten years bent
into pebbly barrels slushed with
sticky containers and other papered and
plastic leavings—

from here out
the wife will see herself in
the shine of my wedding ring
and remember our anniversary
by the calendar on my hands

Scott Farrar Tienken

I Wait for the Day

Anthony,
Mommy's heart is broken,
There are no words to be spoken.
For inside I am bare,
These feelings I cannot share.
You are my life, my love,
And now you're with God above.
I know you are safe in His care,
I wish you were here, for we are a pair.
We were never apart,
And this is tearing up my heart.
I know there will be a day
When we will be one,
How long that will be, I cannot say,
And when it comes,
It will be the best day of my life!

I miss and love you
very much!
Mommy

Rachel E. Giardina

Surrounding Darkness

She sits in the darkness
with nowhere to run
with a longing in her heart
and an innocent grace
Her spirit imprisoned
Her heart is torn in two
she thought age would heal
but her soul just wanders
looking and searching
for all that life holds
there are moments in time
where she just feels lost
lost in the shuffle
lost in the wind
lost in longing
lost in the rain
How long must she wander
How long must she roam
Looking and searching for the unknown

Ruth Smith

In the Winter of My Soul

In the winter of my soul
I felt alone, empty, and cold
As if I were freezing from inside
From the storm I could not hide
Like a seed that could not grow
In the winter of my soul

In the darkness of my mind
I was stumbling around, blind
I was a man without a prayer
There were no answers anywhere
There was no light that could shine
In the darkness of my mind

In the caverns of my heart
Your love ignited a spark
An ember, then a burning flame
And made me feel alive again
I feel your love each day we're apart
In the caverns of my heart

Ken R. Harness

Together

We sat alone on separate shores,
My loneliness mine
And your loneliness yours.
Then fate put her hand in.
It happened by chance
That we found each other—
The seeds of romance.
And now it is time.
We've named the day
When we two will be
Together to stay.
Together at last.
Together forever.
Loneliness, be gone!
Return to us never.
Our hearts flow with love.
We're light as a feather.
It's only because,
We'll at last be together.

David Mark Newcomer

Jewel

Treasures in life
so precious . . . so rare . . .
have found me in you
Every moment with you . . .
a cherished jewel . . .
revealing so many facets
of who you are,
and us . . . together
You, handmade,
crafted by God
glimmer in my presence
in light and in darkness
Be . . . be with me
as we are two jewels
of one necklace
You and I,
each complete as one,
sharing the same strand in life,
giving beauty to one another

Richard Louis Caragol

On Friendship

I realized a gift from the universe
entered my life in quiet form
under the arch of light and love.
Look and find the silent beauty,
only now revealing the balance.
Being now the days gone by
on the way to higher heights,
not to forget, not even sit aside
but enter and be with me today,
help me along the winding way,
and I will aid you as you need.
Know that our dearest dreams
are nearer the truth of ourselves.
Come, my friend. I hear our song,
looking for peace in every heart.
To be ever grateful, ever forgiving,
even as we give each other hope
and accept the gift of friendship
in its own way, its own time.

Franklin Richard Schneider

Dreaming

Let us go
To another place and time
Where my pain and my sorrow
Turns to pleasure and happiness

Let us wake up
In a time
Where we will be strangers
And walk our separate ways
Where we will not hurt each other

Let us disappear
To a secret place
Where our faces will be newborn
And our bodies without judgement

Let us move away
Across country and ocean
And enjoy the sunset
Before we drown in the light
Of the stars

Ragnhild Hansen

Helpless

The rolling of thunder,
This feeling I'm under
Shakes me to my core.
The ground is picking up pace, and
I've got to shield my face
From this sadness I see below.

Each day that drags by
I question myself why—
Why you keep leaving this way.
I'm wondering who really knows
What's eating at you deep in your soul
Where no one is ever invited to stay.

Please, come back and sit a while,
I'll try hard to make you smile
And tell you some silly jokes.
I'd love to hold you right here,
Until that feeling disappears,
And maybe you'll forget you had to go.

Patricia Anne Cinatti

Multiple Personality Disorder

My mind is like a broken glass
Without memories of the past.

In childhood the trauma began
Sexual abuse by a man.

In my mind there are twelve or more
With myself staying as the core.

Each not knowing of the other
Hoping no one would discover.

There's Cathy, Marie, Minnie too;
They all have names like me and you.

Each one developed to survive
The body's way to stay alive.

Crazy, I thought was once to be
Now, doctors call this M.P.D.

Pearl Marie Litke

roses

red and white
never fight
my life is a bed of roses
blue and green
never mean
my life is a bed of roses
see the sharp thorns?
feel the mossy weeds
prick your finger
see ME bleed
you aren't the only one
i have feelings too
i cry those tears
just like you do
now see the whole package
the roses and the thorns
see the ugly weeds
and the petals become worn
here in my bed of roses

Lara Kathlyn Hall

Red Tide

Who lives? Who dies?
Questions asked
By students inside.

Seeping in, it destroys
Plaguing the masses
As an untamed tide.

Bang! Bang! Bang!
Shots fly
Taking no aim of who will die.

Crumpled red on the ground,
Lie students that stain
More than the floor.

A light, a flash
Exposure feeds the plague,
Imparting the next executioner
A hand for the unnatural, eternal fate
Of those to come.

Kelly Michelle Christensen

The Me That No One Ever Sees

Father Time has aged me
My hair is dark and mat
my skin is fairly wrinkled
and my smile is thin and cracked
The clothes I wear are out of date
my style of dress passed on
I wish sometimes of kinder years
when all my friends weren't gone
I've looked into the mirror
to see what others must see
I do admit I throw a fit
or sometimes shed tears openly
I'm sorry for the others
who, as they walk by me
will never know
or try to see
the beauteous soul . . .
the one true me
that's the thing no one ever sees

Renee F. Jackson

Two Dear Friends

In memory of Vicki and Lynn Cole 1980
Today we lost two dear friends
Lord my God it never ends
This dreadful thing called death
You've taken their last breath

It happened one day they say
When our dear friends went away
They were going to the store
They wouldn't be gone just a
minute or more

They came upon the railroad tracks
But I haven't got all the facts
Exactly what happened that day
When our dear friends went away

Today we lost two dear friends
Lord my God it never ends
This dreadful thing called death
You've taken their last breath

Margaret Eleen Jones

If I Were in Charge of the World

If I were in charge of the world
Every God-given day
Would be spent to our advantage
In our own special way

If I were in charge of the world
Every stone that I'd see
Would be whispering to each other
They'd be smiling at me

If I were in charge of the world
The lost souls would be revealed
The sins of them be buried
The next dimension would be sealed

If I were in charge of the world
The seas would be on land
The birds would fly underwater
The fish would swim in the sand

Jesse L. Russell

I Am a Cross

I am a cross
I am nails
His tears

I am a cursing soldier
A crying friend
A hurting mother

I am fear
Love and pain
Hurt and sorrow

I am blood and tears
I am a sacrifice
Your forgiver

A new life for you
I am everything
I am the world around you

I am a cross
I know all your secrets

Jessica Rae Wulf

The Graceful Dancer

The land was cold
My body shivered
The west wind whistled
Like a young child learning to whistle
I watched the sky
Saw a figure of a graceful
dancer
I watched her
moving and changing
into something else
Distraction
My graceful dancer was gone
My heart was saddened
Surely there will
always be
Butterflies, super heroes
dragons
My graceful Dancer
In the clouds

Jessica Rani Buckner

review

as i go through the thoughts,
i think of the lies, i remember the love
and it always makes me cry.
to think of it all
and remember the details
all i can do is review the thoughts
review the lies
review the love
and it always makes me cry.
all the past and every future
i review my life through the glass
and there is regret
there is pain
and it always makes me cry.
now here i lay
and i think,
what have i done
what will i do
all i ever did was review.

Thadyee-Rose Palega

Pain

The pain pulls at my heart,
Having no place to go.
A fountain flowing over is my soul.
I need closure,
I need peace.
Only my God can give me release.
The pain is overwhelming,
The pain is so strong;
I cry out to God,
Hoping he'll hear my song.
Dear God,
Please help me.
Take away this pain,
Clear my soul
Of the storms that rage.
My pain is gone,
My soul is pure;
I know that when I asked,
My God helped me endure.

Blake Rogers

Eve

Lost her
LIFE within a
FILE . . .
EVIL experienced is most
VILE . . . as I
LIVE seeing through the
VEIL . . . accused of using an
ALIAS makes me want to
SAIL A . . .
WAY
YAW: to turn from the planned heading
as a ship fails to keep a steady
COURSE . . . I guess this coincidental
poem is revealing my
RECOURSE . . . we will
SOLVE when we
EVOLVE with
EVE to
LOVE

Shawn O'Neill

Pain and Sorrow

Heart racing, blood boiling.
Red visions of hatred.

Lonely and loveless.
Friends of no substance.

Untouched, unwanted, unloved.
Broken hearts and spiritless souls.

The body is a shell,
I am not human.

Freak of nature,
Not meant for this world.

Wanting to cry, be held.
No one is here or there.

Death is wanted, but will not come.
Sorrow hovers, always near.

Pain continuously stabs me.
Only one regret, I AM ALIVE!

Tristan Michael Gruebel

Innocence

I feel the season lifting
careless in its bends and shifts
The grandeur of uncertainty
a ribbon in your
simplicity of breezes

Unyielding your promises
secrets on the wind
I sense your hindrance
and vacant eclipse

Can I race with your
chances, choices
predestined by autumn's
vague and cleansing life?

Your vibrant colors feed
this child of darkness

mold vigilant shadows into
unprecedented light.

Jocelyn Kara Mawdesley

With and Without

I'm crying inside,
Though you can't see it.

I'm dying inside,
Though I have no physical pain.

I'm screaming in my head,
Though no one can hear my calls.

And living without you
Is life in a nightmare.

I have butterflies in my stomach
That try to break free but can't.

I'm giggling inside,
Like a child is in my soul.

I have hearts circling my head,
Even if they can't be seen.

And spending my life with you
Is life in a dream.

Renee Dianne Collet

Whispers in the Night Frighten Me

Whispers in the night frighten me
When the brightness of the light
Is gone, is it always going to be night
In the darkness, sounds seem so real
The truth of it all is how it feels
By yourself, it's a never ending fight

The lights outside are bright
But inside it's not quite
Light, I have to wait as I kneel
Whispers in the night frighten me

Shadows on the wall have no sight
I try with all of my might
But I just can't deal
With this, everything's so still
So I hold on tight
Whispers in the night frighten me

Christine Creasey Bond

My Wish for You

When I saw a star that fell
Or stood before a wishing well
Was it the first star in the sky
Or the brightest one that caught my eye
In silence I pray my wish come true
While I sleep I dream of you
When those stars would come my way
My wish for you would always stay
I wished upon those lucky stars
As I wondered where you are
If we were really meant to be
You my love would to come to me
Then one night to my surprise
You stood before my very eyes
Next I felt your lips kiss mine
It sent a shiver down my spine
Now I'm lying here next to you
I thank those stars my wish came true

Stephanie L. Woodruff

Awakening

What is that I see . . .
Emerging from the tiny tree?
. . . A knob. . . .
What is that I see . . .
Unveiling its color to me?
Barely peering through the knob . . .
. . . A leaf. . . .
What is that I see . . .
Opening amidst the leaf
In all its majesty?
. . . A bud. . . .
What is that I see . . .
Buzzing and nuzzling that little bud
So happily?
. . . A bee. . . .
What is that I see . . .
Totally enveloping
That tiny tree?
. . . spring. . . .

Barbara Jean Marmion

Together Forever

Your heart hit mine
So then and there I drew the line
We were meant to be together forever
And together forever it shall be

There is no one else like you
You are always kind and true
No matter what
We both got into

The friendship we have
Could never part
Together forever
You're always
Close at heart

Best friends forever
You and me
Together forever
And that's the way it's going to be

Melanie Ann Best

Close to the Edge

When you're close to the edge
and there's nothing else left
but the laughter;
ha, ha, ha . . .
can you smile at the clown,
as he frowns in the mirror of life?
Do you feel his pain
or share his disdain for disaster?
Or understand why
he refuses to cry for himself?
Ah, but wait,
I see a tear,
I see tears,
I feel tears.
Could it be that you're ready?
Your hands are unsteady,
you reach and put out the light.
Put out the light.

David Howard Griffiths

Tenderloin Blues

Nighttime city buses,
passengers bathed in
fluorescent gloom
sit silent,
every corner and crack illuminated,
no one casting a shadow—like the undead
prowling an ancient Carpathian castle.
There were two worlds—worlds apart—
the stark,
bright realism
of the interior
and the impressionist outside
where colored lights
bore through the darkness,
smearing and dripping,
splotching and streaming
onto a dynamic canvas of night.
The bus stops
to take on more sad ghosts.

Terry L. Young

Minutes and Rosary Beads

Minutes and rosary beads
Counted until my watch stopped
No ticking, no praying
Since I made my decision
It did not hurt like it should have
The success stories I read
Told me it would be painful
And deep
They lied
So no one else would follow
The tracks they made in the mire
I stand in the mire
But leave no tracks
Care of indecision
I can hear the mud suck
And gurgle obscenities
As I tremble in remembrance
How can such tiny human feet
Produce such deafening sounds
Like ticking—and praying

Kelly L. Smith

Empty

I found my love
hidden in a corner
underneath a shadowy tree
a weeping willow
so beautiful, yet so sad
the flowers so bright
a beautiful day
the sun shines
a warm breeze blows
I'm so cold
there's a lot of people
but yet it's empty
I think of my love
being lowered in the ground
locked in a box
for all eternity
only to grow empty
like my heart.

Laura Field

Then; Now

Then—
Love is what I felt for you,
While looking in your eyes.
Love is what I felt for you,
When saying our good-byes.
Love is what I felt for you,
When dreams were what we shared.
Love is what I felt for you,
When my fingers combed your hair.
Now—
While looking in your eyes,
I see the pain we've both been through.
When saying our good-byes,
We nod, "ah, good luck to you."
The dreams we had and shared
Lie shattered in the past.
Your hair, I ran my fingers through,
Is now covered with a hat.

Haley Anne Hyatt

Who Am I

Today . . .
I looked across the room
What I saw, I could not believe
I wanted to call you, but . . .
I couldn't get the words out
As the days passed . . .
I grew stronger
As the months passed . . .
I knew I could call you
Then one day
After many, many months . . .
I looked across the room
What I saw, I could not believe
I called you
You looked up and smiled
I knew then, I had to be stronger
Finally, after many months
I knew my mommy's life had just begun

Norma Gutierrez

Love Game

Love is like a ball game
As you step up to bat
You could hit the ball
Or it could miss the bat

One strike you make
Could be the start
Of strike two, which you see
Will be your fault

When the third ball is thrown
And you make a hit
You might get to first base
If you're really quick

But it's your partner
Whom must get a play
For if it's strike three
It's the end of the love game

Vicky R. Messer

Shattered

You slipped and dropped me
to the floor
add some cracks
a thousand more

Now pick me up like nothing's different
Careful boy, I'm feeling bent

You tripped and smashed me
now I'm shattered
Pick up the pieces, use some glue
Right away I'm good as new

You knocked me over
and I fell
strait off the edge
and into hell

You walk away and leave me here
I'll soon get up and start from there

Iris A. Ross-Swisher

To Our Friend

To our friend,
who owns suff'ring and pain,
whose face shows no sign,
but her heart takes the blame.
To our friend,
who will always listen
without ever being a judge,
for the pain that she feels
she covers in her mud.
To our friend,
who will never say a word
about the tears that she hides,
even when the world is
by her side.
To my friend,
let's keep a smile on that face
to help ease the anger that you
always have to face.

Elizabeth Marie Pycior

There Once Was a Time

There once was a time
When I thought you were mine
And our love would last forever
But I guess I was wrong, your love wasn't strong
And now you'll be someone else's
I still love you, babe
I wish I was brave
To take this knowing it's better this way

Joyce Ann Christiansen

The Dance

Masks and feathers
A rustle of dress
A bow, and a gentleman's glove
Weighted limbs
And shifting feet
Music, horribly off key
Bumping and falling
Chunks of flesh roll away
Ligaments detaching from bone
The stench and the madness
As blood streaks the floor
Opulent decay under lights
Drying crust
Lines of gore colored rust
Blending into the tile quite well
With fester and rot
And the last hallow notes
The dance falls into its hole

Nina Elisabeth Verfaillie

Brave

I am not brave
I live in a world
Where I hide my thoughts
Wear a mask of happiness
And play a game of pretend
Until the day is done
And I am home
Alone to think my thoughts
Alone to see the truth

Someday I will be brave
Brave enough to bare my soul
And reveal my heart

But for now
Someday is still the distant future
Too far for mine eyes to see
And too close for my mind to be blind
Someday I will be brave

Sabrina Y. Fan

Alone

No one will talk to me,
No one will listen to me, either.
I feel so very lonely,
No one cares about that, either.

I need someone with me now,
But everyone's too busy.
I only want to feel needed
Before it is too late.

No one seems to need me,
No one acts as though they care,
Can anyone even see me,
Does anyone know I'm there?

I only grow sadder,
But no one will ever know.
Since no one seems to notice me,
I might as well just go.

Krystal Jené Denning

By an Eye of Faith

By an eye of faith I can plainly see
That beautiful mansion God built for me
With gates of pearl and streets of gold
in that beautiful home where will never grow old.

By an eye of faith I plainly see
God's arms open wide to welcome me.
I'll run to his arms and touch his face
and make my home in that Heavenly place.

By an eye of faith I plainly see my sisters
and brothers welcoming me.
We'll no longer take the parting hand,
but we'll make our home in that new land.

Oh! Dear sinners, by an eye of
faith you, too, could see that beautiful
home made for you and me
where the gates are pearl and the streets are gold
in that new home where we'll never grow old.

Mary Ann Hitchcock

1998

A year of tragedy and demands.
A hurt little boy finally becomes a man.
Sadness and tears rolled down his blushed cheeks.
Now he looks back on his losses and defeats.
No understanding why it had to be;
Some things no one should ever have to see.
Friends were taken, tears were shed,
A year always remembered in the heart and in the head.
A hero in the making, a son on the rise,
Now he's just a memory, a great and joyful life.
Happy times, oh, they never came,
But I live on, it's just not the same.
No kisses on the forehead when I'm asleep.
She's gone away, safe in Heaven's keep.
No stone cold stare, the question, "Are you mad?"
Playing on God's court is a boy named Brad.
Great times we shared together, memories best to keep.
Always in my mind, dreams when I sleep.

Donnie E. Egnor

Gone Again

Softly, softly beckoning,
I hear your voice from far away.
Hush the waves are echoing,
you whisper my name upon the breeze.
Look into the dear night sky,
the stars are falling all around.
They frame your face in the moonless night,
and you call to me again.
My heart is reaching out to you,
my soul you already embrace.
I shut my eyes and drift ever closer,
something unnamed pulls me along.
I know that soon the sun will rise,
the night will quickly pass away.
I feel your arms warm around me,
you softly whisper into my ear.
I ope' my eyes to the first light of day,
and quickly does your visage fade away.

Tiffany Anne Ley

Borrowed Angel

In loving memory of Tiffany Danielle Jones (5/21/91-11/15/97)
We borrowed an angel one morning in May.
A small, soft angel, what a glorious day!
She touched the hearts of all she knew;
And her smile glistened, like the morning dew.
Kind words always came from her heart.
She was loyal and true right from the start.
Her touch captured the souls of family and friends,
And only God knew when her time would end.
When angels are borrowed, they must be returned
To God in Heaven; a hard lesson learned.
She's a guardian angel looking down from above,
Watching over us all from eyes filled with love.
She took a part of us to her Heavenly home,
And we are certain she'll never be alone.
But she left more of herself to be adored
Before returning home to meet her Lord.

Pamela Johnston Jones

Reflections

The sound of her voice, the shape of her face
All in my mind, but somehow misplaced
One kind word, a confident look
All of this the Lord took
It seemed like a second, the blink of an eye
I did not even say "good-bye"
Oh, the grief, the anger, the pain
Wrapped up in me all just the same
All those times we would sit and talk
Or even take a little walk
The little things she would do or say
Are not forgotten, but far away
Things at home are not the same
The air of loneliness quickly came
It is hard for us to just pretend
For all those memories just cannot end
So, a part of her will always be
The strongest part I have in me

Tina Louise Walsh

Final Destination

Staring at the ceiling, wondering
What to do,
Do we stay together or finally
Say that we're through?
So much to say, deciding our fate
Can we still save ourselves
Or is it already too late?
Once upon a time love was everlasting
Now it's always passing
Has the mold been cast?
Can we get by the hurt and pain
Into the sunshine, out of the rain?
Searching for an answer, racking my brain,
Driving me insane
'Bout to pop a vein.
Again and again I'm tormented by this bane.
How long shall I be plagued with this question:
What is our final destination?

Delvis D. Dore

Flowers in Heaven

In Heaven the Master has a bouquet,
For which the Lord picks flowers every day.
He only takes the best you see,
This one is just close to you and me.
It is only the most beautiful He finds,
In His heart, He knew we wouldn't mind,
If we only knew what a beautiful place,
And that one day again we would see her face.
If she could, she'd tell us, "Don't cry."
But still yet we would question, "Why?"
"Why her time on Earth didn't last,
And why was she taken from us so fast?"
Even though our hearts are torn,
The Lord knows it takes time to heal and mourn.
We'll never know why the Master needed her, but He made room.
We know her soul in Heaven will forever bloom.
Oh, Lord if you can hear us pray,
Please take care of the rose you received today.

Regina Lorraine Mullins

Your Love in My Heart

Gentle thoughts go through my mind, as I think of you
All my life I've wanted a love so true
From this day forth and each day after, your love is in my heart
In my life, you, my love, have become the most important part
How can I tell you of all the joy you bring to me
I only hope you give us a chance, so I can let you see
How happy you make my heart and how you make me smile
I just know this feeling is going to last a very long while
I will do my best to keep your feelings before my own
With each new day that passes, my love for you has grown
You mean more to me than words can ever say
I want to show you this every single day
Stay in my life and let my heart be only for you
As your heart is mine and forever will be true
Come share my life and let our love become one in you
Allow our love to continue in all that you do
Never forget how much you are loved by me
For your love is in my heart for all eternity

Joan L. Chiles

unseen wings

the truth in reality
and reality's truth
unfamiliar aspect of life
maybe too much thought
or not enough
compensations selfishness isn't so sweet
a veil of ignorance
a bit of nonchalance
combinations cause combustion
ice and fire within
when there is nothing you can do
then a full 360 turns on you
yet the directions you don't seem to find
well, give yourself wings to rise above this illusion
the illusion you know is your reality
doubting you against yourself
you need the touch you can't feel
all you want surrounds you in a way you deny

Autumn Lee Pape

Discovery of Destruction

For years and years they roamed this land,
passing it down from hand to hand.
Until one day their land was attacked,
taken away—never to be given back.
But more than land was taken that day,
their past and their future was taken away.
Their elders were lucky for they did not see
what their tradition was now forced to be.
The intruders were nice, for they gave them land,
but the land was covered with diseased sand.
Destroying the land the natives loved so much,
turning it to dust with every touch.
Their burial mounds which were dear to heart
were destroyed, dug up, and torn apart.
Today it is left for descendents to carry on
the life of their fathers, which must never be gone.
For if it ends, and their spirits leave the land,
That will be the end of all native man.

Marlina Traci Richardson

Vanities of Life

How subtly life's vanities capture and entertain;
How disappointing when vain dreams dissipate into reality.
Only then we do face their hidden evils to
Feel shame and disgrace
For our unloyal, backsliding hearts against
The highest principality.

He warns us in His book of dangers of vanity
Of pitfalls of pride, riches, grand dreams.
But lustful hearts, unwilling to sacrifice,
Reach for heights of glory,
Seeking contentment in status and riches, it seems.

Some go unashamed; unafraid. Youth,
In virginal innocence,
With joyful hearts, in lack of wisdom,
Hurry through each day, seeking fulfillment,
Missing elements of real peace of mind meant
For creatures of God's kingdom.

Betty J. Caldwell Dickens

The Room

She enters and the room lights up
as though happiness does not begin until her arrival
All eyes are on her, as she once again
lays the foundation for their lives
Without uttering a word, their love is spoken
as remembrances of days gone by
lay on the outside of their hearts
like a picture album faded to the naked eye
but vividly colored, like a rainbow in their souls
She will never forget how close she came
to thinking life would be better on her own
outside their lives, outside this room
to thinking of never entering this room again
As her heart closes the door to the other place
where she spent too long
with doubts and tears and forgotten purpose
she is thankful that her wings have been mended
and now she is remembering what it feels like to fly

Marcia K. Ryman

Jesus

Oh, what a sweet name!
Oh, what a peace You give
when only we speak Your name.
Thank You for the times
Your name gave me assurance
and wiped away my tears and fears.
Blessed am I for the victories given me,
through Your sweet name.
As the days come and go,
Thank You for never leaving me
without that name to call on;
and for those outstretched arms of love
to hold me, when seems no one else will.
So when I am in fear,
needing to be held,
Thank You for those open arms
and that always present
Sweet name . . . JESUS

Beth Ann Thompson

You and I

Thoughts turn in my mind
Like the pages of time
Once that I thought so real
Seems to have lost its magical seal
I know that we have a rare and true love
And I will wait to fly, like the white dove
When the moment comes that our love can fly
I know that we will soar into the blue sky
Sometimes I sit and wonder how the story ends
Will we remain lovers or just best friends
What I hope it to be
In time we will only see
When the darkness has settled on the town
I wonder when will your love come around
Maybe all that it seems
Is really nothing but a dream
So, the thoughts keep turning
My love and desire will keep burning

Shelley Gay Reed

Crazy Love

I meet a girl that seems so right,
So I walk up to her that one perfect night.
Her name was Lauren and she seemed so great,
A girl that I would love to take on a date.
So I ask and she smiles and she says yes.
Like every guy I'm stuttering like a mess.
I leave that night being happy as can be.
So I get in my car and put in my key.
I drive away with a smile on my face.
So I put that number in my wallet to be safe.
I look ahead and think of all my luck.
And I didn't even see that truck.
It hit me from the side and I start to cry.
Because I didn't even tell my family or Lauren good-bye.
I'm dying and I'm scared to death.
And I know this will be my last breath.
The man was drunk and he took my life away.
Now I'll have to wait to tell Lauren what I had to say.

Nick D. Acqua

Rejection

What does one whisper on a cold night?
When feelings flare on and do take flight.
On unhallowed ears the words do fall leaving
you the Loneliness fool of all.
Can we be just friends is all I hear
and to me it brings anger and fear.
An from my eye a lonely tear.
Anger 'cause I fear to find no one to love in my time.
Fear that I shall never be told that my love is bold.
To hide myself from the pain I cast love down to disdain.
'Cause it leaves my heart a wreck.
And makes me feel like a speck.
I run and hide from rejection and its painful infection.
Now you know why I have showed no emotion.
Which there is no medicine or potion.
One day the walls may crumble
I may stumble into love. But until that day show its place.
I shall be just a lonely face.

Joshua Louis Steadman

Safe

I stared at a black and white photograph
I found at the bottom of an oil-stained box
I had hid in the attic.
Looking through it to see our two-storied home.
The burnt gold fields, our amber crops, dancing in the wind.
The sun shone just for us,
Welcoming yellow-orange at the dawn.
Fresh white paint coated our house,
Handmade lace curtains kissed the windows.
We piled on our family porch swing after dinner,
Or played jump rope when our chores were done.
Our wheat stretched to the light to grow.

Then, Sorrow
visited us
and stayed.
He let Sorrow move in,
and color our house
and everything else collapsed.

Kaleen R. Covington

Good Love

An eagle flies with the wind beneath its wings,
As I survive with you by my side.
Seasons change from a dullness like death
To a rebirth of new life,
While I also come back to life without you on my mind,
Without you in my heart,
With you no longer by my side.
Though I maintain from day to day,
I can't hide the pain that is seen in my face.
The hurt that is felt in my heart
Turns it cold to the world that surrounds me.
You have shown me doors to my soul
That I never thought would be part of me.
I now know what it feels like to have my heart harden.
While I try to live one day at a time,
I find it hard to live with my heart miles away.
Though it seems as if an eagle may fly for miles,
The wind beneath its wings may leave, as you have.

Samantha M. Wilkins

Society

I'm not fair I'm not here
Like that one who you once knew
My mind is decaying my life is delaying
You ask me the question
that everybody asks, Why?
But yet I have no answer
Wait my mind well it was just a glimpse
All I see is crime
All I see is not much time
All the birds are dying
All the birds are flying To where?
If you must know
To their cages that's all they know
Freedom must scare them
Time is running, Where? Away
Crime is growing, Where? Here
There is not much time

Robert Ryan Dodd

Angel

Dark eyes
Deep like an ocean.
They seem so cold
Show no emotion.

Long hair
Golden and bright
Falls on his shoulders
Reflecting the light.

Large wings
Dividing the sky
He could leave the Earth
But doesn't want to fly.

He's my angel,
He's my guide.
He'll protect me
In the darkest night.

Monica Faith Schneider

Deceitful Dragon

Deceitful dragon
Fangs of fury and hate
Drop thy maiden
And run hither to your nesting ground

Come
Come and taste your own blood
Glimmering blade of might and steel
Ready to drink of your blood

Do not test thy might
Deceitful dragon
I am more powerful than thou
I am more cunning

Breathe your fiery breath
Deflected by my shield of love
Breathe your last breath
Deceitful dragon

Erik Kevin Diamond

Time

Where does the time go?
Will we ever know?

Twenty-four hours in a day.
Most of us wishing them away.

Is it time to go home yet?
Race for time mind set.

Never moment to moment.
Precious time never spent.

What a serious waste,
All the rush and haste.

Only so much time in a day.
We are forever throwing it away.

Enjoy our time each day.
Life seems so much better that way.

Jodi Anne Casselman

Dream Away

The many facets of dreams and dreaming
I lie myself down to sleep,
a time to rest
or take the test.
No longer home,
I see some light,
and now it's out of sight.
The faces change,
the places move,
and I follow an untamed groove.
I can't explain
the picture I see,
another scene there will be.
Now awake,
another day,
I wish to dream away.

Nikolaos James Chivikas

As Long As I Live

As long as I live
I'll be by your side
I'll be your companion
Your friend and your guide

As long as I live
And as long as you care
I'll do anything for you
I'll go anywhere

I'll bring you the sunshine
To chase all your fears
I'll gather up rainbows
To comfort your tears

As long as forever
My love will be true
For as long as I live
I'll love only you

Mary E. K. Manos-Mitchem

No Longer There

It's not the fact I love him
It's not the fact I care
It's just the fact that I now know
He's no longer there

I think of that voice
The voice I found so dear
I fill full of fear
As I hear it very clear

I know that you love me
I know that you care
The only thing you need to know
I'm no longer there

I had told him that I loved him
I had told him that I cared
He had simply said
He's no longer there
Ashley L. Anderson

Dream of Myself

Once again I find myself here—
Alone.
Shadows gathering,
Filling empty spaces.
Snatches of sound,
Distorting echoes of memory,
I can't remember, are they mine?
One clear light—
Shines; a mirror
But I'm not ready to know
Face myself,
Fist flashes out—
Crash!
Glass dances down,
Light bouncing, Illuminating
Gapping hole, jagged edges
Of my life.
Amanda Elizabeth Cesari

Standing There

Thank you, Jesus, for standing there in my place.
Time will tell what truth will see
destroying some their perfect dream

Sharper still their tongues confess
amongst their words ride life's distress

And over and over and over again
I search and find my one true friend

Standing there brave and bold
someone who's golden from days of old

Standing there with prevailing stature
someone so real something of nature

Standing there to save my face
STANDING THERE in my place
Martin Del Merida

Distant Dream

The only thing I see
are letters on a screen,
yet as real as you and I,
she is my distant dream.

I cannot hear her elegant voice,
but I'm sure it's soft and sweet.
The expressions that she makes,
sweeping me off my feet.

How can we be so far apart
and so close at the same time,
truly takes my breath away
and astonishes my mind.

I cannot kiss her tender lips
or hold her close to me,
yet maybe someday this distant dream
will be a close reality!
Travis Alan Gelinas

Night Eyes

Your cologne fills the air
As you touch my arm
The night eyes see
But pose no harm
Your lips touch mine
As I am passed by fear
The night eyes see
But don't interfere
Your kiss so gentle
I want to cry
The night eyes see
And wonder why
How good you are
To pose such love
And as always
The night eyes see
From far above
Whitney Nichole Fowlkes

Look

I look at your eyes,
and what do I see?
You,
looking back at me.

I look at your heart,
and what do I see?
You,
loving me.

I look at your soul,
and what do I see?
You,
a part of me.

I look at your mirror,
and what do I see?
You,
and me.
T. L. Bubonovich

On the Beach in May

On the beach in May
on a warm breezy day
I saw a
mare and a foal
with coats of gold
that shimmered in the
morning sun
their white manes
and tails
blew in the breeze like
silk banners and
the crystal blue sea
lapped at
their feet as
the sun rose
into the
sky.

Amber Renee Wilson

My Only Love

I walked into the room
And our eyes met
For the first time in so long

I was only there a short time
But I felt something
And you did, too

Now we are miles apart
Both of us scared
And the longing is too much

But when you say those words
I know you mean them

If fate is meant for us
I will wait forever
To be with you
And hear those words again

Jenny Marie Cutalo

Ode to a Blankie

When you were born and still brand new
This treasure was a gift to you

As you became a little boy
It was more than just a toy

When it was washed, you really cried
And wouldn't stop until it dried

For 30 years I've kept it safe
And stored it in a special place

The time has gone too fast for me
Like yesterday it seems to be

But on the day you wed, I swore
I'd give it back forevermore

And now you have my gift to you
I hope you know I love you, too.

Diane E. Kanavy

Always Follow Your Heart

Always follow your heart,
Instead of using your mind,
It will lead you in the right direction,
New hope for you it shall find.

No matter what you desire,
No matter how hard it may seem,
Always follow your heart,
Never be afraid to dream.

Always follow your heart,
Let it open your eyes,
Nothing is unachievable,
So always reach for the skies.

Once you've reached your goals,
Never forget your heart,
Always remember what got you here,
And with it never part.

Ryan M. Smothers

My Infinite Dream

For Jason

Long ago, I made you love me
In my infinite dream of you.
Long ago, you ran from me
In my infinite truth of you.

Time passed, and you did not speak
In may infinite truth of you.
Time passed, and in my mind you loved me
In my infinite dream of you.

It is now, and you love me
In my infinite dream of you.
It is now, and you have made me happy
In my infinite truth of you.

Terri M. Gilbert

To Fly

I wish I could fly.
I would fly high in the sky.
I would be free as a bird.
I would just fly.
I'd fly over the trees.
And up to the sky.
I'd be free as a bird I would just fly.
So in the rays that make first light.
When the dawn is to take flight.
I will end my life and set it free.
So now my soul can fly free.
Now I will go high in the sky.
And be free as a bird.
I will just fly.

James E. Wilson

Walk on By

As I see you walking by
I sit here and wonder why
I wonder why you make me cry
why can't you look me in the eye

I try not to think about you
I try not to care
but you don't know how hard it is
when I see her playing with your hair

We broke up
and it's clear to me
that we were never
meant to be

But now I'm tough
and I'm not going to cry
So go on, go away
Walk on By

Julie Michelle Farrar

Thoughts

Why the world is slowly turning,
Why my heart is steadily burning,
What questions hath we asked we hear,
We write, we look, we stop and stare.
Write only what we hath in our hearts,
And keep our mind clear of evil thoughts.
Why doth that task seem so hard to do,
When all my thoughts seem to drift to you?
I cannot think lest hath I write,
Of all the things that within me fight.

Shasta Michelle Brinner

Memorial Day

A tradition born after the Civil War
Flowers and flags from shore to shore
Hearing the echoes of voices callin'
Haunted by memories of those who've fallen
A day for tears of joy and tears of sorrow
For those who gave their lives for a freer tomorrow
Flowers, new and bursting, cut down in their prime
Courageous souls martyred before their time
The plaintive bugler's call from yesterday
Honors the valiant spirit of Memorial Day.

Jason Matthew Romano

A Mountain Dream

A dream . . . on top of the tallest
mountain surrounded by beautiful pine,
cedar, and tamarack.
Just on the edge of a soft, green
meadow overgrown with grasses and
wildflowers . . . daisies, bluebells, and yellowbells.
A creek, the sound of water, as it trickles
over the rocks, trout hide in the
shadows beneath the overgrowth.
Mist rises, as the sun slowly dries
the morning dew.
Deer nibble at the new grass sprouts,
as the birds above look for
perfect nesting material to raise their family.
Our log home, very simple, with a
porch on the front and two rockers to spend
our time watching and listening to all the
sights and sounds of the world around us.

Cheryl A. Schmidt

Even God Cries

Remove this tear from my face
There is no crying in this lofty place
I shed one single tear
Which rolls down my face at a delicate pace
Falls through the sky like angels fear
Past the clouds as the ground nears
It tosses about and turns once more
Before striking the Earth at the precise core
The ground shakes, no one is anymore
God shed one tear, I will shed no more

Alex M. Zinn

Staten Island Ferry

The Staten Island ferry from Manhattan
is like the last scene of a movie,
when the camera pans slowly away
from the city where all the action took place.
I turn my head from bright lights of buildings
toward bright lights of bridges
and wonder whether to think it all beautiful
or mourn the waste of starlight.

Unable to decide, I focus on the people,
melange of tourists, bums, commuters,
and wonder once again,
"Are they beautiful or are they all a waste of life?"
A man is preaching Jesus loudly:
"A'some of you are a-listenin', butchya still a'don't a'HEAR'AH!"
A German woman calls out to her friend,
then cameras flash as Lady Liberty comes into sight. . . .

"Yes, she is beautiful," I decide.

Eileen Mary McDermott

Essentially Enigma

I will draw you in a dervish
swirl from palette onto paper
cream and dimple hungry
for the shape-and-hue emergence
of you from rapid dabs and strokes
by brushes coarse for vital form
and background fine for definition
of the porous contour, detail hid
inside the mystery of your face

I whirl around unsteadied
by your eyes, brown on the canvas
watching every line and mark
I make to fill demanding empty spaces
like a judgment needing eyebrows
and the shape of mouth to cast a verdict
on my fever rush of colors stroked
in the flurried brightness of deluded acts
to catch the essentials of enigma

Frank Faust

Better

It is just as easy for a child to feel love, as it is for a child
to feel fear and anger; and this is the natural response when a child
witnesses and becomes the victim of abuse.

Yet somehow . . . beyond . . . even this pain . . . the greatest sadness
is the secrecy and denial, which brings to life shame.

A child's anger with no place to go will be turned inward,
no longer does the child look around to find reason and justification
for the pain inside, instead the child believes that her sadness
comes from her own inadequacy.
That she is not good enough to deserve better.

Let me describe the child's room . . . it has dark walls
and holds in the air every emotion, which tries to be denied;
the walls surround you wherever you go, and in this room
every word you hear reminds you that you are not good enough . . .
not in any way . . . for anything.

You may fall to your knees with tears being the only words you can speak.
Let these tears heal you, for this is the expression,
which breaks through secrecy and denial and allows room
for the Holy Spirit to be your strength,
for it is within these bounds that the birth of forgiveness and love
can come about.

Janet M. Russo

The Sounds of London—Tribute to Princess Diana

The people of London are weeping in sorrow,
because they have lost a Princess, a princess by the name of Diana.
Diana—what a wonderful person she was in her generosity
to the human race and to her royal subjects.
She gave love from the bottom of her heart to children
and the very sick and shut-in; she fought for cures for diseases,
and made contributions to various funds.
"The Sounds of London" are the people's opinions on their
emotions and thoughts on Princess Diana,
who brought sunshine and happiness into their hearts.

"The Sounds of London" is therefore a tribute to Princess Diana
who died young before her humanitarian work was completely finished.
Now, she has gone home to be with her master; hopefully,
all of us will see her again along with the creator.

Anthony Taylor

Reminiscence

I remember those misguided feelings and thoughts;
Those desperate notions that were brought into starless nights.
I remember those beliefs that couldn't be bought,
But there was always something you could say to make everything all right.

I remember the quickened beat of my hesitant heart,
And the secluded love being pulled into the light.
I remember that beginning, that brand new start,
My love called me an angel tonight.

Hilary Patrick

Endurance

Tall, young trees growing on a tropical beach,
Just starting to bend towards the force of the tradewinds,
Other trees have succumbed to the winds and the tides with
Their roots exposed to the elements just marking time.
The oldest trees have become gnarled and twisted into strange
Shapes by the ocean tides and winds,
By bending with the wind, these trees survived with their
Pride and dignity intact well past their prime.

People are like these trees, bending toward changes in life;
Those who do not bend will break.
Some people have their lives sucked dry of everything valuable,
leaving nothing to keep them upright.
Others not only bend towards change and grow with it,
But have an attitude towards life to never forsake,
These people have kept their pride and dignity intact,
Life's experiences enriching them with wisdom and a glowing light.

Margaret White

Dream

To dream is to live in a world filled with happiness, hope, and peace.
To believe in hope gives us a reason to live,
for happiness mankind cries out for
so the world can live together in peace.

Glenda Johana Perez

I Will . . .

I will never hurt you.
I will never lie.
I promise forever I will be by your side.
No one will take me or even attempt to try.
I will love you forever as long as you never hurt me, or make me cry.
We will be best friends until the end, our friendship will never die.
You can trust me to never turn my back and hide.

Bobbie Jo Lynn Dokken

Jealousy

And exactly who are you?
It is I, with envy that is uneasy.
Ashamed that I neglected to speak but was it not in my eyes, my heart?
Who, I ask, are you?
Who asked for him to share?
His feelings, he exposed . . . forthright . . . a conviction, I presume.
Damnation, I declare!
I need not ask again.
It is you.
There's no life that knows of you who hasn't but once felt his way.
The blame I do take, but my eyes and my heart, they would not say.
The words, they would not come.
I scream . . . and nothing.
Now with fierce eyes, my heart pleads, don't let it be too late.
Fearful my words spatter, inept.
I beg your mercy, another go.
I liked it best when eyes were mute and this heart did not ache
. . . quietly sitting and subdued.
This witness, evasive and true, wretched for catching sight of you.

Diana Marie Foltz

A Son

The Doctor said "a healthy boy" and momma's big tears flow.
Daddy's standing close and proud
with a great big smile and glow.
Grandma and Grandpa's peeking through
to see their pride and joy and racing to the
telephone to tell them it's a boy!
Two years have passed and I have learned,
little boys do cry. I try to explain his words,
but all he asks is why? That sneaky smile that
little hug, he taps me on the shoulder.
Then I say those familiar words: wait 'til you get older!
A car stops and out he goes running through the door.
Leaving momma standing there because kisses he gives no more.
He's grown up now and left our home, remembering all he can . . .
I have lost my blue-eyed boy, but gained a great big man.
There's many pleasures in being a momma,
a lot of heartaches just trying to understand,
but the greatest pleasure in being a momma is . . .
HE IS MY #1 FAN!

Sandy Linn Sevenski

The Magnificence of an Autumn Night

I stood alone one brisk autumn night.
With
my head full of adolescent dreams and the

beauty of the heavens in my sight. The
smell of wonder filled the air and the brisk

wind caressed my hair. The strength of
preteen romanticism overcame me.
My only intention in life was to keep weary
travelers away from the scarlet herald's troubled sea.
All my life I had felt pain from wearing my heart on my sleeve,
this was the
first time it felt good for my young passion to flow inside of me.
I always reminisce on this night with my heart filled nostalgic glee
because this is when my path to
manhood began to become clear enough to see.

Kofi Ablode Modey

Love

Love is a feeling that is so simple,
but so very hard to explain.
You can ask a million people
and no answer will remain the same.
Sometimes we get confused between love and infatuation,
is it because of the touch or the sensation?
We are placed into people's lives for many different reasons
and we will only understand why at the end of our season.
Before I witnessed love, I was prepared to die,
because it felt like I had experience everything that is out there to try
But now I have felt love my life would not be complete
until I can share that feeling with the special woman that's mine to keep.

Reginald LeMar Hicks

Reflection of Life

Have you ever looked in the mirror and seen the reflection of life?

Does it remind you of your mother's smile?
Or, does it look like your father's eyes?

Maybe, your daughter's excitement over the
new flowers blooming in her special little garden.

Or do you see your grandfather's wisdom
reflecting like a beacon or a glare that won't go away.

I once saw my son standing next to me even
though he wasn't there at all . . . he has been gone for some time now.

I sometimes stand in my mirror watching and
listening for signs of life that dictate my divine mission

To become a vessel of love which is thus, a reflection eternal.

Paul M. Faber

Circles

Walk around me now in a moment that seems last forever with you.
Look into your eyes and see all I see in you.
Needing something and not knowing what
while I stand before you, offering myself to you.
You take me in and throw me out.
You build me up, then I tumble down.
You had so much to say but no words came out.
I show up before you and you smile at me and talk small talk.
Once in a while, revealing more about who you really are.
What would you do if I fell in love with all that you are?
Would you be surprised if you walk around in circles in my head?
Take my thoughts away from anything and everything else.
Wrap me up in your world and fill my soul with meaningless thoughts.
Throw me over your shoulders, carry me away,
just as long as you never let me down.

Amber Lee Hallam

American Woman

An American woman should be very grateful and happy.
To think what happens to women in other countries,
We can be proud that we have a heard voice,
Instead of being locked up with no freedom of choice.
We should be proud of all the progress we've made,
From behind our husbands, kept in the shade.
For many years we have been silenced and beaten,
We faced a lot of hard times and unfair treatment.
But what they fail to realize,
We have our eyes set on a greater prize.
We have grace, style, brains, and beauty.
We are more than just the average cutie.
We are princesses, future queens of the world.
It doesn't matter if we like to wear pearls.
So for the non-American women who have not yet learned of this truth,
Teach them that they should be someone of importance, too.

Lanell Renea Howell

I Lost That Chance

I love you, but I can't trust you
I want you, but I can't have you
'Cause I lost that chance
That chance to love you
I scared you away and now you're gone
You're not coming back
There's no more love here
'Cause I lost that chance to love you
And it's all my fault
I'm wishing you were here but you're not
'Cause I know I messed things up for good
You'll go find someone else
'Cause you gave up on me
I want to say I'm sorry but I can't
You won't listen to me
'Cause you are really mad, and I understand
I love you, but I can't trust you
I want you, but I can't have you
'Cause I lost that chance, that chance to love you, and it's all my fault.

Megan Taylor Forman

Release Me

O Lord, Release me, Release me from the bondage of my heart.
I can feel you opening my heart, bit by bit, piece by piece.
The release of your love, flowing out of my heart,
through the tears in my eyes falling over my face.
Not tears of sadness or despair, but tears of joy, happiness and love.
Tears of knowing I will be able to love fully with my heart again.
Tears of thankfulness, mercy and grace.
The release of tears in finding the love of my life.

Jacquelyn Suzanne Cappadoro

Words

I'm sitting here with tears in my eyes,
wondering if this life I have is nothing but a pack of lies.
Is it always my fault with something I've said,
or is it being around me that you dread?
I wake up in the mornings with my heart on a string,
Just wondering what kind of day it's going to bring.

I try to give you hugs, kisses, and write you little love wishes.

Then you slam them to the ground and stomp them with all your might.
And once again I'm wondering what I didn't do right.
Why do you have to bring me such pain
With all those words you always rage?
Someday I hope that this will all change,
And my dreams once again will be within range.
I hope to grab them, hold them, and cherish them tight,
so in the end everything will once again be all right.

Tina Leblang

My Son

The day my son was born my heart was taken out and put into my hands,
God blessed my heart and taught it to walk and talk and stand.
He allowed me to love and raise his child and mine,
Only time would tell the reason or rhyme.
He was a very joyful boy and he liked to play,
Playing got him in trouble each and every day.
Nothing dampened his spirits or took his joy.
I'll tell everyone that the one with joy is my baby boy!

Karen Hathecock Smith

The First Time

The first time I saw you, my heart skipped a beat.
My mind said hello but my lips couldn't speak.
The first time I met you, I was nervous as could be.
Your beauty had me captured,
you are gorgeous, don't you see.
The first time I talked to you, your voice, I had never heard.
It's a voice like that of angels pleasing with every word.
The first time I held your hand, I thought how beautiful,
smooth and soft, it felt like I was flying, my head was held aloft.
The first time I hugged you, I felt your embrace.
You felt so wonderful, you made my heart race.
The first time I missed you, I was gone a short time.
But all I could think of was you on my mind.
The first time I kissed you, I trembled, I shook, and my heart fluttered too.
And I knew in that instant, I truly loved you.

James Ira Whitney Jr.

You Have Helped

You have helped and you don't know it.
Just the little things that count so very much.
They don't seem very big after I look at them although they are.
You helped when my parents were split up and my life was a mess.
You were there to tell me it would get better, when I thought it was over.
You were there to listen when I couldn't talk to them.
I wanted to tell you that you helped me very much, and I am glad.

Billie Joe Powers

Searching

My whole life has been a search.
A search of where I belong. A search of myself.
A search of my faith. A search for true love.
Could it be you? I have found many things I have searched for,
but one still eludes me, true love. Could it be you?
The search has left me broken many times, and still I search.
Could it be you? The search has left me half not whole,
and still I search. Could it be you?
The search has left me tired and low, and still I search.
Could it be you? The search has tested all other searches in my life, and still I search. Could it be you?
The search has left me hopeful, excited, anxious, and still I search.
Could it be you? One day the search will be complete and so will I, and I will search no more. It will be you!

    Christina Ann Wood

So Alone

I never felt so alone in all my life.
When you're born, they carry you.
When you die, they bury you.
In between, you're on your own.
Life is a hard thing to do and harder still to leave.
So many a days I am lost without knowing love,
Without knowing life until I met you.
No more fears, nor tears, only joy knowing someone like you cared.
I miss your loving touch, your laughter, your warm eyes, your gentle whisper.
I will go on, even if my tears are only but my fears living without you.
Now I stand here all alone by your grave.
I can hear your voice whisper, "I LOVE YOU."
One day we will be together.
Through it all God will let us be as one again.

    Marie J. Walker

Holocaust: A Letter to Mommy

They captured me, lots and lots of men.
There were so many, way more than ten.
Took us to this strange, old camp; scary, dreary, dark, and damp.
Why did they take me away from you? So far away, but in the camp, too.
People crying, sad and crying. In the streets they're sick and dying.
Mommy, I don't like it here. Nothing inside me, only fear.
They don't treat us very nice. In the streets are rats and mice.
I had a friend. She went away, left on the train and I thought she'd come back someday.
No one comes back when they leave on the train. So many tears fall like rain.
Hello, Mommy, I'll write you a letter. If I draw you a picture, will you feel better?
Why am I being punished for being a Jew? I miss you and Daddy, too.
Please, don't get onto that train. I look into eyes and see lots of pain.
Tell Daddy I love him, hope to see you again. If not, then good-bye.
Please, Mommy, don't cry.

    Jordan Nicole Hirsch

Poet
Profiles

ACOSTA, TAMMY
[a.] Fullerton, GA [title] "Nana" [pers.] This poem was written about someone very special in my life— my nana, Hildred Grace Coppock. It reflects how much I love her and how her death affected me. I will never forget her. She will always hold a special place in my heart. I love you Nana!

ACREY, D. J.
[a.] Snyder, OK [title] "What the Future Holds" [pers.] This poem is dedicated to my children, Christal and Dennis, and to my loving lifelong partner, Kim. Without them I would not be the person I am. I love each of you completely. This is also dedicated to my mother for standing by me when I tried pushing her away. Thank you, Mom, for always believing in me.

ADAMS, DANIEL
[a.] Tow, TX [title] "Mom" [pers.] My mother is the most genuinely good person that I have ever known or met. I hope that in some way this poem shows my appreciation of her and the gifts that she has given me. Indeed, the very gift of life is enough, but she has shared so much more—love, kindness, humor, and compassion, just to name a few. I hope that this communicates my love and thanks to my mother, Margaret, and reminds others to remember to thank their parents for the gifts they've given.

ADAMS, MEG
[a.] Venice, FL [title] "The Friend I Always Needed and Sister I've Always Wanted" [pers.] I am thirteen years old and I live in Venice, Florida. This poem was written to my best friend and "Blood Sister" for her birthday and as a congrats for making confirmation. I don't know what I would do without Heather—that's what this poem is about! I love poetry! Poetry is what I do when I need a break from life. Poetry plays a big part in my life, and I really enjoy it!

AHMAD, SHAMA
[a.] Sugar Land, TX [title] "The Cherokee" [pers.] This poem was a class assignment that our teacher gave us after reading about the native Americans. I was in seventh grade. What hurt me most is how they were being slowly wiped out from their homebound. Throughout history, people, have been punished most cruelly for who they are: African, Americans, Jews, Muslims, Hutus, and that's only a few. I know that the human race is better than that. In the words of Anne Frank, "In spite of everything, I still believe that people are really good at heart."

AKINS, NICOLE
[a.] Fort Worth, TX [title] "Purple Dragon Dreams" [pers.] I wrote this poem for my four children, Korshaya, Jamil, Kiana, and Carlyn. My love of dragons and fantasy also inspired this poem. I hope you have enjoyed it as much as I enjoyed writing it.

AL-SAND, KHALID
[a.] Riyadh, Kingdom of Saudi Arabia [title] "Apple Seeds" [pers.] Dr. Khalid Abu Al Saud is a multicultural man, born in Indonesia in 1944. He studied medicine in Germany. Currently living in Saudi Arabia, he speaks German, English, Arabic and some Indonesian languages. His concerns about the future, his family, the planet Earth, and human civilizations have forced him to write his thoughts in the form of political books and poems. Although he does not consider himself a poet, he has written the following: *The World Government, Islamic Democratic Constitution, The Survival Strategy for Muslim Countries in the 21st Century, The Path of Prosperity for Muslim Countries in the 21st Century,* and the poems, "Diwan Al Aulamah," and "Diwan Takaya Aser Aulamah."

ALFORD, PATSY
[a.] Gaylord, MI [title] "The Stillness" [pers.] I am a 55-year-old retired homemaker and live with my husband in Northern Michigan. The stillness is a

reflection of my emotion upon the death of my former spouse. My poetry is a revelation of my most private thoughts and feelings that I find difficult to share verbally. Yet I believe it to be a vital part of my legacy that all those who have touched my life in any fashion should know the imprint they left behind. Hopefully my poetry will do the same to those I leave behind.

ALKANOVICH, NATALIE
[a.] Brooklyn, NY [title] "Move On" [pers.] Writing poetry for me is expressing the feelings that cannot be said. This poem is about my first love, whom I thought was my "the one," but things didn't work out. However no matter what, that special person will always be in my heart because he will always be my first love. I cannot imagine my life without him but I know that I must move on! I am only 17 and I have a lot more things coming up in my life, so if something is meant to be, it will be! I'd like to dedicate this poem to the one and only M.S!

ALLEN, DIANNE
[a.] Lakes Entrance, Australia [title] "I Find Comfort" [pers.] This poem was written for a very special friend of mine. With my exploration of the Internet, I have discovered the world has become a smaller place. I have made some wonderful friends with whom I normally would not have had the opportunity to come in contact. This friend has been an inspiration for me and will always remain very special. My poetry is never planned; it always comes to me very suddenly. I'm glad I was able to put this one to paper as a tribute to true friendship.

ALLEN, MONIQUE
[a.] Columbia, MO [title] "Just Another Blak Witch" [pers.] This poem was written by a sixteen-year-old Afro-American Female from Kansas City, MO—the inner-city that is. Now twenty, I have always wanted to be involved in school but I had unreliable support, as my family members were workers and sleepers. No excuse, but I was in love with a rebellious young man from the time I was eleven to when I was eighteen, which contained so much adventure and pain. My parents wanted to protect me, but by doing so they sheltered me, as line two states. I couldn't learn—the school I attended barely was teaching us simple things like grammar for papers and other needed academics. I was feeling unimportant but I knew I was important, as line one states. This poem was originally written to be a rap, so it has so many rhythms encoded that this can sometimes sound like a war. The meaning of life was for me a Christian perspective, whatever Aba or Yahweh placed in my heart, but it was going to require a lot of growing pain, as lines nine through eleven states. I go from first person "I," to first person "we," as in "us young women," line twelve.

ALLMAN, D. LORAINE
[a.] Guin, AL [title] "Give Her Back" [pers.] Her name is Glinda. The poem is inspired by her. She had been very pivotal in my life, and I wanted to honor her for her bravery and strength and unbelievable faith. Poetry is an emotional release, spiritual in a way, for me. Glinda has mentored to me to get my life in order, by teaching me to rely on the inner spirit. Her knowledge of things eternal and her sharing that knowledge with me, binds me to more expression with pen and ink. Her struggle and her overcoming lead me through my life and the realization that all is possible through the Son. This poem is dedicated to her, Glinda Scott, and all the other women who have journeyed past cancer, and the lives that they have touched with their phenomenal strength.

ALLTOP, ERIN
[a.] Gainesville, FL [title] "I Am" [pers.] I've always been looking for some way to express myself. I'm not one to open up to people very often. I'm 12 years old and in the seventh grade, an average girl from Gainesville, FL. My mom sent in my poem that was originally a class assignment. I was stunned when she

gave me that envelope saying my poem was to be published. I've found that I can open up to paper better than people. I don't try to write good poetry— I just write from the heart.

ALVARADO, JOSEPH
[a.] Saginaw, MI [title] "From the Stars" [pers.] I wrote this for my daughter, Bryanna. She is the love that will blaze across the sky long after I am gone— that is what love is.

ALVAREZ, CELIA
[a.] Brooklyn, NY [title] "Joe" [pers.] My name is Celia Antonia Alvarez. I am fourteen years old. I wrote this poem for Taylorr, who was like a father to me. I love him with all my heart and soul. The reason he reminds me of the show is because it was showing before he died the day he died. Lines 17-18 mean that Joe was very childish and loved kids. Therefore, when the kids are playing in the snow, a part of Joe is in every one of them.

ALVI, RIDA
[a.] Karachi, Pakistan [title] "I Love You" [pers.] This poem is a tribute to my parents for what I am today— it is because of them. Whoever I am, however I am— it is all due to them. This is a simple and insufficient thank you to my parents from a 15-year-old daughter.

AMARAN, ARTHI
[a.] Salem, India [title] "Untitled" [pers.] "There is dissolution . . . of thoughts dissolving into words and words being sculpted by thoughts. The process continues . . . and from this emerges poetry." I owe my present to my mother and my friends who encouraged those initial stammerings for expression to grow, through life, to become meaningful expressions.

AMGAR, PATRICK
[a.] St. Laurent, QC [title] "Farewell" [pers.] This poem was created through the sheer happiness and love I had for one special person. Even apart, she inspires me.

AMIN, ANIL
[a.] Vancouver, BC [title] "Light" [pers.] I would like to dedicate this poem to my friends and family: Jamie Phillips, Anton Lim, Wilson Wong, Jonathan Fon, Grandon Gerne, Nico Ciarniello, James Wong, Peter St. James, Sharon Ko, Kate Wong, Joyce Cheng, Krista Poon, Isabel Chen, Tiffany Schneider, Vanessa Chow, Peter Chiu, Kamo Lau, Sam Chu, Steph Ng, Alex Cowan, Jeffrey Wong, Gregory Chong, Melanie Nakhla, Dominic Dobrezensky, Darren Lee, Jack Wang, Brock Clancy, Samuel Lee, Alec Merkt, Valen Ng, Darren Shun, Derek Hou, Candice Wei, Goldy Busayapong, Nunu Busayapong, Matt Carona, Kevin Chang, Mom, Dad, Bro, Shera, and most of all . . . Mr. Weibe, my creative writing teacher!

AMOLSCH, DOLORES
[a.] Westland, MI [title] "Hug Me, Daddy" [pers.] This poem I wrote, "Hug Me, Daddy" is very important to me. It was the death of my father that inspired me to write it. I am having a real hard time dealing with his passing. He was everything to me. Parents are the backbone of life, and losing one is tough. My mom is still alive and well. I hug her every chance I get but I miss hugging my dad. I hope I can at least touch one life with my poem. Hug someone today and every day if you can. Hugs are very powerful.

ANAND, MO
[a.] Farmington Hills, MI [title] "Ghost Monkey" [pers.] The poem, "Ghost Monkey," is a symbolic poem about the horrific nightmares I had as a child. Today, those nightmares are gone, but the memories remain. Most of my poetry comes from different aspects of my life. I feel that my personal experiences in life are easier to express in a poetic manner. Whether a situation is sad or happy, I feel this is the

way the world will know how I feel, and that is the most important thing to me.

ANDERSEN, LORI

[title] Farmingdale, NY [title] "Touch" [pers.] I wrote this poem at a very important transition in my life. I was having a hard time adjusting to the different situations that life handed me. As always when I'm in an uncomfortable situation or place in my life, I take out my journal and write. Writing has always been therapy for me and it enables me to express my feelings on paper, whereas I may never be able to express them in words. My dream has always been to be published in a book, and I'm thrilled that my dream has now come true.

ANDERSON, ASHLEY

[a.] Muncie, IN [title] "No Longer There" [pers.] I wrote this poem about four months before I actually decided to turn it in for the contest. I thought that my poem would never get anywhere, but as you can see, it did. So to all of you, if you have a dream of being something or accomplishing something, don't ever give up. I hope you enjoy my poem.

ANDERSON, JOAN

[a.] Woodbridge, VA [title] "Impressions of My Friend" [pers.] I was born into the multi-talented family of Kenneth and Lucille Ellis. The fourth of five children reared on a farm in Cheltenham, MD, I inherited my musical talent from Dad and my poetic talent from Mom. I have four wonderful, loving children, Debbie, Lester, Kim, and Kristi, two fine stepchildren, ten beautiful, intelligent grandchildren, and four delightful step-grandchildren. Over the years, whenever I've had problems expressing emotions. I would turn to poetry. Through poetry, I am able to express myself freely, sharing my feelings and thoughts without reservation.

ANDERSON, MATTHEW

[a.] Brooklyn, NY [title] "Hidden Meanings" [pers.] Word is as sacred as is man himself. The word is the expression of man's mind. The hidden meanings behind man have the world confused and subjected to the ideas of wicked shepherds who mislead the sheep. Minds are confused as many are led astray from themselves. There will come from the oppressed masses a deficient awakening to the reality of self. Motivation for my work stems from the need for a resurrection of the minds and spirits of Black Americans who have not recovered from the mental death of the slave experience. Our history has meaning that shall no longer be hidden.

ARANHA, ALISON

[a.] Dubai, United Arab Emirates [title] "When I was Young" [pers.] As a child, I used to sit down and write silly little poems that consisted of five or eight lines maximum. They were called "My Cat" and "My Parrot," etc. . . I can write when I am inspired. I enjoy writing stories but I haven't had a lot of time to be able to concentrate fully. "When I Was Young . . . " is a true poem, something that happened to me when I was young and something that still happens to me now, at the age of 16. As the last line of my poem says, "I now hold the key, I put an end to my misery." That is precisely what I have done. No one in my family writes, but I don't know how to thank my parents, Jerome and Dona Aranha, and my sweetheart of a brother, Alister, for their continuous support and encouragement every step of the way towards the road of success.

ARAUJO, JOY

[a.] Indianapolis, IN [title] "Whom Do I Love?" [pers.] The meaning behind this poem is very simple—when you are down, just keep thinking of the one you love. Think how great that love is and how extraordinary your heart feels. Never forget that feeling. Always think to yourself, "whom do I love?" This will

enable you to never lose sight of how great life is. When I first started writing poetry at age nine, I wrote of love. I still do because I have never forgotten the feeling. I just keep thinking, "whom do I love?"

ARCHDEACON, KRISTEN

[a] Hamilton, OH [title] "Tumor" [pers.] I feel that poetry is an exceptional way to express emotions. My poem is a depiction of how quickly and unexpectedly life can end. I feel that we should live life to its fullest. Rather than dwelling on the negative aspects in our lives, we should dwell on the positive aspects. While I haven't had the personal experience of losing a loved one to cancer, I know people that have; it devastated them. I pray to God that someday a cure will be found for cancer.

ARCHIBALD, GINA

[a.] Warner Robins, GA [title] "Heaven Just Could Not Wait" [title] "Heaven Just Could Not Wait" [pers.] This poem is an adoring tribute to my little boy, Caleb. Born with renal failure, Caleb surpassed all obstacles to enter this world and bless us with his life. Through prayers that spanned the globe, God lent us this precious baby for five months, four of which were spent in the ICU of an Atlanta hospital. This poem was written the day after he went home to be with Jesus and serves as a lasting, loving memorial to a child who touched thousands of lives, never speaking a word. My son, may God hold you close until we met again.

ARCHONDOUS, ALLYSA

[a.] Sacramento, CA [title] "Halloween" [pers.] My name is Allysa Archondous. I'm 11 years old and I wrote "Halloween" when I was nine. It sat in my bedroom for two years. Almost all of my life I've wanted to be a world famous poet and author and be a graduate of Harvard University. This is an enormous step for me, and I hope by being published, "Halloween" will show the fun and joy you can find in expressing yourself with poetry.

ARD, STEPHANIE

[a.] Slocomb, AL [title] "You Could've Been Mine" [pers.] Exploring the many social issues that are present in today's society is one of the reasons I wrote. Poetry is a wonderful outlet for expression, and I use it often. This poem explores a very controversial subject, and it is an effort on my part to relate to those who have gone through such an experience.

ARINZE, YENTEL

[a.] Flushing, NY [title] "Vacuum" [pers.] Poetry is an expression of my true, deep rooted being. I recently got married, but my husband resides in my birth country, Nigeria, and I here. I became so engulfed with emotions each time I remembered how I could not feel or touch him when I wanted. I wrote "Vacuum" to express my feelings, the anticipation for future reunions with my honey who is the utmost blessing in my life. I hope others who have the same or similar scenarios will feel the vast emotions of the human soul.

ARNETT, PAUL

[a.] Boise, ID [title] "Are You My Friend?" [pers.] I have played with poetry in my lifetime. It has now become a passion of expression where I can tell family friends and acquaintances how much I love life with all its joys and trials. I'm married to Ruth, and our union has blessed us with six great children who are now blessing us with grandchildren. I am blessed by family, friends, and life! All that I am, I owe to them but especially to Ruth (my love), Paul, Jennifer, Sarah, Joshua, Amy, and Rachel (my reason for life), and my six grandchildren who continue to amaze me.

AROTIN, JOSEPH

[a.] Brooklyn, OH [title] "Unseen, Unheard" [pers.] I wrote this poem to show just how powerful words can be, how it's possible to feel so strongly for people you've never met, just by the written word—a dedica-

tion to on-line friends everywhere. I've written poetry since I was about 12 years old, and nothing makes me happier than sharing my thoughts with my family, my friends, and anyone who is touched by my written words.

ARRINGTON, WILLIAM

[a.] Tucson, AZ [title] "How Do I Write a Letter to My Wife?" [pers.] Born and raised in Texas, I graduated from high school in Columbus, Indiana. One of my early teachers encouraged me to write poetry and songs. I am currently a student at the University of Arizona. Poetry reflects momentary images of life, which transcends generations. My poem reveals a person struggling to understand how to apologize to his wife for improper conduct during a domestic dispute. Seeking forgiveness, trouble took the long, winding road of love. This road raised a question in trying to find the right answer for proper healing. I hope this poem serves as an inspiration to others.

ASHRAF, AZAD

[a.] Tarrytown, KY [title] "Last Kiss" [pers.] I believe every person in the world expresses themselves in verse somewhere in their lives. Some people pay attention to those verses and some don't. I am glad that I got caught by someone. I would love to dedicate this poem to my parents, Ashraf and Nessa, who helped me see the world from East to West, North to South, and across Africa where I have learned and explored. I hope this poem will bring peace of mind that will travel through time. I was born in Dhaka, Bangladesh, educated in Dhaka, UK, and the USA, and I am currently residing in New York.

ASRIYAN, NARINE

[a.] Parma Heights, OH [title] "Careless Driving" [pers.] I always loved to write; even as a child, my favorite hobbies were reading and writing. I wrote many poems before and after "Careless Driving." The day I wrote this particular poem, I was feeling tied up with all the negative forces of life. I wanted to go out and not have any responsibilities to worry about. "Careless Driving" is about having freedom and feeling good about life. It is very emotional, but at the end there is a little humor that shows what I felt at that time. I hope you enjoy my poem and I wish you the best in life.

ATHERTON, GREGORY

[a.] Woodland Hills, CA [title] "A Daughter's Return" [pers.] As a divorced father, I left home when Allison was only one. The courts allowed visitation, and I didn't miss one in ten years. Somewhere along the way, for whatever reason, we grew apart. At age eleven, she didn't want to see me. I almost lost her. I was left alone and saddened to the core of my hear, for five long years. I have little faith in our courts. As she matured, slowly, but surely, her heart returned. Hence, the poem "A Daughter's Return" was born to express the love and pride that this writer feels for his daughter.

AULDS, RHONDA

[a.] Farmerville, LA [title] "Like an Ocean" [pers.] Women experience many changes, struggles, and challenges, and with them all come many emotions. However, through them all we become stronger and wiser and have so much more to give, so many hidden treasures of the heart. I compare our beauty with that of an ocean.

AUTEN, BEVERLY

[a.] Tulsa, OK [title] "Reflection" [pers.] Writing has always been a release for me, an escape from everything that requires attention. I'm very honored and grateful to be acknowledged in this publication. It's more than enough thanks to know others relate to thoughts that are so personal.

AVITTATHOOR, SUBBARAMAN

[a.] Kuwait [title] "Stages of Human Life" [pers.] This poem is an Ode to Almighty, my grandparents,

parents, in-laws, teachers, relatives, friends, our son, and equally to my wife, all of whom have extended their support to me from time to time to reach this stage. If human life can be accepted as light of vein which is eternal, then can we consider this poem as a tune to our life because of its truthfulness?

AXTELL, SANDRA
[a.] Palmer, AK [title] "Circles" [pers.] "Circles" was inspired by climatic waves of devastation inflicted upon this magnificent planet called Earth. Through varying degrees, mankind debased his charge, undermining its fragile balance. The egregious affront distressing essential global attributes, spawned circles of destruction. I have been married to Bruce Axtell for thirty-one years, and have been living in Alaska two-and-a-half decades, inspired by both entities. An obsequious love of poetry unremittingly enlightens that deeper part of me through reading and writing many faceted varieties of verse. Deep within the abyss of writers, mirrors inspired creativity called artistic bent. Protecting that fragile font, it flows as a river, satisfying their thirsty souls.

AYLWARD, BETH
[a.] Dickens, NE [title] "Love" [pers.] I live in a small Nebraska town as the adopted only child of Mike and Julie. Since I first learned to piece together sentences, writing has been an escape for me. Poetry is my favorite way to get my thoughts out onto paper and is extremely therapeutic.

BACAJOL, VALERIA
[a.] Island Lake, IL [title] "Get Scared" [pers.] In my eyes, everyone is a poet. Most people find it difficult to put a poem together because they think they can't do it. All you really have to do is write down your feelings, even if they doesn't rhyme. Poetry is life that is written down. It's something that comes from the heart. The poem I wrote, "Get Scared," was written for a reason. All my friends told me that I was now a different person, that I wasn't Val anymore. Poetry is how I let all my emotions out without crying or fighting.

BAECHLER, GRAHAM
[a.] Ayr, Ontario [title] "Wrinkles" [pers.] The poem, "Wrinkles," is a simple example of expression in an alternate communicative form. Poetry has allowed me as a person and as a young writer to express and legitimize different ideas and personal passions.

BAILEY, RITA
[a.] Spencer, IN [title] "Dreams" [pers.] I wrote this poem many years ago and have written poetry for many years. I love to write about my family as they are such great friends, and my friends that are like family to me. In poetry I can see and write about all the wonders of this great world God has created for all of us.

BAILEY, SAMANTHA
[a.] Brook, IN [title] "The Rose" [pers.] While growing up, I was teased as a child. Throughout this "traumatic" time, my parents, Douglas and Brenda Bailey, taught me that true beauty is held within. It is because of my loving and wonderful parents that I have the outlook on life I do today. The publication of this poem couldn't have been possible without the encouragement of my parents and brother, Joshua Bailey, as well as my fiance, Nicholas Snodgrass, and my seventh grade English teacher, Mrs. Carey. I thank you all for your words of encouragement.

BAILLIO, NATALIE
[a.] Rio Rancho, NM [title] "Beautiful Butterfly" [pers.] My name is Ashley Baillio. I am 16 years old. I'm a sophomore at Moriarty High School which is in New Mexico. I love animals. I have seven horses and a fish. I spend most of my time being a teenager and just living life. I'm a huge softball fan. Right now, I'm playing first base for my school (Go Pintos!) Fame and fortune are two major goals in life. I guess

you could say I'm like any other kid at my age. I wrote this poem for one of my classes for extra credit. My mom saw my poem and sent it in, and that's where my life is currently at right now.

BALDO, CLYDE
[a.] New York, NY [title] "Random Waters" [pers.] This poem is about the magnificence of being moved and affected by a beautiful special soul. It is a privilege to vigilantly love someone and to let them know how much they touch you. My gratitude and appreciation are limitless. My amazement is that one day she appeared, and the day before I hadn't known her. I thank her for sharing herself with me. Thank you, Carey, for your sweetness, your passion, your wackiness, your courage, and your infinite beauty!

BALL, CLIFF
[a.] Canyon, TX [title] "Wind" [pers.] This poem was inspired when we had a day in the Texas Panhandle when there were 65 mph winds, and I figured, why not write this poem? I don't normally like writing poetry. I usually write science fiction. I've had one short story published in a religious magazine ten years ago after taking creative writing in high school and won third in the nation for it. My hope is that I become a successful author.

BANGHART, ARTIS
[a.] Windsor, CO [title] "The Coming One" [pers.] This poem is a treasure to me because it came to me during a time of prayer. It is an expression of my expectation.

BARNES, GWENDA
[a.] Nevada, TX [title] "Friends Are Like Flowers" [pers.] I am a forty-two-year-old single mother. I love music, dancing, singing, and reading. I am a nurse by profession. I live with my 16-year-old son. I have always loved making songs and poetry and hope that I can continue to write, for it is a reflection of our sons.

BARNES, JENNIFER
[a.] Norfolk, United Kingdom [title] "Memories" [pers.] I am 19 years old and have two brothers, Jonathan and Matthew, and two sisters, Sarah and Emma. My parents names are Geoffrey and Christine. I think that all poetry is very special. When I write poetry, I don't think it, I feel it, it's like a silent voice. Poetry can be very emotional, and there is so much we can learn from it. I am really proud and lucky that my poem got published, so that I have the opportunity to share it with others.

BARNETT, DAVID
[a.] Wantima, Australia [title] "Other Things . . . " [pers.] Writing has been such an integral part of my life. I could never imagine not ever doing it. I have been composing poetry and music for so many years that it almost becomes second nature. I truly believe it is a special gift that should be shared with the whole world and not kept hidden away . It is still, after all this time, a constant source of amazement to me.

BARNOW, TARA
[a.] Columbus, KS [title] "Grandpa's Battle" [pers.] I wrote this poem when my grandfather's cancer came back. At Christmas I was surprised how ill he was, yet the enjoyment of the holidays was shown on his face. I was glad to see his mind off of the situation, but sad to think what would happen if the experimental treatments didn't work. My grandfather has given me an appreciation for life that I wouldn't have learned if it weren't for this disease and his fight. I am grateful for what my grandfather has taught me throughout his lifetime. I am hopeful that his health will continue to improve.

BARRETT, JOSEPH
[a.] Solana Beach, CA [title] "Anne, Will, Out . . . " [pers.] This poem is dedicated to the memory of my grandma, who after a long battle with an unknown disease, decided to explore the other side. I hope you have found peace.

BARTH, ALBRECHT
[a.] Bonn, Germany [title] "New Land" [pers.] In my opinion, poetry is an art that can give answers to important questions in life, which no scientist can provide. Of course, it may also face people with new questions. My poem tells about the mixed emotions of a man searching for meanings. He looks for a new land but feels that he can only find it inside himself. I lived in different countries, but I met no one who had an answer for everybody. At present, I am studying Spanish literature. I think that possible answers to life's mysteries can often be found between the lines.

BARTLETT, MARJORIE
[a.] Holly Hill, FL [title] "It Hurts Too Much to Remember and It Hurts Too Much to Forget" [pers.] In looking back and to the future, I have remembered fragments of sadness, regret, joy, love, and hope as expressed in this, my original poem.

BASHKIN, JAMES
[a.] St. Louis, MO [title] "The Encounter" [pers.] I wrote this poem to my dad when I was 15 years old, in response to an argument about my long hair. I am a scientist, and write technical material on a regular basis, but rarely, though increasingly, try creative writing. I dedicate this to Stanley Bashkin.

BATCHELOR, JOSHUA
[a.] Kittery, ME [title] "Dear God" [pers.] All of the gifts and talents we have are gifts from God. I have found that the best way to thank someone for a gift is to use to the best of my ability. Without God, we would not exist, much less have the talents He has given us. I hope this poem touches you the way that it touched me when I wrote it. God Bless you all.

BEARD, JACQUELINE
[a.] Burke, VA [title] "To Say" [pers.] My poem, "To Say," was written especially for my dad. He is a great inspiration to me and always supports me. When I write poetry I feel like I am in my own world, a world parallel to ours, a magical place.

BEARDEN, STEPHEN
[a.] Kent, WA [title] "Wedding Day" [pers.] My gift of the written word is credited to the Lord. It has been the best way to express my feelings. I dedicate "Wedding Day" to my wonderful wife. Without her support and true love, I would never have the inspiration to follow my dreams. Though we were married in Nevada, and the snow did not fall, this poem still was true to my heart. During our exchange of vows, I could see every word in her eyes. Thank you Jeannette, and I will continue the pursuit of acting writing, and singing. I love you. Also, thank you to my mother for her support as well. Mom, I did it!

BECK, STEPHANIE
[a.] Conroe, TX [title] "The Daddy I Loved But Never New" [pers.] This poem is special to me because it's about my father. I have been writing poetry since I was eight years old. Now I am 16 and still writing. My father's death hurt me deeply and reunited me with my family on his side. Four years later, my very good friend, Justin Dvorak, died. As much as love, happiness, and joy affect a writer, death and sadness do as well. Shine on, you crazy diamond. I'm in high school at Oakridge High in Conroe, TX, working at a grocery store at present, and I hope to be a poet and also to write short stories.

BEENE, JAMIE
[a.] Mantachie, MS [title] "Friends" [pers.] I dedicate this poem to Courtney Jade Emmous, Kayla Pasey, Shay Turner, Persha Thomas, Cortnei Franks, Sam Mears, Mary Durham, Mr. Jamie Dill, and Ronnie Gholston. I thought of my friends and how much we fight and then the way we love. My mom, Sheila, told me how well I write, and I decided to write poems. I wrote twenty-seven poems that have not been pub-

lished. I hope on publishing more poems one day. I hope that I publish books also. Maybe I'll get a lucky streak and begin a series! Thanks to Eric Hutcheson!

BEHRAVESH, ASHLEIGH
[a.] Millbrae, CA [title] "My Love" [pers.] This poem symbolizes my best work. One person inspired me to write this poem. He knows who he is. Anyway, I am fourteen and live in Millbrae, California. I attend Burlingame Intermediate School. When I first entered this contest, I thought it was just for fun. I was overjoyed when I got the letter saying that they had chosen my poem to be published. This poem is about love between two people. My advice to anyone is that if you really love someone, try to hang on to him or her. I'd like to say hi to all my friends—they mean a lot to me and help me through hard times. Laurie, Jon, Allie, Izzy, and to all my other friends, I love you all!

DELLAMY, HOPE
[a.] Port Hadock, WA [title] "Heartbreak" [pers.] My poetry and art is all about relationships. We are defined and remembered by how we affect others, good or bad. We also remember others by how we are treated, and most of my poems speak of my reflection on the dynamics of my own personal relationships. As an artist, after this union was dissolved rudely, I felt as if someone dumped brush cleaner on my newly painted canvas. In the end, I learned that although a canvas is smeared, it is free to be worked into the real masterpiece; mistakes are life's genuine second chances.

BELTZ, ROGER
[a.] Niles, OH [title] "The Final Journey" [pers.]. A native of Ohio, I graduated from the Pennsylvania State University with a Masters of Clinical Health Educational. This poem commemorates someone very important in my life—my father. His strength and courage have been inspirational to me, and this poem is my way of remembering him and expressing my love for the way he lived his life. As a health-care professional and college instructor, I recognize the therapeutic benefits of writing poetry. I have used poetry as a form of alternative medicine and I strongly believe poetry can argument many standard health treatments. Roger has been listed in the *Outstanding Men of America* Journals for his Wellness Promotion and Community Service.

BEST, MELANIE
[a.] Highland, NY [title] "Together Forever" [pers.] My name is Melanie Best. I am 14 years old and I live in New York. I have been writing poems for about two years now and I love writing them. I even wrote one for my father when he passed away that my mother read to everyone at church. Poems express the way I feel—some are happy and some are sad. They say a song can tell you how a person feels—well a poem can go deeper into your feelings and show the emotions within.

BEYER, AMANDA
[a.] La Center, WA [title] "With Love" [pers.] I wrote this poem for no reason except to tell my best friend, Stephanie, how much she means to me. She's always been there, believing me when I didn't believe in myself—that has touched me more than anything. I truly cherish her friendship and love. This poem may be brief but it still holds a lot of sentimental value. I'd just like to thank Steph for all the inspiration. I love you, Girlie!

BICKNELL, GAIL
[a.] Charleston, NH [title] "A New Beginning" [pers.] Writing poetry has always been a wonderful outlet for me. This particular poem reflects on my surviving some difficult times. I will be eternally grateful for all my supportive friends and family members, particularly my children, Deborah and David, who have always believed in me and been the "wind beneath my wings." Thank you for paving the way for me to reach out for help. A special thank you to the "stranger" who

came into my life, opening doors I never knew existed. You truly are a Sir Galahad and were instrumental in giving me the gift of "a new beginning."

BIESINGER, BRENDA
[a.] Londesborough, ON [title] "Challenge" [pers.] My life is based on my family. They are my inspiration of every challenge that we face each and every day. The happiness and sorrows that we have faced together only bring us closer together. My happiness comes from their success in life.

BINSTEAD, JOHANNA
[a.] Kelowna, BC [title] "This Something Special" [pers.] I am a single mom of two beautiful girls, fifteen and five. This poem was written at a time when my oldest and I had to be apart for awhile. It's an expression of feelings from a mother, her overwhelming love for her daughter, and the love she knows the daughter has for her. I write my poetry based on my feelings and my emotions at the time. My oldest daughter is very special to me even if she doesn't think so. She is a typical teen, very stubborn and with closed ears, so I have expressed my feelings with pen and paper.

BIRCH, SAMANTHA
[a.] Bay City, MI [title] "Friendship" [pers.] Samantha Birch was born on January 27th 1989, in Bay City, Michigan. I live with my mother and I have one older brother and one younger sister. I have a cat at my mother's house. I attend Thomas Lincoln Handy Middle School and I'm in the sixth grade with advanced math and language arts. I enjoy basketball, rollerblading, skateboarding, soccer, and gymnastics. I also enjoy listening to music, writing poetry, and shopping at the mall. In my free time I like to go to my grandparents house and I also like to go on the Internet.

BIRDSONG, MELISSA
[a.] Vicksburg, MS [title] "My Sunshine" [pers.] Poetry, in any form, has become a very special part of my life. I enjoy writing what is in my heart. Also, I enjoy directing myself to different places internally so that I can pull from many different views and moods. This poem will always be special to me, as it is my first poem. My inspiration? My best friend and soul mate, the love of my life. He truly is my sunshine.

BIRK, JAIME
[a.] Oceanside, NY [title] "Good-Bye" [pers.] My poem, "Good-Bye," is a poem written in memory of my aunt. She lives on only in my heart and memory, and my poems are my way of keeping her alive. I write most of my poems about her because she was very special to me. It is not fair that she had to die; it is not fair that anyone has to die. This poem is my way of expressing my innermost feelings. It is my way of holding on to the bond we shared and it is my way of telling my aunt, "good-bye."

BIRKHOLZ, MAXWELL, JR.
[a.] New Rockford, ND [title] "Why?" [pers.] This poem is my first honest try of writing; it seemed to come so easily to me because this poem expresses my true feelings, mostly pertaining to my somewhat inability to find that one "special person" to share my life with. Even with lots of friends, there is still an empty spot in my heart, and that is what this poem is about.

BISHOP, JACKIE
[a.] Potsdam, NY [title] "Untitled" [pers.] I have written and published other poems under my maiden name Jackie Smith. I have been married to my wonderful husband for two years now. I hope to have my B.A. in Psychology by next December and then go on to graduate school and a family. I love writing. Without it, my soul feels dead. I am currently writing a book and cannot wait to help people and be a soccer mom. That is living poetry.

BIVINS, SUE
[a.] Baltimore, MD [title] "The Lady of the Rainbow Light" [pers.] Family and friends encouraged me to write after I had a mild stroke and stress moods. I love to read poetry and children's books. I have improved in motor skills and stress control. I am retired. In Baltimore schools and libraries, I share my poetry as a mentor.

BLACK, JAMESE
[a.] Winston Salem, NC [title] "Her Dad's Dream" [pers.] Thank you, Daddy, for being my number one man. This is for Rev. James Robert Morris, (1933)-1998).

BLAIR, DENISE
[a.] Keizer, OR [title] "Midnight Prayer" [pers.] I believe family is the most important aspect in life. Through the good and the bad, they will always be there. This is for the two most important people in my life, my daughters, Nakeea and Nicole, without whom my life would be empty. Mommy loves you!

BLAIR, SHIRLEY CAROLYN
[a.] Scottsdale, AZ [title] "Me" [pers.] I live in Scottsdale, AZ. I have two daughters, Pamela and Terri, who are very dear to me. My father, Hayes, is deceased. My mother's name is Opal. I have five sisters and eight grandchildren. This poem came to me from within at a period in my life when I was interested in learning the meaning of life and its origin. Also, I am interested in music and art and am into drawing and painting. Poetry is important to me, and someday I would like to write a book. Thank you for selecting my poem for your book.

BLANCO, CHRISTINE
[a.] Bellflower, CA [title] "Mesmerized" [pers.] Poetry is a way I am able to express myself. Without it, I am unknown to the world. Language in art form gives a sense of structure to the world of communication. Art gives the world a more complex yet beautiful meaning to life. Beauty influences leading emotions. Emotions are the true sense of what it is to be human.

BLANDON, KENNETH
[a.] Miami, FL [title] "Jesus" [pers.] Rather odd how I was inspired to write this poem. I was watching a video on paintings and noticed most of them had Jesus at his crucifixion. I began to write on paper as though I were speaking to the Son of God himself. "Jesus" is the first complete poem I wrote and submitted, never thinking it would get published. The only flaw I find with poetry itself is that only a fraction of what you are really feeling can be expressed. I wish to thank the One from above for this gift, Jesus for being my savior, and Poetry.com for allowing my piece of expression to be shared with many wonderful people out there.

BLAYLOCK, MICHAEL
[a.] Cincinnati, OH [title] "Reality of Luck" [pers.] My poetry is a direct reflection of my instilled values, values which have come from family, friends, and even strangers, for all have been my teachers at one time of another, as I have been a teacher to others. My philosophical attitude is the result of lessons learned and earned throughout my lifetime. I share my truly wonderful life with my wife, Debi. Together we've had twenty-one plus joyous years of learning and loving. She has been my inspiration for many poems. My closing thought for you is, love your life, it may be the only one you get.

BLEVINS, KANDIE
[a.] Brandenbury, KY [title] "Sobriety" [pers.] This poem was written in celebration of my husbands first AA birthday. It comes from the heart of a spouse who has seen the triumph of "successful recovery" through active participation in a 12-step program.

BLEVINS, SHANNON
[a.] Rosemont, WV [title] "Time to Pray" [pers.] This poem is my personal testimony of surrendering to Jesus Christ, the one who came to Earth to die on a cross for my sins, that I may have life everlasting, not only for me but everyone who believes upon the name Jesus. My poem portrays my Heavenly Father knowing me and living me enough to be patient with me. I encourage all who read my poem to come to know Jesus and love as he has and still does, love us. My hope is that when my poems are read, they uplift, encourage, and even bring smiles. The poems I write are from my heart. I hope you enjoy them.

BOGATITUS, KEVIN
[a.] Schererville, IN [title] "Free Fall" [pers.] Poetry is one of the purest forms of expression and a way of sharing my experiences with the world. This piece was inspired by a beautiful girl who recently stole my heart and it captures a moment in time when I found myself welcoming the changes she brought on within me. I realized I was falling in love, and this is my way of returning to her a portion of the beauty she beings me. I hope others can relate to this poem and share some of her beauty. I love you, Heather!

BOLES, KENNETH
[a.] Winston Salem, NC [pers.] The story of Hannah is true. Yes, even the bugs on the wall. I met him at a nursing home while doing some volunteer work. I am always amazed at the aged who manage to keep their quiet dignity while their bodies slowly fail them. Hannah was alone with only a sister several states away. Blind for at least forty years, he showed no self-pity or bitterness. When he awoke in the hospital, his friend had been arrested. Having cleared his friend, he had no idea who shot him. No one was ever brought to trial. The guilty never paid. Or did they? . . .

BOLTZ, MAGGIE
[a.] Columbus, OH [title] "Desire" [pers.] I am the sister of Eugene C. Mays who also has a poem in this volume. He has authored many chop books over the years. I have one called "Presents of Mind."

BONADIO, EDWARD
[a.] Gilbert, AR [title] "Voices" [pers.] The poem, "Voices," was written to coincide with a book that I published. "Voices" is a story about good and evil in this world and its effect on man.

BOOKER, BETTY
[a.] Southmayd, TX [title] "Molly" [pers.] This poem is about the loss of our dog, Molly, whom we considered one of our children. Her death hit me hard, and writing this poem helped me to say good-bye. I had not written anything since high school. I thank Mrs. Martin, my English teacher, for the inspiration she gave me and for caring. My husband and I have been married for nearly sixteen years. Our children are grown and have families of their own.

BORDE, BETTY
[a.] Arlington, TX [title] "Loving You" [pers.] This poem was written by my now deceased husband. It was his way of asking me to marry him. We married in May 16, 1981. He passed away October 10, 1998 at the age of 49. He was a very poetic and compassionate man. He wrote other poems throughout our marriage; it was his way of expressing his love for me.

BOURGEOIS, JAIME
[a.] Shannock, RI [title] "Just Like Me" [pers.] I like to capture the feeling of a moment in my poetry in a way that is easily understood. I believe that's what makes a good poem. I think that if a reader can relate to something I have written then I have accomplished something great. That is not to say that I am great though. It's not words that makes me great; it's the actions that support them. This poem showed a time when I felt alone, a feeling I know many share. I hope

that it does not depress anyone because I'm doing very well. You too can get through your hard times.

BOYD, AFTON
[a.] Stafford, VA [title] "Not the Same" [pers.] I write poetry a lot. I love music, and whenever I write a poem, I'm tapping a beat inside my head. I wrote this poem when someone influential in my life hurt me. It shows, I think, that when you free a bird, it doesn't always come back. No matter how early in your life, you can still feel love and pain. I hope this poem means something to anyone who reads it.

BOYD, SHARI
[a.] Thornile WA, Australia [title] "Time to Come" [pers.] "Time to Come" was written over 10 years ago after the loss of a relative. I'm elated it is to be published in "Stepping Stones." I dedicated this poem to my mom—she has been there for me all my life. I love her dearly. Mom, this is for you. Love, Shari.

BOYLES, WINIFRED
[a.] Las Vegas, NV [title] "A Place to Live—A Place to Love" [pers.] This poem is dedicated to my father, Winifeld Hungerford. Everyone loved him. He inspired me to write because he was such a wonderful man, caring and helping others and having a good sense of humor.

BOZURICH, DANIEL
[a.] Harper's Ferry, WV [title] "God's Garden" [pers.] This is a poem about my grandma. My grandma was an inspiration to me. She always told me to do the right thing, make something of yourself. Well, Grandma, I did. I used your life to help my life. I will never forget her. She wasn't just my grandma—she was my best friend. If you have someone special in your life, this is your poem.

BRAAKSMA, ERIC
[a] Lelystad, Netherlands [title] "Capital Fear" [pers.] Eric Braaksma is the pseudonym for Erick Brauksman, a 35-year-old Dutch citizen. Although not his native tongue, he prefers writing poetry and prose in English. His interest in English language and literature has always been vast. His favorite authors include Robert Howard, Auden, Dylan Thomas, Tolkien, and Milne. Erick works as an IT professional and enjoys his moments off with his wife, Anna, and their six-month-old son, Jan. When writing, the experience is like painting with words, attempting to reach out with not just story line, but the undescribable feeling triggered by the magic of poetry . . . and some prose.

BRAY, CARRIE
[a.] West Lafayette, IN [title] "What I Know" [pers.] We spend our whole lives learning and striving to achieve our goals. After 19 years of learning, working, and experiencing the world around me, the only thing that I know is for my faith to share "What I Know" with you.

BRILL, ROBERT, III
[a] Luray, VA [title] "Walk of Life" [pers.] I live in a small town located in Virginia called Luray. The death of my father in 1998 to colon cancer inspired this poem. I hope others who have lost loved ones have spent as much time with them as possible. My father and I were very close, and he will always hold a special place in my heart.

BRINSON, ALBERT JR.
[a.] Alto, GA [title] "My Heartbeat Finally Came" [pers.] I think poetry is a way of expressing yourself above and beyond the norm. You can express yourself in such away that only the few can understand. Poetry is a big part of my pagan upbringing and religion. There are no limits to poetry. You can write about what ever inspires you. True poetry comes from within. I think poetry is made from three elements—heart, inspiration, and desire. I believe people who

write poetry see the world and life differently than people who don't.

BROOKS, SHANNON
[a.] Liverpool, NY [title] "Shackles to Wings" [pers.] Poetry is a sacred means of expression, whether you're expressing love, hurt, or hate, poetry can help us deal with and freely relinquish our emotions. Some of my most popular poems are "The Day the Sun Stopped Shining" (the dedication to the loss of a love) and also a song that I wrote, entitled "When Rose Petals Fall" (a ballad of hurt and rejection). My biggest inspiration as a poet and songwriter always and forever will be Melissa Etheridge. I believe our goal as poets is to touch the hearts, lives, and emotions of all who dare to dream.

BROWN, ALBERT
[a.] Rexburg, ID [title] "Little Joe" [pers.] I write about everything, but I prefer to write from heartfelt feelings and true experiences. I started writing in 1996 because a grandson, Dillon Finn, aspiring to be a singer, inspired me to write. He is now thirteen years old and pursuing his dream. "Little Joe" is a true story of the youngest son of my elder brother. Joseph's father a special man died before Joseph understood how special he was and at the time when Joseph needed him most. The poem is an accurate account of Joseph after his father's death until and including his own untimely death.

BROWN, EUGENE
[a.] Philadelphia, PA [title] "Raindrops of Love" [pers.] I wrote rain drops of love on Valentine's Day. I was thinking how lucky and blessed I was to be alive, the special support I had in my life from my wife, Linda, and my mother and father, Corrine and Eugene Brown Sr., and how I battled back from a brain injury.

BROWN, KATIE
[a.] Lincoln Park, MI [title] "Forgiving [pers.] I feel this poem really described what my best friend and I went through last year. It was a rough time because some certain "obstacles" were in our way. But we always managed to overcome them. Together, I think we can get through anything. I love you, LRM. I feel poems express how I feel. I'm not good at speaking my feelings, so writing them in verse gives me more freedom and expression.

BROWN, KIMBERLY
[a.] Oak Harbor, WA [title] "A World of Confusion" [pers.] I am a 29-year-old mother of two, suffering from panic attacks, depression, and constant pain. Writing has played an important role in my life as I struggle through everyday life. It is my way of expressing my thoughts, feelings, and over all, a view of my life.

BROWNLEE, DANTE
[a.] Philadelphia, PA [title] "Grandmom" [pers.] This poem means a lot to me. It was especially written for my grandmother, Mary Wilson. She took care of me mostly all of my life. I never can thank her enough for that so this is one of my ways of saying thank you. To me, poetry is a gift that everyone has. You just have to know how to use it.

BROWNLEE, SARA
[a.] Roebuck, SC [title] "My Special Children" [pers.] I am an independent living skills instructor for the S.C. School for the Deaf and Blind. I am in my 29th year, working directly with the blind. My student holds a very special place in my heart. To me, they are "Poetry in Motion." My personal commitment to my students—to give love, provide adaptations, be patient, forever supporting each one in their journey to their independence. I am a mother of two sons, and the grandmother of twin grandson. My hobbies are floral arranging, writing, bowling, dancing, and helping others.

BRUCKER, KATHY
[a.] Toledo, OH [title] "He's Gone" [pers.] My poetry is an expression of my joys, fears, and heartaches. By writing, I am able to share my emotions with others who may also be experiencing the same feelings. Putting words on paper is a need to possibly help someone else. It is my legacy to my loved ones.

BRUCKSCHEN, CHRISTI LYN
[a.] Manitowoc, WI [title] "Crashing Waves" [pers.] Christi lives in rural Wisconsin with her parents, Mark and Deb, and her two sisters, Lisa and Stephanie. Writing is one of Christi's talents, accompanied by her musical and athletic abilities. Christi sings in her church choir and plays the violin and piano. She also enjoys volleyball and soft ball. In her spare time, she enjoys traveling, shopping, eating out, reading, spending some time on the computer, playing with her Sheltie (Mindy), and just being a pre-teen.

BUCKMAN, ANGELA
[a.] Lemon Grove, CA [pers.] This poem means a lot to me, and I hope it means a lot to other people out there. It's about finding out who you are and what is really important to you. We must reveal our true selves to be completely happy. Sometimes we give this advice but we don't give it to the most important person—ourselves.

BUDNICK, GINGER
[a.] Manchester, MO [title] "To the Garden" [pers.] I look forward to sharing more of what life has to offer with those that are special to me and touch my heart. For those that know me, this is only the beginning of my own book, *Reading from a Heart, Learning from a Soul.*

BURHUS, MARIA
[a.] Central City, NE [title] "Life" [pers.] I chose to write this poem because I feel life is the most important thing in life. If others say that other things are more important, how can that be? I say if there were not life, then that more important thing would not be there! I dedicate my poem to my mom, Glenda Burhus, and Mike Abernathy because what they taught me I still remember!

BURNS, ANDREA
[a.] York, SC [title] "Dark Angel" [pers.] For me, poetry is a very special way of releasing my true inner feelings. Nearly all of the verses I set down with love both everlasting and unrequited. They reveal the very personal side of my heart and are a direct window into my soul . Interpretation, however, is left solely to the reader and their imagination. I believe that the understanding of poetry has a direct connection with the life experiences of those who view it.

BURROUGHS, OLLIE
[a.] Oklahoma City, OK [title] "I've Seen" [pers.] After two tours in Vietnam with the Navy, and about sixteen years on the police dept. I was working the late shift, thinking about my life and wrote this poem.

BUTLER, BRANDON
[a.] Littleton, CO [title] "Imprisoned" [pers.] I wrote this poem while staring through the bars of a Colorado State Prison. I was amazed at how most inmates had no remorse or even cared that they were incarcerated. This is what inspired me to write "Imprisoned." I have put forth the best of my abilities to change my life and I am attending college now to become a youth counselor. Maybe I can keep just one kid from being on the wrong side of the fence. I thank the Lord for his help in my change.

BUTTS, FAITH
[a.] Brown Mills, NJ [title] "I Am Woman" [pers.] I love to write poems, especially when I am inspired.

Every poem I write is special. The inspiration for this poem was from a friend. My friend is a strong woman whom I admire. I felt a poem about her would be the perfect way to express my admiration.

BYCZYNSKI, ROBERT
[a.] Houston, TX [title] "Summer Storm" [pers.] It is sometimes a total surprise to me, in my reaction to what my mind has accomplished, in reviewing this creative poetry. It is similar, I expect, to an out-of-body experience, as if part of my mind and body transferred to the paper by osmosis! Although in no way is there an attempt to equate myself to the great creative inventors, one cannot help but wonder if Galileo with his first look through his telescope, or the Wright brothers with first flight were all subjected to the same exhilaration over their accomplishments. Did the caveman in his observation of the heavens, also become awestruck by nature's fury? I expect he did! I was educated at Kelly High School in Chicago, IL. I have been a technical instructor at USAF for 40 of years Computer Maintenance. My hobbies include camping, fishing, astronomy oil painting, gardening, etc. . . . But instead of my being part of all of these, creative poetry displays "part of me!"

BYRD, NICHOLAUS
[a.] Kent, WA [title] "Experience" [pers.] In my life I have experienced many situations which have opened my eyes to what it means to be Nic Byrd. I wrote this poem originally as an assignment for my English teacher/hippie, Tom Brush. I dedicate this poem to all the people in my life who constantly challenged me to be different and unique. I hope this poem can open other people's minds to themselves, digging deep beyond logic and reason and into their own feelings and personalities. I end my statement with a dedication to Jimi Hendrix, Brad Nowell, John Lennon, Bob Marley, Tom Braon, Kim McClung, Dick Johnson, Kathy Swain (Mom), and myself, as I have finally found all I ever wanted, almost.

CAGG, BRETT
[a.] Saint Joseph, MO [title] "Choose" [pers.] My name is Brett Allen Cagg. I'm 14. This was my first work of poetry. I now have ten poems. I started writing poetry in March 2001. The person who has helped me most is my uncle, Richard Cagg. I hope to keep on writing poetry for years to come; this is my best poem so far. I hope you enjoy it. This is the first poem that came from lessons I have learned and experienced. This has been a great experience and this is not the end of where I want to go. Watch for me.

CAGLE, WILLIAM
[a.] Niles, MI [title] "Where Am I?" [pers.] Have you ever had a conflict within yourself? A conflict that, no matter how hard you try, you can't settle? Just when you think you have it figured out, you realize you don't. You wonder how you got there. You wonder what the outcome will be. It's something that you think about so much it all most drives you crazy. You try and try and try to figure it out, but still it is left unresolved. It just goes around in your head like a merry-go-round and all you want is for the ride to be over.

CAIN, KATHLENE
[a.] Matherville, IL [title] "Lonely" [pers.] After years of drug and alcohol abuse and making all the wrong choices, I finally hit rock bottom and did the unthinkable. I am now serving a three-year-sentence in a State Prison. This poem, along with several others, was written while I was waiting to be transferred. Since I have been here, I have been working very hard to change my life, and when the end of my time here comes to an end, despite my past, I know I can make it.

CALDERON, KRYSTAL
[a.] Dallas, TX [title] "From Where You Stand" [pers.] I am very proud to have my poem in a book. I am 14 and live in Dallas, TX. This poem is special to me because it is my very first poem that has accomplished anything. I would like to say hi my family, Ben, Gina, Benji, Benjamin, and Furnelius.

CALI, MICHAEL
[a.] Barre, MA [title] "Silence Embrace?" [pers.] Being a young writer, my experience is limited. I wrote this poem about a girl I met and fell in love with. I always treated her like a goddess and never got anything in return. When she broke up with me, we didn't speak to each other for two months. That's what is about—silence used as a powerful weapon. Love is a strength and mischievous emotion. Nobody can prepare for it, but you can learn how to control it when necessary.

CALLAN, COSPER
[a.] Anthony, NM [title] "Close to You" [pers.] Well, I'm 15 years old, and I kind of picked up poetry when I learned to play the guitar. This poem, "Close to You," was written about my girlfriend of a year-and-a-half. I guess I just wanted her to know how much I care.

CAMPANIONI, OMAR
[a.] Oakland, CA [title] "Self-Image" [pers.] This poem was part of my fifth grade class assignment. Originally I thought writing poetry was not my thing, until my mom, Christina, grandmother, Carmen, sister, Christina, and my uncle, John, helped me get started. Now I really like writing. I would encourage other kids my age to write poetry for the fun of it. Thanks to my family for their patience and to my teacher, Mrs. Jill Reese of Kaiser Middle School for encouraging and believing in me. Thanks, Mrs. Reese, for introducing us to poetry.

CANCLINI, MORGAN
[a.] Arlington, TX [title] "Almost Like Nod" [pers.] "Writing Poetry!" I exclaimed while sitting in my fourth period English class. I did not want to do this seemingly boring assignment. While riding home from school, I was complaining about it to my mom when the most beautiful instrumental song came on the radio. I knew I had to write a poem about it so others would be emotionally moved, just as I had. My feelings easily flowed onto the page, and I realized then poetry was my passion. I am grateful for this opportunity to share my passion with others and I can only hope you will pass on "this happiness that I've found" to the world.

CANNATTA, LORRAINE
[a.] East Haddam, CT [title] "Moments Anew" [pers.] I have been writing poetry since age 11. This poem is about the mystery of parenting. I wrote this poem when my 22-year-old son went to volunteer in an orphanage in Guatemala. I left my job in the medical field and found myself in a career search and in the empty nest. I never had the courage to show anyone my poetry, till now. Once I took the risk to leave a secure career, I found myself writing daily. I have spent the last year of my forties writing stories and poetry. I am so honored to have my poetry acknowledged. Thank you for this wonderful affirmation.

CANNON, CORY
[a.] Willis, TX [title] "Only One Man" [pers.] I am a fourteen-year-old Christian Homeschooler and I live in the small country town of Willis, Texas. I am a part of a family of seven, and we live on a seventeen-acre farm. I am the second oldest in my family and I believe that each one of my family members possess a certain talent passed down to them by our many ancestors. I believe that my poetic skills were passed down to my father's father and I feel the poetry is a great way to express myself. I mainly write poetry to make a point or to show something, and my poem "Only One Man" was written to show the almighty divinity of Jesus Christ.

CANU, KRISTINA
[a.] Denver, CO [title] "Life's Seasons"] It's hard to say what really inspires you to write the things you do. I never thought I would ever have the courage to share my work in such a large way. This is why I would like to dedicate this publication to my wonderful husband, Mike, for believing in me and giving me that final push to share myself with the world. Also, a special thanks to my family who has been so supportive, especially to my mother, Virginia, for showing me how to express myself through the art of poetry. I love you all!

CAPPADORO, JACQUELYN
[a] Lake Worth, FL [title] "Release Me" [pers.] This poem has two sides. One is filled with despair, the other is filled with joy. I was struggling with many issues when a friend suggested I go to church. I accepted, and once there, I received Jesus as my personal Lord and Savior. At that time, I wrote half of this poem. A year later, I wrote the rest. It reminds me of the love our Lord has for us, even when we are suffering and not walking in his ways.

CAPS, ANN
[a.] Neptune Beach, FL [title] "Awake" [pers.] Written at the age of seventeen, this poem describes the yearning to exist in a perfect world where all is blissful. It is a satirical representation of the real world.

CARACOL, LINDA
[a.] Kamuela, HI [title] "Love" [pers.] This is my special poem and a gift to my children. They have been my inspiration. Verna, Vera, Raquel, Rochelle, and Vince, you are very special in my life.

CARAGOL, RICHARD
[a.] Alamo, CA [title] "Jewel" [pers.] Richard, former Sedona resident, currently resides in Northern California with his partner and love of his life, Nancy, for whom "Jewel" was written. He has a 16-year-old son, Spenger, who is a talented artist, musician, and snowboarder. Sharing many common interests, they enjoy complimenting one anothers' abilities. As an architect, investor, poet, and writer, Richard draws his inspiration from nature, romance, human emotion, and life's experiences. For him, art, the creative process is put-of-body. "Poetry is a matter of painting with words," depicting vivid imaginings where uniqueness and familiarity co-exist upon each reader's canvas.

CARAVETTA, RACHEL
[a.] Patterson, NY [title] "Miss You When You're Far and Love You When You're Near" [pers.] I feel that poetry is a way for me to express myself and outline the impact of things that happen in my life. I am thankful to my grandfather who has been my inspiration and my teacher. "Miss You When You've Far and Love You When You've Near" is one of many poems I have written over the past several years that expresses what I was feeling when I first met my husband, whom I love very much.

CARDEN, LISA
[a.] Winchester, VA [title] "Rainy Days" [pers.] My name is Lisa Carden and I am 12 years old. My hobbies are signing, dancing, drawing, traveling, and having a good time with my family. I'm responsible and get good grades. I have a 10-year-old sister and an eight-year-old half-brother, whom I never see. I was born in Germany and lived there until I was 11 years old, then I moved here. Now I speak German and English. I wrote my first poem in fifth grade in Germany and since then I have been good at imagining poems in my head. I have also written and told many made-up stories all my life.

CARL, LYNNIE
[a.] Herndon, PA [title] "Angels Are Watching" [pers.] The poem, "Angels Are Watching" is written about my angels that are watching me. On March 22, 1998,

I lost my two cousins, a loved one, and five close friends in a horrible cabin fire. This was the worst experience of my life, and I miss them so much every day. My loved ones were wonderful, caring people. They had so many dreams to fulfill and never took things for granted. So please remember my dear angels, Toby West, David West, Kip Snyder, Hainy, Jasson Herrold, Amanda, Toni, and Tyrone Wehry, I love all of you so much and I will always know that My "angels are watching."

CARNEVALE, MARY
[a.] Jackson, NJ [title] "Caring Mother" [pers.] This poem means a lot to me. This shows how much my mom really means to me. I think a poem is a great way to express your feelings to someone you love. There will be no other mom better than mine. I love you, Mom.

CARR, TRICIA
[a.] Buffalo, NY [title] "My Friends" [pers.] This poem is extremely important to me. I wrote it for my best friends, Jenny Hartwell, Margo Thomas, and Tabitha Fiorello. They mean the world to me, and I wanted to show them how much I cared by writing them this poem. Jenny, Margo, and Tab—I love you guys.

CARTER, CHARLOTTE
[a.] Plant City, FL [title] "Christmas" [pers.] It has been my pleasure to write for many reasons. Each word I have put to paper was inspired by the way others have touched my life. Thus it has afforded me the opportunity to touch others in some small way. Whether it has brought compassion, love, or happiness, I am fortunate in that I am able to express myself in verse. My poem, "Christmas," was meant for that purpose, to bring a smile to someone who had touched my life. I would like to thank all those many people who have inspired me to write.

CASSELMAN, JODI
[a.] Worcester, MA [title] "Time" [pers.] Writing is a way for your soul to talk to the rest of the world. I have to keep a pen and pad always handy. I carry both in my car. I love poems or poetry that speak to you and move you. I have a love for quotes also. "Happiness is not always getting what you want, but wanting what you have," by an unknown author, is my favorite.

CESTARO, CHRISTINE
[a.] Rockerville, Centre, NY [title] "Me" [pers.] I'm eleven, going to South Side Middle School in Rockerville, Centre, L.I., N.Y. When I was little I loved writing. Through the years, I loved it more and more. In sixth grade, my teacher, Mrs. Shivers, introduced me to poetry, which I fell in love with. I wrote this poem because I had many questions entering middle school, but no answers. Now I love middle school; the questions don't even come up. If I were to give advice to someone, I'd say "Don't think, just imagine. Let the pen flow, you're got a poem!"

CHAVERS, ZERLINDA
[a.] Beldon, MS [title] "I Remember" [pers.] All forms of writing, whether poetry, novels, songwriting or journals, give the author an outlet for expression. Thoughts and emotions are sometimes energetic and blissful, then other times dark and sorrowful. We as humans experience both. Writing is a tool that brings the human spirit together, being a voice for our thoughts and emotions. "I Remember" is a reflection of the love I shared with someone who has left my life and a monument to our short time together.

CHAVIS, CHASITY
[a.] Little Rock, SC [title] "I Still Wonder" [pers.] This poem is one that I dedicate to my brother, Brent. He died of cancer in 1996 at the age of three. I am 12 and I love to write. When I can't talk about my brother or his death, I write about it. I thought maybe I would share something from my heart. I hope others can relate and understand my point of view, and I hope you enjoy my poem.

CHEATHEM, CLEM
[a.] Phoenix, AZ [title] "Eye of the Mind" [pers.] This poem is very special to me because I wonder about the thoughts in the minds of my daughters, now three and four years old, 20 years from now. What will their minds see?

CHEW, RICHARD
[a.] Singapore [title] "Life Incomplete" [pers.] When I was 17 years old, I fell in love with a classmate. We used to reach poems to each other whenever we were alone together. She died two years later of an illness. For 42 years, I never fell in love again until last year when I came across this lady while I was participating in an electronic forum for shares-investors. Hence this poem. Would I ever meet her, know her real identity, have her as my wife? I was born on August seventh, 1940 of Chinese parentage but a Singaporean by birth. My father, a civilian, was executed by the Japanese Occupation Force—just for being Chinese. Life was difficult for my family, especially my mother. But things changed for the better after I completed my studies and got a job. I spent most part of my life giving private tuition in the English language to students in the Secondary School level, (ages between 12 and 19 years).

CHILES, JOAN
[a.] New Braunfels, TX [title] "Your Love in My Heart" [pers.] My family is very important to me. I have wonderful parents who have taught me how to love. I have eight brothers and sisters, and we are very close. God has blessed me with the true love in my heart, my husband. My inspiration for writing comes from all the blessings God has given me.

CHIVIKAS, NIKOLAOS
[a.] Grand Blanc, MI [title] "Dream Away" [pers.] I attended Purie University in West Lafayette, IN. I received my Bachelor of Liberal Arts in December of 1996, majoring in English, creative writing, and professional writing, and minoring in communication.

CHRISTIANSEN, JOYCE
[a.] Costa Mesa, CA [title] "There Once Was a Time" [pers.] This poem was one I had written when I was in high school. I guess you could say it was my first love. I have always enjoyed writing poetry, and my children also enjoy writing. It is a way of writing feelings and sometimes expressing what you can't always say. Writing your feelings is sometimes so much easier.

CICCONE, MELISSA
[a.] Brewster, NY [title] "Reading the News" [pers.] Adolescent years are times of anguish, joy, insecurity, and maturing. These years when a child turns to a young adult are some of the most difficult. My poem reflects the strife felt by many when they are growing up.

CILIBERTO, MICHAEL
[a.] Wickliffe, OH [title] "Medieval Nights" [pers.] I guess you can say we all dream. When I was little I dreamed about dragons and knights. I dreamed I was in a world where I was the hero. When we were kids we all played somewhere—in that special place where our imagination could run wild. Mine was in the backyard. That is where I would get lost in my dreams, in my own world.

CINATTI, PATRICIA
[a.] Woodside, NY [title] "Helpless" [pers.] The inspiration for this poem comes from observing life itself, how we all watch helplessly as someone dear to us tries to overcome their adversity in life. I hope whoever reads this will always be there to help that broken spirit.

CLARK, ALISON
[a.] Marietta, GA [title] "My Search for Me" [pers.] Poetry allows me to express myself in a way I never thought possible. This poem means so much because

it reminds me that no matter what trials are set before me, I can overcome them. Most of all, I know that happiness is always waiting just around the corner. I hope my poem can convey a message to anyone who thinks things will never get any better. Your strength from within will always pull you through.

CLARKE, GARY
[a.] Philadelphia, PA [title] "You Are" [pers.] Of the hundreds of poems I have written over the years, "You Are" is one of my favorites. Many who have read it tell me what a wonderfully spiritual poem it is, and although I can understand their interpretation, it was not written as such. I was inspired to write it after an amazing evening with my girlfriend, Joyce. She is the kind of woman you just can't stop thinking about. I love her very much.

CLAUDE, ANDREW
[a.] Nekoosa, WI [title] "The Horsemen" [pers.] I wrote this poem for a friend of mine who was going through a rough time. Her constant strength, intelligence, grace, and beauty have been a great inspiration to me in the short time I have known her, giving me the courage to face death itself. I am eternally grateful to her.

CLAXTON, DEREK
[a.] Athens, AL [pers.] This poem was created while I was taking summer classes at the University of Alabama in 1999. Many times, I would awaken from the sound of a midnight train while sleeping in the dormitories. The midnight train became my motivation for the poem. However, I believe the poem is written and structured in such a way to provide for a different interpretation, the struggle with madness.

CLAYTON, BRANDY
[a.] Weirton, WV [title] "Personality" [pers.] This poem is written for people to take a good look at themselves and others. I believe that there would be less hate and harm if we all loved for what's on the inside. This is dedicated for all the schools so they may have less hate and hurt and shootings.

CODRINGTON, CHANLAH
[a.] Houston, TX [title] "What I Want" [pers.] This poem commemorates a very special young lady in my life, Tsungi Zhou, my first true love, "Shmily."

COLE, VICTORIA
[a.] Scio, OH [title] "Desert Storm" [pers.] This poem has my innermost feelings of what I believed my brother was feeling at this very special time. My twin brother served nine months over in the desert during the holidays, Christmas, Thanksgiving, and the New Year. He still has this poem and the letter that I had wrote along with it. Our country was at war with Iraq. My heart went out to all of these men serving our country now and forever. Their strength and courage were inspirational to me. My twin brother is very important in my life and this was my way of sharing his experience with the world. I would like to say thank you to the military men whom served our country during the war of Desert Storm.

COLEMAN, KAREN
[a.] Richton Park, IL [title] "As I Await Your Call" [pers.] I write poetry because that is my way of touching hearts and souls. My poetry helps people rediscover their emotions and more importantly, themselves. If I can change someone's life through my writing, it's worth more than anything to me.

COLLINS, AERON
[a.] Thornton, CO [title] "Reunited" [pers.] This is a poem that is dear to my heart. It is about a love that is expressed physically in a beautiful way. I wrote this when my husband and I came back together after a long separation in our marriage. It just shows how beautiful and fulfilling love can really be.

COLLINS, SHELLEY
[a.] Pocatello, ID [title] "God" [pers.] This poem shows just how much I love and appreciate all that God's has done for me. As I was writing this poem, I decided that I would write what I would tell non-believers who, I would hope, would come to know and worship God. Hopefully they would then share the "good news" with others. The one thing I want most in life is for everyone to know what God has done for us and to love and trust Him with all of our hearts.

COLMAN, ANDREW
[a.] Winnipeg, MB [title] "What Is the Truth?" [pers.] This poem has only had meaning to me very recently. I wrote it and the experience happened and it could be not be more true. I enjoyed writing this and other poems all inspired by my friends, so thanks to my two best friends for inspiring me to write my poems.

COMBS, JENNA
[a.] "Hampstead, NC [title] "One Wish" [pers.] There's not much to my poem. I was checking my e-mail and I found a hyperlink to Poetry.com, so I went there and wrote the poem. I just entered it for fun, seeing I had nothing else to do. I would have never thought it would be published in a book. This poem was written for my boyfriend, Brad. I don't have an occupation, because I am only thirteen and in seventh grade. I enjoy things like sports, friends, my boyfriend, shopping, and music. I hope you enjoy my poem.

CONAWAY, TERESA
[a.] "Coeburn, VA [title] "Mother . . . My Friend" [pers.] I have always been interested in poetry since I was in high school. However, when my mom was killed in a car wreck in 1983, in the truck which I was driving, I wanted to dedicate something to her because we was best friends. She was always there for me when I needed her, now in spirit. When I read the poem, I think about our love for each other.

COOK, SARAH
[a.] Grayslake, IL [title] "Breakfast in Bed" [pers.] "Breakfast in Bed" is a tribute to the gentle, quiet spirits of so many women around the world. Daily, they grind their coffee so that it is freshly brewed for their men. As their beautiful breakfasts are presented, their hope for neatness and order is lost. Orange juice and ketchup spill into each other, just as the women's delicate boundaries are wiped away by the passion between them and their men. This is dedicated to Jeanie Carter, a woman clothed in dignity and strength, and to Tom Deaver, who brings his woman breakfast in bed! I wrote to honor God and Cari.

COONTZ, BOBBIE
[a.] Scotland, MD [title] "Remember Me . . ." [pers.] I first got the idea to write this poem after writing the eulogy for my uncle's funeral. This poem was a way to let out all of the hurt I felt deep within. I believe that if people read this poem when they lose someone they care about, it will help them to feel a lot better about death. Although this is not my first poem, I believe it is the most heartfelt and remarkable piece of work I have written.

COPE, LYNDA
[a.] Wodonga, Australia [title] "Lost" [pers.] My poem reflects the inner child inside all of us who suppresses her fears and insecurities during waking life, but cannot protect us while we sleep, when our memories can come back to haunt us, drowning us in our past. I am a software engineer. my hobbies include caring for injured wildlife and writing poetry.

COPEMAN, JASHANA
[a.] Evart, MI [title] "Always Greater" [pers.] Writing has always been natural for me, a wonderful gift God has given me, and one I'm very thankful for. In fact, it is a way for me to reach Him at times. I hope one day for writing to be a successful profession for me. If not,

I'll continue expressing myself through paper, just as I do now. Words are often inefficient for me, so I turn to paper, where my true feelings pour out. Perhaps one day writing will be my career, but only with the wonderful support of my friends, family, and through God's grace.

CORCORAN, DENNIS
[a.] Howell, NJ [title] "Because of You" [pers.] I don't think of myself as a poet, but sometimes I find that emotion has crafted words to be my most powerful expression. I wrote with the hope of revealing that emotion in a manner that can be captured by others.

CORMIER, KEVIN
[a.] Lake Charles, LA [title] "Me and My Unborn" pers.] This poem is dedicated to all women who know the experience like it was yesterday. I don't have any sisters, but this poem came to me in a vision. I picked up a pen and paper and somehow, millions spoke through me. "Me and My Unborn" is not merely words on paper, but an ugly monster that we must defeat. If we are going to defeat violence in schools, churches, and abroad, we must start defeating it in our homes. Mothers, embrace your daughters with unceasing love; just as you needed it then, they need it now. Poetry is life.

CORNEILLE, IAN
[a.] Tacoma, WA [title] "Heavy Rain" [pers.] I am Ian Corneille a thirteen-year-old resident of Tacoma, WA. I was born on March 1, 1988. On my last report card, I am got a 4.0 GPA (grade point average) at Mason Middle School. I would like to thank my school and all my friends and family, especially Rhys Crane who illustrates his poetry. In "Heavy Rain," the heavy rain represents problems we all face in life; you can't ignore them because they "pour" bark on you. The only way to deal with these problems is to to be prepared and to have a solution such as an umbrella.

CORNWELL, JOHNNIE
[a.] Arthur, IL [title] "The Kiss I Miss" [pers.] I was searching for words at a troubled time. Poetry means many things, yet can convey the simplest of ideas. In high school, I wrote some very good poems and I felt myself return to those times when I wrote this.

COST, JENNIFER
[a.] Indianapolis, IN [title] "Gracing the Heavens" [pers.] Without knowing Bob Baldschun, one would not be fully impacted by this poem. Mr. Baldschun was my piano teacher for seven years. He died in his sleep at the end of my seventh year. He was a very religious man and he played the organ at his church. He was a perfectionist because he had played piano his whole life. He was never married. His wife was his music, and his students were his children. At last count, he had over 120 students. Even if you didn't know him, this poem could still be powerful. My family, especially my mother and father, Eldon and Julia Cost, have been very supportive of every endeavor, and I couldn't have done anything without them.

COTA, CHRISTINA
[a.] Sunrise Beach, MO [title] "I'll Love You Forever" [pers.] I wrote this poem based on my imagination and the romance between me and my boyfriend, Stephen Melvin. I love poetry—it's been my life since I was in Melissa Salesman's class in sixth grade. So far, I've been writing poetry for four years. I live with my mom and stepfather, Jay. I have a baby sister named Jayme, and two older siblings, Casey and Cheryl. My step family shows me what it is like to have a family and what a family is for and all about; for the first time in my life, I feel like I belong to a family. My friends that never disowned me and understood me, mean a lot. My whole life is my inspiration for poetry. I love you God, Stephen, and family.

COTMAN, YINDRA
[a.] Brooklyn, NY [title] "Elegantly Wasted" [pers.] Prologue: Incessant scribbling by candlelight is more of a lullaby than an interruption these days. Furiously recording each moment of her own private history, she studies me as if memorizing my every breath. The look is suspiciously smug, softened by a barely discernible smile. I often wonder if I am the hero of the villain of these testaments. I settle back into sleep, leaving her to preserve our most recent memories, our solace a heavy ether like cloud. Turning over, I pause, eavesdropping, hoping to decipher the faint whisper of her thoughts.

COUCH, JANET
[a.] Atlanta, GA [title] "The Touch of Your Love" [pers.] This poem was written during a period of time when two lonely hearts found each other. Once together, they re-discovered and shared feelings of love and passion that they thought were forgotten and would never experience again. This poem is an expression of those awakened feelings.

COURTRIGHT, SHERRY
[a.] Portland, OR [title] "Imagine" [pers.] Poetry is an inspiration of words to guide us. I feel that God gave me a gift of words to inspire myself and others. With this inspiration, I live my life believing in myself and the dreams that can come true . With God and my family and friend, all things are possible. Life is a gift; share it with others with words of joy, love, sorrow, wisdom, truth, and spirituality. I hope my words inspire others to dream and believe.

COWLES, HEATHER
[a.] Noblesville, IN [title["The Night of Demon Dreams" [pers.] Poetry is a gate, a gate that opens to the garden of imagination and fruitful exploration of one's inner being. Having been blessed with the heart of a poet, I know the meaning behind the words and oral dictations that some only see as boredom-filled speeches. I am very grateful to be able to express myself with the open-mindedness of a true lover of words. Poetry is the key to exposing the evil deeds, unfortunate shortcomings, and unexplainable love and desire to those who do not have the resources to expose these things themselves.

COX, ANGIE
[a.] Westerville, OH [title] "Michael" [pers.] My name is Angie. I'm 15 and from Westerville, Ohio When I got the letter from Poetry.com, I never expected it to say my poem would be published. Of all my poems I've written, this has to be the most meaningful. You've heard of writing from the heart—well, that's exactly what I did. This poem is about a good friend I lost. I had a hard time getting over him. I wrote it to let him know I'll never forget him. Now that it is in this book he will be remembered by everyone who reads it.

CRAWFORD, JULIA
[a.] Runaway Bay, TX [title] "Killing Love" [pers.] I was born June 29, 1984. I'm finishing my Junior year in high school. I'm currently a waitress at a restaurant called Rita's Cafe (my first job). I live with my grandparents whom I love very much. They give me lots of love and support. Poetry and art both play an important role in my life. They allow me to release and express bottled up feelings and emotions. I think everyone should have something like that in their life.

CRAY, NED
[a.] Fort Lauderdale, FL [title] "Sailor's Lust" [pers.] Ned Cray is a tailor and professional mariner who has been singing and writing verse for many years. The current focus of his work is connecting the inner and outer experiences of life. Ned lives in Florida and cruises his sailboat, "Otter," along the East Coast and Bahamas. Look for him singing his songs in the ODJCURR Taverns in remote places.

CREWS, LAVONNE
[a.] Altamonte Springs, FL [title] "Loss of a Hero, Dale Earnhardt" [pers.] We all need a hero, someone who touches us and makes us strive to be the best. For more than a decade, my hero was Dale Earnhardt. As much as it hurt to say good-bye, I'm grateful for all the wonderful memories he has left me.

CROSBY, JOE, III
[a.] Spokane, WA [title] "Dream" [pers.] This poem was written after my wife separated from me. I was feeling low and talking to God, when I started to reminisce about a night spent with my wife. It was a night of pure unbridled love and passion, before the child, careers, school, etc. . . . So I put all the thoughts together to become "Dream." I don't think we fall out of love; we just forget how to have fun in love.

CROSSLEY, DOLLY
[a.] Hurst, TX [title] "Winter Weather" [pers.] "Winter Weather" was written for my students as we stood looking out of our classroom window. Is there a better way to begin the writing of any style than with poetry? Learning to express emotions, probing moods and senses, and using words creatively and economically is a wonderful way to explore our language. Reading and writing poetry taps the imagination and opens the flow of thought. I have a B.S. and M.A. from North Texas University. I was Teacher of the Year at both Highland Park ISD, where I taught 30 years, and NTU. I enjoy reading, writing, movies, plays, museums, family, and friends.

CROUSE, SHANNON
[a.] Swansboro, NC [title] "A Flower Like Me . . ." [pers.] I have always loved to write poems. I write for what I feel and make it seem different in someone else's eyes at the same time. I love nature and I am saved by the blood of Jesus so I wanted to incorporate both aspects at the same time, while explaining how I feel. This is not a children's poem even though it may look like it. When you take it to heart, it is so much more.

CROYBAKER, SARAH
[a] Bremerton, WA [title] "impoverished" [pers.] I wrote this poem when I was in the service. Two things happened to me there for which I will always be grateful. First there was having my birth son, Patrick, and my friendship with his wonderful family. Patrick taught me to strive to be the person I believed could be. The second was meeting my loving husband, Danny, who gives me support and who continues to be confident in me. Both are an inspiration. Thank you to Patrick and your family, and to Danny, my husband.

CRUZ, MARTHA
[a.] Bronx, NY [title] "Family and Friends" [pers.] I love to read poetry. I wrote this poem for someone very dear to my heart. This person knows how much he means to me. I like to write what comes from the heart to share with my family and friends. I love you.

CUELLAR, SUZANNE
[a.] Vernon, TX [title] "On Father's Day" [pers.] This poem is in the honor of my wonderful father, Alfred Cuellar Jr. He has done so many things for me, and I love him very much. I hope the public enjoys my poem and I hope it is remembered forever. Writing poetry is one of my ways of showing my feelings. I'm 18 years old and I'm a senior at the Vernon High School. I love to read, write, sing, dance, and go to dances. I am a mother of beautiful baby girl named Francesca Renee Delos Santos, and she was born on January 23, 2001 at Vernon, Texas.

CULVER, STEVEN
[a.] Indianapolis, IN [title] "Heroes" [pers.] In writing my poem, "Heroes," I'm trying to express my deep appreciation to my parents. The love they gave us, all through our childhood, was never doubted and never

missed. "Heroes" is the only title that my poem could have been named. They were and always will be my heroes.

CURTIS-MAKI, CHARLENE
[a.] Hayward, WI [title] "Season of Love" [pers.] In my background, I loved religion and philosophy. I believe in the divinity of Almighty God. Currently, I work in an area of the medical field. I love gardening, bicycling, walking, and camping and tieing my thoughts to what our nature offers. My desire is to have more time for these thoughts to be written down. I appreciate this opportunity and privilege to have a poem in this publication.

CUSHMAN, DEBORAH
[a.] San Diego, CA [title] "My True Hope" [pers.] I wrote this poem at a very important time in my life. I have always written poetry because it helps calm me and brings my thought to light. This particular poem was written for a very special person who means the world to me. Thank you, Chris.

CUSHMAN, SHILO
[a.] Albion, Me [title] "Give Thanks" [pers.] I am a fourteen-year-old student at Lawrence High School. I live in a rural town in Maine. What draws me to poetry is the emotion that comes from it. When I read poetry I can almost feel what the poet is feeling. When I write poetry I put all my emotion into every word. I write what I think is true and what I think people know. "Give Thanks" is the first real poem that I have ever written, and I hope to be writing much more as my life goes on.

CYRUS, BRYAN
[a.] Arkansas City, KS [title] "The Stranger" [pers.] In my opinion, poetry is a way to bypass the mind and enter the deepest fears, desires, and heartaches of the soul.

DACK, RUTH
[a.] Norfolk, United Kingdom [title] "The Decision" [pers.] This poem was written shortly after I decided to take a year out from college to gain some experience in the world. For me, poetry is a way of expressing my emotions in an individual and creative format. My other interests include theatre, which in a similar way to poetry is an expressive medium. That I enjoy greatly. Expression is an important part of my life as it helps me become more at ease with who I am.

DAISEY, DEREK
[a.] Cape Coral, FL [title] "The Love I Can't Feel" [pers.] I would like to thank everyone who has never let me give up in the past, such as Owen and Kerrie. I would also like to thank my cousin, Kyle, who got me into writing. I dedicate this to Melissa Roskowski, the girl who made it possible for me to write this poem and the many others I have written. I love you! I want to thank my teachers for encouraging me, especially my parents, who take time to read and listen. I want to thank Poetry.com for taking my poem and publishing it.

DALE, JOHN, III
[a.] Van Lear, KY [title] "The Race" [pers.] My poetry is just something I do when I feel the need to write about something. I've written about many things—family, friends, and work. I never thought of being published, but I think it is an honor. I have been a police officer for twenty-two years. I live in a small Kentucky city in the mountains of East Kentucky. I am married and have four grown children, and two grandchildren. I wish to thank my lovely wife for submitting my poem. Without her, it would have never went beyond the local paper.

DANIEL, CARMENE
[a.] Belton, MO [title] "Velvet Rose" [pers.] I see poetry in all that God created—flowers, children, and every living thing. I see God in everyday life. I have written many poems, but to have one published for other people to read is an honor.

DANTHONY, JOLYNNE
[a.] Imperial, MO [title] "An Angel's Touch" [pers.]
I believe we grow each day through our experiences, hopes, and dreams. Each person that touches our lives has the ability to change it forever. It is my hope that my writing reflects these beliefs. Born in St. Louis and raised by a loving family, I still had to do things the hard way. As a recovering alcoholic, I need all the angels I can get and daily thank God for them.

DARGAN, ZONA
[a.] Beeville, TX [title] "Ready" [pers.] First of all, I give God all the glory, honor, and praise because He is the source of my life from day to day. I am so thankful for this great opportunity. It's great joy to see that we are in unity. I wrote this poem during a time of storm. With mixed emotions, I was in despair, wondering if God really did care. I gave it some thought, becoming aware that someday I will meet him in the air. As time came a running, I had to prepare. It was time to get ready for He did care. I have been so inspired by God to go all the way with him even if I didn't have a car or money to pay. As a child, I would always write. It's a hidden gift that I will let arise after writing this poem during my moments of despair.

DARRO, YVONNE
[a.] Peoria, AZ [title] "Teardrops" [pers.] This is dedicated to my four boys, Jason, Christopher, Sammy, and Seth. This poem is only a part of the pain I feel living my life without them. However I have faith and I believe that one day God will give us a second chance to become best friends!

DAVID, MARYLINE
[a.] London, UK [title] "The Abyss" [pers.] This poem is dedicated to Nigel, my husband of nine years. The word "love" does not adequately describe what I feel for him—as an abyss has unfathomable depths, so too does my love. As you continue in this life, always look for happiness and peace of mind. May you find it on your journey.

DAVIS, E., II
[a.] Washington, DC [title] "Beauty in Confusion" [pers.] Native has published a volume entitled *Anger, Acknowledgement and Acceptance (Blatant Honesty)*. While raised in an urban setting, his cathasis was writing, regardless of the lack of support. He is living evidence testifying to the positive influences of teachers. His wish is to convey an in-your-face style to the world on subjects ranging from social injustice to love. He is a ruffian turned writer; such is life.

DAVIS, ELSIE
[a.] Lexington, KY [title] "Always with You" [pers.] I am currently writing a book for my grandchildren about my life and some of their ancestors. I intend to add this poem to their book to give them comfort when I am no longer with them physically. I grew up in Casey County, KY (Liberty) in the backwoods of that area, quite poor. I raised three children (successful/honest) alone. I did not go to Jewish High School I but went to nursing college at the age of 31. I have worked in most phases of Health Care with emphasis mostly in emergency medicine. Currently, I am a licensed Realtor and a certified Polygraph Examiner (Forensic Psychophysiologist).

DAVIS, LILLIAN
[a.] Bangelore, India [title] "Judicial System" [pers.] This work voices the anguish of the thousands of women who have passed through the portals of divorce courts in a third world country, all of us victims of a degrading and Archaic Judicial System. My writing is a very personal perspective, drawing on several vivid experiences from each phase of my life, expressing the joy, the pain, and the wonder of finally discovering myself as a woman. The journey has been and continues to be a priceless education. My two sons and life's ever changing kaleidoscope will always be my source of inspiration.

DAVY, WILLIAM
[a.] Buffalo Grove, IL [title] "Your Birthday" [pers.] Poetry has become a therapeutic method for me. My poems generally deal with an event in my life. I wrote his poem when I was recalling a good event that I had with my girlfriend. We had already broken up but this poem helped to bring me closure.

DE GUZMAN, JOYCE
[a.] Corona, CA [title] "Hard to Accept" [pers.] This poem is dedicated to Ethan Lara, a man who will always have a special place in my heart and whom I will love forever.

DE LOS SANTOS, JOHN
[a.] Lewisville, TX [title] "Sent by Grace" [pers.] Poetry has always been a big part of my life, as well as music, theater, and anything else you can imagine having to do with the arts. The story behind this poem is really simple. You know what it's like to talk to someone and not be able to get them out of your head. That's what it's like. Thank you for this wonderful opportunity to share my work with the rest of the world.

DECARLO, MARYANN
[a.] Gilbertville, PA [title] "Stolen Innocence" [pers.] This poem was created from the sorrow I feel for all who have suffered from the evil of their lost childhood, but have been able to overcome such horrendous odds and find balance and happiness. I applaud them. I will forever be indebted to Joseph, my best friend and husband of 39 years for his understanding and compassion. Living in Gilbertsville, PA, we are especially proud of our six grown children and the nine, loving energetic grandchildren who fill our lives with wonder and love.

DEETS, SHAWN
[a.] Alto, NM [title] "Reflections" [pers.] I am actually a songwriter/musician. Some of my poems start out as songs, and some of my songs start out as poems. This poem was the number one choice by the majority of people that viewed my work. It is very interesting because it works as a song as well as it does a poem. I like to describe feelings, certain points in time, and visual scenery from a different point of view, incorporating metaphors and different thought patterns. There are many hidden meanings in all of my work.

DEGRAY, ALI
[a.] Palm Beach, FL [title] "The Little Boy in Khaki Pants" [pers.] I was in a happy, hyper mood when I wrote this! I was bouncing around in my sixth grade English class (I am almost twelve!), so I wrote this poem. I prefer poetry that makes you smile automatically to poems that really make you contemplate depression and sadness. Life is too short! I dedicate this to my classmates, my mommy, Ruthie, Laury, Will (my awesome brother!), Bridget, Amber, and Lilly (bff!) and every other happy and supportive person that's ever been there for me!

DEL SONTRO, STACEY
[a.] Lake Hiawatha, NJ [title] "Every Minute" [pers.] I'm only 13 years old, but this poem truly came from the heart. I was inspired by love. I may not be in love, but I know many people are. I hope I can inspire people not to leave their loved ones because I know that a broken heart isn't easy to deal with. What I hope to get through to people is, if you ever love someone, don't leave them because it could hurt their feelings. Love is a valuable thing and it shouldn't be a game. If you love someone, don't make it a game, because love isn't a game.

DEMCHENKO, LIA
[a.] Brooklyn, NY [title] "I Will Survive (The Holocaust)" [pers.] The Holocaust was one of the most horrible times to live in throughout the history of the world. I admire the strength the people had portrayed in order to overcome that nightmare. I wrote this

poem to commemorate the hardships in their life. I enjoy writing poems that hold a meaning towards my life and to the life of others. Having the opportunity to express the past, as well as trying words and feelings, brings a lot to mind, and I hope to continue to revive the memories of the past through my feelings, my thoughts, and my words.

DENNING, KRYSTAL
[a.] Royersford, PA [title] "Alone" [pers.] I am part of a big family of eight. My sisters and brothers, Tiffany, Josh, Kiera, Taylor, and Cayla are a big inspiration to my writing. My favorite poet is Robert Frost. In my spare time, I love to read, write, act, sing, and watch movies. My all-time favorite actress is Julia Roberts. I love to listen to music, (especially the Backstreet Boys. When I grow up, I want to be either a detective or a singer.

DEPERI, JONATHAN
[a.] Plano, TX [title] "I Do Love Thee" [pers.] The world is a place where few things remain eternal. True love is one of these precious few things. It embraces not only the world but the entire universe. Everything imbued with the locator's divine spark has love. I wrote this poem in praise of my first and truest love, Mary. May she live forever.

DEPOMA, STEPHANIE
[a.] Mesquite, TX [title] "Binding Friendship" [pers.] This poem was written by Stephanie in 1981 when she was a high school sophomore for her best friend. Since then, Stephanie has written much more poetry, as well as several songs, and has competed in many contests for songwriters in the Dallas/Fort Worth area. She has also sang the National Anthem two seasons in a row for the Dallas Stars Hockey Team in 2000 and 2001. She is interested in publishing the rest of the poetry in addition to shopping around a demo CD to Nashville and L.A.

DERR, KEARA
[a.] Selingrove, PA [title] "One Minute" [pers.] Becoming a poet right away is something I did not do. It all started when a devastating event happened in my life, and I expressed my feelings in words and phrases on a piece of paper. My family and friends enjoyed my feelings, or what would be called poems. I invented many poems afterwards. I wrote "One Minute" to inform others they may not be the only ones thinking about the future, and most importantly, that just because someone believes they're going to do something or not, the next minute, or even days, months, or years, they might change their minds. I do this, along with my family and friends, and it's okay. Actually, it's wonderful to think about the choices I make. I discovered that by doing so, I understood why and how I was going to do these things. I will continue to set my feelings free to the people who want to hear them. Nothing anyone does can separate me and my love for poetry.

DESMARAIS, CLAUDETTE
[a.] Briston, VT [title] "Why" [pers.] The story behind my poems comes from a longtime crush that I had on a boy from the third grade. This crush that I had lasted until the boy graduated high school. I was in love and three years of age kept us apart. The sadness I felt in my heart ached to be with him someday. Although we were friends and neighbors, I had always longed for more. Reading this poem today even after 20 plus years, my heart tingles at the thought.

DEVERS, CATHY
[a.] Pauma Valley, CA [title] "Gram" [pers.] I'm 17 years old. I attend Valley Center High School located in Valley Center, CA. I am a senior. While in English class, I had to memorize a sonnet or make up my own. I decided to create my own in memory of my grandma who died April 12, 2000. I also wrote this in order to get my feelings out and to let everyone reading "Gram"

know how much my Gram means to me. My family liked the poem so much that it was engraved on my Gram's headstone.

DEVORE, DEB
[a.] Olney Springs, CO [title] "Why?" [pers.] My innermost feelings are expressed through my poetry. This poem is for everyone who has had that special person touch their heart.

DIAZ, VERONICA
[a.] Sarasota, FL [title] "I See You . . ." [pers.] "I See You . . ." was meant as a reflection on life, missing out on the obvious choice because we are too busy with the "chase." This poem represented an era that changed and turned life upside down for me. Yet the satisfaction of a memory for someone brought back a smile and set everything in place. The only request to you, the reader is to realize and value the friendship of those around and pay close attention to the details. For one day you will look and wonder . . . what if? Then you will continue life with that one regret that came too late.

DIBBLE, ALEX, JR.
[a] Orangeburg, SC [title] "In Your Eyes" [pers.] After the loss of a very dear friend, I longed for a new companion, but I was afraid to commit myself again. Putting my thoughts and feelings in poetry is like therapy for me. I was born in Iowa, but now I reside in Wolftom, SC. I work in a department store in the receiving department.

DICKENS, BETTY
[a.] East Point, GA [title] "Vanities of Life" [pers.] To me, poetry is a way of expressing feelings not always easy to express in person. As I get older, musings of the past reflect, in the mirror of my mind, many surfacing feelings of nostalgia, regret, or guilt. Writing these feelings is sort of like "confession" to mankind and God and it is a "revisiting" of morable moments. I also use poetry to record my personal analysis of other people, of my relationships in love, in life, in spiritual experiences, and of my own self-analysis.

DILLON, KATEY
[a.] Summerfield, FL [title] "One More Day" [pers.] This poem was inspired by just about everything. I would like to dedicate this poem to my grandfather, Doc Garner. I love him more than anything, or anybody, in the world.

DIMAURO, NICOLE
[a.] Waldorf, MD [title] "Life is Full of Changes" [pers.] This poem is about my life and all the changes I have made in 11 years. I think that any kid my age can relate to the things in my poem, except for the line that says "From Waldorf to Queens." I moved from New York to Waldorf, Maryland when I was younger. Before I wrote my last couple of lines, I had to think about change. I realized that change is good and is something that everyone goes through. I look forward to the future and all the changes that are still to come my way!

DINGWALL, TRUDIE
[a.] Saint Louis, MO [title] "My Cyber-Buddy" [pers.] As a new member of AOL in 1996, making lots of new friend in chat rooms, I experienced the bitter and the sweet aspects of such anonymous bonding, which inspired me to write this poem. I am a very philosophical person, rather than a poetic one. If something grabs me deeply in the center of my being, inspiration will move me to put my thoughts on paper. My spelling at times leaves a lot to be desired, as English is my second language. I was born and educated in Germany at a very turbulent time in history, which right there lays the foundation to form one's own philosophy in life in order to survive intact.

DISALVO-BLACK, ANTONIO
[a.] Pueblo, CO [title] "Kristen" [pers.] I live in Pueblo, Colorado. I attend South High, where I spend the majority of my free time with my friends, Charles, Jason Conrad, Tom, Georgia, Bobby, and Josh. I am 17 and love life. This poem is about my feelings for the woman whose name is the title. She always loves to read my poetry and supports me 100 percent. I care very deeply for her. My poetry is based on my life experiences and dreams. All this influences me, as does my religion, which is often misjudged. I am Wiccan, more commonly known as a witch.

DIVEL, TONY
[a.] Lemoyne, PA [title] "Drifted" [pers.] "Drifted" is a poem about a person who runs from problems and hardships that occur in their life instead of facing them. This person then decides to move and escape their problems. Everything seems well at first, until he encounters new hardships. Then he escapes again only to find that one will end up with problems wherever one goes.

DODD, ROBERT
[a.] Anza, CA [title] "Society" [pers.] I feel that my ability to write poetry is a gift that God has given me. My poem, "Society," discusses how society is getting worse. My inspiration for writing poetry was a poet named Jim Carroll. I started writing poetry when I read his work. My hobbies are playing football, surfing, and spending time with my girlfriend, April Lopez. My uncle died from cancer May 4, 2001. I promised him that I would succeed in life, so I have many goals to accomplish. One of those goals is being a famous poet and author. I'd like to thank my father, David, my mother, Linda, my grandparents, brothers, sister, my uncle, Chris, my girlfriend, April, Jesus Christ, and everybody else for helping me in this life.

DOHERTY, FAITH
[a.] Bloomington, IN [title] "If I Were to Tell You" [pers.] For me, poetry is to always express what you're feeling. It is also a way to tell people something that you don't know how to say in person. I believe when you're writing poetry, you should have restrictions or guidelines. A poem isn't about how many lines it has; a poem is whatever you make it about, and it doesn't have to be about anything. Poems reflect who you are, what you're feeling, and what your experiences have been.

DOLENTE, JIMMY
[a.] Staten Island, NY [title] "A Poem by Me" My name is James John Bolloli, but my friends and family call me Jimmy. I was eight years old and in the third grade. This was my first attempt at poetry. My mom sent my poem in for me, and the rest is history.

DOLOR, PARIDA BIANCA
[a.] Las Pinas, Philippines [title] "Broken Friendship" [pers.] Writing poems is one of my hobbies. It was not really my intention to write a specific poem like "Broken Friendship." It was just so sudden that a verse related to this poem came to my mind, so I started developing that idea. It has always been my desire to find an opportunity for my artistic creation to be published and become available to the public. As a result, I became so proud of myself. So I'm now beginning to face the new challenge coming on my way. It's just my hobby to write poems. Writing poems is the way I express myself. My parents are Paciano Dolor and Florida Matuloy Dolor. I am their third offspring. Froylan, Divine Grace, Francis Paolo, and Ardianne are my brothers and sisters. I am currently taking up my second year as a high school student at Blessed Trinity School. Writing poems and playing musical instruments are my hobbies. My philosophical point of view is to study well while still young because good ideas are being developed during our younger years.

DONAHUE, JASON
[a.] Winchester, KY [title] "Time" [pers.] Poetry expresses how I feel about my life and dreams. To share this with others is the best gift I can give. I hope my poems live forever in the hearts of those they reach and have reached. I enjoy writing poems that have meaning for children. In the poem, "Time," the last line means time is always changing. This is true because by looking at what time it is, before you can say it, it has already changed. I give thanks to all those who support me and my wonderful family.

DORAN, AMANDA
[a.] Brick, NJ [title] "The Glass Ceiling" [pers.] I was the Brick Township High School Class of 1998 and the Georgian Court College Class of 2001. I have a BA in English, a BA in Religions Studies, and a Minor in Philosophy. I would like to dedicate this publication of "The Glass Ceiling" to my sophomore English teacher, Miss Lisa Heller. Miss Heller, you taught me to love writing, and for that I am eternally grateful. You have shaped the rest of my life.

DORE, DELVIS
[a.] Peoria, IL [title] "Final Destination" [pers.] "Final Destination" is special to me because it tells of the agony I endured, deciding to stay with my girl or not. My poem relieved a lot of stress, as I was dealing with my problem by myself. After writing poetry for six years, it just became natural to use a poem to express my feelings. I only wish things were different and I didn't have to write this poem.

DORHAM-PIPKINS, LORNA
[a.] San Francisco, CA [title] "The Heart" [pers.] Lorna is a born-again Christian wife of a Bishop, and a mother of eight children. She is very blessed with seven sons, ages six to thirty-three. Her one and only daughter is 24. She is proud and excited to be the grandmother of five, ages one to six years. With children born from four different decades and clothed in her right mind, she knows the Lord Jesus is alive and well. Glory to His precious name. In the 60's, 70's, 80's, and 90's, all the children are a blessing, and I am very grateful the Lord Jesus allowed me the privilege to be wife and mother and grandmother. I thank Him most of all for my strong family background. My dad and mom are very loving and caring so I learned watching them. They enjoy being great-grandparents.

DOROUGH, MELISSA
[a.] Lone Grove, OK [title] "The End" [pers.] Hello, I'm Melissa and I'm 14 years old. I live in the sooner state. I'm a BSB fan so that's why I'm using a pen name. The poem is about a couple. The girlfriend found out her boyfriend was cheating on her, and she died of a broken heart. Her last words, "I kept my word . . . did you?" was meant to haunt him because he wronged her, and now he can't right the wrong.

DOUGLAS, BRIONY
[a.] Sydney, Australia [title] "Martin Luther King— Be Brave" [pers.] Martin Luther King's bravery inspired us all. I am a 14-year-old girl from Sydney, Australia and I decided to use my poem as a message. My poem is a representation of what I believe Martin Luther King would have told people had he lived to continue his fight for racial tolerance. It's a basic message to be brave and never lose sight of the big picture while trying to overcome challenges, a vision for a better future.

DOWLING, CYNTHIA
[a.] Columbia Cross Roads, PA [title] "Tell Me Why" [pers.] "Tell Me Why" is one of the first poems that I have written and that is to be published. I wrote this poem in memory of my father, who died when I was ten years old. Five years later, I have my first poem published. Wow, I never thought this would happen and I'm glad it did. I want to thank my eighth grade teacher, Mr. Beck, for letting me look at poetry in a

different way. In addition, I would like to thank my mother and everyone else for helping me with everything. Thanks to everyone!

DOWN, HELEN
[a.] Brisbane, Australia [title] "Nothing Changes" [pers.] This is one of my first poems written only this year. It was based on the Australian climate where nothing changes. I have always loved poetry but never sat down to write until this year, 2001. Thank you for choosing my poem.

DRESCHER, ASCHLEE
[a.] Port Orchard, WA [title] "All Alone Where No One Can Hear"[pers.] There are many ways to see into someone's soul and mind. Poetry has been my gateway to a connection with the world and myself. I've overcome many obstacles in my life and have hidden myself in the process, but now I want the world to know what I think. Maybe, somehow, my words and thoughts will touch someone and hopefully change them for the better or teach them something about themselves. There have been many people supporting me and helping me along my way, and maybe someday, through my words, I can tell them how much I truly love them.

DUCA, JANE
[a.] Cary, NC [title] "To Be or Not to Be" [pers.] Poetry is life itself as it comes from the depth of my soul. My teachers have been my life experiences, people, events, nature, animals and my spirituality that I have held to throughout my life which has inspired the words to flow like a spring of water. I see beauty in all creation. It gives me great joy to write my poems for whose eyes may fall upon them and maybe someone will be touched from the depth of their soul and be inspired to find their passion and love in this beautiful world.

DUKE, CHARLES
[a.] Richland Hills, TX [title] "After All, He Lived It" [pers.] This poem was written in memory of my grandfather, Owsley. My mother, through the years, always said about him, "He doesn't need to preach about good—after all he lives it every day." Paw Paw Owsley was the smartest man I ever knew, and this is an abbreviated version of the poem I wrote for his eulogy. As a singer, I have dealt with verbiage most of my life. This poem was both rewarding and accurate. Don't let my only regret be yours—tell someone all of the things you feel about them while they are still here.

DUNCAN, ANNA
[a.] Mentone, CA [title] "Love Set Me Free" [pers.] This poem was written with a special person in mind but is for everyone. I believe that most people will find a point in their life when they have a need to receive attention. It doesn't matter who pays the attention. So this poem is dedicated to anyone who is longing. Poetry is an expression of the soul. I hope you enjoyed this.

DUNLAP, AMBER
[a.] Del Rio, TX [title] "Not Today!" [pers.] I wrote this because of an assignment that was given to me by my teacher. We had to read an article from a magazine and write a poem about it. When I saw the article about the little boy named Mason who almost drowned, I knew I was destined to write about him. His parents revived him after he had been swept away by the water, all because he wanted to see the "fishies." I am 14 and am in the eighth grade. I am very proud and honored to have had my poem published.

DUNNELL, MARY A.
[a.] Udall, KS [title] "Smile" [pers.] At my retirement party, the speaker's final statement was, "we will always remember your smile." That memory was the inspiration for the poem "Smile."

DUPERE, STEVE
[a.] Amesbury, MA [title] "Time Forever, Forever Time" [pers.] Time is a mere measuring stick in the scheme of eternity. Where there is eternity, there can be no time. Where there is time, there can be no eternity. Each exists, in and of themselves, yet neither can exist in the presence of the other.

DUTTON, STEPHANIE
[a.] Ludington, MI [title] "Lost in a World of Daydreams" [pers.] Even though I'm only 11, (almost twelve), I think that I write pretty good poems. "Lost in a World of Daydreams" is one of the first poems I whipped up on my computer that isn't short or humorous. Shel Silverstein is a children's poetry writer of humorous things. His books inspired me. I am thinking about writing a poem about when my grandpa died, once this contest is over. I didn't think my poem would make it very far. Now I believe in myself and my poem. I think that I like poetry because I like art and music. They're similar in many ways.

DUTY, MARIO
[a.] Fort Worth, TX [title] "Celestial Downfall" [pers.] I feel that we have to understand and overstand the world. We can all get something from poetry. My whole life has revolved around emotions and taking heed. If you pay attention to your feelings, you are already a poet. I write poetry to teach, to express myself, and most important, to see things through other people's eyes, just to get a better understanding. I'm glad I've gotten this opportunity to speak my piece. I do this so you will want to be "never ignorant to getting goals accomplished." Thanks to my family and friends who have supported me since day one. Thank you, Father.

EARLEY, JANEAN
[a.] Las Vegas, NV [title] "A Teardrop Falls" [pers.] This poem has a very special meaning to me. It is a poem about unconditional love. This is the kind of love I hold for my husband, who encouraged me to submit this for publication. One week prior to his death, we received the confirmation letter from I.L.P. that this poem was selected for publication. This is a tribute to my beloved husband . . . forever and always.

EASLEY, ASHLEY
[a.] Las Vegas, NV [title] "My Annoying Mother" [pers.] My name is Ashley Easley and I am thirteen years old. I feel that this poem describes my mother very well. I know that she sounds bad but really she isn't. The reason she acts the way she does is because she wants to be part of my life forever. You've seen the way teenagers talk back to their parents and hit them—well, she doesn't want that to happen to me, and I don't either. That's why I wrote this poem, because it shows how much she loves me and how much I love her.

EDGHILL, THOMAS
[a.] Brooklyn, NY [title] "Wilted Egos" [pers.] Although I am not an avid follower or reader of the poetic form, I would, from time to time, find some poetry to be meaningful. I don't especially like poetry that rambles on with gibberish. Although poetry should be abstract, some styles are completely incomprehensible. I like to think of myself as a natural writer, a word processor artist. I have written just one short-short story (unpublished), but it has received rave reviews from my family, friends,and co-workers. I wrote the poem "Wilted Egos" on a dare, and to my surprise I received that wonderful congratulatory letter from the sponsors at Poetry.com (International Library of Poetry)! Having this poem published will certainly inspire me to write more, although I don't particularly like the form.

EGNOR, DONNIE
[a.] Paulding, OH [title] "1998" [pers.] Well, I'm a twenty-one-year-old male from a small town in Ohio, called the Paulding. The year 1998 was the year I graduated from PHS. That year our county lost a handful of teenagers in accidents. The first was Brad Dangler, a very well-known boy in our community. Another was Kathleen Gray, whom I had worked with at a pizza establishment in Paulding. These two deaths were very hard for me, especially occurring in a year that was supposed to be so joyous for me and my classmates. So this was written in early 1999 in memory of all that we lost. In ending, this poem is dedicated to Brad, Kathy, David, Tony, Willie, Brandon and Brad. You all are missed and loved, and we'll see you on the other side.

EL-KHUFFASH, AHMED
[a.] Hawalili, Kuwait [title] "Here Are the Unbreathing" [pers.] I have discovered quite by accident that I seem to have a skill for poetry. I submitted this poem to Poetry.com,, and I must say I was surprised when I found out it would be published a month after submitting it! Now I try to write poetry on a regular basis.

ELARIONOFF , LANCELOT, JR.
[a.] Norfolk, VA [title] "Only Yesterday" [pers.] This poem is a reflection of what I would feel if my wife, Brooke, were not in my life, a life made more enjoyable by her laughter, strengthened by her resolve, and ultimately blessed by her presence. For you, Brooke, I would chase rainbows to capture the essence of purple, enjoying the comfort of each others's company beneath a canopy of stars, only to do it all over again when we greet the sunrise in each other's arms. If all else fails, I would eat the fresh green beans and tomatoes from your garden and pretend to like it.

ELLIGSON, KAREN
[a.] Snow Hill, MD [title] "The Ache of Good-Bye" [pers.] Loosing my grandfather was very hard. Yet one thing he (and my grandmother) gave us was a godly example of how to deal with hardship. He taught us to lean on the One who will never leave us. And I am so grateful I can have the confidence of seeing my Pop-Pop again in Heaven.

ELLIS, LINDA
[a.] Boise, ID [title] "Gift From God" [pers.] I wrote this poem for my siblings, after my mother passed away. Along with this poem, I gave them a picture that was taken on the Friday before she died. In the sky was a lone cloud with a rainbow in it. My aunt had taken the picture, and the rainbow was in the shape of an angel. We prayed that day for comfort and support to make it through this difficult time. My mother was a fantastic artist who loved the beauty of God's creation. It has been difficult, but we live on with her memories and her paintings.

ELLIS, WILLEM
[a.] Excelsior, MN [title] "Happiness" [pers.] My name is Willem Ellis, and I was born on August 31, 1989. I am 11 years old and I am in sixth grade. I like to read, write, do math, and play video games. I learned how to write and understand poetry in fourth grade. I dedicate this poem to my teacher, Mr. Knaus, who showed me what poetry is all about. Thank you!

ELLISON, GRAHAM
[a.] North York, ON [title] "Myself" [pers.] When I find myself in a mood for self-reflection, the creative mind often takes over. At such times, I will sketch something present at that moment or I will take up a pen and put my thoughts to paper. That is what took place when I wrote the poem, "Myself." I was thinking of how I present a facade to the world and very few people get the chance to see below, hence, the thought process found throughout the poem. I am a teacher by profession. I have found that I have the ability to instill such a creative process in my students. Many have realized their abilities for art and writing, having spent time in my class. I find this an ideal way to reach children, fostering confidence and self-worth.

ENGLISH, LADONNA
[a.] Louisiana, MO [title] "Wingless Flight" [pers.] Horses are the perfect subjects for poetry. Their gentle grace, rhythmic motion, and powerful beauty are a feast for the senses.

ERRICKSON, WAYNE
[a.] North Plainfield, NJ [title] "A Father's Love" [pers.] A lot of times we write about what we feel. Since I'm in education, I deal with many feelings from many different individuals as well as my own. I tell them that if something is bothering you and you can't talk about it, then writing about it is the next best thing. I would love to put a book together of children's poems. It may become good therapy for all our children. I also lead and wish to be an example, and the best example I can give the children as well as my daughter is that it is okay to express what you feel in any way you can. There are many problems in our society, but the biggest problem is that we don't communicate about them. I plan to send more in the future because there is much more to talk about. So please stay tuned!

ESQUIVEL, VICTORIA
[a.] Revere, MA [title] "I Have a Dream, Too" [pers.] The world is large and full of great artists. I am 11 years old and I am so glad that I have been given this opportunity to have one of my poems published so the world can peek into my soul. This work is only a small way for me to let the world know that I see you how you are and I have a gift to share with you. My mother, I love you. You are great. You have given me life and passed your talent onto me. I will give it back, but to the whole world.

ESTES, GREGORY
[a.] Titusville, FL [title] "Complete" [pers.] This is the greatest honor. I appreciate the interest and attention my poem has received. A true honor! I never intended to be a poet much less have the opportunity to be published. I owe all this to my family and friends who gave me the inspiration to write these words. I especially want to thank James S. Estes for agonizing through countless reading sessions with me, just for me to say, "You don't like it!" I want to give my greatest thought to Nicole, my love, who even when I did not know of her, were the reasons behind my writings.

ESTES, JANET
[a.] Garland, TX [title] "Emotional Snapshots" [pers.] My first grandson died suddenly of SIDS at the age of nine weeks. Not only did I support my daughter through her grief, I also had to deal with my all-encompassing grief. I wrote a poem five months after Devin's death to describe the brief, emotional memories that my body would allow me to experience, and shortened it for this contest. The longer version is located at http://sids-network.org/fg/snapshots. I then created and maintained an on-line sight devoted to helping anyone suffering the loss of an infant. Contact me to join (infanlos-owner@taex001.tamu.edu).

EVANS, DEIRDRE
[a.] Mobile, AL [title] "A Warning to the 'Next Generation'" [pers.] My poem, "A Warning to the 'Next Generation,'" was part of an extra credit assignment. You see, I'm a 14 year old eighth grade student, and in my school, the teachers give extra credit assignments at least once every quarter. I didn't need the extra credit, but the teacher said I could do it anyway. The theme for the poem was, "A Beacon to the Future." The theme really made me think about what's going on today and how it will affect our future. I hope the poem will help people understand that something has to be done.

EVANS, RANDI
[a.] Warrensburg, NY [title] "Justin of NSYNC" [pers.] My name is Randi Lyn Evans. I am an eighteen-year-old girl who has experienced multiple medical problems since birth. I live on a special formula called Neocate, and I am on a special diet. This treatment has helped a lot. I still continue to have other medical problems that haven't been resolved. One of these issues is that I am visually impaired which limits the activities I can do. My interests include drawing, poetry writing, basketball, and NSYNC. These help me to take my mind off my pain and worries.

EVJENE, DIANE
[a.] North Hollywood, CA [pers.] "Lady-Girl" is a poem inspired by God and given to me by Him. Writing it has helped me realize that even I have been given a distinctive inner beauty all my own. What I most enjoy about this poem is that it evokes a smile upon its readers. I believe it has been and will be a source of encouragement to all. Thank you for giving me the opportunity of sharing it with your publication and its readers.

EWERT, MELINDA
[a.] Hays, KS [title] "Dark Train" [pers.] This poem is about the one thing we all have or will experience at some point in our life—loneliness. The train represents the lonely feeling and the humility that loneliness can bring. Although unpleasant, these times in my life have brought me to a greater awareness of who I am and the depth of my soul. I believe the difficult times in my life have bettered me. We can choose to make them our friend by which we choose to endure and overcome. Before we know it, the train is gone, and life goes on to a new plateau.

FABER, PAUL
[a.] Atlanta, GA [title] "Reflection of Life" [pers.] My poem represents the irony of our humanistic search for the truth and meaning of life. The irony occurs in our inability to look within ourselves and embrace the essence of our relationships with others. Live to love and love to live.

FAGAN, JANET
[a.] Eastcote, Middlesex, England [title] "Our Handyman's Retirement" [pers.] I didn't start writing poetry until four years ago, until I was thirty-nine years old. I find it very relaxing after a long day looking after elderly people. I am married to Patsy Fagan, the first ever U.K. professional snooker champion of 1977. We live in Eastcoke, Middlesex, England. I wish I could win just one poet competition, or any competition to feel what it is like to be picked or chosen as number one, but just having my poems published so other people can read them is an achievement in itself.

FAHRENBRUCH, BARBARA
[a.] Milliliken, CO [title] "The Book of My Colors" My name is Barbara. I live in beautiful Colorado with my husband, Rod, and our two handsome sons, Riely and Russell. We all love camping very much and we enjoy watching the sun set over the wonderful rocky mountains. My poems from, *The Book of Many Colors*, began when I was 12 years old with the color yellow. I had planned on trying to publish this as a children's book but I had never gotten up the nerve. Thanks to my best friend, Michele, and this poetry contest, I have the confidence I need to pursue my book.

FAILLE, ERYN
[a.] Norwich, CT [title] "It's You" [pers.] This poem is special to me because it describes how I felt towards not only one person, but several people in my life that were giving me a hard time. I hope others as well can relate to it. Poetry is a way out for me. It's my escape from reality. This is how I express my feelings and get my thoughts out of my mind. It is also a great way to relax but at the same time educate yourself. Poetry is a talent, and not everyone has it. I am thankful for it and I hope you enjoyed!

FAIN, BENNY
[a.] San Angelo, TX [title] "Lost Love" [pers.] Since the tenth grade, I have been writing poetry and short stories. It's a time when the inner soul is in touch with the conscious being. The goodness of people inspires me to write, as does that walk across a field of colorful blooms, or the bursting colors of the horizon as the sun bids farewell for another day. I'm that 46-year-old man who returned to school at Angelo State University in San Angelo, Texas. Since I am such an advocate for our youth I found college life a blessing. Eventually I was voted as student body vice president and the following year president of the student body. I won a majority of the youth's vote because I refused to accept the limitations of a so-called generation gap. I'm the proud father of a son, Nathan Fain. My son writes excellent poetry. My wonderful wife and the mother of our son is Darlene. Everyone is looking for the fountain of youth. Stop looking, as it has been in front of you all your life. Staying in touch and working with our youth is the fountain of youth of one's heart.

FARIAS, TORI
[a.] Hollister, CA [title] "Almost Always Never" [pers.] This poem is important to me because I was inspired to write it during a most difficult time in my life. The story behind this poem is just one problem I was facing during my late-adolescent years. I don't think my poem is very complicated to decipher at all. It is obvious what I am saying and even more obvious to those who have been through the same thing. I am extremely honored to have been able to share my artistic abilities with everyone and I hope that they can be understood as well as appreciated.

FARRELL, SHANNON
[a.] Niagara Falls, Ontario [title] "Family Pets" [pers.] Poems are very special to me because they let me express how I feel, like my poem "Family Pets." I love animals; they have so much character, especially the pets in my family. I'm 10 years old and I am so happy my poem is going into this book. It's not just my family that likes my writing. My mom tells me to never be afraid to express myself. She also says it's up to me to find my dreams, and for her to guide me into the right direction, until I'm old enough to find my own way.

FAUCHER, REBECCA
[a.] Campbell, BC [title] "Broken" [pers.] This just proves all my friends were right—you need to get published and allow others to enjoy your words. After years of writing my thoughts on paper, I have achieved one of my life's greatest desires—to have a poem published. "Broken" represents the crumbling of my first love, that moment when it's ending but you struggle so hard to keep the love going. However, every cloud has a silver lining—mine did!

FELDMANN, PAUL
[a.] Savannah, GA [title] "Lost in Dementia" [pers.] I've never written seriously, prior to this poem. After a fall, in which my wife was seriously injured, a sudden change occurred in her behavior. The physician's diagnosis of Dementia, or possibly early Alzheimers, was a tremendous shock to myself and our family. Suddenly, my bride of forty-six years was a stranger who depended on me for nearly everything. I remembered how she had cared for me after I had undergone heart surgery. As I wrote the poem, I thought of the reality of one's wedding vows. Now it is my turn.

FENN, ANGELA
[a.] Sandy Creek, NY [title] "Once for Me" [pers.] This poem wasn't written in the sense that I've lost love and am looking back, but rather that I have someone whom I love with all my heart. If for some reason this was taken from me, I could still know that I am the luckiest person alive to have had that, just

once, just once more than I could ever ask for, a realization that I could cherish every moment. God only knows when it all will be taken away. Don't save the best for last or the best will never come. Nickface, I love you and thank you.

FERGUSON, CLAUDETTE L.
[a.] Harrison, AR [title] "No Going Back" [pers.] This poem was written shortly after the death of my mother. I lived far away from my brothers and sisters, who were fortunate to live in the same town, and both of my children were away from home. At the time this was written, I felt very much alone and found, at that point, able to lean on what my childhood in a small town with a loving family had meant to me. This made it possible for me to face the tomorrows that followed, knowing that nothing would ever be the same.

FERGUSON, RUTH
[a.] Westport, CT [title] "Provided" [pers.] I have been a governor of transcendental meditation for thirty years and have had Gita studies in my home weekly, plus approximately fifteen hundred people for whom entering my home was like entering another world.

FERREBEE, VICTOR
[a.] Forest Hill, WV [title] "A New Best Friend" [pers.] When I started 12th grade, a very good friend and I got into a very big fight, and I couldn't go until I made amends. I was so happy when I gave her this poem and we become the best of friends again.

FERREIRA, ELIZABETH
[a.] Rio de Janeiro, Brazil [title] "Exist or Exit" [pers.] Writing poetry came late into my life. My experience was limited to academic papers in my area of studies (anthropology). In 1966, a book of mine came out. It was the result of my project of oral history using testimonies of women who had been political activists under the military regime in Brazil (1964-1985), and had been imprisoned and tortured. Certainly the impact of their stories changed me, but at the time I did not know in what sense. Now I do. A year later, at the age of 53, I wrote my first poems. This is one of them.

FERRELL, ALLISON
[a.] Quincy, MI [title] "A Pillow and a Blanket" [pers.] I always feel strange when people talk about the extravagant mansion they will own in Heaven. I think, "Why would you spend eternity in a house when you could be sitting at the feet of the creator of the universe?" I am the kind of person who thinks about things, then expresses them in words. For me, there is no doubt. If I had an eternity to spend anywhere, I would choose to bask in the radiant love of the one who knows me better than I know myself, and who continues to hide me under the shadows of his wing.

FERRO, MICHELINA
[a.] Monroe, NY [title] "Mother, I Don't Remember You" [pers.] This poem is in memory of my mother who left me when I was two years old. Mother, I want to thank you for giving me this precious life. Although I am afflicted with Parkinson's Disease, I still thank God for every day that he gives me, days that I can share with my loved ones, Michael, Denise, Carol, and my four sisters and two brothers. Mother, your inspiration gives me the chance to share my inner feelings with everyone who has the chance to read my poem.

FETZER, CARA
[a.] Coatesville, PA [title] "Friend" [pers.] This poem means a lot to me. I wrote it because kids should know what a friend really is. Picking friends is not easy. I hope you enjoy my poem.

FICO, PIERA
[a.] Reading, MA [title] "Just Another Day" [pers.] I thank God each day for my husband, Franco, and my

two precious daughters, Dina and Sarma, for not making each day "just another day," and making all my dreams come true! I wrote this poem for a dear friend who's about to go to the alter as a sacrificial lamb, in order to please her parents. I will always keep her in my prayers! Life is too precious to not live it to the fullest and make all your dreams come true!

FIELDS, BROCK
[a.] Lucasville, OH [title] "The Hand of Pain" [pers.] The poem, "The Hand of Pain," represents the overwhelming distress that I felt before I became saved. At a time when the concept of a great, loving God seemed to be a mere myth, I was lost and full of pain. When in such a state, people try to escape it by doing things that only fool them by mimicking happiness and, in actuality, push them farther into ignorance and the misery. I learned that the sky isn't the place to look, because God must be sought from within. It's a process, with the only true cure being God.

FIORONI, PAUL
[a.] Odessa, TX [title] "Creature of Magic" [pers.] This poem truly fills me with a sense of imagination and wonder, as you really feel the true magic and love which is all around us. Faith is a powerful tool, and being able to express my faith through poetry is a very spiritual and moving feeling. I hope all those who read this are filled with this same awesome sense of magic and prayer.

FISCHER, NATALIE
[a.] Modesto, CA [title] "Clouds" [pers.] I started writing when I was three years old, and ever since then I haven't been able to stop. Over the years, my writing has matured, and I am currently writing books. I love to read and I know that soon I will be living in the hallway because my books will take over. I am thirteen years old and turning fourteen in July. I really hope you enjoyed my poem, "Clouds."

FISHER, VANCE
[a.] Midwest City, OK [title] "Happy Cow Disease" [pers.] I was born in Buffalo, NY in 1970. Impressively handsome and intelligent, yet humble, I, Mr. Vance A. Fisher, have never been recognized as the unbelievably creative and insightful human being as I am until now. I would like to dedicate my poetic contribution to this book to my fiance, Wendy Michelle Torrance, and my son ,Vance H. Fisher, for they are truly the happiness of my life. I think we need to learn how to laugh at ourselves before we learn to make fun of others.

FLAGG, LARRY
[a.] Bowie, MD [title] "Happy Birthday, Mom" [pers.] My gift comes from God, my inspiration started with Mom. She was the encourager. Ella Pearl Flagg a very special lady indeed. God took her home in 1999. This poem was written while she was alive, and will serve as a permanent record of her love.

FLEMING, KAREN M.
[a.] Carson City, NV [title] "Distant Fire" [pers.] I have been writing poetry since I was ten years old. I also play guitar and sing. I enjoy spending time applying poetry to music. This poem is my favorite. My inspiration comes from the realization that happens when we look inside ourselves for light and truth to benefit us in our spiritual growth. Conquering and embracing our fear gives us courage and strength. We are here to remember who we are, to experience, to learn, and most of all, to come from a place of love, not from a place of fear.

FLOYD, RENEE
[a.] Redwood City, CA [title] "Separated Now" [pers.] Anyone who has ever been through an unsuccessful relationship will relate to this poem. Such an experience led to the writing of this poem, and I am truly grateful to have poetry as such a useful emotional

outlet. I thank Jesse for presenting me with this opportunity; I still love him with all my heart.

FOLTZ, DIANA
[a.] Columbus, OH [title] "Jealousy" [pers.] This was my first real attempt at poetry. I am a big fan, however, and my favorite poet has to be Dorothy Parker for her cynicism. "Jealousy" came about when a friend forwarded a poem to me that she had received from a co-worker. It was a desperate attempt to show her that I too could share my thoughts and feelings creatively. My hope is that everyone who reads this has at least once in their life been as fortunate to know someone like my friend. I dedication this poem to Dina.

FORCE, ROBERT
[a.] Orlando, FL [title] "A Mother in Heaven" [pers.] I love poetry and writing. It is a wonderful form of expression. It is easy to write things that are from the heart. I feel that "A Mother in Heaven is a poem to which everyone can relate. This particular poem is very close to my heart. I would love to publish more and I am also working on a novel right now.

FORD, ALANA RENEE
[a.] Chula Vista, CA [title] "True Love" [pers.] As a thirteen-year-old, San Diego native, I usually write poetry to express the emotion that I am feeling at the moment. My poem represents the feeling of losing a loved one. Quite often, emotions are hard to put into words. I want people to be able to read it and say, "That's exactly how I feel, felt." I wrote this poem after I had heard that my inspiration and role model, Michael Cuccione (singer/actor), had passed away. I tried to place myself in the shoes of someone who has experienced the loss of someone close to them.

FORESTER, FREDA
[a.] Chattanooga, TN [title] "Together" [pers.] I wrote this poem for my husband, Ed, on our 18th wedding anniversary. We met in 1949, when I was 14 and he was 18 years old. We knew from the beginning our lives would be spent together. On May 16, 2001, we will celebrate our 49th wedding anniversary with our three children and all our grandchildren. We look forward to spending our twilight years together.

FORMAN, MEGAN
[a.] Lockport, NY [title] "I Lost That Chance" [pers.] I am only twelve years old, so people can't believe the way I write, especially about love. The theme for this poem just popped into my head. My poem is about a girl falling in love with a boy and then running away from it because she wasn't sure if he mean it when he said he loved her. She just didn't want to get hurt. Then she has second thoughts about it because she finds that she is actually willing to take that risk, but it is too late, and she has lost the chance to have him.

FORNEY, TRICIA
a.] Fairfield, OH [title] "Dusk" [pers.] Thanks to the believers. "You can do it, " she would tell me. Sometimes I believed her and sometimes I wondered why she believed in my writing talent. Yet she had faith in me . . . the faith that helped me to take a leap in life and discover myself through my writing. Believe in someone and watch dreams come true!

FORTSAKIS, MICHAEL
[a.] Los Angeles, CA [title] "A Father's Pain" [pers.] For me, writing is a gift that is priceless. Not only do I enjoy the finished product, but writing is a release that leaves me rested and satisfied. I wrote "A Father's Pain" to help me deal with the extreme pain of not seeing my children on a daily basis. I work in Los Angeles in the security industry. My hope is that I will be able to write full time one day.

FOSTER, DANIELLE
[a.] Winona, MN [title] "The Words I Speak" [pers.] The subject for this poem came to me while I was

listening to the radio. It pretty much explains itself. I'm not putting down all music, just the negative ones toward others. I'm pretty much a Backstreet Boys fan, but that has nothing to do with my opinion on these songs. I like a lot of other bands and music too. My other hobbies include soccer, reading, chatting with my buds on ICQ, and of course, guys. I have many people I look up to—my friends, family and my grandmother that lives in Brooklyn, New York. My favorite quote, "Silence is golden, but laughing is more fun!" Gotta bounce! Me!

FOSTER, MYST
[a.] Qualicum, BC [title] "Soul Fire" [pers.] My inspiration for my writings came when I met my soul mate. It is a magic that fills every part me, every minute of each day and night. I write for him.

FRANCO, VINCENT
[a.] Seaford, NY [title] "Family Treasure" [pers.] Family Treasure is one of many poems I wrote to express a way of life dedicated to family. Our family reaches out to cousins, including lifelong friends, establishing special party celebrations as an excuse to bring us together. Love and happiness are obvious whenever we get together to honor someone or celebrate a special event. This poem pays tribute to leisure devoted to family, utilizing rhyme to measure non-material treasures of life. My immediate family—our eleven grandchildren, daughter, and three sons with their spouses meet regularly. I am a retired public school administrator who enjoys painting, sport activities, writing, and poetry.

FRASER, PAMELA
[a.] Taylor, MI [title] "On Marriage" [pers.] Poetry is my gift to my children and grandchildren. It is also the key to my heart and the way I can always remember those who have made a difference in my life. My poetry will preserve all the cherished memories living inside my heart. I believe we all possess this gift and ability. I just wish we weren't so shy in sharing it.

FREEMAN, GIGI
[a.] Salt Lake City, UT [a.] "New Awakening" [pers.] This poem was written for a very special friend of mine. It shares my thoughts of encouragement through life's trials. I hope this inspires others to feel secure at their times of need.

GALBAN, DAVID
[a.] Pompana, FL [title] "Reminiscences" [pers.] Sometimes in life we have to face changes, we have to experience situations that arouse awareness in us of a need, a need to express our inner feelings. Poetry appears as an answer to that need.

GALLAGHER, VICTORIA
[a.] Wilmington, DE [title] "The Vision" [pers.] I do not know where the poetry gene came from in my family nor do I know how the writing gets to the page so wonderfully. All I know is that I love sharing this gift with the world, and I hope to keep sharing. Writing this poem was a wonderful experience for me. It was the first poem I wrote which I truly liked once I read it afterwards. I hope to write many more, and hopefully they can also be printed in a book like this one.

GANT, RUTH
[a.] Toms River, NJ [title] "Right Before Valentine's Day" [pers.] Although I never considered myself a poet, putting my emotions on paper has always been an outlet for me, not only to express myself, but also as a healing experience. Whether or not the words come from joy or pain or sorrow, or just fun, it is an incredible form of expression. This poem was very therapeutic to me when I wrote it, because of my need to get through a difficult time, but also now that I can look back and know that I became a stronger person because of events in my life. For others to be able to relate to any kind of poetry validates their feelings at

different times in their lives, which is why poetry is important to me.

GARCIA, IGNACIO JR.
[a.] Jasper, TX [title] "The Flamenco Guitar" [pers.] Writing poetry has always been easy for me. I read them in books, learned them in school, but it was my mother who planted that seed as she read them to me when I was about two or three. Today I write these words of prose, to make me feel better I suppose, to express what I feel deep inside, unseen moods or unreasonable emotions I so conveniently hide. Whenever I look over my past struggles and strives, I realize I've been writing about feelings that will someday effect people's lives.

GARRISON, SUSAN
[a.] Wichita, KS [title] "Life" [pers.] I listen and waken when my savior calls during the still silence of the night. Many prayers are revealed and answered during this time of dwelling with my God. My writings and poems are in response to his awesome calling and in obedience to his word. I look forward to God's presence in my life. What a mighty God I serve!

GAWRYLA, LORRIE
[a.] State College, PA [title] "A Child's Hope" [pers.] "A Child's Hope" was inspired by my recent trip to the country of El Salvador. I performed medical assessments during a medical clinic of Hope for Kids Inc. provided for the earthquake victims. It was hard to remain objective when one witnesses hundreds of children and families homeless with medical needs and lacking the basic essentials for survival. Hope for kids is a non-profit charitable organization that provides specialized care for abandoned and homeless children in the U.S. and El Salvador. Find out more about us at hopeforkidsinc.org.

GEPALAGA, CHERYL
[a.] Hercules, CA [title] "Dream" [pers.] People often say things they do not mean. Apologies are made and accepted but the hurt often remains hidden. People may also dream of things related to their relationship or life. Sometimes it's not always convenient to vocally express these desires. In dreams, there are no boundaries. It has always been easier for me to express my feelings in verse. My high school boyfriend whom I later married, Anthony Gepalaga, was a huge inspiration. My high school friends, especially Git Maboloc, were also a big part of my writing. I put their joys and sadness on paper. It often made it easy to deal the problems at hand. It was proof that someone else understood exactly what he or she was going through. I am honored to share one of my poems with the world.

GIARDINA, RACHEL
[a.] Highland, NY [title] "I Wait for the Day" [pers.] I started writing poetry in April 2000, when my son was in the hospital fighting for his life at five years old. I never thought about writing, but one night while I was watching over him, all these thoughts were running through my mind, and I picked up my notebook and started writing my thoughts, prayers, and feelings down on paper. All of my poetry has a special meaning to me. My son is no longer with us, and the poetry I write and have written is based on him and my loss. I feel my being able to write poetry was a gift sent from God and Anthony Jr. I am not able to tell him face to face how much I miss him and love him very much so I write it in my poetry.

GIBASON, KRISTIN
[a.] Phoenix, AZ [title] "Kisses" [pers.] My name is Kristin Gibason. I'm fourteen years old and a Christian. One of my favorite things to do is go to church because I love getting to know the Lord. One teacher that inspires me most to just do it and to be outgoing is Mrs. Carter. She is the best teacher I have had and probably will have. This sums up a little bit about me. I hope you enjoy my poem.

GIBSON, JOHN
[a.] Lavonia, GA [title] "Hope" [pers.] The life brings so many unpredictable times. With everything that goes on in the world, we get so wrapped up that we seem to forget about the most important things in our lives. We never know how we affect another's life or how much life we actually have left. I think we should live life to the fullest. No matter what you are dealt with next, through good times and bad, there is always hope.

GIBSON, MARY
[a.] Clarksville, TN [title] "Love Is" [pers.] I wrote this poem because I believe that too many people do not really understand the true meaning of love. Poetry allows me to share the message that is in my heart. Every time I sit down and write, the words seem to come out on paper. This poem is just one example. I hope to one day become a writer and get my work published. This is my goal—to write and become a public speaker. I am currently seeking my degree in Secondary Education at the Austin Peay State University here in Clarksville, TN.

GIBSON, SHANNON
[a.] Richmond, VA [title] "The Real Reality" [pers.] I'm 16 years old and in the 11th grade. I play basketball and golf and write poetry. Writing poetry is a way to express one's inner feelings through words. This poem, "The Real Reality," makes you think about life. This poem doesn't deal with family, friends, or love. It is a poem to make people think. I would like to dedicate this poem to my parents, family, friends and most of all, God.

GILBERT, NANCY
[a.] Mexico, NY [title] "My Heart" [pers.] I feel that poetry is a beautiful way of expressing what's in your heart. I was inspired to write this poem by a very special person who came into my life and touched my heart so lovingly and so tenderly at a time of great loss and loneliness. He picked me up and held my hand, showing me the beauty in the world and helping me to gain the courage to go forward and live life once again. To him, I will be forever grateful!

GILL, BELENDA
[a.] Newell, WV [title] "Maybe Someday" [pers.] I wrote the poem "Maybe Someday" at a point in my life when I felt at my wit's end. It was before I met my wonderful husband, Bernie, when my daughter, Connie, and my son, Chucky, and I were living in New Cumberland WV. I enjoy writing about my feelings. I wrote a poem called "My Man" which is sort of a continuance of the poem "Maybe Someday." "My Man" tells about me finding my husband Bernie. I feel that writing is my way of telling how I feel, sometimes in a poem or a short story, sometimes even in a children's book. I am also a grandmother of two beautiful little girls, Catelyn and MycKenzie.

GIORDANO, PEARL
[a.] Mililani, HI [title] "Flower Child" [pers.] Daughters are one of life's many blessings. I was blessed with Tabitha and Samantha. I dedicate my poem, "Flower Child," to my buds. You are truly my flowers in the garden of life. Always remember, I love you forever and a day.

GIULIANO, ANTHONY
[a.] Bronx, NY [title] "Living Life's Path" [pers.] I have inherited my gift for writing from my father. Even though he didn't attend school, he was famous in a little town in Italy for his rhymes. I've been inspired by my friends at the Greenwich Health Center to continue to write, for it is an expression of my feelings. At this time in my life I am 74 and retired with a lung problem, and that is why I attend the State Center. My close friends all have health problems, but seeing us together, we have so much fun and inspire each other each other so much, you would never know we were ill. Dedicated to all my friends at Greenwich Health.

GLADIN, LISA
[a.] Sellersburg, IN [title] "Dreaming" [pers.] Poetry is me. It is what moves my soul. Poetry is how my soul speaks. I've only let my step-mom read my poetry, and after the first, she said, "girl, there is poetry in you, so let it out and if you do, you will be more free than you have been," and well, I did and I am. Thanks, Mom.

GOEPPINGER, EDNA
[a.] Tulsa, OK [title] "Teachers Are So Great" [pers.] How did I come up with the poem, "Teachers," for my daughter? My daughter came from school very upset. She said to me, "Why do I need to read and write and add in school?" This was the answer to her questions; the poem says it all. I hope teachers and school children enjoy, "Teachers Are So Great," as much as I enjoyed writing it! My hobbies are going to the Tulsa Zoo, spending time with friends, fishing, camping, and writing short children's books.

GOFFE, CYRIL
[a.] Compton, CA [title] "Let Peace Reign—Are We Our Brothers Keeper or Usurper?" [pers.] I have always enjoyed writing poetry. I would like to dedicate this poem to my family in the hope that the world will become a better and kinder place for all.

GONZALEZ, TIFFANY
[a.] Fairmont, WV [title] "The Light of Day, Mr. Tyler Ray"[pers.] This is a poem dedicated to the Garber and Snyder families in Pennsylvania and West Virginia. It was a way to express the love and joy for a six-and-a-half-year-old boy who tragically died in an accident. Truly, he's an angel touching many lives throughout his years. This is never an easy situation, but with the gift of poetry I could share my feelings with the family in a way that made sense to me. Sometimes relating in verse helps me put life into perspective and gives me the opportunity to grow as a person.

GOODEN, JOHNNY, JR.
[a.] East Providence, RI [title] "Silence" [pers.] My grandmother taught me to love, my mother instilled family unity, and my father epitomized strength and courage in times of adversity. Poetry is a figurative language utilized to create images. I have learned to listen to my heart, and what I write are simply the echoes from within.

GORHAM, JERRY
[a.] Memphis, TN [title] "When Dona Comes This Way" [pers.] This poem is a testament to the fondness of the heart and its oftentimes disquieted countenance. My approach to poetry is one of sheer enjoyment and intellectual cogitation. Poetry provides the ideal medium for the kind of versatility of expression my mental voices seem to thrive on in my celebration of life through personal and vicarious experience. Poetry is a voice always speaking within me, younger than the age of my time, yet wiser than the scope of my personal vision. Through poetry, I can explore the affinity of man with man, without regard to space, time, spirituality, or tradition.

GORNEAULT, GARY
[a.] Wolcott, CT [title] "Silence" [pers.] Poetry is one of the most ancient forms of expression. It was an art that was orally passed down for generation to generation long before there was writing. Today, although it is presented more in the written form than oral, it remains a symbolism of one's emotion and imagination. I am very proud to be part of this ancient art. To all poets, and those who read their work, let us continue to keep this art alive.

GOWEN, CLIFFORD
[a.] Burley, ID [title] "Love Will Show" [pers.] This poem expresses the turmoil I went through with my first marriage. This poem also expresses how my love is today, and as of today, the love is great. I just hope this poem will touch people in a special way. I was the youngest of my family along with my two older brothers. I have experienced so many things while growing upon our small farm. I do love my four kids, three girls and one boy. Now I am 41 and I enjoy writing certain parts of my life and turning them into poems.

GRAHAM, JOYCE
[a.] Jamaica, West Indies [title] "Let It Flow" [pers.] Poetry is my life line to sanity, the energizer that keeps me going and it is my sweet tooth. This is dedicated to mother, Agnes Graham, my daughter, Teresie, and my son, Leroy. I was born on February 21, 1957 in Westmoreland and am presently living at St. Catherine, Jamaica, West Indies. My hobbies are reading, writing poems and songs, and gardening. This is specially dedicated to all the countries of the world, especially to my island, Jamaica.

GRANT, KENNETH
[a.] Norwalk, CA [title] "The Shroud" [pers.] This poem was written during summer vacation in Lake Tahoe. It came out of my awe and appreciation for the eternal nature of all that I was observing. People came and people go, but all of God's creation stands as a testament of creative genius. Each poem I write is intended to express a particular feeling or emotion that grows out of the joy I feel in being alive. God has give us a wonderful planet, if we only take the time from our busy schedule to take it all in.

GRAY, DR. DOVIE
[a.] Decatur, GA [title] "The Gatlinburg Experience" [pers.] Dr. Dovie Wesley is a motivational speaker and an educator. She was inspired to write this particular poem after seeing Gatlinburgh and its beauty in the heart of winter. The annual January trip with over 40 plus co-workers and friends has become a religious retreat. Dr. Gray is intrigued with the wonders of the God's creations. Dr. Gray is available for speaking engagements. "A vision not shared is a lost reality" is her original motto.

GREEN, ERIC
[a.] Bryson City, NC [title] "Always for You" [pers.] I am a teenager who just had a love for poetry. I have written several poems but I have my favorite ones and my favorite authors. I know that poems of love are from people's point of view, but it should be able to teach you something. My poetry is my way of expressing myself, but it is not the only way I do it. I wrote this poem for a certain someone, but all of them have a story behind them.

GREEN, STEPHEN
[a.] Washington, DC [title] "XtremeDaPoet" [pers.] "XtremeDaPoet" is one of my touching poems. It describes what I see going on in the lives of many people today. It's like people killing themselves and thinking God approves it. As humans, we can be perfect but we need to destroy this image of the human mentality and enter into perfection. This is something I pray for even in my own life.

GREENE, BRIAN
[a.] Yadkinville, NC [title] "The Never-Ending Race" [pers.] I am 12 years old and in the seventh grade. I attend Courtney Elementary School. My poem is about Dale Earnhardt. To me, he was like a family member. He was a hero, just like my Dad. Poetry helps me express my feelings—when I am happy or when I am sad, I can find words to express it. My hobbies are painting, poetry, and riding my two-wheeler with my cousins Charlie, Cody, and Hartey.

GRIFFITH, BRETT
[a.] Ontario, NY [title] "The Voices" [pers.] Poetry was a gift from my high school English teacher. She saw that I was having problems and showed me a way to get them out. This poem is about the fight I had with myself. I wanted to come home, but I thought I let my family down by not making something of myself. It's the ongoing battle that everyone faces—wondering, am I worthy?

GRIFFITHS, DAVID
[a.] Bergenfield, NJ [title] "Close to the Edge" [pers.] David Griffiths is an Englishman living and working in New Jersey. This poem was originally penned in 1981 as a lyric. The subject is isolation and despair leading to suicide. It is not based on any personal experience or insight of the author. Despite its introspective view, it is one of the only poems that the author has sought to publish.

GRIMM, ANGELA
[a.] Pine Bluff, AR [title] "Overwrought Shortcoming" [pers.] I wrote this poem at a time when I felt so alone and misunderstood. Though I wrote this poem a few years ago, I still fell those same emotions at times. Being able to jot down my feelings and getting recognized for it is truly a gift. I have no special words of wisdom to share—the only message I can give is, be true to yourself and be honest with others, and everything will turn out fine. I love you 124/412 (They know who they are).

GRINTON, DARA
[a.] Taylorsville, NC [title] "Shenandoah" [pers.] I wrote this poem when I was at a turning point in my life. To me, there is nothing more wonderful than giving people like me a piece of my soul. My dream is to be a writer, and now I feel like I am on the way to achieving that dream. Thanks, and keep reading.

GROVER, ANDREW
[a.] Springvale, ME [title] "Dreams Not Experienced" [pers.] Mediocrity can be achieved in any individual's life span but to excel determination and mental clarity. The subconscious realm sees situations as finite with limited opportunities. Poetry supercedes this subconscious realm into a world where excellence is the norm.

GRUVER, PHIL
[a.] Bethlehem, PA [title] "Memories of One" [pers.] I am now a senior in high school. My sister passed away when I was in eighth grade. I wrote this poem to remember her. My teacher encouraged me to write poetry. I felt this poem helped me to express my feelings about her more deeply.

GRZESKOWIAK II, ANTHONY
[a.] South Lyon, MI [title] "Lost a Child's Wish" [pers.] This poem was the first one I ever wrote and is also the one that means the most to me. Being 20 years old and having all of the responsibilities of an adult comes flying at you is hard. This poem expresses the feelings I had when I was hit with these responsibilities. It represents the child in all of us that is trying to come back out.

GUASTELLA, SARA
[a.] Cheshire, CT [title] "My Little Angel" [pers.] "My Little Angel" was written for my special needs daughter, Amber. Though she was born with many challenges, she was also born with a great gift, a gift of strength, love, and hope. Her light has shone upon many people and has touched many lives, especially mine. I love you, my baby girl.

GUETERMAN, FILICIA
[a.] Apex, NC [title] "A Father's Love" [pers.] I wish for every reader that each person will "feel" the words and relate to the message. I chose not to explain why or who I may write poetry; my goal is that it "moves" you and brings about some emotion within each of you and take what you feel and read!

GUREVICH, SVETLAND
[a.] Toronto, ON [title] "In Front of the Mirror" [pers.] When I feel lonely, I look into my soul, take what I see there and put it into words. Although "In Front of the

Mirror" has no rhymes, it is a reflection of my thoughts and feelings. Therefore, it is poetry in its true sense.

GUTSCH, BONNIE
[a.] Soldotna, AK [title] "The Forest of Youth" [pers.] I am truly blessed to have been born into a family that possesses boundless talent in the wonderful world of artistic expression. I remember picking up a pen and paper at age four and I haven't set them down since. My inspiration is and will continue to be fed by my supportive family, the beauty of Earth, and the power of imagination.

HAECK, BIANCA
[a.] Dove Canyon, CA [title] "Lost" [pers.] I feel that poetry is something personal, something that was sparked off by a memory or event that had happened. The poem that I wrote was about how tremendously painful it was to lose my grandfather. He and I were close, and to lose him so suddenly was dreadful to me, being only nine years old at the time. This inspired me a few years later to write "Lost," as a dedication, and a final farewell. So this goes out to all those who have lost someone they loved. Remember, death is merely a phase of life.

HAGLUND, KIRSTEN
[a.] Pelican Rapids, MN [title] "Afraid" [pers.] My name is Kirsten Haglund. I live in Pelican Rapids, MN. I am 14 years old and in eighth grade. My family consists of my mom, Mia, my dad, Jamie, and my eight-year-old brother, Stephan. My hobbies are rollerblading, talking on the phone, hanging out with my friends, singing, and being on the computer (Internet, chatting, games). The sports I like are volleyball, basketball, track, swimming, and football. The reason I wrote this poem is because I have had some experiences in life where some things didn't go exactly as I wanted them to, but the way things go may turn out to be better in the end.

HALL, DARLEAN
[a.] San Jose, CA [title] "Life's Game" [pers.] I write this poem when I was 16 and just starting to find the confusion of growing up pressing in on my life. I dedicate this one to Terry Hart Hill, the father of my daughter, Jona Renea.

HALL, ELIZABETH
[a.] Hanford, CA [title] "Life Is a Gift" [pers.] My poem was inspired by years of contemplation with those particular questions in mind. Is life a gift or a test? I feel it is a combination of the two with the predominating element being that of the precious gift of life. I feel my poem may be an inspiration to others' gift of life. I feel my poem may be an inspiration to others who might have had the same spiritual struggles I have had in my youth and young adulthood life. Live life to the fullest. Touch everyone's life in a positive way if you can, use your given talents to their fullest potential, and share them with others.

HALL, LARA
[a.] Boise, ID [title] "Roses" [pers.] It is a great honor to be published. I am only thirteen, and poetry is my way of expressing my feelings. This poem is about a girl I know. Everyone tells her how she has the perfect life. One day, I was over at her house, and she burst out crying. She told me her parents were getting a divorce. I realized then, nobody's life is perfect. This poem is an expression of her life. This is to you, Kaelynne.

HAMILTON, JENNIFER
[a.] Elkton, VA [title] "Delusions" [pers.] Poetry isn't a gift, but to write well you must have a passion for it. It's something that is emotionally driven. When writing, we should feel strongly for what we're writing about. No matter how successful we become in life, we must never forget our friends. I'd like to say a special thank you to Rick Ramos for all the encouragement he's given me. I also would like to thank my

family for all their support. I couldn't have done it without them.

HAMILTON, PAULINE
[a.] Grand Rapids, MI [title] "The Struggle of a Woman" [pers.] It was Mother's day, and I thought about all the children who were given away like myself or placed in foster homes. Life can be cruel to people who know nothing about showing or receiving love. For us, there is very little hope of having a meaningful relationship. I was fortunate to have people who believed in me and encouraged me to get an education. I want to thank my best friend, Edward Campbell, and his family for their encouragement. I also extend my heartfelt gratitude to my two children, Samantha and Kimani, for the joys that they have brought to my life.

HAMILTON, REBECCA
[a.] Abilene, TX [title] "Montana" [pers.] The poem, Montana, is very special to me because Montana has been my home from the time I was five until I was 13, when I moved to Texas. I like to ride horses and hang out with my friends. I am a freshman at Clyde High School and I make fairly good grades. I like to write letters, stories and poems and lots of other stuff. I am very caring and friendly and last but not least, I love my family. I also have five brothers and sisters. I am the baby of the family but I am not spoiled.

HAMMOND, STEPHANIE
[a.] Sharon Hill, PA [title] "I Found Me" [pers.] I use my poetry as a means of cleansing. Sometimes my verses purify like fire and mirrors the burning in my soul. At other times, my words flow in and out like the tide and reflect my philosophy of self. "I Found Me" was definitely a purification by water.

HANEY, ANNA
[a.] Elizabeth, WV [title] "Trapped" [pers.] I was introduced to poetry in a one-room school during the early 60's. I grew up on a farm, and poetry was a means to make farm life appear more exciting. I would dream up poems in my head to offset laboring farm chores. As I got older, I wrote poetry to express my innermost thoughts and feelings to special people in my life. I am a registered nurse, and this poem is a tribute to the strength of patients as they regain their normal lifestyle.

HANNAN, KHOANDKAK
[a.] Farwaniya, Kuwait [title] "My Outgoing Colleague" [pers.] Born in Bangladesh, I am an engineer by profession. My wife is Lucy, my son is Shaon, and my daughter is Choyon. Having been a resident of Kuwait since 1981, I have met many colleagues and friends of different origins. This poem was written on a special occasion that a colleague left for his country forever. Certainly the moment was unique in its perpetual measure. However the feeling was great in myself, and I sketched that with the words of my finest care. About poetry I shall mention that it is the fairest mode of expression that demands and pays love, truth, and beauty eternally and universally.

HANSEN, RAGNHILD
[a.] Korsor, Denmark [title] "Dreaming" [pers.] When I began writing poetry at the age of 13, I never thought that it would lead to this. It would have seemed unreal. But now, at the age of 22, it is nevertheless extremely real. I cannot even begin to explain how I feel or what poetry means to me. It is like lightening striking from a clear, blue sky. I realize that God has given me a gift, and that it is now up to me to make the best of it. I dedicate "Dreaming" to everyone who has the courage to believe in themselves.

HARNER, DON
[a.] Stockton, CA [title] "Tree" [pers.] Poetry has always been an outlet for me. Although I do not write as much as I'd like, I find great therapy in the times

when I do. Nature is a great inspiration to me. I appreciate the simple things like trees, rocks, and mountain streams which bring me comfort and help me to remember my place in the universe. I don't see nature as something to be squandered and used up, but rather as something to preserve and take joy in. I dedicate this poem to my wife, Trisha, for whom trees are the most wondrous of nature's miracles.

HARPSTER, HELEN
[a.] Tyrone, PA [title] "My Mother" [pers.] The poem, "My Mother," reflects exactly what kind of a special person my mother was. She was a very important and special person who helped to mold my life. I will always be indebted to her for the many years of hard work, great strength, courageous and everlasting love she gave to me and to the rest of my family. I dedicate this poem to my precious mother who has since gone home to be with the Lord.

HARRINGTON, TAMARA
[a.] Baltimore, MD [title] "My Love for You" [pers.] Poetry is the best way for me to express what I am feeling at that precise moment—love, anger, or depression. My poem portrays my feelings for my boyfriend as a lover and how being just friends would not be enough. He is the best friend a girl could have in her life—helping me get through any and everything in life, and I love him for it. Poetry helps me show others what is going on in my head, and perhaps my poems could help others do the same when they are not able to find the right words.

HARRIS, JENNIFER
[a.] Buffalo, NY [title] "Purple" [pers.] I have been writing since sixth grade. I normally write about animals but when I wrote about my favorite color, purple, I was surprised at how easily the words came. I have since then used poetry and short stories to express my feelings. I feel writing is a great outlet for emotions as it allows me to put down exactly how I feel. Writing for me relieves stress and calms my inner feelings.

HARRIS, PHILICIA
[a.] Buffalo, NY [title] "The Nightmare of You" [pers.] I feel poetry is a gift; one that should be treasured. For me, poetry is the one way to show the reality of my existence without telling my entire life story. I like being a mystery; I don't want anyone to know what I'll write about next. I would also like to think of myself as being unpredictable. I don't want anyone planning my next move. Poetry allows me to state myself to the world yet still remain a mystery to many.

HARRISON, TERRI
[a.] Gonzales, TX [title] "Where Has She Gone?" [pers.] I am the mother of four beautiful children. In them, I find so much humor. When I seem to get overwhelmed with the everyday aspects of life, I find myself writing poetry about the funny side of parenthood. Sometimes I write of a more serious nature, but I enjoy these funny little memories, set to verse. And to my children, Sarah, Brooke, Kristyn, and Garrett, I leave a piece of my heart, etched in a poem to remind them of the joy and inspiration that they have brought into my life.

HARSHBARGER, ASHLEY
[a.] Xenia, OH [title] "Love" [pers.] This poem means a lot to me, because I dream of being in love with someone. My friend inspired me to write this, and I'm glad I did. I write poetry quite a lot. It is an honor for my poem. I read poetry often. Of course I think poetry is beautiful. I would like to thank the International Library of Poetry. I am a huge anime fan . My slogan is "Tsukino hikari wa ai no message," originally said by Naoko Takaevchi. The translation is, "The moonlight is a message of love!" Most of all, I would like to thank all of the readers of my poem and my friend, James. Sayonara!

HART, JENNENE
[a.] Sicklerville, OH [title] "More Time" [pers.] This poem was written for the loss of a very close friend of mine, Carlos, 21, 1979-2000. He meant the world to me. When his life was taken, I was completely devastated. I then decided to write some words on paper. I found myself writing words that came from deep within me. Finally, I produced this poem. From his death, I was able to reach inside of myself and explore my emotions. Even though Carlos is gone from this world, he will be in my heart and in my thoughts forever. This poem was written in July of 2000 in memory of Carlos.

HART, MARK
[a.] Miami, FL [title] "Ode to Burning of Age" [pers.] I have an immense respect for words and poetry. They quench the innermost feelings' need to be understood. With age comes the understanding of many things. This includes a deeper knowledge of pain through our experiences. However, the pain of love always seems to burn anew. Like an innocent child, we become vulnerable to feeling it for the first time—every time. Feeling it again, for the first time, sparked "Ode to Burning of Age."

HARTER, SARAH
[a.] Altoona, PA [title] "And God Said" [pers.] For those of you who not know me by Sarah, you know me as Sally. I'm a down-to-Earth sort of person. To me, a smile from a stranger is worth more than gold. I enjoy cuddling up with a good movie and my best buddy. Sing to me of love, sing to me great spirit Earth. Show what you're made of. I truly believe if you have faith you can move mountains, and good things will come.

HARTFORD, JARED
[a.] Tillamook, OR [title] "This One Girl" [pers.] I am currently a freshman in college seeking a major in business. I wrote this poem for my girlfriend, who before I met her was fighting anorexia. After she won the fight with anorexia, depression set in. I wrote for her to let her know that I understand what she is going through, and also that she doesn't need to worry, because I will be by her side through it all.

HARTMAN, HEATHER
[a.] Lemoore, CA [title] "Heartbreaker II" [pers.] The poem, "Heartbreaker II," means a lot to me. I feel that the poem can be shared with others. It is about losing someone that I just can't get over. This is just a beautiful poem that I can't explain. It belongs in my heart and with others who feel the same way. I think when people write poems they are expressing themselves. I think the best way to express yourself is on paper. I have been writing poems ever since I was young and I can't find anything that makes me happier. Thanks for giving me a chance to show my poem to the world.

HARWOOD, RICK
[a.] Glenfield, Australia [title] "Bonnie's Tree" [pers.] I was born and raised in Sydney, Australia. This poem was inspired by the beautiful poetry of my friend, Nicole G. McDougal. Her poem, "For Bonnie," told the story of the planting of Bonnie's tree. I'd like to start by thanking her. Also I'd like to thank my mother, who taught me to express myself creatively without restraint, as well as my family and friends for inspiring and encouraging me to write the things I do. Without you, there would be no one to write for and nothing to write about. I love you all.

HASHIM, NORISAH
[a.] Wichita, KS [title] "When We're Apart" [pers.] Created from deep inside, this poem lamented for the lost love of a mother whom I've never known or seen since childhood and the search for the true and sincere love of a separated husband for the happiness of another woman. I feel I am born a loser. These are emotions best shown through a poem.

HATZIDIMITRIOU, KIKI
[a.] Toronto, OH [title] "You" [pers.] Every poem I write represents my feelings. Every day, every hour, a new poem in my life. . . . "You" was written while I was feeling strong, indifferently, free!

HAUER, DIANE
[a.] Stratford, NJ [title] "Flight" [pers.] One day, back before the war broke up Yugoslavia, I was there, sitting on a rock, on a mountainside. The sun was warm, and a soft breeze was like a message. I relaxed and started letting my mind wander. I tried not to control it. I saw a great many things—the valley, darkness, light, a woman tending her herd of cattle. The feelings were deep and raw—pain, joy, and grief were among them. When I awoke, I was still trying to absorb all that my mind saw. So I started writing it down. "Flight" is what came out.

HAWKINS, AMELIA
[a.] Provo, UT [title] "Echoes" [pers.] "Echoes" is dedicated to Lehi community, Mesa, Arizona, and to all those, like myself, who lived there, but who where moved elsewhere for the sake of the much-needed free way. This place, where I grew up, is forever in my heart even though it can no longer be seen.

HAWN, JASON
[a.] Mishawaka, IN [title] "Really Miss You" [pers.] I am a musician by heart but I have always felt I had a gift for lyrics. This poem was actually a song I wrote for a friend who was leaving for college. Writing has always been the way that I liked to express my love for people, and I hope that others can relate to the feelings I express in my words.

HEAD, TROY
[pers.] Louisville, KY [title] "Days of Your Dreaming" Troy Thomas Head is a 32-year-old student of architecture, painting, and poetry. He has discovered that each discipline not only overlaps, but moreover, engages and enhances the others. This synergy, Troy finds most satisfying to his innermost being. This has grown into the inspiration for his life and paints the color of his soul violet. This keeps him alive and kicking, and forever optimistic.

HECHT, DANNY, JR.
[a] Broomfield, CO [title] "Valentine" [pers.] This is a poem for my wife, Gina, who encourages me and inspires every thought I have. I love my wife and family.

HECKAMAN, SHAWNA
[a.] Mishawaka, IN [title] "In the Night" [pers.] All my life, poetry has had a special meaning to me. There is no better way to express one's feelings than by a poem. "In the Night" tells my feelings toward my boyfriend, Adrian. To me, poems are a way to calm a person and give them a certain feeling of peace and comfort. I am 15 years old, and that proves that no matter what your age is, you may have the ability to write a poem. I love the night, which is why I chose to use nighttime features, such as the stars and the moon.

HEDGLIN, ADAM JAMES
[a.] Bothell, WA [title] "This is Not Good-bye" [pers.] Poetry plays a big part in my life as it allows me to address certain issues and share them with others. This certain poem refers to school shootings. This issue is very important to me as it is to many others, and somehow sometime soon we are going to find a way to stop it. Even step counts toward a better outcome. The first step is figuring out where to begin.

HEE, HUIWEN
[a] Singapore [title] "Prayer" [pers.] "Prayer" is actually one of numerous poems which I wrote under my Lord and Savior's divine inspiration. He has worked in ways that I cannot express. He has given me this chance to contribute here. God truly gives back tenfold what is offered to Him, and I only hope and pray that you, upon reading this poem, will be similarly touched by my Saviour, Brother, Redeemer, and Friend, Jesus Christ. Thank you and I pray that God blesses you in a personal way today.

HEISINGER, CHARLES R., JR.
[a.] High Ridge, MO [title] "Thinking of You" [pers.] This poem was originally inspired by my first love in January, 1992, but it was written on March 13, 1998. I like to write after the fact. With age, it just gets better, just like wine. All of my poem are written from heart and from personal experiences I have been through. Since falling in love again, I now know that this poem applies to all true love. To this date, I have written 13 poems. I dedicate this poem to those two who have changed my life.

HELMS, DANNY
[a.] Kodiak, AK [title] "Loss of Someone Special" [pers.] This poem is very special to me; even though I would like to keep this poem anonymous. This poem gave me the strength and will. I hope that others who have lost someone special can relate to my poem and perhaps share it with those who are dear to them.

HELOU, GEORGE
[a.] Yagoona, Australia [title] "Jewels of Time" [pers.] This poem was inspired by my love for the greatness and divinity within all people. We create our reality, and the only truth I subscribe to is the knowledge that we are unconditionally loved and we are given the same power to realize our dreams as we are given the ability to dream them. My purpose in this life is to communicate the knowledge that our attitudes create powerful magnetic fields that attract circumstances equal to our expectations. This is to the God within and never without.

HENDERSON, TOMMYE
[a.] Little Rock, AZ [title] "Just Be" [pers.] Through continued evolvement of my interest and learning experiences related to nature, the poems surface for expression. Native American culture and lore have contributed greatly to my feelings of connectedness which relates to what I perceived as Mother Nature. Symbolism of "Just Be" speaks of visual beauty of the mountain lake home of my friend, Gray Ghostly, plus our philosophies about life. The deep desire to express my philosophies via symbolism plus the love of nature's subtle and yet dramatic beauty has flowed intensely from my heart to the printed word since early winter.

HENEGAR, RICHARD
[a.] Daleville, VA [title] "I Am Like a Star" [pers.] For me, poetry is a way of expression, a way of talking about things. I'm a sophomore in high school, an all-state sprinter, and a poet on the side. I also enjoy singing. A lot of my poems may sometimes turn into songs. They all have their separate meanings but this poem seems to be my favorite for a reason I can't explain.

HEPP, DAVID
[a.] Huntington Beach, CA [title] "The Bard's Tale of Darkness" [pers.] "The Bard's Tale of Darkness" was created through a medieval fantasy adventure novel that I recently finished, but have not yet published. This poem is a Bard's song told to warn adventurers from pursuing a very deadly beast for their hope to gain fame and fortune. I have a beautiful family here in California, and my success will become theirs. I hope to be able to continue my writing full on with poetry, short stories, and novels that I have written and will continue to write. II hope the publication of my poem is the first successful step in order for my dreams of being an accomplished writer to come true.

HERNANDEZ, ALONZO
[a.] Evans, CO [title] "Seeing What Is Behind" [pers.] Throughout my life, I have noticed that the world keeps revolving, and us, well, we revolve with it. We've invented something we call "time" to quantify

those revolutions by hours, minutes, and seconds, thus making us believe we can control it to our whim. However, the truth is that the world moves at its own bowl, inflexible and serene. Let's move along with it. I dedicate this piece not only to my friends and family, Raul, Corrine, Amanda, and Nata, but to the "old" which in my opinion holds the key to time. Most of all I dedicate this to Jehova, for without him I am nothing; with him I have everything.

HERNANDEZ, ATHENA
[a.] Lathrop, MO [title] "Why?" [pers.] I love poetry! It is like a passion for me. I get my feelings out on paper through poetry, feelings that I normally would have locked up inside.

HERRERA, DEBRA
[a.] Tukwila, WA [title] "I Remember Mama" [pers.] This poem was a first time effort, with my inspiration coming from my granddaughter, Casandra, who has been a blessing and a joy.

HERREWEGH, HAROLD
[a.] Rotterdam, The Netherlands [title] "Pilgrimage" [pers.] My poems are very personal thoughts and ideas. I try to make a nice package in the form of language around them. Finding the deeper meaning of feeling, thoughts, and events is what inspires me most of the times to write. My poems are usually a summary. Sometimes a poem just pops into my head, sometimes I write very deliberately. However, they are all very special to me, and I hope people will enjoy reading them and that they will be touched by them.

HEYEN, ERIC
[a.] Lincoln, NE [title] "Beer Can Parade" [pers.] I have always been the shy and quiet type about what I am thinking or feeling. Poetry has always been my way of giving the world some idea as to the chaos in my head. I would like to thank KC, for showing me that one geeky kid can make a difference, and also TS, my inspiration.

HIBBLER, MOLLIE
[a.] Indianola, MS [title] "Do You Want Me?" [pers.] I give all thanks and praise to God who has given me the talent and ability to travel the road which leads to fulfilling one of my biggest dreams, writing poetry. I love expressing myself in verse. I enjoy putting feelings and emotions in writing. Ever since third grade I have been writing short stories and poems, and have always dreamed of being published.

HICKS, REGINALD
[a.] Richmond, VA [title] "Love" [pers.] My poem was created strictly from my heart. I was very confused about love because I had never witnessed love. The day that love intended my heart for someone other than my family was a day that I viewed life through virgin eyes. I pray that everyone who reads my poem will find significance and understand my love.

HICKS, RONALD
[a.] Mobile, AL [title] "More Than Conquerors" [pers.] The Bible states, "My people are destroyed for lack of knowledge" (Hosea 4:16). The poem, "More Than Conquerors," conveys to mankind that we are more than just carnal creatures. I wanted to make people think about who they really are and what they were predestined to do in their lives. Even though we are individuals with special talents, we should come together as one and use our talents for the betterment of mankind. Most importantly, the force that resides around us, the Holy Spirit, enables us to accomplish all things, and that makes us more than just conquerors.

HICKS, SHAWN
[a.] Tabb, VA [title] "Admiring Star" [pers.] This poem was written to a beautiful women who swept away my heart. I was basically telling her that she was the only one whom I wanted to be with out of the entire world, and I asked her if she was feeling the same way. I truly miss you and love you, Dawn Aycock.

HICKSON, GENETRA
[a.] Gary, IN [title] "This Word, Love" [pers.] "This Word, Love" come to me when I was thinking about love and how many people take it for granted. Knowing unconditional love and true meaning makes me think of Jesus. God is love; God spoke about the word love. Love came into existence and was planted in the hearts of those that believe. If you failed to find out where "This Word Love" originated from then you will never understand the true meaning of love. Poetry is a gift given to me by God. I look to Him first, then the words follow.

HILL, HEATHER
[a.] Cuyler, NY [title] "A Journey" [pers.] I thank God for the gifts my parents have given me. Do not take for granted the talents with which God has blessed you. A friend of mine had drifted back into my life. Happy with no worries, we sat up all night together on a hill, waiting for the sun to rise, as if we had stepped out of the world and were watching it from above. I dedicate this poem to Abner Oviedo, because he was and is the inspiration behind it. I thank him for giving me light behind darkness and for our beautiful daughter, Andaria Frederique.

HINMAN, KELLY
[a.] Orlando, FL [pers.] The basis of this poem is about what I have learned while raising my four children, Bruce Paul, Cody Daniel, Joshua Keith, and Zachary Austin. These four are my pride and joy. I am 28 years old and have lived in Florida all of my life. I have been married for eight years to a wonderful supportive man. My hobby is my poetry. It is my outlet from the daily stresses.

HINNERSHITZ, FELICIA
[a.] Merchantville, FL [title] "Remembering" [pers.] I wrote this poem because Michael Cuccione was a person who touched me and many others. His death left me very sad, and the way to express my feelings was to write this poem. I hope that this poem means as much to others as it does to me. Keep Michael's spirit alive always. Love yaz, Felicia Hinershite.

HINSON, ANDREA
[a.] Ambrose, GA [title] "Distance" [pers.] I am the youngest daughter of Rev. Hugh and Sarah Hinson of Ambrose, GA. I believe poetry is a window into one's innermost thoughts and expressions. Poetry is a way that I can fully express my deepest feelings, without feeling guilty about it.

HIRONAKA, SHANE
[a.] Hilo, HI [title] "That's Life" [pers.] To me, poetry is an expression releasing your deepest feelings from your heart. This verse was actually a rap I wrote and performed. This poem was written after my good friend passed away. It expressed my frustration towards the world and questioned life itself. This poem released my anger and made me realize that life is a gift, and we have to accept everything, even the bad. I would like to thank my friends and family back in Hawaii. Rip-A.C, "You don't know what you have got till it's gone."

HIRSCH, JORDAN
[a.] Michigan City, IN [title] "Holocaust: A Letter to Mommy" [pers.] I started learning about the Holocaust when I was really little because I'm Jewish. About three years ago, when I was 11, I was reading a book about the Holocaust, and the tragedy of it inspired me to write my poem. My current project is a book.

HITCHCOCK, MARY
[a.] Kalamazoo, MI [title] "By an Eye of Faith" [pers.] This poem came to me one night as I was working under stress. I kept praying to God to give me the strength to get through the night. As I prayed, God gave me these words. I hope these words will be a blessing to others.

HOAGLAND, CHERIE
[a.] Mercerville, NJ [title] "Prepared" [pers.] Poetry is one of God's gifts. Each of us is given a heart that stores deep feelings and emotions. One must quiet himself, tune in, and open it to connect with that which is there. Then those feelings can be placed on paper, where, like water flowing peacefully over rocks in a stream, they can flow through the hearts of many. Many extreme changes have occurred recently in my life. My wonderful faith in the Lord has allowed me to adapt to each challenge with courage, knowing that it's just another part of His plan!

HOAGLAND, GLENDA LOUISE
[a.] Detroit, MI [title] "My Hideaway" [pers.] This poem was written in 1981 when I moved into my first apartment as a single mother. Across from my window was a beautiful meadow that inspired me. I have been writing poetry since I was 15 years old (I am now 51). It is a source of peace and freedom for me, truly a gift from God.

HOLDAWAY, KATHLEEN
[a.] Lawrenceville, GA [title] "Inaudible" [pers.] Poetry is my expression of the depths of human emotion, the spirit with each of us and our journey. By sharing this gift, my intention is to help others know they are not alone in the process of discovering who they are created to be. As the layers of all pull away, and the true self emerges, there are depths to our sorrows that words alone cannot express and heights to the joy we can't begin to imagine. Poetry is my vehicle to reveal this to a world in transformation. My goal is to honor God and to stir the spirit within each of us.

HOLEMAN, KIMBERLY
8[a.] Kuttawa, KY [title] "Infinity and Beyond" [pers.] This poem has a special meaning to me. I wrote this poem after my fiancé and I separated. It was a hard and difficult time for both of us. I would tell him I love you, "to infinity and beyond." That is where the title of my poem came from. I hope you enjoy reading my poem and will want to share it with others. I have learned that you need to love, laugh, and be happy in a relationship.

HOLLINSHEAD, SHERRI
[a.] Bronson, FL [title] "Time Standing Still" pers.] "Time Standing Still" is very special to me because it is about a creek at my parent's house in the woods which is absolutely breathtaking. If you are a believer in the beauty God has created, this place is a little piece of Heaven. Therefore I would like to dedicate this poem to my parents, Devon and Judy Fowler, who not only live in a beautiful place, but who are beautiful themselves. I love you both!

HOLMES, CHRISTOPHER
[a.] Montgomery, AL [title] "This Race" [pers.] This poem was written when I was extremely depressed, with thoughts of committing suicide. I was thirty years old, with no idea of who I was or where I was going. I'd seem to be all right around others, but inside I was dying. I guess you could call me "The Great Pretender." I truly believe anyone can relate to this poem. Sometimes you're up; sometimes you're down. I guess it's part of the roller-coaster ride we call life.

HONZA, BRANDON
[a.] Columbia, MD [title] "The Pillow" [pers.] To me, poetry is a way to release and express my feelings and emotions to those close to me. "The Pillow" deals with the smell that I have associated with a person dear to me. Even though she was no longer in my company, I was still able to smell her. This brought back many thoughts and emotions. I immediately

started to write. Kind emotions live longer. I would like to dedicate this poem, my first published poem, to all those who believed I had what it takes to be published.

HORTON, MARK
[a.] Denver, CO [title] "The Faith to Leap" [pers.] My words reflects passages in my life. They help me to share with others the passions and emotions I can sometimes not find the with spoken word alone. The following passage resonates for me a profound sense power that captures one's heart and inspires the courage to face our fears. They are not my words, but they are from someone I admire. Life is either a daring adventure, or nothing. To keep our faces toward change in the presence of fate is strength undefeatable.

HOSEIN, NERISSA
[a.] Sanfernan, Trinidad [title] "My Light" [pers.] The beauty of a poem lies in the emotion it expresses. It is amazing to have a feeling powerful enough to inspire creativity, something so strong that it must be shared and immortalized. I have always felt that words give us that kind of immortality. They capture pieces of our lives and preserve them for eternity. These words were never meant to be a poetic verse. I was simply trying to tell someone very special what was in my heart. Thank you Brian . . . for being my inspiration.

HUDSON, HANNAH
[a.] Fairfax, VA [title] "Angel Wings" [pers.] I have always loved poetry. It is a wonderful thing that you can put thoughts and dreams into a beautiful piece of writing. In 1997, my grandfather died, and my grandmother has been very sad at times. I wrote this poem about her but I also put at the end that I also see an angel that has loved me and watched me all of my life because that is what she is to me. Thank you for including my poem in this book.

HUDSON, LORRAINE
[a.] Milton, DE [title] "March Promises" [pers.] I am an artist, writer, and musician of an unique style. My paintings, writing, and music form a diamond of many facets creating a journey to the infinite. I reside near Milton, Delaware and am currently working on a book which will be illustrated with my latest art. I also am composing and writing theater. The arts are a way of conveying my message—One People One Planet One Universe Extending to Infinity! I live life to its fullest and revel in its beauty.

HULSE, MEREDITH
[a] Scarborough, MA [title] "Harvest Basket" [pers.] Often my writings begin, as "Harvest Basket" did, welling up in my subconscious mind in the twilight between asleep and awake, when dream images and insights are still available and malleable to restructuring by my wakening consciousness of them. I experience them as gifts rather than as products. They are rather like gift kits, however. Once I have received them, I have to work long and hard on them. Each poem, once conceived, is asking to be born through my labor.

HUTCHINSON, MARLENA
[a.] Leitchfield, KY [title] "Husband" [pers.] This poem was written for my husband whom I love dearly. I never knew what love really meant until I began to love him. Tyrone is the missing part with whom I feel complete. My four sons and I know the true meaning of family. Japheth, Jacinth, Javan, Jalen, Mom, Brittney, Lydia and James, I did it! I have one published! Thanks, Lord, for the true ability to love and to write my poems. Thanks to everyone who has encouraged me.

HYNES, DENISE
[a.] Whitter, CA [title] "Living in My Head" [pers.] This poem reflects what it feels like to suffer with manic depressive disorder at times. It's like living in a world with two people inside you. One side is happy and gay and the other side is gloomy and gray.

HYSELL, RON
[a.] West Palm Beach, FL [title] "The Quiet in You" [pers.] This poem is about my wife, Denise. She's a very shy and quiet person. I can't always tell what she is thinking, but I can usually tell how she feels by the look in her eyes. She's a very wonderful person.

IDEMUDIA, IZIEGBE
[a.] Benin City, Nigeria [title] "Unstable Suns We Are" [pers.] I was born on the fifth of September 1975 in Benin City, Nigeria. I am a graduate of Mathematics with Economics (R.S.C.). A lyricist, psalmist, I work with "United Nations of Youth Network Nigeria" as a zonal coordinator. I write for pleasure. I feel poetry is the melody of the soul that expresses feelings, ideas . . . about all that comprises our world. I hope all who will read these poems will share with me that "Time is irreversible and won't shed a tear for wasted days, for this tomorrow shining far away waits for none but brings changes to our lives in the fading days."

ILES, BERTHA
a.] Bronson, MI [title] "A Crow Named Hope" [pers.] I write poems to express my love for the beauty that fills our lives and to express my love for my beautiful children and their families. They think they are fun, and that is enough encouragement for me. Everything has its own beauty, even a crow named hope.

INGRAM, ERIKA
[a.] Littleton, CO [title] "Love" [pers.] This poem basically portrays what I thought my first love was going to be like. Who knew my first love was actually going to turn out like this! This is the first poem I've written that I was actually proud of, and I can't wait to share the rest of my works with the world.

INMAN, ALLISON
[a.] Fork Union, VA [title] "My Dog Harley" [pers.] I am nine years old. I have been writing poems for a year. I would like to be a poet when I get older and I love writing poems because it is fun and exciting. This poem is dedicated to my granny who is up in Heaven, whom I love and miss very much.

IRELAND, HAROLD
[a.] Wildwood, NJ [title] "The Hummingbird's Secret" [pers.] From my heart I could not speak. Moments alone we never shared. How could you know it was love in the air? Silence whispers deep within my ear. I write that you always knew. I write because you are my inspiration. If we never talk, how else can I tell you that I love you? Boo! I dedicate this one to Hue.

JACKSON, CHRISTOPHER
[a.] Sauk Village, IL [title] "Poetry" [pers.] This is dedicated first to God without whom this would not be possible. To my wife who is truly an important and inspiration part of life, "I love you, Booh." This is also to my mom, brothers, and my own children. This poem describes how my writing makes me feel. My love for poetry is deeply rooted and heartfelt. It helps me to express my innermost thoughts and feelings. I love to walk and will write about almost anything. My inspiration started my sophomore year in high school. It now has turned into a part of my life. I cherish, appreciate, and thank God for my gift. As I continue to write I hope that I will bless and influence someone's life and inspire people to know that there's a little poet in all of us.

JACKSON, RACHEL
[a.] Saint Albans, WV [title] "Waiting" [pers.] The talent I have is a gift from God. The passing of my grandmother is when I discovered my talent. It was the persistence and encouragement of my parents that kept me inspired to pursue my God-given talent. This poem means a lot to me. I took myself back into the heart of a paralyzed person. I thought about their feelings and how things are for someone confined to a wheelchair.

JACKSON, SHERRY
[a.] Jersey Village, TX [title] "Michael is Seven!" [pers.] This poem about my grandson, Michael, is one of seven poems I've written about him. Each year on his birthday, I write a poem about that particular birthday, surround it with pictures of him, and then frame it and give it to my daughter. This particular year, they relocated to New York from Texas, and we were seriously considering moving to New York to be closer. I feel that one day, when Michael is much older, he will look back on all the poems I've written about him and know just how very much his grandmother loves him!

JACOBSEN, TRACY
[a.] Riverside, CA [title] "Depends on the Day . . ." [pers.] "Depends on the Day . . ." was one of the many poems I write due to a feeling, emotion, or time in my life that inspires me to write at that moment. I'm a "Survivor" of Depression, not yet as good as I was or as good as I'll be, but, well on my way. I know anyone that lives and shares my disease knows just what I mean by, "Depends on the Day." My wish for this, poem and all others that I write is that it will help them through a time in their life or to simply let them know they're not alone in their suffering. "God Bless."

JADHAV, AMITA
[a.] Kolhapur, India [title] "Earthquake" [pers.] This is my very first poem, and I am singularly honored that the ILP has found it fit for publication. The devastating earthquake which shook India on January 26, 2001, killing thousands, is the tragic inspiration for this dirge. The pain and anguish of a people who have faced this epic calamity with dignity and fortitude is humbling for the rest of us who were spared. I admire my parents who also went through several hardships but never let us feel the rough edges of life. My personal philosophy is, "you are only an attitude away from success."

JAMEUS, BRIDGET
[a.] Sudbury, ON [title] "To a Rich Man from a Poor Girl!" [pers.] We are worlds apart, but inside, we're much alike. While growing up, you filled my fantasies and fueled my desires. You were my prince from the fairies of fairy tales; you awakened my soul and imagination. The sin that I had talked about was that these feelings were never shared with you; instead, it was silenced by the ignorance of others. Thus, may the worlds between rich men and poor girls crumble with time so no other will feel as I did. Thanks, for the memories you and yours gave; they mean a great deal.

JANSON, KENNY
[a.] West Farmington, Ohio [title] "Great Dad!" [pers.] This poem is one of the poems I wrote for my father. I was 11 when he passed away. Now I'm 12 and I'm writing many things for him. I love animals and I have a lot of them in my home. I go to school in Bloomfield. I have many hobbies, playing on the computer among them. I love to be outdoors because each day seems to bring something new. Thank you, everyone, for your help, and I hope you enjoy this poem.

JARVIS, MARY
[a.] Park Hills, MO [title] "Bill" [pers.] Bill, the youngest of three sons and one daughter, was a delight to be around, always doing something and having many friends. He was just like a boy wading creeks fishing, picking mushroom, and flowers for Mom. I started young writing poetry. I have written many and have had some published. I wish for this poem to be enjoyed.

JENKINS, DARRELL
[a.] Taylorsville, NC [title] "Owed to Mom" [pers.] There is always one person who adds encouragement and enthusiasm to a life, the one who says the right words to keep you going when you feel like quitting, to keep you trying when you feel like a failure, and to keep you smiling when you feel like crying. My mom

was the person who was always there for me. My poem lets others know my gratitude to her since I can no longer tell her. Lois Jenkins left enough memories behind to carry a loving son through the difficult times in his life.

JENSEN, BELLEZA
[a.] Austin, MN [title] "Forever" [pers.] I am registered nurse who believes writing is a good way to express negatives and positives and is a healthy way to deal with some of life's difficulties.

JENSEN, DEBRA
[a.] Lund, NV [title] "My Knitted Afghan of Many Colors" [pers.] My poem is a collaboration of my two loves. I have crocheted and knitted for many years, and my thoughts always end up in poetry. Coming from a small town in Nevada, there is a lot of time to devote to these two loves. My friends have complimented me on both of these hobbies in the past.

JENSEN, JOHANNA M.
[a.] Hutchinson, MN [title] "My Son Dan" [pers.] This poem was written in the first days after my son was killed in a car accident. Dan was 18 years old when he died. It expresses the grief a mother experiences when she loses a child. She begs for God's help to go on.

JETT, LINDA
[a.] Lakeland, FL [title] "Deserted Places" [pers.] The gift of poetry is something to be shared with others, to inspire thoughts and emotions deep within the heart, to encourage goals set in life and knowing they can be obtained, leaving your mark in the world.

JOHNSON, BILL
[a.] Las Vegas, NV [title] "Secret Thoughts" [pers.] This poem is one of many I have written which draws upon a reflection of my many feelings of emotion. Throughout our lifetime, there are such quiet times we encounter that hold a memory we relish, as I have done with this one.

JOHNSON, CRAIG
[a.] Lauderhill, FL [title] "No Peace of Mind" [pers.] When I was writing this poem, the thoughts came one after the other. It took me just over an hour to complete the poem. These were thoughts I have always had. My poem talks about not finding any peace of mind, which sometimes we all go through. There is always something or someone to think about, usually a positive feeling, but not long term. This poem expresses deep thoughts that will always change, but never die.

JOHNSON, ERIC
[a.] Sand Springs, OK [title] "Thunderstorms" [pers.] I am 14 years old and in the eighth grade, at Keystone Middle School in Sand Springs, OK. I would like to give special thanks to the following, my aunt, Sandy Utley, for believing in me and telling me about Poetry.com, my teacher, Angie Spradlin, for the guidance with my poetry writing, my stepmom, Tresa Johnson, for believing in me and giving my poetry to people to read, my mom, Karin Gowdy, for supporting my writing, and my dad, Brian Johnson, who has always been there for me.

JOHNSON, HAFFEZAH
[a.] Bronx, NY [title] "Mothers and Fathers" [pers.] This poem came to mind because I wanted fathers to understand the emotional impact they have on their children when they are not around. You have to understand my mother raised my sister and I on her own with no help whatsoever from my father. Although, my mother tried her very best to be a mother and a father to my sister and I, there will always be a void because my father was never around to see his children become young and productive adults. However, I have come to the understanding at the end of the

day that my father is still my father and I will always love him.

JOHNSON, MICHELLE
[a.] Fort Worth, TX [title] "What Do You See?" [pers.] This poem was born out of my struggle to realize the truth—I am created in God's image and not anyone else's. My validity as a human being is not based upon pigmentation but upon the fact that God loves me.

JOHNSON, NICKOLAS
[a.] Frackville, PA [title] "When People Die" [pers.] I am 11 years old and in a fifth grade class. I wrote this poem when my mom's boyfriend, my good friend, Joe Cincilla, died. It was a very difficult time for everyone, and I decided to put the feelings in a poem. It was hard for me to handle his death, so I hope you like my poem.

JOINER, SEAN
[a.] Augusta, GA [title] "Long Lost Love" [pers.] The story behind this poem is that hope is a wonderful thing. We are all faced with heartache at some point, but to hope to regain what was once lost is worth every tear. Many people never find love, and when you have it, you never want to let it go. This poem was written for a special woman I had in my life. To everyone else, maybe you will be as blessed as me to know true love at all costs. God bless you all.

JONES, AMY
[.a] Birmingham, AL [title] "Christmas Given" [pers.] My writings are an expression of my life—the spirituality and friendships I have made along my journey. My plans are to move and relocate to London, somewhere near the Victoria Embankment, in order that I may be able to walk upon Westminster Bridge every day and every night for the rest of my life and continue my writings there.

JONES, DEBBIE
[a.] Silver Point, TN "Someday"[pers.] Each piece of poetry I write is inspired by my father above. The poem, "Someday," is quiet special to me. It came to me shortly after the brutal death of a dear friend. It was a way of consoling my grief and remembering her. All of the poetry I write is of a spiritual nature and mirrors outwardly the essence of my faith and the peace of my soul. God is the joy of my life and the inspiration for my words.

JONES, JENI
[a.] Orem, UT [title] "The Stranger" [pers.] Poetry, for me, is a way of expressing myself. I feel very close to my savior and wanted to portray the gentleness and kindness of his being. I also wanted to portray the power of his amazing and miraculous ability to help people.

JONES, PAIGE
[a.] Fall River, MA [title] "In-Between" [pers.] This is for all of us struggling with mental illness, and it is the only poem I've ever written. I wrote it while in patient at McClean Hospital. When the doors are looked, your mind gets creative.

JONES, PAMELA
[a.] Mooresville, NC [title] "Borrowed Angel" [pers.] I wrote "Borrowed Angel" after the loss of my six-and-a-half-year-old daughter, Tiffany Danielle, following a two year battle with cancer. She was the strongest and most courageous soul I've ever had the privilege of knowing.

JONES, SHELIA
[a.] Raleigh, NC [title] "The Soccer Player" [pers.] What little writing I have done comes from my heart, and "The Soccer Player" is no exception. The original poem, much longer in length, was written as a Christmas gift for the soccer player in my life. You may appreciate it a little more to know that this particular athlete plays in an "over 40" league. I hope you enjoy reading it as much as I enjoyed writing it.

JONSDOTTER, MATT
[a.] Durham, NC [title] "Various Shades of Blue" [pers.] This being my first publication, I must mention the people who inspired me. First and foremost, I want to thank my mom for always supporting my creativity. I would also like to thank my English teachers, Ms. Kobik, for introducing me to poetry, Ms. Duffner, for helping me to think differently; and Ms. Panley, for encouraging me to get published. Lastly, I want to thank my best friend, Laura Brooke Ashley. If for anyone, this poem was written for her. She has shown me things about myself that I never knew and has given me the free-flowing feelings that inspire me to write. Thanks.

JORDAN, MARLA
[a.] Gardena, CA [title] "Mother" [pers.] I praise God for giving me the perfect mother who inspires me.

JOSEPH, DEBORAH
[a.] Huntsville, AL [title] "Sea of Turmoil" [pers.] I love to write poetry because I find myself able to bare my soul while I am writing a particular poem. Poetry becomes as much a part of me as life itself. "Sea of Turmoil" was written during a time of tremendous sadness and overwhelming upheaval in my life. My Lord saw me through this period of time, and I became stronger than ever before. For me, writing poetry is a way to express how I feel. It is a testament to who I am, and my thoughts and feelings become real when I put them on paper.

JOYCE, PATRICIA
[a.] Beverly Hills, CA [title] "Answer My Prayer" [pers.] In this poem I found myself still grieving an arduous, failed marriage. I prayed for blessings of a more fulfilling personal life. Three weeks later, I was diagnosed with breast cancer. My world was dramatically transformed. I am grateful for the love, compassion, and care from my parents, Sadie, and John Joyce, my family, friends and doctors at Cedars Sinai Medical Center in Los Angeles. Additionally, I must give special recognition to my surgeon, Dennis L. Wood. His dedication to medicine and his friendship have taught me to find my balance and harmony again. The Lord works in mysterious ways.

KALLFELZ, WILLIAM
[a.] Clarkesville, GA [title] "The Lightning's Lesson" [pers.] I owe inspiration and motivation for this piece to a very talented human being and accomplished poet, Corrie Amestoy. I was composing a letter to her about the soul, and out came the poem within a matter of minutes. I myself am a professor of physics and I have also studied theology. I believe this poem reflects what I have learned and my outlook on life. Life is very short, and we're here for a reason, but we can never be fully aware of the meaning of this and everything. Indeed, "we see through the glass very darkly."

KAMARA, AMINATA
[a.] Columbia, MD [title] "A Mother Defined" [pers.] This poem is dedicated to and was inspired by my mother, a woman of integrity, courage, and strength. Though she did not give birth to me, she raised me as though I was her own. It is because of her that I am the person I am today. Being a woman of such significant influence is "a mother defined."

KANE, KATHLEEN
[a.] Philadelphia, PA [title] "Self Portrait" [pers.] My passion is writing, and I am an artist as well. I think the two are intertwined. This poem is about myself; it speaks of my past relationships and my sensitivity as a poet of 18 years. It refers to a diamond that has and should have many facets, pureness of heart being the most important, for seeking to be understood is to understand.

KANG, BEE HUA
[a.] Singapore [pers.] "At the End of All Our Strivings" is one of a collection of poems I've penned for my first publication titled *2001 Diary for Today's Men and Women: Inspirational Thoughts for Everyday Issues.* This piece of work aims to help lessen the severity of the daily grind and hopes to bring hope, joy, and comfort to the reader and to promote love among the human kind. I would like to express my deep gratitude to Poetry.com for endorsing my work. It was a very delightful surprise for a first time writer!

KARLSGODT, ADAM
[a.] La Mesa, CA [title] "The Search" [pers.] Life is about opportunities. The successful ones are those who seize them and hold them with a passion. We constantly are living in a society where the margin for error is so small that with one mistake, the force of Lucifer would be staring through your pale eyes with the need to take you. This poem came to me with the meaningful advice that I take from my grandfather, Erling, and the passionate love from my grandmother, Vernette. Thank you.

KARPINSKI, JENNIFER
[a.] Beltsville, MD [title] "A Tale of Tears" [pers.] This poem is dedicated to one of my best friends. I wrote this poem to give her hope through her tough times end. I hope that it touched not only her but many people.

KAWAII, SAKANA
[a.] Bellevue, WA [title] "Stay Silent" [pers.] Something about me the dark side of life appeals to me. Most of my poems have no real root in my life. I just write them to honor or mock those in my life that catch my attention positively or negatively.

KAZILBASH, ZEHRA
[a.] Karachi, Pakistan [pers.] I started writing poems when I was in grade eight. At that time it was only a way of expressing myself, but as I grew up I understood that it's not just self expression, it's how I look at life. When I wrote "World of Silence" I was only expressing my feelings towards the world around me. I feel that poetry is a very light medium of expression yet it makes a very subtle impression on the readers. One can say a lot more in a poem than maybe they could otherwise. I hope those who read this poem can link themselves with it. I live in Kalachi, Pakistan and I am a student of the Association of Chartered Certified Accountants, UK. Though I am doing distant studies, I always wanted to have a foreign degree. I also want to do a degree in TV direction and production from abroad. I live with my parents, and my brother is studying in Australia.

KEEN, EVE
[a.] Euclid, OH [title] "The Ultra Sound" [pers.] I am a registered nurse from Cleveland Ohio. All of my poetry is an expression of personal feelings or experience. It has proved to be a therapeutic release in difficult times. I would like to dedicate this poem to all single mothers who have the courage to raise wonderful children in the absence of a partner. My philosophy in this life can best be summed up with a quote by Lee Iococca: "We are continuously faced by great opportunities, brilliantly disguised as insoluble problems."

KELLER, CORTNEY
[a.] Sarasota, FL [title] "Ungrateful [pers.] Poetry is my God-given gift. I enjoy writing all kinds of poetry. Most of my poetry comes from my heart at certain times of my life. It's a way to express my feelings and emotions. I hope this ability to have my voice heard will someday turn into profession. I see writing poetry as a wonderful way to earn a living and spend a lifetime. "Ungrateful" is dedicated to my wonderful mother and best friend to show her my love and gratitude. Thank you so much for publishing my poem!

KELLER, JACQUELINE
[a.] Columbus, GA [title] "Dreams" [pers.] Ever mystifying, dreams are a constant part of my life. They are so real sometimes, I have remembered a portion after awakening and contacted the person in the dream just to satisfy myself they were all right. One such dream was of my son calling to me one night. I sat up in bed thinking he was downstairs, though he lived several miles away. I answered him aloud, and when there was no response, I went downstairs to see why he was there. The dream was that real. Then I realized I had been dreaming and returned to bed mystified.

KELLOGG, SHARON
[a.] Gambrills, MD [title] "The Morning Commute" [pers.] I wrote this poem shortly after accepting a paralegal position in Baltimore City, Maryland. I actually composed the poem in its entirely while riding the light rail one morning. I had recently medically retired from the Army as a Patriot Missile Officer and this was my first true commuting experience. My interest in poetry was encouraged by my "Grandpa K" who gave me his old poetry books from his personal library. I aspire to write children's books and to become a lawyer.

KELLOGG, SHERRI
[a.] Bridgewater Corners, VT [title] "Employment of Hell" [pers.] I have always loved to write. I was working at a Postal Distribution Center when I was inspired to write this poem. I would like to thank my friend, Vinnie Eppler, and my family—Stuart, my husband, and Abby, Josh, and Nick, my children, for believing in me.

KELSO, JENNIFER
[a.] Forest Grove, OR [title] "The Missing Person" [pers.] One night I was lying in my bed and I just had this urge to write about my ex-boyfriend. I had no clue what to write, but while I was sitting there, it came to me. That's how I came up with this poem, "The Missing Person." It's about my ex-boyfriend, Jesse. We didn't go out long, but after we broke up, I realized how much I care about him and how much he means to me. He still does to this day! He doesn't know how much I care about him, and I don't know if he ever will.

KENLY, MISTY
[a.] Gainesville, TX [title] "My Hero" [pers.] To me, poetry is an emotional outlet. I was very upset when I found out that Mr. Dodson would no longer be our band director. I had only known him for five months and already I thought very highly of the man. I still do. He had the courage to teach and befriend us and then to let us go. This poem is to say thank you for everything you've done.

KENNE, KENDRA
[a.] Rochester, MN [title] "You" [pers.] I have decided to write about the best emotion and the most knowledgeable feeling of mine. I once had a man that touched my soul, and I touched his, but some things can't last. In this poem, I am expressing my love for him. This wonderful man is Ale Franz. I know that I shall love him until the day that I die and so I would like to dedicate this poem to him.

KENT, STEVEN
[a.] Copiague, NY [title] "The Reoccurring Smile" [pers.] My poem, "The Reoccurring Smile," was written for a special person in my life. She was going through some tough times, losing someone very dear to her. This poem was to get her to know that no matter how bad things may get, they'll always get better. I live in Copiague, NY and I write periodically when I don't exactly know how to say or describe something. Writing makes it easier to express myself to others. I'd like to thank Laurie Mayer for giving me inspiration to use my pen again to release my mind, heart, and soul.

KENYON, CAROL
[a.] Clementon, NJ [title] "Kayla" [pers.] Poetry gives me the opportunity to express myself so that my family may know my inner thoughts. I am the mother of six wonderful children. By name, they are Donna Grace, Sharon Beale, Billy Dobson, Patricia Dobson, Lee Kenyon, and Matt Kenyon. I also have 12 grandchildren. I enjoy crafts, painting and poetry, but most of all, my husband, Ed, and my children. My extended enjoyments include singing in the church choir and serving the Lord, Jesus Christ, who is my Savior and number one in my life.

KETTER, CURTISS
[a.] Lomira, WI [title] "My Flower" [pers.] Poetry is about love, and this is why I dedicate this poem to the woman I love. I love you with all my heart, Kim! I will love you always!

KHAN, BAKHTOWER
[a.] Karachi, Pakistan [title] "Good Child" [pers.] I guess it was my O levels that made me come up with a poem like "Good child." This poem rejuvenates my memories from when I was a kid. Although I haven't had much interest in poetry I am beginning to really love it. Having the ability to write good poems is a gift and also the best way to express one's innermost feelings.

KIM, JANGWOO
[a.] McLean, VA [title] "My Family" [pers.] I was happy that I had the opportunity to share my poem with somebody. Sometimes, I feel that poetry is a messenger from God who obeys my order. He informs people of the expression of my heart. This poem, "My Family," shows how much I love my family. I often yell at them but later I always regret what I've done and scold myself,"Ah, this wasn't what I meant!" Even so, I've never told them that I love them. I just don't have the courage to speak the word, "love." But here, my faithful messenger delivers it to people, including my family.

KIMMEL, TARIE
[a.] Ashland, PA [title] "Beauty Unseen" [pers.] All my life I've always cared about how I'm seen in the eyes of those around me. My friends, Nikki, Amy, Carmella, and my mom have helped me see the importance of all that I hold inside. They inspired me to write "Beauty Unseen." Without them in my life, it might have never been written. I hope my poem helps others to see the beauty within themselves.

KINGSTON, ANN
[a.] Indianapolis, IN [title] "Playboy" [pers.] I am an older runner who becomes creative outside, close to nature. Each season brings the joy of writing for poetry, stories, and songs. I tell people I write with my legs.

KISER, JAMIE
[a.] Milford, NY [title] "Things That Stacey and Julie Have Taught Me! [pers.] This poem is very special to me. It talks about the most important things, both funny and serious, that my best friends, Stacey and Julie Gordon, have taught me. I first met them at Word of Life in Upstate, NY. Hey guys, I'll never forget that summer or you!

KLEINMEIER, JOAN
[a.] Lake Worth, FL [title] "Night" [pers.] My poetry always reflects what I am feeling at that time. I have always been able to express myself better by writing than by telling someone how I feel. I love to write. My writing is a part of me so it is very special to me. I feel at peace and I've completed either a poem or short story that I've been working on.

KLEMONS, STEPHANIE
[a.] New Brunswick, NJ [title] "Within the Sea of Tranquility" [pers.] I am a dancer, singer, actress, and currently a freshman at Rutgers University on partial scholarship as a Biology-Genetics major. I believe

that "true art" is that which creates an inconspicuous yet opportune connection between the outside world and the bell jar. A "true artist" is one who can detect and appreciate this as another step toward mental and spiritual enlightenment. This is dedicated to my mother, Janet, who has been my everything, my father, Ira, who has taught me more than I can thank him for, any brother, Adam, whose sincerity and sensitivity and drive inspires me every day, and my best friend, Katie, whose love for life burns like an inextinguishable flame.

KNOTTS, JENNIFER
[a.] Cedar Rapids, IA [title] "Once Lovers" [pers.] I love poetry. I love to write it and I love to read it. I feel it's a great way to express yourself. Your anger, love, heartache, betrayal, etc . . . it can all be said in a poem. The great thing about poetry is it can be whatever you want it to be. You can say as much or as little as you want, and it still makes sense. I feel that most people relate to this poem. It's about the feelings of first love, the joy, the fun, the laughter, and finally the heartache once it's over.

KOEHL, MICHELLE
[a.] Dayton, TX [title] "Why Me and My Family?" [pers.] I wrote this poem one night when I was upset. It talks about this young woman who wrote a suicide note (the poem) saying that this man killed her family. When she came home and realized what happened, she overdosed on pills. It is a sad poem but it is everyday life. It gives a point of view of what happens when you do drugs. Well, I am going to tell you a little about myself. I am fourteen years old and in the eighth grade. My best friend is Meghan Nammett. She was with me when I wrote this poem.

KOH, HANNA J.
[a.] Los Angeles, CA [title] "The Greatest Play" [pers.] This poem was written when I was twelve. Evidently, I did sedate myself, almost too successfully with melancholy's stupor. Now is no exception. Still, life is that profile elaborate stage set for a fleeting binge. Quite ridiculous I know, but I don't judge anymore. There is no light there, and angst is gross. My Savior, Jesus, and my James keep me from unfavorable emotions. I do my best, and that's all that is really needed. I was dancing when I was twelve.

KOHL, JARED
[a.] Charleston, SC [title] "Sarah" [pers.] This poem speaks about the woman I love—she means the world to me. I would like to thank my mother, Nancy, my father, Dan, and my sister, Ashlyn for encouraging me in my writing. They give me so much love and support in everything I do academically, in sporting events, and in the decisions I make in my life. I couldn't do anything without their help and love. To my family, thank you, and I love you all with all my heart and soul. To Sarah, "you are, and always will be my soul mate, I love you."

KOK WEI, LIM
[a] Gadong, Brunei [title] "The Rite of Choosing" [pers.] In life we always have to make choices, and more often than not, they are difficult ones. My poem is not about making the right or wrong choice but the inability to make a choice. "Grab your chances," they all said. But what of the risk involved, the humiliation to be endured. In the process of saving ourselves from hurt, we usually take a step back and hide. But later, we are bound to regret not daring to stand up and make the choice that was in our hearts all along. Thanks to Poetry.com for providing this wonderful opportunity for me to express myself.

KOMOROWSKI, DAVID
[a.] North Royalton, OH [title] "Our Ever-Shrinking World" [pers.] I really started writing my poems when I met and married my wife, Nancy, as she was my inspiration. I also would include poems on special days to my family and friends in their cards. However, I wrote "Our Ever-Shrining World" shortly after my father-in-law, Leonard Grateful, who has past away seven years ago. I was sitting at a Bingo game waiting for it to start with my wife, Nancy, and my mother-in-law, Catherine Grateful. Poetry is my way of expressing my feelings inside about a person, place, thing, or loved one. Since this time we now have lost my mother-in-law, Catherine Grateful suddenly. But I still have my wife, Nancy, and my son, Brian Zaccardelli and my mother, Hattie Komorowski, who have all said that I have a special talent. I live in North Royalton, Ohio with my family. I went through 12 years of school, fought in the Vietnam War in the Air Force, and also was a corrections officer in Cleveland, Ohio. I now work at Orbit Industries Inc. in Middleburgh Hts., Ohio as a metal technician. My hobbies are basically doing any type of craft with my wife, Nancy, reading books, playing hand-held games, woodworking, and writing poetry.

KOONCE, LESLIE
[a.] Midland, KY [title] "Love" [pers.] Fist of all, I would like to dedicate this poem to my family and to every person in Muhlenberg County, KY. Without them I wouldn't know what love is and I couldn't have possibly had the drive to write "Love." All of my poetry reflects how I see someone or something. I live in the rural community of Midland in Muhlenberg County, Kentucky. During high school I developed a rare gift of loving to write and being able to write well. I would like to personally thank my Junior English teacher, Kathy Sparks, at Muhlenberg North High School for believing in my writing abilities and pushing my will to believe in myself.

KOREN, TROY
[a.] Metairie, LA [title] "Bestefar" [pers.] My grandfather has always been like a father to me. He is one of the greatest people you could ever know. So when he became very ill, and the doctors did not think he would make it through the weekend, I sat down and thought for a couple at hours, and in those hours I had multiple feelings about this situation. The only way I couldn't tell everyone how I felt was to write it down. This poem, "Bestefar," was a prayer to God to keep my grandfather here on Earth, and I believed it helped. I hope others who are in the same situation I was can relate to my feelings, and maybe my poem can help them.

KOROWAJSKI, ANIA
[a.] Arvada, CO [title] "Love" [pers.] This special poem says something about the man I used to be with. Even though I am only thirteen, I never thought that I would actually get into a book with poems in it. This means very much to me. "Love" is my work of art. Love is not just a four letter word that can be thrown around.

KOVACH, BRITNI
[a.] Phoenix, AZ [title] "Becoming One" [pers.] To me, poetry is a way to express your feelings, thoughts, and dreams. This poem wasn't written from experience, but from my feelings about soul mates. I believe that you can also express your thoughts and feelings through reading poems. Therefore I write poems that I think others can relate to. Every poem holds a special message or meaning that is meant to touch someone's heart. It maybe clearly stated or deeply hidden, but if it's needed badly enough, it will be found!

KOWALEWSKI, LOIS
[a.] Phoenix, AZ [title] "Commitment to the Lord" [pers.] Poetry is a gift from God. I can express myself more sincerely by writing a poem. God gave the gift to my dad, first, then to me. My Dad is 92 (as of 2001) and still writing beautiful poems! Growing up, I only knew of God, but now I have a personal relationship with him. I love God with all my heart and I pray that others will open their eyes to him. He is my Lord, Savior, Redeemer, and Comforter! Jesus died for all of us and forgave our sins. Why not repent? If you died tonight . . . where would you go?

KRIVKA, SUE
[a.] Austin, TX [title] "Keep a Watch" [pers.] I am a widow. Our family had a farm. We had bees. Oh! How sweet and fresh the honeycomb. Oh! The stings! Honey can sweeten all problems and anger. What beauty and health it adds to your life! The Bible is full of honey, in Prov. 15:1 Prov. 24: 13-14, and many more. Our family was a unit.

KULL, TENNA
[a.] Lake Havasu City, AZ [title] "Sleigh Bells" [pers.] My life took off at the age of 11 years. I ran a small 200 and had 40 different animals, wild and tame. I am a swimmer and a bowler. I ran a daycare of over 40 children. I still care for the wild and tame animals. I teach others who can't read. I do stained glass. My day starts at 4:00 a.m. and ends at 1:00 a.m. I am in junior college with one year to go.

KUMAR, PRASHANT
[a.] New Delhi, India [title] "Triumph" [pers.] This poem was written about two decades back at two hours past midnight . It was a dark winter night, and the thing farthest from me was sleep. As I lay in bed, restless, pondering over the purpose of life, my thoughts suddenly began to take definite shape. Without losing a moment, I put pen to paper, and what followed was this poem.

KUSNERY, WAYNE
[a] Suttons Bay, MI [title] "Forgiveness" [pers.] Ten years have past, and it's time to move on. I've fallen in love with Svetlana. Soon she will leave her beautiful Crimea and come to me. Our lives wil be like some story book romance, maybe like Nicholas and Aleksandra! As now we stand in front of a small castle, "Swallow's Nest," in Leelanau, "Land of Delight." We will wake to the morning sunrise over Grand Traverse Bay. It is our little castle on the hill, and we know that this love is forever.

LACOMB, SHIRLEY
[a.] Amarillo, TX [title] "My Husband" [pers.] When my husband passed away, I wrote this for his funeral. To me it is a way to help myself express my love for him. He was my friend, my sweetheart, my lover, and at times my enemy. Through him he showed me how to live my life to the fullest. He gave me five wonderful children and 14 grandbabies to help me make it the rest of the way without him. He was a wonderful person who only lived to be 54 year. old. Everyone loved him so much. It is my way of telling him thank you for being so special to me. I know that his love will live on through me and our children and I thank God every day for letting me have him in my life for as long as I did. I hope everyone can find a love as wonderful as his. And so I will say thank you, Jimmy, for loving me.

LAMBRIANIDOU, GALATIA
[a.] Limassol, Cyprus [title] "Midnight-Desperation" [pers.] Poetry means everything to me. It's a way to escape life. I'm a family doctor. I constantly see people suffer or die after a hard day's work. Once, when I had returned home late, I was sitting in my bedroom thinking and then I decided to write this poem. I guess it was my desperation coming out.

LANCASTER-MURPHY, KRYSTLE
[a.] Wichita, KS [title] "Together Once Again" [pers.] This poem has a very special place in my heart. This poem was written in memory of Branden Murphy and Brandon Abshire. Branden Murphy was my best friend as well as my brother. When he died, it devastated me, until eventually Brandon Abshire took over his place, never trying to take his place, but being there for me. Six years after my brother died, Brandon also died. In my lifetime I have lost two brothers. This poem was written for Brandon Abshire's family, and also mine. Brandon Abshire and I were never related, but like my brother he changed my life and showed me love.

LANDE, JARDENA
[a.] Zurich, Switzerland [title] "Miss You, Love You, Need You, Want You!" [pers.] This poem is very important to me because it is dedicated to my boyfriend, Itamar. Meeting him is the best thing that could have happened to me in my life. He is the most precious person that there is. He means everything to me. I want to thank him for everything he did and still does for me. I can't describe what I feel for him; it is the deepest love that exists. Itamar, I love you more than everything in this world and I want to spend the rest of my life with you. You are just perfect for me!

LANDES, MEGAN
[a.] Fork Union, VA [title] "PerfectHalo17" [pers.] To me, poetry is a great release. Like a great catharsis at the end of a tragedy, poetry is my quiet after the storm. You don't have to be a certain person to write—just be yourself. That is the most truthful statement in the world. Don't worry what others think.

LANE, KERRY
[a.] Corpus Christi, TX [title] "Casey" [pers.] This poem is an exact account of an incident that changed my life forever. I refused to believe that my son would be taken from me and yet I realized the hopelessness of not knowing what to do or how to make the pain go away. I most earnestly believe that all of the prayers during those 18 days brought my son back to me. Today he has not a single side effect as a result of the meningitis. Thank God. Kerry Lane is a 17 years veteran of Law Enforcement in Nueces Co. Texas. He is 38 years old and he and his wife Cathy, have three beautiful children, Kaleb, 14, Casey, 11, and Baby Keri, six, who are the greatest part of his life's fulfillment.

LANE, RHETA
[a.] Oklahoma City, OK [title] "For His Sake" [pers.] This poem was written for my true love. We were together for many years and we have a son with eyes of brown. My true love has died now, but I think of him often. Sometimes I can remember that feeling of total love. It takes my breath away and brings a smile to my lips and a tears to my eyes. If you've ever known it, you can imagine it again and bring that awesome feeling back for a fleeting second. I've moved on now, but I believe there is only one.

LARSON, CLARICE
[a.] Belmont, CA [title] "Forever Friends" [pers.] I wrote this poem nineteen years ago after the death of my best friend. Not a day goes by that I don't remember her. We went through the most important times in life together. We made a promise to name our firstborn daughter after one another. Unfortunately, Carmen was taken before she married and had children. After many years, I gave birth to Carmen Clarice Larson, fulfilling both promises made so many years ago by two best friends.

LATONA, THOMAS ANDREW
[a.] Milwaukee, WI [title] "Thankful Friend" [pers.] I believe poetry is one of God's gifts, a way to express the deepest emotions of the soul. Throughout my life I have learned never to take anything for granted, especially family and friends. "Thankful Friend" was written for a very special and close friend. I put it into a Christmas card that I gave to her. It was intended to show that the bond of friendship is a very special gift which I will always treasure and to simply thank her for being a true friend just because of who she is inside.

LAUTERIO, MICHAEL
[a.] Hanford, CA [title] "A Starlit Night" [pers.] I would like to thank you for the publication of my poetry. The story behind my poetry is life, people, and the world. In a nut shell. This is the meaning poetry has in my life. It has meaning because publishers like yourself took the bull by the horns. My teachers never didn't—in high school all they said was that I would never get anywhere with my writings or my poems or

short stories. I never had a teacher say to me that I would get anywhere. They know who they are!

LAWRENCE, JEROME
[a.] Los Angeles, CA [title] "Sunshine" [pers.] This poem is dedicated to the young lady who showed me the sun and moon really exist. Poetry has always been within me. My grandmother was a poetic storyteller, and her one and only child, my mother, is a poet in her own special way. I also would like to express my gratitude to a special friend that took me for a walk and gave me a reason to write. Poetry is in all of us—it is just a matter of time until we realize it.

LAWRENCE, JOSHUA
[a.] La Place, LA [title] "One's Own Fantasy" [pers.] Hi, I'm Joshua Stevan Lawrence, writer of "One's Own Fantasy." I am a 15 year old Freshman at Varnado High School in Louisiana. I've been writing for about five years but have been interested in journalism all through school. My mother has always encouraged and inspired me to write. Ashley Brumfield brought out a lot of my feelings, so I must mention her. All of the poetry or songs that I have written have been based on inspirations and depressions, but mostly things that prove a point. My greatest dream is to publish my own book and become an author.

LAWRENCE, MELISSA
[a.] Winter Park, FL [title] "Future Baby" [pers.] I wrote this poem when I was nine years old, about my "future baby" sister. I was so excited when my stepmom and father were expecting their first baby. And guess what . . . they did have another one!

LAWRENCE, ZACHARY
[a.] Mammoth Lake, CA [title] "Goose Shoes" [pers.] Poetry is a very important gift that was given to me when I first learned how to write. All 18 years of my life have been filled with many thoughts that, I believe, need to be brought to life. In my case, these thoughts are given breath through my music and, of course, my poetry. Soon, I will be moving to Durango, Colorado to start my first year of college. I will always love writing. It is a habit that I will never quit.

LAWSON, STEPHEN
[a.] North Cape May, NJ [title] "Cursed" [pers.] This poem is very special to me. It is based on my belief that love truly does transcend time and that two souls are truly only halves of the greater whole. I dedicate my poem to anyone who has lost a love. I hope you find it again soon. If you do not then remember, there is always next time. Blessings to you and your love!

LEAHEW, BECKY
[a.] Baldwin City, KS [title] "Daddy" [pers.] I find poetry to be an easier way to say how I feel. This poem lets go of anger about my past, but also reminds me of where I came from. Each person gains their talents from experiences in their past. Mine comes from the loneliness of my childhood. Yet now I am rich for I have friends who care; the success I gain can only come from the support of them. So here's to the late night camp fires out by the lake.

LEASURE, JENNIFER
[a.] Wichita, KS [title] "My Wonderful Husband" [pers.] "My Wonderful Husband" is a tribute to the man who makes my life complete. Don makes me a better person. He has helped me understand what true love is.

LEBLANG, TINA
[a.] Sistern Lakes, MI [title] "Words" [pers.] This poem was written with my beloved mother in mind. She is and has been going through a very difficult time in her life. Thinking of her and the way she might be feeling brought me the words I needed to say. Maybe there is someone else who needs to express their feelings but really can't find the words they need. I

have been writing poetry since I can remember. My brother writes and so does my father. However, the two people I write about most are my darling husband, John, and my beautiful son, Christopher. These two people are my life, and I cherish them.

LEE, KIMBERLY
[a.] Marble Hill, MO [title] "All These Years" [pers.] I wrote "All These Years" for speech class my senior year in high school. It was at the time I wrote it. I was inspired by a close friend of mine. We at the time hadn't seen each other in quite a number of years. The best way I can describe what the poem means is the way too often friends got tossed by the wind, separated for years on end. Too often they lose a golden opportunity to become so much close. But the most important thing is to keep each other close in both of your hearts because you never know what fate may hold. One day, a reunion may be written in the stars.

LEGRANDE, BRUCE
[a.] Omaha, NE [title] "Breath of Fresh Air" [pers.] I think most of us in life have experienced the feelings of being castaways in the "sea of love." We wander aimlessly with a pain inside that is hard to describe. Eventually, like a breath of fresh air, we meet someone who brings feelings of excitement, passion, and love into our empty and broken hearts. I feel this is what life is all about . . . love! We should never abandon it, but strive to keep it alive in this world, giving our love freely to one another till the end of time. for the greatest of these is love!

LEINO, BRENDA
[a.] Lewiston, ME [title] "Dotty the Angel" [pers.] This poem is very special to me, as it was written to help my friend Michael Dube to deal with the death of his girlfriend, Dorothy Shoko Murphy, Dotty, as all of her friends referred to her. This was my way to help Michael Deal with his loss.

LEOLICH, JUDY
[a.] International Falls, MN [title] "How?" [pers.] Judy (Dahlvang) Leolich resides with her daughter, Alicia, in International Falls, Minnesota, "The Icebox of the Nation." She is very involved in local politics and causes. Judy has a genuine love for live theatre and has acted in many plays in International Falls and Ft. Richardson, AK. Judy has always had a passion for writing poetry and song lyrics, and has used that gift to create personalized singing telegrams. Through her writing, Judy wishes to communicate hope for this troubled world, and the belief that with love we can heal our children's lost and wounded spirits. They are our hopes for tomorrow!

LEON, NOEL
[a.] Little Rock, AZ [title] "Me in the Mirror" [pers.] I was 13 last summer when I wrote this poem. It came out in one burst as my family bustled around the house. It was accepted as a cornerstone of a theatrical production of a summer theatre program I was enrolled in. It was a very special experience for me. I am thrilled it has been selected for this anthology.

LEVEN, YANIV
[a.] Rosh Ha Ayin, Israel [title] "2 a.m." [pers.] Did I create? Did I? The statues, they looked, they saw! They, in their quiet sleep, create. A mass played by backs infinite genius plays the mood in my creation. I create to be created.

LEWIS, BRENDA
[a.] Yucaipa, CA [title] "Angel Sent" [pers.] This poem was written after my brother-in-law was in the hospital. After surgery, he got a Staph infection and double pneumonia which become so bad the doctors gave him a 50/50 chance of surviving. He was completely unaware of who or what was around him. He was in the hospital over a month. I could not be there for my sister and brother-in-law every day so I

sat and created this poem for them. After a long recovery, he is fine now.

LEWIS, JOYCE
[a.] Toledo, OH [pers.] I enjoy writing poetry, for it is therapeutic to be lost in a God-given gift. I wrote "Dove" for my goddaughter to give as a gift to a friend. In order to write it, I had to think of my only child, Jake Tyler Bergan. My inspirations come through my daily walk with Jesus. He anoints me with his Holy Spirit, giving my life direction and instruction. Only through the grace of God and great parents have I been a teacher for the past 13 years. I dedicate my life to God, and surrender all my earthly possessions. My life would be incomplete if I did not take the time to thank my parents, Odestin and Wilbur Lewis Sr., my sisters, Gloria and Jennifer, my brothers, Robert, Wilbur Jr. and their families, my grandparents, godparents, godmother, Margaret (Williams) Carter, and a host of relatives and friends.

LEWIS, LUSTER
[a.] Duncanville, TX [title] "To Be Thy Valentine: (Italian Sonnet)" [pers.] I lament the first forty-three years of my life without eloquent expressions in verse. I spent those years creating with my hands. Those years will never compare with the seven years of deep satisfaction I've derived from the creative expressions of my mind, spirit, and soul. Most of my waking thoughts are filtered through my poetic nature, which recently annexed my dream thoughts as well. I aspire not to fame, beauty, or worth, for these things are transient. Rather, expressions of my deepest feelings in verse are timeless and eternal.

LIMBAUGH, ASHLEIGH
[a.] Murfreesboro, TN [title] "Dad" [pers.] My poem is about my relationship with my father. Obviously, I was very angry when I wrote it. I think poetry is many different things. Poetry can be funny, sad, relaxing, energizing, or healing. "Dad" was very much about healing. My mom's name is Janita, and my little brother's name is Taylor. I have a step-dad named Mark, my real Dad's name is Greg, and my stepmom's name is Barbie. My hobbies are soccer and cheerleading. I've played soccer since kindergarten. I've been cheering on my elementary school (GC Braves!). I've also been on a competition squad (Go Eagles!). Now I'm on my high school squad (Go Warriors!). I'm 13 and I hope to become famous someday. Just kidding—I don't know what I want to do.

LINDSAY, CAROLE
[a.] Calgary, AB [title] "Home" [pers.] We grew up in a large home in a small city in Saskatchewan, Canada. Mom's natural gift for interior decorating transformed our home into our castle. As we all moved away, my parents moved into a smaller place. While back for a visit, I drove by the first place I called home, only to see that the new owners had neglected it and allowed it to fall to ruin. It truly broke my heart.

LINE, GAIL
[a.] Hancock, MI [title] "50th Anniversary" [pers.] Poetry is a gift that I seem to have developed over the years. I try to concentrate on the people, event, or life's happenings for inspiration. I have a God-given gift that I want to share with others. I see this opportunity as a new stepping stone for my path in life. I have shared my poetry with family and friends and now I wish to share it in *Stepping Stones.*

LINTON, MARCIA
[a.] Kingston, Jamaica [title] "Blessings from Above" [pers.] This poem originated out of the realization that releasing or sharing unconditionally what I have to those in need, returns to me the fulfillment of my own immediate needs. To me, poetry is very important as it creatively release my thoughts and feelings into words that radiate light into the hearts and minds of my fellowmen.

LIVELY, TINA
[a.] Timmins, ON [title] "Who Am I?" [pers.] This poem was inspired by my fiancé, Pierre. He has allowed me to experience so many events in my life, and stood by me through good and bad times. This is for you, my love.

LOANZON, JENNIFER
[a.] Columbus AFB, MS [title] "A Memo from My Heart" [pers.] This poem was written and dedicated to a very dear person in my life. I had troubles expressing my emotions in person so I thought to write them down. I know many people feel the same way I do about their loved ones and I hope to share my poem with them to help express their feelings to that "special someone" in their life.

LONG, JULIE
[a.] Beech Island, SC [title] "Poet's Words" [pers.] My poetry is very special to me. Poetry is an escape, an adventure, a way out of the world, and into myself. I consider poetry and the talent to write a gift, a miracle. I am thankful for my talent and the chance to share it. Above all, poetry is a way to express emotions and better understand one's views and the way one feels. Poetry shall be forever shared!

LOPEZ, ANDREA
[a.] Port Saint Lucie, FL [title] "Far beyond the Stars" [pers.] This poem was actually the first poem that I really wrote. Music inspired me to write this poem. I was trying to write about what I could see far beyond the stars . . . far beyond our imagination . . . far beyond our universe. I imagined it as Heavenly visions. I was trying to write about beyond what the eyes could see, trace out my imagination with it. When I'm writing, I just can't stop sometimes. There's too much exploding in my mind that I have to let down on paper. I want to show others what I see. My cousin was the one who lead me to writing when I was seven. She told me to write in diaries, and the more I wrote diaries, the more it lead me to poetry. I didn't realize that while I was writing poetry, I fell into this completely different world, like magic, almost. And I still feel that way with my poetry. I hope if I get my imagination out there, people will enjoy it. This is a vision of my own.

LOPEZ, ANNA
[a.] Kingsville, TX [title] "May Age Invoke Me Gracefully" [pers.] I am an eighteen-year-old Hispanic girl, who has been writing poetry for the greater part of her life. Poetry is a beautiful art form. Here in "May Age Invoke Me Gracefully," I subtly voice admiration for my mother. On the verge of high school graduation, I can only hope to graduate to her level of wisdom. I feel I have shaken off my shroud of youth-oriented vanity, and that is what I aimed to express in "May Age Invoke Me Gracefully." Perhaps readers will see more of me in the future!

LOPEZ, JANICE
[a.] Union City, NJ [title] "Love Is Like the Seed of a Rose" [pers.] To begin with, I love poetry. My poems always reflect my life, and I get inspired mostly when I am sad. As for this poem, it speaks for itself. Love always starts off beautifully, but unfortunately always has an end. I currently reside in Northern, NJ. I am a Medical Assistant and becoming an RN soon.

LORD-LLOYD, DOROTHY
[a.] Oakley, CA [title] "Sun Sets in the Sky" [pers.] Poetry comes naturally for me. Each time that I may feel that I am all alone or that some things in life are too big to handle, I can look to my savior in Heaven and he will speak to me through poetry. I may not understand the message given to me through a poem right away but later I reread it and there's always a message. The "Sun Sets in the Sky" talks about letting go of each worry and each why and starting each day anew. Let our Savior handle all the strife, and we will be okay. As for you, the readers, I wish you a healing through my poem as it has helped me. God bless.

LOUNSBURY, CHERYL
[a.] Torrington, CT [title] "Dreamer" [pers.] Words cannot express how happy I am that a poem that I wrote is going to be in a book that thousands of people are going to read. This particular poem was something that I wrote in my eighth grade English class. The topic was dreams. Basically my poem means in a dream you don't have to face the problems of everyday life and you can dream about anything because only you will know about it. I want to thank the International Library of Poetry for publishing my poem.

LOVELESS, LAURA
[a.] Billings, MT [title] "Don't Cry" [pers.] To me, poetry is a very important form of self-expression and also a powerful way to express my feelings to others. Writing is a cathartic experience and is a way for me to pour emotions out of my heart and onto paper where they become easier to sort through and confront. My poem "Don't Cry" was written for someone very special to me and expresses my admiration for her strength despite her youth and my hope that she will be able to nurture the strength to carry on.

LOWTHER, GLORIA
[a.] Billings, MT [title] "Nature's Masterpiece" [pers.] I thought of this poem while driving to town from the country one morning. I have written lots of poems, but none meant as much as this one. I was thinking of my children and grandchildren, of how much God has blessed me with love. Just about that time I saw a blue bird. The country has so much beauty, you see it everywhere you go. I think of God's hand putting every little thing in just the right spot. I enjoy writing poems and hope to be able to write for many years to come.

LUNA, JENNIFER
[a.] Princeton, WV [title] "Just Another Day" [pers.] This poem is very special to me, as are the rest of my poems. All of my writings come from deep inside my heart. Writing has always been an escape from everything around me and a chance to express my feelings freely to myself. Now, I share this with everyone, hoping that it will help someone else like it has helped me. Thank you, R.P. for the inspiration. With you in mind, hopefully I can continue to do what I love. I urge everyone else to do the same. Live out your dreams, or you'll never know what you're missing out on.

LUNSFORD, KRISTINA
[a.] Lathrop. CA [title] "A Wrinkle in Time—Take a Breath" [pers.] I started writing poems while asleep two years ago. The only thing I can credit this too is finding my father after 34 years of not knowing him. This emotional release catapulted into a book I am writing, titled *From the Heavens above.* "A Wrinkle in Time—Take a Breath," published in this wonderful book, *Stepping Stones,* will also be in my book, along with close to 60 other animal and spiritual poems. I am finding that writing poems is such a wonderful way to share your expressions of the heart.

LYLE, ABBE
[a.] San Jose, CA [title] "Hummingbird" [pers.] "Hummingbird" reflects our yearning to "escape," but we must search within to find ourselves. Poetry is my creative outlet and my source of inspiration. I honor my six beautiful children, my exceptional husband, my family, and my close friends with this poem. You all allow me to be. Namaste!

LYONS, PATTI
[a.] Howell, NJ [title] "Tissue" [pers.] Some of my favorite things are cheese, coconut, artichoke, piano, horses, and dolphins. My dad is Steve, my mom is Janet, I am an only child, and my best friend is Belle Spangle. I am 12 years old and in seventh grade.

M.., C.

[a] Dover, PA [title] "not" [pers.] You could say I'm not your average teenager. Writing poetry is something I love doing; it's a tension reliever, as well as a form of expression that can have underlying messages (but not always). I think I wrote this poem to say things aren't always what we want them to be.

MacDONALD, CAMERON

[a.] Addison, TX [title] "No Smile Today" [pers.] The poem, "No Smile Today," was written to preserve the memory of Jhing, a young lady whose smile and kind words warmed and stole my heart. This poem is the last in a collection of five. To me, these words express a portrait of her, and when I read them I can see her smile.

MacKENZIE, SHANNON

[a.] San Juan Capistrano, CA [title] "I Am a Watcher" [pers.] This poem is very special to me because I wrote it in high school when everyone is worried about making themselves look better, instead of bettering themselves. It reminds me to focus on my future instead of the opinions of others.

MacKEY, SANDRA

[a.] Roswell, GA [title] "The Ghost of Memphis" [pers.] This is the fifth poem that I've had published in an anthology. It's a great feeling to see my words in print! By day, I am an Administrative Assistant for Kimberly Clark. By night, I am a writer (I've had one book published), and poet. I have four grown children, three grandchildren and two birds. I teach a ladies' Bible Class and hold motivational workshops in my "spare" time. I believe that an active mind and busy hands keep a person young, healthy, and happy. Elvis has been a life-long hobby, and this poem is for the fans who miss his amazing presence.

MAFFIA, CARMELLA

[a.] Bay Shore, NY [title] "Someday in a Dream" [pers.] I have always enjoyed writing poetry, for cards, special occasions and even jokes. This poem was written as part of a story I wrote years ago. This poem is dedicated to my husband of almost 42 years, who is still my dream.

MAGDALENA, MARIA

[a.] West Jakarta, India [title] "Throb of my Miss" [pers.] This poem is my special one for me, because it comes from my feelings. It tells about someone who is falling in love with a man who lives far away, separated from her by ocean and continent. We kept in touch for a year and we also met once. After that we separated again and contacted each other again by e-mail. Sometimes I would never get his reply because his work kept him so busy. We phoned rarely. Although in e-mail he seems serious about our relationship, he has never told me he loves me. He always seems caring, worried, and concerned about everything concerning me, but although I have told him my feelings, I don't know about his feelings for me. Sometimes I miss his voice and the sight of him and I just want to hear him say that he loves me. This poem is a message, a message I wish to share about our feelings when we are far away from someone we love.

MALDONADO, BANESA

[a.] Pacoima, CA [title] "Cage of Love" [pers.] From the depths of need and despair, my feelings of love transcend in "Cage of Love" manifesting my "passion, seduction, and corporal give." In a sexual, sensual, outcast, and modern woman's point of view, this poem describes my desire and willingness to capture a beloved. Prohibited love it was, submission and patience were factors that gave boost to this romance. "Cage of Love" is a synonym of freedom to be loved and it is also an expectation that promised that love is immortal.

MALEY, SCOTT

[a.] Perth, Australia [title] "Footprints" [pers.] My definition of poets are those few with the ability to carefully observe their surroundings and translate their thoughts into words by creatively interpreting their imagination. The meaning of my poem will depend upon each reader. For me, it relates to a combination of themes. These bring loneliness, isolation, insignificance, escapism, and death even, or perhaps I'm just lost. I'll leave it to you to find my voice.

MALLOZZI, SARAH

[a.] Yorktown Heights, NY [title] "Strings of Our Hearts" [pers.] Writing poetry is my way of letting people know how I feel. I wrote this poem at a difficult time in my relationship with my boyfriend. We were apart for many reasons but we did everything we could to stay together. I love him very much and I know he loves me too. I wrote this poem while I was thinking of him and I want him to know that our hearts beat as one, and I will never let that fall apart. So Ricky, this poem is dedicated to you. Don't ever forget that I love you.

MALOHN, ANGELA

[a.] Toledo, OH [title] "To You" [pers.] This poem is dedicated to my father who passed away from cancer. He was an inspiration to me in everything he did. I can't express in words what my father meant to me, but this poem was my attempt. I love you, dad. This is in loving memory of Paul Malohn, February 15, 2001.

MALTBA, MELEA

[a.] Midland, NC [title] "How Can We Grow As One?" [pers.] Poetry is my outlet. Through poetry, I can explore my feelings and concerns about the world around me. My husband, Michael, and our children are a great source of inspiration. I hope all the readers of this book enjoy the emotion and each poem because poetry is from the heart.

MANNING, MALISA RENEE

[a.] Green Bay, WI [title] "Little Kittie" [pers.] I wrote this poem to tell how much I enjoyed my past childhood with my cats. They always spark something inside of me that makes me love them. The example of "Little kittie in the tree, little kittie on my knee," is an example of when my kitten, T.C., climbed a tree and we could not get him down. When we did, I took him in my lap and hugged him, thankful he was with me. I started writing and getting interested in poetry in fourth grade when we had a poetry night. I have liked poetry ever since.

MANOS-MITCHEM, MARY

[a] Fairview Park, OH [title] "As Long As I Live" [pers.] I enjoy writing poetry to express my feelings. I want to show my love for my husband, Terry, and my joy and amazement over my daughters, Alexis and Emma. I understand the wisdom of my mom and dad, John and Linda Manos, the friendship of my brother, Mike, and the special love of my sister, Mindy. Without the love and support of my entire family, I wouldn't be me.

MANZI, MIKE

[a.] Mamaroneck, NY [title] "Heart of Gold" [pers.] I have always been able to write poems. Most of the time it was a short poem for a friend, or a school project. Recently I have started to write poems to convey my thoughts and opinions on various subjects and events. I also write poems to express myself to others when I find it difficult to use the spoken word. "Heart of Gold" is an example of one of these poems and is dedicated to someone special to me.

MARBUT, LAURA

[a.] San Antonio, TX [title] "The Empty Heart" [pers.] Writing is a treasure that passed down from my grandfather who had his own book, "The Weeping God," published. I find writing poetry therapeutic and in my case quite spontaneous. I never know when

a flood of words may come upon me and I'll find myself writing away on any scrap of paper within reach, allowing it to flow without much thoughts. I enjoy the process of writing, and if it happens that someone enjoys reading it . . . all the better.

MARTEINA, JILLYVETTE

[a.] Columbus, OH [title] "Wonder" [pers.] This particular poem came to me at a very vulnerable and emotional time in my life. When I put those words on paper, they came straight from my heart. Those were my feelings of recent experiences that at that particular time I was dealing with. Writing has always been a way for me to express myself completely and totally whether I'm writing poems, songs, or in my journal. I've always had a journal I write in every day. I've always said one day I'm going to write a book of my life and it's going to be a best seller.

MARTIN, BRYAN

[a.] Washington, DC [title] "The Wilderness" [pers.] "Poetry" is one of our most precious gift of life which I have always admired. I wrote this poem mainly because I am from an area of the world that is known to be a wilderness—Africa. Everyone else in the world believes that Africa is a jungle of some sort. Of course, people living in Africa know that this is not the case. I have two parents, Dumisile Nxumalo Martin, my mother, and William Martin, my father. My mother is from a small country in Southern Africa known as Swaziland. We now live in Zimbabwe, and I attend school at the Harave International School. I am 14 years old . Poetry should be something that is taught to our children's children's children. It is something that should never be forgotten.

MARTINEZ, MONA

[a.] Newark, NJ [title] "Forever More" [pers.] I dedicate this poem to my mother, a brilliant writer as well as a wonderful mother. She encouraged me to start writing poems at an early age. I'd like to thank God for giving me the gift of writing poetry for others to enjoy. I also want to thank my mother and sister for always being by my side. I hope my poem touches a part of your hearts as it did mine when I wrote it. May God bless you all.

MASSENGILL, KELSIE

[a.] Oakville, CT [title] "January First" [pers.] My poem, " January First," is very personal to me. I was only five when my father died, and I truly didn't understand what the word, death, meant. Now that I'm older, those memories are coming back to me. I would like to thank my English teacher, Mrs. Brown, my family, and my friends for encouraging me to pour my heart and soul out. And to my father . . . I love you, Daddy!

MASUSOCK, HEATHER

[a.] Glenside, PA [title] "A Runner's Life" [pers.] "A Runner's Life" is special to me because it symbolizes everything it takes to become a great runner. Poetry and running are two things that I have acquired both a talent and an interest towards, and when someone has a talent for something they should use it to their fullest potential. I like to use poetry as a path for my self expression, and things that are important to me. I hope my poem will inspire not just runners but all athletes to believe in themselves and follow their dreams.

MATTHEWS, ARCHIE M.

[a.] Yakima, WA [title] "A Sticker In My Boot" [pers.] I would like to dedicate this poem to my mother, Frieda F. Matthews, for always loving us boys and being sure we were always well supplied with plastic army men and my father, Archie H. Matthews, for always putting up with them wherever he found them. This is also to my own children, Archie Matthews and Brittany Deanne Matthews, whom I shall always love and cherish. "Poetry and stories shared around the fire is that which we in my family shall never tire."

MATURO, JESSICA
[a.] New Castle, PA [title] "Merlin" [pers.] This poem is important to me for many reasons. One of them is my grandmother. She awoke the interest inside me for Arthurian literature. She told me to read the three book series by Mary Stewart *The Crystal Cave, The Hollow Hills,* and *The Last Enchantment.* Another reason this poem is important and special to me would have be my "love "for Merlin! I could go on and on about this but I'll stop here. Thanks!

McGILVRAY, ROBERT
[a.] Marlborough, MA [title] "Friends" [pers.] This poem is my way of keeping alive a memory of my best friend. A friendship comes out of nowhere, and grows until fully understood by two. Poetry seems to me a sincere form of expression of one's innermost thoughts.

McALLISTER, JOHN
[a.] Hacienda Heights, CA [title] "Good-Byes" [pers.] The phenomenon of death, an essential component and partial definition of life itself, assumes many facets. In youth, it is a faint abstraction. In middle age, it becomes a distant reality. In old age, "His" dark specter hovers, constant, casting a shadow over the path ahead. Then, when "Death's Door" swings wide, and his bony finger beckons, we must often say, "good-bye" to a loved one, relinquishing our roles of provider, nurturer, protector, and lover, giving those tasks to God, alone. Thereupon, we experience many emotions and perceptions, beginning with denial! Thus, this poem deals with that phase of mourning.

McCAGE, LULA
[a.] Panama, OK [title] "Growing Up" [pers.] This poem came to me at 2:00 a.m. after working the evening shift. I am the mother of nine children, six of them adopted. Each one of them is very special to me. The youngest one recently married, and my husband and I are alone for the first time in our 39 years of marriage. We look forward to visiting with our children, grandchildren, and great-grandchildren.

McFARLANE, PHYLLIS
[a.] Windsor, ON [title] "No You and I" [pers.] Poetry is putting into words what the eye sees and the ears hear. Senses become thoughts on paper. It is a hope that the reader will see, hear, or feel the perceptions of the writer. Thank you to a family whose kindness and generosity opened their doors to those in need. It is of these people I write. What a tribute to them and what an honor to have a second submission in print!

McGINNIS, ROBERT
[a.] Walnut Creek, CA [title] "Lord of the Dance" [pers.] One day, while feeling depressed, a vision of dancing in a club came over me. My emotions soared, and my pen began to write all that I saw. When I was done, my depression had lifted and I had a piece of artwork I could be proud of.

McIVOR, THOMAS
[a] Plymouth, MA [title] "Lonely Boats" [pers.] Ever since grammar school, I've shown an interest in writing. I love to write short stories and to let my imagination take me to uncharted territories. As I moved onto junior high school, I found an interest in writing poetry. Writing poetry is an excellent way for me to express my feelings. Now writing gives me a way to release the many emotions of adolescence. My mother has been writing all her life. My father also likes to write poetry and songs. How could I have not fallen in love with writing? I've been surrounded by it my whole life!

McKENZIE-JONES, MARGARET
[a] Springville, TN [title] "Two Dear Friends" [pers.] This poem was written in memory of Lynn and Vicki Cole on February 15, 1980.

McKINNEY, BEKAH
[a.] Gig Harbor, WA [title] "So Willing to Die" [pers.] This poem is written about a very important part of me—my best friend. As our friendship has become stronger through the three years we have known each other, her body has become weaker with the disease of cystic fibrosis. I believe she is my angel. At times when she goes away to the hospitals, I feel as if part of me is missing. No matter the long days and endless nights, I will sit by her side through thick and thin. She is my life, my hope, and my inspiration, and she will always be with me as my guardian angel.

McKINNEY, TERI A.
[a.] Hesperus, CO [title] "Loving Chance" [pers.] I was born and raised in Durango, CO and will always consider it as home. I believe poetry comes from deep within the soul. I write from life's experiences. I do my best writing after a turning point in my life. The bumpier the road travelled, the better my writing captures the mood. I believe the best way to tell someone how you feel is with a poem.

McMULLEN, MICHELE
[a.] Vancouver, British Columbia [title] "Promised Dance" [pers.] Poetry, from my perspective, is a unique demonstration of the ability to reflect creativity, imagination, and love through words. My poem, "Promised Dance," portrays the introduction and first dance for my fiancé and me. It was a night that captured my heart, and the love that we share grows stronger each day. Expressing my feelings through poetry has allowed me to see through some difficult periods as well. Writing poetry has always been, and will continue to be, a regular part of my life.

McPHEE, WANDA
[a.] Miami, FL [title] "I Miss You" [pers.] On July 30th 2000, I left the Bahamas and everything familiar to pursue a bachelor's degree in Fine Arts in the United States. As you can imagine, the transition was hard, but what was even worse, was the fact that my best friend and confidante, my husband, George, could not take the journey with me. Though we called each other constantly, and he came to see me whenever he could, we both missed each other dreadfully. It was out of these feelings of deep longing for each other that the poem, "I Miss you," was born.

McQUAID, WILLIAM
[a.] Newburyport, MA [title] "Lost" [pers.] This poem represents the lowest point of my life. Subsequent writings depict my ascension out of the depths of despair into which I had fallen. I have dedicated each writing to the "special angel" who's friendship and caring have healed and inspired me. Thank you, my angel.

McROBBIE, MARGARET
[a.] Syracuse, NY [title] "Hey, Mister" [pers.] In order to appreciate our similarities, we must first (as a nation) learn to accept our differences. My name is Margaret Elizabeth McRobbie. I am the daughter of Robert and Kathleen McRobbie. Growing up in a large family of five children, my parents have instilled in my siblings and me the notion that regardless of race, creed, gender, financial status, and other classes that separate us as a society, our family would maintain moral standards. After receiving two degrees at Norfolk State University, I presently teach in the Syracuse City School district in hopes to spread my message. In August 2000, I gave birth to my son, Ephesus From Jr. I pray he, too, will carry on my ideas to influence the positive in all people.

MECHEM, JESSIE
[a.] Wa Keeney, KS [title] "Lost and Unseen" [pers.] To me, poetry is words that form all of my emotions or perspectives that flow onto paper. They help me understand what I am feeling or thinking at that moment. One thing that I enjoy about poetry is that the poem's value varies according to the reader. I

hope that "Lost and Unseen" touches a place in your soul and invokes new perspectives in your life.

MEKONNEN, SOLOMN
[a.] Addis Ababa, Ethiopia [title] "Born Free" [pers.] Freedom is one's mind. It is not given from outside. If you expect others to let you free, you are loosing it. The only person who could defend the freedom you have by nature is you. Despite this fact, some dictators claim on your freedom. I wrote "Born Free" as a reaction to them. Poetry gives me the power to air out the feelings in my heart. It's my beat. I am a graduate in economics, a bank employee, and a freelance TV journalist. I have published a Volume of poetry in Amharic.

MELANCON, CHERIE
[a.] New Orleans, LA [title] "If I Wanted To" [pers.] Cherrie Rita Melancon was born in New Orleans, Louisiana on June 16, 1971. "If I Wanted To" is the first of her original works to be published. She is currently working on a collection of poetry titled *Loving You for Baked Potatoes* which she hopes to be accepted for publication. Also the author of "New Orleans, Take Me Home" and "Grey Sweatpants, November Morning," she feels confident in her future as a poet and hopes to someday to continue her education. She is getting married to Arthur Franz IV, also a writer, in February 2002. They will reside in New Orleans.

MEREDITH, LACY
[a.] Carlisle, AZ [title] "What Does That Mean?" [pers.] I wrote this poem because I really like this guy. He is my best friend, but I am starting to have a lot of new feelings for him. I wanted to ask him all these questions, and what they mean to him. I also wanted to tell him that I think I might be falling in love. I couldn't ever get up enough courage to ask him so I wrote this poem so I could show him. I put it on-line so he could go read it. I told him about it, and he said he would go read it. I was hoping he would tell me if he liked it or not. He hasn't said anything to me yet. Hopefully he will soon.

MERRILL, SHARON
[a.] West Palm Beach, FL [title] "Missing You" [pers.] This poem was written for Mr. John M.W. Smith, "My Loving Brit." Thank you, for sharing your love and now our new life together. John has inspired me to continue with my poetry, and for this I will be forever grateful. Poetry has become my way of communicating, when the "right words" elude me at the appropriate time. My poems are an attempt at giving you a glimpse inside my heart and soul. I hope I have succeeded with my poem, "Missing You." I thoroughly enjoy expressing my feelings, whatever they may be, through my poetry.

MERRITT, AARON
[a.] Gahanna, Oh, [title]["Me, We, Us, You [pers.] Hello, my name is Aaron, and I have been writing for about two years or so. I never thought I would get something of mine published in a book. I'm 17 and in 11th grade at the Gahanna High School. After college I hope to become a high school teacher. I really don't know what to say that would really explain me in this, so have a nice day and don't do anything I wouldn't.

MESSER, VICKY
[a.] Pontotoc, MS [title] "Love Game" [pers.] I'm from Mississippi, a simply country girl. We played softball every summer. That is where most of us girls found that special guy who made our hearts pound with joy. This poem was inspired by those memories of my youth and those wonderful summer ball games that were worth playing just to see a special guy smile. Thanks to my mom and dad for providing a way to get to the games and the materials to play ball. Thanks for the memories, Ann and John Rush, from your daughter, Vicky.

MIALE, DANNY
[a.] Pompano Beach, FL [title] "The Courtyards of Quann" [pers.] My name is Danny Miahe. I am 17 years old. I have a strong passion for playing guitar and writing poetry.

MIGNOGNA, MIKEY
[a.] Baltimore, MD [title] "Hair" [pers.] This is my first attempt at writing poetry . I realized how rewarding it was when writing it actually caused me to laugh. Hair! What was I thinking?

MIKULKA, BETH
[a.] Lexington Park, MD [title] "My Zachariah" [pers.] Dedicated to my love, my Zachariah, this poem attempts to depict the experience he invokes inside me. He awakens my soul, inspiring me in directions I never expect. I gain focus when he is near. The last three-and-a-half years, filled with more good days than bad, have proved richer than I thought possible. And so, hopefully, this poem expresses to the world what he means to me. However, sometimes words just don't do!

MILLER, COREY NGOZI
[a.] Rex, GA [title] "Tomorrow" [pers.] The name I have chosen, "Ngozi," of Ibo origin, means blessed, and blessed I am, in spirit and in family. The faith I possess in my Creator is unsurpassed by any other. My creator has shown me through growth, both spirit and psychological, that there always exists an alternative if the heart and mind are willing, that if we believe strongly enough in one another, supporting are another, no accomplishment shall be too great. Peace be with you and all your endeavors.

MILLER, JEANIE
[a.] Apollo, PA [title] "Even the Deer" [pers.] Ever since I learned how to write, I have loved writing poetry. I took out my frustrations by running off to a secluded spot in the forest and writing, scribbling down anything and everything. I could just sit down and relax amongst all that God has made and forget about my troubles. This particular poem, "Even the Deer," was created on one of these outings and was turned in for an assignment at school. It spoke of the beauty that was created all around us and how people sometimes take advantage of all they have. But even animals know to give gratitude where it is due. I wanted to prove to the world that very few have respect for the gifts around us. Hopefully, I can make at least one person come to this realization.

MILLER, RANDY
[a.] Andrews, TX [title] "Miss Kitty, What Do You Say?" [pers.] My poetry is inspired by the love of my life, Miss Kitty, now my wife. Together, we have children a' plenty, starting at two years to past twenty. From our granddaughters, Angel, Dana, and Shiane, our daughters Brittay, Randi, Lacosta, and Leeann, and then our sons, Jimmy, John, and Robert, you can see Kitty and I are true romantics at heart. Our hobbies are horses, dancing, and roller skating. Imagine a cowboy on wheels—what a mistake! This pretty well sums it up I suppose, so on that note, I reckon I'll close.

MILLER, RAY
[a.] Bradenton, FL [title] "How Long?" [pers.] The artist lives with wife, Gladys, in the Tampa Bay area of Florida. They enjoy boating, fishing, and "glorious sunsets." His works include several poems, a screen play, and he is presently working on a collection of short stories.

MILLER, SANDY
[a.] Alamogordo, NM [title] "Sisters Are Special" [pers.] I was inspired to write this poem by my two sisters, Amy and Julie. We are much more than sisters—we are friends! I grew up in Calhoun, GA but I now live in New Mexico. I think poetry brings out feelings we have for certain things, whether it be people, scenery, or a special vacation place. It brings out who we are and how we feel. I hope if you have a sister or even a brother, you let them know each day what they mean to you. I also have three step sisters who mean a lot to me, Jinny, Anita, and Rita. Thank God for sisters!

MILLER, TINA
[a.] Montrose, MI [title] "A Man with a Big Heart" [pers.] This poem is a contribution to my dad whom I lost four-and-a-half months ago. He always helped anyway that he could. He was also a big believer in family. Sometimes we look back wondering what good qualities we've gotten from our parents. Well, Dad, you left me with your good sense of humor and you helped me become a fighter. My Dad was a brave fighter until the end. So here's to you, Dad. I'll always remember the important advice you always gave me. I will not take any wooden nickles. With love always, your daughter, Tina.

MIRANDA, BARBARA
[a.] Orange, CA [title] "Yours" [pers.] I wrote "Yours" for someone special in my life. I enjoy writing poetry, putting my feelings into words. I often find that writing my feelings is easier than actual words. I hope you enjoy it. This is for Brian, Kevin, and Stacey Twist, my beloved children.

MITCHELL, RENEE
[a.] Lake Forest, CA [pers.] I wrote this poem during a low period in my life. Being able to express myself allowed me to focus on the situation which brought me relief and made me feel so much better. I am striving to always enjoy life and to become a better person. Poetry helps me do just that. I currently reside in Lake Forest, CA.

MITROVIC, JACKIE
[a.] Franklin, VA [title] "I Was Here . . . " [pers.] I got the gift of poetry from my mother, Ivanka. As a professional of International Literature, she taught me to express my thoughts in a more sophisticated challenging and unusual way, than ordinary everyday words are able to say. I graduated with a Mechanical Engineering degree from the University of Belgrade, Yugoslavia. My father, Strahinja, as a doctor, taught me to love life and people. My sister, Jasmina, gave me a courage, strength, and support whenever I need it. My beloved husband, Nesa, our wonderful boys Andro and Djuro, and our little princess, Simonida, give me inexhaustible scores of love, inspiration, and happiness.

MODEY, KOFI
[a.] Memphis, TN [title] "The Magnificence of an Autumn Night" [pers.] The theme of this poem came from a special place in my heart. It symbolized the time in my life I went from childhood to manhood. In junior high school I was always teased about the way I looked, because I am the son of immigrants from Ghana in West Africa. This was the point where the teasing didn't hurt any longer. Poetry has always been a median for expressing the artistic vision I see in my mind from time to time. I think everyone has a little poetic literary ability inside of them; it just takes a special situation to unlock it.

MONTESSI, GINO
[a.] Chula Vista, CA [title] "My Brother" [pers.] I admire and respect my older brother, which is reflected in my poem. I was 14 years old when I wrote this, and I chose poetry because my brother, Hugo, writes wonderful poems himself. He has inspired me to explore poetry as a means of expressing myself. Another way the two of us enjoy creating is through cooking. Although we are both good cooks, I think I have begun to surpass Hugo's skills in the kitchen. I am grateful to Hugo and all my family for encouraging me in my interests. I hope they are proud of me.

MOORE, AMBER
[a.] Keavy, KY [title] "The Rain" [pers.] This poem represents all the despair that people fee when they want to do something, but are afraid to try because of all the chances that they might have to take. However, there will always be one person who throws caution to the wind and does it anyway.

MOORE, DENISE
[a.] Plano, TX [title] "Heartbeat" [pers.] This poem was dedicated to my son, William Hunter Moore. He is the joy of my life. His birth and being has been a true inspiration. I am thankful for my gift of poetry given to me by my father. Through his love of scripture and verse, I have been blessed. This is dedicated to all of my ancestors with their ability to express themselves through verse.

MOORE, MARISA
[a.] Rockledge, FL [title] "The Truth Within" [pers.] This poem is close to my heart because of what it represents. This is the first time I ever attempted to write a poem. My aunt and I decided to be creative one night, and we wrote this poem together. I am not a poet, or do I try to be. I'm just myself and in the past year I have had a lot of hard times, which are the meaning behind this poem. Most people like to talk about all of the great things, but I'm not like that because life is not always great and this is my way of expressing my emotions.

MOORE, SHERENE
[a.] Oxford, MS [title] "Missing You" [pers.] My inspiration for this poem was my dear best friend, Sandy. She was going through a very rough time in her life, and my goal was to prove to her beyond any doubts that my love and support would be there during her greatest time of need and that it would never fade with time. She tells me often that I have achieved my goal.

MORAN, ERIN
[a.] Arlington, VA [title] "The Curse of Life" [pers.] Janis Joplin once sang, "Freedom's just another word for nothing left to lose." When you pour your heart and soul onto a piece of paper for all the world to see, you have nothing left to lose. Poetry is my freedom.

MORAN, REBA
[a.] Theodore, AL [title] "Love's Touch" [pers.] My poetry is an expression of my innermost thoughts and feelings. Without my poetry, I'd probably keep everything balled up inside me and I'd go insane. It's a wonderful release for me.

MORENO, LINDA
[a.] Twenty-Nine Palms, CA [title] "Take My Hand" [pers.] I dedicate this poem to my first love. After our falling out, he got into some heavy drugs. I couldn't let a person I cared for so much throw his life away. I wrote "Take My Hand" to inspire him and also to let him know someone cares and to never give up. After realizing how much better he can do, he took the first step and asked for help. He's now living at a place he loves and has a good paying job. He thanked me for caring so much and told me he couldn't get through it alone.

MORI, ROSMI
[a.] Singapore [title] "Obsessive Love" [pers.] Ever since my secondary school days in Raffles Girls (Singapore) School, I have loved English literature and poetry. Now, as Head of the Department of English at Teck Whye Primary School (Singapore), I try to inculcate the love for poetry in my pupils. The publication of my poem in this anthology will certainly help to inspire my pupils to write poetry too. This poem is dedicated to the man I love, who inspired me to write this poem and to receive this honor.

MORISON, AYNNE
[a.] Manassas, VA [title] "The Belly Dancer" [pers.] I came to Middle Eastern dancing as physical therapy

after leg surgery. Now in my third year, I do it for the joy and support I've found in our troupe. "Hips Accepted!" American Tribal Belly Dance Troupe of Sterling, Virginia has given me a venue to express myself, just as poetry has. In the mix of Celtic and Native peoples that make up my heritage, there as always been the storyteller. My great-grandmother, Ella Francis Simms, was published in a poetry journal in the 1920s. Ella Francis' cousin, William Jennings Bryant, was a bit better known.

MORISSEAU, SAPHIA
[a.] Brooklyn, NY [title] "Not by Your Lonesome" [pers.] Poetry is my passion. It is my form of expression. I am a sophomore at Suny New Paltz, soon to be a junior. I have been writing poetry since high school. My subjects range from romance to religion, hopes, dreams, and depression. I like to share my poetry on open-mike nights. In addition to writing poetry, I love to dance. The only difference is when I get older, I may not be able to dance as much but I will always write. All of my accomplishments are dedicated to God. Without Him, none of this would be possible. With God I am not by my lonesome.

MORRELL, CHANNON
[a.] Southfield, MI [title] "Bonded for Life" [pers.] I am a sophomore student at Detroit Country Day High School in Birmingham, MI. In my free time, I enjoy reading, writing, shopping, and listening to music. I deem that poetry is a way to sincerely show true feelings in all its originality, uniqueness, and affection. Writing poetry is a way for me to achieve serenity and relax, and a way for me to tell the world how I feel. Being able to express myself in a much characterized way has given me a talent that I am very proud of.

MORRIS, SAMANTHA
[a.] Orlando, FL [title] "Beautiful Day" [pers.] The story behind this poem is actually that most people don't pay attention to nature. I was outside when I noticed all of this. My friends and family inspired me and helped me. They tell me that I write good poetry. They all wish me good luck, and tell me I can be whatever I want to be. I also want to thank God for giving me this gift that I have to write poetry and for making me notice how beautiful nature is.

MORRIS, WANDA
[a.] Eccles, WV [title] "Black Rose" [pers.] "Black Rose" was written to remind me that life is a gift, and the people in your life are as well. I am 17 years old, and I live in West Virginia. On November 2, 2000, my father had a massive stroke. It hit hard on everyone in our family, and it effected me because I was so close to him. This event was an inspiration for me. So I would like to dedicate this poem to my father and my whole family. I love you all, Freddie Morris and family.

MORSCH, IAN
[a] Augusta, NJ [title] "one thousand ill-faded wishes and kisses" [pers.] I am 19 years old and live in rural New Jersey. My poem is a collage of memories from last summer. It does mean something, indeed. The limit on words and such was very difficult—it mostly upset the system of the poem—but I am honored the message was still able to be appreciated.

MOSELEY, CAITLIN
[a.] Fairbanks, AK [title] "Evyn" [pers.] I feel surprised that I can just take the facts about someone and turn it into poetry. Though I knew that poetry doesn't have to rhyme, I still make mine rhyme. I am ten years old going on eleven, and I feel good about it. Though I am still young and people put me down for everything I do, I am still self-confident about things that I do like violin, poetry, and singing. I feel good about my poetry, and I still encourage people to do the things they give up on.

MOSES, DELORES
[a.] Riceville, TN [title] "The Only Thing We Need" [pers.] I just feel like God was leading me to write this poem.

MOSHER, JENNA
[a.] Nevada, MO [title] "Daddy" [pers.] Poetry, for me, is a way to express how I feel. I write when I have something to say, and I don't know how to say it out loud. I wrote this poem about my daddy a few days after his funeral. Losing my dad at fourteen was a hard time for me. I had so many things that I wanted him to hear. So, I sat down in a mournful rage and wrote to him. After I had finished, I felt much better. I knew that he was proud of me. I knew he heard the words I wrote.

MOULDERS, THERESA
[a.] Houston, TX [title] "Be Free" [pers.] I wrote this poem when I was 12. It was a time in my life, where I was confused of who I was. I was told I was adopted, my mother was dead, and my father never wanted me. I became depressed; I wanted to die. I realize I was not alone, but very much loved by my parents Mr. and Mrs. Moulders, who raised me from six months old. They loved me, they loved me forever. I became free after that.

MOUTSOS, SAMANTHA
[a.] Vero Beach, FL [title] "When Is It Time?" [pers.] I love writing poetry. It's something in which you can be you; you don't have to pretend or hide. Poetry is honest. It's something I use to let things out, whether I'm sad, angry, or happy. This poem I wrote speaks for itself. This person just wants to disappear into the world, to hide forever. I'm sure many people can relate to this poem and I hope they do; I know I can.

MUHAMMAD, KALIMAH
[a.] Austin, TX [title] "Have You Got the Vision" [pers.] The poem was inspired by the Holy Spirit; God gave me this poem which was suppose to be a song. My friend, Steve, also encouraged me to enter it in the poetry contest on the Internet. I thank God for blessing me with the talent to write songs and poetry, and allowing me to share it with the world. Hopefully this poem will inspire people to trust in God, and look to him for help in finding their own unique God-given vision.

MULLINS, REGINA
[a.] Buckeye Lake, OH [title] "Flowers in Heaven" [pers.] I wrote this poem as a memorial for Anita Johnson, a close friend who died in her early forties of an aneurysm of the heart. She was unbelievably cheerful, good hearted, and a devout Christian. She was always taking care of her family and others, and her sudden death left a great void in the lives of her family and friends. This is the first time I have written poetry, but I found the effort and result comforting in my sorrow. Anita was truly an inspiration, and through this poem I hope she will be forever memorialized in our hearts.

MULVANEY, KIMBERLY
[a.] Topeka, KS [title] "Society's Child" [pers.] Poetry, like all forms of art, is a deep desire within the artist that must find an outward expression. "Society's Child" is an expression of inner frustration with people who are so busy living their daily lives that they never take the time to look inside themselves. This inner frustration leads to a quiet rebellion against "the norm," which surfaces in the realization that it's all right to be myself. I don't have to be like everyone else. I've been writing poetry since I was a young teen. I feel that it's not only therapeutic, but pleasurable as well.

MURDOCK, JEAN
[a.] Dubois, WY [title] "Pronghorn on the Highway" [pers.] I am seventy-six, going on twenty. I spent most of my life in the wind river mountains of northwest Wyoming. I wrote my first poem at age nine. My grandfather homesteaded in Wyoming.

MURRAY, CAITLIN
[a.] St. Louis, MO [title] "Advice Untaken" [pers.] Everyone has a special talent, but not everyone is as lucky to find it right away. I'm blessed because I have found my gift, and I get to share it with so many other people. I am also blessed to have such a loving, supportive mother to encourage me to share my gift. This poem is to tell others, especially people around my age, that advice given by your parents and sometimes friends can make life a lot easier.

MYERS, LUCAS
[a.] Woodinville, WA [title] "Gone Fishin'" [pers.] What can I say? I took a marine biology class and felt bad for fish. The rest is history. Oh, wait, that's too cliche, oh well, it's not like I'm a poet or anything.

MYERS, TRISTA
[a.] Imperial, NE [title] "Love?" [pers.] Poetry is like a canvas to an artist, or notes to a musician. It expresses my inner most feelings. The words to this poem flowed like the tears I cried for my best friend when he moved away. He will forever remain in my heart.

NADERI, NADER
[a.] Fredricton, NB, Canada [title] "A Red, Red Rose" [pers.] I am a wood lover and wood worker. However, since I have met my better half, Mansoureh, she put a real rose taste in my life. I thank her, I dedicate this poem to her and her rosy feeling.

NAHAL, DENNIS
[a.] Rensselaer, NY [title] "Wedding Whisper" [pers.] "Wedding Whisper" was written as a song for my cousin, Thea Denise Davis, at her wedding to Robert Osborne. It holds a special place in my heart as well as in the hearts' of my family. I have been writing poetry, lyrics, and composing my own music for several years. I currently attend Siena College, working on a degree in political science. I also work part time selling cellular phones. Much of my free time is spent at home composing songs and creating CDs on my computer.

NAHINURK, ERIKA
[a.] Grand Forks, ND [title] "AIDS" [pers.] This poem is very important to me. I saw the AIDS quilt at my university last year. It got me thinking about these suffering people. That is how my poem came about. I am a senior at the University of North Dakota in Grand Forks. I am working on a psychology degree.

NANAMKIN, HALLYE (FLORES)
[a.] Coulee Dam, WA [title] "A Friend" [pers.] This poem is about me. I was stabbed in the back by my best friend. I'm an 18-year-old female. I am a married senior, attending Lake Roosevelt High School in Coulee Dam, Washington. I'm going to attend college and major in Accounting and General Business. I want to become a certified public accountant (CPA). I love to play volleyball, ride/raise race horses, and spend time with my family and friends.

NAZARENUS, SHERYL
[a.] Englewood, CO" [pers.] Poetry has always helped me find my way. Life is just one of those things that help me to write and express my feelings. My faith in God keeps everything in perspective. We all have our days and this poem helps me to remember to take life day by day. I hope everyone will live life day to day in the fullest.

NEDAL, JENS
[a.] Vienna, Austria [title] "Soulbound" [pers.] Poetry happens along the greater moments of happiness, sadness or when awe at this life overwhelms us, about our personal greater insights. Words put into shape this way remain within us though they may fade. All that matters is the moment contained within the essence of those words. I live in Vienna, Europe. A programmer at work, a life's artist for the rest of the

time. Curiosity and challenge can be counted as some of the key drives in my life, plus affection for nature and animals.

NEILL, DEBBIE
[a.] Wantirna South, Australia [title] "Waiting for the Ghost" [pers.] Poetry is a language that, if you are fluent in it, you experience your emotions threefold. It allows me to assemble the jigsaw puzzle that is confusion. In order to see the bigger picture, it promotes understanding and to those that influence you, it is a thank you. I started writing at the age of twelve. Now four years later, I still find it an excellent outlet. Someday I hope to publish my full collection, in the hope that someone will relate to it and enjoy it.

NELLES, MILLIE
[a.] Calgary, AB, Canada [title] "Three Valley Gap" [pers.] "Three Valley Gap" is an excerpt taken from a poem I wrote about a breathtaking place located in British Columbia, Canada. Three Valley Gap Lake Chateau, owned by Gordon and Ethel Bell, is nestled at the point where three valleys meet and are surrounded by the Canadian Rocky Mountains. My great Uncle Walter Moberly, an explorer and surveyor, discovered Eagle Pass in 1865. Walter named this pass "Eagle Pass," and the lake was named "Lake of Three Valleys." Used by the C.P.R. Railway in 1886 and by the Trans Canada Hwy. in 1962, this pass contributed greatly to unifying Canada.

NELSON, MANDIE
[a.] Vandergrift, PA [title] "Open Doors" [pers.] This poem, "Open Doors," is to a very special person in my life, Brett Shoner. It's dedicated to him, because we are so close and in reality, I feel that words can express the way I feel about him.

NELSON, MICAYLA
[a.] Saint Charles, MO [title] "Kingdom" [pers.] I dedicate my achievement to my friends and family. Thank you to my mother for being my angel for the past 16 years. Thank you, Mr. Meier, for being an excellent mentor and friend, and teaching me to put my thoughts onto paper. Thank you, Meagan, for being the best friend any girl could hope for. And thank you, Chris, for inspiring me in every aspect, and making me the luckiest girl in the world. I love you the most, baby.

NEMIA, ELIZABETH
[a.] Harrisburg, PA [title] "One Breath" [pers.] This poem embodies a great deal of my perspective on life and my religion. Every day I thank God for giving me a chance to experience life and all of its glory. I simply feel privileged to be able to be a part of, what I believe to be, God's grandest creation, Earth. Sometimes I try to hold the beauty of Earth inside, yet at times it proves to be too much. I hope my poem will inspire others to simply understand and appreciate what God has given to them, because life truly is one of the greatest gifts of all.

NESTER, TRISH
[a.] Wapakoneta, OH [title] "Scott" [pers.] My husband, Wayne, our daughter, Kristin, and I was devastated when we lost our only son, her only brother, 24-year-old Scott, in a four-wheeler accident. Scott had a big heart, lots of friends and is sadly missed by everyone. He continued giving even after his death by being an organ donor. His courage, goodness, and smile was well-known to family and friends. This poem is my way of honoring him and sharing his life with the world. I hope that others can relate to my love for my only son, and perhaps share my poem with their loved ones.

NETTI, DAVID
[a.] Mansfield, OH [title] "The Coming Reunion" [pers.] At a large family reunion I was asked to speak some appropriate thoughts from the bible. It is a family where love is shown and where family gatherings always begin with the reading of the bible. There were those of the family who were missing—both parents as well as children, young mothers, and fathers and people who passed away. As I thought of the responsibility of speaking, I penned the poem, "The Coming Reunion." There will always be those missing from earthly reunions, but in my thoughts I looked ahead to a day that is coming when there will be a reunion which will never end and all the family members who have gone before will be there.

NETZEL, AMY
[a.] Pembroke, NC [title] "I'm Scared" [pers.] When a child experiences many sorrowful days and many lonely nights, that child may grow to be an adult who longs very deeply to embrace happiness and love. These longings are what my poem speaks of. Hurt and confused are states of being that the soul refuses to accept. The result is that people become scared to show who they are. Becoming scared is the soul's way of letting us know that life can be better if we are brave. I dedicate this poem to my best friend, DBE. He has shown me that I can be brave.

NEUHARTH, KART
[a.] Lodi, CA [title] "Mikey" [pers.] During my third year in Pepperdine University, I had the honor of roaming with Michael McGehee, an aspiring writer and poet. His unique attitude and charisma inspired me to write this poem about him, and the alternate state of consciousness he enters when he is writing. Poetry has always been special to me, but it has never meant as much as it did whilst I was attending school in Heidelberg (Tori, Maya, and Arlene: This sentence was for you). I must also give kudos to my best friend and compatriot, Steven Drouink, for making my life worth writing poetry about.

NEUMANN, CRYSTAL
[a.] Fremont, CA [title] "Tears" [pers.] This poem is very special to me. It is dedicated to my daughter's godfather, my close friend. He has recently passed away, but remains in my heart. His precious memories will never fade for he brought laughter to so many. I hope that others who have lost someone dear can relate to my poem and share it with others.

NEUROHR, KATHERINE
[a.] Dallas, TX [title] "Never through Years" [pers.] I believe poetry is a great way to express one's inner most feelings. I wrote "Never through Years," not only as a school assignment, but a tribute to e. e. cummings, whose poetry inspired me greatly. Like cummings, my expression of feelings in this poem is difficult to explain, but the words create images in moods which are very effective. I come from a family of nine where it is sometimes difficult to make your feelings known. Poetry gives me an outlet to express myself.

NEWCOMER, DAVID
[a.] Olympia, WA [title] "Together" [pers.] This poem was one that I wrote during a time in my life when I met my life-partner, prior to which I had been going through a bad time of depression and loneliness. I found that writing poetry helps to express emotion for me, and helps to chase the blues away.

NGUGI, SIMON
[a.] Lowell, MA [title] "Show Me the Way, Lord" [pers.] Whenever the urge of creativity challenges me, I always pick up the gauntlet and write. This poem has since been my very personal prayer. The impetus behind were the challenges I faced as a Catholic Youth Leader in Kenya. It was through the thick and thin while heading the Secretariat at St. Luke's right through to my position at the National Catholic Youth Council that I discovered the joy of working and helping others for the glory of God. I pay tribute to my mom, Mrs. Teresia Ngugi, and my late dad, Mr. John Ngugi, who always urged me on. To my brother, Joel, who is a poet of exceptional promise; I am grateful. To my other brothers and sisters, Lucy, Monica, Julius, Paul, Peter, James, Margaret, Sylvia and Rodah—I will always be grateful. I can never forget father's Francis and John for their encouragement. Lastly, for very personal reasons, I am grateful to Miss Salome W. Valentine. I dedicate this poem to all of the above people.

NGUYEN, JIMMY
[a.] Waipahu, HI [title] "Endless Search" [pers.] I wrote this poem during a personal crisis in my life. It was a time of chaos and confusion, which led me to write poetry. Since "Endless Search," has shown success, I will probably write lots more in the future. Poetry helped me become more in tune with God. I am grateful to the readers who have shown appreciation of "Endless Search." Poetry will hopefully become more accessible to the public, because it can heal deep inner wounds.

NGUYEN, MAI
[a.] Lubbock, TX [title] "Your Love Is . . . " [pers.] I dedicate this poem to my boyfriend, Nick. He is the true love of my life, my soul mate. He told me that he wants to spend an eternity with me. So I took pen, paper, and my God-given talent, and wrote all my feelings down in numerous poems. Of course, I could never put to words the way Nick makes me feel (only God could know that). He is everything I could ever ask for and so much more. I not only thank God for my ability to write poetry, I also thank Him for bringing Nick into my life.

NICHOLS, DARLENE
[a.] Howe, TX [title] "Leaving the Laughter Behind" [pers.] This poem is dedicated to my son's memory. Troy Chatham Nichols 9-13-80—8-11-2000.

NOLAN, SALLY L.
[a.] Lubbock, TX [title] "Ode to Love" [pers.] I am 10 years old. I wrote this poem in honor of my Great-Grandfather. He was the most important and influential man in my life. As he looks down from Heaven, I hope he knows I love and miss him.

NOONEY, CHARLES
[a.] Ladonia, TX [title] "Of Thought and Time" [pers.] I am a 46-year-old, retired from chemical work and EMS. I am currently a student majoring in social work and sociology at a Texas University. I have written poetry most of my life. Now I write poetry to share with everyone. Some of my poems reflect an intense emotion followed by a positive emotion or solution, while others are based on a particular moment in time and life experiences. The gift that has long eluded me has returned. To James Kerr (the original family poet) and Robert Frost, my inspirations to my writing poetry. Thank you!

NORONHA, CHARLOTTE
[a.] Kuwait [title] "Solitude" [pers.] It is such a delight to identify my true talents! Apart from music and art, I enjoy writing poetry. A poem begins in delight and ends in wisdom. Our life is what our thoughts make it. From the brain, and the brain alone, arise our pleasures, joys, laughter, and jests as well as our sorrow, pain, grief, and tears. I do hope all those who read "Solitude" will receive genuine pleasure!

NORRIS, JEWEL
[a.] Laurel, MS [title] "As You Go" [pers.] I am a mother, grandmother, and a nurse. In my later years, God has given me the gift of poetry. I write poems that tell a story. They are true events that have touched my life or those dear to me. They are an expression of my inner most feelings. "As You Go" was written for an outstanding co-worker who was resigning.

NWOKO, STACIE
[a.] Chicago, IL [title] "Who I Am" [pers.] My poems portray my feelings, mainly the ones that I can only

express on paper. I started writing poems, because sometimes I could only explain myself in phrases and I could only give a meaning to life with a title. This poem describes my motto which is "I'll always be me, no matter what others think." I have a sister named Scrabeth and she writes lovely poems. She is a big idol to me, because she's helped me to learn the meaning of writing poems. I live in Chicago, this great big city, I sometimes feel closed in by all the excitement, but that's where my poems come in. They help me to see inside of me and I ignore the outside world. That's not the easiest thing to do though, being in eight grade. I am so happy to have the pleasure of being chosen to have my poem published.

OAKCRUM, LEWIS
[a.] Clinton, MD [title] "The Touch of an Angel" [pers.] This poem is an attempt to capture, in few words, the months of being in the presence of a lady whom God must smile at every day. My daughter, Joy, was the first person to inspire me to write poetry. I'm certain other people who have special people in their lives can relate to this poem.

OCATE, YOUSUF RONILO
[a.] Jeddah, Saudi Arabia [title] "Happy Birthday" [pers.] Mothers are unsung heroes that we sometimes fail to recognize. Here's a poem verbalizing a thought only a mother can convey to her child. Birthdays are special days; we recollect those growing years being witnessed by somebody close to our hearts. Being taken for granted sometimes (if not most of the time), mothers never fail us. I can only imagine how great their unconditional love is toward their children. My wish is that this poem reminds each and every one of us that we'll always be that "little you" in our mother's hearts—no matter what.

ODOM, LINDA
[a.] Fresno, CA [title] "Food for Thoughts" [pers.] After years of putting my thoughts on paper, which was easy, to share these thoughts was a hard decision to make. This poem is about the psych of gaining weight. After losing the same twenty pounds a dozen times, I can read this and think back to focus on the action and reaction. My thoughts have themes of friends, relationships, love, and faith. The feedback after sharing with a few friends has encouraged me to share with more people who can identify with things we all face a one time or another. To find encouragement and hope, whether it be the battle of weight management, the powerful feeling of love, or the strength one can find in faith.

OKAI, LYNDA
[a.] Philadelphia, PA [title] "Heart Break" [pers.] The daughter of a renowned African poet, Atukwei Okai, and a mother who is an artist and designer, Korkor-Botor, I derive my artistic abilities from my parents. Born in Iowa City, 1979, I spent my childhood in my homeland, Ghana. In the fall of 1999, I enrolled at Temple University, Pennsylvania, to pursue a bachelor's degree in political science and history after successfully completing the International Baccalaureate. I am the second of five sisters: Kordei, Klorkai, Klorisoo, Korle-Fofo. My father's poetry largely influenced my love for the art. I write out of inspiration and the need to conscientize society to existing vices. The world lends an eager ear to the voices within through poetry.

ONASSIS, LANA MARIE
[a.] Merrimack, NH [title] "Seashore De-Lights" [pers.] This poem is about what I enjoy as an artist and a person. I find there is a great feeling of peace that can be found when near the ocean. I hope that this poem will give you that same feeling of peace it gives me, and that it will enrich, in some way, the lives of those who read it. Enjoy!

OROZCO, RAFAEL
[a.] Santa Ana, CA [title] "The Venetian Rose" [pers.] This poem is for Ms. Moniaforch, a great friend. I write intuitively, so I cannot consider myself a proper poet. My love for the written sentiment gave me courage to submit this poem. Thanks for sharing it and Gloria A. Dios.

OSAKOWICZ, MICHAEL
[a.] Norwalk, CT [title] "Simply in Love" [pers.] Anyone can be a poet with the right inspiration. Kerin Towne, my one and only love, has given me the inspiration to write, "Simply in Love." Kerin is my soul mate, and has given me the greatest gift one can give to another person, the gift of love. This poem, along with my love, is my gift in return. Love stimulates and excites sense in a person, and in writing this poem I tried to capture that. Keri, you will always be in my heart.

OSTER, JOHN
[a.] Palm Springs, CA [title] "Just Like Me" [pers.] The inspiration for "Just Like Me" is the beauty and mystery of rainbows, which appear to have a spectrum of clearly defined colors, but in fact are an infinite spectrum of all colors and shades. The parallel in the world with its people of all colors and shades (in personality as well as skin color) is never lost to me. The rainbow also reminds me that there is so much more to life than we'll ever know or experience.

OUTLAW, ALEXIS
[a.]Chestnut Ridge, NY [tile] "Untitled" [pers.] I am 16 years old, and I am from the Bronx in New York City. Right now, I am in a Residential Treatment Center. I've been living here for two years now. I attend high school at Spring Valley High School. My poem is about me and what I am going through right now. In the poem, I talk about the staff at my group home, my family, and myself. I feel that I am by myself and trying to get away from all the hurt. I don't like it at my group home because half of the staff doesn't care about the students. It is also a very uncomfortable place. My family has never really been there for me. I am trying to do the right thing and then I end up making it worse for myself. I use writing and other hobbies to express myself because it helps me.

OUTLAW, WANDA
[a.] Washington, DC [title] "I Am Rescued" [pers.] There is always that someone in your life who is a warrior spirit. You cry with them. You both consume joy and pain together; you fight many battles together. You cannot help but breathe together. I created this piece for that spirit partner in my life. He keeps me in the inner recesses of his heart. He who rescues me on time and in time—God bless him for he is divine!

OWL, WHITE
[a.] Yellville, AR [title] "Rose Marie" [pers.] I am a descendant of the Oneida Nation. Inspiration for my poetry is received while listening to the "Silence." I place in poetry the wisdom and teachings from the Ancestors, and the animal, plant, and mineral kingdoms. I provide Native American teachings, ceremonies, and lodges at Turtle Island, in the Ozark Mountains of Arkansas, where I lives. The poem "Rose Marie" was written after receiving an e-mail from a young woman whose grandmother had dropped her robe and passed to the spirit world. This poem is dedicated to Rose Marie, Grandmother, and Rose Marie, Granddaughter.

OZOBIALU, VIVIENNE
[a.] Lagos, Nigeria [title] "Kaleidoscope" [pers.] "Kaleidoscope," much like the scientific instrument, summarizes my deep belief in the importance of my existence, though ordinary it seems. It expresses the hope in my heart even in my hopeless situations. Poetry has been a medium of release and expressions ever since I was 11 years old. Poetry is a window to

my very soul and yearnings. After 11 years of writing poetry and dreaming of being published, the dream has finally come true. I wish to acknowledge my family; my mom, Mrs. P. Ozobialu; my siblings, Kingsley, Linda, and Nneka; and my friend, Mike. I am a student in the university, studying law in Nigeria, where I was born and raised. My hobbies are reading, writing stories and poems, and listening to music.

PAGE, DELECIA
[a.] Chicago, IL [title] "Fathers" [pers.] I feel that poetry is an excellent form of expression for the soul. For what better way to express your innermost emotions be they, love, hope, happiness, or even anger in as much as anger may become a wonderful tool of inspiration when released in poetry. I personally rely on poetry as my personal tool for self-expression and relaxation.

PAIGE, JUBILEE
[a.] Belleville, KS [title] "Side by Side" [pers.] I wrote this poem in dedication to all of those who have experienced the blessing of a true friend. It is my belief that there are individuals that tend to brightly score one's life, but after a while they may fade and pass. However, true friends make eternal impressions upon the heart that will never be forgotten. True friends will forever shine in your life and it is my advice to never let go. In turn, you will prove to be a true friend yourself. I thank God for my friends, the stars of my life!

PALEGA, THADYEE ROSE
[a.] Hartford, CT [title] "Review" [pers.] Poetry has always moved me, and I have always used it as an outlet being that I don't express myself emotionally. I know I can always express myself in words. I believe this is healthy, because the words, as in any other story or song, form a picture in one's head and after rereading what I have written I can see the problem or a solution in a different perspective. Then I can take everything head on philosophically and the outcome is always a positive end.

PALMER, NATHAN
[a.] Clovis, NM [title] "Journey through Life" [pers.] This was my first time writing poetry. I know this poem means a lot to me and everyone who will read. It tells of a life and the way you should feel about it. It speaks to a person and his inner-self, like an alter ego, who is always there when you need him. The poem is about a man and his best friend, which in fact turns out to be himself. He realizes that when no one's around, you always have yourself. Remember, never wait 'til it's too late to show your true feelings.

PARKER, DAVID
[a.] Timpson, TX [title] "Satan Whispers" [pers.] This piece speaks of the unending struggle that we all face every day. With every decision we make, and every situation we react to, we choose between good and evil. We must always remember in making these decisions, that a half truth is a complete lie. And while Satan whispers in our ear, God sits mute upon his throne waiting for us to turn to him and ask his guidance.

PATRICK, HILARY
[a.] Hubbard, OH [title] "Reminiscence" [pers.] Hilary Patrick is a sixteen-year-old sophomore at Hubbard High School in northeastern Ohio. She enjoys skating, reading fiction novels, playing video games, and writing from time to time out of inspiration. "Reminiscence" was originally written in response to a poetry assignment in her honors English class. She never imagined that in submitting this poem, a personal favorite, that she would be published for the first time. She would like to dedicate "Reminiscence" to her beloved friend for whom this poem was written, and also her family for their continued support.

PECK, ROSALIE
[a.] Marysville, CA [title] "Confusion" [pers.] Writing poetry has allowed me to express the inner me, my thoughts, and feelings. With each poem I write I learn a little more about myself and grow from it. I know poetry isn't my best quality, but none-the-less I value it very much.

PELC, DEBBIE
[a.] Croswell, MI [title] "My Stinky Shoes" [pers.] Debbie wrote, "My Stinky Shoes" at a time when she had a very bleak outlook on life. She's made many mistakes, but has had the strength and determination to learn from her past, now trusting God with her future. Though she used to think her life was irrelevant, she currently lives by the philosophy recorded by Paul in Philippines 1:20-26. Her greatest ambition is to share God with the world through her writing, artwork, and her life.

PELLAM, GARY
[a.] Emporium, PA [title] "Wandering Thoughts" [pers.] Poetry is emotions frozen in time, recorded as history for the world to read. I was fascinated with the rhyming word at a very young age, and it became very natural for me.

PERAINO, KEITH
[a.] Staten Island, NY [title] "Just Fall in Love" [pers.] This poem was written from an inspiration that I had in regards to almost losing the woman that I love. Sometimes I am unable to express to her in words how I feel, and I express it in verse instead.

PEREZ, BALLEN
[a.] Las Vegas, NV [title] "If You Were Mine" [pers.] This poem was written for people who have found love, lost love, and found it once again. Poetry was introduced to me in basic training by a bunkmate who would write beautiful words to his girlfriend. When I showed my admiration, he encouraged me to try it. I was on guard duty when I attempted my first poem and never stopped since. I'd like to dedicate this book to my mother, who pointed me down the path of sobriety; to Paula, who took pity on me and became my wife; and to Karen, whose humor has kept our friendship flourishing.

PEREZ, GLENDA
[a.] Fort Smith, AR [title] "Dream" [pers.] This poem is actually hope for anyone or anybody that sometimes believes and hopes that someday all people will live in peace. Many try to maintain their hopes and happiness believing that it will bring peace to the whole world. It has been difficult to share poems with many people, but this is a very good start.

PERRY, JAMES
[a.] Columbus, OH [title] "Honor and Pride" [pers.] Jim was the father of four natural children and four step-children he raised teaching the responsibilities of life. He taught wisdom, honor, pride, and respect. Jim died shortly after I submitted this poem he wrote for me as a child. He knew the submission of this poem was my way to show my pride in him. He penned this poem for me when I was ten years old, in the fall of 1967. I am the eldest of his children, and at the time of the writing I was a Girl Scout. I was being honored for an accomplishment I had struggled to achieve. Dad wanted to show his encouragement and pride in me, so he took to pen and paper to share his feelings by writing me this poem. Jim wasn't one to speak openly of his feelings, and he didn't feel confident in his writing abilities. But he showed his love for his family through his poetry. He left us a legacy of love, honor, wisdom, inspiration, laughter, and pride.

PERRY, PAMELA
[a.] Tuttle, OK [title] "Clear in Thought, Clear in Sound" [pers.] "Clear in Thought, Clear in Sound" is extremely special to me. It talks about my troubles with speech when I was younger. I wrote this poem in the 4th grade. I spent my youth not talking, because I couldn't say "r's" correctly. I would spend hours and hours practicing. I was very proud of myself when I could talk correctly. This poem shows my happiness. I'm glad that people enjoy my poem so much.

PESOK, YANIR
[a.] New Haven, CT [title] "Like a Little Bird" [pers.] This poem is my first poem that I wrote. I wrote this poem after I received a broken heart from a relationship that I really thought that is going to work out. I was depressed and my father, that also write poems, encouraged me to write what I felt at that time. With this poem, and another one that followed, I tried to explain my love to her. Unfortunately, this didn't work out and I am still looking for my love.

PETERSHEIM, BENJAMIN
[a.] Granville, OH [title] "My Father's Eyes" [pers.] I am a 15-year-old boy in the 9th grade at Granville High School. My father was killed in a freak accident on August 4, 2000. On his way to work at 10:15 p.m., he hit a 1,200 pound Black Angus bull that had gotten loose from a farm. I was very blessed in that he was the best father. So many kids do not have the luxury of such a relationship. I am thankful for my 15 years with a great dad. I will always remember and miss "My Father's Eyes."

PETRUCCI, KENJI
[a.] Chesapeake, VA [title] "It's All My Fault" [pers.] I'm a 17-year-old guy in a band called Fairground. We're still in high school, and music is our lives. This is actually a song, and these are the lyrics. It's about a girl, one who can be very confusing and very sensitive. We had something going between us, but one day I did something to upset her. I had such deep feelings for this girl and I felt so sorry for what I did that I put it to paper and gave it to her. I'm not one for admitting I'm wrong, so there's a lot of feeling and sincerity in this.

PHELAN, PAUL
[a.] Bridgewater, VA [title] "Be Silent and Listen" [pers.] Diagnosed with incurable cancer a year ago, Paul began writing poetry to thank his treatment team and friends who prayed to life his spirit. Looking at Christ on the cross, he prayed, "My God, why have you forsaken me?" Silent, a thought came. "You will be a better person now. Better than you were before. Trust me!" Paul is now in remission and his heartfelt poetry has lifted the spirits of his many readers. He is the son of Paul and Majorie Phelan. He has a wife, Cecelia, and four children, Rita, Andrew, Veronica, and Daniel.

PHILLIPS, ANTHONY
[a.] Gainesboro, TN [title] "In Memory of Michael" [pers.] The death of my brother was so overwhelming: I needed a release for the unbearable pain in my heart. "In Memory of Michael" reminds me to take more seriously the people God choose to place in my life. For just as the plants in a field fall and disappear once they fulfill their purpose, so do the people we love and care for. Nothing in life lasts forever. Memories, we can no longer make with our loved ones, and memories made we cannot see with our eyes, but yet they play over and over in our hearts and minds.

PHILLIPS, DIANE
[a.] St. Louis, MO [title] "A Champion" [pers.] I feel my poetry is a gift from Father God. My poem, "A Champion," was inspired by the Holy Spirit to write for a close friend's relative who had just lost her mom. I enjoy writing poems to help encourage family and friends during difficult times, I am a licensed clinical school social worker and work with behaviorally disordered teenagers. Some of my hobbies are traveling, singing, and working on my Internet ministry. I love life, church, reading the Bible, praying for others, and most of all spending time with my Lord, Savior, Jesus Christ.

PIERCE, JODY
[a.] Kettle Falls, WA [title] "The Messenger's Path" [pers.] This poem is about life, courage, beauty, strength, nobility, humanity, and death. It is my first poem to be published, and hopefully not my last.

PIERRE, ANGEL
[a.] Decatur, GA [title] "Sensual Inhalation" [pers.] My poetry is a blessing from God. In "Sensual Inhalation," I share a very intimate side of myself that was inspired by my husband. Romance is a very lovely subject, and one that I enjoy exploring in every depth. Every poem I write involves feelings that are special and unique. I treasure every poem I read and write, and hope my poems are precious to others.

PIERRE, ROSELYN ANN
[a.] Houston, TX [title] "The Grief of Death" [pers.] I've been writing poetry for many years. Poetry has been a true part of my expression. It is a gift that allows me to uplift, edify, and express creativity through the written word. This poem, "The Grief of Death," is very special to me; it has expressed my inner most feelings during the death of my dear mother. I hope that others who have experienced the death of close loved ones or friends can find consolation and tranquility in this poem.

PINION, CECILIA
[a.] Shawnee, OK [title] "The Mask of Truth" [pers.] This poem was written at a time in my life when I looked at everyone around me and could only see false faces. I thought I was different, yet when I looked in the mirror my reflection was like a mask to cover up all that felt unreal, or anything I didn't want to see. I would like to thank my granny, my Uncle Joe, my parents, and my grandparents. A special thanks to all of my friends and family who have believed in me. Extra special thanks go to Cary Gregory, who never had to wear a mask.

PINKHAM, JEROMY W.
[a.] Olathe, Kansas [title] "What We Share" [pers.] This poem is meant for those separated by physical distance, but are forever mated in their souls. Time and distance can not weaken, diminish, or even kill true love. The most wonderful and beautiful things can be shared by any person, anywhere, no matter what circumstances separate them physically.

PIRACHA, KIRAN
[a.] Karachi, Pakistan [title] "You Are the One I Chose . . . " [pers.] This poem is a simple piece of wisdom. I hope it will help a lot of people understand that love in all its forms has a special purpose to serve; which is to contribute to our growth and help us become wiser. More often than not, the emotional turmoil and mental agony that we undergo while in love is not a result of love itself but stems from our lack of understanding as to what love really is.

PIRET, EDITH
[a.] Amherst, NY [title] "Such Love" [pers.] I consider poetry a joy of the spirit that feeds our souls, and touches others in a very special way. Poetry can speak to those we love who are still with us, or we can write of those who have gone on, evoking treasures of their own special memories.

PITTENGER, DANIEL
[a.] Menomonee Falls, WI [title] "Life's Cruel" [pers.] I wrote this poem in a depressing time in my life. Nothing seemed to be going right. I had troubles with the law and my family. But now I have had a chance to see a new light thanks to my family and friends, but especially to my wife, Robyn. I love her so much and she has brought joy to my life. I hope this poem will encourage others to talk about how they feel with the ones they love.

PIZZI, NICHOLAS
[a.] Whiteman, MO [title] "The Racehorse" [pers.] I never thought that any of my writing would find its way into publication. I'd like to thank Chelsea for always believing in me, and never turning her back. I'm sorry I can't be with you.

PLACE, SIMONE
[a.] Ringwood, VIC, Australia [title] "CFS/M.E.—A Sufferer's Nightmare" [pers.] I wrote this poem on behalf of my daughter, Simone (now 17). Unfortunately Simone, Dux of her primary school in Elon, Iris, Melbourne, and then "Student Achiever of the Year" in her first three years at Camberworll High School, fell ill in 1997 with CFS. She is now on a disability pension, a tragedy. I've also written "Valentine to My Wife, Dianne," "Caress of the Moon or King of the Night Sky," "Birth of an Island," and "Tasmania, Emerald Isle of Australia."

PLANTE, EVELYNE
[a.] Bethel Island, CA [title] "Escape of the Mind" [pers.] "Escape of the Mind" came about during meditation. After a hard day, I like to relax and read poetry. It gives me a peace of mind. I just think of something beautiful and my mind takes it from there. Writing poetry is a good way to get rid of stress. To me poetry is a work of art. A painting bares the soul of the artist and a poem tells of the inner most feelings of the person behind the pen. It doesn't matter, if it's good or badly written, they are all beautiful, because the true feelings are there. Poetry gives a meaning to "baring your soul."

POLETSKI, TRISTA
[a.] Eureka, CA [title] "Untitled" [pers.] I'm so happy that I was picked. I think when you sent the news to me my mom was more excited than me. I thank you so much, but now I want to tell you about me. On April, 24, 2001 I will turn ten. I love my room and my favorite subjects in school are math and writing. I love writing, and I wrote other poems and stories. I am very happy I was published.

POLITIS, JASON
[a.] Riner, VA [title] "It Could Happen to You" [pers.] My poem was written just a few days after my friend was killed in a car accident while riding with a drunk driver. I never really wrote much before this, and I enjoyed doing it. The last thing I thought I would be doing with my spare time is writing. This poem is very important to me, because it shows a period of hurt in my life, the day my best friend died.

POLKINGHORN, ALLISON
[a.] San Ramon, CA [title] "Sing to Me" [pers.] I've waited a long time for this recognition to my poetry, and I'm thrilled about this privilege. "Sing to Me" is about the essential need for companionship, it's the heart's appeal for that person to come and amend with the response of a smile. I'm a college student working towards a degree in English. I hope to teach high school English and continue to develop as a writer. With words and my need to help and teach others, I will continue to strive toward more achievements with my writing. Remember to reach for others, you never know, you may pull back the friend of a lifetime.

POOTA, OLIVIA
[a.] West Bloomfield, MI [title] "My Father, My Life" [pers.] Anything can happen to me right now, and I wouldn't be afraid. For the biggest fear is fear itself. For me, the biggest fear is losing someone very close to me again. My dad died on January 1, 1999. The unforgettable day will remain in my mind forever. Most importantly I'll never forget the happy, sad, and joyful memories my father shared with my family and I. I'll always miss him. I'll always love him. But now I know, I have a guardian angel very close and dear to me.

PORTWINE, MARGARET
[a.] Clarion, IA [title] "It Will Be" [pers.] This is a third in a trilogy of peace: "Maybe," "Then," and "It Will Be." This is dedicated to all who love peace and sing our song. Thanks, Ron, for the Nantucket Sleigh Ride.

POSEY, LADONYA
[a.] Detroit, MI [title] "To Imagine a Perfect Person" [pers.] This poem was inspired by a dream. The dream was a gift from the Lord to inspire and to encourage me to be me. We all want to belong, we all want to fit in but I never did. I have always felt alone in this world no matter who was around, no one understood me. Through the pain of the loneliness I prayed, and out of my prayer came this dream. And out of the dream came this poem. I have come to know we are never alone.

POTOCHAR, CARLEE
[a.] Monroe Township, NJ [title] "Grandma" [pers.] I feel that poetry is an excellent way to let out feelings that have been bottled up inside. One of my close friends, Anika, once told me of her grandmother's death. This inspired me to write "Grandma" for her. Many other poems I've written have also been the results of a friend's inspiration. I also enjoy writing about special occasions and to special friends. If by reading my poems people can feel more comfortable in expressing their feelings and emotions, then my goal is achieved.

POULTON, STEPHANIE
[a.] Joplin, MO [title] "Doors" [pers.] This poem is very special to me, it was written about a man I corresponded with who was in prison at the time. He brought out the best in me and it helped us both to get through the time he was in jail.

POWELL, JESSICA KATHRYN
[a.] Foley, MN [title] Untitled [pers.] This poem is the first poem I ever wrote. It's special to me because I wrote it on the day I got out of the behavioral health unit in the hospital for overdosing. It is my outlet for pain, anger, frustration, and happiness—my escape.

POWER, MANDY
[a.] Wareham, MA [title] "Snowy Sunrise" [pers.] I have been writing poems for about ten years now, and I love sharing my work. Poetry has always been a very important part of my life; it helps me express my innermost secrets. I would like to dedicate this poem to my husband, Rick, for helping me realize true love cannot be hidden and for making all my dreams come true.

PRATT, ALYSSA
[a.] Austin, MN [title] "Who Wants 'Em" [pers.] I feel that poetry is something not everyone can do, only my sister has an interest in writing poetry. I do love writing it. I mainly wrote my poem to show people that, deep down inside, by someone somewhere, they are loved.

PRATT, TRISHA ANN
[a.] Austin, MN [title] "My Life" [pers.] All of my poems mean a lot to me because they are the real emotions that go through my head. I am a junior in high school, and teens usually get stressed, and I just write poems when I get stressed out, angry, or sad.

PROSKURNIA, LORI ANN
[a.] Matawan, NJ [title] "Picture Perfect" [pers.] Poetry has been a part of my life and heart since I was 13. It is my freedom—a freedom I can't imagine living without! I wish for the world to enjoy my poetry as much as I enjoy writing it.

PROULX, KAREN
[a.] Fall River, MA [title] "The Great Purification" [pers.] As a young girl, my mother would call me her little philosopher because of the way I perceived life. "The Great Purification" was inspired by my niece Kerry, born with Down's Syndrome. She lives every day with life-threatening complications. Kerry, with her constant struggle for life, never ceases to fill our home with an abundance of love and laughter. My children and granddaughter also inspired "The Great Purification," by showing me the true meaning of their unconditional love. Together, our home is truly blessed.

PROWANT, CHRIS
[a.] Pendleton, OR [title] "Sometimes" [pers.] Poetry is one of my favorite forms of art. I never imagined I would ever get anything of mine published or recognized in any way. I'm pleased with this opportunity to share my art with whomever should choose to read it. Some of my favorite writers and poets include D. A. Levy, Hermann Hesse, Samuel Beckett, and Hunter S. Thompson. I am a fan of nearly every artistic medium. I believe in existentialism and enjoy avant-garde forms of expression. I am currently very interested in film-making, theater, and writing.

PRYOR, CHRISTINA
[a.] Chicago, IL [title] "Are You There?" [pers.] I am a second-year student at North Park University, in Chicago, Illinois. I have finally realized that writing is my gift. I wrote this poem when I doubted my gift. Every person who has searched and yet remained in quest, I challenge you to seek again. Just because you didn't see it doesn't mean it wasn't there. To you I say: Look with your eyes, search with your heart, and feel with your spirit; only then will the relation appear. I dedicate this, my first published work, to my mother. My accomplishments are because of you and your endless display of a Godly mother's love. You are my inspiration.

PUAH, MIMI
[a.] Kuala Lumpur, Malaysia [title] "Ode to Vincent" [pers.] I believe that human life is just like a piece of virgin white cloth since birth. As we journey into adulthood, the events of our lives are etched and painted upon that cloth. Each piece of verse I write is an embroidery of distinctive events in my life, inspired by the people who love me and who I love. For "Ode to Vincent," I was inspired by the song "Vincent" (by Don McLean) and by Van Gogh himself. To me, Vincent's fabric of life is coarse to the feel yet fine, so grey to the eyes yet colorful . . . simply beautiful.

QUALKENBUSH, MICHELLE
[a.] Shoals, IN [title] "Dad" [pers.] I was inspired to write this poem on the morning of my father's funeral. I loved him very much. I have always loved poetry, but have never done anything in the way of writing it until now. In the past few months I have been inspired (I believe by God) to put thoughts, which otherwise might have been hard for me to express, on paper, about people, events, etc. I have a master's degree in elementary education and have taught for 26 years. I live in southern Indiana with my husband, Dennis, and four children, Aimee, Joe, Stephen, and Leah.

QUINN, AMBER
[a.] Greensburg, PA [title] "Removed" [pers.] You all laugh because I'm different. I laugh because you're all the same.

RADER, SHELBY
[a.] Irvine, KY [title] "Friends" [pers.] I wrote about what I think is the best thing you could ever have, friends. Without the support of friends, their friendship, and their kindness, your life would go nowhere. Your friends always have your back in case anything happens. You can have no material objects, money, or anything else everyone always goes nuts over to have and still have a great life, if you have friends. If you have a true friend, you'll always have a true friendship and anything else you can wish for. You can always reach the stars.

RAFFERTY, DOROTHY
[a.] Colfax, WA [title] "A Daughter's Prayer" [pers.] I'm proud to say I wrote this poem in 1982. I loved my

mother very much. She raised kids by herself, four boys and one girl. I was the youngest. My brothers' dad died when Mama was three months along with their fourth child. She married my dad three years later. He died several years later, while I was still little, so Mama had to be mother and dad to us kids, which was no easy job. She was the best mother anybody could have ask for. All my brothers were musically inclined, and so was I. My mother always encouraged me not to give up on anything I did.

RAFT, LAUREN
[a.] Bloomfield Hills, MI [title] "Memories" [pers.] I love to write poems and journal entries. I wrote this poem in memory of my grandmother Connie Raft, who I loved very much! She taught me a lot about strength and family honor and love. I miss her every day. This one's for you, Grau-Connie, I hope you like it! I love you.

RAHMAN, MAHFOOZUR
[a.] Dhaka, Bangladesh [title] "The Rains" [pers.] The monsoon is the stuff of life in the Gangetic plains of Bengal, bringing life to the parched earth where the peasant now sows seeds, hoping for a harvest. The rains arrive, heralded by the thunder and the winds, inducing thoughts and casting images to the reflective minds that are both magical and mystical. At such a time that the rains fall incessantly, to add to the flows that eventually merge with the sea, the poet sees the drops of rains as teardrops of eternal tragedy that befalls man. He knows, however, that all these drops will merge in a stream to meet the sea, as souls separated will eventually unite in a divine repository. The rains are but teardrops of the heavens, purging the sorrows of life's eternal tragedies, renewing life in all its majesty, uniting souls for yet another golden harvest.

RAMACHANDRAN, VENKATESWARAN
[a.] Kuala Lumpur, Malaysia [title] "Ode to a Beautiful Girl" [pers.] Writing poetry is more than a hobby—it drives my creative thinking. I write often on occasions, very specific or just generally. "Ode to a Beautiful Girl" was written as a gift to one of my former colleagues who has been supportive, helpful, and friendly in my working life. This was written on the spur of the moment on her birthday and presented to her. I live in Kuala Lumpur, Malaysia, with my wife, parents, and sister and work as a systems consultant with an IT company. Writing poetry helps me relieve some of the tension usually found in a complex and intensive software environment, where tight deadlines are the norm. I have written a collection of poems so far, and I hope to publish it some day in the not too distant future, even as I add to my collection.

RAMIREZ, ANDREW
[a.] Madera, CA [title] "Gone, but Not Forgotten" [pers.] Written on the death of my wife's grandmother, I presented this poem to my father-in-law in the hope that I could, in some small way, console a man I greatly admired in a time of severe grief. To be able to express my admiration for Grandma and at the same time do something for my father-in-law brought to me why I started writing poetry. Poetry can be a special and powerful force, and I hope anyone reading this verse can relate to its universal message, that our loved ones never really leave us.

RAMIREZ, GABRIELA
[a.] Scottsdale, AZ [title] "The Silencer" [pers.] I was extremely happy and felt very privileged, when I was informed that my poem was to be published. I am 13, and I'm not afraid to write about death. Death, to me, only becomes real if you are forgotten. I believe this is why so many people are frightened of death. They are actually fearful that their existence will not be remembered by future generations. Death is just the release of the soul. I take pleasure in sharing my poem with others, and I enjoy writing about reality and the occasional harshness of life. Life is what it is.

RAMOS, TRISTAN
[a.] Garden Grove, CA [title] "Change" [pers.] I first began to write this poem about November 2000, right before winter break. I had spent the night at a friend's house, and his sister, who I had not seen for ages, was there. His sister, the subject of my poem, has always inspired me to write, but she and I are hardly friends. She is something of a secret inspiration. Nevertheless, all of the events featured in the poem actually did happen. The phone calls, the front door, and the morning on the couch all happened. Inspiration comes from the weirdest places—just look.

RATHORE, NASHWA
[a.] Jeddah, Saudi Arabia [title] "The Witches!" [pers.] Poetry holds a special place in my life. For me, it is the best means of expressing my thoughts and feelings. I wrote this poem in 1999 when I was 16, and this is one of my favorite poems. It is based on a dream I've been having for the past six or seven years. At first no one knew about this dream, because I didn't know how to tell anyone about it. I guess I found the best way to do it easily.

RAWHOOF, KELLY
[a.] Waukegan, IL [title] "Love" [pers.] My poem is simply about the love I had for someone. I will never forget him, and I hope that others have or will have a love like that. James W. was my total inspiration for "Love," and I thank him. My other thanks go to my uncle Dale and Anjie for getting me my first poetry book. It made me realize how beautiful poetry is and what I could do with it. Thank you, Mom, Dad, and Amanda, for everything. I also want to thank Mr. Richter, my literature teacher, for helping me understand what poems mean.

RAWLS, TRACY
[a.] Lake Elsinore, CA [title] "A Dog of My Own" [pers.] I wrote this at one time because I had wanted a dog. I thought this would help my cause. I enjoy poetry and felt this would be a good way to tell my parents. It worked!

RAY, EUNICE
[a.] Balderton, UK [title] "The Cherubs in the Sky" [pers.] I started to write poetry when my pony, Piccolo, was put to sleep. The words just whirled around in my head, so I wrote them down in verse. It helped to ease my sorrow. Now I write verses about my life and found it also helps other people who have been through the same experiences as I have. I love my animals, the countryside, and talking to people about their culture, etc. The great inspirations in my life are my fiancee, Cheg, and Michael Flatley. Flatley is a great Creator, who encourages people to never give up on their dreams.

RAYMAN, JACQUELINE
[a.] Riverdale, MD [title] "Love of My Life" [pers.] Poetry, to me, is an escape out of this world and into another, where I can just feel free to let my emotions run wild. This poem is very special to me, as it is dedicated to someone who is very dear and means a lot to me. Telling someone "I love you" in a poem is a beautiful way of sharing one's innermost feelings. I just hope that others who have special people in their lives can relate in some way to my poem and perhaps share it with their loved ones.

REAVES, CURTIS
[a.] [title] "Touching" [pers.] This poem was written early one morning. I could not sleep and had on my mind my soon-to-be wife, Karen. We met online and have come to know we have each other. She is the most wonderful woman I have ever met. (Karen, I love you, baby!) As for me, I am a mature (57), easygoing gentleman with a great sense of humor, the divorced father of three really great young men and the doting granddad of three boys (no girls in sight ...yet). I enjoy exercise, running, and weight-lifting,

reading, writing, museums, plays, music, and stimulating conversation. I love poetry, both reading it and attempting to write it. I would like nothing better than to one day participate in a poetry slam.

REECE, SHARON
[a.] Powder Springs, GA [title] "Perfect Love" [pers.] This poem simply describes my undying devotion to finding the perfect relationship between two people, the way God meant it to be. Through failed previous relationships and dreams that have fallen apart, I have learned that the perfect love must be one sent from Heaven. To all the people who feel the same way I do, I say, "Keep looking upward."

REES, BARB
[a.] Powell River, BC [title] "The Piper by the Sea" [pers.] I live on the rugged west coast of British Columbia, surrounded by poetry in motion. While living in Victoria, enjoying the crashing surf on the rocks, I was struck by the haunting notes of a piper practicing down there. It was like being transported back in time to another land. That's how poetry has always struck me and filled my heart with its ability to take me to other places and dreams. Being a dreamer, poetry lets me express that in words.

REINHECKEL, STEPHEN
[a.] Stow, MA [title] "The Hunger" [pers.] Words have always been very spiritual to me. Whether reading them or writing, I can draw a sense of being. The inspiration for what I write comes from within and is driven by a special person in my life. She is my heart, my soul, and my guiding light. Without her I truly would be lost, and this is my special gift to her.

RENE, LINDA
[a.] Sarasota, FL [title] "Distant Love" [pers.] This poem was written 27 years ago when I was 15 years old. I had a huge crush on a man eight years my senior. I think all young girls embrace these feelings at one time or another. It can be a painful experience, though it's all part of growing up. "Distant Love" is a keepsake of my past and the words of a young girl's infatuation.

RETTINO, DANIELLE
[a.] Totowa, NJ [title] "Poetry in Life" [pers.] I think poetry is a gift that all people possess. Some just need to know how to find it. Poetry is a very big part of my life at the moment. I have written many poems in my life, but my poem "Flowers" is one of my favorites, because it was the very first poem I ever wrote.

REUVENI, TALI
[a.] Mazkeret-Batya, Israel [title] "Eve" [pers.] As a writer and singer/songwriter, I've written "Eve" from a feminine point of view, although "Eve" is about a universal self-search regarding life's mysteries and riddles. "Eve" celebrates life. She starts out very young and naive, but by the time she finds her answers to her own existence (given to her by nature itself, with all of its glory), she is calm, whole, and complete. Her life-circle has been universally accomplished.

REVERCOMB, TERESA ANN
[a.] Kihei, HI [title] "The Soul's Kiss" [pers.] Through the gift of poetry, I both discover and reveal my truth. The most intimate relationship I have is that with pen and paper.

RHAULT, JAMIE
[a.] Bristol, CT [title] "Love Is to Trust" [pers.] My poem is inspired by my experiences and is for someone who believes that, beyond all the bad relationships a lot of people have, there is still hope for more good things in life. My poem expresses the way I feel about that special someone close to me, although that person didn't really understand the love and trust they could have had. Some people can't express themselves out loud or even understand the love they have, and then they are gone. I hope someone can relate to my poem and experience the love and trust that comes their way.

RHINES, EVA
[a.] Barrie, ON [title] "New Beginnings" [pers.] My inspiration for this poem was my sister, Viola. It is dedicated to her and all the persons seeking courage to extricate themselves from unsatisfying and selfish relationships.

RHYNE, PAUL
[a.] Sauk Village, IL [title] "The Strings of Love" [pers.] The gift of poetry I have comes from my inspiration and can be expressed in many areas. Sometimes just one word will make me think precious thoughts, which I save with ink. I like to write about love, the natural world around us, and human nature. Write what you feel, even if it doesn't rhyme; search for the rhyming words later. Never rush your poetry! Find me on the web—peace to all.

RICHARDSON, AMANDA
[a.] Mooringsport, LA [title] "Painted Dreams" [pers.] Poetry is words of the soul. I have been writing poetry since I was about 11. Poetry gives me a good feeling inside and really expands my point of view on many situations. I could sit and read poetry all day. I am 15 years old and cannot wait to write many more poems.

RICHARDSON, RENEE
[a.] Paige, TX [title] "The Good Old Days" [pers.] This poem was inspired by the life of my grandparents. They were hardworking, farming people who were happy with the simple pleasures that life offered. They taught me to value family, friends, and God. There was always time for food, family, and fellowship. As each generation passes, some of the past is lost. Lost is time, time for the simple pleasures; just to pause a moment to smell a rose is such a luxury. People just don't have time. Are we better off? With all the newfangled thrills to entertain us? I think not. I think we are victims of a society that pressures us to press on. We are not considered successful, unless we're involved in the never-ending rat race of life. It is my hope that maybe people will see that happiness can be found within their own families; it's waiting there, just as it has always been.

RICKY, SCOTT
[a.] Lincoln, NE [title] "Mission Statement" [pers.] This poem is very special to me. It was written while I was in the Army, deployed to Kosovo for seven months. This poem is for all of those who serve in the United States military, especially those on deployment. We will appreciate your dedication to our country. Thank you, Mom, for all your support. Kellie, I love you! In closing, just one question remains unanswered: Kellie, will you marry me?

RIEDEL, FELICIA
[a.] Colorado Springs, CO [title] "Heart Constellation" [pers.] I am originally from California, but I call Hawaii home. I graduated from King Kekauliko High School in 1999. This poem was written with a tinge of mad, crazy frustration. It seems, most often, that when I need to sit down and write so desperately, all the thoughts are racing around in my head so hazardously I can't catch even one to express on paper. The ones not caught become lost forever, instead of living on forever. I not only love to write, I need to write. It is my outlet, my sanity—or, maybe, my insanity.

RILEY, CATHY
[a.] Hiram, GA [title] "Marine" [pers.] This poem is in dedication to my husband, who has always been a shining example of who and what a Marine is. His love and dedication, shown through the years, inspired this poem. I wrote this poem remembering our years together and his retirement speech. Our lives together have been filled with many blessings, and, had it not been for the corps, we may had not met. I hope that all who read this enjoy it as much as I do—the few, the proud, the Marines, simple but true, Semper Fi.

RIVERA, JENNIFER
[a.] Bronxville, NY [title] "Angel in Disguise" [pers.] This poem is dedicated to the goddess in my life—the mom of whom I am proud—the woman who gave me life. Today, as I stride through life with all that I've accomplished, I can only say, with great honor, I owe it to my mom. No words exist in this world that could ever express the deep emotion of gratitude that I have for the woman who made me whole. To you, Mom, I dedicate "Angel in Disguise," for you gave me life and will to live. In this world, you are my angel, my God—the mother I adore.

ROBBINS, DONNA
[a.] Wilmington, NC [title] "To Silky, My Best Friend" [pers.] Silky was my best friend from four weeks old until the day she went gently to sleep in my arms at the age of 15, my Labrador retriever, my one true friend forever.

ROBERSON, CARMELLA
[a.] Absecon, NJ [title] "Ebony" [pers.] Poetry is my way of expressing myself creatively and artistically. I color my thoughts with words. I began writing poetry when I was in fourth grade. Many poets, like Maya Angelou, Shel Silverstein, and Edgar Allan Poe, inspired me. This particular poem is special to me because it describes me. I want to be a light that shines on the world in lyrical verse. In my free time, I enjoy reading, writing, and exercising. I dedicate this poem to the memory of my grandmother, who also inspired me to write and compares with the characteristics described in the poem.

ROBERTS, AGNES
[a.] Stamford, CT [title] "The Birds" [pers.] Birdwatching is one of the many hobbies that brings me joy. All God's creatures do, but birds are my favorite. Looking at them soaring upward into the sky, creating a standard way of moving, helps me to understand how free they really are. Another aspect of liking birds is I whistle a lot. When the birds chirp, I chirp back with my whistling sounds, and so I became inspired to write "The Birds."

ROBERTS, BRILUND
[a.] Memphis, TN [title] "A Present State of Mind" [pers.] The substance of this poem is a collection of the best words that came to me to capture how I felt in a split second of one random day—untouched, alone in the world, neglected by the human race. I don't think that there is a greater punishment. At least it was only temporary.

ROBERTS, DEAN
[a.] Northants, UK [title] "Nothing to Lose" [pers.] This poem was originally a verse to one of my songs. The story behind it is basically this: A new love from abroad has entered my life and has given me the drive to follow my feelings. Writing is not only a hobby of mine but a career ambition. Music is a big part of my life. To write lyrics and hear them along with music as a profession would be a dream. As I live in the U.K., another of my aspirations is to study in the U.S. This would be a great opportunity for my future. All I need is a sponsor.

ROBERTS, JEREMY
[a.] Wilmington, CA [title] "[pers.] "Is There a Word?" was inspired by a woman more amazing than any I have ever met. I met Natalie Sara Sunami online, August 17, while working graveyard. That is what's meant by "an unconventional route." She, in that first conversation, captivated me. Ever since that August 2000 night, she has been my first waking thought and last conscious fantasy every day. I've tried to express to her, through some method, the extent of my feelings for her. This poem is my way of opening my heart to only her. This poem is, and always will be, for you, Mija.

ROBERTS, RUSSELL
[a.] Azle, TX [title] "Alone in Sorrow" [pers.] I just want to thank my mother, Elaine, and my father, Michael, for always giving me support and encouragement. I hope children of the future will be fortunate enough to have parents as great as mine.

ROBINSON, BRITNEY
[a.] Los Angeles, CA [title] Untitled [pers.] I came to live with my great-aunt when I was seven. I am now 13. This poem is dedicated to her because they are her words to me. In December 1999, she was diagnosed with ovarian cancer. I say to her now, "Stay strong." I will go through life using these words.

ROBINSON, DORINDA
[a.] Chagrin Falls, OH [title] "He Runs" [pers.] The poem "He Runs" was written at the encouragement of my husband, Paris, who pushes me toward excellence in my life. I am happily married, and the mother of three wonderful children who I love deeply, my son, Erick Jason, and my two daughters, Lisa Michelle and Veronica Nichole. They are all (along with my grandson, Daniel) the inspiration in my life. "He Runs" is special because it is about a treasured pet my husband gave to me, one in which I delight. More than that, he represents a free spirit created by God, perfect in every way.

ROBINSON, HENRY
(a.] Orange Park, FL [title] "Life is Hard" [pers.] This poem is very inspirational to me. The poem "Life Is Hard" inspires me to keep my head when times become unbearable. I was inspired to write poems by my tenth-grade English teacher, who told me that I had a talent for writing poems, and by the love of my mother and my girlfriend. If it had not been for them, I do not think I would still be writing poems.

ROCHE, STEVE
[a.] Alamogordo, NM [title] "Revelation" [pers.] I only recently began writing. This selection is my first publication. It is about a woman that means the world to me. The problem is I cannot have her. The fact that she is my life and not in it is the irony of the selection.

ROCKWELL, THOMAS
[a.] Denver, CO [title] "The Flames of the Storm" [pers.] Poetry, to me, is an expression of feelings in partial thoughts, references from one thought to another. This poem is about a singular event in nature, as nature reaffirms our strength of will, albeit we are a miniature, but integral, part of all that occurs. I live in the mountains west of Denver and am inspired by my now deceased father's love of the wilderness and my grandfather's stories. My great-uncle Norman Rockwell's paintings and sketches have always influenced me.

RODE, SANJAY
[a.] Pittsburgh, PA [title] "Gift" [pers.] Poetry is a medium to endure. I inherit creativity from my father. I want to express my heartfelt gratitude for such an awesome source as existence. Our open hearts can feel the bliss of being. I hope the reader will experience the closeness of rich nature while experiencing this poem. You can reach me online.

RODRIGUEZ, VICTOR
[a.] Toledo, OH [title] "A Real Man" [pers.] I am pleased to dedicate this to my children, Victor, Jr., Audrianna, and Vicki. I thank God for the gift he has given me. I am a man of riches, not of gold, but many friends. I thank them all, but most of all you, Miss Tina Chandler and Norma Velasquez, for being there for me.

ROGERS, SUSAN
[a.] Lumberton, NC [title] "Death" [pers.] Hi, my name is Susan and I submitted my poem "Death" with hopes of its getting published. I don't like to write

poetry with a fake attitude, such as "I am feeling down, so I will write a depressed poem." Now some people are taken aback by my vocabulary. I am a seventh grader at Orrum Middle School. I live with my mom and stepdad next to my grandparents. My cousins, Kayln and Keri, and my loved ones are proud of me. I hope you find delight, and I hope you feel my feelings when you read my poem "Death."

ROGERS, TONI
[a.] Harrison, AR [title] "Lingua Enlightenment" [pers.] I, as an English teacher, try to instill in my students the might of language. As an educator, I am often witness to some form of pupil conflict. Students, pent up with frustration, will fight physical battles to answer friction, or, feeling bullied, they will shy away from confrontation entirely. Either way, they end up disliking themselves at the end of the day. My mission is to show them that they need only the self-confidence to settle struggles with words, they need only like themselves enough to give others control over their self-worths.

ROHRBAUGH, DONNA
[a.] Newalla, OK [title] "Little Girl" [pers.] I wrote that when my daughter was five just for her; it was fun for me. Her name is Sherri. My name is Donna Rohrbaugh. I'm a waitress by trade. I'm married 15 years. I write from the heart and the head.

ROSE, JAMIE
[a.] Phoenix, AZ [title] "The Dream" [pers.] Poetry to me is a gift—you either have it or you don't. The poem I have written is "The Dream." This poem is about a girl who likes a guy who is out of her reach, and she dreams about him all the time. I also have written poems about death, friendship, love, and the world. Not only do I enjoy writing poetry, I love to read it. I hope everyone enjoys my poem as much as I enjoyed writing it.

ROSENBERG, JANETTA
[a] Overland Park, KS [title] "At the End of the Rainbow" [pers.] This poem tells a story of two loves, my husband and I. One has a background of child abuse and torture, the other is a Holocaust survivor. They met and fell in love at Lake Tahoe, with the rainbow and birds flying overhead. They finally can set aside the sorrows of the past and find happiness. I may be moving to Las Vegas in September 2001.

ROSSITZ, DOROTHY
[a.] Oliverea, NY [title] "To Laurel" [pers.] I have been writing poetry for as long as I can remember. Poetry is a wonderful way to express your feelings. "To Laurel" is one of the few poems that I have written that actually rhymes. Sometimes we forget to take a moment to tell people how much they mean to us. This poem was my way to tell my best friend how much she really means to me.

ROY, CONNIE
[a.] Millville, CA [title] "Seasons" [pers.] Poems come to me in the night, and I have to write them down, or they are gone from memory. I love nature and wild things. I live where I can see many beautiful animals and creatures to study. I share my poems with those who I feel need encouragement or just a little bright spot in their day. Most of my poems are of a spiritual nature and hold a lot of meaning for me, as they come from my own experience.

RUBIO, CHRISTEN
[a.] Granite Shoals, TX [title] "Pure Elves" [pers.] I am eight years old but will be nine on May 9. I love wrestling, tae kwon do, video games, reading, music, and swimming. I will have completed the third grade this year. I like to do construction with my papa and art with my mom. You can always find me building imaginary worlds in my sandbox, or you will find me curled in a chair reading. I play tennis, roller blade, or

just play with my pet dumbo rats. I have a min pin dog named Cindarella. We sleep together every night. She loves to snuggle. My poem tells about the world I would like to take adventures to. My family encourages me to use my imagination sometimes and the real world other times.

RUIZ, ASHLEY
[a.] Philadelphia, PA [title] Untitled [pers.] I have been inspired by what I have learned about my culture to write this poem. I wrote this poem because it has helped me cope and understand that it is of utmost importance to get to know someone instead of judging them by the color of their skin. I am very proud, blessed, and thankful for who I am.

RUPERT, PATRICIA
[a.] Lake Charles, LA [title] "Masked Angels" [pers.] I've always been a "wonderer," thinking about all there is and even what we don't know for certain. Is everything really as it seems? Have we all faded? You probably have no idea what I'm rambling about. Maybe I'm too young to be thinking about so many things some adults never bother with, but maybe I'm some midlife woman stuck in a child's body. There's just so much in and outside of the world to think about, so many things I'll never know, never understand, never touch or even dream about. You might feel sad about it, I know, but I like it. I love being a "wonderer."

RUSSELL, JESSE
[a.] Kalamazoo, MI [title] "If I Were in Charge of the World" [pers.] I am 16 years old, and I am living in Michigan. I've been writing poetry for as long as I can remember. It comes to me naturally. Writing poetry is one of my forms of art. I will be submitting as many poems as possible to poetry.com, and I am looking forward to it. I dedicate my work to my mother and family.

RUSSUM, MICHAEL
[a.] Portland, OR [pers.] I am a 19-year-old high school graduate from Portland, Oregon. I started writing poetry because it allowed me to explain my feelings more completely and to use my imagination freely. Real-life situations have inspired and are continuing to inspire me to write. I hope "Close Your Eyes" ignites a spark in a couple's minds or helps someone convey their love in a poetic fashion.

RYAAN, DEE
[a.] Deland, FL [title] "Take Me Home" [pers.] This poem is dedicated to my dear mother. She suffered many weeks and months before passing. She had breast cancer, which later invaded her bones. I believe if she could have spoken, these would have been her words. I am so excited about this, my first poem chosen for publishing. It truly gives me a boost to continue my love of writing.

SAHAGUN, GISELA
[a.] San Mateo, CA [title] "Moment of Passion" [pers.] I would not have written this poem if it wasn't for the love my parents have for each other. They have been married for 21 years and love each other more each day. When I wrote this poem, I was young and believed they were forced to get married. I now understand it was a deep love that joined these two souls together and has kept them as one for so long. I thank my parents for all the love and support they have given me, and I know someday I, too, will find my happy ending.

SAINTSURIN, JEAN
[a.] Miami, FL [title] "Picnic at Flamingo Park" [pers.] I am always dreaming of becoming a poet. I have a real passion for poetry. Therefore, at age 19, I wrote my first poem, "Miserable Life." I was born in Jeremie, Haiti, and graduated from high school. My college education has been put on hold. This coming summer, I will be majoring in criminal justice. Poetry is my soul, just as oxygen is in blood to activate life.

I was admiring nature and wrote "Picnic at Flamingo Park." In honor of my beloved children, Dwinnell, Jeffery, and Kristen, I dedicate this poem. My philosophy is to keep the dream and reality alive.

SALAZAR, DEBORAH
[a.] Dallas, TX [title] "Roses" [pers.] I am speaking to my son, Joshua. I want him to plant different kinds of colored roses in our garden, before he starts a new life. I can look at them and remember him. It also reminds me of my mother, about the talks we used to have. She would say roses are for dead people. My husband, Roy, and Joshua bring me different colors of roses. Joshua did plant different kinds of roses in our garden. I want the world to know I love my son, Joshua! He is very special to me and God.

SALMON, DIEGO
[a.] Chicago, IL [title] "As I Am Looking at Your Face" [pers.] Dear Vika, as I am looking at the picture you gave me, "I am looking at your face" and at your immortal beauty, which you share with me every day.

SALTALAMACHIA, DANIELLE
[a.] Newburgh, NY [title] "Forever" [pers.] This poem was written about a very special person in my life. It is about my Papa, who just recently passed away. After all the grief and pain in the knowing that he's gone, I realized that he will always be alive and have a special place in my heart.

SAMAROO, NINA
[a.] Harrison, NJ [title] "Life" [pers.] This poem is an ambition for guidance in our children who are unfortunately deprived beyond comprehension. I was lost and did demented things. I learned that striving to find what I lack inside is what makes me a stronger person. Regardless of age, I believe everyone needs guidance and attention. If we attempt to see the cause, we can know where to start to find clarifications.

SANCHEZ, CHRISTOPHER
[a.] Lake Kiowa, TX [title] "Laughter" [pers.] Poetry is what helps me get through the week. Every time I start getting angry, I sit alone and start writing away. My poem, "Laughter," means a lot and is very special to me. I would like to dedicate this poem to some of my very close friends (Jamie, Jennifer, Sam, Janette, Taylor, Lisa, Ryan, Margee, Karla) and also to a very special teacher, Mr. "G". I dedicated this poem to you all to show you that anything and everything can make you laugh. You just have to find it inside of yourself. I love you all!

SANDERFORD, RICHARD
[a.] Rolesville, NC [title] "The One for You" [pers.] This poem is dedicated to two beautiful women in my life. The first is my mom, Marie, who raised me as a single mom. I was, of course, a child and didn't have a clue about how hard it must have been. The second lady is Jennifer, who made me realize how hard it is to be a single mom. I love and respect both of you. Jenn, that someone for you is me. This poem is also the basis of a song called "Single Mom."

SANDFORD, DEREK
[a.] Dublin, Ireland [title] "Sweet 16" [pers.] I write a lot about World War I; both my grandfathers were in the trenches in France. My favorite poet is Siegfried Sassoon. I also admire Wordsworth, Coleridge, and Tennyson. My favorite Irish poet is W. B. Yeats. I have been writing poetry since 1978. I will be 46 on May 27, 2001. My favorite hobbies are going to the cinema, reading books, and watching my beloved team, Liverpool, play soccer on the television. My favorite authors are Ernest Hemingway, Mary Higgins-Clark, and Graham Greene.

SANDGATHE, TERRY
[a.] Black Diamond, AB [title] "Leaving" [pers.] I never ever thought about writing poetry until I met the

lady I wrote "Leaving" to, and since then I think about nothing else. I hope it conveys at least a fraction of my feelings and moves someone else as well.

SANKO, CHRISTINE
[a.] Rancho Santa, CA [title] "Red Roses, Red Roses" [pers.] Giving red roses to someone close to you is another way of saying "I love you!" Receiving them is knowing you're loved by somebody special. When you walk into the room and see them, they remind you of being loved so. I was touched by this poem and thought, as I wrote the words, to take each day as it comes and not to take anything or anyone's love for granted.

SANNI, GBOYEGA
[a.] Ames, IA [title] "Artistic Wizardry" [pers.] The story behind the poem is this: Surfing the web idly, I came across the contest. Then I thought to myself, "Isn't this about creativity for an artist? A whiz would be great at this! Hmm . . . I'll write a poem about the computer, used with artistic wizardry." Thus, you can see where the title of the poem came from. My hobbies are composing music, playing the piano, singing, making cartoons, and reading books on philosophy and psychology. My personal quotes is "Poetic verse is the chalice of expression that souls thirst for and gain from, conducting human spirit with harmonic reed, in one end, the reality of illusions, beneath, above, and behind, utterings from the very brim of life."

SARTORE, BETTE
[a.] Melbourne, Australia [title] "The Seeker" [pers.] Powerful emotions are evoked when we start to search for our own truth. I was inspired to write "The Seeker" by those compelling emotions that don't let you give up and don't allow you to cover up your feelings. I am the mother of an autistic child and helping him to search for his own truth and allowing him to be the seeker is my greatest challenge.

SAUNDERS, SHELBY
[a.] Lexington, NC [title] "For Someone Special" [pers.] It is very special to me. The poem expresses so much love, so many thoughts and cares I have for my husband, my two sons, and all of my family. You know, we never say "I love you" enough, but those five words, "Little things mean most of all," are the most precious blessings that could be inspired. I hope my poem will inspire others who have very special loved ones in their lives, that it will always be remembered and never be forgotten. "These little things mean most of all."

SAVOIE, DONNA L.
[a.] Carencro, LA [title] "In Loving Memory" [pers.] The poem "In Loving Memory" was written for my husband, Michael L. Savoie, age 46, who passed away in June 2000. Michael taught me a lot about life. He was a very kind and gentle person. He never spoke unkind words of anyone. I would like to live my life in the way he would be proud of, being more like him and letting him live though me. When Michael fell sick in September 1999, I took a leave of absence to take care of him. I told him I would walk every step of this illness with him and never left his side for nine months. He was someone I will always love.

SAWYER, SHAMEKA
[a.] Philadelphia, PA [title] "Memories" [pers.] This poem reflects my feelings about stumbling across life's mishaps without proper guidance. This poem explains how I felt about not knowing the truth about life and its struggles. My mother taught me a lot about life, but she didn't teach me about living life.

SAWYER, TOM
[a.] Carrying Place, ON [title] "A Mother's Love" [pers.] I wrote this poem for a very special woman in my life. I wrote it for her to read aloud every night to her unborn child. It was a means of expressing their

inexplicable bond and a means for me to share in this bond. The writing of this poem allows us to freeze the moment in time to enjoy again and again.

SCALF, DONALD
[a.] Indianapolis, IN [title] "Take Me Back" [pers.] I am 71 years old and only recently began to write with the encouragement of a special friend. Writing is a newfound pleasure for each day, giving opportunity for self-expression. Given time, I would like to write a novel. The poem "Take Me Back" expresses an awareness that we cannot take back our youth, but we can make dreams come true in the present time.

SCHIAVO, STEPHEN
[a.] College Station, TX [title] "Again" [pers.] This poem is about a person who is very special to me. She is everything that a man would want in a woman. She is intelligent, fun, honest, devoted, and beautiful. More importantly, she is the first person to introduce me to God, and I am convinced that He put her into my life for that reason. She was only a part of my life for a year, but the impact she made will last forever. Even though we have gone our separate ways, only one person knows what will happen in the future (Matthew 21: 21-22).

SCHMIDT, ALBERT
[a.] Kansas City, MO [title] "Supreme Court Judges" [pers.] Shortly after prayer in schools was eliminated, the tragic news about students shooting students in public schools inspired me to write the poem "Supreme Court Judges." It appears to me that there has been a significant increase in school violence, sometimes resulting in death and destruction. Policymakers may have to reevaluate their decisions and the potential impact they have had on students and the public school system.

SCHMIDT, DANIELLE
[a.] Evansville, IN [title] "New Love" [pers.] Our intense bond allows us to express our thoughts without words and to know what the other is feeling with a simple touch. When the time came to speak the truth, it was hard for me to say it and to say it right. This was my only way to express how you affect me both mentally and physically. Our lives have taken different paths, and it feels like the moments we now share are ones we are stealing from this busy world. When I am with you, I forget there is an entire world out there.

SCHMITT, EMILY
[a.] Winder, GA [title] "Gold" [pers.] I'm 17, a senior at Winder Barrow High School, survivor of a critical car crash, a cynic, and a pessimist, but above all I nurture a deep appreciation for written language and use it any way I can. I've been writing short fiction works since I was 12, and writing—be it poetry, music, or short pieces of literature—will always have an extreme importance in my life. My poem "Gold" deals with my own feelings of inadequacy in this world and the yearning to be perfect, golden. However, being imperfect is a part of our roles as human beings.

SCHMITT, MICHELE
[a.] Raymond, WA [title] "Always Pretty, Always Beautiful" [pers.] This poem is in dedication to and in memory of my mother, Linda Stanturf, and to all those people who are in a fight for their lives. Cancer is a devastating disease. Friends, family members, and even the folks who are unknown to many of us, I willingly send my love, thoughts, and prayers to you during this fight for your lives. May God be with you and your family members during this time.

SCHNEIDER, IRENE
[a.] Bowie, MD [title] "Who Is He" [pers.] I am a wife to Bill, mother of Troy and Stephanie, grandma to K. J. and Rhiannon, and sister to Ed. We are a middle-class family living in the suburbs Washington, D.C. I

am a small business owner who has always enjoyed personal development and the spiritual journey of life. My brother and I had lost contact with each other as children and recently have been afforded the opportunity to live life together again. I enjoy gardening with my husband and spending time with our children and grandchildren. My family is my life's energy! Writing has always been a dream for me.

SCHNEIDER, MONICA
[a.] San Antonio, TX [title] "Angel" [pers.] Poetry was a gift from my mom, and my mom was a gift from God. Both these gifts are very important to me, and I cannot imagine life without them. Neither can I imagine a life without God. My love for my mom is incredibly big, and so is God's love for me. My poem, "Angel," deals with his love and how he protects his children, no matter what. I hope that others learn how endless God's love is and that they find their way to the Father, just as I found mine.

SCHOENER, ROY
[a.] Bridgeville, DE [title] "Left Alone" [pers.] I'm a 54-year-old self-styled philosopher, poet, author, outdoors man, and Kidney transplant patient, still searching for my niche in life. My idea of heaven is a remote mountain cabin on a trout stream with my wife and my animals.

SCHRADER, NICK
[a.] West Charlton, NY [title] "Trust in Me" [pers.] This is one of my first poems written for everyone who feels alone in this world. Poetry may very well be a gift, to me it is. Thank you, Amanda Peterson, you are the soul reason that my love for poetry was created; you unearthed what little talent and have. Thank you.

SCHUCK, CYNTHIA
[a.] FPO, AP [title] "Heart Whisperings" [pers.] "Heart Whisperings" is written for and dedicated to my mom and dad, Doline and Jim Whitney; my children, Holly, Brandon, Adam, and Brent; and my entire family. Teaching in Japan became an opportunity for me in August 2000. This is the only time I have lived out of Kansas, and away from my beloved family. This poem, hopefully, relays to them an important message. Although Japan contains many ornamental and sacred sites to see, and interesting customs to experience, my heart whispers daily to me of Kansas and family that waits for me there.

SCHULTZ, INGRID
[a.] Great Falls, VA [title] "Who I Am" [pers.] This poem served as an introduction to my college applications. Without this poem I would not be where I am today. It gave me a unique and personal way of answering the question of describing myself.

SCHUSTER, RHONDA
[a.] Hackensack, NJ [title] "In Difference" [pers.] I'm a singer and songwriter, who believes in freedom of diversity and respect for all my living things. In this poem, I felt the music should be heard in the words. There are many poems and songs in this heart.

SCOTT, CARL
[a.] Largo, FL [title] "I Just Know" [pers.] This poem was written with a spirit of gratitude for God's provision of such a wonderful woman to love cherish, and the woman who daily blesses me with so much. These mere words can't fully describe all that I feel for her, but they are intended to convey my sincere, heartfelt thoughts. Those thoughts in short are: My dearest Rhonda, I love you now, forever, and always no matter what life brings our way!

SCOTT KING, GLORIA
[a.] San Rafael, NM [title] "God Bless Christmas" [pers.] Thank you for selecting my poem, "God Bless Christmas." I am a 71-year-old widowed lady who has been writing for many years for family and friends. I have many unpublished poems; I hope to put them

into book form to leave to my heritage. Being a minority, I feel it is a double honor for me and my race. I would like to thank Dixie Diaz, the Librarian at Mother Whiteside Library in Grants, New Mexico, who did an excellent job on the art work, as I am not familiar with the use of computers.

SCUDERI, JENNIFER
[a.] Burnsville, MN [title] "Invisible Angel" [pers.] Open your mind and heart to people, no matter what new ideas they bring to your life. When you look closely and without prejudice, you might see something wonderful that you never knew could exist for you. Thank you to those who taught me to really see people.

SEABAUGH, GLEN
[a.] Lakewood, CO [title] "Purple Sunrise" [pers.] This poem was inspired by the time spent with a loved one, beneath the purple sky that hung above Mt. Hood in Portland, OR, on Christmas morning of 2000. From the east a rising eclipse had magnified an endless purple sky blanketing the western horizon. I reminisce and sometimes wonder if what we had witnessed were the Northern Lights. Only such perfect company and timing with mother nature could have created a feeling like that. It was truly beautiful, and I thank the world for that moment.

SECHRIST, ANGELA MARABETH
[a.] Warren, MI [title] "Infidelity vs. Faithful Living an Acrostic" [pers.] I have been writing in journals for over 15 years. Writing soothes me. Writing reveals who I am and who I don't want to be. This poem was the "love child," conceived by unlikely lovers. Infidelity pursued faithful relentlessly. In her moment of weakness, she was seduced. His forbidden nature beguiled her. The lovers soon discovered they would have no peace together. They quickly parted to find new lovers. Unfortunately, they both chose you! Ultimately, who will you give yourself to, infidelity or faithful living?

SEN, RIYA
[a.] Boston, MA [title] "The Seraph" [pers.] Some of the most significant things in our lives are unplanned or unwanted. The poem, "The Seraph," depicts the emotions of a woman looking down upon her cherubic child, who was the product of a rape. There are incidents, objects, and people in our lives who we need to accept, and this poem portrays this woman's struggle with being reminded every day of an experience she'd much rather forget. The value of acceptance is something I've been taught by both my parents and siblings. They are the true inspiration for the words conceived by my pen, my thoughts, and my passions.

SEVENSKI, SANDY
[a.] Charlotte, MI [title] "A Son" [pers.] This poem was written from true feelings of watching my son grow up in front of my eyes. This is dedicated to my son, Michael, who is truly my number one fan. I believe in him and know his life will be full of happiness and love. I am a mother of four wonderful grown-ups, Renee, Michael, Cami, and Ryan. I have been married for 34 years to my husband, Mike. I have worked with Eaton Intermediate school district for 21 years. I enjoy writing poetry, because it always reflects true feelings of life.

SEWARD, SIERRA
[a.] Flandreau, SD [title] "Going and Returning" [pers.] Poetry is very beautiful. I am only 13 years old, and I can't believe I made it. I wrote this poem for all of those people who are lost. Running away is not the answer; go back to where you started, and try to work out your problems. I would like to thank my family and friends, for they are the ones who inspired me.

SHAHAK, ANTOINETTE
[a.] Glendora, CA [title] "Allow Me"

SHAIKH, HADEEL
[a.] Jeddah, Saudi Arabia [title] "Cold" [pers.] Through my poetry, I can abandon the structures of decorum and surpass the confines of my life. Not being a native speaker of English is no hindrance, because my words are driven by the forces of my feelings, feelings veiled from the world. The essence of which can be glimpsed only through my poetry. This poem is in dedication of my two sons, I hope they are always sheltered from the cold, the coldness which instigated this poem.

SHAKESPEARE, SHAWNA
[a.] Hamburg, PA [title] "Dear Mama" [pers.] I started writing poetry to express my feelings in a different way! I had not been the best of daughters, so I wrote this poem to my mother, Lori Shakespeare. The poem, "Dear Mama," allowed me to tell her how much I really do love her. Poetry is a wonderful way to let somebody know how much you care about them. I have two other poems in books. I'm very thankful I can write poetry to express my inner feelings. Thank you, everyone, for taking the time to read my poem! Everybody has a talent, and they should use it!

SHARMA, PAULINE
[a.] Bergenfield, NJ [title] "Just a Number" [pers.] I was born on June 21, 1951, in New Delhi, India. I have been happily married to Parvesh Sharma for 29 years. I am a mother of two wonderful children, Geetanjali and Yugant. I am a product of the schools where English was the second language, however I am grateful to my English teachers, Mr. Kaushik and Mrs. A. Singh for a job well done. Thanks to Dr. Schmidtberger, my college professor, and all my friends for the encouragement. I graduated with honors from Safdarjang Hospital, School of Nursing in 1972. I worked in AIIMS as an ICU nurse before coming to the US in 1983. Currently I am employed at NY Presbyterian hospital as an I.C.U.R.N. Recently I caught the "poetic bug" after reading Emily Dickinson's and Robert Frost's poems. I love reading, gardening, cooking, dancing, and entertaining friends. I would like to dedicate this poem to all who survived from or perished in the massive earthquake of India in the year 2001.

SHARP, BERNICE
[a.] Vashon, WA [title] "A Northwest Evening" [pers.] This poem was an inspiration by having all these beauties to enjoy daily. I am a nature lover. When my husband, our young daughter, and I moved to beautiful Vashon Island in Washington State, we were surrounded by the beauty of magnificent Mt. Rainier, the Cascade and Olympic Mountains, and beautiful beaches, and lush greenery of all kinds. I am always in awe of all these wonders. When our daughter got married and moved away, and then my husband passed away, I was unable to leave this marvelous scenery. I became inspired to put how I feel into the words of a poem.

SHARP, BRENTSTON
[a.] Huntsville, AL [title] "Blinded" [pers.] This poem is, of course, about a lost love—not really lost but just misguided. She did blind me with a love that I will never forget. For this reason, this poem was written for her.

SHARP, JANET MARIE
[a.] Asheville, NC [title] "My Best Friend" [pers.] Poetry is a powerful art form. I wrote this poem for my Dad's 75th birthday on December 7, 1998. In March of 1999, my Dad was diagnosed with bladder cancer. During his surgery, I kept reciting his poem over and over in my mind. It comforted me to remember all of the times we had shared. Today, my Dad is a cancer survivor. It means a great deal to me that my Dad will see this poem in print. I come from a family that believes in sharing. This poem has allowed me to share my Dad with everyone.

SHARP, SEBASTIAN
[a.] Calgary, Canada [title] "Above" [pers.] I am a 14-year-old Australian, currently residing in Calgary, AB. I would like to dedicate this poem to my family for introducing me to the world of the arts. My parents have taken me from play to play, movie to movie, have bought me book after book, and have taken me all over the world. My sister, Caitlin, introduced me to all the good poets and authors in the world, particularly Sylvia Plath, who inspires me on a daily basis.

SHEEHAN, REGINA
[a.] Waynesville, NC [title] "See Only Me" [pers.] I make my home in western North Carolina. It is a beautiful place to live. This poem is for my sweet husband, Michael. I love sharing life with you and our wonderful children. Jesus, thank you for my inspiration.

SHEPHERD, SAMANTHA
[a.] Gillette, WY [title] "Back in the Old Days" [pers.] Samantha's is currently 11 years old. She and her family lived on her uncle's ranch most of her life, where she learned to ride horses and work cattle. Samantha loves the western way of life, which is her motivation for western poetry.

SHIPLEY, KAREN
[a.] Fowlerville, MI [title] "The Abyss" [pers.] My parents are Marilyn and Elgin Simmerson. I was born in Beausetour Manitoba, Canada, on June 7, 1956. I was raised in Lake Wilcox, Ontario, Canada. I have two older sisters, Janet Lynn Lewis and Patrica Simmerson. My younger brothers are Daniel, David, and James Simmerson. I am currently residing in Michigan with my husband, Bob Shipley. "The Abyss" comes from a part of life when so much that was important to me was lost. Maybe someday what was lost will return. Thanks, Mom, for encouraging my writing. I may not be able to sing like you could, but I can write. Mom, love ya.

SHIRLEY, AMANDA
[a.] Irmo, SC [title] "You Are Like" [pers.] I wrote this poem for my grandmother as a gift. She is very special to me and so are my poems. Actually this was my first poem I ever wrote, but the love put into it, the joy I had in giving it to her, and seeing what it meant to her, showed me what I can do when I allow my heart to guide my hand in writing poems.

SHWAIKI, NANCY
[a.] Chicago, IL [title] "Why Has the World Turned Around on Me?" [pers.] I believe poems are best when written from the heart. It makes them emotionally true and readers can actually feel what the poet is writing. All my poems are emotional and extremely deep, they hold special parts of my life. Poetry is the best way to express one's self, and I am thankful that I was blessed with this gift. I would like to thank my family: Nelly, Ruth, Riwayda, Sam, and Samia, especially my mother, Blanca, for giving me love and strength to continue to succeed in life.

SIAW-LATTEY, KWASI
[a] Richardson, TX [title] "Success" [pers.] Growing up in a poor African family in Ghana, my goal to succeed in life could only be achieved through patience and endurance. This poem becomes a "Philosophical Formula" for anyone who dreams about a successful future. This and many other original works will be published soon.

SICARD, RICHARD
[a.] Johnston, RI [title] "Dad" [pers.] This poem is very special to me, because I come from a very large family—three boys, and five girls. I wrote this to my dad, because I could never express my feelings to him in any other way. Through this poem, I expressed to him how I felt. I'm glad I did this, because he recently passed away. Before I wrote this poem, we really weren't close and this poem helped us to see eye to

eye. Everyone tells me I'm just like him. He also, was a middle son. This poem is dedicated in the loving memory of Arthur Raymond Sicard (1933-1999).

SICKLE, CLIFFORD
[a.] Bartlesville, OK [title] "Steadfast Love" [pers.] This free verse was written to celebrate the 50th wedding anniversary of Mavis and Keith Bau, my sister and brother-in-law. It reflects how I perceive who they are and their relationship with each other.

SILVA, PEDRO
[a.] Flower Mound, TX [title] "Blue Sky" [pers.] I am from Portugal, and I moved to Texas in 1996 to start college. This poem is the result of one of my class assignments. By now it means much more to me than just a class assignment. Every time I read this poem, I remind myself that sometimes we look but we don't really see, and when we want to see there is nothing to look at.

SIMMONS, ASHLEY
[a.] San Bernardin, CA [title] "And It Makes It Hard to Think" [pers.] This poem means a lot to me. It's mostly just about love and how easy it can get taken away from you. It's also saying how you shouldn't lose hope, even if you can't think anymore. That's the one way we're all the same, because of our pain. Even a 14-year-old can experience it. We just have to get through it and start thinking.

SIMMONS, KELLI
[a.] Tillamook, OR [title] "Thank You, CP" [pers.] I am the assistant teacher with teacher, "CP." We have had three years together as friends and as a team. We've really had fun, learned from and gotten to know one another. She is caring, supportive, "hysterically funny," and inspirational. Most of all, she's been like my second mother. She has really taught me a lot. She's moving this year, and I am truly going to miss her. So, to her, I dedicate the recognition of my poem, with truth and love. I'm 25 years old, and have written poems since I was 12. Every poem I write is true to my life and the people in them. Thank you to everyone who has helped me through the hardships of life.

SINCLAIR, WILLIAM
[a.] High Ridge, MO [title] "Another Day in Hell" [pers.] My poems are my deepest thoughts. "Another Day in Hell" is about someone who I thought once loved me. I write poetry in my spare time or when I'm sad. Some days the words come easily to my mind. This poem is about someone close to my heart. I can't touch them anymore.

SINGLETON, KATHRYN
[a.] Garner, NC [title] "Pamela Christine Finch" [pers.] This poem is one of several bird poems I have written. They are all true stories of birds and their families as they go about their day. This particular bird, Pamela Christine Finch, made her bed in the early evening in the upper corner of the carport of a close friend of mine. She would fly away very early in the morning, and I began wondering just what she did while she was away from her comfortable nighttime perch. Her name came to me as my friend and I were leaving for a bridal shower for one of my co-workers whose name is Pamela Christine. The bird herself provided her own last name. She was a finch.

SKAALERUD, LISE
[a.] Naples, FL [title] "Anger" [pers.] To me, poetry is a visual way of capturing the essence of a moment. It's a world of its own. The growth I am doing as a human being is an eternal source of inspiration for my poems. I love to explore the different levels of poetry, letting the language frame the psychological or spiritual content. This poem reflects an attempts to increase my emotional intelligence by taking control of the anger.

SKINNER, PATRICIA
[a.] Clarksburg, WV [title] "The Dreamers" [pers.] This poem was written for a very special man I had met on the Internet. We share a bond of friendship that words cannot explain. I believe God has blessed me with a special gift of expression through poetry, and I hope my words can touch others. Poetry allows me to express the emotions and feelings I have deep inside, and helps me sort through the thoughts running through my mind. As a single mother of three, the ability to put my feelings into words helps keep me balanced and focused on what is important.

SLATER, ROSE
[a.] Athens, TN [title] "Poetry" [pers.] This poem was inspired after reading about the life of John Bunyon, who wrote the classic, "Pilgrim's Progress." It is said that during a time of imprisonment for his faith, Bunyon could find nothing on which to write his thoughts other than a "potato sack." This was the inspiration for the words, "an item to write on, and an item to write with." My greatest inspiration comes from God, my dearest friend, and from my loving and supportive family. I love to write! I write everything from poetry to children's books of which I hope to have published.

SLAUGHTER, ANITA
[a.] Dixon Springs, TN [title] "Quiet Place" [pers.] My father named me after Anita Carter. She was the daughter of the famous Mabelle Carter who performed on the Grand Ole Opry. My father loved more than ever to hear Anita Carter sing. It always saddened me that I was not gifted with a singing voice. Yet, words on paper were easy for me. When my father read "Quiet Place," he cried. It was his wish that somehow I have this poem printed. Unfortunately, he passed away. I could never sing for my father. Yet, before he died, he knew that one gift was traded for another.

SLAVIS, CHARLES, JR
[a.] Millersburg, OH [title] "Eternity" [pers.] I became aware of our race through time in high school. Existence is our slot in time. As we pass by each other, the only constant is change. I created future projection flying to Vietnam. I visualized myself flying back home and projected myself to that point in time. Of course it took a year in time and many adventures to yet there, or was it just an instant? Given eternity, our lives are an instant, and a year is a small part of that instant. I have to run; time is short!

SLAYBACK, RACHEL
[a.] Ider, AL [title] "Remember God" [pers] Even though a controversial subject, I believe that God is the one and only thing that inspired me to write this poem. I am thankful and very privileged to have been brought up in a loving family that took me to church every Sunday morning. I cherish the opportunity that I had to learn about God. In this poem, I am merely trying to express the unconditional love he had for the world, yet in so much pain while he died for our sins. I appreciate this opportunity to share my own vision with the world.

SLUSS, JOAN
[a.] Woodbridge, VA [title] "The Compassionate Jesus" [pers.] I am the second daughter and fifth child of Sydney and Gladys (Easter) Banks. I came to the United States in 1956 following my marriage to Elmer G. Sluss in 1954. I have four children and eight grandchildren. I converted to Christianity in 1957, and my deep faith in Jesus Christ as Savior, friend, advocate, and counselor has sustained me down through the years. Verse has been the modem for working through the difficult experiences of life and bringing closure to an event or problem.

SMALLEY, NANCY
[a.] Apple Valley, CA [title] "Vietnam" [pers.] This poem reminds me of my brother, Richard, and the horror I felt watching him pull away and thinking of all the young men on their way to Vietnam, who might never return! I was only 13 at the time, but my whole life was turned upside down. When I write poetry I usually write from personal experiences. I write from the heart about life's lessons, and hope to touch others with my thoughts.

SMART, KATHRYN
[a.] Roy, UT [title] "What Is a Dream?" [pers.] This poem is special to me, because I knew that I had done a good job of writing it. Lots of people have read my poem, and they're hoping as I am, that my poem will do well. I come from a large family. I'm often expected to do as well as my older siblings. It has always been hard to do things the older kids haven't done. Even now it's hard, because I have their school reputation to live up to. I want to thank my aunt and my English teacher. To both of you, thank you! You both helped me so much.

SMART, TIM, JR.
[a.] Campobello, SC [title] "Who Am I" [pers.] As a young adolescent, I had the opportunity to become involved with a local volunteer Fire Department. This allowed me to see the dedication and love which certain people in the community have for their fellow citizens. This job is very rewarding to the individual, but it is also very emotionally fatiguing. Due to the relationship I have had in the field of emergency response, I have made it my goal to some day become a paramedic. I want to give back to those who have given so much to others. I give credit to my parents for the Christian background.

SMITH, AMANDA
[a.] Aurora, CO [title] "For Michael" [pers.] This poem was written for my fiance, Michael Palo. I wrote it for him when we got together. He proposed almost two months later. We are planning on having the wedding in December. I love him with all my heart and so much more. He is everything to me. I only hope others can find the kind of love and joy that we have. Love is a precious gift that is meant to be cherished. For those who find it, there is no other feeling quite like it. For those who don't, my prayers are with you forever and always.

SMITH, ANGELA
[a.] Wallace, KS [title] "Will You Be My Eternal Love?" [pers.] I enjoy writing my own poetry in my spare time; it often helps me get my true feelings out when I can't express them in words. I wrote this poem in my college English class a couple of summers ago using "magnetic words." At the time, I never even dreamed that this poem would have the honor of being published. I hope someday to dedicate "Will You Be My Eternal Love?" to my future eternal love.

SMITH, ANNETTE
[a.] San Diego, CA [title] "My Many Lives" [pers.] I am 65 years old, and poetry has been an important means of expression for me all my life. I also love words and music together, and to write lyrics for songs that express thoughts and feelings about human interaction and relationships.

SMITH, JAY
[a.] Houston, TX [title] "When Bluebonnets Grew" [pers.] A poem is like a piece of art, though the medium used are simple words. A poem is not meant to tantalize the eye, but the mind of the reader, by touching on past remembrances, thoughts, and emotions. The poem, "When Bluebonnets Grew," is an attempt to express my feelings after a day of watching my son play among the Texas hill country wild flowers. Seeing the joy and wonder on his face is something any parent that loves their children can relate to.

The emotion of an experience such as this is what I hoped to capture in this work.

SMITH, KAREN

[a.] Indianapolis, IN [title] "My Son" [pers.] My son was born 16 years ago. He is a blessing and a miracle. He has taught me more about life and people than I can ever teach him. He brings joy to everyone who meets him. Looking at him you would never believe that he came close to dying at birth.

SMITH, MICHELLE

[a.] West Sacrame, CA [title] "Remember" [pers.] I want to dedicate this poem to every young girl in the world who has no father, yet still has one living with her. I hope my poem reaches out to every girl who knows my pain, be she thirteen, like me, or ninety. I am so glad to share my poem with the world.

SMITH, PAUL

[a.] Gasport, NY [title] "Thoughts" [pers.] This poem came to me as a inspiration from someone who truly is special. She amplifies beauty in her own and unique way. Her thoughts are always cherished and held in the highest regard. This poem is dedicated to Stephanie Meindl.

SMITH, ROSZALIA

[a.] Columbus, MS [title] "Why Did I Get Pregnant?" [pers.] My inspiration to write "Why Did I Get Pregnant?" came from the struggle placed on my heart to save my daughter, Sabrina Butler, from this sweet old justice system, she was taken, tried and placed on death row, for a crime she didn't commit. My greatest fear was to lose my child that I had carried for nine months. Then in 1995 through my constant fighting, prayers, and devotion, she was released. My hobbies are singing, dancing, and playing the piano. We live in little town called Columbus, Mississippi, but the ghost of her trial still haunts me and my family.

SMITH, RUTH

[a.] Garrett, IN [title] "Surrounding Darkness" [pers.] I am currently finishing my second year of college. I am majoring in youth, adult, and family services. I learned at an early age the importance of reading and the written word. Writing is my way of expressing my feelings and life experiences. It is my desire for people to gain enjoyment from my writings.

SMYTH, MICHAEL

[a.] Ireland [title] "Bartra" [pers.] I find poetry helps me to express my true feelings, the soft loving ones particularly. This poem is very meaningful to me. I wrote it and rewrote it at a very special time in my life. I had come out of a marriage, and was finding it very difficult to accept the end of the relationship. I was attending a counselor and after each session I walked on Bartra Strand, sometimes feeling very alone, confused, and afraid. The sound and sight of the sea got me in touch with my true feelings and emotions, and inspired me to pen those lines. That was nine years ago almost today. I'm leading a full happy life, and have come out the other side of that dark tunnel. I'm a retired post-primary teacher, and I work a few days a week in a hotel.

SNELLER, KASSIE

[a.] Pella, IA [title] "best friends forever" [pers.] The death of one of my best friends inspired me to write this poem about him. He was killed in a head-on collision with a semi while he was roller blading. He died at age 13. His death has taught me to appreciate what I have, and to never leave on a bad note with a loved one. Just because I am 14 does not mean I don't know what love is. I will always love him. I would like to thank my family, Cornie, Brenda, John, Casey, and my best friend for having faith in me. I hope everyone who reads this can feel somewhat how I feel about this poem.

SNIDAL, MYRTLE

[a] Nanoose, Canada [title] "Memories" [pers.] This poem was written with memories of my grandmother, a dear lady who was always so special to me during my growing years. If not for Gran, I would have failed in reaching my goals. She was always there to give encouragement, and help me reach those goals; she gave me a secure future. My wish for all young would be that they could also find a Gran as loving and helpful as mine. Gran was one dear lady. In all my tomorrows, she will never be forgotten.

SNYDER, BOB

[a.] New Castle, PA [title] "Walk Me to the Bend" [pers.] My thoughts in this poem are really a composite of each person's struggle with good and evil, and the forces leashed upon us by just being human. Having once studied for the priesthood, I was immersed in the mystical and metaphysical. I enjoy the speculative thoughts of St. Augustine, yet the simplicity of Francis of Assisi. My parents fought the good fight in this struggle, and both died a peaceful death. I seek the same resolution of peace in my writings and poetry.

SNYDER, NICK

[a.] Martinsburg, PA [title] "Searcher" [pers.] Poetry and songwriting are emotional and spiritual outlets for me. "Searcher" is actually much longer than the portion I submitted. It expresses the way both Christians and non-Christians feel a they search through life for truth and joy. The truth that I have come to know is that there is a God and He died so that we would not have to go through this life in misery and confusion. Joy is the life that he would have us live. I hope people who read it can relate and know that life doesn't have to be like this.

SOPPELSA, ALYSA

[a.] Lawrence, MI [title] "Rain" [pers.] This poem was an assignment in my class. I wrote about the rain, because rainy days always make me sad. I'm 12 years old, and I have an older brother, and an older sister, Trina. We live in a small town in MI with our mom and dad. I'm very proud to have received the honor of being published in this book.

SOSIN, HELENA

[a.] North Miami, FL [title] "None Negotiables" [pers.] My late father, a Polish social activist, did imbue my soul with the ideal attitude of human nobility, brotherhood, and care for all forms of life. It would be worse than the second world war, for him, to see our indignant metamorphosis. We are killing each other. If not with knifes and bullets, then by the blind ignorance and lack of care for these among whom we walk. We thrush our Mother Earth. He, my father, would ask: "What have you done to yourself homo sapiens?" A suicidal matricide of our planet is not away of progress.

SOUCY, JACQUELINE

[a.] Oceanside, CA [title] "Eternal Bond for Life" [pers.] It is an privilege having my art recognized and entered in print. My inspiration is Robert, my true love. Although I have written poems in the past my love for him makes the words flow from my heart and soul. Someone very dear to me once said, true love transcends all earthly bounds, truer words were never spoken. The bonds between God's Creation (the flower), its sustenance (sun, water, soil), and seed (eternal life) mirrors that of man. God's Creation (man) his sustenance (love, faith in God), and eternal life (soul). God Bless you, all.

SPARKS, JENNIFER

[a.] Cincinnati, OH [title] "Why?" [pers.] I was thirteen years old when I wrote this poem. I attend St. Ignatius School in Cincinnati, Ohio. Almost two years ago, I was inspired to start writing poems by reading my older sister's poems. At the time, I was

going through some emotional times in my life, and I basically just let it all out by picking up a pen and paper. Ever since then, I write about anything or anyone I can think of, journalizing many of my thoughts. It is one of my favorite things to do. I am very thankful that I got this opportunity to have my poem published.

ST. ANDREW, STACY

[a.] Wayne, MI [title] "Real Me" [pers.] The poem I wrote describes how I feel about love. It simply says that if you really love me and give me the time, you will get to know all of me. I wrote this poem because I was thinking about Brandon Dickerson and everything that has happened to me. My name is Stacy Lynn St. Andrew. I was born on August 20, 1985. I live in Wayne, Michigan. I go to school at Wayne Memorial High. I'm a freshmen there. I want to be a singer and a dancer one day, or a writer. I'd like to thank a couple of people for saying I can win no matter what. Thanks Canaice, Cassie, Devaun, Nicole, Jessi, Mirromirro, and to the rest of my peps. I love you all. Thanks!

STAFRACE, MARCO

[a.] Paola, Malta [title] "Universe of Love" [pers.] I am a 17-year-old man from Malta, and I am currently single. I usually write poems to loved ones when I am in a relationship. Poems are the voice when I cannot speak, when words are not enough to describe something as precious as love, because everybody needs love in their life. A poem is the best gift that one can give to a loved one, because they describe their true emotions, and that in what this poem is all about.

STANT, MELISSA

[a.] Brigantine, NJ [title] "What Happened" [pers.] For me, words cannot always be spoken, so writing became my escape. It has helped me come to terms with all of the joys and sadness the world has to offer. I would like to thank my husband, Dominick, for giving me the confidence to share my work with others, and for believing in me when I found it difficult to believe in myself.

STAPLES, ERIKA

[a.] Summerville, SC [title] "The Point to Die Is Death" [pers.] I like to write poetry as if I were in someone else's shoes. If I were ever to publish a book, I would dedicate it to my mother, Kimberly Moore. She and my sister, Nicole, mean the world to me. I love my life, yet I like writing poetry about things that happen to other people. To me, poetry expresses feelings. My inspiration comes from all the good poems I have read. I am grateful to have my poetry published with many others. When I have things on my mind, I write. It is so much easier to express myself. This poem is about someone I know who shot himself.

STARWALT, LINDSEY

[a.] Mount Carmel, IL [title] "Waiting" [pers.] This poem is written to explain the type of love that everyone dreams for, but that cannot always be found. This verse is a reminder to be patient with love. It will come to each and everyone when they least expect it, and they will be happier than ever. I wrote this poem at a time in my life where I doubted that I would ever find love or vice versa. After writing my feelings down, I realized that love isn't a prize to be won, but a beauty of life to enjoy. I hope that by reading this poem people will have the courage to listen to God and wait for love patiently.

STEED, CHREE

[a.] San Antonio, MS [title] "My Guardian Angel" [pers.] My mother raised me by herself all my life. I have seen her struggle to provide for us. She was my inspiration for this poem. Even though my mother is still with me on earth, she has always been my "Guardian Angel." My mother is very special to me and any opportunity I have to honor her is but a small portion of what she's given to me. Not only is she my mother, she is my best friend. This poem is dedicated to my mother, my true "Guardian Angel," Ronda Steed. I love you, Mom.

STEELE, ROBIN

[a.] Laingsburg, MI [title] "Good Ol' #3" [pers.] I feel very fortunate to have had my poem selected. Although I consider myself a singer/songwriter, I cannot express my gratitude. I'd like to dedicate this to my mother, who inspired me because of her loyalty as a fan of Dale Earnhardt, and Nascar racing. My poem is about inspiration, it's a way of letting go, and understanding that the "race must go on!" I'd also like to thank my children, Tarence, Nash, Lyric, and Jessica; my husband, Dennis; and my father, Robert. They have always been my biggest fans, and I thank them. Most of all, thanks to the International Library of Poetry. God bless and God speed, Dale Earnhardt!

STEPP, ROBBY

[a.] Carthage, TN [title] "Tick-Tock Clock" [pers.] In my own eyes, I have always been a failure. I was never good enough, and I could not live up to my own expectations. The poem, "Tick-Tock Clock," was just a way of expressing the thoughts and feelings I was going through at the time. As I looked at the finished copy I finally realized the reason behind my writings. I, unlike most people, do not write to express my feelings to the world. Instead, I write to express my feelings to myself. I use poetry as a means of communication with my soul.

STERWERF, CHRISTY

[a.] Milan, IN [title] "God Took a Great Man" [pers.] This poem is very special to me. I would like to dedicate it to my cousin and his family. He was taken by God on July 26, 1999. He was a nice, handsome young man. Writing this poem helped me express my innermost feelings. We all miss him very much. We know he is all right, because he is in God's hands forever.

STILLWELL, RYAN

[a.] Mammoth Lake, CA [title] "Awakening" [pers.] This is one of the most special works of poetry in my collection. This poem shows the exhilaration that I feel about the future. I feel an awakening that is pervading the global consciousness. It can be seen not only in my work, or this book, but more and more in the chance coincidences that are having serious impacts on all of our lives. My poem, chosen to be published in this book, shows this understanding. I offer this poem up to the Creator in hopes that it will be a spark toward universal consciousness.

STOKES, LINDA

[a.] Santa Rosa, CA [title] "Love Nets" [pers.] This poem was written on Valentine's Day for "Andy." We met through an ad online. Our relationship—the things we have in common, as well as our differences—has been so unique and wonderful that we feel we are two sides of the same coin.

STOLZ, TINA

[a.] Dix Hills, NY [title] "Secrets" [pers.] I've considered myself a writer for years now. I started writing in kindergarten as soon as I could spell. Now I can just consider myself a published writer. (It's some sort of justification, or maybe proof, for the rest of the world, you know?) Writing is the best way to get all the crazy stuff floating around inside my head out. This poem was written while listening to comforting "ancient" music and drinking lots of chamomile tea. Tea does wonders for the imagination, but so does the imagination.

STONECYPHER, PATRICIA

[a.] Jamestown, CA [title] "Friends" [pers.] As far back as my earliest memories, mother nature has always beckoned me and been a vivid part of my life. I discovered great comfort within her grasp and soon realized words flowed from my heart and answers could be found. When I was within her reach, her strength was my strength, her comfort quieted my soul. I could lie quietly and let myself be enshrouded in her embrace. I have not been blessed with children of my own, so I mentor and tutor whenever I can, hoping to be an inspiration to those whose lives touch mine. I daily endeavor to practice random acts of kindness and, at the very least, to bring a smile to someone's heart in the same way that others have touched mine.

STOUT, LORI

[a.] Savannah, GA [title] "Life Lost" [pers.] "Life Lost" was written for my brother, Jerry Ray Kinsey, who was taken from us entirely too soon. Being younger than he was, I often looked to him for guidance. We did not always agree, but I always loved him for who he was. I hope that these words will bring joy to those who read them, as they have for myself and my family. It is an honor to have my poem included in this volume of works. I am proud; I know my brother is as well.

STRUNK, JUDY

[a.] Euless, TX [title] "I Can't Breathe" [pers.] I come from an artistic family. My dad painted, and my mother writes limericks. My brother, son, and grandson are very good artists. My granddaughter and I have always been creative people, doing many different crafts. I have never really written poetry. I guess in times of family crisis and frustration, an unseen hand guides your thoughts to paper for all to see. Maybe other families are going through the same situation, and maybe they will realize that they are not alone.

STUBBS, ELIZABETH

[a.] Bennettsville, SC [title] "Winter Calls" [pers.] I love writing poetry but am somewhat modest. In writing, I find the words from my innermost feelings. "Winter Calls" is special in that I had to feel the seasons. I felt the need to defend nature as I would for all things misunderstood, especially people. As a nature lover, I give her feelings in a way to which we (as people) can relate. Sometimes the beauty is hidden and can only be seen within the decay that we must enter. I wish for more time to write; in time, I do believe I could find the beauty in all things.

STUMPFF, CHARLOTTE

[a.] Mountain Grove, MO [title] "Our Brightest Star" [pers.] I'd like to dedicate this poem to the loving memory of Jessica Summer Stoddard. My poem tells about how my family and how I lost an angel. At the age of three weeks, she left us for her heavenly home. She left my family sweet memories, but a lost love. Through this poem I share her spirit and my family's love for her. I hope you all enjoy this poem as much as my family and I!

SUAREZ, KAYZIM

[a.] Somerville, MA [title] "What Else Is There to Do" [pers.] Life has many things in store for us, and through our experiences we can find truth and happiness. Poetry has always been a way for me to feel. Ever since I was a little girl, my own father's poetry has inspired me. Now, I use this inspiration to deal with and share my experiences with the world. I hope that my verses can console another's soul just like they've consoled mine. This poem is just one of many that I have written during heartache. I dedicated it to my past. Sometimes you just have to say good-bye.

SUCILLON, SHARON

[a.] Roy, UT [title] "The River of Hope" [pers.] Poetry has been a way for me to express those feelings too close to my heart, which up to now have been reserved for family members. Music and poetry have saturated my life from the time I was born. All my family members are gifted singers or musicians. My momma instilled in me a love of singing and playing the piano and was my biggest poetry fan. Recently, I took on conquering fears that haunted me. With God's help I have overcome my fear of deep water and learned to swim. Opening myself through poetry has been another big step.

SULLENGER, REBECKA

[a.] Albany, MO [title] "Dear Lord" [pers.] This poem was written the morning after we had last our 19-year-old son in a car accident. It expresses the pain, anger, frustration, and just sheer helplessness that I've felt since. When you lose a loved one, especially a child, it is very hard to let go. My comfort is that he is in God's care. He is a special young man who will always be with me, and I look forward to the day down the road when I can wrap him in my arms once again.

SWANSON, JASON

[a.] Hillsboro, ND [title] "Life Unfolding" [pers.] This poem came to me one night as I was thinking of the things that have gone on in my life. It deals with my divorce and getting custody of my daughter, Carissa, and not giving up.

SWIFT, AMANDA

[a.] Martin, GA [title] "Gloria's Poem" [pers.] This poem is dear to me, because I wrote it for my grandmother Gloria. She had cancer, and it was very difficult for our family to cope with. Then I wrote this poem for her, to cheer her up. I have a wonderful husband and three little boys. I write poems in my spare time. I am a housewife, and I am a Christian. A poem shows your true feelings. This poem shows my feelings for cancer and that with God by your side you can overcome anything. My grandmother has been cancer-free for two years.

TACKETT, RENEA

[a.] West Union, OH [title] "Angels" [pers.] My name is Renea Tackett, and I'm 14 years old. The person who inspired me to write my poem was my friend. My idea came from God. Without God I would be nothing. I thank God for the breath of life that was given to me, to write about his angels. The Almighty God is very real, and I thank Him for His many blessings.

TAI, NIKKI

[a.] New York, NY [title] "Hiding" [pers.] Poetry is so much a part of my life. Times of happiness, sadness, even music, are poetry to me. "Hiding" is one of my moments of inspiration while listening to the silence of an empty room. I wrote this trying to capture the loneliness of a confused and broken heart. I write poems, like this one, hoping to capture the depth of emotion and share it with others.

TAKIEDDIN, SARA

[a] Boston, MA [title] "Rain, Oh, Rain" [pers.] This poem has a funny story behind it. My ex-boyfriend and I challenged each other to see who was the better poet. A mutual friend chose the topic, and I set a deadline. I almost lost due to my lack of ideas. I guess the pressure got to me and got me going. I actually won, and, as the loser, my ex had to clean my apartment for a month. I guess living in Boston, where it rains a lot, motivated me to write about rain. God bless!

TALBOTT, LAURA

[a.] Timonium, MD [title] "The Promise of May" [pers.] Dad, you kissed my cheek, and I was gone, and though the petals fall, the apple tree will bloom again, and I will never stop asking the time of day. I love you!

TAMBORRA, MARYBETH

[a.] Salem, CT [title] "Mystery" [pers.] Poetry means a lot; there is nothing with more depth then a unique poem written from the soul. This poem, to me, is just the beginning of what we don't know of our mysterious world. We won't realize many of these things until after we are deceased. I would like to thank my grandmother Mary Terese Tamborra and my sisters for the inspiration and strength they have given me.

TANEMORI, TAKASHI THOMAS
[a.] Lafayette, CA [title] "My Only Gift" [pers.] A survivor of Hiroshima, I was controlled by the desire to take vengeance on Americans. Yet, looking back, the "path of Hiroshima" taught me a most important truth. We who have lost the most in war are also the ones who have the most to gain by putting aside feelings of revenge, learning to forgive, and making peace with our painful past. I finally understand that going beyond my personal suffering and helping others leads to healing. It is only when we look with "a vision of the heart" that we are at last able to "see."

TAVITIAN, ANNETTE
[a.] Killarney Heights, Australia [title] "Alone I Know" [pers.] Poetry comes from within the heart. Experiences have encouraged me to share my work and remind me how much of a gift life really is. This poem signifies how painful it can oftentimes be when a long-term relationship comes to an end. As sad as it can be, being apart from that special someone, you learn to move on and put the past behind you. I believe if we go on regretting things that once happened, then we lead very empty and unfulfilling lives.

TAYLOR, BILL
[a.] Cordova, IL [title] "Who's Free?" [pers.] For 43 years on Earth, my view was always different, especially my ability to change the lyrics of songs as fast as you could sing them. . . . Without the support of family and friends, I wouldn't be able to to have the confidence to do it. May God take care of those who touched my life and left us too early. This poem is for you. I will use this gift to wake the living.

TAYLOR, LYNDA
[a.] Severna Park, MD [title] "Alone" [pers.] I started writing classes about six years ago. In one of my classes we were asked to write a poem. "Alone" was one of them. I had already started writing a mainstream novel, *Tony With a Why?*, then decided to expand my plot into a trilogy. "Alone" seems to fit perfectly at the end of *Emma's Diary*, the second book of the trilogy. I hope the ideas continue to flow, like a tranquil babbling brook to my mind, fulfilling my life, and, someday, when they are published, give pleasure to others.

TAYLOR, WALTON
[a.] Poca, WV [title] "Mom and Dad" [pers.] This poem is in honor and memory of my beloved mom and dad, who touched the hearts of and were dearly loved by everyone they met during their lifetimes. I am honored and proud that you would publish their poem, so that it might bring comfort and relief to others who also might be suffering the pain of losing a loved one. Thelma K. and Joseph P. Taylor, both now deceased, lived in Poca, West Virginia.

TEEPLE, GIFFARD
[a.] Evanston, IL [title] "Smiling Eyes" [pers.] Merely observing Geri, my heart wrote this poem. Despite circumstances that prevented my even getting to know her, I still fell in love. Seven months later, there was no change; yet all the world has changed. So sayeth Anonymous.

TEIK, CHEAH
[a.] Prai, Malaysia [title] "Never Really Ends" [pers.] My full name is Cheah Cheng Teik. You can address me as Mr. Cheah (Cheah is my family name) or you can just call me Cheng Teik. (Cheng is my generation name, Teik is my actual name.) My favorite quote is "Appreciate the simple things, see how beautiful life is." You are welcome to sign the guest book at my web site. My nickname is Ricamy. Experience prompted me to write "Never Really Ends." I have observed people unfortunately in trouble, hinting that, besides studies and work, most people have not learned to live a favorable lifestyle.

TELESCA, LEONARD
[a.] Old Tappan, NJ [title] "The Dove" [pers.] Love is a powerful emotion. At times, it can be very difficult to express. That difficulty inspired me to write this poem and to help myself and others express how they truly feel.

TENNENT, SARAH
[a.] Bowie, MD [title] "From the Outside" [pers.] Poetry has been a passion of mine for as long as I can remember. Even though many of my poems, including "From the Outside," have very dark themes, the vast majority of them have no basis in reality for me personally and are simply products of my imagination. My favorite poets are Sylvia Plath, Dorothy Parker, Walt Whitman, and Lord Byron, and other major influences include songwriters such as Fiona Apple, Tora MacLean, Juliana Hatfield, and Lisa Loeb. I hope to pursue poetry in college and beyond, as well as songwriting, psychology, and theater.

TERMO, LAWRENCE
[a.] Flushing, NY [title] "I Should Have Painted the Road Grey" [pers.] I had a nervous breakdown in 1967 and suffered for a long time. A friend was trying to assure me that when I got well life would be this marvelous carnival ride. It took me a long time to accept the reality that life consists of ups and downs, despite one's mental health. Rather than searching for a magical fantasy, I would have done better to appreciate the tender mercies of life. Now I do. By appreciating that there is good to be found in the simple things, I enjoy every day and have stopped searching for the Garden of Eden that a total life just is not.

THEIS, SHARON
[a.] Rockwood, MI [title] "Just Right" [pers.] Growing up in the heart of middle Tennessee, I've been inspired to write poetry all my life. My home and family were a great inspiration. This time I chose to write about my best friend, my husband. We've shared almost 18 years together so far, and I mean every word in this poem. My husband is the love of my life. I hope God grants us many more years together. Life is "just right" with him.

THERIAULT, CAROLYN
[a.] Bristol, CT [title] "Good-Bye" [pers.] Poetry has an amazing effect on me. It allows me to channel my emotions positively. God gives all people gifts; this happens to be one of mine. Anything can be done with God's help and the right inspiration.

THIES, CAROL
[a.] Interlochen, MI [title] "House in the Clearing" [pers.] I would like to dedicate my poem "House in the Clearing" to my two daughters, Kimberly Kay and Kerri Lynn, who have fond memories of their very first house; and to my husband, Robert, who made this house a happy home and memory for them.

THOMAS, LEAH
[a.] Chickasha, OK [title] "Roger" [pers.] This poem is very special to me. It is about one of my biggest crushes so far. I felt I was competing with Lammie for his attention. Although he does not go to my school anymore, we still keep in touch by phone. Roger will always have a special place in my heart.

THOMAS, LYNDA
[a.] Boca Raton, FL [title] "Be Assured" [pers.] My name is Lynda Thomas. I am a licensed massage therapist in Boca Raton, Florida. I wrote this poem for William J. Henry, Jr. (Bill). Bill is my significant other—he lost his father when he was only 11 years old. He misses his dad and mom. However, they await his arrival one day in Heaven. Bill can "be assured," thanks be to Christ. I want to acknowledge my parents, Jack and Yvonne, and my children, John and Murray and Bill, all of whom I love deeply.

THOMAS, MARK
[a.] Palmer, AK [title] "The Traveler" [pers.] I am the Traveler. The mystery behind my 18 years of travel could only be explained through my poems. Living on a ranch in the wilderness of Alaska has allowed extreme discipline of the mind. This has greatly inspired my talent as a musician and a poet. My inspiration comes from God my creator.

THOMPSON, KRISTINA
[a.] Iowa City, IA [title] "Powerless" [pers.] This was written for a person who is very special to me. Poetry allows me to express my feelings in a deeper state. It comes more from the heart in poetry. I hope to allow all the couples who are in relationships where emotional expression is hard to remind each other how strong love can be.

THOMPSON, TREVOR
[a.] Jacksonville, OR [title] "Sunset" [pers.] This poem is actually the second one I have written (out of four). Poetry comes almost naturally to me, but I have never had anything worth writing about until my one love, Paige Noel, showed up and swept me away to a dreamland. I could not have done this without her, or my mother. I love you both. You mean the world to me, and I could never live without you.

THOMPSON, VALDON
[a.] Arlington, TX [title] "Oh, Where Could That Gorgeous Sun Be?" [pers.] I was at work during lunch break, staring outside at the gloomy sky. I remembered how fun it is to see people having fun and enjoying those beautiful sunny days, which led me to writing "Oh, Where Could That Gorgeous Sun Be?" in dedication to those beautiful days out in the sun. My name is Valdon Thompson. I am 22 years old and currently live in Arlington, Texas. Poetry is my way of expression. It is how I show my feelings best.

THOMSON, DARYL
[a] Nottingham, UK [title] "Exist to Me" [pers.] This poem, although not about her, is dedicated to my sister, Dawn. My childhood was a fountain of inspiration and unconditional support. "Exist to Me" is a poem about the unknown aspects of my love, my heartache, and my journey. Although unknown to me, I do not doubt or deny it exists in essence, just not in form at present.

THORNTON, CHRISTOPHER
[a.] Vista, CA [title] "Stars" [pers.] My poem was written after my friends, Lonni and Shawn, told me that I should write a poem about the night sky. I enjoy writing poetry, because it is a good way to express marvel for God's creation. I'd like to thank Lonni, Shawn, and my English teacher, Ms. Zeaman.

THORNTON, VIRGINIA
[a] Weaubleau, MO [title] "God's Love" [pers.] I am a 78-year-old great-grandmother. My husband, Johnny, and I recently celebrated 60 years together. We have two sons, four living grandchildren, and two beautiful granddaughters who are with God. We have eight great-grandchildren. I am a member of Hope Well Baptist Church in Quincy, Missouri. Our pastor is Ken Bolton, a God-inspired young man. Poetry has always been a part of my life. God puts the words in my head and I write them down for Him. I praise God with my poems.

TICE, CHRISTOPHER
[a.] Wilmington, NC [title] "Fear" [pers.] Poetry is a gift. It is an art that has come to mean a lot to me lately. While many of my friends and other poets try to use free verse, my gift remains in the traditional styles. I wrote "Fear" after one day, thinking about how terrifying it would be to spend my life completely alone.

TILLOTSON, KATHERINE
[a.] Bedford, TX [title] "Why?" [pers.] I feel that poetry is a good way to express your feelings whenever you want to. It allows you to say exactly what you feel and not have anyone talk back to you at that moment. I also feel very naked when someone else reads it. I think sometimes that's just what you need to get across the point that something is important to you. That's why I wrote this poem about my friend Patrick, who killed himself. I miss him a lot, and this is how I feel about his choices.

TINSLEY, LUCINDA
[a.] Bakersfield, CA [title] "Daddy" [pers.] I wish to dedicate this poem to my real father. With all my heart and soul, may you rest in peace and may your memory live on through my words in this poem (love, Cynda Bear). I hope my poem will touch the hearts of all of those who read it. It is written with love and admiration. I would also like to thank my daughter, Heather, and my husband, Randy, for always encouraging me to continue to express my heart, spirit, and soul through the magical words of poetry.

TOLLIVER, DUSTIN
[a.] Fort Wainright, AK [title] "Why Do Angels Cry?" [pers.] I wrote this poem for a special person in my life after I saw tears fall from her eyes. To see her cry would surely make me cry. I want her to know I would never make her cry, because I truly love her, and, patiently waiting, I hope in time she will love me. This person means the world to me, and I hope she knows that now.

TOME, ALEX
[a.] Point of Rocks, MD [title] "Split" [pers.] I dedicate my poem "Split" to all those who need to find their inner selves and paths in life. Poetry is my outlet, my life force; without poetry, my body is a husk, lifeless and fragile.

TOMESCU, ALINA
[a.] Cluj-Napoca, Romania [title] "To My Love" [pers.] I'm a Transylvanian Leo, born in 1986, and I go to a bilingual Romanian-English school in a city called Cluj-Napoca. Poetry, music, drawing, and the Internet are my passions. The verse "To My Love" is precious to me, as it shows the wishes and dreams of a heart that's been struck by love. In my view, poetry is a blurry mirror of existence, a refuge in which we all are somehow dependent.

TORO, STEPHANIE
[a.] Germantown, MD [title] "I Am Me" [pers.] Poetry is my personal outlet for anger, frustration, and sorrow. Life is sometimes hard to deal with, and being able to express this through poetry is something I value greatly. This poem, to me, illustrates the importance of being yourself, who you are inside. If you can accept yourself the way you are and not care what other people think, you will live a very honest and happy life, during which you can be true to yourself.

TRAGER, SCOTT
[a.] Wellington, OH [title] "My Journey" [pers.] This poem is about the feelings that accompany the trials of life. My poetry is a way for me to deal with my feelings. I hope you enjoy it. My life is very colorful. Sometimes the colors aren't beautiful. These are the moments that make my poetry mine.

TRAIL, STACIE
[a.] Batesville, AR [title] "Why?" [pers.] This poem is about my first love. I enjoy reading and writing poetry. My inspiration comes from important events in my life. I usually have to experience strong emotional events to write a poem. I am currently finishing my second year of college. I hope someone else can relate to this poem as I do.

TROJAN, BETHANY
[a.] Dearborn Heights, MI [title] "My Special Friend" [pers.] The story behind the poem is my younger brother, Noah Webster. By the time he turned three, we knew he was special. Right around his third birthday came the confirmation, when he was diagnosed as autistic. Noah is now turning six, and he shows us something new every day. I have always enjoyed creative writing, and this was a chance to bring two of my loves together. The poem is dedicated to my brother and special friend, Noah Webster.

TURNER, DIANA
[a.] Beavercreek, OH [title] "Grandpa, May You Rest in Peace" [pers.] This poem was written to express my feelings of love and sadness following the death of someone I loved very much, my grandpa. This special person was the motivation behind this poem. He passed away at home after a short battle against cancer in March 2001, prompting me to write this poem. I was proud to be able to express my love for my grandpa by reading this poem at his funeral. Poetry gave me to the opportunity to express my love for my grandpa in a special way and to share those feelings with others.

TURNER, RICKEY
[a.] Ayer, MA [title] "I Hope" [pers.] I would like to thank my family for their support and encouragement. I would also like to thank all the people who believed in me, including my fifth-and sixth-grade teachers, Mrs. Z, Mrs. D., and Mrs. B, for their inspiration.

UDDIN, KHALID
[a.] Fords, NJ [title] "[pers.] For me, poetry is something that symbolizes a culmination of thoughts, feelings, opinions, and emotions. It gives me an opportunity to tell an intricate story in a matter of sentences. This poem reflects an idealization of what we all seek, putting gender aside. Everyone has an image of the perfect person in their mind, someone who they hope to meet or have already found. I believe we all need this person in our lives, whether we are thriving from their support or from the hope of meeting them.

UNITHOMMAN PARAMBIL, BENNY
[a.] Auckland, New Zealand [title] "Journey" [pers.] When everyone left me, the story began. I felt quite lonely. Like a streak in the darkness, Lisa, who was in the same situation, came to me. She made me laugh and think and lifted my sunken soul with words like "You have worth, hang in there." That night, after our long conversation, I felt so light in my mind and so happy in my heart that my poetic spirit spontaneously overflowed. The bliss, the strength, and everything I am wishing her are my own affirmation, too. Like a light in the night she came and disappeared.

UYAN, MARILYN
[a.] Monterey Park, CA [title] "Noble Retreat" [pers.] This piece was inspired by the author's strong faith in survival, especially in matters of the heart. With divine direction and guidance (and one's unconditional acceptance thereof), success will always be within reach. In the final analysis, triumph comes as a reward for sacrifice and determination, anchored in the person's trust in the Almighty. I heartily dedicate "Noble Retreat" to Him . . . the gift giver and savior; my son, Leester Clark; my daughter, Majonelle; my mom; to two very special people closest to my heart; to my relatives and friends; and to all of you . . . precious poetry readers who I believe are one with me in my view of success as translated into this poem.

VALLADE, PAUL, JR.
[a] Romulus, MI [title] "Friend" [pers.] I was born in Germany, and my father is in the army, so I travel and see many places. This poem, called "Friend," comes from the respect I have for the friends that have come and gone during my travels, like Danny, Ben, Samantha, and Brendon. They know who they are.

My sixth-grade teacher, Ms. Baptiste in Kentucky, pushed hard for my poetry, so I owe her much gratitude. Two years later, the power of poetry is spilling from me. Poetry is how I express what I see in life.

VAN EREM, ASHLEY
[a.] Jamestown, ND [title] "Pegasus" [pers.] My poetry is very important to me, as it helps me express what I feel. I can show my appreciation of nature and life; I can also write when I feel upset or angry. My poem, "Pegasus," symbolizes my love of life, and my other poems also help remind people of the importance of expression in any way that makes you happy or makes you feel comfortable.

VAN TUYLE, JEAN
[a.] Pasadena, CA [title] "Rain" [pers.] The California rain in February is a monsoon, day and night on end, but with it is the promise of those first magnificent roses, big as cabbages with the right amount of sunshine and the blessed rain.

VAN WELL, MARILYN
[a.] Akron, CO [title] "My Friend Has a Garden" [pers.] I have written poetry since childhood. I was inspired the most while seated behind the cook stove in our kitchen. Over the years I have written several poems for those who have lost loved ones. I have had to pull over, while driving, to record the words of a poem flowing through me. We farm gals always made trips to each other's gardens to admire what grew there. That is how "My Friend Has a Garden" came to be.

VANCAMP, MONDAY
[a.] Hamilton, ON [title] "At Last" [pers.] A Canadian resident all his life, the author is making his first public attempt at poetry. He is a shy introverted man when it comes to sharing his inner feelings. He usually expresses himself in his volunteer work, which recently was elevated to coach a mentally and physically challenged baseball team. The author enjoys all sports, bridge, golf, and the company of good friends.

VANHOOSER, YOLANDA
[a.] Buford, GA [title] "Daughter" [pers.] I have four daughters. Each one is special in her own way. I watched each one grow to become a loving, compassionate, and caring woman. This poem is a mere expression and reflection of what I saw in each one during her youth. God blessed me with these girls, and it's by his love and grace that they are the way they are today.

VELTKAMP, JACOB
[a.] Stevenson, WA [title] "Rain" [pers.] When I was in sixth grade, I had a school assignment to write a poem about the rain for the local Gorge Rain Festival. Basically, I wrote what I knew. I feel this poem has little to do with the rain and more to do with how I feel about myself.

VEREEN, JOHNIE, III
[a.] Oak Island, NC [title] "To Be" [pers.] Johnie Vereen, III is a lifelong North Carolina coastal resident. Because he has been exposed to beautiful beaches, long cool nights, and wonderful family and people of this region to influence his writing, you will find a keen sense of life in his expression and pen.

VIERRA, DAN
[a.] Stockton, CA [title] "Mountain of Knowledge" [pers.] Poetry is only one of my outlets for my passion. I also enjoy making music, drawing, and graphic design. I own a small company called Creations by the Created, where I design logos, flyers, business cards, etc. If you would like to find out more, you can find me on the Internet. On the other hand, I would like to thank my parents; my girlfriend, Emily; my friends, Kevin, Ruth, and Mike Canada; and everyone else who has believed in me over the years. I promise there will be more to come from me in the near future.

VILLANUEVA, ANDRE

[a.] Birmingham, AL [title] "Revelation, 8/12/98" [pers.] I used to hate poetry. I thought it was for lazy writers. I thought it was sacrilegious to the religion of the Almighty story. When the obligations started piling up in my life, however, I decided to (gasp!) try my hand at poetry. Well, it's several years later, and I am a full-fledged convert to poetry. I've joined the heathens. I've written hundreds of the darned things. I'm addicted. Give me a pill. . . . Give me the cure. I cannot stop. Help me!

VIRGIN, ANDREW

[a.] [title] "Letter to Father" [pers.] This poem expresses my true feelings for my father at a time when things were not so good. My family had barely enough money to make it by. My mother had moved out. ("Ran away" is a better term for it.) To top that off, I was seriously struggling with my own sexuality. My father was overwhelming, mentally abusive. Basically, I had no escape and no outlet for emotions. Poetry, I think, helped cure me.

VIRTUE, SERENE

[a.] Denver, CO [title] "Crying Eyes" [pers.] I am 13 years old and I'm in eighth grade. For fun I like to play volleyball and baseball and swim. I wrote this poem because, when I heard about the Holocaust, I was deeply affected. We should never forget about what happened to the people, and we should always keep them in our heart.

VIVIAN, MARRIS

[a.] Dodgeville, WI [title] "My Love" [pers.] I wrote this poem over 40 years ago when I was dating the woman I later married. Now we are celebrating our fortieth wedding anniversary, so I believe there is a very special power in poetry.

WADDELL, JAN

[a.] Natoma, KS [title] "Recognition" [pers.] My love for poetry I attribute to my Scots-Irish ancestry. Most of my work is about journeying inward, as I believe life to be a spirit quest. Being a native Kansan, both my love of nature and of the Native American culture are very important influences in my writing.

WAGGONER, LELA

[a.] Lake Oswego, OR [title] "Time" [pers.] This poem came from my heart. It was written about one month before my daughter's birthday. I do not consider myself a poet. This poem was written during one of many grieving times I have gone through. You see, I lost my daughter during childbirth. It has been a very hard three years since her death. I just want to let anyone who has gone through this know that I understand your pain. I also want you to know that if you hang in there, no matter how hard it seems, it will get better. God bless you all.

WALDRON, HARMONY

[a.] Apopka, FL [title] "Hidden Away" [pers.] I wrote this poem when I was 15 years old for someone who is and always will be very special to me: my ex-boyfriend. I also wrote this poem because I was inspired by my mother. She inspires me to do a lot of things. Writing just happens to be one that I love to do.

WALKER, DL

[a.] Pasadena, TX [title] "Strain in My Brain" [pers.] To me all my poems are very special. I'm always writing new ones. I have enough for my own book of poems. I write poems, stories, and music. I sing and play guitar and drums. I love writing something new; it makes me very happy that someone likes my work. I know my writing comes from my family, but God made me who I am. Sometimes I see something, and it just hits me to write about whatever. I'd like to share a line from the words of a word man: Words come down like a rainbow of love, making emotion out of life and living.

WALKER, DWIGHT

[a.] Belton, MO [title] "Sunlight and Shadows" [pers.] Being strong amidst struggles is how my family raised me to be a man. I give because of that love. Love transcends even self. Sunlight and shadows teach me how to appreciate all things and to realize not to forget about self. Without me, these moments would not be possible. Sunlight and shadows exist together, like the words of this poem. The same applies to the family. Not even the pain that arises from these feelings can alter them. Although some people can't identify with these moments, with belief in love, we can understand its passion and power and its pain.

WALKER, MARIE

[a.] San Diego, CA [title] "So Alone" [pers.] I feel that poetry is the world to expression. I wrote this poem about a feeling of love lost. So many times we seek out our soul mates and then, once found (if ever found), we could lose it all in a moment. I am so pleased to be a part of all of this. My poem is dedicated to all those who found true love and then lost it in a moment.

WALKER, WENFRED

[a.] Los Angeles, CA [title] "You Are Joy" [pers.] I think Malcolm X addressed America at a time when the hatred and bigotry was too often accepted and ignored by many. In candid language, he addressed the issue of how black America felt and continues to feel when we must cope with unresolved racism and discrimination. White America, you took humanity and life away from black people. We are still trying desperately to regain what we were and what we had. Please encourage us, help us, and, above all, love us, and we will try to do the same with you.

WALLS, SHARON

[a.] Toano, VA [title] "Moments" [pers.] Verse has always played an important part of my upbringing. Tragedy didn't avoid my childhood, and death was certainly no stranger. Instead of fearing the inevitable, I applied myself to verse. Death is not an end, but a new beginning. My mother led our family through the trying times we encountered. She granted us an understanding by providing us strength. Her courage and determination were gifts to all who knew her. My hope is, with this poem, she may somehow realize that verses continue and poetry hasn't ceased.

WALSH, TINA

[a.] Patchogue, NY [title] "Reflections" [pers.] The poem "Reflections" was written when I was 18, right after my mother died from cancer. This was my goodbye to her. I hope all who have lost someone close will know they are always with them, making them stronger.

WAN RAMLI, WAN

[a] Kajang, Malaysia [title] "Wish Comes True" [pers.] This poem is very special to me, as it talks about wishes. Most people wish for a lot of things, but not all of them get their wishes granted. This verse tells a story of a person who lives in depression but is wishing for happiness by praying to God. I hope that anyone reading this poem will relate it to their own lives and perhaps be guided to their own happiness.

WARD, WILLA

[a.] Rio Rancho, NM [title] "Shores" [pers.] Poetry is a wondrous gift that has been bestowed upon me. Like most of us, my written word and spoken word differ greatly, and I am always amazed that the words do come for me. Like thieves in the night, the words creep up on me when I least expect it and leave in their wake the beauty of their might. Poetry takes hold of my heart, mind, and hand when I least expect it. All of us have a bit of poet in us; learn to pick up that pen when you feel compelled. Our lives are pure poetry, are they not?

WARREN, STERLING

[a.] Burtonsville, MD [title] "I Was There" [pers.] Poetry is not only a reflection of my creativity, but of everything about me. It is a reflection of my beliefs, my morals, my fears, my hopes, and my dreams. These things are all expressed through every line, through each verse. With this poem, I wanted to go back and explore where I came from and how I feel connected to the struggles and triumphs of my people. I thought about some of the most defining moments in history and how they not only influenced my life, but the lives of many people.

WATTS, NICOLE

[a.] Yokosuka, Japan [title] "The Voyage of Christopher Columbus" [pers.] This was a school assignment my dad helped me with. I am in the fifth grade at Sullivans School, Yokosuka Navy Base, Japan. I like poetry very much, and to be a finalist on my first entry is great. Dad, thank you for your ideas; without you this wouldn't be possible. Mom, thank you for your patience. I love you both. Sammi, thank you for sharing this moment; I love you. All of your support and family time contributed to this accomplishment.

WATTS, SHERYL

[a.] Apple Valley, CA [title] "Good-Bye" [pers.] I share a common ground with poetry; we are both misunderstood.

WEAKLY, JUSTIN

[a.] Pocatello, ID [title] "Me and a Shaggy-Coated Zebra" [pers.] I am 13 years old, in eighth grade, and I go to a one-room school. Writing is not one of my favorite activities, like reading, but I do like this poem. I wrote is as a language arts assignment. I think I would have to thank Mrs. Fry, my teacher, for her patience with me and her encouragement to complete all her writing assignments.

WEBBER, CYNTHIA JOY

[a.] Oshawa, ON [title] "And I Smile" [pers.] This poem was written and dedicated to my boyfriend, Paul, who, with gentle patience, taught me to believe in love again. To me, poetry is essential in life, for without it we would have no reason for self-expression. Poetry thrives in any age, under any circumstance. The many societies of the world use it to convey their truest feelings; by this means, we gain valuable insight on the culture and heritage of the people. To the one who inspired this poem . . . I love you, my precious. Without you, my soul would cease to dance.

WEBER, CORRIE

[a.] Commerce Township, MI [title] "Lady from Leeds" [pers.] I wrote this in math when we were doing a poetry lesson. This poem means a lot to me. I love writing poetry. I am honored to have my poem published.

WESSLING, MICHAEL, SR.

[a.] [title] "The Little Girl I Knew" [pers.] The poetry I write comes from the hidden thoughts and feelings I possess inside. I believe other people can relate, but are unable to put into words or really show what their hearts and souls want to illuminate. I hope my poems touch the people who read them. Poetry enables a small mark of existence in anyone's life. Michael W. Wessling, Sr. is a technical engineer from Columbus, Ohio. He has an associate's degree in electrical engineering, and his hobbies include handyman projects, music, puzzles, cooking, and, of course, poetry!

WEST, ANGELA

[a.] Elma, WA [title] "Gameboy versus Homework" [pers.] Hi, my name is Angela Marie West. I write poetry as a way of getting my feelings out. I am 13 years old, the oldest kid in a family of five that includes my father, Martin; mother, Kathy; 11-year-old sister, Daniel; and five-year-old brother, Charlie, who has autism. We are all silly and goofy. They are my main source of inspiration. My hobbies are track and singing, not to mention 4-H. We have six cat and eight dogs. My wiener dog, Joey, is my greatest source of joy. Thank you for reading my poem. My mom inspired it.

WHEATLEY, ANGELIC

[a.] Singapore, Republic of Singapore [title] Untitled [pers.] I am a mother of three children, ages 20, 19, and nine. I am 42 years of age, married to a man who is in the army. I am teaching kindergarten and also Sunday School in church. This is my first attempt to write a poem after meditating on God for one of my difficult catechism lessons.

WHEELER, KATIE

[a.] Lima, OH [title] "Seasons" [pers.] Poetry is a gift I got from my Grandpa Leland and my Aunt Shannon. I've been interested in writing poems ever since I was a little girl. This is like a dream come true! I've always wanted one of my poems published, and it finally happened! My poem is about how all the seasons have something in common and how I like all of the seasons. That's why it's here to stay. I hope everyone can have at least someone in their life to teach them poetry and the wonders of it!

WHITE, MARGARET

[a.] Rochelle, IL [title] "Endurance" [pers.] I am a single mother raising two children. This poem reflects not only how I have learned to look at life but what I have observed in others. My poetry reflects my experiences, and I hope others feel inspiration from my words.

WHITE, PHILLIP

[a.] Mt. Pleasant, SC [title] "The Daffodil" [pers.] This poem is one of many I wrote some years ago that I remember with fondness. It is a short, simple poem. I hope the meaning you find in it lightens your heart and puts a smile on your face.

WHITE, TREMAIN

[a.] Houston, TX [title] "What to Do with You" [pers.] Poetry, to me, is just as much a means to self-knowledge as it is to self-expression. This, in turn, helps us to better understand each other as we draw inward to better understand ourselves. For me, it is a chance to strip away the appearances that I normally hold up and see myself for what I am—human. Through poetry, I am able to simplify those emotions, and from there I can remove myself from my own hiding place and truly relate who I am to the rest of the world. No mask, boundless, we are all just the same, just as good, just as bad, just as distracted. "What to do with You" is a poem that deals with struggles and self-expression and appearances. It also shows how, through the process or realization, one becomes stripped down, so that one first can relate to oneself as well as to others.

WHITNEY, JAMES

[a.] Huntsville, AL [title] "[pers.] This poem is a very special poem, and I dedicate it to my very best friend in the whole world, for it is she who inspired the words for this. She and the love we have shared have been so special to me. Because of her and what she has put in my heart, I am able to write something that I can share with others, to make others aware of the love that is out there for them if they just look. I dedicate this poem to my love, my wife, Melody Rose Whitney. May God bless you all.

WHITTAKER, JIMMIE

[a] Stockton, Ca [title] "A New Lullaby" [pers.] Originally from Illinois, I now reside two hours from San Francisco, California. Upon moving here four years ago, I immediately felt a strong sense of contentment, as if I had just arrived home after a long tiresome journey. Sometimes we all need a change of scenery or a different perspective to help us wake up. I hope that one day we will all realize how insignificant we are to this world, and how our being alive is

such a wonderful gift. Maybe then we can develop a heightened sense of consciousness and stop all the needless violence.

WILBUR, FRANCES P.

[a.] Cupertino, CA [title] "Death of a Wild Duck" [pers.] My love of poetry and nature comes from my parents, both of whom were educators. My father was also a botanist with a deep love of nature. Every summer our family piled into the car, and we took a trip together. We visited national parks, historical sites, factories, and mines. Once we saw a band of wild horses. Another time I saw some duck hunters, during hunting season. This poem grew out of that experience.

WILDES, ASHLEY

[a.] Pitman, NJ [title] "Headache and French" [pers.] I'm 14 years old. I was in French class one day, and I got a headache. That's when I started writing, and I came up with "Headache and French." I try to write something every day. After my aunt died of cancer, I got more involved in music and writing. I'm in band and choir, I play guitar and flute. Writing is my passion, and I hope one day I can become a writer. I can't draw, so I paint my pictures with words.

WILEY, MICHAEL JOHN

[a.] Tucson, AZ [title] "Domingo" [pers.] Poetry is like a springboard that launches the spirit through time and space. It is more than a flight of fancy or a tour through the imagination. There is a real and tangible world within the experience of poetry, an incident that is encased by feeling and remains existent unto the very end. A good poet knows this and therefore magically crafts a tool that may yield the nature of such sensation. This poem is about a very short moment in my recent past. The location is Coyoacan, Mexico City, on a typical Sunday afternoon near the market plaza.

WILKERSON, ANTHONY

[a.] Newport, NC [title] "Unforeseen Promises" [pers.] I thank God for my grandmother Sybil Turner; my mother, Pearl Billet; and my wife, Kelly Wilkerson, who have always inspired and supported me in all aspects of life. They have helped to create the person I am today. I am also inspired by life's ironic behavior, which always keeps things interesting.

WILLIAMS, CASEY

[a.] Pueblo, CO [title] "A Day's Wait" [pers.] I wrote this poem for anyone who has to wait for their wife or husband to come home, to keep with them for what it is worth. I am 13, in seventh grade. I really didn't know I had a talent for writing poems, but I was inspired by William Shakespeare, and I got some of my titles from other things to give me something to write about.

WILLIAMS, GLENN

[a.] Chicago, IL [title] "When A Tear Drops" [pers.] I feel that poetry is a way to express my deepest emotions. This poem is actually dedicated to me and a dramatic change I had in my life. "When a Tear Drops" was written to give inspiration and to remind me that I always have to stay positive, no matter what the situation is. Poetry satisfies my soul, and it helps to keep me whole. After reading this poem I hope the reader feels encouraged and realizes that there is a chance; things are going to get better. Poetry is a gift from God, and I will cherish it for the rest of my life.

WILLIAMS, KAREN

[a.] Santa Monica, CA [title] "Ponder" [pers.] I was born in Scotland as Karen Marie McGauley. This poem means so much to me, as I wrote it at a time in my life when I almost lost someone very close to me, and as people that have been close to me have passed on. I find that this poem has given me a little strength to deal with the sadness of loss. I would like to dedicate this poem to all who read it in the hope that

perhaps it will bring you a little faith, a little hope, and a little healing in your time of need.

WILLIAMS, WILSON

[a.] Detroit, MI [title] "One Dozen Scented Silk Roses" [pers.] Poetry is my hourglass of life and God-given gift. This poem was inspired by a magazine ad to order some special flowers. I thought, "Wow, flowers that will last forever! How wonderful it would be if relationships did the same!" I was born in Wilmington, North Carolina. After graduation, I enlisted in the United States Navy. My poetic seed was planted in my mind by my oldest brother. In 1984, I created my pen name, Sir Quevon. I am the proud father of three beautiful daughters. I am pursuing higher education and publication of my book, *Quevon's Quest, My Poetic Journey.*

WILLIS, ALICIA LEIGH

[a.] Laguna Beach, CA [title] "White Fantasy" [pers.] Alicia Leigh Willis is an actress now living in Venice, California. She was a regular on the soap opera *Another World*, playing Ali Fowler, and has frequently appeared on the television show, *7th Heaven*. Alicia has enjoyed writing poetry since she was a child, and "White Fantasy" was a dream she had one night. She awoke afterward and wrote it down. It has remained one of her favorite poems.

WILSON, JACQUELINE

[a.] Troy, MI [title] "Simple Joy" [pers.] Almost all of my poetry is simply my feelings in words. I believe that I inherited my fascination with poetry from my father. He wrote several poems for my younger brother and me. I would definitely say that those poems inspired me as well as some famous poets. In this I also want to say "Thank you" and "I love you" to my family.

WILSON, JENNY

[a.] Boone, NC [title] "The Best Friend" [pers.] I feel that the poetry that I write is a gift from God. It is sort of funny because I can't write it when I want to, only when the lines wake me up out of a sound sleep. I have been writing poetry for six years now. I consider it to be my way of expressing my feelings. In my opinion, it is also my way of thanking someone in my life. I wrote "The Best Friend" for my best friend, Shannon Coyle. Over the past couple of years I have faced some really bad times, and she was there with me through everything. Therefore, I wrote this poem in her honor just to let her know that I owe my thanks to her and that I love her with all my heart.

WILSON, KASY

[a.] Midlothian, TX [title] "Danger" [pers.] Poetry is very special to me. I feel that it is a gift. Poetry has been inspirational for me. Without the support of my family and friends, I would not have given a second glance at my poetry.

WILSON, NATHALIE

[a.] Austin, TX [title] "The Room" [pers.] I was living with a friend and her 15-year-old daughter. I was almost 20 years old and was completely miserable, because my friend's daughter would pretend to be an angel before her and be the devil incarnate behind her. One day, she said some really horrible things that made me cry. I cried not only because the words hurt me but because I was never treated that way before. I wished I were back home in Jamaica where I had my own space and self-respect. The hurt inspired me to write this poem, craving solitude with all my heart.

WILSON, RHONDA

[a.] Buddina, Australia [title] "A Friend" [pers.] The poem was written by me at the age of 13 when my best friend, Wendy, died of cancer. It was my farewell to her, as I was not permitted to attend her funeral. She was a very special person and extremely important to me and still very much is an important part of my life.

WINKELS, KATHRYN
[a.] Greer, SC [title] "One" [pers.] I've been writing for my benefit only, and in secret, for almost 30 years. Every emotion I've had has been scribbled on anything I could get my hands on. I credit my mother for this, because she's always encouraged me to open up my inner self to the rest of the world. I'm so grateful to my sons, Christopher and Tim, for making it possible for me to do just that.

WINTERFELD, JOLENE
[a.] Sioux City, IA [title] "A Friend I Never Knew" [pers.] Growing up in a small town such as mine, the death of a youth can affect everyone, even those who did not know him or her personally. When a young man from my town was killed in an accident, the whole town was aggrieved. Even those people who did not know him, such as I, experienced remorse in some way. I felt as though I had lost a friend. Maybe I did not know him then, but possibly someday I would have. This poem is for anyone who has lost someone they may or may not have even known.

WITHERSPOON, RON
[a.] Salt Lake City, UT [title] "Freedom" [pers.] I have been writing poetry as a way of expressing my emotions for over 30 years. Poetry has been my way of dealing with my fears, my anger, and my depression. It expresses loves and my hates. This poem was written out of anger at the political right, which seems to have nothing to do other than to tell people what they cannot do. "Freedom" is about the freedom this country was founded on, which has now been taken away.

WOHLGEMUTH, PEGGY
[a.] Quitman, GA [title] "In Love" [pers.] Poetry is a gift that was given to me by God. I was inspired to write poems after receiving one from my boyfriend, finding it romantic to express thoughts and feelings that way. I wrote "In Love" for my boyfriend after knowing him for only 18 days. I believe that the affections we share come from God above, which is the reason I give thanks to Him in my poem. Our love would not exist without the love of God, for He has brought us together.

WOMBLE, MARY
[a.] San Antonio, TX [title] "My Friend" [pers.] My poem, initially, was written for a close friend. I had rewritten the last few verses, so those don't apply to her. Fortunately she is still with us. It was with her in mind that I started this poem. Edna is a rare find, a good friend—a real friend. She has suffered so much but always takes time for someone else's problems. When you meet her, you don't forget her. To you, Edna, I dedicate this poem. Thank you for being there for me. I'm so glad I can call you my friend.

WONG, JUN HAO
[a.] Evergreen Park, Singapore [title] "Home" [pers.] I wrote this poem because I just love my home. Whenever I feel down, I just come home. Coming home after school also helps me to relax. I love my family when they are all at home with me. I hope that others feel the same way, too, and I dedicate this poem to those who love going home. I hope they will share this poem with their loved ones and everyone they know.

WONG, WARREN
[a.] Vancouver, BC [title] "Darkness Abode" [pers.] Poetry is the written language of the soul. I'm so happy I am blessed with one that writes so well. I can only hope my poetry permeates the souls of others and brings them some sort of joy, or sorrow, or anger, whichever I am trying to convey. For now, enjoy poetry, for it lives within us all.

WOOD, GLENDA
[a.] Santa Rosa Beach, FL [title] "Connection" [pers.] This poem was written at a beautiful retreat site in Maui, Hawaii. Everything—people, nature, spirit—

seemed to be connected. I loved to train, and when I do, I relax and get more in touch with myself.

WOODY, JAMES
[a.] Carthage, MO [title] "Your Flame" [pers.] I have never really loved poetry with a passion, but I just one day picked up a pencil and started writing in the middle of school. I don't know where it came from, but this poem just came so naturally. I wrote some others but haven't entered them yet.

WOOLF, LINDSEY
[a.] Houston, TX [title] "Frustration" [pers.] As a teenager, frustration is constantly part of my life. Sometimes these feelings grow until they feel unbearable, and I feel like giving up altogether. Through the expression of these feelings, I have learned to deal with and overcome the harder parts of life. Frustration (along with many similar aggravations, too) will come to pass.

WORRILOW, EDDIE
[a.] Wilmington, DE [title] "M.M" [pers.] When I first made this poem, "M.M.," it was for my ninth grade English class. Here it is, nearly one-and-a-half years later, published in a book. I am very proud of my poem. As a child, I loved to watch Mickey Mouse, and I still do. I thought this poem expressed my, and everyone else's, feelings about the lovable, big-eared mouse we've all grown up with. I hope you enjoyed reading my poem as much as I enjoyed writing it.

WULF, JESSICA
[a.] Thornton, CO [title] "I Am a Cross" [pers.] The story behind my poem is that I was told by my language arts teacher to write a poetry book. We were told to write a few different types of poems. . . . Poetry has a great meaning to me; it is an amazing way with words that my dad passed on to me. This poem specifically has a very religious meaning to me. My mother, Janet, is one of my best friends; she has always been there for me and I for her. My dad is the one I got my sense of humor and way with words from. My very weird, odd, little brother is annoying yet sweet. I'm a citizen of Thornton, Colorado, and I attend Century Middle School. My hobbies are rollerblading, bike riding, swimming, and just hanging out with my friends. I have not yet come across an occupation, but my dad is working on getting me a summer job at a local skating rink. On a personal note, I am very honored and excited to receive such a wonderful offer. I'm very thankful for having this wonderful opportunity.

WUST, DANIELLE
[a.] Chalmette, LA [title] "Love?" [pers.] Danielle Wust is a 13-year-old student at Hannan School in Chalmette, Louisiana. She enjoys dancing, talking on the Internet, and writing poetry. She hopes to become a writer or psychologist.

YARBROUGH, GAYLE
[a.] Hitchcock, TX [title] "At the Ranch" [pers.] This poem was written for and inspired by my good friend, Johnny Sellers, and his abundant love of nature. The beauty of a South Texas ranch and the wildlife there will never be forgotten. I will always be grateful to Johnny for showing me this special place and for giving me the opportunity to experience and know it. Through this poem I was able to capture my feelings for the moment and keep them for a lifetime.

YASIKA, BRADLEY
[a.] Raymond, NH [title] "Lizee's Poem" [pers.] I never thought in my wildest dreams that I would be a published poet. This has opened a door for me that otherwise may have remained closed. To express your feelings in words, you must be able to bare your soul. This is not easy to do, especially when you face possible criticism or the harsh reality of rejection. I travel for my work as a construction supervisor and

have spent a considerable amount of time separated from my wife; thus the inspiration for "Lizee's Poem." I will continue to look for inspiration, and I will continue to bare my soul.

YATES, SOUMAIA
[a.] Windsor, VT [title] "The Demons in My Head" [pers.] At 36 years of age, depression has taken a big part of my life away in the last few years. Diagnosed as manic depressive in my early twenties, I've stayed in many a suite, in different psychiatric words. Plagued with hallucinations, both visual and audio, I've started writing poems to describe what was happening in my life. "The Demons in My Head" is my first attempt at poetry.

YAU, KWOK YUK
[a.] Surrey, BC [pers.] Born in Hong Kong on June 17, 1936, I was educated and worked in Hong Kong until 1992, in which year I migrated to Canada. At the University of Hong Kong, I received my B.A. with honors in 1962, a postgraduate diploma in education in 1963, and my M.A. in 1971. I took up the teaching profession after graduation from the university. I had served the St. Catharine's School for Girls, K.T., in Hong Kong from 1966 to 1985. Then I was appointed principal of the T.W.G.H.S. Wong Fung Ling College in Hong Kong until 1992, in which year I retired and left Hong Kong. I had published two books of Chinese poetry written by me, namely the *Hsien-yin Chi* (1983) and the *Hsien-yin Xu-chi* (1992). I also had published a booklet of my Chinese paintings in 1990. Since 1994, I have tried to write English poems. My wife is Lai Ching Chan (Cecilia), who had been a primary school teacher in Hong Kong. She is a Chinese painting artist.

YOUNG, IAN
[a.] Redondo Beach, CA [title] "Untitled" [pers.] My mom had a hard time raising me, to say the least. Nothing ever came easy to us, and she had to fight tooth and nail for everything we got. She had to make a lot of stressful decisions, and, looking back, she has expressed her regret for the way in which she handled certain situations. I wrote this poem for her, so she might realize I can share those regrets; she could not have done a better job. It was my father's wish that I somehow have this poem printed. Unfortunately, he passed away. I could never sing for my father; yet, before he died, he knew that one gift was traded for another.

YOUNG, MARCIA
[a.] Bethlehem, GA [title] "Tomorrow" [pers.] I believe that poetry is an outpouring of passionate emotions that have been held in captivity inside the human heart and soul. Born and raised in a small Georgia town, my two children and my two grandchildren are the loves of my life. By profession, I am a teacher, one who tries to help shape the future by inspiring today's youth to develop their intelligence, talent, creativity, and sense of humor. Through faith, I look inside myself, and my poems just seem to flow naturally, a gift from the Creator who made me.

YUHICO, RICCI
[a.] Miami, FL [title] "Simplicity" [pers.] People always take things for granted. Rarely does anyone stop to admire the elegance of the simplest things. I had a dream before I wrote my poem that it was my last day alive, and I stopped to marvel at every single thing. I found more than thousands of ways to describe them, the majesty of it all, and how I couldn't believe I never noticed it before.

ZAGHIAN, KHALIL
[a.] Valley Village, CA [title] "My Best Friend, the Love of My Life" [pers.] Writing poems is one of the many artistic ways by which I can uniquely and effectively express myself and can describe my thoughts and feelings in the purest, most imaginative, and most creative form. The inspiration for this poem is my loving girlfriend, April. With her, I hope to

develop a true spiritual, emotional, and physical union. The beginning of this poem describes the power of our first kiss, which helped our friendship to blossom into something much more intimate. The last three lines of the poem represent the connection of love that we will ultimately experience after marriage.

ZAIDI, FIZZA

[a.] Jeddah, Saudi Arabia [title] "All above the Sky" [pers.] We are a small family. Currently we are based in Jeddah, Saudi Arabia. I love poems. I will not say that poetry writing is my hobby, because it comes to me naturally without any prior intention or planning. It has no place . . . no time. I feel this poem is the result of my continuous inquiry about so many natural wonders.

ZALESKI, JILLIAN

[a.] Lake Charles, LA [title] "Freedom"

ZEDAN, AHMED HASSANAIN

[a.] Riyadh, Saudi Arabia [title] "Questions!" [pers.] To be a poet is a great honor. It's God's gift to lucky and special people, but those who recognize and taste poetry are the greatest of all. I write my poems mainly in Arabic. As I am an electronic telephone exchanges and computerized telecom systems engineer, I write also in English. A poet can write in any language he knows, because of his rhythmic and poetic soul. Poetry is the most real part of my life; it's my existence, in brief. I like fishing, cooking, traveling, teaching, and all creative works. The strangest thing about my life is that all its practical aspects, such as my studies, are merely scientific, even my job in Saudi Telecom. Company. I'm Egyptian, working and living in Saudi Arabia. I write about many subjects, like literature, prose, and thinking. Writing is my wonderful life. I'm a very productive writer if encouraged.

ZIC, CAROL

[a.] Las Cruces, NM [title] "It Ain't Easy Being Married!" [pers.] Born a poor white child, bereft of legitimacy, I seemed destined for a deprived, socially unacceptable life. Once school started, I embraced education with a passion that still exists. Through childhood and adolescence, I fought twin demons of poverty and sexual abuse and read everything for comfort until, scarred but undefeated, adulthood arrived. I joined the U.S. Navy WAVES and was honorably discharged. College and theater beckoned. Acting and a legal career flourished, as did marriage and five children. In middle-age, jobs in Europe and South America enticed, and, suddenly, hello, senior citizen! Oh, yeah? You ain't seen nothing yet!

ZOKA, ZOONA

[a.] London, UK [title] "[pers.] I wrote my first poem, when I was seven years old, with the help of my mother. She always encouraged me to write and read; therefore, writing poems and short stories was my way of motivating and expressing myself. My parents have made me what I am today, with their support and unconditional love. I thank you, Mumma and Daddy. I hope I'll make you proud one day. I would like to dedicate my poem to my parents; my brother, Zumma; my sisters, Lailomah and Natasha; my aunt, Gona; my brother-in-law, Razi; and my grandparents.

ZUCKER, SCOTT

[a.] Northridge, CA [title] "My Existence Is . . . " [pers.] Poetry is an art form that allows me to express myself in a unique way, which I have found impossible in any other art form. It enables me to deliver an expression of emotion simply through the use of abstract images. In this poem I make use of the literary device known as allegory. I do so with the use of a fish, paralleling it to human relationships and emotions in terms of novelty. I hope you are able to see through the allegory in this poem and appreciate it for its deeper meaning.

Index
of
Poets

Index